RICHARD A. BURRIDGE is Dean of King's
College London, where he is also Director of
New Testament Studies. His other books include
Four Gospels, One Jesus? and *What Are the Gospels?
A Comparison with Graeco-Roman Biography.*

IMITATING JESUS

IMITATING JESUS

An Inclusive Approach to New Testament Ethics

Richard A. Burridge

WILLIAM B. EERDMANS PUBLISHING COMPANY
GRAND RAPIDS, MICHIGAN / CAMBRIDGE, U.K.

Published 2007 by
Wm. B. Eerdmans Publishing Co.
2140 Oak Industrial Drive N.E., Grand Rapids, Michigan 49505 /
P.O. Box 163, Cambridge CB3 9PU U.K.
www.eerdmans.com

Printed in the United States of America

12 11 10 09 08   7 6 5 4 3 2

Library of Congress Cataloging-in-Publication Data

Burridge, Richard A., 1955-
   Imitating Jesus: an inclusive approach to New Testament ethics / Richard A. Burridge.
       p.   cm.
   Includes bibliographical references and index.
   ISBN 978-0-8028-4458-3 (cloth: alk. paper)
   1. Ethics in the Bible.   2. Bible. N.T. — Criticism, interpretation, etc.
   3. Jesus Christ — Example.   I. Title.

   BS2545.E8B87   2007
   241 — dc22

                                                          2007030015

To Archbishop Desmond Tutu
and all the rainbow people
of South Africa,

  who taught me that interpreting the Bible
   can be a matter of life or death —
    or even more important than that!

Contents

Preface and Acknowledgements

'So, if you were given some space to write again and research some new area, what would you like to look at?' It seemed an innocent enough question at the time — but I little thought that it would take me over a decade to answer it! It was a sultry Louisiana evening in November 1996, and we were relaxing in the academically unlikely setting of an open-air hot tub on the roof of a New Orleans hotel. Professor Ian Markham, a colleague from previous years at Exeter University, but then at Liverpool Hope University College, had encouraged me to go with him to the extraordinary gathering which is the joint Annual Meeting of the American Academy of Religion and the Society of Biblical Literature. Every autumn just before Thanksgiving, some 10,000 academics from biblical, theological and religious studies gather together for thousands of papers and hundreds of seminars and meetings. I found the whole event quite mind-blowing, and it made me reflect upon my first couple of years as Dean of King's College London. Now that I had settled in to its challenges, perhaps it was time to start a new research project. Under Ian's probing questions, ideas began to swirl around like the bubbles in the Jacuzzi, exploring possibilities about how I might apply all my previous work on the biographical genre of the gospels to the vexed question of how the New Testament is used in ethics today. The following autumn at the 1997 AAR/SBL meeting in San Francisco, I started discussions about publishing a book with Sam Eerdmans of William B. Eerdmans Publishing Company about this work, and we have continued such meetings every autumn since then. I guess that neither of us realized that my wider duties as Dean of King's would make sustained regular academic research difficult so that it would take me so long, or that the project would change so much along the way.

xiv

On the other hand, being Dean of King's has also provided marvellous opportunities to consider how the New Testament has been used in ethics and has taken this book in directions I could never have realized at the start. First and most important has been the connection of the College with Southern Africa which has come about through decades of our training South African clergy, especially those denied education under apartheid because of their colour, and sending them back home to work for a better future. I first visited that beautiful land to represent King's at the retirement of our most famous alumnus, Desmond Tutu, as Archbishop of Cape Town in June 1996. When I was invited by his successor, Archbishop Njongonkulu Ndungane, also an alumnus of King's, to give clergy schools and lay training in Cape Town, I realised that this would give me a unique chance to research at first hand how the New Testament had been studied and used both to support apartheid and to critique it in the struggle for liberation. I was given study leave from King's to spend three months, March to May 1998, researching and teaching in universities and churches across that country.

I am particularly grateful to Archbishop Desmond Tutu for inviting me to visit him and to interview him in the middle of the Truth and Reconciliation process. I want to thank all those who showed me such generous hospitality, especially the Very Reverend Rowan Smith (another former King's student), Dean of St George's Cathedral, Cape Town, for inviting me to preach through Holy Week, Good Friday and Easter; the Reverend Terry Lester and his wife Colleen, who have been such good friends; the Reverend John Stubbs who organized my accommodation and transport and arranged for me to give clergy conferences and lay training events across the diocese of Cape Town; the Right Reverend David Beetge and his wife Carol for their hospitality for me and my family, for a memorable stay in the Kruger Park, and for arranging clergy schools across Johannesburg and the High Veld. It has been an honour subsequently to represent Bishop David and his diocese as Commissary for the High Veld back in England. I am also grateful to academic colleagues who invited me to visit various universities to give papers and to learn from stimulating debate about the Bible in South Africa: Professors Bernard Combrink and Jan Botha at Stellenbosch; Dirkie Smit and Denise Ackerman at the University of the Western Cape; Steve Martin and the Research Institute on Christianity in South Africa (RICSA) at the University of Cape Town; Gerald West and Bev Haddad at the University of Kwa-Zulu Natal, Pietermaritzburg; Jan van der Watt, Andries van Aarde and Stefan Joubert at the University of Pretoria; Louise Kretzschmar at the University of South Africa (UNISA). It was through these events in churches and universities that the ideas contained in this book were first developed. Thereafter, it has been a joy to be able to return to South Africa regularly and to continue to teach and debate this material, enjoying the hospitality of Archbishop Desmond and Leah Tutu, Bishop David and Carol Beetge, Terry and Colleen Lester, Gerald West and Jan van der Watt, without all of whom this book would never have appeared. I gladly dedicate this book to the rainbow people of South Africa, who have taught the rest of the world so much about how to interpret the New Testament in the midst of some of the most challenging ethical situations of recent history.

Another major influence has been the opportunity to discuss this material at international conferences. If the book had its origins in the meeting of the Society of Biblical Literature in New Orleans, 1996, some of its central ideas were first aired in papers at subsequent SBL meetings, especially 'Imitation and Moral Communities in Reading Pauline Ethics Today' at Nashville, 2000, 'Being Biblical: Reading the New Testament in South Africa under Apartheid' at San Antonio, 2004, and 'Imitating Jesus: Handling the Diversity of Ethical Material within the New Testament' at Washington, DC, 2006. I also benefited greatly from belonging to the seminar on New Testament ethics within the annual meetings of the Society of New Testament Studies (SNTS), chaired by Professors Richard Hays, Wolfgang Schrage and Andreas Lindemann, especially the opportunity to present my central thesis at SNTS in Copenhagen, August 1998. The visit of SNTS to Pretoria in August 1999 allowed me to unite my academic studies with the South African context, especially in the following conference at Hammanskraal. Back home, the British New Testament Conference has also been a great source of encouragement and inspiration, particularly through its Seminar on Hermeneutics and Interpretation: Theory and Practice, which I had the privilege of chairing from 1998 to 2004; again, material in this book was first delivered in papers such as 'Bridging the Gap: New Testament Ethics Today' at Bristol in September 1999 and 'A Biographical Approach to New Testament Ethics', the opening plenary address at Liverpool, 2005. In addition, I have given papers at staff and postgraduate research seminars in various universities, including Professor Christopher Rowland's seminar at the University of Oxford, summer 1998; Liverpool Hope University College, June 1999; London Bible College, May 2000; Ridley Hall Cambridge, November 2000; Exeter University, November 2002, as well as on several occasions in the biblical research seminar here at King's College London. I am grateful to all those who participated in such conferences and seminars, and who responded to my papers, whose questions helped to sharpen my thinking.

The third main context for this research on how the New Testament is used in ethics today has been in various church training events, conferences, theological societies and lectures, including the Pinner Association of Churches Lent Course, 1999; Guildford Diocesan Training Day, March 1999; Kensington

Diocesan Area Training Day, March 1999; Willesden Diocesan Area Training Day, April 1999; Islington Deanery Chapter Conference, May 1999; Chelmsford Diocese Training Days, June 1999; Truro Theological Society, October 1999; Peterborough Theological Society, January 2002; All Saints, Fulham, London, March 2002; Leicester Theological Society, March 2003; the Anglican Institute at St Michael and St George Church, St Louis, Missouri, USA, March 2003; St Louis Diocesan Study Day, Missouri, USA, March 2003; Norwich Diocesan Study Day, April 2004; Kensington Area Clergy Conference, Merville, France, September 2004; Barking Episcopal Area, Chelmsford, October 2004; Hartford Seminary, CT, USA, February 2006; the Cheyneygates Seminar, Westminster Abbey, June 2006. I was also privileged to be able to teach this material at a Summer School for Regent College, Vancouver, BC, July-August 2003, a week's residential conference for Hereford Diocese, April 2004 and for Fuller Theological Seminary Summer School, Los Angeles, July 2007. It has also formed a backdrop for our discussions within the Bishop of Southwark's Theological Issues Group looking at how we interpret the Bible today, which I have been honoured to chair since 2004. It also forms the main substance of 'Being Biblical? Slavery, Sexuality and the Inclusive Community', the 22nd Eric Symes Abbot Lecture, at Westminster Abbey and Keble College, Oxford, May 2007. Again, I want to express my thanks to those who attended all these events and asked penetrating questions which sent me back to my research!

An earlier and shorter version of my material on Mark's gospel in Chapter IV was first published as 'Imitating Mark's Jesus: Imagination, Scripture, and Inclusion in Biblical Ethics Today', in honour of Professor Christopher Bryan in *Sewanee Theological Review* 50.1 (Christmas 2006), pp. 11-31.

Clearly, such a long and wide-ranging project is bound to affect all of an author's family, friends and colleagues. I am indebted to Professor Arthur Lucas, the previous Principal of King's College London, who first granted me the study leave to start the project, and Professor Rick Trainor, the current Principal, for allowing me to finish it. Present and former colleagues in New Testament in the Department of Theology and Religious Studies at King's gave critical encouragement and stimulating questions, including Professors Graham Stanton and Judith Lieu, Francis Watson, Doug Campbell, Eddie Adams and Lutz Doering. The burden of my absences has been carried uncomplainingly by the rest of my team in the Dean's Office and Chaplaincy, especially by the Reverend Tim Ditchfield, the College Chaplain, and by various secretaries over the period, including Alison Shapton, Frances Pattman, Lara White and Clare Dowding, who has also proved to be a sharp-eyed proofreader. Anna Cope did a huge amount of the basic research legwork as my research assistant in the early years, the results of which proved to be immensely useful all the way through to the end of the project; it was an honour to play a small part in supporting her along the path to her own doctorate, not to mention being ordained and married, now as the Reverend Doctor Anna Poulson.

Father Christopher Lowe of the Community of the Resurrection and himself a regular visitor to South Africa guided my spiritual exercises through the initial periods of research, but sadly did not live to see the project completed; may he rest in peace. Many others have supported me with 'ghostly counsel', especially the Reverends Gordon Oliver and Ken Leech and Sister Kathleen Hopkins, as well as those who have been part of my prayer circle, praying for me to complete this book, including the Reverends Nick Holtam, Dave Tomlinson, Giles Legood, Malcolm Doney, Martin Wroe; the Very Reverend Vivienne Faull; Doctor Christopher Southgate, Justin Butcher, Andy Harrison, Judy Wren, and Don Arthurson. In addition to her thoughts, prayers and friendship, Jane Pendarves once again provided much editorial and stylistic assistance, for which I have been hugely grateful.

I am especially indebted to those who have read various drafts of these chapters at different times and returned them with corrections and further suggestions, especially the Right Reverend Tom Wright and Professor David Horrell, both of whom tried to help me understand Paul a little better! I have benefited so much from their own work and have appreciated their concern for mine. Professor Richard Hays has been constantly generous with his interest in and reactions to my responses to his own seminal work on New Testament ethics. My dialogue with all three has been crucial for the development of my ideas, including the areas where we still disagree, or when I have not heeded their advice; the mistakes are mine.

As the project began with a visit to the USA with Ian Markham, it is fitting that he should have invited me to spend my most recent study leave in 2006 to complete the book at Hartford Seminary, Connecticut, where he was then Dean. His encouragement and belief in this work kept me going when I was tempted to despair, and his probing questions always generated new ideas, even without a hot tub. Lesley, his wife, provided generous hospitality in their home and was kindly patient of my monopolising her husband with yet more draft chapters; I am also grateful to Luke Markham for allowing me to turn his playroom into a study and making sure that I had written my daily allotment of words before being allowed any dinner!

Sam Eerdmans has proved to be the most patient of publishers, and has allowed the project to change and develop into a completely different book; his concern and friendship have been vital. Within Eerdmans, I am very grateful also to Mike Thompson for his interest and support, and more latterly to Milt Essenburg for finally showing me what a copy editor can and should do. Meanwhile, Bill Eerdmans himself demonstrated the importance of jazz and blues clubs for publishing, as well as being long-suffering to this author.

Finally, once again it is my family who have paid the price of my absences at the laptop or on the research. My daughters, Rebecca and Sarah, can hardly remember the time before Dad became preoccupied with The Book. I missed them terribly when I was away, and was delighted that they were at least able to join in on trips to South Africa and to Vancouver. As with all my writing, my wife Sue has been the constant star, coping with my ups and downs, encouraging me and even reading endless drafts. Without her love and support, it would have never have been finished.

I hope I have been sufficiently inclusive in my thanks to everyone in academe and the church, in South Africa, the USA and in Britain. The research on this project and the writing of the book have demonstrated beyond all doubt the importance of the community of those who want to follow Jesus not just in his ethical teaching, but more importantly in his all-embracing acceptance of others. Thank you to all those whose acceptance of me and my work on this project have shown me what it means to imitate Jesus today.

Holy Week, 2007   RICHARD A. BURRIDGE

Abbreviations

ANRW	*Aufstieg und Niedergang der römischen Welt*
BETL	*Bibliotheca Ephemeridum Theologicarum Lovaniensium*
BJRL	*Bulletin of the John Rylands Library*
BTB	*Biblical Theology Bulletin*
BZNW	Beihefte zur Zeitschrift für die neutestamentliche Wissenschaft
CBQ	*Catholic Biblical Quarterly*
EvT	*Evangelische Theologie*
ExpT	*Expository Times*
HTR	*Harvard Theological Review*
ICC	International Critical Commentary
JAAR	*Journal of the American Academy of Religion*
JBL	*Journal of Biblical Literature*
JBLMS	Journal of Biblical Literature Monograph Series
JR	*Journal of Religion*
JSNT	*Journal for the Study of the New Testament*
JSNTSS	Journal for the Study of the New Testament Supplement Series
JSOT	*Journal for the Study of the Old Testament*
JSOTSS	Journal for the Study of the Old Testament Supplement Series
JTSA	*Journal of Theology for Southern Africa*
LNTS	London New Testament Studies
NIGTC	New International Greek Testament Commentary
NovT	*Novum Testamentum*
NovTSup	Novum Testamentum Supplements
NTS	*New Testament Studies*
SBL	Society of Biblical Literature

SBLDS	Society of Biblical Literature Dissertation Series
SBLSBS	Society of Biblical Literature Sources for Biblical Study
SBT	Studies in Biblical Theology
SJT	*Scottish Journal of Theology*
SNTS	Society for New Testament Studies
SNTSMS	Society for New Testament Studies Monograph Series
SWJT	*Southwestern Journal of Theology*
WUNT	Wissenschaftliche Untersuchungen zum Neuen Testament
ZNW	*Zeitschrift für die neutestamentliche Wissenschaft*
ZTK	*Zeitschrift für Theologie und Kirche*

I. Being 'Biblical':
Contexts and Starting Points

Controversies about how to apply the Bible to moral issues and ethical debate have always raged throughout the history of the Christian church. These have been over issues as diverse as relationships between Christians and Jews, or with pagans within the early church, or with Muslims and those of other faiths in our multicultural world today. The use of the Bible has been at the centre of arguments within denominational groupings and of separations between Christians, such as the Orthodox–Roman Catholic schism in 1054, the Catholic-Protestant debate at the Reformation and the subsequent history of splits and new Protestant churches since that time. In political affairs, the Bible has been utilized in support for or antagonism against kings, rulers and states, and provided justification for imperial expansion (such as the Conquistadores, or colonization), warfare (both wars between countries and internal civil wars), slavery and racism, and many other abuses of which Christians are now ashamed. Yet at the time, those who took a different view of scripture and criticized the official line were often accused of selling out the faith, or giving in to the liberal 'spirit of the age'.

Most significantly in the twentieth century, the Dutch Reformed Church in South Africa provided a clear reading of 'human relations . . . in the light of scripture' in support of the doctrine of 'separate development'.[1] It is tempting to dismiss this 'biblical' justification of apartheid as a mere pretext to justify the

---

1. *Human Relations and the South African Scene in the Light of Scripture*, Dutch Reformed Church, Cape Town–Pretoria, 1976. Afrikaans report entitled *Ras, Volk en Nasie en Volker-everhoudinge in die lig van die Skrif*, approved and accepted by the General Synod of the Dutch Reformed Church in October 1974.

1

control of the rich resources of South Africa by a white minority, arising from a crude racial prejudice, but such an easy answer is both unfair to the DRC and flies in the face of the historical record. In fact, the argument that apartheid had a 'biblical' basis was developed over many years in a scripturally based church in the reformed Protestant tradition, backed up by various excellent faculties of biblical studies and theology in major universities such as Pretoria or Stellenbosch. As Prior notes, 'Although *apartheid* became a term that evoked virtually universal opprobrium, it was deployed within an ideological frame-work which derived from a particular form of Christian nationalism which looked to the biblical paradigm as its ultimate, Godly-assured justification'.[2] The Nationalist Government saw themselves as Christians, representing a 'spe-cial people' who had been particularly called and chosen by God. Seeing them-selves as a bastion against atheistic communism, the Afrikaners characterized their white critics as 'liberals' and black opponents as 'terrorists'. Other Chris-tians who sought to use the Bible to critique apartheid were accused of defend-ing atheism and violence, and were subject to all the rigours of the 'total strat-egy' of an oppressive police state. Even Archbishop Desmond Tutu in his capacity then as General Secretary of the South African Council of Churches had to undergo detailed legal scrutiny by the Eloff Commission in 1982.[3] Yet now, only a few years later, it is hard to credit that prayerful, faithful Christians could have believed that this evil system was 'biblical'.

Therefore, any attempt to reflect upon the use of the Bible in ethics should begin and end with a frank recognition of this shameful episode in recent his-tory. We have adduced it here at the start of this book as the most contempo-rary classic case of 'biblical justification' for something now widely seen as un-ethical, and it is hard to think of a better example to which to apply any study of biblical ethics. Therefore, we shall return to it in much more detail in the final chapter of this book as a test-case, or 'thought-laboratory', in which to examine the conclusions of this present study to see if they can withstand the hermeneu-tical challenge of recent South African history.

However, South Africa is only the most recent example of a recurrent theme throughout the history of the church, as traced in our opening paragraph. What is significant is that often both or all sides claim to be 'biblical' and accuse their opponents of being hidebound by the tradition or betraying it, selling out to the

2. Michael Prior, *The Bible and Colonialism: A Moral Critique* (Sheffield: Sheffield Academic Press, 1997), pp. 287-88, his italics.

3. Archbishop Desmond Tutu, *The Rainbow People of God: South Africa's Victory over Apartheid,* ed. John Allen (London: Bantam, 1995), see pp. 53-78 for the full text of his submission to the Commission; John Allen, *Rabble-Rouser for Peace: The Authorised Biography of Desmond Tutu* (London: Rider, 2006), pp. 197-98 has further discussion of this investigation.

contemporary world and the spirit of the age, frequently employing other terms such as 'conservative' or 'liberal'. The claim to be 'scriptural' is often linked to a desire to be holy and pure, to preserve the community from error, heresy or sin, and so those who want to be 'biblical' can be, or appear to be, 'exclusive' in their attitude towards those with whom they disagree. On the other hand, those who want to, or claim to, be 'inclusive' are open to the accusation that they have abandoned scripture. Thus Philip Turner, former Dean of Berkeley Divinity School at Yale, criticises recent decisions in the Episcopal Church of the USA: 'In place of the complex God revealed in Christ Jesus, a God of both judgment and mercy, a God whose law is meant to govern human life, we now have a God who is love and inclusion without remainder. The projected God of the liberal tradition is, in the end, no more than an affirmer of preferences'.[4]

It is all too easy to recognize these attitudes in our contemporary debates in some churches about, for example, homosexuality or the role of women in church leadership. In many circles today, there is endless debate about the 'biblical' viewpoint on such issues, and whether it means that we should be 'inclusive' or 'exclusive'. This book will not be yet another volume about those issues, nor does it grapple directly with them. This is not because we have no interest in such issues. It is because these debates are so strongly felt and vehemently argued that it is hard for each side to listen to the arguments of others, and even harder to accept that one's opponents might also be faithful Christians who read their Bibles and believe that they are guided by prayer and the Holy Spirit, despite their different views.

However, in another sense, this book *is* all about such issues — for it is an attempt to take a step back from contemporary debates and look directly at the New Testament, what ethical material it might contain and how we should read these books today. Throughout this study we shall examine whether the demands to be 'biblical' or 'inclusive' are really incompatible, or whether this might not be a false dichotomy.

It is also in facing these sorts of issues that this book will make its particular contribution. As we shall demonstrate shortly, many surveys of New Testament ethics remain simply that — surveys — and never grapple with how they might be applied to the contemporary world. Indeed, it might be argued that, during the apartheid era, many South African New Testament scholars concentrated on the study of ancient interpretation of the text, through things like rhetoric, perhaps to avoid the difficulties of contemporary application under a police state.[5] It is harder to explain why so many other writers elsewhere in the

---

4. Philip Turner, 'The Episcopal Preference', *First Things* 137 (November 2003), pp. 28-33.

5. See, for example, D. J. Smit, 'The Ethics of Interpretation — and South Africa', *Scriptura* 33

contemporary world simply describe the ethics of the New Testament with no discussion of today.

A second, more unusual, feature of our approach will be an insistence on the priority of the person of Jesus of Nazareth. We shall also soon see that many other studies concentrate simply on the ethics of the New Testament writers, partly because of the difficulty of reconstructing the historical Jesus, and partly for the good literary reason of beginning with the final form of the text. However, we want to assert that the key to understanding the New Testament has to be the person of Jesus, and that therefore he is the correct person and place with which to begin as well as to end.

This is because, while literary theory rightly concentrates upon the final form of the text, it also requires attention to its genre or genres — which have been mostly ignored by other writers in this field. In response, we will argue that the biographical genre of the canonical gospels redirects our gaze back to begin with the historical Jesus, and in particular to a stress upon both his deeds and his words, his activities as well as his teachings. Furthermore, although the apostle Paul is writing letters in the genre of epistles, he also presumes an underlying narrative about the entire event of Jesus' life, death and resurrection. Finally, Paul and the writers of the gospels derive both from the Jewish tradition of *ma'aseh,* or precedent, and from the Graeco-Roman habit of *mimesis,* an insistence upon the imitation of Jesus through a narrative of his words and deeds as the way to lead a moral life or reflect upon ethical issues.

In order to do this, we will need to begin this opening chapter with a survey of the field of New Testament ethics to demonstrate these three assertions about our particular approach, applying New Testament ethics to today, through the person of Jesus, with attention to the biographical genre of the gospels with their narrative of his deeds and words. Secondly, as befits a biographical approach to ethics, we will then go on to explain something of how this book came to be written and the contexts within which it emerged, including the author's own setting. Finally, we shall return to the genre of ancient biography to demonstrate why, against the arguments of many other scholars, we insist on beginning any study of New Testament ethics with Jesus.

(1990), pp. 29-43; idem, 'A Story of Contextual Hermeneutics and the Integrity of New Testament Interpretation in South Africa', *Neotestamentica* 28.2 (1994), pp. 265-89; Jan Botha, 'Aspects of the Rhetoric of South African New Testament Scholarship anno 1992', *Scriptura* 46 (1993), pp. 80-99.

1. The scholarly context of the debate

Therefore we now turn to a review of the major work in the field of New Testament ethics to demonstrate that it is not only South African scholars who have been guilty of avoiding the moral and political challenges of the contemporary world. Furthermore, we have suggested that many writers also tend to avoid dealing with the person of Jesus, seeing him as more of a problem than a resource for ethics. In addition, we hope to show that both of these features arise from a widespread lack of attention to genre, which is what gives us both the focus upon Jesus and the application for today. For easier arrangement, we shall look at both national and denominational groupings of scholars.

a. British scholarship

The first Hulsean lectures to be delivered at the University of Cambridge after their limitation to members of Church of England clergy was removed were given by C. A. Anderson Scott and published in 1930 as *New Testament Ethics: An Introduction.*[6] After five lectures on Jesus and Paul, his final lecture, 'Limitations and Their Removal', did at least include some consideration of Christians and the state, economics, and war. However, Dewar's *An Outline of New Testament Ethics* in 1949 simply worked its way through Jesus, the Holy Spirit, Paul, John and the rest of the New Testament with no application to today. Leslie Houlden's classic study covered an enormous amount of ground in a short compass, moving from an introductory attempt to outline the overall 'shape' of New Testament ethics through a study of the individual writers to discuss some particular ethical problems of the first century (divorce, political obedience, wealth and toleration); however, he did conclude with a ten-page discussion about 'the use' of the New Testament today, although this was mostly about methodology rather than specific issues.[7] On our other key issue, he begins his account by explaining his method of concentrating upon the New Testament writers, rather than with Jesus himself, who can only 'be found at the end not at the beginning of an inquiry'.[8] When he does come to examine Jesus in his penultimate chapter, it is as 'the Lord' of the New Testament writers with all the difficulties of reconstructing his voice: 'The Church had to build up the rule-book which Jesus had

6. C. A. Anderson Scott, *New Testament Ethics: An Introduction* (Cambridge: Cambridge University Press, 1930).

7. J. L. Houlden, *Ethics and the New Testament* (Oxford: Oxford University Press, 1973, and frequent reprints, e.g., Edinburgh: T&T Clark, 1992).

8. Houlden, *Ethics and the New Testament*, p. 4.

failed to provide, and thereby it imperilled its hold on the clarity of Jesus' message'.[9] There is, not surprisingly, nothing really about genre in this book, but the fact that it has remained in print, with various different publishers, as a key text over more than three decades is a tribute to its incisive comprehensiveness.

b. German studies

Houlden's approach was in criticism of Schnackenburg, who paved the way for a flood of German studies with his *The Moral Teaching of the New Testament,* which did begin with a major concentration on the moral demands of Jesus, and then moved through a general study of the early church to consider the moral teaching of Paul, John, James, 1 Peter, Hebrews and Rev. 2–3.[10] Schrage's huge *Ethics of the New Testament* has quickly become the standard text in the German tradition; it also begins with a systematic treatment of the ethics of Jesus and then goes on to the earliest congregations, the gospels, Paul, James, John, Hebrews and Revelation. It is carefully done, with historical-critical and theological analysis — but there is no attempt at any application to today.[11] A similar approach is followed by Schulz in his even larger treatment,[12] while Merklein organized the twenty-nine articles in the Festschrift honouring Schnackenburg to the same structure, again with nothing about today.[13] Lohse sought 'a middle way' between this standard account of each New Testament writer or book in turn and a purely systematic approach by including both aspects in his *Theological Ethics of the New Testament.*[14] In his turn, Marxsen claims not to want to 'present an "Ethics of the New Testament"' (p. xii) because of the differences among the writings; since ethics is an aspect of theology, he undertakes an historical, linguistic and systematic exegesis and analysis of the 'ethics oriented towards Jesus', and those of Paul, and the developments of these in other New Testament writings; he alone within the German tradi-

---

9. Houlden, *Ethics and the New Testament,* pp. 101-14; quotation from p. 114.

10. R. Schnackenburg, *The Moral Teaching of the New Testament,* trans. J. Holland-Smith and W. J. O'Hara from the German 2nd edn. of 1962 (New York: Herder and Herder, 1965); see Houlden, *Ethics and the New Testament,* pp. 4-5 for his criticism of Schnackenburg beginning with Jesus.

11. W. Schrage, *The Ethics of the New Testament,* trans. David E. Green (German edn. Göttingen: Vandenhoeck & Ruprecht, 1982; Philadelphia: Fortress, 1988).

12. S. Schulz, *Neutestamentliche Ethik* (Zurich: TVZ, 1987).

13. H. Merklein, ed., *Neues Testament und Ethik* (Freiburg: Herder, 1989).

14. E. Lohse, *Theological Ethics of the New Testament,* trans. M. Eugene Boring (Minneapolis: Fortress, 1991).

tion concludes with a brief treatment of the problem of founding a Christian ethic today on the New Testament, but it is only a couple of pages.[15]

c. In the United States of America

Across the Atlantic, J. T. Sanders followed the same sequence of working through the main New Testament witnesses, with particular attention to eschatology, and caused some reactions to his conclusions that neither Jesus, nor the early church, nor the New Testament helps us 'develop coherent ethical positions' today.[16] Goldsmith does want to help people hear the different ethical voices in the New Testament in his study of eight writers, but again the concentration is on the texts, with only a brief conclusion about the problems of applying them to today.[17] F. J. Matera, however, sets his face against both synchronic and diachronic approaches to New Testament ethics, preferring a literary study of the 'ethical legacies' of Jesus and Paul only, looking at the gospels and letters in turn. While he is clearly aware of the generic differences between the gospels and epistles, Matera does not deal with their genre, nor with either the historical Jesus or the authentic Paul, merely describing the ethics of each New Testament book in turn. He does conclude with seven brief theses about the moral life arising from the study, but he 'does not engage in hermeneutical questions about the normative value of the moral teaching in the writings of the New Testament'.[18] Blount provides a distinctive reading of New Testament ethics from the perspective of African Americans by reading through the lens of antebellum slaves. However attractive to the slaves the person of Jesus was, he was mediated through the gospels, and so after the discussion of his use of the lens of liberation to 'reconfigure' ethics, Blount moves through a useful discussion of the Synoptics, John, Paul and, more unusually, Revelation. He concludes by saying that he had intended to apply all of this to 'the most pressing ethical issues which presently face us', such as marriage and sexuality, economics and the state, but has come to the realization that this 'would contradict everything' for which his book stands. So he returns instead

15. W. Marxsen, *New Testament Foundations for Christian Ethics,* trans. O. C. Dean, Jr. (Minneapolis: Fortress/Edinburgh: T&T Clark, 1993); see pp. 310-12.

16. J. T. Sanders, *Ethics in the New Testament* (London: SCM, 1975); the preface to the second edition (1986) defends himself against some reviews, but still maintains his basic conclusion that 'Jesus provides no guide for ethics today' (p. xiv; see similarly, p. 130).

17. Dale Goldsmith, *New Testament Ethics: An Introduction* (Elgin, IL: Brethren, 1988).

18. F. J. Matera, *New Testament Ethics* (Louisville: Westminster John Knox, 1996); quotation from p. 9.

to some final reflections on the different cultural lenses through which New Testament ethics can be read.[19] Swartley's book is rather different in that it is not an attempt to produce a comprehensive account of New Testament ethics, but rather to trace 'the missing peace' within such studies. Chapter 1 does begin with tracing the role of peace in the preaching of the kingdom of God by the historical Jesus, but thereafter his main concern is with 'the final form' of the New Testament books from the gospels and Acts through the letters of Paul and the other epistles to the book of Revelation. The concluding three thematic chapters reflect upon the role of peace in discipleship, moral character and moral formation, which has clear implications for peacemaking today, although these are not worked out in particular detail.[20]

d. Roman Catholic and Orthodox work

There has been a greater interest in the use of the Bible in ethics among Roman Catholics since Vatican II declared that Catholic moral theology 'should be more thoroughly nourished by scriptural teaching'.[21] Josef Blank considers the standard stress on the plurality of ethics contained in the New Testament, but sees a unity in the command to love.[22] Curran and McCormick have analysed the link in four stages, looking at the original meaning of the text, its meaning today and how it relates to different approaches within moral theology and to the other sources of moral guidance, such as reason and tradition.[23] However, from a Protestant perspective, Hauerwas criticised McCormick for stressing natural law and reason rather than deriving an ethic from Jesus or the revelation in the scriptural narrative.[24] On the other hand, the Catholic Biblical Asso-

19. Brian K. Blount, *Then the Whisper Put on Flesh: New Testament Ethics in an African American Context* (Nashville: Abingdon, 2001); quotations from pp. 185-86.

20. Willard M. Swartley, *Covenant of Peace: The Missing Peace in New Testament Theology and Ethics* (Grand Rapids: Eerdmans, 2006).

21. The Decree on Priestly Formation, *Optatam Totius*, 16, promulgated Oct. 28, 1965; *The Documents of Vatican II*, ed. Walter M. Abbott, S.J. (London: Geoffrey Chapman, 1966), p. 452.

22. Josef Blank, 'Unity and Plurality in New Testament Ethics', in *Christian Ethics: Uniformity, Universality, Pluralism*, eds. J. Pohier and R. Mieth, *Concilium* 150 (New York: Seabury, 1981), pp. 65-71.

23. Charles E. Curran and Richard A. McCormick, S.J., eds., *Readings in Moral Theology No. 4: The Use of Scripture in Moral Theology* (New York: Paulist, 1984); see pp. vi-vii.

24. See, for example, S. Hauerwas, *A Community of Character* (Notre Dame, IN: University of Notre Dame Press, 1981), p. 39; idem, *The Peaceable Kingdom* (London: SCM, 1984), pp. 59-60, 64; for further critique, see Michael E. Allsopp, 'The Role of Sacred Scripture in Richard A. McCormick's Ethics', *Chicago Studies* 35.2 (1996), pp. 185-96.

ciation set up a Task Force on New Testament Ethics, some of whose papers were published as *Christian Biblical Ethics,* concentrating mainly on issues of method, with a number of case studies on specific texts.[25] Collins collected a number of his articles together deliberately as a response to the call of Vatican II to explore the scriptures and ethics within a Catholic perspective.[26] Spohn updated and expanded his study on the use of scripture in Christian ethics, which includes Bonhoeffer and Barth, natural law traditions, liberation theologians, narrative approaches of people like Hauerwas, and the response to love, as in H. Richard Niebuhr.[27] However, this is still at the level of method and hermeneutical theory, what Bretzke calls the 'second stage' of the response to Vatican II's call; this methodology needs to be worked out better, but also to go on to a third stage of 'concrete application to the particularities of Christian ethics'.[28] Spohn also responded to the call of Vatican II. He notes that 'in the pre–Vatican II Catholicism in which I was raised, the person of Jesus played an important role in devotional life while being largely ignored in Catholic moral theology'. Therefore his next book was a deliberate attempt to combine biblical studies, especially work on the historical Jesus, with the Catholic tradition of virtue ethics and relate both to contemporary spiritual practices, especially the Jesuit use of imaginative engagement with the text.[29] It is interesting that Guroian's treatment on the Bible and ethics from an Orthodox perspective stresses the importance of the ecclesial and liturgical context leading to a 'typological hermeneutic', yet it includes how this might affect a concrete issue, that of surrogacy in the 'Baby M' case.[30]

e. Worldwide

Thus it can be argued that a clear direction has been established in British, German and American scholarship, as well as within Roman Catholic writings, that

25. Robert J. Daly, S.J., ed., *Christian Biblical Ethics. From Biblical Revelation to Contemporary Christian Praxis: Method and Content* (New York: Paulist, 1984).

26. Raymond F. Collins, *Christian Morality: Biblical Foundations* (Notre Dame, IN: University of Notre Dame Press, 1986).

27. William C. Spohn, *What Are They Saying about Scripture and Ethics?* (New York: Paulist, 1984; 2nd rev. edn., 1995).

28. James T. Bretzke, S.J., 'Scripture: The "Soul" of Moral Theology? — The Second Stage', *Irish Theological Quarterly* 60.4 (1994), pp. 259-71; quotation from p. 270.

29. William C. Spohn, *Go and Do Likewise: Jesus and Ethics* (New York: Continuum, 1999); quotation from p. 185.

30. Vigen Guroian, 'Bible and Ethics: An Ecclesial and Liturgical Interpretation', *Journal of Religious Ethics* 18.1 (1990), pp. 129-57.

the proper study of New Testament ethics is an analysis of its main writings; with a few honourable exceptions such as Schrage and Spohn, most scholars concentrate on the final form of the books to the detriment of any serious consideration of Jesus. Furthermore, any attempt to relate it to today will be a brief conclusion about the problems or methods of so doing, rather than anything about its specific content.

This same approach is reflected elsewhere. Thus in Scandinavia, Gerhardsson looked at the ethos of the whole Bible, while Moxnes argued that the particularity of the New Testament makes it difficult to be 'directly applied to our situation' universally.[31] In Italy, Segalla looked at both the story of ethics in the New Testament and the hermeneutical and methodological problems.[32] From France, Léon-Dufour does stand out somewhat from the trend in the way he begins with the 'fundamental experience of Jesus' in his preaching of the kingdom of God; however, his method is rather undermined by his outdated contrasting of the Synoptics with the Fourth Gospel in every chapter; however, he is to be commended for his attempt to engage 'the realities of this world', such as money, sexuality and society, towards the end of the book, although they are not worked out in detail.[33] Various review articles summarizing and analysing many of the above books translated these ideas and approaches into Norwegian (Moxnes), Spanish (Verdes) and German (Horn).[34] Similar review articles in more general journals introduced such books to wider audiences from various traditions, Catholic, liberal and evangelical, on both sides of the Atlantic, such as those by Perkins, Hays, Platten and Wright.[35] Therefore it should not be surprising that this overall approach of ignoring Jesus and contemporary application was also communicated in South Africa under apartheid through articles written both by those from out-

31. B. Gerhardsson, *The Ethos of the Bible*, trans. S. Westerholm (Philadelphia: Fortress, 1981/ London: DLT, 1982); H. Moxnes, 'New Testament Ethics — Universal or Particular?' *Studia Theologia* 47 (1993), pp. 153-68; quotation from p. 163.

32. G. Segalla, *Introduzione all' etica del Nuovo Testamento*, Biblioteca Bíblica 2 (Brescia: Queriniana, 1989).

33. Xavier Léon-Dufour, *To Act according to the Gospel* (Peabody, MA: Hendrickson, 2005).

34. H. Moxnes, 'Eskatologisk eksistens: Nytestamentlige bidrag til etikken', *Norsk Teologisk Tidsskrift* 92 (Oslo, 1991), pp. 1-13; L. A. Verdes, 'Las Eticas Bíblicas del Nuevo Testamento', *Estudios Biblicos* 48.1 (Madrid, 1990), pp. 113-36; F. W. Horn, 'Ethik des Neuen Testaments 1982-1992', *Theologische Rundschau* 60 (Tübingen, 1995), pp. 32-86.

35. Pheme Perkins, 'New Testament Ethics: Questions and Contexts', *Religious Studies Review* 10.4 (1984), pp. 321-27; R. B. Hays, 'Recent Books on New Testament Ethics', *Quarterly Review* 6.4 (1986), pp. 13-30; Stephen Platten, 'The Biblical Critic and Moral Theologian', *King's Theological Review* 12.1 (1989), pp. 11-17; Chris Wright, 'Biblical Ethics: A Survey of the Last Decade', *Themelios* 18 (1993), pp. 15-19.

side the country, such as Strecker (from Göttingen), and from within it, like Hartin (from Witwatersrand).[36]

f. Evangelical approaches

Evangelicals are traditionally committed to the person of Jesus and to the authority of scripture for everything, and so one would expect them to be different and actually to use the Bible in ethics, starting with Jesus' words. Unfortunately, the temptation has often been to do so in a naive or uncritical manner, simply reading off from the text with an 'answer for today'. However, the last few decades have seen significant developments in this area. In the 1970s, a young evangelical described as a 'recently appointed tutor at Wycliffe Hall, Oxford', Oliver M. T. O'Donovan, argued for the 'Possibility of a Biblical Ethic' and 'Towards an Interpretation of Biblical Ethics' in which he displayed the theological concerns which would lead not much later to his appointment as Regius Professor of Moral and Pastoral Theology at Oxford.[37] He then held this post with distinction for the next quarter of a century, writing several key works on ethics.[38] Meanwhile, Howard Marshall was urging his fellow evangelicals who assume that the Bible is relevant and authoritative for ethics to face the problems in using it today; he urged a middle path between extreme biblicism and the approaches of Nineham, Bultmann, Houlden and J. T. Sanders by looking at the 'underlying theological and ethical principles' behind any biblical exhortation.[39] R. E. O. White's work *Biblical Ethics*, on the other hand, was rather uncritical and never reached through to today, even with its companion volume, *The Insights of History*.[40]

In contrast, Verhey's *The Great Reversal* sought to combine a respect for the authority of scripture with critical scholarship in his comprehensive treatment

36. Georg Strecker, 'The Importance of New Testament Ethics Today', *Journal of Theology for Southern Africa* 25 (1978), pp. 31-40; Patrick Hartin, 'New Testament Ethics: Some Trends in More Recent Research', *JTSA* 59 (1987), pp. 35-41.

37. O. M. T. O'Donovan, 'The Possibility of a Biblical Ethic', *Theological Students Fellowship Bulletin* 67 (1973), pp. 15-23; idem, 'Towards an Interpretation of Biblical Ethics: The Tyndale Biblical Theology Lecture 1975', *Tyndale Bulletin* 27 (1976), pp. 54-78.

38. Oliver O'Donovan, *Resurrection and Moral Order: An Outline for Evangelical Ethics* (Leicester: IVP, 1986); idem, *The Desire of the Nations* (Cambridge: Cambridge University Press, 1995); idem, *The Ways of Judgment: The Bampton Lectures, 2003* (Grand Rapids: Eerdmans, 2005).

39. I. Howard Marshall, 'Using the Bible in Ethics', in *Essays in Evangelical Social Ethics*, ed. David F. Wright (Exeter: Paternoster, 1978), pp. 39-55; quotation from p. 50.

40. R. E. O. White, *Biblical Ethics* (Exeter: Paternoster, 1979); idem, *The Insights of History* (Exeter: Paternoster, 1981); republished together as *Christian Ethics* (Leominster: Gracewing/ Macon, GA: Mercer University Press, 1994).

of the ethical material found in Jesus, the early church and the New Testament writings, ending with a major section on the hermeneutical issue of how we might use the Bible today, although not actually getting to any specific issues.[41] Birch and Rasmussen also want to 'bridge the gap between biblical studies and Christian ethics' in their discussion of the moral life in the Christian community and their examination of decision making and scriptural authority.[42] While these books grapple with the hermeneutical and methodological questions, there is still little in them about what actual content New Testament ethics might bring to today's moral issues. D. C. Jones' study, *Biblical Christian Ethics,* defines it as 'a way of life that conforms to the will of God as revealed in Christ and the holy scriptures', which, after a study of love and the Ten Commandments, does conclude with two chapters on the family, marriage and divorce.[43]

g. Historical and sociological enquiry

Thus this survey so far has shown that there was an explosion of books and articles about New Testament ethics in the last couple of decades of the twentieth century, but that the majority contain only analyses of the ethical material found in the books of the New Testament, often to the neglect of Jesus himself. Some do conclude with some discussion of whether and how this material might be used today, but there is little (if anything) about which aspects of New Testament ethics might impinge on the issues facing us.

Indeed, others argue that we cannot bridge this gap at all. Thus Wayne Meeks (from Yale) began his presidential address to the Society of Biblical Literature in November 1985 by stressing the importance of not confusing historical research into early Christian ethics with later ethical discourse, including our own day. He wanted to confine his study to 'historical inquiry only'. Such historical enquiry concerns the 'history of communities' and the 'moral universe of the first Christian groups'. He followed up this lecture with two books concentrating on the early Christian communities a couple of centuries around the writing of the New Testament, but, once again, ignoring Jesus.[44] Others, too, such as Moxnes and

41. Allen Verhey, *The Great Reversal: Ethics and the New Testament* (Grand Rapids: Eerdmans, 1984).

42. Bruce C. Birch and Larry L. Rasmussen, *Bible and Ethics in the Christian Life,* rev. and exp. edn. (Minneapolis: Augsburg, 1989), p. 7.

43. D. C. Jones, *Biblical Christian Ethics* (Grand Rapids: Baker, 1994), p. 16.

44. W. A. Meeks, 'Understanding Early Christian Ethics', *JBL* 105.1 (1986), pp. 3-11; p. 3; idem, *The Moral World of the First Christians* (London: SPCK, 1987); *The Origins of Christian Morality* (New Haven, CT: Yale University Press, 1993).

Theissen, have followed this sociological, community-based approach.[45] Ian Mc-Donald has built upon his work, *Biblical Interpretation and Christian Ethics*, with a study of the early Christian communities in the Jewish, Hellenistic and Christian 'crucible' of the first century, but once again refers only to the 'remembered' or 'recollected' teachings of Jesus who started it all off.[46] He concludes that Christian morality today needs to be forged in the crucible of our world — but how and what the New Testament might contribute is not described. So these approaches based on early Christian communities get us no further back towards Jesus nor any closer forward to today than did the historical.

h. More recent application to today

Yet the paradox is that people today, outside the Christian church as much, if not more, than within, still go on talking about Jesus as 'a great moral teacher', up there in the popular pantheon with Socrates, Buddha and so forth.[47] On the other hand, many books on contemporary ethical dilemmas fail to include, let alone grapple with, the New Testament material at all. After all this outpouring of scholarship upon the subject of the ethics of the New Testament writings, it is high time that this gulf between Jesus and today's moral issues was bridged. Interestingly, Leander Keck, also from Yale, gave his presidential address to the SBL ten years after Meeks'; in it he stressed that 'the defining feature of New Testament Ethics is its orientation to an event, namely, the event of Jesus', and so he called for a 'rethinking of New Testament Ethics'.[48]

Therefore, this survey must conclude with a few writers in the last decade or so who have actually begun the process of connecting the New Testament, especially the material about Jesus, with some ethical issues today. Stephen Mott set out to convince an (evangelical?) readership which accepts the authority of the Bible about the need for social involvement and justice, looking at evangelism, attitudes towards government, civil disobedience and violence.[49] Although some of his handling of the text, especially in such broad general terms, has been

---

45. H. Moxnes, 'New Testament Ethics — Universal or Particular?' *Studia Theologia* 47 (1993), pp. 153-68; G. Theissen, *Social Reality and the Early Christians: Theology, Ethics and the World of the New Testament,* trans. M. Kohl (Minneapolis: Fortress/Edinburgh: T&T Clark, 1993).

46. J. I. H. McDonald, *Biblical Interpretation and Christian Ethics* (Cambridge: Cambridge University Press, 1993); idem, *The Crucible of Christian Morality* (London: Routledge, 1998); the index to the latter does not even include 'Jesus'!

47. See A. McGrath, 'In What Way Can Jesus Be a Moral Example for Christians?' *Journal of the Evangelical Theological Society* 34 (1991), pp. 289-98.

48. L. E. Keck, 'Rethinking "New Testament Ethics"', *JBL* 115.1 (1996), pp. 3-16; p. 10.

49. Stephen C. Mott, *Biblical Ethics and Social Change* (Oxford: Oxford University Press, 1982).

criticised, his attempt to relate the Bible to today has been widely welcomed. Similarly, Richard Longenecker attempted to relate the New Testament to social ethics today, beginning with some hermeneutical discussion which leads to the idea of 'the principles of the gospel'; then he applied Gal. 3.28 to racism, slavery and sexism.[50] It is a good attempt in a brief compass, but New Testament social ethics includes more than one verse of Paul, important though Gal. 3.28 is; this takes us back to our observation about the absence of Jesus in much scholarship on New Testament ethics. Equally, the issues of today are more manifold than these three topics. Countryman has a similarly limited focus in his more extended treatment of sexual ethics in the New Testament and their implications for today; by concentrating on the concepts of purity and property, he developed an interesting and original reading of the texts and raises a wide range of sexual ethical issues at the end.[51] However, at the same time, his concern for purity and property leads him to consider them in the context of Judaism and the ancient Mediterranean, Acts, the four gospels and Paul's writings, without much about Jesus himself. His new edition, updated after nearly twenty years, includes an important new chapter about other principles of sexual ethics in the New Testament, erotic relationships, the social and cultural context, creation ethics and liberation theology, but again with little on Jesus.[52]

After these essays' more limited scope, we come to Richard Hays' comprehensive attempt to analyse both the 'moral vision of the New Testament' and the hermeneutical problems of applying it to today, concluding with consideration of five contemporary issues (violence, divorce, homosexuality, anti-Judaism and abortion), which are notable for arising out of their context in contemporary American debate rather than being the most central topics of the New Testament.[53] From the point of view of our three issues, it is significant that Hays begins with Paul and the four canonical gospels before asking, after 150 pages, in an excursus, 'Why not begin with Jesus?' His answer, as noted with others above, relates to the problems of the historical reconstruction of Jesus, so he supplies his own brief attempt in a couple of pages.[54] While this book reflects Hays' background as a Pauline scholar and its American context, it has quickly established

50. Richard N. Longenecker, *New Testament Social Ethics for Today* (Grand Rapids: Eerdmans, 1984).

51. L. William Countryman, *Dirt, Greed and Sex: Sexual Ethics in the New Testament and Their Implications for Today* (Philadelphia: Fortress, 1988/London: SCM, 1989).

52. L. William Countryman, *Dirt, Greed and Sex: Sexual Ethics in the New Testament and Their Implications for Today*, rev. 2nd edn. (Minneapolis: Fortress, 2007).

53. Richard B. Hays, *The Moral Vision of the New Testament: A Contemporary Introduction to New Testament Ethics* (San Francisco: HarperSanFrancisco/Edinburgh: T&T Clark, 1996).

54. Hays, *The Moral Vision of the New Testament*, pp. 158-68.

itself as the classic treatment and has been widely appreciated.[55] Therefore, it is a key text with which we will be in dialogue throughout this study.

Writing since Hays, Stassen and Gushee also share our surprise at 'the evasion of Jesus' in Christian ethics; in particular they note that 'the teachings and practices of Jesus . . . are routinely ignored or misinterpreted in the preaching and teaching ministry of the churches and in Christian scholarship in ethics'.[56] Therefore they begin with Jesus' proclamation of the 'reign of God' as summed up in the Sermon on the Mount, which they then apply in detail to various ethical issues of violence, life and death, marriage and sexuality, love, justice, economics and politics. In this weighty and detailed treatment, the writers attempt two of our three concerns, namely some attention to Jesus and application to today, and for this they are to be applauded. Regrettably, the absence of any treatment of genre leads to the abstraction of the Sermon on the Mount from its narrative context within Matthew's gospel; the result is that the 'practices of Jesus', to which they referred at the start, are ignored here as well.

After dealing with the content of New Testament ethics and the hermeneutical issues in his earlier work, more recently Verhey has produced two books of application to today. In *Remembering Jesus,* he seeks to bring together scriptural material about Jesus in the church as 'a community of moral discourse' to handle particular issues of sickness and healing, liberation and sexuality, justice and generosity and, lastly, politics and theocracy, in an engaging and helpful way.[57] His other book is even more practically based as he seeks to

55. See, for instance, the reviews by Francis Watson in *Studies in Christian Ethics* 10.2 (1997), pp. 94-99; Markus Bockmuehl, *ExpT* 109 (1997-98), p. 86; F. J. Matera in *Theological Studies* 58 (1997), pp. 537-39; Colin Hart in *Anvil* 14.4 (1997), pp. 320-21; James T. Bretzke in *Theology Today* 55.1 (April 1998), pp. 97-98; Richard A. Burridge in *JTSA* 102 (1998), pp. 71-73; Richard A. Burridge in *Theology* 101 (799) (1998), pp. 54-55; C. Freedman Sleeper in *Interpretation* 52.2 (April 1998), pp. 200-202; Richard A. Young in *Journal of the Evangelical Theological Society* 42.1 (March 1999), pp. 136-38; and the review articles by Luke Timothy Johnson, 'Why Scripture Isn't Enough', *Commonweal* 124.11 (1997), pp. 23-25; William C. Spohn, 'Is There Such a Thing as New Testament Ethics? A Review Essay of R. B. Hays' *The Moral Vision of the New Testament*', *Christian Century* 114 (May 1997), pp. 525-31; Judith Gundry-Volf, 'Putting the *Moral Vision of the New Testament* into Focus: A Review', *Bulletin for Biblical Research* 9 (1999), pp. 277-87; the most critical reaction is by Dale Martin in *JBL* 117 (1998), pp. 358-60, which makes a number of important points, despite its somewhat intemperate language; he returns to his criticism also in Dale B. Martin, *Sex and the Single Savior: Gender and Sexuality in Biblical Interpretation* (Louisville: Westminster John Knox, 2006), pp. 29-31; see also Horrell's discussion of Hays in David G. Horrell, *Solidarity and Difference: A Contemporary Reading of Paul's Ethics* (London: T&T Clark, 2005), pp. 34-40.

56. Glen H. Stassen and David P. Gushee, *Kingdom Ethics: Following Jesus in Contemporary Context* (Downers Grove, IL: IVP, 2003), p. xi.

57. Allen Verhey, *Remembering Jesus: Christian Community, Scripture, and the Moral Life* (Grand Rapids: Eerdmans, 2002).

apply biblical teaching as a whole (not just New Testament or Jesus material) to specific medical issues like the human genome, stem cell research, assisted reproduction, euthanasia and so forth.[58]

In conclusion, it is significant that after this exhaustive survey of scholarship from around the world and across the various traditions, it is only more recently that a few scholars like Hays and Verhey have really attempted to bridge the gap between the New Testament ethical material and the multiple nature of moral issues today. Furthermore, even Hays follows the more usual habit of not starting with Jesus, but concentrates instead on the final finished form of Paul and the gospels. Finally, practically no one has addressed the issue of genre or faced the fact that the New Testament is simply *not* an ethical treatise or book of moral instructions. Since these three aspects have dominated my own work and writing over the last couple of decades, we now need to turn to this particular author's own context.

2. The personal context of this project

Since this book will advocate a biographical approach to ethics, it may be helpful to set this project within the context of the author's own biography. For over thirty years, I have been studying the New Testament in its literary setting within the first-century world of classical literature, particularly in terms of the relationship of the gospels to ancient biography. This started with my first degree, in classics, which excited and interested me in the whole area of literary theory and the ancient historical context. After leaving Oxford, I became a classics teacher, but I was also involved in helping with the school chaplaincy, which led me to give General Studies courses on how a classicist might view the New Testament material. Then, as part of my later theological education and training for ordination, I was able to work on a doctorate on the literary genre of the canonical gospels, trying to set them within the literary environment of the ancient Mediterranean. I continued this combination through my academic teaching both at Exeter University and at King's College London, following up the Christological implications of the biographical genre of the gospels with their concentration on the person of Jesus. This stress of how we might read and teach the person of Jesus through the gospels in a way that is relevant for today has also informed all my writing, including my previous books. At the same time, I have also been writing, teaching and speaking about ethics and

58. Allen Verhey, *Reading the Bible in the Strange World of Medicine* (Grand Rapids: Eerdmans, 2003).

moral issues. This project is therefore an attempt to bring these various fields — of Jesus and the gospels, genre and literary theory, ethics and a concern for the world today — all together, particularly since the above review of the literature has demonstrated that it is precisely these three aspects which seem to be overlooked by many scholars in this area of how we use the New Testament in ethics today.

a. Biblical debate

I grew up and was educated in the English local parish church school tradition, going on to a Cathedral School for secondary education, with its catholic stress on the sacraments, the evangelical emphasis on the Bible and a liberal concern for the contemporary world. As an undergraduate I trained as a lay Reader for the Church of England. A decade later I was ordained, undertaking ministry in both local churches and in universities. Over this period, I was nurtured and formed within the evangelical tradition of taking the Bible seriously and seeking to apply it as the authority and guide for today. Thus my academic background means that I cannot accept the one extreme of simply reading straight off from the text to today's issues, while my life of faith means that these documents can never be of merely archaeological interest at the other extreme. In my work among the churches, and especially over more than a decade representing the University of London in the General Synod of the Church of England, I have heard many debates between those who claim that their views are the only ones which are 'biblical' or 'scriptural' and those who argue that these writings are outdated or cannot be applied to today. At academic conferences of the Society for New Testament Studies (SNTS) and the Society of Biblical Literature (SBL), I have heard the same issue recur repeatedly in various papers and presentations. Through my travels and invitations to preach and teach abroad, I have become aware of its significance for churches across Europe and the United States as different Christian traditions have grappled with ethical debate and contemporary moral issues. Therefore this practical need to apply the New Testament ethical material today, arising from my work and ministry, has impacted upon my academic study and research to drive this project.

b. South Africa

The other significant context over the last decade while I have been reflecting on this project has been my involvement with Africa. I have been privileged to be involved a little with theological education in West Africa, and to see how the church and ministry training might face the issue of inculturation there, both through visiting Ghana for an Anglican Communion partners-in-mission consultation and subsequently bringing postgraduates from there to supervise their doctorates at King's College London. Even more significant has been the honour of continuing the tradition of the Dean of King's working in partnership with South Africa, which goes back over many decades to sponsoring the training of many South Africans in London, including Archbishop Desmond Tutu.[59] Over the last ten years or so since the birth of the new democracy there, I have visited South Africa regularly to work with both the churches and the universities. I have undertaken research and given lectures in various university theological departments which spanned the different racial, linguistic and social groupings of the old South Africa under apartheid, as well as doing clergy training across several dioceses, in my capacity as Commissary for the Bishop of the High Veld (the area between east Johannesburg and Swaziland). I was also able to visit and interview Archbishop Desmond Tutu on a number of occasions, including at the Truth and Reconciliation Commission, as well as hosting him as Visiting Professor in Post-Conflict Societies for a term back at King's in spring 2004.

South Africa is, nominally at least, a highly Christian country, with perhaps 70 percent of the population actively involved in church. As we have already noted, over the last century the Bible has been applied to today in various ways, both to support apartheid and in the struggle for liberation and the new multiracial South Africa. Throughout this period, New Testament study has thrived in South African universities, and I was able to be closely involved in the first visit of the SNTS to Africa for its annual conference, at the University of Pretoria in 1999, which included a following conference with African biblical scholars at Hammanskraal.[60] Meanwhile, the New Testament continues to be used regularly in South Africa outside academia, in churches and colleges, cities and townships, urban or rural settings, again often as an authority or guide for today.[61] South Africa has therefore provided the backdrop and context for my thinking throughout this project, and so we shall return to it again in the final

59. See Allen, *Rabble-Rouser for Peace*, pp. 77-99; Richard A. Burridge, 'Praying at 125mph', in *Tutu As I Know Him: On a Personal Note*, ed. Lavinia Crawford-Browne (Roggebaai: Umuzi, Random House, 2006), pp. 89-93; see also Janet Dyson, 'Students at King's', in the same volume, pp. 24-28.

60. Subsequently published as *Interpreting the New Testament in Africa*, eds. Mary Getui, Tinyiko Maluleke and Justin Ukpong (Nairobi: Acton, 2001).

61. See especially the work of Gerald West from the University of Kwa Zulu Natal, and his Ujamaa Centre, as discussed in Chapter VIII, sect. 6.d, pp. 402-4 below.

chapter as our 'test-case' against which to examine whatever conclusions emerge from this study.

Thus my own personal struggle to read the gospels today in the light of their biographical presentation of Jesus and to apply New Testament ethical material to contemporary moral issues is repeated in many situations in both church and academic contexts around the world. However much some academics may protest, people will go on using the New Testament for ethical guidance, while, on the other hand, the critical questions about this process continue to be asked, however uncomfortable some Christians may find that. What both sides need, therefore, is to find the right way in for a proper method for this application today.

3. The biographical context of the gospels' genre

It is remarkable that, despite the outpouring of scholarly work upon New Testament ethics, nobody has grappled with the obvious basic fact that the New Testament is not itself an ethical work in the manner, say, of Aristotle's *Nicomachean Ethics,* nor does it contain any books written in the genre of ethical treatise. So why is there this obsession with New Testament ethics? It clearly has something to do with the popular assessment of Jesus as one of the world's great moral teachers, as well as fact that throughout the last two millennia, people have used its teachings to argue about ethical issues, despite this not being its literary form. Therefore, in the last section of this introductory chapter, we shall consider these questions about the role of Jesus and the genre of the New Testament books to see if we might find a way to be able to use the New Testament material in ethical debate today.

a. Can we start or finish with Jesus?

Our earlier discussion of the literature revealed that in contrast to the more 'popular' approach, particularly in some evangelical writings, of concentrating on 'What would Jesus say?' in a naive or uncritical manner, most scholars, with one or two exceptions, do not discuss the ethics of Jesus at all. Thus, at one extreme, Wayne Meeks notes, 'I do not have a chapter on "the ethics of Jesus" . . . it is both elusive . . . and beside the point'; his task is to describe the 'moral world' of the first Christians.[62] In his next book, Meeks portrays himself as an 'ethnographer'

---

62. Meeks, *Moral World,* p. 16.

out to interpret the *ethnos* which was the early church; thus the only time Jesus even gets mentioned is in his accounts of the 'stories of Jesus' told by Paul and the evangelists.[63] Shifting his metaphor, Meeks describes his work more in archaeological terms as 'some preliminary trenches . . . not a complete excavation,'[64] so it is perhaps not surprising, though still disappointing, that he does not reach bedrock! Matera agrees with him: 'The work of historical reconstruction is not the primary object of New Testament ethics. Indeed it is not even the proper prolegomenon to this discipline'. He too uses the archaeological metaphor to argue that excavations 'start with the most recent stratum and then work back to what is earlier'. Like Meeks, Matera never actually gets down that far, but will confine himself to the 'ethical legacy' of Jesus in each of the gospels.[65] As noted above, Richard Hays takes nearly 160 pages before he gets round to asking 'Why not begin with Jesus?' He prefers to start with the New Testament canonical witness since the attempt to reconstruct the historical Jesus is beset with so many problems, particularly in the light of the versions produced by the 'Jesus Seminar' (a group based mainly in the USA committed to a critical reconstruction of Jesus).[66] In order to avoid mistaking our own 'subjectivity and cultural bias' for the historical Jesus behind the text, Hays moves from using the text for historical reconstruction to concentrate instead on its relationship with the reader.[67]

So, according to such approaches, if we are to talk of the ethics of Jesus at all, it should only be at the end of the process. Leslie Houlden stresses that Jesus may be at the centre of the New Testament writings — but for that reason we cannot start with him; instead we have to start by understanding all the different writers' views of him and the development of the traditions: 'Jesus, in other words, is to be found at the end not at the beginning of an inquiry'.[68] Marxsen thinks we cannot read the historical Jesus straight off the text, but his work on the redaction of the gospel writers is an attempt to allow us to find the 'ethics oriented toward Jesus', having made allowances for the interpretation of the evangelists and other writers.[69] J. T. Sanders did begin his original account with

63. Meeks, *Origins*, pp. 8-11; 195-207.
64. Meeks, *Origins*, p. 17.
65. Matera, *NT Ethics*, pp. 7-8.
66. Hays, *The Moral Vision*, Chapter 7, 'Excursus: The Role of "the Historical Jesus" in New Testament Ethics', pp. 158-68.
67. Although when it is necessary for his argument, for example, over anti-Judaism, Hays is quite willing to use the 'historical' reconstructions of modern scholars (see pp. 154-55 and pp. 407-43) — a criticism which is also noted by Watson's review in *Studies in Christian Ethics* 10.2 (1997), pp. 94-99, especially pp. 96 and 98.
68. Houlden, *Ethics and the NT*, p. 4.
69. W. Marxsen, *New Testament Foundations*, pp. 28-59.

Jesus, but in his revised edition he has changed his mind, saying that 'what should be done' is to start with the Synoptic gospels and work back through the tradition 'to see what could be made of Jesus'.[70] Ian McDonald also begins with the early Christian communities, but he is going around in more of a circle, working his way back through Q and Mark to what the early church 'remembered' or 'recollected' of Jesus' teachings, but then he quickly moves back out again into the ideas of the ancient world.[71]

After all the books not dealing with Jesus, or doing so only at the end of the enquiry, it is significant (and brave?) that both Schrage and Verhey do begin with Jesus. Schrage devotes over one hundred pages to 'Jesus' eschatological ethics' and only then moves to the gospels and to Paul and the rest of the New Testament, which shares this 'theological or christological foundation'.[72] Verhey also starts with the 'ethic of Jesus' to understand 'the origin and impetus of the moral tradition' which develops that 'this Jesus is Lord'.[73] In response to the concerns of Houlden and Marxsen, both writers still use historical-critical methods in their treatment of Jesus.

This is surely the right place to begin. Admittedly, Meeks and Matera are correct in their metaphor that archaeologists begin digging with the most recent layer and work down to the earliest in their excavations — and any attempt to excavate the ethics of Jesus must similarly work *backwards* from the text and evidence. However, when the archaeological report is written up, it will often begin by describing the bottom layer first: what is crucial is why this site was settled in the first place, or the reasons why there is anything there at all. Only then do they trace the story *forward* to show how the building, the site or the city grew and developed from these earliest beginnings. The same process is true for us. We cannot avoid the hard work of critical exploration and reconstruction, but in this attempt to relate New Testament ethics to today, we must begin with Keck's 'event of Jesus', which starts it all off.[74] Without this, there is nothing there at all. Only from this beginning, in the person and teaching of Jesus, can we trace the story forward through the gospels and the letters, as the impact of Jesus is demonstrated by their central Christological concerns. After that process, like the archaeologist following the development right through to the modern level of the concrete surface, so we may come to today's specific ethical issues and the use of the Bible in places like South Africa under apartheid.

70. J. T. Sanders, *Ethics in the NT*, 2nd edn., p. xii.

71. McDonald, *The Crucible of Christian Morality;* see the plan of his approach outlined on pp. 10-11.

72. Schrage, *The Ethics of the NT,* pp. 13-115; quotation from p. 8.

73. Verhey, *Great Reversal,* p. 4.

74. Keck, 'Rethinking "New Testament Ethics"', p. 10.

b. Historical and literary approaches to the gospels

Therefore, the next question must be how we get back to the earliest layer of the person and teaching of Jesus. As the brief description of the personal context revealed above, such a relatively unusual, Christological, Jesus-centred approach to using the New Testament in ethics arises out of my previous work on the gospels. Therefore, we need to go back a little, and work out what kind of books the gospels are and how they portray Jesus of Nazareth.

Central to all communication theory is the threefold model of transmitter-communication-receiver. Thus literary critics can speak of a triangle of relationships in reading — the author, the text and the reader. Obviously, 'author' includes everyone who has to do with the production of the text — author or authors, editors or revisers, those who have formed or passed on the material until it reaches its final form — while 'reader' includes everyone who has to do with its reception, which goes beyond the modern individual silent reader to the audience who may listen to the text being read, or who watch its performance, or the group within which the text is preserved and handed on. In between author and audience, however, comes the crucial question of the communication itself — what is the nature of the text, and how does it function?

Alongside the triangle of relationships of author, text and reader, we want to place a second triangle of images of reading: windows, mirrors and stained glass. Much historical-critical study of the gospels treats the gospels as though they are some kind of *window* through which modern readers and scholars can look back at what lies 'behind' or 'beyond' the text — the world of the author, or of those who produced the text. Thus both the Quest for the Historical Jesus and the New Quest of Käsemann and others used the gospels as 'windows' through which they looked for material about Jesus himself.[75] This is also true of the so-called Third Quest, locating Jesus within Judaism from Vermes through Sanders to Wright, as well as the accounts coming from the likes of Crossan and the Jesus Seminar.[76] If such scholars use the gospels as 'windows' onto the historical Jesus, many form critics used them as windows onto the

---

75. A. Schweitzer, *Geschichte der Leben-Jesu-Forschung* (Tübingen: Mohr, 1906); ET *The Quest of the Historical Jesus* (London: A & C Black, 1954); J. M. Robinson, *A New Quest of the Historical Jesus*, SBT 25 (London: SCM, 1959).

76. G. Vermes, *Jesus the Jew* (London: Collins, 1973); E. P. Sanders, *Jesus and Judaism* (London: SCM, 1985); N. T. Wright, *Christian Origins and the Question of God*: vol. 1, *The New Testament and the People of God* (London: SPCK, 1992); vol. 2, *Jesus and the Victory of God* (London: SPCK, 1996); J. D. Crossan, *The Historical Jesus: The Life of a Mediterranean Jewish Peasant* (San Francisco: HarperCollins/Edinburgh: T&T Clark, 1991); R. W. Funk, R. W. Hoover and the Jesus Seminar, *The Five Gospels: The Search for the Authentic Words of Jesus* (New York: Macmillan, 1993).

early churches in the search for their *Sitz im Leben,* while redaction critics and proponents of sociological analysis have looked through them to the 'communities' within which and for which they were written — notably, of course, all the work on the Johannine community.[77]

However, in recent decades there has been a reaction to this use of the gospels as 'windows' to look through at what lies behind the text. After all, we do not know who wrote them, or when, or for whom. What historical critics think they see *behind* the text may just be their own concerns reflected from *in front of* the text. Thus many modern literary approaches view texts as more like *mirrors* than windows. The quest for the author and authorial intention, and for the group or community which may have produced an ancient text are all merely puzzling reflections of our own presuppositions. In reality, we simply have the text and the reader. Thus the structuralist Roland Barthes could speak of 'the death of the author', allowing us to concentrate solely on reader and text: he concludes, 'The birth of the reader must be at the cost of the death of the Author'.[78] Furthermore, while the historical methods tended to dismember the texts to get behind them, such literary approaches focus on the final form of the text as a unified whole. Meaning is not to be discerned by the mistaken attempt to discover the author's intention, or the historical context; it may be controlled by the text itself, or in more radical criticism any meaning the reader finds reflected in the text is acceptable. Such reader-response approaches draw heavily on the work of Wolfgang Iser and Stanley Fish.[79] In reply, Kevin Vanhoozer has attempted both to 'resurrect' the author and 'reform' the reader.[80]

c. The genre of the gospels and Graeco-Roman biography

Both approaches, by concentrating on the author at one end or the reader at the other, tend to ignore the question of the genre of the text as a whole as the

77. For a critique of such community approaches, see *The Gospels for All Christians,* ed. R. Bauckham (Grand Rapids: Eerdmans/Edinburgh: T&T Clark, 1998), including my chapter 'About People, by People, for People', pp. 113-45 on the implications of the biographical hypothesis for gospel audiences.

78. Roland Barthes, 'La Mort de l'auteur', *Mantéia* 5 (1968), ET 'The Death of the Author', in *Image, Music, Text,* trans. Stephen Heath (London: Fontana, 1977), pp. 142-48.

79. See Wolfgang Iser, *The Implied Reader: Patterns of Communication in Prose Fiction from Bunyan to Beckett* (Baltimore: John Hopkins University Press, 1974); idem, *The Art of Reading* (Baltimore: John Hopkins University Press, 1978); Stanley Fish, *Is There a Text in This Class? The Authority of Interpretive Communities* (Cambridge, MA: Harvard University Press, 1980).

80. Kevin J. Vanhoozer, *Is There a Meaning in This Text? The Bible, the Reader and the Morality of Literary Knowledge* (Grand Rapids: Zondervan, 1998).

means of communication between them. Thus some people describe the gospels as 'tragic' or 'dramatic', without recognising that they do not contain any of the formal elements required for ancient drama, such as being in verse, using a chorus and actors and so forth. Such 'adjectival' descriptions of a work are really about its *mode;* thus something which is written in the genre of a 'biography' or an 'epistle' may be tragic or dramatic or historical or elegiac in its mode. Others may say that the gospels are really 'about God' or 'teach the faith', which is true at one level of *content;* but works in other genres, such as epistles, or sermons, or films, may also be 'about God' and 'teach the faith'. A work's genre is communicated though a variety of 'generic features' which include aspects of both form and content to help the reader or audience recognize what the genre is. This is important since genre is a crucial convention for both the composition and interpretation of works: we do not listen to a fairy story in the same way as to a news broadcast!

In my doctoral research, I compared the gospels with ancient 'lives' *(bioi* or *vitae);* the term 'biography' does not appear until the ninth century, and carries too many modern associations. This demonstrated that the gospels share all the same generic features as ancient biographies. They are prose narratives of a medium length (10,000-20,000 words, about the number able to be fitted on a single scroll), with only a bare chronological structure of the subject's birth or arrival on the public scene and their death; in between, they contain stories, sayings and anecdotes about the person, with a constant focus on their words and deeds. The various narrative threads usually come to a climax at the subject's death where they reveal their true character, do their greatest deed or die according to the beliefs expressed earlier in their words. The gospels thus belong to this genre.[81] This means that they need to be interpreted in a biographical way, as an account of Jesus told through the ancient method of narrating a person's deeds and words, in which stories are combined with speeches and sayings, culminating in describing their death to reveal the author's understanding of them.

Thus, to return to our previous images, the gospels are neither clear glass windows, through which we have an unimpeded view of the historical Jesus and the evangelists' communities lying 'behind' them, nor are they mirrors, which merely reflect whatever we bring 'in front of' them. They are more like *stained glass.* It is of course true that one can look through stained glass to what

---

81. For further discussion of this, see Richard A. Burridge, *What Are the Gospels? A Comparison with Graeco-Roman Biography,* SNTSMS 70 (Cambridge: Cambridge University Press, 1992), especially pp. 26-54 on genre theory and pp. 109-259 on the generic features manifested in both ancient lives and the gospels; rev. 2nd ed. (Grand Rapids: Eerdmans, 2004), pp. 25-52 and 105-307.

lies on the other side — but it can be indistinct and coloured by the glass. Equally one can use stained glass for reflection as in a mirror — but again it will be unclear, and likely to colour all we see. However, the main point about stained glass is the picture *within* the glass, how the artist has composed it in a limited space and used the conventions about depicting the hero or saint, what has been included and what left out. Similarly, of course, the gospels can be used for historical research into the person of Jesus or possible reconstructions of the early church — but the results will always lack definition and be coloured by the evangelists' interests and intentions. They can also be used to reflect upon our contemporary concerns, as we intend to do later in this book, but allowance always must be made for their own colouring, as well as the need to beware of introducing a reflection of our own concerns into the picture. But first and foremost, the gospels are narrative accounts written within the conventions of ancient biography, on a limited canvas, with some things included and others omitted, in order to bring out each evangelist's particular portrait of Jesus' ministry and teaching, his deeds and words, his life, death and resurrection. Therefore, every gospel passage or pericope is part of the evangelist's depiction of Jesus — and is to be interpreted in that way. Christology is thus the biographical key to the gospels' hermeneutic.

d. Biographical narratives of Jesus' words and deeds

The first implication of this biographical-narrative approach to the gospels relates to the popular view, already mentioned, of Jesus as a great moral teacher, often mediated through Hollywood epic or films about Jesus. In contrast, the biographical hypothesis makes it clear that the gospels are not just, or even primarily, collections of Jesus' teachings. Such documents did exist, such as the *Gospel of Thomas,* which were just lists of sayings, with no narrative about Jesus' life, actions — or even his death. Many later Gnostic gospels, such as the *Apocryphon of James* or *Dialogue of the Saviour,* have even less connection with his life, being primarily revelatory discourses delivered by the risen saviour. It is probable that Q, the source scholars assume was shared by Matthew and Luke (*Quelle,* or 'source' in German, which gives it its abbreviated name), if existed as a document, was a similar collection of sayings with little or no narrative setting. It is notable that Matthew tends to gather the Q teachings together in his sermons and discourses, while Luke often supplies a narrative context for the Q sayings. These tendencies of both evangelists suggest an absence of narrative in Q itself. Furthermore, Matthew and Luke have no shared Q material in their narratives of Jesus' Passion, implying that such a Passion narrative too is missing from Q.[82] Such 'sayings-collections', of course, miss the other aspect of ancient biographies, namely the narrative of the subject's deeds and activities which provides the context for the sayings.

It is thus not surprising that some New Testament scholars who give priority to Q and *Thomas* as the earliest evidence for the historical Jesus end up stressing his role as a teacher or dispenser of wisdom sayings in the manner of an ancient Hellenistic sage or a wandering Cynic, more than a Jewish prophet.[83] Burton Mack developed this idea with his account of Jesus as a wandering teacher based upon his reconstruction of the earliest levels of Q as opposed to Mark's later distorting narrative.[84] On top of this, Crossan's added stress on *Thomas* and other collections of sayings leads naturally to his portrait of Jesus as a teacher expounding what Crossan calls his 'brokerless kingdom'.[85] Such views have two main implications for Jesus' ethics. First his teaching is seen as sociopolitical rather than apocalyptic; Crossan's 'brokerless' Jesus undermines the power structures and '-isms' of the Roman empire. Second, its wisdom-philosophical base means that Jesus' teaching is directed more towards the imagination and mind — 'look at it like this', like eastern riddles — than at the heart and will — 'repent and believe', like the words of old Jewish prophets. This is all a result of giving Q and *Thomas* priority over the canonical gospels, putting the focus simply on Jesus' teaching, like that of any other wisdom teacher, but the consequence is the lack of narration of Jesus' deeds as found in the gospels.

What is more surprising is that many approaches to the ethics of Jesus within a more Jewish background also treat the canonical gospels as though

82. Larry W. Hurtado, *Lord Jesus Christ: Devotion to Jesus in Earliest Christianity* (Grand Rapids: Eerdmans, 2003), pp. 274-76 debates my linking of Q and *Thomas*, and argues that there is a 'narrative substructure' underlying Q's arrangement, pp. 244-48; while this may be true, it remains the case that Q's genre is likely to be closer to a sayings collection than to a continuous prose narrative like ancient biography.

83. See F. Gerald Downing, *Christ and the Cynics: Jesus and Other Radical Preachers in First-Century Tradition*, JSOT Manuals 4 (Sheffield: Sheffield Academic Press, 1988); see also Downing's other writings, especially his 'Cynics and Christians', *NTS*, 30 (1984), pp. 584-93; 'Ears to Hear', in *Alternative Approaches to New Testament Study*, ed. A. E. Harvey (London: SPCK, 1985), pp. 97-121; 'The Social Contexts of Jesus the Teacher: Construction or Reconstruction', *NTS* 33 (1987), pp. 439-51.

84. Burton L. Mack, *A Myth of Innocence: Mark and Christian Origins* (Philadelphia: Fortress, 1988); idem, *The Lost Gospel: The Book of Q and Christian Origins* (San Francisco: HarperCollins, 1993) and 'Q and a Cynic-Like Jesus', in William E. Arnal and Michel Desjardins (eds.), *Whose Historical Jesus?* Studies in Christianity and Judaism 7 (Waterloo, ON: Wilfrid Laurier University Press, 1997), pp. 25-36.

85. Crossan, The *Historical Jesus*; idem, *Jesus Parallels: A Workbook for the Jesus Tradition*, 2nd edn. (Philadelphia: Fortress, 1991).

they were simply like these collections of sayings and concentrate only on his teaching and words. This often involves a debate about whether his ethics are derived from wisdom traditions or from Jewish eschatology.[86] The stress on teaching is obvious within the sapiential tradition, but those who stress the eschatological background also see Jesus as a teacher. Thus, even scholars as keen on eschatology as Chilton and McDonald can begin their work with, 'Jesus of Nazareth is probably most famous, among believers and non-believers, as a teacher of morality'.[87] Equally, Lohse's 'Christological grounding of early Christian ethics' stresses the 'words of the Lord', concentrating on Jesus' sayings and parables.[88] Schrage's huge treatment of 'Jesus' eschatological ethics' similarly concentrates on his sayings and teaching, and it is the 'sayings of Jesus' which get taken into the 'ethical beginnings in the earliest congregations'.[89] From the other side of the Atlantic, Verhey also describes the 'ethic of Jesus' predominantly through his teaching; even when he examines the 'tradition of Jesus' words and deeds' in the 'beginnings of a moral tradition', the emphasis is squarely on the words rather than the deeds.[90] Thus, whether Jesus' teaching is seen as a form of wisdom or based on Jewish apocalyptic or eschatology, such a stress on the teaching itself means that the biographical link of words and deeds, of Jesus' teaching with the rest of his life, is lost.

On the other hand, there is a strong Protestant tradition which reacts against the picture of Jesus as just a good moral teacher. Instead, this approach stresses the saving work of Jesus through his cross, death and resurrection, reading the gospels through Paul's emphasis on Jesus' death and resurrection. Such a focus on Jesus as Saviour ignores both his teaching and the narrative of his deeds and activities, and ends up treating the gospels, in the words of Kähler's famous dictum, as a 'passion narrative with an extended introduction'.[91]

Thus the reconstructions of Jesus as a Hellenistic philosopher or wandering Cynic, together with traditional approaches to his ethics through Jewish

86. See, for example, G. Theissen and A. Merz, *The Historical Jesus: A Comprehensive Guide*, trans. John Bowden (London: SCM, 1998), pp. 348 and 372-81; W. C. Spohn, 'Jesus and Christian Ethics', *Theological Studies* 56 (1995), pp. 92-107, especially the section, 'Subversive Sage or Eschatological Prophet?', pp. 96-101.

87. B. Chilton and J. I. H. McDonald, *Jesus and the Ethics of the Kingdom* (London: SPCK, 1987), p. 1.

88. Lohse, *Theological Ethics*, pp. 25-32.

89. Schrage, *Ethics of the NT*, pp. 18-115, 122-26.

90. Verhey, *Great Reversal*, pp. 6-33, 34-61.

91. M. Kähler, *The So-Called Historical Jesus and the Historic, Biblical Christ* (Philadelphia: Fortress, 1964), p. 80, n. 11.

sapiential or apocalyptic teachings, as well as an evangelical stress simply on his saving death and resurrection, all have this in common, that they have completely missed the biographical narrative of the gospels within which the sayings and teachings, and his sacrificial death, have all been set. Against all of these approaches, the biographical genre of the gospels stands full square with its emphasis on the totality of the portrait in the narrative. Central to all ancient lives is that the picture of the subject is built up through both their words *and* their deeds, through the anecdotes and stories as much as through their sayings or speeches. Furthermore, both the deeds and the words lead up to the account of the person's death, which is often dealt with in some extended detail in ancient lives, as it is in the gospels; often it will also reveal something further about the person's life, or bring the author's major themes to a climax. So to find the heart of Jesus' ethic, we need to consider both his ethical teaching *and* his actual practice. As Luke puts it at the start of Acts, 'In the first book, I wrote about all that Jesus began to do and teach', ἤρξατο ὁ Ἰησοῦς ποιεῖν τε καὶ διδάσκειν (Acts 1.1). This means, therefore, that we will have to look at Jesus' sayings and sermons, but also at his actions, in healing, miracles, and the events narrated, especially over his final days, in order to grasp the full depiction of the evangelists' portraits if we are properly to understand how Jesus' ethics fit into this.

e. The depiction of character within a biographical narrative

The second implication of the biographical genre of the gospels to be considered concerns how other ancient lives are used for ethical instruction. The first thing to notice is that it is not the sole, or even primary purpose of classical biography. Authors tend to use philosophical dialogue or treatise for this, as in the works of Plato and Aristotle. Instead, the primary purpose of ancient biography is to describe a person's life and death according to the particular understanding of the author. Thus both Philo and Lucian want their readers to know what kind of person their subject was: τοιοῦτος μὲν ὁ βίος, Philo, *Moses* 2.292; ὁποίος ἐκεῖνος ἀνὴρ ἐγένετο, Lucian, *Demonax* 67. Similar statements about wanting to inform people about the person and to preserve their memory can be found in many *bioi*. Such intentions were often expressed in a context of debate or argument about someone, and ancient lives were regularly used in polemic and apologetic, to defend or attack a person, or their opponents (see, for example, Xenophon, *Agesilaus* 2.21 or Tacitus, *Agricola* 42.4).

Naturally, to fulfil such aims, *bioi* would include accounts of the person's ideas or teachings, including their ethics when appropriate. Sometimes the ethics of the author can also be seen, as in Plutarch's moral view of the universe (see *Cato Minor* 9.5; 44.7-8; 53.2). Furthermore, Plutarch makes explicit his intention to portray his subject's moral character (*Cato Minor* 24.1; 37.5) and to encourage others to develop their own moral character by imitating their virtues and avoiding their vices (*Pericles* 1; *Aemilius Paullus* 1). Similarly, Xenophon's picture of Agesilaus is an example, παράδειγμα, for others to follow to become better people (ἀνδραγαθίαν ἀσκεῖν, *Agesilaus* 10.2). Such ethical exemplary motives are also expressed by Isocrates (*Evagoras* 73–81) and Lucian (*Demonax* 2).[92] Therefore, although ethical instruction may not be the primary aim of ancient biography, it is clear that such Lives share the purpose of *mimesis*, or imitation, in common with much other classical literature.

These purposes are fulfilled in the author's portrait of the person through their words and deeds, combining sayings and speeches with stories and anecdotes. Obviously, an account of a philosopher like Demonax or a tragedian like Euripides will include more on their teachings and ideas, but there are still the stories and anecdotes in which these are placed. On the other hand, the lives of statesmen and generals like Agesilaus or Agricola are bound to have more on their deeds and actions, but they still include sayings and speeches, as in Agricola's oration before the battle of Mons Graupius (Tacitus, *Agricola* 33–34). Similarly, such active lives will tend to be more chronologically structured, while others are arranged more by topic, such as Satyrus' account of Euripides' ideas on philosophy, religion, women, politics and so forth, while Philo looks at Moses as a king, lawgiver, priest and prophet. While a few *bioi* make an attempt to cover the whole life equally, most concentrate on a particular period which best displays the subject's character, such as Agesilaus' Persian campaign of 396-394 BC (*Agesilaus* 1.6–2.16) or Agricola's battle of Mons Graupius (*Agricola* 29–39). In particular, there is often an extended concentration on the person's final days or death to sum up their life, and to see how they lived out their teaching or displayed their character in the ultimate test; this takes up nearly a tenth of the *Agricola* (43–46), over a sixth of the *Cato Minor* (56–73) and a quarter of Philostratus' *Apollonius of Tyana* (7.1–8.31).[93] Often it is in this final crisis that the real lesson for imitation can be found.

So other ancient *bioi* would lead us not to expect a detailed representation of Jesus' ethical teaching in the gospels, but rather a mixed account of his deeds and words, combining an outline chronology with a topical arrangement to con-

92. See Burridge, *What Are the Gospels?* (1992), pp. 149-52 and 185-88 for further discussion of the purposes of ancient biography; pp. 145-48 and 180-83 in the 2nd edn. (2004).

93. For a full treatment of these lives, see Burridge, *What Are the Gospels?* (1992), Chapters 6 and 7, pp. 128-90; pp. 124-84 in the 2nd edn. (2004).

centrate on his public ministry, culminating in his death. This is, of course, exactly what we do find. Thus Mark often refers to Jesus as a 'teacher' (1.21-22; 1.39; 4.1-2; 6.6; 6.34), but he has surprisingly little actual teaching, beyond the parables section in 4.1-32; he concentrates more on Jesus' mighty acts and his interactions with people. Matthew does have five large sections of Jesus' teaching (5–7; 10; 13.1-52; 18; 24–25), but they are interspersed with stories of his healings and activities. Luke's structure, moving from the ministry in Galilee (4.14–9.50) through the journey to Jerusalem (9.51–19.27), allows him to combine words and deeds along the way. Similarly, John's combination of signs and discourses reflects not separate hypothetical sources (as in the reconstructions of Bultmann and others) but this typical biographical approach of deeds and words. Finally, they all lead to a stress on Jesus' last week and death in precisely the manner of other *bioi*. Therefore we might also expect that the gospels would share their ethical purpose to encourage their readers to imitate Jesus as their subject.

Given this Christological key to interpreting the gospels, in another book I provided a symbolic reading of each portrait, using the traditional images of the human face, lion, ox and eagle.[94] The lion can be used as an image of Mark's picture of Jesus bounding on stage, rushing around, roaring enigmatically, getting into conflicts and eventually dying terribly alone and bounding off again to Galilee, leaving an empty tomb and further enigma. The human face depicts Matthew's Teacher of Israel with his long sermons, being rejected and forming a new community of faith. The ox, the patient beast of burden of Luke, cares for all, especially the outcasts, up to and including his sacrificial death, while the high-flying, far-seeing, all-knowing eagle of John depicts Jesus always totally in control. Thus we have both unity and diversity in these four portraits, and each gospel's Christology is the key to its interpretation. There are many implications of such a narrative reading, such as the relationship between 'his story' and 'history' and how the plurality within the canon (which itself has the idea of 'limit') provides both a stimulus and a control for further Christological development.[95] However, it is the implications for New Testament ethics of this Christological focus through the biographical genre of the gospels which will concern us in this study. Therefore we need to start with Jesus and to keep the focus on both his words and deeds, his teachings and his example; when we move on to the study of both Paul and the canonical gospels, again we will always start with Jesus, by examining their Christology first and what the ethical

94. Richard A. Burridge, *Four Gospels, One Jesus? A Symbolic Reading* (London: SPCK/Grand Rapids: Eerdmans, 1994; rev. and updated edn., 2005).

95. For further discussion of these implications, see *Four Gospels, One Jesus?*, Chapter 6, pp. 163-79 (1994); 165-82 in the 2nd edn. (2005).

implications of that might be for their purpose in writing, especially looking for suggestions of *mimesis,* imitating Jesus.

Therefore this brief analysis of the genre(s) of the New Testament and the gospels in particular has revealed that they are not primarily written in the genre of ethical instruction. First and foremost, the whole of the New Testament is about Jesus of Nazareth and what God has brought about through his deeds and words, life, death and resurrection. Without him as the catalyst, there would be no New Testament, and no Christian church, let alone Christian ethics. Therefore he is the correct place to begin our study of the ethical material in the New Testament, even if that is relatively unusual among other scholars writing in this field.

Also, proper attention to genre can liberate us from using the texts as windows or mirrors in the manner of traditional historical critics and modern literary readers. The particular genre of the canonical gospels belongs amongst ancient *bioi,* biographical accounts of people's lives, told through their deeds and words, up to and including a full account of their death. Too many studies of the ethics of Jesus have concentrated solely upon his words, his sayings and teachings, and have missed the important biographical narrative context in which they are recorded.

Finally, while such ancient *bioi* were not primarily written simply for ethical purposes, nonetheless most of them included their relevant teachings or sayings with an ethical dimension to their narrative account of the person's life, often for the purposes of *mimesis,* imitation of a good example to follow, or a bad one to avoid. The gospels should therefore be interpreted accordingly, as similar biographical narratives which include ethics to help people follow and imitate Jesus.

4. Conclusion

In this introductory chapter, we have set New Testament ethics within its academic context in the disciplines of New Testament Studies and Ethics and also in the context of the debates which are taking place in both church and university settings about the use of the Bible today. Our survey of the literature has shown that the vast majority of works on New Testament ethics concentrate almost exclusively on the ethical material within the New Testament; any attempt to relate it to today may include a brief consideration of the problems in so doing and possible methodologies, but little by way of actual content or application. Furthermore, very few scholars begin by considering the ethics of Jesus, and the majority argue that this is not possible at all.

This is curious given that many people still talk of Jesus of Nazareth as a great moral teacher and claim to use or follow his ethics today. Therefore, we have proposed a Christological focus for this study of New Testament ethics arising out of my previous studies on genre. The biographical genre of the gospels suggests that we need to look at the whole narrative of Jesus' life and death, and include his deeds, actions and example alongside his teachings and words to determine his ethics. We have considered the objections of many scholars that one cannot describe the ethics of Jesus at all, or at least can do so only at the end of a long critical analysis, like digging down to the earliest level of an archaeological excavation. While recognizing and making use of the hard work being done by historical critics, we propose to outline first the development of New Testament ethics from its primary level, the event which started it all off, namely the deeds and words of Jesus, his life, death and resurrection. In our chronological reconstruction, we shall then come up to the next layer, to see how the 'Jesus-event' impacted upon Paul as evidenced by the large body of letters bearing his name, to examine whether he was himself a follower of Jesus, or the founder of a whole new ethic and religion. Here too, therefore, we will need to begin with Jesus, with Paul's Christological understanding of him and the narrative about Jesus' deeds and words, life and death which undergirds Paul's theology and writing. After this, we shall come to the most recent level, that of the four gospels, taken in turn and in presumed chronological order, and following the same Christological analysis as used for both Jesus and Paul.

Finally, it is only after all of this that we can come right up to the contemporary level to examine how all this ethical material in the New Testament was used in South Africa under the apartheid regime as our test-case for what it might mean to be 'biblical' today. In a worldwide context where people in churches and universities from Europe to America, from South Africa through the developing nations, claim that their ethical viewpoint is 'biblical', it is important to undertake this process to find out what the ethical material New Testament does contain, and how we might use that, if at all, in following and imitating Jesus today.

II. Jesus of Nazareth:
Great Moral Teacher or Friend of Sinners?

In the opening chapter, we saw that relatively few academic writers on New Testament ethics begin with Jesus, and those exceptions who do, tend to concentrate mainly upon his teaching. However, we have argued that we should start with the whole event of the life of Jesus, looking at both his deeds and words, his activity as well as his teaching, as *the* primary event which starts the entire process which will eventually lead to the formation of the New Testament. Of course, we do so while recognizing that our main access to him and to his ethics is through that very New Testament, especially the gospels, which themselves come from the latest layers in the developing tradition, but also by considering the impact Jesus had upon Paul of Tarsus, causing him to compose his various epistles, which also contain some ethical material.

Furthermore, we stressed the importance of literary genre in the interpretation of texts. In attempting to reconstruct the ethics of Jesus, we have to remember that the gospels and the letters are not primarily ethical texts in the manner of, say, Aristotle's *Nicomachean Ethics*. This obvious, but often overlooked, fact is true of the entire New Testament. As Keck notes, 'The vocabulary of ethics used in the major philosophical traditions is generally absent from the New Testament'.[1]

On the other hand, there is what Goldsmith terms the 'common assumption that Jesus was primarily, or most importantly, a teacher of morality'.[2] Admittedly,

1. L. E. Keck, 'Rethinking "New Testament Ethics"', *JBL* 115.1 (1996), pp. 3-16, esp. p. 9.

2. Dale Goldsmith, *New Testament Ethics: An Introduction* (Elgin, IL: Brethren, 1988), Appendix 1, 'Jesus the Teacher', pp. 177-80; quotation from p. 177; see also 'Jesus Christ Was the World's Greatest Teacher of Righteousness', in C. W. Carter and R. D. Thompson, *The Biblical Ethic of Love*, American University Studies Series 7: Theology and Religion 79 (New York: Lang, 1990), p. 128.

Jesus is regularly called 'rabbi' or teacher in the gospels (e.g., Matt. 26.25, 49; Mark 9.5; 10.51; 11.21; 14.45; John 1.38, 49; 3.2, 26; 4.31; 6.25; 9.2; 11.8; 20.16). But he is not portrayed as just a moral teacher, despite so many people's estimation of him as such today. Essentially, the 'rabbi' is a religious teacher, and Jesus' ethical material cannot be separated from the rest of his teaching about God. Thus neither the gospels nor the epistles contain a comprehensive treatment, or even outline, of Jesus' ethical teaching in itself. Further, in such biographical works as the gospels, Jesus' teaching cannot be separated from the rest of his life and work. Similarly, in the epistles, we shall see that the ethical material is essentially integrated within their wider theological message, which is itself Christological, focussed upon what God has done in and through Jesus of Nazareth.

In this chapter, therefore, while we shall outline the main features of Jesus' ethical teaching, we will also go on to consider the ethical implications of his deeds and actions. Then, after dealing with Paul in the next chapter, we will finally be able to examine the effect of each evangelist's interpretation of Jesus and his ethics in their respective biographical narratives. However, before we can do that, we need to begin with a little historical excavation.

1. Beginning with the historical Jesus

We saw in the previous chapter how Meeks and Matera use the archaeological metaphor to argue that the historical Jesus, as the earliest layer, is actually the last to be brought to the light, and, in fact, neither of them actually digs down that deep, preferring simply to examine the more recent layers of the early Christians' ethical material in the first Christian communities of Paul and the gospels.[3] While we recognized that the hard work of digging down has to be done first, our approach contends that it is only the preliminary to telling the story of the development from the earliest layer to today. However, unfortunately, we cannot undertake a complete excavation here ourselves. It is a long, detailed, and painstaking task, which has occupied New Testament scholarship for the last couple of centuries from the original Quest for the Historical Jesus in the days of Schweizer, through the New Quest of Käsemann and others, to the so-called Third Quest, from Vermes to the Jesus Seminar.[4] Regrettably, it is

3. W. A. Meeks, *The Origins of Christian Morality* (New Haven, CT: Yale University Press, 1993), p. 17; F. J. Matera, *New Testament Ethics* (Louisville: Westminster John Knox, 1996), pp. 7-8; also J. L. Houlden, *Ethics and the New Testament* (Oxford: Oxford University Press, 1973, and frequent reprints, e.g., Edinburgh: T&T Clark, 1992), p. 4; see further our discussion above in Chapter I, pp. 19-21, nn. 62-65.

4. A. Schweitzer, *Geschichte der Leben-Jesu-Forschung* (Tübingen: Mohr, 1906); ET *The Quest*

also true that there is no agreement about all the details which emerge from the dig, as is shown in the massive reconstructions by the likes of Crossan, Sanders, Wright, Theissen, Meier and many others.[5] This is the main reason why Hays,

---

of the Historical Jesus (London: A & C Black, 1954); J. M. Robinson, *A New Quest of the Historical Jesus,* SBT 25 (London: SCM, 1959); G. Vermes, *Jesus the Jew* (London: Collins, 1973); R. W. Funk, R. W. Hoover and the Jesus Seminar, *The Five Gospels: The Search for the Authentic Words of Jesus* (New York: Macmillan, 1993); for a full coverage of many of the major writers and topics, see the collection *The Historical Jesus in Recent Research,* ed. James D. G. Dunn and Scot McKnight, Sources for Biblical and Theological Study (Winona Lake, IN: Eisenbrauns, 2005); see also A. E. Harvey, *Jesus and the Constraints of History* (London: Duckworth, 1982); William E. Arnal and Michel Desjardins (eds.), *Whose Historical Jesus?* Studies in Christianity and Judaism 7 (Waterloo, ON: Wilfrid Laurier University Press, 1997); Christopher Tuckett, 'Sources and Methods', and James Carleton Paget, 'Quests for the Historical Jesus', both in *The Cambridge Companion to Jesus,* ed. Markus Bockmuehl (Cambridge: Cambridge University Press, 2001), pp. 121-37 and 138-55; Scot McKnight, 'Jesus of Nazareth', in *The Face of New Testament Studies: A Survey of Recent Research,* ed. Scot McKnight and Grant R. Osborne (Grand Rapids: Baker Academic, 2004), pp. 149-76; James D. G. Dunn, *A New Perspective on Jesus: What the Quest for the Historical Jesus Missed* (Grand Rapids: Baker/London: SPCK, 2005); Carl R. Holladay, *A Critical Introduction to the New Testament: Interpreting the Message and Meaning of Jesus Christ* (Nashville: Abingdon, 2005), esp. chap. 5, 'From the Gospels to Jesus', pp. 77-103, or pp. 103-45 in the expanded CD version; Christopher Tuckett, 'Does the "Historical Jesus" Belong within a "New Testament Theology"?' in *The Nature of New Testament Theology: Essays in Honour of Robert Morgan,* ed. Christopher Rowland and Christopher Tuckett (Oxford: Blackwell, 2006), pp. 231-47.

5. See, for example, J. D. Crossan, *The Historical Jesus: The Life of a Mediterranean Jewish Peasant* (San Francisco: HarperCollins/Edinburgh: T&T Clark, 1991); J. D. Crossan, *Jesus: A Revolutionary Biography* (San Francisco: HarperSan Francisco, 1994); E. P. Sanders, *Jesus and Judaism* (London: SCM, 1985); E. P. Sanders, *The Historical Figure of Jesus* (London: Penguin, 1993); N. T. Wright, *Christian Origins and the Question of God:* vol. 1, *The New Testament and the People of God* (London: SPCK, 1992); vol. 2, *Jesus and the Victory of God* (1996); vol. 3, *The Resurrection of the Son of God* (2003); idem, *The Original Jesus: The Life and Vision of a Revolutionary* (Oxford: Lion/Grand Rapids: Eerdmans, 1996); Marcus J. Borg and N. T. Wright, *The Meaning of Jesus: Two Visions* (San Francisco: HarperSanFrancisco, 1999); G. Theissen, *The Shadow of the Galilean: The Quest of the Historical Jesus in Narrative Form* (London: SCM, 1987); G. Theissen and A. Merz, *The Historical Jesus: A Comprehensive Guide,* trans. John Bowden (London: SCM, 1998); John P. Meier, *A Marginal Jew: Rethinking the Historical Jesus:* vol. 1, *The Roots of the Problem and the Person* (New York: Doubleday, 1991); vol. 2, *Mentor, Message and Miracles* (1994); vol. 3: *Companions and Competitors* (2001); see also Marcus J. Borg, *Jesus, a New Vision: Spirit, Culture, and the Life of Discipleship* (San Francisco: Harper, 1987); Richard A. Horsley, *Jesus and the Spiral of Violence: Popular Jewish Resistance in Roman Palestine* (San Francisco: Harper, 1987); Markus Bockmuehl, *This Jesus: Martyr, Lord, Messiah* (Edinburgh: T&T Clark, 1994); Robert W. Funk, *Honest to Jesus: Jesus for a New Millennium* (San Francisco: HarperSanFrancisco, 1996); Gregory J. Riley, *One Jesus, Many Christs: How Jesus Inspired Not One True Christianity, But Many* (San Francisco: HarperSanFrancisco, 1997); Paul W. Barnett, *Jesus and the Logic of History* (Grand Rapids: Eerdmans, 1997); Martin Forward, *Jesus: A Short Biography* (Oxford: Oneworld, 1998); James D. G. Dunn, *Jesus Remembered* (Grand Rapids: Eerdmans, 2003); Sean Freyne, *Jesus, A Jewish Galilean: A New Reading of the Jesus-Story* (London: T&T Clark, 2004).

lamenting that 'efforts to reconstruct the historical Jesus have been beset by subjectivity and cultural bias', does not start with Jesus, or even consider his ethics in any depth.[6]

Yet we do need to provide at least a brief sketch to establish our twofold approach of considering 'words and deeds', that is, looking at both Jesus' teaching and his main activity: in this respect, there is some surprising unanimity. Thereafter, we will need to be alert to the critical, historical issues as we go on through the development of the story of Jesus.

a. Jesus of Nazareth existed as an historical figure

Keck's 'rethinking of New Testament Ethics' stressed that 'the defining feature of New Testament Ethics is its orientation to an event, namely, the event of Jesus'.[7] Any archaeologist will look for the reason which started the site — a bridging point over a river, defensive capacity on a hill, agricultural potential and the like. Equally, the historian needs to posit a cause for any event, something to have started it all. Without the fact of Jesus' existence, there is no reason for the New Testament at all, let alone its ethics. There is nothing to start the development of the Christian church and no reason for this attempt to use the New Testament in ethics today. The 'Jesus event' started it all, and if that is not accepted, we can stop now.

In fact, not only did Jesus of Nazareth exist, but there is a reasonable body of evidence for his existence, both in the New Testament and in noncanonical sources like *Thomas,* Jewish-Christian gospels (those of the *Nazarenes, Ebionites, Hebrews*) and fragments of other gospels (like *Secret Mark* and *Peter*). In addition, there is the non-Christian evidence of Josephus (*Antiquities* 18.63-64; 20.200), rabbinic sources (e.g., *b. Sanhedrin* 43a), and the Roman writers Pliny (*Epistles* 10.96), Tacitus (*Annals* 15.44) and Suetonius (*Claudius* 25.4).[8]

---

6. Richard B. Hays, *The Moral Vision of the New Testament: A Contemporary Introduction to New Testament Ethics* (San Francisco: HarperSanFrancisco/Edinburgh: T&T Clark, 1996), pp. 158-61, quotation from p. 159; compare this with the handling of this issue in William C. Spohn, *Go and Do Likewise: Jesus and Ethics* (New York: Continuum, 1999), pp. 16-23.

7. Keck, 'Rethinking "New Testament Ethics"', p. 10.

8. For these texts and discussion about their interpretation, see Theissen and Merz, *Historical Jesus*, pp. 17-124; see also Meier, *A Marginal Jew:* vol. 1, *The Roots of the Problem and the Person*, pp. 56-166; James D. G. Dunn, *The Evidence for Jesus* (London: SCM, 1985).

b. Jesus was a teacher with a mixed following

We have stressed that it is not enough simply to look at Jesus' teaching, but that the ancient biographical focus gave great importance to the narrative of a person's life and activity. This mixture of deeds and words is also recognized in the non-Christian evidence cited above, where Josephus, rabbinic and Roman sources all agree that Jesus was some kind of religious teacher, who attracted a following, particularly among the sorts of people of whom these sources do not approve! While the exact texts of some of the sources and their meaning are debated, these two basic facts about Jesus' teaching and his followers are clear, and are accepted by historical Jesus scholars right across the spectrum.

Thus while the debate between Crossan and the Jesus Seminar on the one hand and Sanders and Wright on the other may centre on whether Jesus' sayings were like Hellenistic Cynic wisdom or Jewish restoration eschatology, the fact that Jesus went around teaching things about 'the kingdom' is undisputed.[9] Equally, they agree that such teaching was worked out in an open acceptance of a wide variety of people of dubious ethical backgrounds. Thus Crossan talks of Jesus' ministry among the 'nobodies' and 'undesirables', and of his combining healings and eatings, which he calls provocatively 'magic and meal'; he concludes his account of Jesus thus: 'His strategy . . . was the combination of *free healing and common eating.* . . . Miracle and parable, healing and eating were calculated to force individuals into unmediated physical and spiritual contact with God and . . . one another. He announced, in other words, the brokerless kingdom of God.'[10] Similarly, Sanders links Jesus' teaching and actions: 'The concrete behaviour . . . was Jesus' association with sinners, which correlates with the sayings which call sinners and promise them the kingdom. In common with many modern interpreters, I shall later argue that such behaviour and sayings were characteristic of Jesus'.[11] Finally, Wright comments, 'There is a more or less universal consensus among scholars — something as rare as snow in midsummer, and no doubt similarly transitory — that Jesus offered a welcome to, and shared meals with "sinners".'[12] His pessimism about this agreement is probably sardonic, for this combination of Jesus as a teacher who accepted and ate with ordinary people is clearly established across the different historical reconstructions and provides us with sufficient firm historical bedrock from which to proceed.

9. For a discussion of why the Jesus Seminar began with Jesus' sayings rather than his actions, see Lane C. McGaughy, 'Words before Deeds: Why Start with the Sayings?' *Forum,* new series 1.2 (Fall 1998), pp. 387-99.

10. Crossan, *Historical Jesus,* pp. 265-353; quotation from p. 422 (his italics).

11. E. P. Sanders, *Jesus and Judaism,* p. 5.

12. Wright, *Jesus and Victory of God,* p. 264.

c. A brief outline of Jesus' life

We have established enough to begin our study of Jesus' words and deeds, his ethical teaching and his attitude to other people, and, in one sense, need to provide no more foundation or analysis of the lowest level. However, for the sake of completeness, it may be helpful to give a brief outline of which version of the developing story seems most likely. It has already been noted how different scholars' reconstructions of the historical Jesus depend somewhat upon their presuppositions about the sources and evidence. Thus Crossan's account depends upon his analysis of the sources with the earliest level (AD 30-60) including *Thomas,* Q and various noncanonical gospels, while the second layer (60-80) contains *Secret Mark,* then Mark, revised *Thomas,* and others, with the other canonical gospels appearing only in the third or even fourth stages.[13] While such an approach may be shared by some other members of the Jesus Seminar, it has not persuaded most British and German scholars, who tend to hold to the traditional sequence of Q and Mark first, followed by Matthew and Luke, and then by John towards the end of the first century AD, with *Thomas* and the noncanonical gospels all coming later.[14] This dating sequence also seems much more likely to me, and this, together with the need to consider Jesus in his Jewish-Palestinian setting, means that we will tend to follow more the arguments put forward by those involved in the 'third quest'.

It is remarkable also how, despite the enormous and detailed treatments by scholars like Sanders, Wright and Theissen, their general conclusions and outlines of Jesus contain the same basic facts, which are also those found in the canonical gospels:[15]

- Jesus is to be interpreted in the light of his Jewish background, particularly in terms of restoration eschatology.
- he was involved with John the Baptist, and influenced by him, in his preaching of the kingdom and repentance.
- he then moved out on his own and was seen by many as a prophet with an itinerant ministry, gathering a group of followers, including women.
- he preached about and proclaimed the coming of the kingdom.

13. Crossan, *Historical Jesus,* Appendix 1.A, 'Chronological Stratification', pp. 427-34.

14. See the summary chart with dates and periods in Theissen and Merz, *Historical Jesus,* p. 59.

15. For ease of reference, see E. P. Sanders' list of conclusions in *Jesus and Judaism,* pp. 326-27 or his 'Outline of Jesus' Life', in *The Historical Figure of Jesus,* pp. 10-14; the 'Short Life of Jesus' in Theissen and Merz, *Historical Jesus,* pp. 569-72; Hays follows similar lines in his 'Proposed Reconstruction', in *Moral Vision,* pp. 162-66; for Wright, see *Jesus and Victory of God,* passim.

- he combined this mission of preaching and teaching with a ministry of healing and accepting people, especially those outside the normal social and religious groups.
- he provoked debate with various groups within Judaism, which led to growing opposition from several sources, which came to a head when he was involved in an incident in the temple at Jerusalem.
- he was arrested and put to death by the Roman authorities on a charge which included both political and religious elements as a kingly pretender or messianic claimant; crucifixion of the leader was a typical Roman response to trouble.
- something happened different from that of other groups in that the death of the leader did not end it all; the claims of Jesus' resurrection from the dead led to the rapid growth of the early Christian communities within Judaism and eventually to the Gentile mission.[16]

Of course, this outline is a simplification. In the case of each of the scholars quoted, the picture is worked out differently, particularly in its details or emphases. However, perhaps this is not so different from the canonical process which led to the basic outline of the one Jesus being described in the four portraits of the gospels;[17] hence Kähler, writing at the end of the nineteenth century, saw the historical critic as a 'fifth evangelist'![18] We shall come to the four particular portraits of the canonical evangelists in due course, but in this chapter we shall concentrate upon the broader picture which emerges of the historical Jesus' deeds and words, using the usual criteria of authenticity, such as dissimilarity, coherence and multiple attestation.[19]

16. From my own personal viewpoint, it was as a student of classical literature and ancient history at Oxford that I came to accept that historically only this explanation provided the necessary cause for the development of the rest of the story of the New Testament, and also the reason for our concern to relate it today.

17. For further discussion on the plurality and unity of Jesus and the four gospels, see Richard A. Burridge, *Four Gospels, One Jesus? A Symbolic Reading* (London: SPCK/Grand Rapids: Eerdmans, 1994; rev. and updated edn., 2005), chap. 6, pp. 163-79 (1994); 165-82 in the 2nd edn. (2005).

18. M. Kähler, *The So-Called Historical Jesus and the Historic, Biblical Christ* (German original, 1892; Philadelphia: Fortress, 1964), p. 62.

19. For discussion of such criteria, see Norman Perrin, *Rediscovering the Teaching of Jesus* (London: SCM, 1967), pp. 37-49; see also Meier, *A Marginal Jew:* Volume 1, *The Roots of the Problem and the Person*, pp. 167-95, or Holladay, *A Critical Introduction to the New Testament*, pp. 91-94, or pp. 123-29 in the expanded CD version.

2. Jesus' ethical teaching — his words

a. The kingdom of God as the centre of Jesus' teaching

'The kingdom of God is at hand; repent and believe the gospel' (Mark 1.15). At the core of Jesus' teaching is a stress on the kingdom of God and a consequent need to repent. When he sends his disciples out on mission, they are to proclaim the same message: 'The kingdom of God has come near to you' (Luke 10.9). Thus it is not surprising that most discussions of the ethics of Jesus begin with this stress on the kingdom — what Schrage calls 'the Kingdom of God as the foundation and horizon of Jesus' ethics'.[20] However, while there is general agreement about the kingdom as the starting point, there is much debate about what it meant, both for Jesus and today, in terms of its background, content, timing and so forth.

God is often portrayed as King in the **Old Testament**.[21] This can be connected with the temple, where Isaiah has a vision of 'the King, the LORD of hosts' (Isa. 6.5). However, this 'King of glory', the 'LORD of hosts' (YHWH Sabaoth) was also King of all the earth, which belongs to him (Ps. 24; see also Pss. 103.19; 145.10-13). This priestly understanding that the God who is worshipped in the temple as King is also Lord of the world undergirds much of the prophets' oracles not just about Israel but concerning all the nations. After the exile in Babylon, the return to Jerusalem was a declaration that 'your God reigns' (Isa. 52.7-10; compare Obad. 20-21 or Zeph. 3.15). Alongside such cultic and political interpretations of God's kingship here and now, eschatological understandings grew up that the time would come when 'the LORD will become king over all the earth' (Zech. 14.9).[22] The development of apocalyptic literature looked forward to when the kingdom of God would replace earthly political kingdoms both in books like Daniel (e.g., 2.26-45; 7) and in intertestamental writings,

20. W. Schrage, *The Ethics of the New Testament*, trans. David E. Green (German edn. Göttingen: Vandenhoeck & Ruprecht, 1982; Philadelphia: Fortress, 1988), p. 18; compare Verhey's opening 'The best starting point for inquiry into the ethic of Jesus is provided by the striking summary of Jesus' teaching which Mark places at the head of his account of Jesus' public ministry . . . Mk. 1.15', Allen Verhey, *The Great Reversal: Ethics and the New Testament* (Grand Rapids: Eerdmans, 1984), p. 11; see also E. Lohse, *Theological Ethics of the New Testament*, trans. M. Eugene Boring (Minneapolis: Fortress, 1991), pp. 39-47; W. Marxsen, *New Testament Foundations for Christian Ethics*, trans. O. C. Dean, Jr. (Minneapolis: Fortress/Edinburgh: T&T Clark, 1993), pp. 62-77; Theissen and Merz, *The Historical Jesus*, pp. 240-80, 376.

21. See G. R. Beasley-Murray, *Jesus and the Kingdom of God* (Grand Rapids: Eerdmans, 1986), pp. 3-35.

22. See Beasley-Murray, *Jesus and the Kingdom of God*, pp. 39-62.

such as *Assumption of Moses* 10 or the Qumran Scrolls' accounts of the victory of the 'children of light' (e.g., 1QM VI.6).[23]

Thus although the kingdom may ultimately have **political or eschatological implications**, the common translation of the Hebrew *malkuth* or the Greek βασιλεία as 'kingdom' can be confusing if it causes people to think that it denotes a place or region like our political kingdoms. Furthermore, given that such masculine language is now seen as exclusive and hierarchical ideas are suspect, 'kingdom' is probably a less helpful translation of what is actually a feminine abstract noun in both Greek and Hebrew. E. P. Sanders prefers to call it 'the reign of God, the "sphere" (whether geographical, temporal or spiritual) where God exercises his power' or 'the ruling power of God'.[24] Many other scholars, such as Merklein and Chilton, agree that it is what happens when God is accepted, when God's 'rule' is acknowledged and welcomed.[25] Yet Kvalbein has criticized such approaches, arguing from its synonyms and antonyms that such a 'reign of God' interpretation ignores the way the phrase βασιλεία τοῦ θεοῦ does include the time and place of salvation, which is God's gift. While Jesus' ethics cannot be derived simply from the 'reign of God', but are rather to be found in the love command and the call to discipleship, the 'kingdom of God' still provides their 'power and motivation'.[26] Swartley stresses the important connection of the 'reign' or 'kingdom of God' and the gospel itself with Jesus' message of 'peace', shalom or εἰρήνη, which he considers underrepresented in much scholarship.[27]

John Riches has explored the political implications of the 'social world' of Jesus, the Jewish 'symbolic universe' of election, covenant, land and temple, in

---

23. See Schrage, *The Ethics of the NT*, p. 18; Verhey, *The Great Reversal*, pp. 12-13; Theissen and Merz, *The Historical Jesus*, pp. 246-51; for a full discussion of the background in the Old Testament, Pseudepigrapha and Qumran, see Meier, *A Marginal Jew: Rethinking the Historical Jesus: Volume 2, Mentor, Message, and Miracles*, pp. 237-88.

24. E. P. Sanders, *Jesus and Judaism* (London: SCM, 1985), pp. 126-27.

25. See H. Merklein, *Die Gottesherrschaft als Handlungsprinzip: Untersuchung zur Ethik Jesu* (Würzburg: Echter, 1981); B. D. Chilton, 'Regnum Dei Deus Est', *SJT* 31 (1978), pp. 261-70; idem, *God in Strength: Jesus' Announcement of the Kingdom* (Sheffield: JSOT Press, 1987) and *Pure Kingdom: Jesus' Vision of God* (Grand Rapids: Eerdmans, 1996); also J. D. Crossan, *The Historical Jesus*, p. 266; Glen H. Stassen and David P. Gushee, *Kingdom Ethics: Following Jesus in Contemporary Context* (Downers Grove, IL: IVP, 2003), pp. 19-31; Dunn, *Jesus Remembered*, pp. 383-487; see also J. P. Louw and E. A. Nida (eds.), *Greek-English Lexicon of the New Testament Based on Semantic Domains* (New York: United Bible Societies, 1988), vol. 1, p. 480.

26. Hans Kvalbein, 'The Kingdom of God in the Ethics of Jesus', *Studia Theologia* 51 (1997), pp. 60-84.

27. Willard M. Swartley, *Covenant of Peace: The Missing Peace in New Testament Theology and Ethics* (Grand Rapids: Eerdmans, 2006), pp. 1-26.

the light of the uprising and destruction of Sepphoris around the time of Jesus' birth; from this, he argues that 'Jesus' use of kingship language' shows that he was 'attuned' to his contemporaries' expectations of an independent Jewish temple state, even if his other teaching on nonviolence indicates that this was not his way.[28] E. P. Sanders' groundbreaking work on 'Jesus and Judaism' has shown how Jesus' preaching of the kingdom of God was linked with 'Jewish restoration eschatology', in which the kingdom would be established not by force of arms but by 'an eschatological miracle' which would include the 'wicked' and sinners who accepted Jesus as king.[29] Following Sanders' lead, many scholars have developed this idea of 'restoration eschatology' further. Particularly important is the work of N. T. Wright, whose immensely detailed treatment has stressed how Jesus' preaching of the kingdom was a retelling of the story of Israel, preparing for the return of YHWH to Zion, which would happen in and through Jesus' own work.[30]

Thus Jesus affirmed **the nearness of the kingdom** in his direct teaching, in his parables and in his actions. Mark's description of Jesus' preaching as 'the kingdom of God has come near' (1.14) has its parallel in Matt. 4.17, who also includes this in his summaries of Jesus' ministry (4.23; 9.35); Luke similarly describes this as Jesus' typical activity in 4.43; 8.1; 9.11. Jesus taught his disciples to pray for the coming of the kingdom in the Lord's Prayer (Matt. 6.10//Luke 11.2) and told people to 'seek his kingdom' (Matt. 6.33//Luke 6.31). The kingdom is likened to many things in Jesus' parables, especially to growing things in parables such as those of the Sower, the Seed Growing Secretly and the Mustard Seed (Mark 4.1-34; Matt. 13.1-52). He constantly warns of the imminence of the kingdom, using images like harvest (Matt. 13.24-30), collecting dues (Mark 12.1-12//Matt. 21.33-43) or settling accounts (Matt. 18.23). The kingdom is also proclaimed in Jesus' activities and deeds such as exorcisms by the spirit or finger of God (Matt. 12.28//Luke 11.20); his healings and miracles are given as a reply to John the Baptist's question whether Jesus is 'the one to come' (Matt. 11.1-6; Luke 7.18-23).[31]

---

28. John K. Riches, 'The Social World of Jesus', *Interpretation* 50.4 (1996), pp. 383-393; see also John Riches, *Jesus and the Transformation of Judaism* (London: DLT, 1980), pp. 87-111.

29. E. P. Sanders, *Jesus and Judaism*, passim; see particularly pp. 123-241 and his conclusions on p. 326; see also his *The Historical Figure of Jesus* (London: Penguin, 1993), pp. 169-204.

30. N. T. Wright, *Christian Origins and the Question of God:* Volume 2, *Jesus and the Victory of God* (London: SPCK, 1996); see esp. pp. 443-74 and his conclusions on pp. 612-653; Wright helpfully gathers all the material about the kingdom of God and analyses it by categories in his Appendix, pp. 663-70.

31. See E. P. Sanders, *Jesus and Judaism*, pp. 135-40 and Marxsen, *New Testament Foundations*, pp. 77-81 for a discussion of these texts.

Furthermore, there is an **urgency** to all the teaching about the kingdom: everything must be sacrificed to gain the treasure of entering the kingdom (Matt. 13.44-46), and any obstacle overcome, even to the point of self-maiming, or the abandonment of riches or sexuality (Mark 9.42-48; 10.21-25; Matt. 19.12). And yet, one must enter it 'like a child' (Mark 10.14-15; Matt. 18.1-5). There are warnings that those who expect to enter the kingdom will find others such as tax collectors or Gentiles going before them (Matt. 21.31; 8.11-12//Luke 13.28-29), and there will be harsh judgement for places that reject the preaching of the kingdom such as Bethsaida and Chorazin (Luke 10.9-16; 11.29-32). Parables liken the judgement of those entering the kingdom to sorting out good fish from bad or sheep from goats (Matt. 13.47-50; 25.31-46). Therefore, from start to finish, the urgency of the message of the kingdom includes spreading the news everywhere and on all occasions (Matt. 4.23), and Jesus continues to teach about the kingdom even after his resurrection (Acts 1.3).

Thus while some of these passages and verses reflect the differing redactions of each evangelist, as we shall discover in subsequent chapters below, the basic outline of the kingdom or reign of God at the centre of the teaching of the historical Jesus is clear from its frequent multiple attestation and its distinctiveness from the rest of the New Testament, such as John and Paul.[32]

b. The eschatological setting of Jesus' ethics

We have seen how the kingdom of God is at the centre of Jesus' teaching as a whole, drawing on both the Old Testament and intertestamental background and linked to the political and religious hopes of the period. His teaching on the kingdom is marked by a sense of urgency coupled with warnings of reward and judgement, so it is not unreasonable to expect ethical implications arising from such teaching. Above all, there is the question of timing; how and when is the kingdom coming, and how does ethics fit into its proclamation?

This area has gone through many swings in critical scholarship between future and realized eschatology, the individual and the corporate, the political and the religious.[33] In **the nineteenth century** the stress on the so-called 'Social

---

32. For a full discussion of all the passages about the kingdom of God, the historical Jesus and their authenticity, see Beasley-Murray, *Jesus and the Kingdom of God*, pp. 71-312; Norman Perrin, *The Kingdom of God in the Teaching of Jesus* (London: SCM, 1963), pp. 158-206, and idem, *Rediscovering the Teaching of Jesus*, esp. pp. 54-108 and 154-206.

33. For a brief survey, see Theissen and Merz, *The Historical Jesus*, pp. 240-45; for a more detailed account, see J. I. H. McDonald, *Biblical Interpretation and Christian Ethics* (Cambridge: Cambridge University Press, 1993), pp. 65-162.

Gospel' concentrated on Jesus as a great moral teacher. Jesus' teaching was seen as a blueprint for restructuring society, to build the kingdom of God here on earth; thus the call of the kingdom involves human effort and activity for the sake of others, as in the work of people like Albrecht Ritschl in Europe and Walter Rauschenbusch in America.[34] In the same social tradition, but against their stress on corporate responsibility, Henry Cadbury argued instead for an individual demand and response.[35]

In contrast to such approaches, Weiss and Schweitzer stressed the **eschatological and apocalyptic framework** of Jesus' thought. Jesus was preparing people for the imminent kingdom of God, which only God could inaugurate through a cosmic cataclysm. The kingdom of God is not something human effort can create on earth; thus Jesus' teaching was only an 'interim ethic', to enable his hearers to prepare themselves to enter the kingdom when it arrived. It is not, therefore, a moral teaching for all time; furthermore, it is called into question by the fact that the kingdom did not, and has not arrived.[36]

Between the wars, while Bultmann accepted this apocalyptic 'myth', he brought it back to **the present** by existentializing the eschatology into an existential decision 'now'. In his view, Jesus 'demythologized' the future expectation into a present experience of God; thus he taught 'not ethics at all in the sense of an intelligible theory valid for all'. There is, therefore, no permanent validity to Jesus' ethical teaching.[37] Meanwhile, Dodd's stress on realized eschatology argued that Jesus' ethics were not interim, but are for those living in the new age, who accept Jesus' announcement that 'the kingdom has already come' (according to his reading of Mark 1.15), that it is now breaking into our present reality.[38]

34. A. Ritschl, 'Instruction in the Christian Religion', in A. Ritschl, *Three Essays*, trans. with an Intro. by Philip Hefner (Philadelphia: Fortress, 1972) sects. 5-10, pp. 222-32; W. Rauschenbusch, 'The Kingdom of God', speech to Cleveland YMCA on January 2, 1913, reprinted in Robert T. Handy (ed.), *The Social Gospel in America, 1870-1920: Gladden, Ely, Rauschenbusch* (Oxford: Oxford University Press, 1966), pp. 264-67; see also Perrin, *The Kingdom of God in the Teaching of Jesus*, pp. 46-49.

35. Henry J. Cadbury, *The Peril of Modernizing Jesus* (London: SPCK 1937); see especially chap. V, 'Limitations of Jesus' Social Teaching', pp. 86-119.

36. J. Weiss, *Die Predigt Jesu vom Reiche Gottes* (Göttingen: Vandenhoeck & Ruprecht, 1892); ET *Jesus' Proclamation of the Kingdom of God* (London: SCM, 1971); A. Schweitzer, *Geschichte der Leben-Jesu-Forschung* (Tübingen: Mohr, 1906); ET *The Quest of the Historical Jesus* (London: A & C Black, 1954); idem, *The Mystery of the Kingdom of God* (London, A & C Black, 1914), pp. 87-99; see also Perrin, *The Kingdom of God in the Teaching of Jesus*, pp. 13-36; Richard H. Hiers, *Jesus and Ethics: Four Interpretations* (Philadelphia: Westminster, 1968), pp. 39-78.

37. R. Bultmann, *Jesus and the Word* (London: Collins, 1958), p. 66; see also pp. 82-97; Perrin, *The Kingdom of God in the Teaching of Jesus*, pp. 112-29; Hiers, *Jesus and Ethics: Four Interpretations*, pp. 79-114.

38. C. H. Dodd, *Gospel and Law*, Bampton Lectures in America 3 (New York: Columbia Uni-

After World War II, the pendulum swung back somewhat through the New Quest for the historical Jesus, through the work of scholars like Dibelius and Käsemann as they interpreted Jesus as an **eschatological prophet**; in an essay in honour of Dodd, Bornkamm considered the effect of the delay of the eschatological cataclysm in his groundbreaking redactional study of Matthew.[39] Other scholars have reemphasised the eschatological dimension. J. T. Sanders argued that Jesus' ethics are so linked to first-century concepts of eschatology that they cannot be used in the 'modern world': 'Jesus does not provide a valid ethics for today'.[40] On the other hand, work by systematic theologians like Moltmann have argued that eschatology can not only be credible today, but also that it provides the grounds for Christian hope.[41]

Meanwhile, Windisch tried to combine the apocalyptic strand in Jesus' teaching with **the wisdom tradition** in his treatment of the Sermon on the Mount.[42] More recently, work by Mack, Crossan and some members of the Jesus Seminar has stressed the wisdom background of Jesus' sayings, giving us a non-apocalyptic, sapiential Jesus.[43] On the other hand, the so-called 'third quest' for the historical Jesus in the work of E. P. Sanders, John Meier and Tom Wright has reaffirmed Jesus' role as an eschatological prophet, with a sense of a future dimension.[44] This has led to a renewed emphasis on the corporate nature of Jesus' ethic; as Wiebe's discussion concludes, a positive response to the

versity Press, 1951), see, for example, p. 60; see also Perrin, *The Kingdom of God in the Teaching of Jesus*, pp. 58-78; Hiers, *Jesus and Ethics: Four Interpretations*, pp. 115-47.

39. G. Bornkamm, 'End Expectation and Church in Matthew', in *Tradition and Interpretation in Matthew*, ed. G. Bornkamm, G. Barth and H. J. Held (London: SCM, 1963, pp. 15-51); original German version 'Endwartung und Kirche im Matthäus-evangelium', in *The Background of the New Testament and Its Eschatology: Studies in Honour of C. H. Dodd*, ed. W. D. Davies and D. Daube (Cambridge: Cambridge University Press, 1956); see also E. Käsemann, *New Testament Questions of Today* (London: SCM, 1969).

40. J. T. Sanders, *Ethics in the New Testament* (London: SCM, 1975); see esp. pp. 1-29, quotation from p. 29.

41. See, for example, J. Moltmann, *Theology of Hope* (London: SCM, 1967); *God in Creation: An Ecological Doctrine of Creation* (London: SCM, 1985).

42. Hans Windisch, *The Meaning of the Sermon on the Mount* (Philadelphia: Westminster, 1951).

43. Burton L. Mack, *A Myth of Innocence: Mark and Christian Origins* (Philadelphia: Fortress, 1988); idem, *The Lost Gospel: The Book of Q and Christian Origins* (San Francisco: HarperCollins, 1993); Crossan, *The Historical Jesus: The Life of a Mediterranean Jewish Peasant;* Funk, Hoover and the Jesus Seminar, *The Five Gospels: The Search for the Authentic Words of Jesus.*

44. E. P. Sanders, *Jesus and Judaism*, see esp. pp. 123-41; idem, *The Historical Figure of Jesus* (London: Penguin, 1993), see esp. pp. 169-88; Meier, *A Marginal Jew: Rethinking the Historical Jesus:* Volume 2, *Mentor, Message, and Miracles*, see esp. pp. 269-70, 289-397; N. T. Wright, *Jesus and the Victory of God*, see esp. pp. 198-243.

kingdom of God is a call to the whole nation of Israel, rather than the individual decision as in the reconstructions of Bultmann or others, and a similar stress emerges from Wright's work.[45]

In fact, despite the swings of the scholarly pendulum, **both future and present** aspects must be retained. As Chilton and McDonald argue, 'When the Kingdom is viewed as a decision for the future which has already been taken, a reconciliation between the eschatological and ethical aspects of Jesus' preaching becomes practicable'; in particular, the parables all show that the future of God is breaking into our present and demands a response now.[46] Similarly, Schrage talks of 'the temporal dialectic of present and future. . . . the simultaneity of present and future is characteristic of Jesus'.[47] We cannot ignore the fact that some texts speak of 'entering' the kingdom in the future (e.g., Mark 9.47; 10.15; Matt. 7.21; 18.3), while others imply that it is here now (Matt. 11.2-6; 12.28). Equally, some suggest that it is the sole activity of God, such as the seed growing 'by itself' (αὐτομάτη), yet requires human labour, in 'putting in the sickle' (Mark 4.28-29). Perhaps both aspects are best summed up in the Lord's Prayer: to pray 'Your kingdom come. Your will be done, on earth as it is in heaven' (Matt. 6.10) commits the one who prays for the coming of God's heavenly rule to live like that in the here and now.

Thus the relationship of eschatology and ethics will require a lot of **dialectic**, for it is both future and present, individual and corporate, political and spiritual, apocalyptic and sapiential. Jesus' ethics, like all his teaching, is to be understood in the light of the *eschaton* — which involves both living as though the kingdom were here now, yet preparing for it, and also living as though God were already King, yet realizing that if or when God's rule is acknowledged universally, ethics will not be needed.

c. Jesus' ethic of response

Whatever view is taken on the kingdom and eschatology, it remains clear that Jesus' ethic, like much of Old Testament ethics, is one which makes a demand and seeks a response in discipleship. So Jesus' ethic cannot be just an interesting way of looking at things, like many forms of wisdom literature or philosophy. Mark summarizes the demand as 'repent and believe the gospel' (1.15); the call

45. B. Wiebe, 'Messianic Ethics: Response to the Kingdom of God', *Interpretation* 45.1 (1991), pp. 29-42; see also N. T. Wright, *Jesus and the Victory of God*, for example, pp. 274-319.

46. Chilton and McDonald, *Jesus and the Ethics of the Kingdom*, see esp. pp. 6-20; quotation from p. 9.

47. Schrage, *The Ethics of the NT*, p. 19.

for μετάνοια is for repentance for the past — not in a wallowing penance, but as a prerequisite for following in discipleship in the present and into God's future. Later in this chapter we shall explore what Jesus seems to have required by way of repentance. Here, however, the emphasis is clearly demonstrated by the next instruction, 'Follow me'. Thus the announcement of the kingdom leads into the call of Simon and Andrew, and then James and John (Mark 1.15-20//Matt. 4.18-22). Their response is to follow 'immediately', using Mark's typical word εὐθύς, 'at once'. However, immediate response is also to be found in other stories of calling disciples in the gospels, such as that of Levi (Mark 2.14//Matt. 9.9; Luke 5.27-28; see also John 1.37-43).

It was the Jewish custom for young men who wanted an education to choose a rabbi with whom to study for a period as part of their training.[48] Here, however, it is Jesus who issues the call and demands a response from people who are apparently engaged in daily life and not even seeking a rabbi. Those who do volunteer on their own accord to follow him are given warnings about its likely cost (Matt. 8.19-22//Luke 9.57-62). While students might live with their rabbi for a period to learn his understanding of the tradition in a stable setting, Jesus' call to an itinerant life was not primarily about education. It is more like the call of the prophets, as Elijah called Elisha (1 Kings 19.19-21), or Josephus' account of people following 'sign prophets' into the wilderness (*Antiquities* 20.97, 167).

Thus Jesus' call fits into the prophetic demand for repentance as a returning to God; his ethic requires a response. It is not about learning philosophy, or wisdom, or even memorizing the oral traditions to learn to be a teacher: action is required, not study. Perrin entitles his chapter on Jesus' ethical teaching, 'Recognition and Response'; 'but "ethics" is a misleading word . . . there is nothing in that teaching about standards of conduct or moral judgements, there is only the urgent call to recognize the challenge of the proclamation and to respond to it. To talk about the "ethical teaching of Jesus" is to talk about something that can only be found by a process of abstraction and deduction from the teaching as a whole'.[49] This can be seen in the parable of the Two Sons, in which the one who actually does what his father asked is praised, not the one who said he would, but did not (Matt. 21.28-31). The demand to follow must take precedence over everything else, even including something like the sacred duty to bury the dead (Matt. 8.22//Luke 9.59-60), which is so distinctive and outra-

48. M. Hengel, *The Charismatic Leader and His Followers* (Edinburgh: T&T Clark, 1981), esp. pp. 51-57; see also Schrage, *The Ethics of the NT*, pp. 46-52; Theissen and Merz, *The Historical Jesus*, pp. 213-17.

49. Perrin, *Rediscovering the Teaching of Jesus*, chap. 3, pp. 109-53 discusses all these relevant passages; quotation taken from p. 109.

geous in that culture that most scholars accept it as historical; Lohse labels it a 'gruffly formulated command' for the 'radical call to discipleship'.[50] The call must take priority over family relationships (Matt. 10.37-38//Luke 14.26). It asks one to give up all possessions (Luke 14.33), sacrificing everything for the sake of the 'pearl of great price' or the treasure (Matt. 13.44-46). It is a personal call to follow Jesus, regardless of the cost or suffering; it means denying oneself and taking up one's cross (Mark 8.34-37). It involves not worrying about food, drink or clothing (Matt. 6.31-33//Luke 12.29-33). The mission charge to take no bag, staff or sandals (Matt. 10.9-10//Luke 10.4) goes beyond even that of the Essenes or the Cynics (see Josephus, *Jewish War* 2.125-26).[51] This is preparing for war — the conflict with evil (Matt. 12.28). Thus the response demanded by Jesus is total, all or nothing.[52]

If the stakes are high and the costs total, there is also a lot about reward and punishment in Jesus' parables and teaching, depending on people's response. The day of judgement will bring punishment and shame to those who are ashamed of Jesus and the loss of eternal life (Mark 8.35-38); the cities who reject him will be worse off than Sodom and Gomorrah (Matt. 10.15; 11.21-22; Luke 10.13-15). Equally, however, there are rewards both in this life and in the age to come for those who do respond, repaying them a 'hundredfold' for family, houses or fields (Mark 10.29-30; see also Matt. 5.3-10; 6.33; 19.23-30; Luke 6.38; 22.28-30). As Keck notes, 'The New Testament writers do not shun reward and punishment as sanctions. The notion that the good is to be done for its own sake, not with an eye on future reward, simply never appears, for New Testament ethics is not oriented toward the good but to God's will, character, and activity as actualized in the Christ-event'.[53]

We shall return to some of these passages in the separate chapters on the evangelists, but even if we have to make some allowances for individual gospels' redactions, the overall picture here is clear. Jesus' ethical teaching is not a separate body of moral instructions, but rather part of his preaching of the eschatological in-breaking of the reign of God, which demands a total and immediate response from his hearers.

---

50. Lohse, *Theological Ethics of the NT,* p. 49.

51. Theissen and Merz, *The Historical Jesus,* pp. 215-16.

52. See further Schrage, *The Ethics of the NT,* pp. 46-52; N. T. Wright, *Jesus and the Victory of God,* pp. 297-304.

53. Keck, 'Rethinking "New Testament Ethics"', p. 14.

d. Responding in community

Finally, it is notable that this response is not simply an individual choice, but is located in the context of a new community. We have already noted Jesus' shocking saying to a would-be discile to leave his dead father unburied (Matt. 8.22// Luke 9.59-60). Other parts of his teaching against family ties would be equally scandalous: on being told that his mother and brothers and sisters are looking for him, he does not go to them as an obedient son should, but rather declares that his new community of those who 'do the will of God' are his mother and brothers and sisters (Mark 3.31-35). As Wright notes, 'In a peasant society, where familial relations provided one's basic identity, it was shocking in the extreme.'[54] This suggestion that their response to Jesus would replace his followers' original family with a new community is borne out in the promise of the 'hundredfold' reward including new families of mothers and fathers, brothers and sisters (Mark 10.29-30). The warning of the woes to come includes the threat of violent strife even within families (Mark 13.9-12). The disciples are not to call anyone 'father', for they are all brothers and sisters, with one Father in heaven (Matt. 23.8-10). Jesus' addressing of God as 'Father' in the Lord's Prayer and elsewhere implies a new family, the family of God (Luke 6.36; 11.2, 13; 12.30).[55] Crossan argues that Jesus' teaching is 'against the patriarchal family . . . the Kingdom against the Mediterranean. But not just against the Mediterranean alone'.[56]

This new community was comprised of all who responded together — and sometimes they made an interesting collection! Jesus was regularly criticised for his table fellowship with sinners, as we shall see when we come to consider his deeds in the next section. However, here in his words he defended this practice vigorously in his teaching (e.g., Mark 2.13-17; Matt. 11.19; Luke 15.1-2; 19.1-10). Wright points out that the comparison of Jesus' disciples to those of John the Baptist or the Pharisees and Jesus' response using the language of bridegroom and bride imply that these new communities were for the renewal of Israel (Mark 2.18-20).[57] This is also reflected in Jesus' community language of 'little flock' (Luke 12.32). Sanders considers the particular calling of a group of twelve disciples to be one of 'the (almost) indisputable facts about Jesus'.[58] The twelve tribes of Israel had ceased to exist as a group after the Assyrian invasion of 734 BC, yet the number retained its symbolic importance. The preservation

---

54. N. T. Wright, *Jesus and the Victory of God,* p. 278; see further pp. 274-78.
55. Theissen and Merz, *The Historical Jesus,* pp. 218-19.
56. Crossan, *The Historical Jesus,* pp. 299-302.
57. N. T. Wright, *Jesus and the Victory of God,* p. 276.
58. E. P. Sanders, *Jesus and Judaism,* p. 101; see further pp. 98-106.

by the early church of Jesus' teachings about the twelve sitting on thrones to judge Israel together with the promise of new families (Matt. 19.28-29) — despite the embarrassment of there only being eleven apostles after Judas' betrayal — is evidence that Jesus saw his followers as a community 'in terms of the eschatological restoration of Israel'.[59] Thus Jesus' ethical teaching is in the prophetic tradition of expecting a response to the sovereign rule of God, and any individual's response is to be worked out within the wider community of God's people who also respond to his call.[60]

e. The law and love

The enormous debate about Jesus' attitude to the law and love cannot be dealt with here in detail, but clearly some examination is needed. At the heart of Jesus' ethics is **the double love command,** to love God and one's neighbour, given in response to a question about the greatest commandment (Mark 12.28-34).[61] Such questions and debates were quite common, and the rabbinic tradition includes similar stories, such as Rabbi Hillel's summary which could be delivered while standing on one leg: 'What is hateful to you, do not do to your neighbour. That is the whole Torah. The rest is commentary. Go and learn!' (*b. Shabbat* 31a, Babylonian Talmud).[62] Jesus' reply brings together two statements from the Old Testament — Deut. 6.5 (the *Shema*) and Lev. 19.18 — and this particular combination seems to be new. While recognizing other contemporary Jewish

59. N. T. Wright, *Jesus and the Victory of God*, p. 300.

60. See also Ian McDonald's stress on the community aspect of ethical response in his *The Crucible of Christian Morality* (London: Routledge, 1998), esp. pp. 85-122.

61. For fuller discussion of the double love command, see V. P. Furnish, *The Love Command in the New Testament* (Nashville: Abingdon, 1972), esp. pp. 22-45; Robert Banks, *Jesus and the Law in the Synoptic Tradition*, SNTSMS 28 (Cambridge: Cambridge University Press, 1975), pp. 164-73; Reginald H. Fuller, 'The Double Commandment of Love: A Test Case for the Criteria of Authenticity', in *Essays on the Love Commandment* by Luise Schottroff, Reginald H. Fuller, Christoph Burchard and M. Jack Suggs (Philadelphia: Fortress, 1978), pp. 41-56; Schrage, *The Ethics of the NT*, pp. 68-87; D. C. Jones, *Biblical Christian Ethics* (Grand Rapids: Baker, 1994), pp. 43-57; Marxsen, *New Testament Foundations*, pp. 95-97; Verhey, *The Great Reversal*, p. 24; Chilton and McDonald, *Jesus and the Ethics of the Kingdom*, pp. 2-3; Theissen and Merz, *The Historical Jesus*, pp. 381-94; Oliver O'Donovan, *Resurrection and Moral Order: An Outline for Evangelical Ethics* (Leicester: IVP, 1994), pp. 226-44.

62. For a comparison of Hillel's comment with Jesus' teaching, see P. S. Alexander, 'Jesus and the Golden Rule', in *Hillel and Jesus: Comparative Studies of Two Major Religious Leaders*, ed. J. H. Charlesworth and L. L. Johns (Minneapolis: Fortress, 1997), pp. 363-88; quotation of *b. Shabbath* 31a from p. 366; also reprinted in *The Historical Jesus in Recent Research*, ed. Dunn and McKnight, pp. 489-508; quotation from p. 491.

summaries of the law, Furnish states that 'nowhere else is there the specific coupling of the two texts from Deut 6.5 and Lev. 19.18 which we find attributed to Jesus'.[63] This dissimilarity argues for the combination to be from the historical Jesus. As we shall discuss further in our later chapters on the evangelists' redactions, Matthew's typical interest in the law is seen in his addition that 'the law and prophets depend' on this double command (Matt. 22.40). In Luke's version (10.25-28) the lawyer is made to give the answer himself, and then he continues with the obvious question, 'Who is my neighbour?' In the Old Testament, 'neighbour' tended to mean fellow Israelite, but the parable of the Good Samaritan in Jesus' reply widens it beyond national boundaries, even to those who are despised (10.29-37). This broadens the scope of Jesus' ethic considerably and stresses the wider community as the place where the response is to be made.[64]

The centrality of love in Jesus' ethics even extends to **the love of enemies**. The Q-saying of Matt. 5.38-48//Luke 6.27-36 goes beyond mere nonretaliation to positive love for enemies, exemplified in turning the other cheek and giving away clothes and goods. Luke includes his version of the 'Golden Rule' here, 'As you would wish people would do to you, do so to them' (Luke 6.31). While a loving attitude even to such outsiders is a central theme for Luke, it can also be found in Matthew's unique material: the practical outworking of love to the poor, hungry, prisoners and the like becomes grounds for the judgement in the parable of the Sheep and Goats (Matt. 25.31-46); according to the Sermon on the Mount, you cannot worship God without loving your brother (Matt. 5.23-24). Thus both what McDonald calls 'the distinctiveness of this new praxis' in Jesus' command to love enemies and its multiple attestation across the sources argue that this is a key feature of the ethics of the historical Jesus.[65] Piper's ex-

---

63. Furnish, *The Love Command*, p. 62; Schrage agrees, *The Ethics of the NT*, pp. 70, 85.

64. See Lohse, *Theological Ethics of the NT*, pp. 52-60; N. T. Wright, *Jesus and the Victory of God*, pp. 304-7; Pheme Perkins, 'Jesus and Ethics', *Theology Today* 52.1 (1995), pp. 49-65, esp. pp. 54-58.

65. McDonald, *Crucible of Christian Morality*, p. 104; on the love of enemies, see also Luise Schottroff, 'Non-Violence and the Love of One's Enemies', in *Essays on the Love Commandment* by Luise Schottroff, Reginald H. Fuller, Christoph Burchard and M. Jack Suggs (Philadelphia: Fortress, 1978), pp. 9-39; A. E. Harvey, *Strenuous Commands: The Ethic of Jesus* (London: SCM/Philadelphia: Trinity Press International, 1990), pp. 96-115; W. M. Swartley (ed.), *The Love of Enemy and Nonretaliation in the New Testament* (Louisville: Westminster John Knox, 1992); G. Theissen, 'Non-violence and Love of Our Enemies (Matthew 5.38-48; Luke 6.27-38)', in his *Social Reality and the Early Christians: Theology, Ethics and the World of the New Testament* (Minneapolis: Fortress, 1992/ Edinburgh: T&T Clark, 1993), pp. 115-57; M. Schöni, 'What More Are You Doing than Others? The Radical Ethics of Jesus', *Near East School of Theology Theological Review* 16.2 (1995), pp. 75-97; Theissen and Merz, *The Historical Jesus*, pp. 390-94; Verhey, *The Great Reversal*, pp. 24-25; Schrage, *The Ethics of the NT*, pp. 73-79.

tensive study concludes that the historical Jesus' teaching is the basis for 'the central command of enemy love' behind both the Synoptic versions and 'the early Christian paraenetic tradition' seen in the epistles (Rom. 12.14, 17-20; 1 Cor. 4.12; 1 Thess. 5.15; 1 Pet. 3.9).[66] Klassen notes that even the Jesus Seminar thought it 'inconceivable' that anyone other than Jesus could have 'made up' this saying![67]

Closely allied to all this is Jesus' stress on **forgiveness**, which is linked to forgiving others in Matt. 5.23-24 and in the Q-saying of forgiving others seven times or seventy times seven in Matt. 18.21-22//Luke 17.4, which leads to Matthew's unique parable of the Unforgiving Servant (18.23-35). This theme of being forgiven as we have forgiven others is repeated in the Lord's Prayer (Matt. 6.12; Luke 11.4). The failure to forgive has dire consequences, as those who do not forgive others will be unable to receive the Father's forgiveness (Matt. 6.15; Mark 11.25-26); mutual forgiveness is matched by not judging others and being judged, leading to the saying about the mote and beam (Luke 6.37-42; Matt. 7.1-5). Such forgiveness is exemplified in Jesus' healing ministry, where forgiving the paralytic's sins enables him to 'get up and walk' (Mark 2.1-12). Similar teaching on forgiveness is also used to defend Jesus' acceptance of sinners (e.g., Luke 7.36-50). No wonder that Luke depicts Jesus dying with such words of forgiveness for enemies and acceptance of sinners on his lips (Luke 23.34, 39-43). Again, therefore, while we will return to Luke's redaction in the separate chapter on Luke-Acts below, this multiple attestation in so many different versions demonstrates that forgiveness is thus another distinctive feature of the ethical teaching of the historical Jesus.[68]

Jesus' **attitude to the law** has been the subject of much debate over recent decades.[69] On an initial reading of the gospels, he seems somewhat different from many others of his time. Unlike the people in many stories contained in

66. John Piper, 'Love Your Enemies': Jesus' Love Command in the Synoptic Gospels and in the Early Christian Paraenesis: A History of the Tradition and Interpretation of Its Uses, SNTSMS 38 (Cambridge: Cambridge University Press, 1979), pp. 171-72.

67. William Klassen, 'The Authenticity of the Command: "Love Your Enemies"', in Authenticating the Words of Jesus, ed. B. Chilton and C. A. Evans (Leiden: Brill, 1999), pp. 385-407, esp. p. 403.

68. See further Donald W. Shriver, Jr., An Ethics for Enemies: Forgiveness in Politics (Oxford: Oxford University Press, 1995), see esp. pp. 33-45.

69. See, for example, Banks, Jesus and the Law in the Synoptic Tradition; John Riches, Jesus and the Transformation of Judaism, pp. 112-44; Harvey, Jesus and the Constraints of History, pp. 36-65; Dunn, Jesus Remembered, pp. 563-83; Peter J. Tomson, 'If this be from Heaven . . .': Jesus and the New Testament Authors in Their Relationship to Judaism (Sheffield: Sheffield Academic Press, 2001), pp. 144-59; William Loader, Jesus' Attitude towards the Law: A Study of the Gospels (Grand Rapids: Eerdmans, 2002), esp. pp. 518-24.

the rabbinic material, Jesus does not debate specific cases and situations, and in particular he is not as concerned about issues of cultic purity, preferring to look for 'the basic purpose of the law . . . the inner intention and desire'.[70] However, this can lead to making too easy a contrast between Jesus and other Jews, with the latter being caricatured as concerned only for casuistry, using the law to gain reward and being legalistic. According to such a view, Jesus is unique in his teaching about grace and love. The work of E. P. Sanders on covenantal nomism and Jesus' setting within contemporary Judaism has changed this caricature of Jewish legalism, hopefully for ever.[71] Furthermore, while Jesus seems to have 'relaxed' some aspects of the law in general, perhaps through an appeal to its 'inner meaning' or love, on other occasions he appears to radicalize or intensify it, and he never really abrogates it.[72] As Loader concludes at the end of his extensive study, 'The earlier forms of the anecdotes . . . all indicate an attitude towards the Law which upholds it, but changes the emphasis in interpreting it.'[73]

Of course, there is the issue of the evangelists' redaction to be faced here, since Matthew in particular has an especial interest in Jesus and the law (see, e.g., Matt. 5.17-48); we shall return to this in more detail in Chapter V below on Matthew's portrait. However, Jesus' relationship to the law is not found solely in Matthew. Even in Mark, Jesus affirms the law and the Ten Commandments to the rich young man (Mark 10.17), and strengthens it beyond even the most conservative interpretation in relationship to divorce (Mark 10.2-9) and marrying again (Mark 10.11-12). In Jesus' teaching on the Sabbath and eating with unclean people we have a clue to his attitude about 'relaxing' the law. The statement that the Sabbath was made for human beings and not vice versa (Mark 2.27) may be taken as programmatic for Jesus.[74] Something similar seems to happen in his criticism of Corban (Mark 7.8-12) or the ritual and sacrificial system (Mark 12.33). The Q-saying on tithing herbs but neglecting justice and love reflects a similarly prophetic sense of priorities (Matt. 23.23//Luke 11.42). This is then developed further in later Matthean redaction, which includes the quotation 'I desire mercy, and not sacrifice' from Hos. 6.6 in his versions of Mark 2.17 and 27

---

70. Millar Burrows, 'Old Testament Ethics and the Ethics of Jesus', in *Essays in Old Testament Ethics: In Memory of J. Phillip Hyatt,* ed. J. L. Crenshaw and J. T. Willis (New York: Ktav, 1974), pp. 227-43, quotation from p. 233; see also Furnish, *The Love Command,* p. 29; Josef Blank, 'Unity and Plurality in New Testament Ethics', in *Christian Ethics: Uniformity, Universality, Pluralism,* ed. J. Pohier and R. Mieth, *Concilium* 150 (New York: Seabury, 1981), pp. 65-71, esp. p. 68.

71. E. P. Sanders, *Jesus and Judaism,* passim, but see pp. 245-69 on Jesus and the law.

72. For Jesus both 'relaxing' and 'intensifying' the law, see Theissen and Merz, *The Historical Jesus,* pp. 359-72.

73. Loader, *Jesus' Attitude towards the Law,* pp. 518-19.

74. See Schrage, *The Ethics of the NT,* p. 53.

(Matt. 9.13; 12.7). To return again to Loader's conclusions, he argues that 'in addressing application of the Law' the earliest traditions 'emphasise the priority of compassion for human needs, of following God's original intention, of ethical behaviour and attitude above ritual and cultic'.[75] In other words, we are back to love.

It is interesting, therefore, to note that Hays, when selecting his key images for New Testament ethics, argues that 'love and liberation are not sufficient'. Not only is love not central to New Testament ethics as a whole, according to Hays, it is not really an image, but more often 'easily debased in popular discourse . . . a cover for all manner of vapid self-indulgence'.[76] However, it is arguable that Hays only demonstrates the importance of his images of 'cross, community and new creation' in Paul and then applies them briefly to the rest of the New Testament.[77] Since references to 'love' are many times more frequent than to 'cross' or 'community', it is debatable whether these images will serve his purpose, even for the whole of the New Testament. Furnish concludes that 'for most of the New Testament writers the love command is . . . *decisive* and *central*'.[78] Similarly, Blank argues that 'the commandment to love provides the fundamental unity in New Testament ethics and . . . *the centre of Christian ethics*'.[79]

Certainly, in relation to Jesus' ethics, love is absolutely crucial — even if we agree with Hays that 'love' means something tougher than many ideas of the 'loving thing to do' today! What can prevent Jesus' teaching from sliding into a vague 'situation ethic' or 'internalized love' is closer attention to how he both strengthens and relaxes the law in an eschatological context. E. P. Sanders is clear that Jesus did not break the law himself or advocate its wholesale transgression (otherwise the later debates in the early church about the law would not have been necessary). However, his radical demands to 'let the dead bury their dead' (Matt. 8.22//Luke 9.60) and the strengthening of the prohibition against divorce on the one hand, and his relaxed acceptance of sinners and healings on the other hand, both make sense in the light of the eschatological crisis when the 'Mosaic dispensation' is no longer 'final or absolutely binding'.[80]

75. Loader, *Jesus' Attitude towards the Law*, p. 519.

76. Hays, *The Moral Vision*, pp. 200-205; quotation from p. 202.

77. Hays, *The Moral Vision*, pp. 19-36 on Paul, 196-98 on the rest of the NT.

78. Furnish, *The Love Command*, p. 200, his italics.

79. Blank, 'Unity and Plurality in New Testament Ethics', p. 70, his italics; see also 'agapeic love is the single thread that links together the ethical teaching of the various New Testament writers', Raymond F. Collins, *Christian Morality: Biblical Foundations* (Notre Dame, IN: University of Notre Dame Press, 1986), p. 42.

80. E. P. Sanders, *Jesus and Judaism*, pp. 267-69.

Wright agrees with this eschatological explanation and develops it further with his understanding of the controversy between Jesus and his Jewish contemporaries being rooted in Jesus' redefinition of the key 'symbols' of Sabbath, food, nation, land and temple. This leads to a 'redefined Torah' in which his 'returned-from-exile people, who had themselves received "mercy" and "forgiveness"', must 'demonstrate the same "mercy" and "forgiveness". . . . Forgiveness lay at the heart of the symbolic praxis which was to characterize his redefined Israel.'[81]

Thus this brief study of Jesus' attitude to love and the law leads us to agree with Lohse's conclusion: 'Therefore, it is not the individual admonitions, for which the study of comparative religion can furnish ample parallel material, which give us the distinctive foundation of ethical instructions in Jesus' teaching. Rather, the foundation is the radicalisation of the love commandment, which Jesus extends to love for one's enemies. In the light of the in-breaking of the kingdom of God this love will clearly illuminate the signs of the incomprehensible mercy of God in the midst of this world'.[82]

Therefore we return to our key point that Jesus' ethical teaching cannot be abstracted from the rest of his overall preaching of the kingdom of God. Jesus is not seeking to interpret the finer points of the law, nor even to provide a new law. As Schrage concludes, 'Beyond all doubt, Jesus denied the Torah the central place it had for Judaism. What matters in the light of the eschaton is not one's attitude toward the Torah but one's attitude toward Jesus' message of the kingdom of God and God's will'.[83] The love of God, which can never be 'vapid' or 'self-indulgent', is breaking into our world here and now to bring about the eschatological restoration of his people under God's gracious reign. Such love, at one and the same time, makes a 'radical and strengthening' demand for a total response, while requiring a more 'relaxed' and open acceptance of all those who respond to God's call in love.

f. An 'impractical' approach to ethical issues?

Thus the centrality of love in the teaching of Jesus does not lead to a vague 'anything goes' ethic nor to a dismantling of the law. It is a consequence of his proclamation of the kingdom of God as the eschatological sovereignty of God is

---

81. N. T. Wright, *Jesus and the Victory of God*, pp. 369-442; quotations from p. 432.

82. Eduard Lohse, 'The Church in Everyday Life: Considerations of the Theological Basis of Ethics in the New Testament', ET in Brian S. Rosner (ed.), *Understanding Paul's Ethics* (Grand Rapids: Eerdmans, 1995), pp. 251-65; quotation from pp. 255-56.

83. Schrage, *The Ethics of the NT*, p. 67.

made manifest in the present through the outpouring of his love. As Harvey puts it, 'Much of the most distinctive moral teaching in the gospels presupposes Jesus' proclamation of the kingdom'.[84] Such preaching requires a wholehearted response rather than a set of ethical instructions. Even when we turn at long last to what Jesus says about practical moral issues, we find that once again his teaching is more about a total response to God than specific commandments.[85]

While he may have taught a more 'relaxed' acceptance of people, at the same time Jesus 'strengthened' many moral areas into a more rigorous ethic. Thus in the area of **marriage and sexuality**, divorce was permitted by the law (Deut. 24.1); Jesus' teaching, however, 'intensified' it by returning to the original intention of 'one flesh' in Gen. 2.24 and thus allowing no divorce.[86] As we shall discover in the individual chapters on the evangelists below, Matthew's qualification 'except for immorality', μὴ ἐπὶ πορνείᾳ (Matt. 19.9, agreeing with the more conservative Jewish tradition as Rabbi Shammai did), is likely to be later redaction, while Mark's uncompromising refusal to accept any grounds for divorce is so distinctive from both contemporary Judaism and the practice of the early church (cp. Paul's exception to Jesus' prohibition in 1 Cor. 7.12-16) that it is extremely likely to go back to the authentic teaching of the historical Jesus (Mark 10.2-12). Similarly, Jesus 'strengthens' ethical teaching about celibacy, commending those who do not marry but become 'eunuchs for the sake of the kingdom of heaven' (Matt. 19.12), another distinctive emphasis in a society where getting married was seen as a duty.[87] Even looking at a woman with a lustful eye is tantamount to adultery (Matt. 5.27)![88]

When the subject turns to **money and possessions**, there are some suggestions in the Old Testament that wealth is a gift from God or a sign of his blessing (e.g., Gen. 13.2; Ps. 112.3; Eccl. 5.19), while other passages do warn of the dangers of riches and urge care for the poor (Deut. 15.1-11; 24.18-22; Ps. 49; Amos 2.6-7; 4.1; 8.4-6). Jesus develops this dimension also, stating that the poor are blessed (Luke 6.20); people are not to save wealth since one cannot

---

84. Harvey, *Strenuous Commands*, p. 192.

85. See Schrage, *The Ethics of the NT*, pp. 87-115 on the 'Concrete Precepts' of Jesus' teaching.

86. A. E. Harvey, 'Genesis versus Deuteronomy? Jesus on Marriage and Divorce', in *The Gospels and the Scriptures of Israel*, ed. Craig A. Evans and W. Richard Stegner, JSNTSS 104 (Sheffield: Sheffield Academic Press, 1994), pp. 55-65; on Jesus' use of Gen 2.24, see the new chap. 12 in L. William Countryman, *Dirt, Greed and Sex: Sexual Ethics in the New Testament and Their Implications for Today* (Minneapolis: Fortress, rev. 2nd edn. 2007); for a full discussion of all the passages, see William Loader, *Sexuality and the Jesus Tradition* (Grand Rapids: Eerdmans, 2005), pp. 61-120.

87. Loader, *Sexuality and the Jesus Tradition*, pp. 121-229.

88. See Banks, *Jesus and the Law in the Synoptic Tradition*, pp. 146-59; Harvey, *Strenuous Commands*, pp. 80-89; Schrage, *The Ethics of the NT*, pp. 91-98; Loader, *Sexuality and the Jesus Tradition*, pp. 9-20.

serve both God and money, so it should be given away (Matt. 6.19-33; Luke 12.22-34). 'How hard it will be for those who have wealth to enter the kingdom of God! . . . It is easier for a camel to go through the eye of a needle than for someone who is rich to enter the kingdom of God.' This runs so counter to the respect given to those who have been 'blessed' with wealth, both in his society and in most ever since, that again it is likely to be the authentic teaching of Jesus; no wonder 'the disciples were perplexed at these words' and 'greatly astounded' (Mark 10.23-27). What Mealand terms 'Jesus' presentation of the challenge to existing values by the supreme worth of the coming Reign of God' is no less demanding in terms of wealth and poverty than it was about sexuality.[89]

The same is true about **war, violence and the power of the state**: in contrast to the *lex talionis* for retribution and God fighting for Israel (Exod. 21.23-25; Deut. 19.21–20.4), Jesus taught nonresistance and nonviolence, to 'turn the other cheek' and to 'put away the sword' (Matt. 5.38-44//Luke 6.27-30; Matt. 26.52). Far from advocating 'holy war' against the Roman occupiers, Jesus counselled obedience to the state and the payment of taxes in the famous aphorism, 'Render to Caesar the things that are Caesar's, and to God the things that are God's' (Mark 12.13-17). We should even be prepared to carry a legionary's pack for two miles, if requisitioned for one (Matt. 5.41)![90] Once again, we hear the same total demand for a complete response to the sovereign reign of God as in the two previous moral experiences.

The well-known antitheses in the Sermon on the Mount — 'You have that it was said . . . but I say to you' (Matt. 5.21-48) — may owe their current form to Matthew's particular interest in the law, coming after the general statement about 'fulfilling the law' (5.17-20), as we shall see when we discuss his redaction in Chapter V below. However, the basic thrust of taking the old commands about basic human moral experiences and intensifying them does fit into this coherent overall ethical voice of the historical Jesus, stressing a rigorous ethic of lifelong sexual fidelity, poverty, nonviolence and obedience. Minear tries to give this teaching shape by grouping the 'Commands of Christ' into nine instructions: 'Let your yes be yes'; 'keep it secret'; 'love and lend'; 'become last of all'; 'sell and give'; 'ask, seek, knock'; 'be carefree'; 'watch and pray'; 'take this and divide among yourselves'.[91] However, these are not really what one might term

---

89. David L. Mealand, *Poverty and Expectation in the Gospels* (London: SPCK, 1980), p. 92; see also Banks, *Jesus and the Law in the Synoptic Tradition*, pp. 159-64; Harvey, *Strenuous Commands*, pp. 116-39; Schrage, *The Ethics of the NT*, pp. 98-107.

90. See Harvey, *Strenuous Commands*, pp. 72-73, 92-106; Schrage, *The Ethics of the NT*, pp. 107-15.

91. Paul S. Minear, *Commands of Christ* (Edinburgh: Saint Andrew Press, 1972).

'moral commandments'; rather, they help to form this overall ethical attitude of a total response to the kingdom of God.

We shall return to the evangelists' redactions of these teachings in the chapters below about each of the gospels. Here we are concerned more with this all-demanding approach which seems to have characterized the teachings of Jesus himself. At this point, however, we must recognize that many people have considered that Jesus' ethics, particularly in the Matthean form of the Sermon on the Mount, are 'impractical' and demand something which is impossible for human beings. As Léon-Dufour puts it, 'The Sermon on the Mount is, in itself, impracticable. As a result, we are invited either to contemplate an illusory ideal or plunge into the depths of guilt.'[92] Similarly, Anthony Harvey terms Jesus' ethics his 'strenuous commands', as he quotes G. K. Chesterton that 'the Christian ideal has not been tried and found wanting. It has been found difficult, and left untried.' He goes on to note that this 'ethic of Jesus' is rather sidelined in the Christian ethical tradition, with its particular stress on moral theology and natural law; indeed, he argues that even the rest of the New Testament seems not to know of these teachings.[93] Spohn equally notes that 'the person of Jesus and the biblical roots of the Christian vocation' were 'largely ignored' in the moral theology of 'pre–Vatican II Catholicism', which preferred the natural law tradition for ethical guidance.[94]

The first question which arises here concerns whether these general ethical teachings of Jesus are meant to be taken literally as practical moral commandments or instructions. Does Jesus expect his disciples to cut off their hands or feet, or pluck out their eyes (Mark 9.43-48), or to 'hate father and mother' (Luke 14.26)? The Matthean version of the latter, 'who loves father or mother more than me' (10.37), reminds us of the importance of recognizing hyperbole and exaggeration. After all, Jesus also spoke about a man with a log in his eye trying to take out somebody else's speck of dust, or of a camel going through the eye of a needle (Matt. 7.3-5//Luke 6.41-42; Mark 10.25)! Having said this, an appeal to Jesus' exaggerated style of speaking as a way of avoiding the challenge of his rigorous ethic seems too easy an answer.

There have been many other attempts to deal with the situation.[95] Even

92. Xavier Léon-Dufour, *To Act according to the Gospel* (Peabody, MA: Hendrickson, 2005), p. 94.

93. Harvey, *Strenuous Commands*, pp. 1, 7, 24.

94. Spohn, *Go and Do Likewise: Jesus and Ethics*, p. 185.

95. For further discussion, see Harvey, *Strenuous Commands*, pp. 7-38; Lohse, *Theological Ethics of the NT*, pp. 61-73; Hans Dieter Betz, *The Sermon on the Mount: A Commentary on the Sermon on the Mount, including the Sermon on the Plain (Matthew 5:3–7:27 and Luke 6:20-49)*, Hermeneia (Minneapolis: Fortress, 1995), pp. 5-43; N. Guillemette, S.J., 'The Sermon on the Mount: Feasible Ethics?', *Landas* 9 (1995), pp. 209-36; Theissen and Merz, *The Historical Jesus*, pp. 394-400.

Matthew's redaction adds the suggestion that the rich young man only needs to sell everything 'if you would be perfect' (Matt. 19.21), though this did not stop Origen, Chrysostom and Basil from trying to follow it all literally! From this stress on 'perfection', some in the early church argued that 'if you can bear the Lord's yoke in its entirety, then you will be perfect, but if that is too much for you, do as much as you can' (*Didache* 6.2). Over the centuries, this led to a distinction between what 'ordinary Christians' were supposed to do (the evangelical 'precepts' or commands), and the 'super league' of the religious orders committed to the vows of poverty, chastity and obedience (the evangelical 'counsels'), expressed most clearly by St Thomas Aquinas (*Summa Theologiae*, 1a.2ae.108.3-4).

As might be expected, the Reformers resisted this attempt to divide the people of God into 'first'- and 'second'-class citizens. Instead, Luther's stress on the 'two kingdoms' applied the distinction to the individual's private sphere where the rigorous demands applied, and to the public sphere where the authorities still had to deal with vengeance, marriage, taxes and so forth. However, even in the personal area, the very impossibility of keeping the commands only serves to drive us to recognize our sin and throw ourselves on God's free grace and mercy.[96] Meanwhile, Léon-Dufour notes how Catholics 'maintained it [this division] incorrectly' until 'John Paul II himself rejected the distinction between "commandments" and "counsels", stressing that we are all called to the perfection that consists in loving our neighbour'.[97]

Another approach recognizes the impossibility of keeping such instructions literally. They are not to be understood as legal codes or commands to be obeyed (as in the Jewish *halakhah*), but as exaggerated standards to inspire us to the best we can be (as story or commentary, *haggadah*). In this way, generations of preachers have applied them more to our inner life of intentions, attitudes and motives, rather than expecting a literal obedience. As Guillemette notes, Jesus does not even keep them himself, getting angry (Matt. 21.12-13 against 5.22), calling Pharisees 'fools' (Matt. 23.17 against 5.22) and not turning the other cheek, but protesting when he is struck (John 18.22-23). Thus he concludes: 'Jesus does not give *directives*, but rather a *direction*.'[98] However, both Matthew and Luke conclude their main accounts of these instructions with the parable of the houses built on rock and sand to stress the importance of acting upon what he says; Luke introduces it with

96. See Schrage, *The Ethics of the NT*, pp. 88-91; Lohse, *Theological Ethics of the NT*, pp. 64-67.

97. Léon-Dufour, *To Act according to the Gospel*, pp. 109-10, quoting the *Catéchisme de l'Église catholique* III, nos. 2052-54 for the distinction, and John Paul II, *Veritatis Splendor* (Milan: Sao Paolo, 1994), no. 18 for its overturning.

98. Guillemette, 'The Sermon on the Mount', pp. 227-28, 231 and 235, his italics.

the clear statement, 'Why do you call me "Lord, Lord" and not do what I tell you?', while Matthew stresses that it is not saying but doing which matters (Matt. 7.21-27//Luke 6.46-49).

Such demands from Jesus for concrete action have always caused some people to take these teachings literally. In a variation upon the 'evangelical precepts' approach of applying them to the totally committed religious, various sectarian movements have embraced them for all their people, and thus withdrawn from the wider life of society, as in the case of the Amish community. Some groups of Anabaptists, Mennonites and Quakers have also followed this approach. More recent advocates of sociological analysis of the New Testament have similarly seen these teachings as practised only by a small group within the early church, namely the 'wandering radicals' or 'itinerant charismatics'. The work of Theissen in particular has stressed that 'only the person who has left home and possession, wife and child, who lets the dead bury their dead, and takes the birds and the lilies of the field as his model . . . can consistently preach renunciation'. Jesus' rigorous ethic does not 'have a situation *in* real life at all' but only '*on the fringes* of normal life'.[99] The existence of such 'wandering charismatics' is demonstrated by the instructions about receiving them in *Didache* 11, and by similar travelling teachers, such as the Cynics. Freyne sets this call 'to abandon all and imitate Jesus' lifestyle' within the Jubilee tradition in Galilee: 'Jesus' radical abandoning of the values of home, family and possessions and his expectation that his followers would do likewise was . . . based on the Jubilee values of total trust in Yahweh's gifts of food, shelter and the necessities of life. Without a context in which prophetic signs act as radical expressions of social critique, such a manifesto could only be regarded as irresponsible'.[100]

Another variant of this approach stresses the eschatological context of Jesus' proclamation of the kingdom of God, and therefore sees his teaching as an 'interim ethic' for the period up to the final cataclysm. As we saw in the section on eschatology and ethics (sect. 2.b above), this approach follows from the stress on eschatology by Weiss and Schweitzer. Clearly, if one believes that the world is going to end tomorrow, then a total renunciation of money, possessions, family, sexuality, offspring, homes and stability does not really matter; it is only when one attempts to put that ethic into practice over centuries and millennia that the difficulties emerge.

99. G. Theissen, 'The Wandering Radicals', in his *Social Reality and the Early Christians: Theology, Ethics and the World of the New Testament* (Minneapolis: Fortress, 1992/Edinburgh: T&T Clark, 1993), pp. 33-59; quotation from p. 40; see also Theissen, 'We have left everything . . . (Mark 10:28)', also in *Social Reality*, pp. 60-93.

100. Freyne, *Jesus, A Jewish Galilean*, p. 118.

The problem with all these attempted 'solutions' is precisely that: Jesus' radical ethic is perceived as a 'problem' or 'difficulty', and the answer is to be found by applying it to a particular small group, or period, or sphere of human life. As Harvey points out, 'The main objection to any approach of this kind is that it fails to account for the continuing attraction and influence of Jesus' ethic'. If his teaching is only for a small group or time, rather than the majority of Christians, it would have ceased to have been 'of interest and importance'.[101] Far from being seen as a 'problem', in fact Jesus' radical ethic and rigorous teaching has continued to challenge and inspire men and women across the world and down the ages, both inside and outside the church. Harvey himself interprets these 'strenuous commands' against the background of prudential wisdom in the ancient world and sees them as a challenge to Jesus' hearers. 'His ethical teaching was not intended to provide a set of rules to regulate the moral conduct of his followers, but rather to challenge us to live "as if" the kingdom were already a reality.'[102] Harvey wrote against the background of the fall of the Berlin Wall and the collapse of the Communist regimes of Eastern Europe; I have undertaken some of this study in the new democratic, post-apartheid South Africa. Both of these extraordinary contexts seem suitable to reflect upon what might happen if more people did live 'as if' these idealistic and radical ethics were indeed practical and feasible!

Thus we return to the central argument of this chapter. Attention to their literary genre reminds us that the gospels are ancient biographies, not coherent ethical treatises; therefore, they must be interpreted primarily as a portrait of a person through their deeds and words. Jesus' ethical teaching is not a separate and discrete set of moral maxims, but part of his proclamation of the kingdom of God as God's reign and sovereignty are recognized in the here and now. It is primarily intended to elicit a wholehearted response from his hearers to live as disciples within the community of others who also respond and follow. In his appeal for the eschatological restoration of the people of God, Jesus intensified the demands of the law with his rigorous ethic of renunciation and self-denial in all the major human ethical experiences, such as money, sex, power, violence and so forth. However, at the same time the central stress in his teaching on love and forgiveness opened the community to the very people who had moral difficulties in these areas. Therefore, as befits a biographical narrative, we must now turn from Jesus' teaching to confront this paradox in his activity and behaviour.

101. Harvey, *Strenuous Commands*, p. 31.
102. Harvey, *Strenuous Commands*, p. 210.

3. Jesus' ethical example — his deeds

We have seen how Jesus announces the kingdom, says that the end of everything is at hand, that it all depends on our response to him and the need to give up everything and follow him; he strengthens the demands of the law so much that many think his ethic is impractical, particularly in the main areas of human moral experience. His teaching is very rigorous and demanding, so we expect him to be the sort of person who has high standards for those around him and whom ordinary fallible human beings would find rather uncomfortable. Accordingly, his rigorous ethical teaching should be set within a narrative of his struggle against those who cannot live up to his demanding standard.

a. 'The Friend of Sinners'

And yet, when we consider his activity, the exact opposite is the case. It was **religious leaders**, the ones with high ethical standards and the guardians of morality, who found him uncomfortable and with whom Jesus finds himself constantly in conflict. Immediately here we encounter the problem of how Jesus' opponents are depicted in the differing accounts in the gospels. At the very least, it is reasonable to assume that some teachers of the law would have debated with the historical Jesus, as Luke shows certain Pharisees inviting Jesus to discussions over dinner (Luke 7.36; 11.37; 14.1). While Luke has some Pharisees warn Jesus that Herod wishes to kill him (Luke 13.31), he still depicts most of them as scoffing at Jesus and being 'lovers of money' (15.1; 16.14). However, the depiction of the Pharisees in Matthew's gospel is much harsher, especially in the diatribe of 'woe to you, scribes and Pharisees' in Matt. 23. It is likely that both this portrait and the characterization of Jesus opponents in John's gospel as simply 'the Jews' reflect the bitterness of the conflicts and separation of synagogue and church in the latter decades of the first century, but such portrayals have led to accusations of anti-Semitism or anti-Jewishness in the gospels.[103] Therefore we shall have to consider each evangelist's redactional material and

103. See further Samuel Sandmel, *Anti-Semitism in the New Testament?* (Philadelphia: Fortress, 1978); Craig A. Evans and Donald A. Hagner (eds.), *Anti-Semitism and Early Christianity: Issues of Polemic and Faith* (Minneapolis: Fortress, 1993); William R. Farmer (ed.), *Anti-Judaism and the Gospels* (Harrisburg, PA: Trinity Press International, 1999); Peter J. Tomson, *'If this be from Heaven...': Jesus and the New Testament Authors in Their Relationship to Judaism* (Sheffield: Sheffield Academic Press, 2001); *Anti-Judaism and the Fourth Gospel: Papers of the Leuven Colloquium, 2000*, ed. R. Bieringer, D. Pollefyt and F. Vandecasteele-Vanneuville (Assen: Royal Van Gorcum, 2001).

attitude towards the Jewish authorities and the Pharisees in turn in our subsequent chapters. E. P. Sanders has done much to counter such 'anti-Semitic' tendencies in his reassessment of Palestinian Judaism and the Pharisees in particular. However, as Wright has argued, Sanders' reconstruction has not totally convinced everyone, nor does it render Jesus' clash with the religious authorities unhistorical[104] — and even Sanders himself recognizes that Jesus' opponents were 'the normal leaders of Judaism' and 'the normally pious'.[105]

Both the four gospels and the great majority of historical reconstructions today agree that one of the main causes of offence which led to opposition to Jesus and to his eventual death arose from **Jesus' table fellowship of eating with tax collectors and sinners.** While Jesus is particularly depicted as a 'friend of sinners' in Luke, it is also there in the call of Levi (Mark 2.13-17; Matt. 9.9-13) and the Q-saying that he was called 'a glutton and a drunkard, a friend of tax collectors and sinners' (Matt. 11.19//Luke 7.34). John is often accused of narrowing Jesus' call to universal love down to 'love one another' in the Christian community, yet even here Jesus is shown searching out those despised across social barriers of gender, race, belief or social status — the Samaritan woman (4.8, 27), the paralytic or the blind man cast out (5.1-14; 9) and the woman in adultery (if 8.1-11 is admitted), as we shall explore in more detail in Chapter VII on John below. Such multiple attestation across the different groupings and types of source material witnesses to the historical reality of Jesus' positive attitude towards 'outsiders' and sinners.

This too is an area which has undergone considerable revision and debate in recent years.[106] The basic fact remains true that while Jesus taught this rigorous, all-demanding ethic, it was the ordinary fallible folk, or even sinners, who flocked to him, among whom he spent his time and from whom he called his followers and disciples. What is more debated is how this is to be interpreted. It used to be accepted that, as Thompson put it, 'This [i.e., Jesus'] challenge to Jewish culture was nowhere more evident than in Jesus' frequent table fellowship with sinners'.[107] Jeremias argued that the 'sinners' were the same as 'the

---

104. N. T. Wright, *Jesus and the Victory of God*, pp. 376-83.

105. E. P. Sanders, *Jesus and Judaism*, pp. 287-88; see pp. 270-93 for full discussion.

106. See, for example, Banks, *Jesus and the Law in the Synoptic Tradition*, pp. 108-13; Marcus J. Borg, *Conflict, Holiness and Politics in the Teachings of Jesus*, Studies in the Bible and Early Christianity, vol. 5 (New York: Edwin Mellen, 1984), pp. 78-95; Richard A. Horsley, *Jesus and the Spiral of Violence: Popular Jewish Resistance in Roman Palestine* (San Francisco: Harper & Row, 1987), pp. 209-45; James D. G. Dunn, *Jesus' Call to Discipleship* (Cambridge: Cambridge University Press, 1992), pp. 62-76; Dunn, *Jesus Remembered*, pp. 526-34, 599-611.

107. James W. Thompson, 'The Ethics of Jesus and the Early Church', in *Christian Social Ethics*, ed. Perry C. Cotham (Grand Rapids: Baker, 1979), pp. 45-59; quotation from p. 50.

people of the land', the *'am ha'aretz* or ordinary folk, and that they would all have been seen as 'impure' by the Pharisees; no Jewish rabbi was as open in accepting them as Jesus.[108] The demand, 'Be holy, for I the LORD your God am holy' (Lev. 19.2), meant that those seeking to keep the law would keep away from those who were not holy or ritually pure, and certainly would not eat with them. This is made clear in the intertestamental literature, such as Jesus ben Sirach's instruction to 'consult with the wise. Let your conversation be with intelligent people . . . about the law of the Most High. Let the righteous be your dinner companions' (Sirach 9.14-16).

Sanders has criticized Jeremias' reconstruction, arguing that it depends upon too easy an identification of the *'am ha'aretz* with actual 'sinners' and that Jesus' offence was not about purity or even forgiveness; it was rather that he offered true 'sinners' admission to the kingdom if they accepted him.[109] Wright also distinguishes between 'sinners' and the 'people of the land', but suggests that 'we are dealing with shadings, not clear and obvious demarcations'.[110] Dunn similarly criticizes Sanders' 'unnuanced view of why individuals might be described as "sinners" within Judaism of that day'; in fact, it could include anybody outside any particular sectarian grouping. Therefore, he concludes that Jesus 'objected against a boundary-drawing within Israel which treated some Israelites as outside the covenant and beyond the grace of God. . . . those regarded as "sinners" by the narrow definitions and scruples of others had to be reaffirmed. Just as the poor were God's special concern, so the excluded and marginalised were of special concern for Jesus' mission.'[111] Even Crossan agrees that Jesus ministered among 'the nobodies' and 'undesirables', including common eating with them, which he terms 'commensality'.[112] Garrison compares Jesus' table fellowship in Luke's gospel with Graeco-Roman symposia but also contrasts his open acceptance of people with the more usual concern for the right guests; he suggests that Paul's warning to the Corinthians that the greedy and drunkards will not inherit the kingdom of God (1 Cor. 6.9-10) and that they should not even eat with such people (1 Cor. 5.11) may represent an attempt to correct a 'misconception' arising from the traditions about Jesus.[113]

108. J. Jeremias, *New Testament Theology 1: The Proclamation of Jesus* (New York: Scribner's/ London: SCM, 1971), pp. 108-13, 121.

109. E. P. Sanders, *Jesus and Judaism*, pp. 174-211.

110. N. T. Wright, *Jesus and the Victory of God*, pp. 264-68; quotation from p. 266.

111. Dunn, *Jesus Remembered*, pp. 528-32; quotations from pp. 529 and 532.

112. Crossan, *The Historical Jesus*, pp. 261-64 on 'open commensality' and 266-82 on 'a kingdom of nobodies' and 'undesirables'; see pp. 261-353 for full discussion.

113. Roman Garrison, *The Graeco-Roman Context of Early Christian Literature*, JSNTSS 137 (Sheffield: Sheffield Academic Press, 1997), pp. 41-47, 87-88.

At this point we need to emphasize this apparent contradiction of the teacher of rigorous ethics consorting with those who might have been seen as immoral. Carapiet, writing from the perspective of ministry among the rejected of Calcutta, describes Jesus' work as being among those who were excluded on cultic or ritual grounds (the sick), moral grounds (prostitutes) and religious or political grounds (tax collectors).[114] In fact, the various grounds are not so easy to distinguish at this time, as political, religious, cultic and moral considerations all merged into one another. Instead of too definite a distinction between 'grounds', or between the 'sinners' and the 'ordinary people', let us concentrate on the key areas of Jesus' rigorous ethical teaching noted above, that is, the major human experiences of money, sex, power, violence and so forth.

In the category of money, we find Jesus appealing to financial collaborators like tax collectors working for the Romans (Levi, Luke 5.27-30; Zacchaeus, Luke 19.1-10). He associated both with the poor and with women like Joanna and Susanna, wealthy enough to help fund his mission (Luke 8.1-3). This latter list also includes Mary Magdalene, who is often described as a prostitute in later traditions, although not in the gospels: all Luke 8.2 says is that she had had 'seven demons cast out of her'. However, Jesus does say that two key types of 'sinners', namely tax gatherers and prostitutes, were those who heard John the Baptist gladly and who would precede the religious leaders into the kingdom of heaven (Matt. 21.31-32). Tax gatherers and prostitutes would also have been concerned about the issues of violence, power and relations with Romans. Rather different views of these areas would have been held by those involved in resistance groups such as the Zealots, as Luke suggests was the case with Simon the Cananaean, and Judas, if Iscariot is connected with *sicarius*, or dagger-carrier[115] — yet they too were among Jesus' disciples (Mark 3.18-19//Luke 6.15-16). On the other hand, Jesus praised a centurion used to the exercise of military power for having faith 'such as I have not found even in Israel' (Matt. 8.5-13// Luke 7.1-10). Thus Jesus accepts many and various people who would have had different problems in the areas of money, sex, violence, the state and power — as well as with each other. Borg concludes that Jesus used table fellowship with such a wide range of people 'as a weapon . . . an acted parable of acceptance . . . an acted parable of what Israel should be, embodying a different understanding of Israel's nature and purpose'.[116]

114. M. Carapiet, 'Jesus and Christian Ethics Today', *Jeevadhara* 23 (Kottayam, Kerala, India, 1993), pp. 437-55; reference to p. 441.

115. *Sicarius* is used for such fighters in Acts 21.38, translated as 'assassins' in the NRSV; for a discussion of Iscariot and *sicarius*, see R. E. Brown, *The Death of the Messiah* (New York: Doubleday, 1994), pp. 1414-15; for a full account of the *sicarii*, see Crossan, *The Historical Jesus*, pp. 117-23.

116. Borg, *Conflict, Holiness and Politics in the Teachings of Jesus*, pp. 82 and 93-94.

The teacher of rigorous ethics did not just spend his time eating and drinking with such ethically dubious characters, but showed his acceptance of them in another major activity, for most of **Jesus' healing ministry** is directed towards such 'outsiders'.[117] Bolt has argued that the 'suppliant' narratives in Mark, of those who come to Jesus for exorcism or healing, are designed to reveal his authority to forgive and heal as the Isaianic servant. When the Israelites came out of Egypt, God promised to preserve them from the diseases with which he plagued the Egyptians if they listened to him, 'for I am the LORD who heals you' (Exod. 15.26); yet they were also warned of disease and affliction if they disobeyed (Deut. 28). Jesus' activity of healing and exorcism against the background of ancient fears of sickness and death was a claim to fulfil the promises of the prophets (Isa. 35.5-6; 42.7; 43.8; 53.4-6; 61.1-3). Thus the unclean spirit is exorcised, the leper healed and the paralytic forgiven his sins and told to get up and walk (Mark 1.21-27, 40-44; 2.1-12).[118] Dillmann derives 'a foundation for a new ethic' from the biblical narratives of Jesus' healing, notably that of the deaf mute (Mark 7.31-37) and the bent woman (Luke 13.10-17).[119] Jesus' acceptance of people included touching those who were ritually impure such as lepers and a haemorrhaging woman (Mark 1.41; 5.25-33) and offering healing to the racially despised such as a Samaritan leper and the Syrophoenician woman (Luke 17.11-19; Mark 7.24-30). Thus Jesus' healing ministry can be seen as an activity consistent with his general acceptance of ordinary people and even sinners and his habit of eating with them. In the same way that Jesus was able to heal sick people rather than being infected by them himself, so his acceptance of those who were 'impure' made them whole rather than polluting himself. Blomberg terms this 'contagious holiness': 'a godly person's holiness rubbing off on and transforming an unclean or unholy person scarcely seems to have been countenanced', yet this is what Jesus' table fellowship and open acceptance of people achieved.[120]

Finally, we must come to the culmination of Jesus' activity, his **death on the**

117. For a full discussion of Jesus' healing ministry, see J. P. Meier, *A Marginal Jew: Rethinking the Historical Jesus:* Volume 2, *Mentor, Message, and Miracles* (New York: Doubleday, 1994), pp. 678-772.

118. Peter G. Bolt, "'. . . With a View to the Forgiveness of Sins": Jesus and Forgiveness in Mark's Gospel', *The Reformed Theological Review* 57.2 (Victoria, Australia, 1998), pp. 53-69; see also Bolt's Ph.D. thesis, 'Do You Not Care That We Are Perishing?' (King's College London, 1997) ; revised for publication as *Jesus' Defeat of Death: Persuading Mark's Early Readers,* SNTSMS 125 (Cambridge: Cambridge University Press, 2004).

119. Rainer Dillmann, 'Aufbruch zu einer neuen Sittlichkeit: Biblisch-narrative Begründung ethischen Handelns', *Theologie und Glaube* 82.1 (Paderborn, 1992), pp. 34-45.

120. Craig L. Blomberg, *Contagious Holiness: Jesus' Meals with Sinners,* New Studies in Biblical Theology (Downers Grove, IL: IVP, 2005); quotation from p. 93.

cross. This was soon seen by early Christians as being 'for sinners', as in Paul's 'while we were still sinners, Christ died for us' (Rom. 5.8). Luke also depicts Jesus forgiving his executioners and offering acceptance as he dies to the thief crucified with him (Luke 23.34, 39-43). Is it possible to say anything about whether or how the historical Jesus foresaw, or even intended, his own death and if it was linked to his attitude towards 'sinners'? This enormous area of debate cannot be discussed fully here, but some relevant comment is required.[121] Most recent discussions concentrate as much on Jesus' activity as his words, anticipating the biographical stress used here. The two key activities which may give us a clue about Jesus' intentions at the end are the incident in the temple and the Last Supper. Sanders considers it quite conceivable or even possible that Jesus could see that his actions would lead to his death and that he saw it 'as that of a martyr who would be vindicated'.[122] As might be expected, Wright goes further, arguing that the Last Supper is 'the key symbol' to the 'intention of Jesus', setting his own death within the context of God's redemption of his people. Wright then links this to Jesus' other action in the temple and to his various sayings and words to demonstrate that Jesus saw his death in terms of redemptive suffering which would bring the victory of God: 'This is how the true exodus will come about. This is how evil will be defeated. This is how sins will be forgiven.'[123]

'For the forgiveness of sins' is also found in Matthew's version of Jesus' eucharistic words over the cup, but this is later redaction of Mark's 'for many' (Matt. 26.28//Mark 14.24). However, the idea that the body and blood are 'for' (ὑπέρ) others also appears in Luke's 'for you' and Paul's handing on of the tradition (Luke 22.19-20; 1 Cor. 11.23-25). After all the table fellowship of eating and drinking with sinners, it is significant that these words also come in the context of a meal. Jeremias' study of the eucharistic words as showing Jesus' interpretation of his death in a Passover context has been widely accepted.[124] Theissen and Merz also see the Last Supper as a symbolic action, linked to his other action in the temple, both indicating a 'new covenant', which soon came to be seen in sacrificial terms.[125]

Further insight into how Jesus may have seen his death may be found in his 'passion predictions' (notably Mark 8.31; 9.31; 10.33-34, and parallels). The Jesus Seminar consider these unhistorical on the grounds that Jesus did not

---

121. See, for example, Dunn, *Jesus Remembered*, pp. 790-824.

122. E. P. Sanders, *Jesus and Judaism*, pp. 326, 332; for a general discussion of Jesus' death, see pp. 294-318.

123. N. T. Wright, *Jesus and the Victory of God*, p. 610; see his discussion, pp. 553-611.

124. J. Jeremias, *The Eucharistic Words of Jesus* (London: SCM, 1966).

125. Theissen and Merz, *The Historical Jesus*, pp. 405-69.

have divine foreknowledge.[126] However, many have responded that Jesus would not have needed supernatural powers to see that his actions were likely to lead to his death; as Brown's careful discussion has argued, while some of the details may reflect later redaction, the basic thrust of Jesus' predictions coheres with what anyone under Roman rule at the time expected, and they are expressed in terms of Old Testament language about the suffering of the righteous, especially prophets: 'A Jesus who would not have thought about any of these things would have been an oddity.'[127] Freyne deduces the same point from the incident 'within the tinder-box that was the Jerusalem temple': 'Jesus cannot have been unaware of the consequences of his symbolic action for his own future.'[128] What is interesting from the point of view of this study is that both Mark 9.31 and 10.33-34 lead into discussions of true greatness, with Jesus' rigorous ethic about the renunciation of power, the importance of being like a child and service, the latter concluding with 'to give his life as a ransom for many' (Mark 9.33-37; 10.35-45). While, once again, the concept of 'ransom' may be later redaction, this saying still includes Jesus' self-giving for others, which does fit with all we have discussed above. Stuhlmacher concludes his study of the passion predictions, the ransom-saying and the institution of the Eucharist thus: 'Jesus knowingly and willingly went to his death. He understood this as a vicarious atoning death for the many, both Israel and the nations. . . . Jesus took suffering and death upon himself out of love for God and humanity.'[129]

Thus we may conclude with the notable fact that the Jesus who taught a rigorous ethic in the areas of key human moral experience, such as money, sex, power and violence, also spent a large part of his time with ordinary people and even 'sinners' with difficulties in these areas. He not only accepted them, ate and drank with them, but also healed them from disease and impurity and probably saw his own death as 'for' them. If the biographical hypothesis about the gospels means anything at all, it must have something to say about this — that Jesus' attitude and actions towards sinful people are as important as his teaching in establishing his ethic. So did he expect them to change, and if so, how?

126. R. W. Funk and R. W. Hoover, *The Five Gospels: The Search for the Authentic Words of Jesus* (New York: Macmillan, 1993).

127. Brown, *Death of the Messiah*, p. 1488; see Appendix VIII, 'Jesus' Predictions of His Passion and Death', pp. 1468-91 for full discussion.

128. Freyne, *Jesus, A Jewish Galilean*, pp. 165-66.

129. Peter Stuhlmacher, 'Jesus' Readiness to Suffer and His Understanding of His Death', in *The Historical Jesus in Recent Research*, ed. Dunn and McKnight, pp. 392-412; quotation from p. 412.

b. Forgiveness and repentance

We have seen that at the heart of Jesus' ethic was the announcement of the kingdom of God and a call to respond: 'Repent and believe the gospel. . . . Follow me' (Mark 1.15, 17). The interesting thing is that he does not spell out what that repentance might mean. Indeed, after the initial summary of Jesus' preaching in Mark 1.15, the word occurs again only in a summary of all the disciples' activity (6.12). Matthew similarly does not use it about Jesus, except for the Q-passages about woes to the cities of Galilee (Matt. 11.20-24//Luke 10.13-15) and the repentance of Nineveh (Matt. 12.41//Luke 11.32). It does not occur in John at all, but it is a little more frequent in Luke as part of Jesus' teaching in 5.32; 13.3, 5; 15.7, 10; 16.30; 17.3-4, culminating in the mission of the disciples to preach 'repentance and forgiveness of sins in his name to all nations' (24.47). Given this uneven distribution, not surprisingly, E. P. Sanders has doubts about claims that repentance is 'central to Jesus' message'.[130]

Forgiveness and repentance are both clearly important in Judaism. The Marcionite attempt to contrast a 'God of wrath' in the Old Testament and a forgiving 'God of love' in the New Testament is nonsense.[131] At Sinai, God was revealed as 'merciful and gracious, slow to anger and abounding in steadfast love and faithfulness . . . forgiving iniquity, transgression and sin' (Exod. 34.6-7).[132] The plea to God's love for forgiveness is basic to many psalms, especially Ps. 51. In the prophets, we have Hosea's daring picture of God's love struggling in his heart and overcoming his anger with Israel, 'for I am God and no mortal' (Hos. 11.1-9). Wright draws attention to the way forgiveness of sins is linked to the return from exile in Isa. 40–55, Jer. 31, 33 and Ezek. 36–37.[133]

Forgiveness, however, involves repentance. Individual sinners among the priests, rulers or people who sinned 'unintentionally' could offer sacrifices, 'and you shall be forgiven' (Lev. 4.1-31; Num. 15.27-29). Deliberate, or 'high-handed' breaking of the commandments, however, led to being 'cut off', or executed (Num. 15.30-36). Individual or occasional trespass was to be dealt with by restitution of what was stolen or defrauded, plus an extra fifth, followed by sacrifice (Lev. 6.1-7), which would have entailed a trip to the temple in Jerusalem. In addition, there was the annual Day of Atonement (Lev. 16.29-34). Thus repentance requires a 'turning back' to God and is evidenced by a turning back to the law and to the covenant through sacrifice in the temple and restitutive action.

---

130. E. P. Sanders, *Jesus and Judaism*, pp. 108-13; see also Dunn, *Jesus Remembered*, pp. 498-99.

131. See L. Gregory Jones, *Embodying Forgiveness: A Theological Analysis* (Grand Rapids: Eerdmans, 1995), pp. 105-10.

132. See Dunn, *Jesus Remembered*, pp. 786-87.

133. N. T. Wright, *Jesus and the Victory of God*, pp. 268-72.

This view is also expressed in the intertestamental literature (e.g., *Psalms of Solomon* 3.9; 9.11-15; 14.1). Other groups within Judaism, such as the Essenes, had their own additional demands and customs, including ritual bathing. At Qumran, to repent meant 'to return to the law of Moses' within that community as a 'covenant of repentance' (CD 16.1-3; 19.16).[134] John the Baptist fits well into this environment. He came 'preaching a baptism of repentance for the forgiveness of sins' (Luke 3.3; cp. Acts 13.24; 19.4). He called people 'vipers' and warned them of the 'wrath to come', offering them a ritual of baptism to demonstrate their repentance; he also expected a change in their behaviour afterwards, that they should 'bear fruits that befit repentance' in very practical terms like sharing food and clothing, and not extorting money (Matt. 3.7-10; Luke 3.7-14).[135]

Although the word 'repent' may not be common in the preaching of Jesus, Wright argues that in many of the parables and the rest of Jesus' teaching, the challenge of his 'different values' and the call to discipleship all implied 'a summons to repentance'.[136] There are Jesus' warnings about what might happen if people or towns do not repent (Luke 13.1-5; Matt. 11.20-24//Luke 10.13-15; Matt. 12.41//Luke 11.32). The parables urge us to sell everything to gain the treasure, or the 'pearl of great price' (Matt 13.44-46); the king's invitation means that people should stop everything else to respond and come to the banquet (Matt. 22.1-10// Luke 14.15-24). Thus it is clear that Jesus expects a total response, but, unlike John the Baptist, he does not give concrete instructions about how his followers are to demonstrate repentance. So Minear talks of no 'single tangible clue as to the precise denotation of the word' and the 'fuzziness of meaning'; thus he sets out to investigate his nine 'commands of Christ'.[137] Verhey agrees that repentance is 'a radical and joyful turning' which is hidden in the 'mystery of the kingdom'. What it 'means more precisely, what its concrete shape is, can only be discerned in the concrete commands of Jesus', which he considers to be six, only three of which overlap with Minear's nine.[138]

It is notable that not only are these calls for repentance couched in such general terms, but that they are all part of Jesus' teaching, which we have already studied. The difficulty comes when we turn to his activity, his deeds. Not only does he not spell out concrete and specific changes of behaviour in the lives of the people with whom he associated, he also requires none of the ritual

134. See Schrage, *The Ethics of the NT*, pp. 41-42; Wiebe, 'Messianic Ethics', p. 37.

135. See E. P. Sanders, *Jesus and Judaism*, pp. 108-9; Theissen and Merz, *The Historical Jesus*, pp. 196-211.

136. N. T. Wright, *Jesus and the Victory of God*, p. 254.

137. Minear, *Commands of Christ*, pp. 22, 27.

138. 'Be last of all'; 'be not anxious'; 'give alms'; 'it shall not be taken from her'; 'forbid them not'; 'judge not'; Verhey, *The Great Reversal*, pp. 16-21.

or other demonstrations of repentance, such as going to the temple, or offering sacrifice — doing what Dunn calls 'bypassing the cult'.[139] Instead, he just accepted people where and as they were. What is more, when criticized for this, he said that God accepted them — and held a party to celebrate! No wonder the religious people with the high ethical standards objected and accused him of being 'a glutton and a drunkard, a friend of tax collectors and sinners' (Matt. 11.19; Mark 2.15-16). In response, he told them parables about lost sheep, lost coins and lost sons — all ending with a party objected to by the elder son, who represented the religious high ethicists (Luke 15).[140] With the medical analogy of the sick needing doctors, Jesus said, 'I came not to call the righteous, but sinners' (Matt. 9.12-13; cp. Mark 2.17).[141] If we include the woman taken in adultery, Jesus refuses to condemn her too (John 8.1-11). O' Malley contrasts the fact that 'Jesus never waxed wroth over a sexual sinner' with 'the eyes of the official church' from Augustine onwards and the probing questions he, as a Jesuit priest, was taught to ask![142]

Here, then, is the problem: Jesus' acceptance of sinners ran contrary to established practice, by not 'requiring repentance as normally understood'. As Sanders puts it: 'There is a puzzle with regard to Jesus' view of sinners: we do not know just how he expected them to live after their acceptance of his message'. Jesus 'simply did not deal in detail with their behaviour and thus could truly be criticized for including the wicked in his "kingdom"'.[143] Sanders suggests that if Jesus did call individuals to repentance, there is little in his teaching about 'national repentance' for Israel as a whole.[144] Tom Wright disagrees, arguing that Jesus' main themes are 'a summons to repentance', including a national call, and sees the forgiveness of sins as 'the return from exile', 'the renewed covenant'.[145] However, he agrees that the scandal was that for Jesus, repentance 'did not involve going to the Temple and offering sacrifice. . . . Jesus offered membership in the renewed people of the covenant god on his own authority and by his own process'.[146]

Whether Jesus' call is interpreted on an individual or national basis, two

139. Dunn, *Jesus Remembered*, pp. 786-88.

140. See Borg, *Conflict, Holiness and Politics in the Teachings of Jesus*, pp. 86-92.

141. See Wiebe, 'Messianic Ethics', p. 38.

142. W. J. O'Malley, S.J., 'The Moral Practice of Jesus', *America* 170.14 (April 1994), pp. 8-11.

143. E. P. Sanders, *Jesus and Judaism*, pp. 206, 283, 323.

144. See E. P. Sanders, *Jesus and Judaism*, pp. 106-111, 200-211 for full discussion.

145. N. T. Wright, *Jesus and the Victory of God*, pp. 246-74, esp. pp. 268-73; Wiebe also argues for a national and community understanding of repentance and response to Jesus, 'Messianic Ethics', pp. 35-41.

146. N. T. Wright, *Jesus and the Victory of God*, p. 257; see also p. 274.

things stand out clearly. First, Jesus spent a lot of time with sinful characters, so much so that he could be called 'the friend of sinners' — and that was meant to be an insult. As the Greek proverb, found in the comic poet Menander, put it, 'Bad company ruins good morals'. Paul even quotes it approvingly and applies it to his readers in 1 Cor. 15.33 — yet Jesus kept bad company while teaching good morals! Secondly, Jesus did not seem to make any ethical preconditions on such sinners joining him; they simply had to respond to his invitation. Nor is it clear what changes he expected afterwards. According to Luke's story, Jesus went into Zacchaeus' house without making any prior demands for repentance or changes of behaviour before he would come for tea — he just went! Afterwards, Zacchaeus does respond by offering to give half his possessions to the poor and to reimburse anyone he defrauded fourfold — but that is his idea in response to Jesus' visit. As a consequence, Jesus declares that 'today salvation has come to this house' and calls Zacchaeus 'a son of Abraham' (Luke 19.1-10). As Wright notes, 'What Zacchaeus would normally have obtained through visiting Jerusalem and participating in the sacrificial cult, Jesus gave him on the spot'.[147] What is more, Zacchaeus does not even follow Jesus' own rigorous ethic of selling *everything* to give to the poor, as laid out a little earlier in this gospel (Luke 12.33; 14.33; 18.22); he still retains the other half of his possessions. Yet Jesus accepts and praises Zacchaeus' decision, rather than criticizing him for not obeying his ethic and selling all.

How are we to square this open acceptance of sinners and what must have appeared as 'pastoral laxity' with Jesus' rigorist ethical teaching? The biographical genre of the gospels means we must hold together Jesus' deeds and words. In fact, such open acceptance of sinners is also there in the teaching, especially the parables about the lost (e.g., Luke 15). Thus both Jesus' teaching and his actions in accepting people without the official forms of repentance have ethical implications: if God forgives people just like that, is this not the end of morality as we know it? No wonder some religious leaders or guardians of morality were offended — and, as the history of the church shows, they have gone on being offended ever since. We have already seen Harvey's observation that the distinctive ethic of Jesus appears to be overlooked in much of the rest of the New Testament and in the history of Christian moral theology.[148] Similarly, even Paul's instructions 'not to associate . . . or even eat' with sinners and that 'bad company ruins good morals' (1 Cor. 5.11; 15.33) seem to ignore Jesus' example.[149]

---

147. N. T. Wright, *Jesus and the Victory of God*, p. 257; see also E. P. Sanders' discussion of this story in his *The Historical Figure of Jesus* (Harmondsworth: Penguin, 1993), pp. 230-36.

148. Harvey, *Strenuous Commands*, pp. 7, 24.

149. See Garrison, *The Graeco-Roman Context of Early Christian Literature*, pp. 41-47, 87-88.

By way of a modern comparison, an attempt by Richard Holloway, then Bishop of Edinburgh, to expound the 'radical, scandalous gospel' of 'forgiveness preceding repentance' from the parable of the Prodigal Son provoked a vigorous attack in the journal of so-called 'traditionalists' in the Church of England, complaining that 'they were being sold a gospel of "love" which did not take seriously the problem of sin, repentance and judgement'.[150] Similar reactions are, of course, both the context for the parable of the Two Sons itself and the consequence of Jesus' acceptance of Zacchaeus (Luke 15.2; 19.7)! Thus, despite his rigorous, all-demanding 'strenuous commands', in fact both Jesus' teaching and his example, in biographical terms, his words and his deeds, cohere in an open acceptance of people, especially sinners. Therefore, we need finally to examine the implications of this for Christian discipleship.

c. Following and imitating Jesus

The central argument of this book arises from the fact that ancient biographies held together both words and deeds in portraying their central subject. We also noted in the opening chapter that many Lives were written explicitly to give an example to others to emulate: thus Xenophon composed his *Agesilaus* to provide a paradigm (παράδειγμα) for others to follow to become better people (ἀνδραγαθίαν ἀσκεῖν, 10.2). Equally, Plutarch aims to provide examples so that by imitating (μίμησις) the virtues and avoiding the vices described, the reader can improve his own moral character (*Pericles* 1; *Aemilius Paullus* 1). Riley points out that 'because the two concepts of words and deeds are intimately linked in the classical tradition and the culture in which Christianity arose', the early Christian movement and texts were presenting 'the life pattern of Jesus and what that represented in the culture of the ancient observer'.[151]

In fact, it is not just the biographical hypothesis which requires us to take this aspect of Jesus' example in the gospels into consideration. The Jews believed that a teacher's example was as important as his words. Thus, in the absence of a ruling by a legal authority, it was permissible to report his actions and to deduce from them what his legal position would be on the matter. This was known as a *ma'aseh* ('precedent'): 'It happened that Rabbi X did such and such'. From the master's action, something of the Torah could be learned. Thus

---

150. Simon Ellis, 'All You Need Is Love', *New Directions* 2.28 (London: Forward in Faith, July 1998), p. 10.

151. Gregory J. Riley, 'Words and Deeds: Jesus as Teacher and Jesus as Pattern of Life', *HTR* 90.4 (1997), pp. 427-36, quotations from pp. 426 and 428; see also his book, *One Jesus, Many Christs*, pp. 59-60 and 61-95.

stories are told of Rabbi Akiba following his master, Rabbi Joshua, into the toilet to see how he relieved himself, and there he learned three things (to sit north and south, to sit, not stand, and to wipe with the left hand, not the right). When Ben 'Azzai expressed some surprise that he should 'take such liberties with your master', R. Akiba explained that 'it was a matter of Torah, and I needed to learn'. Ben 'Azzai then followed R. Akiba into the toilet and learned the same three things, which he duly passed on to R. Judah. Similarly, R. Kahana hid under his master's bed and was so impressed with what is euphemistically termed his master's 'chatting with his wife, and joking and doing what he required' that he cried out, 'One would think that Abba's mouth had never before supped the cup!' When his master, somewhat surprised to find his pupil under the marital bed, told him to get out 'because it is rude', Kahana's reply was also, 'Master, it is Torah, and I need to know'.[152] So the imitation of the master is a way of knowing Torah, and thus becomes an imitation of God.

Jesus' own call to discipleship also included the idea of doing what he was doing, namely, imitating him by joining in his ministry: 'Follow me and I will make you fishers of men' (Mark 1.17). After being with Jesus for a while, the disciples are sent out to imitate him in preaching the kingdom of God, teaching and healing (Matt. 9.35–10.16//Luke 10.1-16).[153] The Baptist scholar R. E. O. White wrote, 'The imitation of Christ is, in truth, the nearest principle in Christianity to a moral absolute'. Although 'the figure of Christ is limned afresh in every age' and the meaning of imitation changes, 'The imitation of Christ remains the heart of the Christian ethic'.[154] It was what drove St. Francis of Assisi to give up everything to follow the example of Jesus. However, as Mealand drily points out, 'It is true that such thoroughgoing imitation of the life of Jesus has more often been praised than practised'![155]

The imitation of Christ was also a great motivation for the work of Mother Theresa in Calcutta, and, writing out of that experience, Carapiet states, 'Christian ethics cannot but primarily be modelled on Jesus Christ whose life and actions are archetypal and paradigmatic' for the church and 'for the life and actions of his future disciples'.[156] McGrath, however, is concerned about what he sees as 'the liberal approach to the ethical significance of Jesus' in which Jesus is

152. *Berakoth* 62a, in *The Babylonian Talmud,* trans. and ed. I. Epstein (London: Soncino, 1958), p. 388.
153. See Schrage, *The Ethics of the NT,* pp. 51-52.
154. R. E. O. White, *Biblical Ethics* (Exeter: Paternoster, 1979/Leominster: Gracewing, 1994), p. 109; see pp. 109-23 for full discussion.
155. Mealand, *Poverty and Expectation in the Gospels,* p. 92.
156. M. Carapiet, 'Jesus and Christian Ethics Today', *Jeevadhara* 23 (Kottayam, Kerala, India, 1993), pp. 442, 449.

a 'moral teacher' or 'moral example'; nothing less than Luther's 'being conformed to Christ' or Calvin's 'being incorporated into Christ' will do.[157] Spohn brings these aspects together by proposing that 'the entire story of Jesus is normative for Christian ethics as its concrete universal'; Jesus thus provides the 'perception' to see 'which features of experience are significant', the 'motivation' for 'how to act' and the 'identity' of 'who we are to become as Christian'.[158] Not surprisingly, therefore, in his next book Spohn specifically tackled how Jesus' life 'can function as a moral paradigm that offers normative guidance for a way of life . . . a normative pattern or exemplar' for us to 'go and do likewise'.[159]

This concern for the imitation of Jesus as exemplar finds its counterpart in current popular moral discussion about the WWJD phenomenon — bracelets with the slogan, 'What Would Jesus Do?' Verhey claims that 'the idea for the bracelets originated some years ago in a youth group in Holland, Michigan, where I live', and quickly moved on to bumper stickers or T-shirts. While the habit can seem trite, Verhey notes that at least his students 'understand that the Christian life is a life of discipleship. They understand that the test for conduct and character in Christian community is the church's memory of Jesus. They understand that to follow Jesus one has to remember him.'[160] The difficulty is that many of today's moral dilemmas concern issues about which Jesus never said or did anything. In response to WWJD, Spencer has tried to provide such questioners with a guide to those areas where Jesus did at least do something.[161]

The main problem comes in deciding what it is we are supposed to imitate in or about Jesus. It cannot be a concrete property like his Jewishness, or maleness, or the colour of his eyes, if it is to be universal. The Jewish tradition that the imitation of the rabbi was an imitation of Torah and thus ultimately an imitation of God reflects the central command in the Torah, 'You shall be holy, for I the LORD your God am holy' (Lev. 19.2). Jesus draws upon this to challenge his hearers to an imitation of God in the Q-passage, 'Be perfect/merciful, therefore, as your heavenly Father is perfect/merciful' (Matt. 5.48; Luke 6.36).[162] These variant readings bring our paradox of the rigorous ethic and the pastoral acceptance together. Matthew's reading, 'Be perfect', could be taken as a summary of

---

157. A. McGrath, 'In What Way Can Jesus Be a Moral Example for Christians?' *Journal of the Evangelical Theological Society* 34 (1991) 289-98.

158. Spohn, 'Jesus and Christian Ethics', pp. 101-7.

159. Spohn, *Go and Do Likewise: Jesus and Ethics*, p. 10.

160. Allen Verhey, *Remembering Jesus: Christian Community, Scripture, and the Moral Life* (Grand Rapids: Eerdmans, 2002), pp. 12-13.

161. F. Scott Spencer, *What Did Jesus Do? Gospel Profiles of Jesus' Personal Conduct* (Harrisburg, PA: Trinity Press International, 2003).

162. M. Burrows, 'Old Testament Ethics and the Ethics of Jesus', pp. 240-41.

our study of Jesus' rigorous and demanding ethical teaching, while Luke's 'Be merciful' encapsulates Jesus' forgiving and accepting behaviour. As we shall see in the two chapters below on these evangelists, it is true that both adjectives reflect their particular redactional interests, but we have demonstrated that both the rigorous teaching and the open acceptance are found together in the ministry, life and death of the historical Jesus. The difficulty comes when we try to imitate both today. Schöni says that 'Christians are frequently caught in a yo-yo game between a highly demanding "law" and a glibly accepted "forgiveness of sins".'[163] Can the two aspects be held together?

First, we have seen that Jesus' ethics are not a set of moral instructions, but rather part of his whole preaching of the kingdom of God, to which a response is sought to his call to wholehearted discipleship in a life lived in community with others who also respond. His teaching also includes the 'rigorous ethic', strengthening the law in the key areas of human moral experience such as money, sex, power and violence. Should we attempt to put these 'strenuous commands' into practice as a way of 'being perfect, as your heavenly Father is perfect'? And yet Jesus ate and drank with, and lived and died for, those who were far from perfect, without apparently requiring them to change their behaviour first or undergo the normal rituals of repentance. The nearest we get to Jesus actually telling anyone to change is 'go and sin no more' to the adulterous woman (John 8.11). We shall also study later the different gospel accounts in which a rich young ruler is challenged by Jesus to sell and give away his possessions in order to follow him; however, in Luke's next chapter, Jesus goes on to commend Zacchaeus who only goes halfway (Luke 18.18-25; 19.1-10). A challenge to change is implicit in the call to repentance and discipleship, but it is never spelled out, or required.

When criticized for this by the guardians of morality, Jesus defends himself with the aphorism, 'Those who are well have no need of a doctor, but those who are sick; I came not to call the righteous, but sinners' (Mark 2.17). This was also true literally in his ministry among the sick, and this may give us a clue. We have seen that Jesus' healing ministry was performed mostly among those who were ordinary people, or even social outcasts or ritually impure through their illness. In his love, he accepted them as they were, touched them and healed them — but that same love did change them for good. Doctors do actually make people better, and Jesus the healer made them well. Similarly, Jesus accepts sinners as they are without any preconditions or requirements for formal repentance. But he still teaches his rigorous ethic: the 'good morals' among 'bad

---

163. M. Schöni, 'What More Are You Doing than Others? The Radical Ethics of Jesus', *Near East School of Theology Theological Review* 16.2 (Beirut, 1995), pp. 75-97; quotation from p. 76.

company' and the call to follow him in discipleship include the challenge to 'get better' and to live a new life. Thus while repentance and change cannot be a prior requisite, it may be a response to the call of Jesus, as was the case with Zacchaeus. As people respond to the call and follow Jesus as disciples, they will hear his demanding ethic and will want to change along the way. To become 'perfect, as your heavenly Father is perfect' is a lifelong process — and perhaps even beyond that.

Borg is unequivocal about Jesus' teaching following the holiness code in Lev. 19: 'Jesus' ethic, in short, was based on an *imitatio dei,* just as the quest for holiness was based on an *imitatio dei.*' However, he goes on to point out that 'the imperative to replace holiness as the content of the *imitatio dei* with mercy and the consequence of this substitution for the historical life of Israel are nowhere so clear' as in this Q-teaching, in which Borg assumes that Luke's version reflects the original.[164] It thus challenges Jesus' hearers to a second imitation of God, 'Be merciful, as your heavenly Father is merciful' (Luke 6.36). However, this stress on mercy is not only to be found in Luke. According to the parable of the Unforgiving Servant found only in Matthew, we are to imitate God in forgiving others as we have been forgiven, and if we do not, then God may imitate our lack of forgiveness back to us (Matt. 18.23-35). Other examples of Jesus' ethical teaching in the Q-material include the instruction, 'Judge not, that you be not judged' with the parable of the Mote and the Beam (Matt. 7.1-5//Luke 6.37-42), while the Lord's Prayer stresses forgiving others as we have been forgiven (Matt. 6.9-15//Mark 11.25-26).[165] Thus to imitate Jesus and follow his example means that people have to emulate his open pastoral acceptance of others, especially those whom some may consider to be 'sinners'. Furthermore, such following and such accepting have to be done within the community of others who also respond, yet who may be very different from ourselves. Shriver sees Jesus as the 'discoverer of social forgiveness', who through his activities of healing, prayer, eating and including 'public enemies' like tax collectors and collaborators within his ministry brought about the new community of forgiveness.[166] As Minear argues, it is only as 'the community of Jesus' followers' respond to him together that the community becomes 'the Church'.[167]

Therefore, to respond to Jesus' preaching that the reign of God is 'at hand' inevitably entails obeying his call to 'follow me' (Mark 1.15, 17). In the Jewish context, disciples would learn to follow their master through imitating his

164. Borg, *Conflict, Holiness and Politics in the Teachings of Jesus,* pp. 125-43; quotations from pp. 125 and 127.

165. See Verhey, *The Great Reversal,* pp. 20-21.

166. Shriver, *An Ethics for Enemies,* pp. 34-45.

167. Minear, *Commands of Christ,* p. 29.

precedent, *ma'aseh,* and in this way learn how to imitate the Torah, and ultimately to become holy even as the Lord is holy. Such imitation, *mimesis,* is also central to much ancient biography, as readers were encouraged to follow the paradigm of the subject's deeds and words. In seeking to follow Jesus, we are called not merely to obey his ethical 'strenuous commands' in the pursuit of holiness, but also to imitate his deeds and his words, which call his hearers to be merciful, reflecting the mercy of God, as revealed in Jesus' own merciful and loving acceptance of everyone, including or especially those whom some considered to be 'sinners', without preconditions. In this way, we learn to 'do what Jesus would do'.

Conclusion

We have argued that any attempt to provide an account of New Testament ethics should start with Jesus as the origin and starting point of the whole enterprise. Accordingly, therefore, our archaeological report has described the earliest level of the main outline about the historical Jesus, drawing upon the various scholarly reconstructions. We established the fact of his existence and the two key points about him which we shall follow through our study, namely that he was a teacher who had a mixed following, including some ethically dubious people. These two aspects are then reflected in the double nature of the ancient biographical genre in which the gospels were composed, that is, a portrayal of the subject through his words and deeds, his life and activity as well as his teaching.

In studying Jesus' ethics, therefore, it is not enough just to outline the main points of his moral teaching, or simply to quote the Sermon on the Mount. His ethics cannot be divorced from his preaching of the kingdom of God, the sovereign rule of God breaking into our world, which requires a wholehearted response within the new community of all who choose to follow. At the heart of Jesus' teaching is the double command to love God and neighbour, including one's enemies, and this is the driving force behind Jesus' attitude towards the law. However, when Jesus does address the major human moral experiences, such as marriage and sexuality, wealth and poverty, war and violence, power and the state, his teachings are very rigorous and all-demanding, to the extent that many people have found them impractical and impossible to keep down through the centuries.

However, such 'strenuous commands' cannot be appreciated separately from his behaviour and activity; a person's words always require the context of their deeds. Both the biographical genre of the gospels on the one hand, and the ancient idea of imitation and Jewish rabbinic precedent on the other suggest that Jesus' teaching must be earthed in his practical example, both of calling people to repentance and discipleship — but also his open pastoral acceptance of sinners, with whom he spent his life and for whom he died. All too often those who apply New Testament ethics to today end up doing one or the other: that is, teaching a rigorist ethic with extreme demands which seem condemnatory and alienate people from the church — or having an open acceptance of sinners and being accused of having no ethics at all! Seeking to follow Jesus in becoming both 'perfect' and 'merciful' as God is perfect and merciful is not an easy balance to maintain, but one we will explore throughout the rest of this book, as we continue our archaeological excavation, coming next to the level of St Paul and his epistles, before finally arriving at the four portrayals of Jesus in the canonical gospels.

III. Paul: Follower or Founder?

We have argued for the importance of beginning any consideration of New Testament ethics with the person of Jesus as the primary event which starts the whole thing going. Because of the biographical nature of the gospels, we have looked at his deeds as well as his words, his example as well as his teaching. Both aspects have to be set within his preaching of the kingdom, the eschatological reign of God and in the light of the relationship between the law and love. In addition, we have discovered an interesting tension between a tendency towards a rigorous, all-demanding ethic in his teaching and an all-embracing acceptance in his pastoral practice. After Jesus, it might be expected that we should go on next to look at the writers of the gospels and their ethics. However, in this report of our excavation, we are following the chronological sequence up from the primary level of Jesus through the various stages of the New Testament, which means that we need to consider Paul and his letters before coming to the gospels.

Upon the foundations of Jesus' words and deeds, teaching and ministry, life and death is constructed the whole of the New Testament. Whatever happened on the third day after his crucifixion, Jesus quickly became the centre for the development of the early Christian communities, who were constituted around individuals' faith in him. There is an opaque level for about fifteen years in the historical stratification at this point. If Pauline scholars are right to identify earlier traditions or credal fragments embedded in his level, such as 1 Cor. 15.3-7 or 1 Tim. 3.16, then we can glimpse the importance of early faith in Jesus of Nazareth as the one whom God has raised from the dead. Also during this time, collections of his sayings and anecdotes together with stories about his deeds and activities were being assembled and passed on, many of which we may find preserved further up the levels in the gospels.

But before then, we find the layer of Paul's letters, whose clarity reveals something of what had been happening in the previous opaque level. The old adage that the teaching *of* Jesus has become the teaching *about* Jesus, and that the preaching of the kingdom turns into the proclamation of the King is nonetheless true for being well worn. For Paul, Christ has become the centre of his theology, which, if any of his autobiographical comments are to be believed, was a major turnaround for him. We have to recognize that Paul includes little direct quotation from or allusion to the earthly life of Jesus, although we shall show later that there is more than is sometimes supposed. Nonetheless, for Paul, everything depends on the whole 'Jesus event', and what God has done in Jesus' life, death and resurrection. This raises the question of continuity: Is Paul the follower of Jesus' teachings and ethics, or is he the founder of a completely new religion?

To guide our exploration of this question, we shall follow a similar sequence to that which arose from our consideration of Jesus' words and deeds. Therefore we shall begin with Christology to see how Jesus' preaching of the kingdom becomes Paul's understanding of the King, that is, how God's sovereign rule is inaugurated in what he has done in Jesus, before going on to consider the setting of Paul's letters and their relationship to his theology, especially eschatology. As with our study of Jesus, this will lead on to the question of the law and the love command, before coming to the practical issues challenging the ethics of Paul's communities. Finally, we shall return to the combination of rigorous ethical teaching and open pastoral acceptance found in Jesus' ethics. This aspect is more difficult in Paul, since the combination of Jesus' words and deeds arose out of the biographical genre of the gospels. Paul's letters share many of the generic features of the epistolary genre, and are therefore more concerned with Paul's words and his teaching than with his example. It is, of course, true that the Acts of the Apostles contains much biographical material about Paul, and about the other leaders of the early church, and that the genre of Acts is closely related to that of the gospels.[1] The relationship between the portrait of Paul in Acts and the historical Paul is much debated and cannot be handled fully here.[2] However, Paul does refer to his own example occasion-

1. For further discussion, see Richard A. Burridge, *What Are the Gospels? A Comparison with Graeco-Roman Biography*, SNTSMS 70 (Cambridge: Cambridge University Press, 1992), pp. 243-46; see the rev. 2nd edn. (Grand Rapids: Eerdmans, 2004), pp. 236-39, and pp. 275-79 for the more recent debate.

2. Wenham argues strongly for the 'historical reliability' of the story of Paul in Acts throughout his *Paul and Jesus: The True Story* (London: SPCK, 2002), see his conclusions on pp. 179-88; for a similarly positive comparison of one speech in Acts and one letter, see Steve Walton, *Leadership and Lifestyle: The Portrait of Paul in the Miletus Speech and 1 Thessalonians*, SNTSMS 108 (Cam-

ally, and so we will consider those passages and his ideas about 'the imitation of Christ' at the end of this chapter.

1. Paul's Christology

It might be thought that we should begin with Paul's theology; after all, by etymology and definition, 'theology' means 'an account or words about God' — and many key books on Paul include the word 'theology' in their title. Thus Dunn starts his monumental treatment, *The Theology of Paul the Apostle,* by saying that we have 'to begin with his belief about God', and a substantial chapter about God follows.[3] However, Dunn next considers the human situation, and then comes to the person of Jesus Christ: 'Christ became the key to understanding God's purpose for humankind, and indeed God himself'[4] — and many of the hundreds of pages which follow are actually about Jesus Christ. But even this Christological emphasis is not enough for Francis Watson, who has criticised Dunn's account as insufficiently Christian and Trinitarian. He argues that, for Paul, God's very deity is shown in his agency, and his identity is understood only in relation to Christ and the Spirit: God is 'the God and Father of our Lord Jesus Christ' (Rom. 15.6; 2 Cor. 1.3; Eph. 1.3).[5] Thus, for Paul, theology is Christology and vice versa. Similarly, Ridderbos may entitle his important book, *Paul: An Outline of His Theology,* but he too moves immediately to Christology: 'The fundamental structure of Paul's preaching is only to be approached from his Christology.'[6] Similar points are made by most major studies of Paul, ranging from scholars like Bornkamm across to E. P. Sanders,[7] and therefore we too will begin with Paul's understanding of Jesus Christ.

---

bridge: Cambridge University Press, 2000); for a more contrasting approach, see John Dominic Crossan and Jonathan L. Reed, *In Search of Paul: How Jesus' Apostle Opposed Rome's Empire with God's Kingdom* (New York: Harper Collins/London: SPCK, 2005), pp. 28-41; for general discussion of the issue, see Carl R. Holladay, *A Critical Introduction to the New Testament: Interpreting the Message and Meaning of Jesus Christ* (Nashville: Abingdon, 2005), pp. 251-55, or pp. 349-53 in the expanded CD version; Bruce N. Fisk, 'Paul: Life and Letters', in *The Face of New Testament Studies: A Survey of Recent Research,* ed. Scot McKnight and Grant R. Osborne (Grand Rapids: Baker Academic, 2004), pp. 283-325, esp. pp. 296-300.

3. James D. G. Dunn, *The Theology of Paul the Apostle* (Grand Rapids: Eerdmans, 1998), pp. 27-50; quotation from p. 28.

4. Dunn, *The Theology of Paul the Apostle,* p. 181.

5. Francis Watson, 'The Triune Divine Identity: Reflections on Pauline God Language, in Disagreement with J. D. G. Dunn', *JSNT* 80 (2000), pp. 99-124; see especially pp. 113-14.

6. Herman Ridderbos, *Paul: An Outline of His Theology* (London: SPCK, 1977), p. 49.

7. 'Jesus Christ himself and salvation . . . form the subject of Paul's proclamation', Günther

a. Jesus reshapes Paul's own biography

This is necessary because Paul's own understanding of himself, his identity and his calling in life all followed from his encounter with the risen Christ on the Damascus road. He begins one of his earliest letters, Galatians, by describing himself as 'Paul an apostle — sent neither by human commission nor from human authorities, but through Jesus Christ and God the Father, who raised him from the dead' (Gal. 1.1). This divine authority comes from his conversion experience, as he goes on to describe in Gal. 1.13-24; furthermore, the other apostles recognize that he has been 'entrusted with the gospel for the uncircumcised' (Gal. 2.1-10). In Phil 3.4-16 he again refers both to his previous life and to the 'surpassing value of knowing Christ Jesus my Lord'. In the later biographical portraits included within his narrative of the early church, Luke emphasizes the significance of the encounter on the Damascus road by describing it no fewer than three times (Acts 9.1-30; 22.1-21; 26.1-18). It is equally central to most scholarly accounts of Paul's life.[8] The popular phrase 'the conversion of St. Paul' suggests (wrongly) that he changed from being a Jew into a Christian, while the more accurate description of 'a calling' still directs our attention to Paul's apostleship to the Gentiles, and his subsequent relationship to his Jewish heritage, which has undergone enormous scholarly debate in recent years.[9] It has also

---

Bornkamm, *Paul* (London: Hodder and Stoughton, 1971), p. 109; Sanders stresses that Paul's conviction, 'Jesus Christ is Lord, that in him God has provided for the salvation of all who believe', is the principal approach to Paul's theology rather than the human condition — see E. P. Sanders, *Paul and Palestinian Judaism* (London: SCM, 1977), pp. 441-42.

8. See Gerd Lüdemann, *Paul, Apostle to the Gentiles: Studies in Chronology* (London: SCM, 1984); Martin Hengel, *The Pre-Christian Paul* (London: SCM, 1991); Martin Hengel and Anna Maria Schwemer, *Paul between Damascus and Antioch: The Unknown Years* (London: SCM, 1997); Rainer Riesner, *Paul's Early Period: Chronology, Mission Strategy, Theology* (Grand Rapids: Eerdmans, 1998); Ben Witherington III, *The Paul Quest: The Renewed Search for the Jew of Tarsus* (Downers Grove, IL: IVP, 1998); Jerome Murphy O'Connor, *Paul: A Critical Life* (Oxford: Clarendon, 1996); idem, *Paul: His Story* (Oxford: Oxford University Press, 2004); John Ashton, *The Religion of Paul the Apostle* (New Haven, CT: Yale University Press, 2000); David G. Horrell, *An Introduction to the Study of Paul* (London: T&T Clark, 2000; 2nd edn. 2006), esp. pp. 27-43; on using Paul's letters to reconstruct his biography, while adopting my suggestion of Acts as a biography of the early church, see Douglas A. Campbell, *The Quest for Paul's Gospel: A Suggested Strategy* (London: T&T Clark, 2005), pp. 20-22.

9. Note Krister Stendahl's essay, 'Call Rather than Conversion', in his collection, *Paul among Jews and Gentiles* (London: SCM, 1977), pp. 7-23; see also W. D. Davies, *Paul and Rabbinic Judaism: Some Rabbinic Elements in Pauline Theology* (London: SPCK, 1948; 3rd edn. 1970); F. F. Bruce, *Paul: Apostle of the Free Spirit* (Exeter: Paternoster, 1977); E. P. Sanders, *Paul and Palestinian Judaism* (London: SCM, 1977); Francis Watson, *Paul, Judaism and the Gentiles: A Sociological Approach*, SNTSMS 56 (Cambridge: Cambridge University Press, 1986); Jürgen Becker, *Paul: Apostle to the Gentiles* (Lou-

provided a focus for discussion about the nature of identity between Christian and Jewish New Testament scholars; interestingly, Segal, for example, still prefers to talk of Paul's 'conversion' as the 'appropriate term'.[10]

b. Jesus reshapes Paul's theology

This encounter with the risen Jesus was not just a turning point in Paul's life, but also in his theology. After listing his Jewish qualifications ('blameless') as the grounds for his 'confidence in the flesh', Paul describes them as 'loss' and 'rubbish', σκύβαλα, compared with 'the surpassing value of knowing Christ Jesus my Lord'; he wants to 'know Christ and the power of his resurrection' and to press on since he has not yet 'reached the goal' (Phil. 3.1-16). From the Damascus road onwards, the significance of Jesus' life, death and resurrection and the implications of new life 'in Christ' are crucial for Paul's understanding of the relationship of God and human beings.[11] Yet despite this concentration upon the person of Jesus, Paul has less stress on Jesus' actual earthly life or ministry: he is more concerned to write about the whole Christ-event. As a consequence, Paul has little of the actual biography of Jesus; as we shall see at the end of this chapter, both Jesus' words and his deeds seem to be rarely mentioned in Paul's letters — with the focus instead being on what God has done through the whole Christ-event and the consequences of that for Paul's understanding of the identity of Jesus.

---

isville: Westminster John Knox, 1993); Terence L. Donaldson, *Paul and the Gentiles: Remapping the Apostle's Convictional World* (Minneapolis: Fortress, 1997); Troels Engberg-Pedersen (ed.), *Paul beyond the Judaism/Hellenism Divide* (Louisville: Westminster John Knox, 2001); S. J. Chester, *Conversion at Corinth* (London: T&T Clark, 2003); for an historical analysis of how Paul's conversion has been interpreted from the time of the early church, see Bruce Corley, 'Interpreting Paul's Conversion — Then and Now' in *The Road from Damascus: The Impact of Paul's Conversion on His Life, Thought, and Ministry*, ed. Richard N. Longenecker (Grand Rapids: Eerdmans, 1997), pp. 1-17.

10. Alan F. Segal, *Paul the Convert: The Apostolate and Apostasy of Saul the Pharisee* (New Haven, CT: Yale University Press, 1990), see pp. 6, 72, for example; also Pinchas Lapide and Peter Stuhlmacher, *Paul: Rabbi and Apostle* (Minneapolis: Augsburg, 1984); L. W. Hurtado, 'Convert, Apostate, or Apostle to the Nations: The "Conversion" of Paul in Recent Scholarship', *Studies in Religion/Sciences Religieuses* 22 (1993), pp. 273-84; Daniel Boyarin, *A Radical Jew: Paul and the Politics of Identity* (Berkeley: University of California Press, 1994).

11. *The Road from Damascus: The Impact of Paul's Conversion on His Life, Thought, and Ministry*, ed. Longenecker, analyses the effect of Paul's conversion on every area; see also the major treatments of Paul already listed above, and J. Christiaan Beker, *Paul the Apostle: The Triumph of God in Life and Thought* (Edinburgh: T&T Clark, 1980); Michael J. Gorman, *Apostle of the Crucified Lord: A Theological Introduction to Paul and His Letters* (Grand Rapids: Eerdmans, 2004); Udo Schnelle, *Apostle Paul: His Life and Theology* (Grand Rapids: Baker Academic, 2005).

c. The narrative of Paul's Christology

However, it is important to note that the absence of the narrative of Jesus' earthly life in Paul does not mean that he has no narrative about Jesus. Hays' doctoral dissertation drew attention to 'the narrative substructure' underlying Paul's thought.[12] N. T. Wright also rejected any idea that Paul 'forswore the story-form' in favour of 'much more abstract terms'; instead, 'the apostle's most emphatically "theological" statements and arguments are in fact expressions of *the essentially Jewish story now redrawn around Jesus*' as he then goes on to demonstrate the interplay of the various multiple and overlapping stories in early Christianity.[13] Similarly, for Ben Witherington, 'Paul refers to four interrelated stories comprising one larger drama: (1) the story of a world gone wrong; (2) the story of Israel in that world; (3) the story of Christ, which arises out of the story of Israel and humankind on the human side of things, but in a larger sense arises out of the very story of God as creator and redeemer; and (4) the story of Christians, including Paul himself, which arises out of all three of these previous stories and is the first full instalment of the story of a world set right again. Christ's story is the hinge, crucial turning point and climax of the entire larger drama, which more than anything else affects how *the* Story will ultimately turn out'.[14] Such narratological approaches to Paul have been widely debated and are increasingly accepted within the mainstream.[15] Thus Wright states in his more recent work, 'The turn to narrative is, in fact, one of the most significant developments which the "new perspective" revolution has precipitated'.[16] Of course, this shift from Christological titles to narrative is not confined solely to Pauline studies, as we have argued elsewhere.[17]

Therefore we return to our central argument from genre that the New Tes-

12. Richard B. Hays, *The Faith of Jesus Christ: The Narrative Substructure of Galatians 3:1–4:11* (Chico: Scholars Press, 1983; 2nd edn., Grand Rapids: Eerdmans, 2002).

13. N. T. Wright, *The New Testament and the People of God* (London: SPCK, 1992), p. 79, his italics.

14. Ben Witherington III, *Paul's Narrative Thought World: The Tapestry of Tragedy and Triumph* (Louisville: Westminster John Knox, 1994), p. 5, his italics; see also Witherington, *The Many Faces of the Christ: The Christologies of the New Testament and Beyond* (New York: Crossroad, 1998), pp. 104-19.

15. See Bruce W. Longenecker (ed.), *Narrative Dynamics in Paul: A Critical Assessment* (Louisville: Westminster John Knox, 2002) for a full analysis and discussion, and also the response from Richard Hays, 'Is Paul's Gospel Narratable?' *JSNT* 27 (2004), pp. 217-39.

16. N. T. Wright, *Paul: Fresh Perspectives* (London: SPCK, 2005), pp. 7-13; quotation from p. 8.

17. Richard A. Burridge, 'From Titles to Stories: A Narrative Approach to the Dynamic Christologies of the New Testament', in *The Person of Christ*, ed. Murray Rae and Stephen R. Holmes (London: T&T Clark, 2005), pp. 37-60.

tament is not primarily an ethical treatise. Paul is writing letters, not doctrine nor ethics, nor even biography — but underlying all his thought is a biographical narrative about Jesus Christ and what God has achieved in him. It is nothing less than the whole biblical story of the creation and fall, the election and history of Israel, leading up to the coming of Jesus, through whose life, death and supremely his resurrection God has provided the means for the salvation of the world. Thus Paul's Christology is set in an inevitably eschatological framework. Jesus Christ is the key pivot of the ages, the means whereby the new age has broken into the present through the death and resurrection of Jesus. We now live 'between the times' awaiting the final consummation of all things in Christ. This can be summed up in one of Paul's most programmatic verses: 'God was in Christ reconciling the world to himself' (2 Cor. 5.19).

d. The language of Paul's Christology

We saw in the last chapter that the kingdom of God was at the heart of Jesus' own preaching, proclaiming the 'rule' or sovereignty' of God. This too is a dynamic and narrative concept. As we noted at the start of this chapter, Paul's Christology is sometimes (mis-)represented as a shift from preaching the kingdom to proclaiming the King; however, if the nexus of the life, death and resurrection of Jesus is the supreme means whereby the 'rule of God' is inaugurated for the whole world, then this 'shift', far from being a radical departure, is in perfect continuity with Jesus. Soards has identified no fewer than fifty-two 'story-elements' within the Pauline Christological narrative about who Jesus is and what God has done in him.[18] Nonetheless, it is still worth abstracting briefly from the narrative the kinds of descriptions Paul uses for Jesus: perhaps Hurtado's phrase 'Christological language and themes' is a better way in than the traditional term of 'titles'.[19] The first is, obviously, the use of 'Christ' itself, which occurs some 270 times in Paul's letters, often almost as a 'surname' for Jesus. However, it is clear that it contains a rich resonance. Tuckett suggests that in Paul's usage, 'Christ' has lost much of its royal, eschatological messianic context, but Wright disagrees, arguing that Paul combines both the religious and political overtones of Messiah.[20] In addition, Paul regularly links 'Christ' to

18. Marion L. Soards, 'Christology of the Pauline Epistles', in Mark Allan Powell and David R. Bauer (eds.), *Who Do You Say That I Am? Essays on Christology in Honor of Jack Dean Kingsbury* (Louisville: Westminster John Knox, 1999), pp. 88-109; see esp. pp. 93-97 for the list.

19. Larry W. Hurtado, *Lord Jesus Christ: Devotion to Jesus in Earliest Christianity* (Grand Rapids: Eerdmans, 2003), p. 98; see pp. 79-153 for his full treatment of Paul's Christology.

20. Christopher M. Tuckett, *Christology and the New Testament: Jesus and His Earliest*

Jesus' death, as in 'Christ crucified' (1 Cor. 1.23; 2.2; Gal. 3.1) or 'the cross of Christ' (1 Cor. 1.17; Phil. 3.18).

Another very frequent term is 'lord', occurring over 200 times, applied to Jesus alongside God in Paul's regular greeting, 'Grace to you and peace from God our Father and the Lord Jesus Christ' (see Rom. 1.7; 1 Cor. 1.3; 2 Cor. 1.2; Gal. 1.3; Phil. 1.2, etc.). That this term carries the implications of divine lordship is clear at the end of the hymn in Philippians, that 'every tongue should confess that Jesus Christ is Lord, to the glory of God the Father' (Phil. 2.11). In addition, the Old Testament and intertestamental figure of Wisdom also contributes to Paul's portrait of Jesus (e.g., 1 Cor. 1.24, 30; 8.6, and in the later Col. 1.15-17). While Dunn accepts that for Paul, *Jesus is the exhaustive embodiment of divine wisdom; all* the divine fullness dwelt in him', he does not see in such passages any suggestion that Paul believed in his preexistence.[21] However, most reactions to Dunn over the last couple of decades have not been convinced, continuing to accept that Paul did have an understanding of Jesus' preexistence.[22] This is also linked with Paul's description of Jesus as the 'Son of God' (Rom. 1.3-4; 5.10; 8.32; Gal. 2.20; 1 Thess. 1.10) whom he 'sent' into the world (e.g., Rom. 8.3; Gal. 4.4, 6). Nonetheless, despite this high Christology, Paul is still careful to stay within Jewish monotheism: only once, in the context of an outburst of praise, does he seem to call Jesus 'God' in Rom 9.5.[23] Overall, his Christology is much more functional than ontological; rather than trying to fit Paul into later Christological debates about who Jesus *is*, it is better to understand his conviction about what Christ has *done,* or rather what God has done through the whole narrative of Jesus' life, death and resurrection, which brings us back to 2 Cor. 5.16-21 again. Furthermore, not only does Paul stress how Jesus participates in the life of God, but he also has a very corporate ap-

Followers (Edinburgh: Edinburgh University Press/Louisville: Westminster John Knox, 2001), p. 46; see pp. 41-69 for his full discussion; N. T. Wright, *Paul: Fresh Perspectives*, pp. 42-50.

21. J. D. G. Dunn, *Christology in the Making* (London: SCM, 2nd edn. 1989), pp. 114-21, 176-96; quotation from p. 195, his italics.

22. Douglas J. Moo, 'The Christology of the Early Pauline Letters', in *Contours of Christology in the New Testament*, ed. Richard N. Longenecker (Grand Rapids: Eerdmans, 2005), pp. 169-92, see esp. pp. 178-79; Tuckett, *Christology and the New Testament*, pp. 63-64; Hurtado, *Lord Jesus Christ*, pp. 118-26; Horrell, *An Introduction to the Study of Paul*, pp. 64-65.

23. The debate about this verse turns on how one punctuates the Greek: most translations, including the NRSV, punctuate it as 'the Christ, who is over all, God blessed for ever', while the NEB (and NRSV second marginal note) prefers to insert a full stop after Christ, so that 'may God supreme over all be blessed for ever' is a separate sentence. However, this translation has not won wide support among New Testament scholars; see, for example, Witherington, *The Many Faces of the Christ*, pp. 107-11; Tuckett, *Christology and the New Testament*, pp. 64-65; Moo, 'The Christology of the Early Pauline Letters', pp. 189-91.

proach to Christology as we all participate in the divine life of Jesus, as the phrase ἐν Χριστῷ, 'in Christ', occurs eighty-three times in the Pauline corpus, of which fifty-eight come in the undisputed letters. We shall return to this stress on participation 'in Christ' later in section 3.c below.

e. Christology and ethics

We also saw in the last chapter that Jesus' preaching of the kingdom or reign of God at the centre of his message meant that his ethic was more a response to what God was doing than a list of do's and don't's. Our study here has now shown that Jesus, as the means whereby God is inaugurating his rule, is the centre of Paul's theology, and therefore our response to what God has done in Christ is at the heart of Paul's ethic. Thus any study of Paul's ethics must also start with this Christological focus. While Kilner argues that Paul's ethics are 'God-centred', this 'God-centred ethics is more specifically a Christ-centred ethics'.[24] Schrage takes this further: 'The starting point and basis for Paul's ethics is the saving eschatological event of Jesus' death and resurrection.'[25] Leslie Houlden also notes that 'this Christological basis for ethics is one of the two most striking and distinctive features of Paul's teaching' — the other one being his eschatological convictions.[26] There is almost universal scholarly agreement on both sides of the Atlantic, from scholars such as Hays to Lohse, that 'Paul grounds his ethics in his Christology'.[27] Even when Paul seems to use earlier Christological material such as hymns, he is concerned not with arguing for or against any one Christological ontological position, but rather, according to Stephen Fowl, he repeats the narrative of the 'story of Jesus' in order 'to support . . . ethical positions'.[28]

Thus the Christological heart of Paul's theology inevitably means that we

24. John F. Kilner, 'A Pauline Approach to Ethical Decision-Making', *Interpretation* 43 (1989), pp. 366-79; quotation from p. 369.

25. W. Schrage, *The Ethics of the New Testament* (Philadelphia: Fortress, 1988), p. 172.

26. J. L. Houlden, 'Paul, Ethical Teaching of', in *A New Dictionary of Christian Ethics*, ed. J. Macquarrie and J. Childress (London: SCM, 1967; 2nd edn. 1986), p. 457; see also J. L. Houlden, *Ethics and the New Testament* (Harmondsworth: Penguin, 1973), pp. 26-27.

27. Richard B. Hays, 'Christology and Ethics in Galatians: The Law of Christ', *CBQ* 49 (1987), pp. 268-90, quotation from p. 289; Eduard Lohse, *Theological Ethics of the New Testament* (Minneapolis: Fortress, 1991), p. 107.

28. Stephen E. Fowl, *The Story of Christ in the Ethics of Paul*, JSNTSS 36 (Sheffield: Sheffield Academic Press, 1990), p. 20, and see pp. 198-202; Fowl develops this further in his 'Christology and Ethics in Philippians 2:5-11', in *Where Christology Began: Essays on Philippians 2*, ed. R. P. Martin and B. J. Dodd (Louisville: Westminster John Knox, 1998), pp. 140-53.

must have a Christ-centred approach to his ethics, which is rooted in the whole biographical narrative underlying his theological thought rather than merely looking at specific texts at the end of his letters. Such an approach coheres well with the development of our argument so far in this book that we must begin New Testament ethics with the person of Jesus, and his preaching and teaching as well as his example. Now that we are moving into Paul's letters before we come to the gospel writers, we must continue with this Christological focus for our study.

2. Paul's letters in their setting

a. The letters

'He was no more a systematic moralist than a systematic theologian.'[29] Our Jesus-centred approach arose out of the biographical genre of the gospels. Equally, R. E. O. White's assessment of Paul is a consequence of the genre of his writings — letters. The fact that he writes letters means that the issues with which he deals are contemporary and contingent; this is best demonstrated in his comments, such as 'concerning the matters about which you wrote' (1 Cor. 7.1). Matera calls them '"occasional" writings; that is, Paul wrote to answer specific questions raised by the churches and in response to problems they faced'.[30] Sometimes his communities wrote and asked questions first; but on other occasions, Paul writes to tell them what he thought they needed to know in the situation they were facing. Our difficulty is that we do not have letters from Paul's early Christian communities with their questions, or any external evidence about their problems. Instead, we have to glean the situation from what Paul says and how he replies — like hearing only one half of a telephone conversation and guessing the other! Thus Paul is not writing a single complete ethical primer any more than a systematic theology, but rather addresses a mixture of contingent queries, over a period of some considerable time, utilising a wide variety of sources, as we shall see shortly. This means that there are bound to be variations, at the very least, in the way he handles issues and in the things he says.

Secondly, there is much debate about which letters are authentic, that is, written by Paul himself. Most books on Pauline ethics — indeed, on his theology and work in general — assume that seven letters are genuine: Romans, 1 and 2 Corinthians, Galatians, Philippians, 1 Thessalonians and Philemon.

---

29. R. E. O. White, *Christian Ethics* (Leominster: Gracewing, 1994), p. 134.
30. F. J. Matera, *New Testament Ethics* (Louisville: Westminster John Knox, 1996), p. 120.

Even here, only Romans actually comes from Paul alone (Rom. 1.1); other people are mentioned with Paul in the opening salutations, such as 'Paul and Timothy' (2 Cor. 1.1; Phil. 1.1; Col. 1.1; Phlm. 1.1) or 'Paul, Timothy and Silas', also known as Silvanus (1 and 2 Thess. 1.1), or 'Paul and Sosthenes' (1 Cor. 1.1).[31] Then there is what Dunn calls 'the afterwave, or tail of the comet, or, better, the school or studio of Paul'.[32] Thus there is continuing argument about the authorship of Ephesians, Colossians and 2 Thessalonians, while most scholars agree that the so-called 'Pastoral Letters' — 1 and 2 Timothy, and Titus — are actually post-Pauline, although this does not necessarily mean that they are without value for understanding the Pauline tradition.

It might be helpful at this point to include a brief word of introduction about each letter.[33] Matera begins with the letters to the **Thessalonians**, since 1 Thessalonians is probably the earliest of Paul's letters, dating from around AD 50, and he includes 2 Thessalonians, regardless of the debate about its date and authorship, because of its similar content.[34] In the first letter, Paul writes to encourage the church he founded there, to assure them of his concern for them and to give them some ethical instructions about living an holy life as well as teaching them about the final coming of Christ. The second letter contains further material about the coming, and commends Paul's example for how to live. **Galatians** was also probably written in this early period (although some date it in the mid 50s) to deal with a crisis in Galatia caused by some people teaching that Christians need to be circumcised and keep the law.[35] Paul defends his understanding of the gospel and his apostleship against such 'Judaizers' with an account of freedom in Christ, and concludes with the ethical implications of that for his readers' lives. The letters to the **Corinthians** probably date from the mid 50s.[36] 1 Corinthians teaches the readers how to be a Christian community, an-

31. On Paul's methods of writing and his assistants, see E. Randolph Richards, *Paul and First-Century Letter Writing: Secretaries, Composition and Collection* (Downers Grove, IL: IVP, 2004).

32. James D. G. Dunn, *The Theology of Paul the Apostle* (Grand Rapids: Eerdmans, 1998), p. 13.

33. For a good recent survey of each letter in turn, considering the 'story behind' it (its background, setting, authorship), the 'story within' (its account of the story of Jesus and its contents) and the 'story in front of the letter' (some readings of it by others), see Gorman, *Apostle of the Crucified Lord: A Theological Introduction to Paul and His Letters*, pp. 146-579; see similarly the introduction to each letter in Holladay, *A Critical Introduction to the New Testament*, pp. 263-444, or pp. 365-633 in the expanded CD version.

34. Matera, *NT Ethics*, p. 123; see also Ernest Best, *The First and Second Epistles to the Thessalonians* (London: A & C Black, 1972); F. F. Bruce, *1 and 2 Thessalonians*, Word Biblical Commentary, vol. 45 (Waco, TX: Word, 1982).

35. Hans Dieter Betz, *Galatians*, Hermeneia (Philadelphia: Fortress, 1979); F. F. Bruce, *The Epistle to the Galatians: A Commentary on the Greek Text*, NIGTC (Exeter: Paternoster, 1982).

36. C. K. Barrett, *A Commentary on the First Epistle to the Corinthians*, 2nd edn. (London:

swering their questions with instructions about unity, morality, sexuality, food offered to idols, worship and spiritual gifts, communion and the resurrection. This results in further correspondence, and 2 Corinthians may be a mixture of several letters in which Paul seeks to defend his apostleship and his relationship with the church at Corinth, again commending his own personal example of living. **Philippians** is written by Paul from prison, either in Caesarea or Ephesus in the mid 50s, or from Rome in the early 60s, to exhort his readers to live a life worthy of Christ's example.[37] The personal letter to **Philemon**, also written from prison but curiously omitted by Matera,[38] asks him to receive back a runaway slave, Onesimus, out of Christian love. The epistle to the **Romans**, probably written in the mid/late 50s, is generally agreed to be the fullest expression of his theology, though it remains a specific letter rather than a treatise.[39] Paul sets out his gospel message, of God's salvation offered to everyone, Jews and Gentiles alike, in what he has done in Christ (1–8); he then deals with the consequences of this for Israel and the Jews (9–11) and for how Christians should live, with very practical ethical instructions (12–15) and his greetings (16). Scholars are divided about the authorship of **Colossians** and **Ephesians**, which appear to be closely related. These letters have clear links with the rest of Paul's writings, but scholars note the differences of style and vocabulary as well as theological emphasis (arguably containing a 'higher' Christology and a more realized eschatology). Some scholars suggest that this puts the letters further, towards the end of Paul's life, and/or implies that they were written by or with one of his colleagues, while others argue for pseudepigraphal composition shortly after his death; opinion is roughly split down the middle over Colossians, while rather fewer consider Ephesians to be authentic.[40] However, most New Testament scholars do accept

---

A & C Black, 1971); C. K. Barrett, *A Commentary on the Second Epistle to the Corinthians* (London: A & C Black, 1973); Richard B. Hays, *First Corinthians,* Interpretation (Louisville: John Knox, 1997); Anthony C. Thiselton, *1 Corinthians,* NIGTC (Grand Rapids: Eerdmans, 2000).

37. Peter T. O'Brien, *Commentary on Philippians,* NIGTC (Grand Rapids: Eerdmans, 1991); Markus Bockmuehl, *The Epistle to the Philippians,* 4th edn. (London: A & C Black, 1997); Gerald F. Hawthorne, *Philippians,* Word Biblical Commentary, vol. 43, rev. Ralph P. Martin (Nashville: Nelson, 2004).

38. Matera, *NT Ethics,* p. 122 says that this is because he deals with slavery elsewhere; for Philemon, see Eduard Lohse, *Colossians and Philemon,* Hermeneia (Philadelphia: Fortress, 1971).

39. C. E. B. Cranfield, *The Epistle to the Romans,* ICC, 2 vols. (Edinburgh: T&T Clark, 1975, 1979); J. D. G. Dunn, *Romans,* Word Biblical Commentary, 2 vols., 38 and 38A (Milton Keynes: Word, 1991); Joseph A. Fitzmyer, S.J., *Romans: A New Translation with Introduction and Commentary,* Anchor Bible 33 (New York: Doubleday, 1993).

40. See, for example, Gorman, *Apostle of the Crucified Lord: A Theological Introduction to Paul and His Letters,* pp. 476-78 and 501-5; Fisk, 'Paul: Life and Letters', in *The Face of New Testament Studies,* ed. McKnight and Osborne, pp. 283-96.

that the differences found in the **Pastoral Letters** (1 and 2 Timothy and Titus), especially the concern for church order and polity and the different style, mean that they are later, even if they may preserve some authentic material about Paul and his concerns for the younger leaders coming after him.[41] While we will make occasional reference to these later letters in this chapter, we shall concentrate for the most part on the undisputed seven epistles. Similar strategies are adopted by most scholars writing on Pauline ethics.[42]

Thus all of these letters seek to respond to specific situations facing the early Christian communities by drawing upon Paul's theological understanding of what God has done in Christ and its practical implications for his readers — which means that his ethics is bound up with the rest of his thinking and writing, and with the particular concerns of his churches.

b. Old Testament and Jewish sources

It is clear that Paul draws on a variety of sources for his ethics, including both Jewish and Greek ideas, past and present. His use of the Old Testament, in particular, is much disputed among scholars. On the face of it, Paul is explicit about the importance of the Hebrew scriptures for providing ethical guidance: 'For whatever was written in former days was written for our instruction' (Rom. 15:4; see also 1 Cor. 10.11). Thus he uses the phrase 'for it is written' to quote 'vengeance is mine' from Deut. 32.35 in Rom. 12.19, or 'one flesh', Gen. 2.24, in 1 Cor. 6.16; similarly he introduces Exod. 16.18 into 2 Cor. 8.15 and Ps. 112.9 in 2 Cor. 9.9. However, these instances alone do not settle the case. Even Rosner, at the start of his attempt to demonstrate Paul's use of the Old Testament as a source for his ethical teaching, has to recognise that less than a fifth of Paul's quotations of the scriptures occur in his ethical sec-

41. See Stanley E. Porter (ed.), *The Pauline Canon, Pauline Studies*, vol. 1 (Leiden: Brill, 2004); also George W. Knight III, *The Pastoral Epistles: A Commentary on the Greek Text*, NIGTC (Grand Rapids: Eerdmans, 1992); Martin Dibelius and Hans Conzelmann, *The Pastoral Epistles*, Hermeneia (Philadelphia: Fortress, 1972).

42. See Schrage, *The Ethics of the NT*, p. 167; Matera, *NT Ethics*, pp. 120-22; V. P. Furnish, *Theology and Ethics in Paul* (Nashville: Abingdon, 1968), pp. 11-12; A. Verhey, *The Great Reversal* (Grand Rapids: Eerdmans, 1984), p. 103; R. Mohrlang, *Matthew and Paul: A Comparison of Ethical Perspectives*, SNTSMS 48 (Cambridge: Cambridge University Press, 1984), pp. 3-4; J. P. Sampley, *Walking between the Times: Paul's Moral Reasoning* (Minneapolis: Fortress, 1991), p. 2; B. S. Rosner *Understanding Paul's Ethics* (Grand Rapids: Eerdmans, 1995), pp. 3-4; R. B. Hays, *The Moral Vision of the New Testament* (San Francisco: HarperCollins, 1996/Edinburgh: T&T Clark, 1997), pp. 60-61; David G. Horrell, *Solidarity and Difference: A Contemporary Reading of Paul's Ethics* (London: T&T Clark, 2005), p. 1.

tions.[43] Von Harnack's analysis demonstrated that six of the letters (1 and 2 Thessalonians, Colossians, Philemon, Ephesians and Philippians) do not use the Old Testament for ethical instruction; the quotations in Galatians and Romans are explained by the special circumstances of the debate with the Judaizers, although this is less obvious a reason for the quotations in 1 and 2 Corinthians. Instead, the gospel and the Spirit form the basis for Paul's ethics.[44] Similarly negative conclusions about the Old Testament as a source for Paul's ethics are held by many scholars up to the present time.[45]

On the other hand, there has been a major reassessment of Paul's relationship with Judaism in recent decades, particularly after the groundbreaking work of E. P. Sanders.[46] Bockmuehl has shown that the Noachide Commandments (about idolatry, sexual immorality and blood offences) may have crystallized in rabbinic work only in the second century, but were very important earlier in the Second Temple period; he sees their influence not only in Acts 15 but also on Paul's ethics.[47] Holtz argues that Paul's ethical teaching comes out of a Jewish background which sees everything as originating from the Torah: 'Even for Paul the Torah represents the only norm of life and its order represents the order of the wholesome life.'[48] Rosner specifically tackles 1 Cor. 5–7 as a test-case because von Harnack believed that it had no relation to the Old Testament: his analysis looks at parallels with Ezra, Moses, Joseph and the Torah itself and concludes that Paul has a 'positive orientation towards the Scriptures, especially in matters of Christian conduct'; they are indeed 'written for our instruction (1 Cor. 10.11)'.[49] While Rosner probably tries to argue for too much and some of his links are more convincing than others, his work has been widely received as

43. Brian S. Rosner, *Paul, Scripture, and Ethics: A Study of 1 Corinthians 5–7* (Leiden: Brill, 1994), pp. 7-8, 188-89.

44. Adolf von Harnack, 'Das Alte Testament in den paulinischen Briefen und in den paulinischen Gemeinden', *Sitzungsberichte der preussischen Akademie der Wissenschaften* (Berlin, 1928), pp. 124-41; ET 'The Old Testament in the Pauline Letters and in the Pauline Churches', in *Understanding Paul's Ethics*, ed. Rosner, pp. 27-49.

45. See Rosner, *Paul, Scripture, and Ethics*, pp. 3-9 for a list and details.

46. E. P. Sanders, *Paul and Palestinian Judaism* (London: SCM, 1977); idem, *Paul, the Law, and the Jewish People* (Philadelphia: Fortress, 1983); idem, *Paul* (Oxford: Oxford University Press, 1991).

47. M. Bockmuehl, 'The Noachide Commandments and New Testament Ethics with Special Reference to Acts 15 and Pauline Halakhah', *Revue Biblique* 102 (1995), pp. 72-101; repr. as Bockmuehl, *Jewish Law in Gentile Churches: Halakhah and the Beginning of Christian Public Ethics* (Edinburgh: T&T Clark, 2000), pp. 145-73.

48. T. Holtz, 'Zur Frage der inhaltlichen Weisungen bei Paulus', *Theologische Literaturzeitung* 106 (1981), pp. 385-400; ET 'The Question of the Content of Paul's Instructions', in *Understanding Paul's Ethics*, ed. Rosner, pp. 51-71; quotation from p. 69.

49. Rosner, *Paul, Scripture, and Ethics*, p. 194.

an important corrective to the approach of von Harnack and others opposed to Paul's use of the Old Testament. Hays has recently applied his previous work on the 'echoes of scripture' as constitutive of Paul's worldview to his ethics; although the scriptures appear to have a less direct role in his ethical sections, they 'play a major role in shaping Paul's moral vision', providing 'the overarching narrative framework for the moral life'.[50] In other words, we do not necessarily have to find a specific reference to an Old Testament text, but rather allusions to the interlocking stories which we discussed earlier. A slight corrective to this comes from Tuckett, who recognizes Paul's use of Old Testament scripture, but wants to limit its significance more directly to the text quoted; instead, 'far more central to Paul's argument here are the twin (or connected) appeals to the person of Jesus and to the figure of himself as an apostle as paradigms for Christian existence'.[51]

A resolution of these differing approaches may be found from our first point above: we noted that all of Paul's theology is essentially Christological, and the same is true of his use of the Hebrew scriptures. Furnish's analysis shows that Paul appeals to the Old Testament, but not in a casuistic manner to find specific texts or answers; instead it provides the 'scriptural witness to the history of God's dealings with his people' — which has now reached its fulfilment in Christ. Equally, Paul is well aware of intertestamental material, apocalyptic writings and contemporary Rabbinic Judaism — all of which adds to the 'perspective from which he interprets the whole event of God's act in Christ'.[52] Hooker agrees: for Paul 'Christ himself is the key to the meaning of scripture . . . all scripture can be used, because it is all Christological'.[53] Similar conclusions are reached by Verhey and Schrage at the end of their analyses of Paul's use of the Old Testament also.[54] Thus, like the rest of Paul's theology, after his experience of Jesus on the Damascus road, everything, including the ancient scriptures, now has to be interpreted in the light of what God has achieved in him.

50. Richard B. Hays, *Echoes of Scripture in the Letters of Paul* (New Haven, CT: Yale University Press, 1989); idem, 'The Role of Scripture in Paul's Ethics', in E. H. Lovering, Jr. and J. L. Sumney (eds.), *Theology and Ethics in Paul and His Interpreters: Essays in Honor of Victor Paul Furnish* (Nashville: Abingdon, 1996), pp. 30-47; quotation from p. 46; see also Hays' review of Rosner's *Paul, Scripture, and Ethics* in *Westminster Theological Journal* 58 (1996), pp. 313-16.

51. Christopher M. Tuckett, 'Paul, Scripture and Ethics: Some Reflections', *NTS* 46 (2000), pp. 403-24; quotation from p. 423.

52. V. P. Furnish, *Theology and Ethics in Paul* (Nashville: Abingdon, 1968), pp. 1-44; quotations from pp. 34 and 42-43.

53. M. D. Hooker, 'Beyond the Things That Are Written? St Paul's Use of Scripture', in her *From Adam to Christ* (Cambridge: Cambridge University Press, 1990), pp. 139-54; quotation from pp. 152-53.

54. Schrage, *The Ethics of the NT,* pp. 204-7; Verhey, *The Great Reversal,* p. 110.

c. The contemporary Hellenistic world

The other major source for Paul's ethics is the contemporary Hellenistic world around him and his readers. Once again, some confusion is apparent from an initial reading of the texts. On the one hand, Paul tells his readers not to be 'conformed to this world' (Rom. 12.2), which suggests a world-denying ethic. Yet, on the other hand, the opening chapters of the same letter, Rom. 1–2, imply that there are moral norms in the world, known to people in the creation so they are without excuse (1.19-20) with 'what the law requires written on their hearts to which their own conscience also bears witness' (2.15). Both the idea of and the word 'conscience', συνείδησις, are Greek, with no equivalent in Hebrew. However, Paul uses it here, as well as regularly in the Corinthian correspondence, which is further indication of its Greek background (see 1 Cor. 8.7-12; 10.25-29; 2 Cor. 1.12; 4.2; 5.11).[55] Other Hellenistic concepts include 'freedom', ἐλευθερία (1 Cor. 10.29; Gal. 5.1, 13), and 'self-sufficiency', αὐτάρκεια (2 Cor. 9.8). The shift of the latter from the Stoic idea of 'self-sufficient' into being 'content' in trusting God 'who strengthens me' in Phil. 4.11-13 is a good example of the way Paul takes contemporary ethical ideas and transforms them. A few verses earlier, Paul gives us a list of 'virtues' upon which to think — true, serious, just, pure, lovely, well spoken of — most of which are words very rare in his letters, yet common in contemporary ethics (Phil. 4.8). He tells his readers to think upon virtue and praise, ἀρετὴ καὶ . . . ἔπαινος, again developing typical Greek concepts.[56]

Paul also uses Stoic metaphors of life as an athletic game or war (e.g., 1 Cor. 9.25; 2 Cor. 10.3). He quotes the proverb, 'Bad company ruins good morals' (1 Cor. 15.33), which is preserved in fragment 218 of the comic poet Menander's *Thais* — although Paul may just have known it from common quotation.[57] 'Household codes', *Haustafeln*, are another piece of ethical instruction from Hellenistic literature, which can be traced back as far as Aristotle's *Politics*, book 1.[58] Two good examples of modified codes occur in Eph. 5.21–6.9 and Col. 3.18–4.1, although there are none in the undisputed letters of Paul. Whether they are by Paul or not, this is another example in the Pauline tradition of the use and adaptation of Hellenistic sources for ethical instruction.

55. See Furnish, *Theology and Ethics in Paul*, pp. 47-48, 228-30.

56. On Paul and virtue, see J. Ian H. McDonald, 'The Crucible of Pauline Ethics', *Studies in World Christianity* 3.1 (1997), pp. 1-21, esp. pp. 2-8.

57. See Furnish, *Theology and Ethics in Paul*, pp. 45-47.

58. See D. L. Balch, 'Household Codes', in *Greco-Roman Literature and the New Testament: Selected Forms and Genres*, ed. D. E. Aune, SBLSBS 21 (Atlanta: Scholars Press, 1988), pp. 25-50; also J. Ian H. McDonald, *The Crucible of Christian Morality* (London: Routledge, 1998), pp. 162-65.

Recent decades have seen the development of a large amount of study of the social context of the New Testament, and Paul's letters in particular.[59] Meeks and McDonald have particularly sought to apply these methods to New Testament ethics in their reconstructions of the 'crucible' or 'moral world' of the early Christian communities, including some possible sources for Paul's ethical material.[60] A fuller understanding of the social background of first-century morality helps us not only to see some of Paul's sources for his ethics, but also to notice when he diverges from contemporary understanding. For instance, the idea of 'humility', ταπεινοφροσύνη, and the concepts of being abased or humbled are seen negatively in the Hellenistic ethical tradition, almost as a vice. However, for Paul this is a supreme virtue as characterised by Christ's humbling himself for us (Phil. 2.8), and so we should also 'in humility count others better' than ourselves and 'associate with the humble' (Phil. 2.3; Rom. 12.16). As with Paul's use of the Old Testament as a source for his ethics, so too with his contemporary Hellenistic culture: 'Again the crucial influence is Christology', concludes Schrage.[61] The impact of his Graeco-Roman setting on Paul is crucial and contributes much to his ethical teaching — but always to serve his understanding of what God has done in Christ and the practical implications of this for his readers.

A mixture of Jewish and Hellenistic backgrounds can also be seen in Paul's use of the early paraenetic tradition, especially in the lists of virtues and vices. Such lists were common in both cultures, and Paul includes a number of them, addressing his readers as 'my children' or 'brothers and sisters' (e.g., Gal. 4.19; Phil. 4.1). There are more vice lists and they are longer: Rom. 1.29-31; 13.13; 1 Cor. 5.10-11; 6.9-10; 2 Cor. 12.20; Gal. 5.19-21; Col. 3.5, 8.[62] Lists of virtues occur in 2 Cor. 6.6; Gal. 5.22-23; Phil. 4.8; Col. 3.12. In particular, the contrast between 'the works of the flesh' and 'the fruit of the Spirit' in Gal. 5.16-24 shows that these are not just lists for human moral endeavour, but rather the practical outworking of the new life 'in Christ' enabled by the power of the Holy Spirit.[63]

---

59. See David G. Horrell (ed.), *Social-Scientific Approaches to New Testament Interpretation* (Edinburgh: T&T Clark, 1999); Gerd Theissen, *The Social Setting of Pauline Christianity* (Edinburgh: T&T Clark, 1982); Wayne A. Meeks, *The First Urban Christians: The Social World of the Apostle Paul* (New Haven, CT: Yale University Press, 1983).

60. Wayne Meeks, *The Moral World of the First Christians* (London: SPCK, 1987) and *The Origins of Christian Morality* (New Haven, CT: Yale University Press, 1993); McDonald, 'The Crucible of Pauline Ethics' and *The Crucible of Christian Morality*.

61. Schrage, *The Ethics of the NT*, p. 201.

62. See B. J. Oropeza, 'Situational Immorality: Paul's "Vice Lists" at Corinth', *ExpT* 110.1 (October 1998), pp. 9-11.

63. For discussion of Paul's paraenesis and the lists, see Furnish, *Theology and Ethics in Paul*,

Thus, whether he is drawing upon Jewish or Hellenistic sources, the Hebrew scriptures or contemporary moral teaching, Paul maintains his Christological focus, adapting and transforming whatever is available to instruct his audiences in the ethical implications of all that God has done in Christ. This is his focus, rather than quoting Jesus' own ethical teaching, of which there is surprisingly little in Paul's letters — as we shall discover in our more detailed examination at the end of this chapter. At this point, it is sufficient to conclude that the search for the sources of Paul's ethics has revealed a wide range of diverse backgrounds. The debate about whether his ethic is Jewish or Hellenistic is essentially sterile — for it is both and more. The whole world of the first century was syncretistic in its mixture of cultures and ideas, and Paul could not help but be influenced by them all. However, all of them had to serve his primary goal: after his experience on the Damascus road, Paul was gripped by the way all of Israel's history had come to its climax in Christ, who was the fulfilment of Gentile hopes as well. Therefore, he can make use of any of these sources in his attempt to make the new life in Christ a reality in the experience of his readers.

3. Ethics, eschatology and theology

a. Separation or integration?

In Romans and Galatians, the ethical material comes in the second part of each letter and deals with specific issues asked by Paul's correspondents or pertaining to their situation. This tendency can also be discerned in some other letters (e.g., 1 Thessalonians) and in the later Paulines (e.g., Ephesians). The question immediately arises about the relationship of this material to the earlier doctrinal teaching and whether it is separate from it.

Dibelius argued that the ethical material at the end of the letters was little more than contemporary Hellenistic paraenesis, inserted to provide moral guidance in the absence of an early Christian ethic, which was not needed in the expectation of the immediacy of the second coming.[64] Dibelius' account has been subsequently disputed, but a similar separation is perpetuated in many analyses of individual letters, such as Betz' commentary on Galatians.[65]

---

pp. 68-92; Verhey, *The Great Reversal,* pp. 109-10; and Dunn, *The Theology of Paul the Apostle,* pp. 661-65.

64. M. Dibelius, *A Fresh Approach to the New Testament and Early Christian Literature* (Hertford: Ivor Nicholson and Watson, 1936).

65. H. D. Betz, *Galatians,* Hermeneia (Philadelphia: Fortress, 1979); see p. 292.

Meanwhile, J. T. Sanders argues that Paul's eschatology combined with his mixture of sources just makes him 'inconsistent' in his ethics.[66] His namesake, E. P. Sanders, has been responsible for the major reassessment of Palestinian Judaism in terms of 'covenantal nomism', where keeping the law is a response to the grace of God as a way of 'staying in', rather than 'getting in' by good works. He argues that 'Paul could readily hold together the "juristic" and "participatory" categories', but that while Christ is the means of salvation, the law still gives moral guidance to Christians for the 'good deeds . . . the condition of remaining "in"'.[67] This division in Sanders' approach between salvation and the moral life, it has been argued, leads to an incoherence in Paul between his theology and his ethics.[68]

On the other hand, many argue that, in general terms, theology and ethics are inextricably linked: thus Marxsen maintains that 'ethics is an integral part of theology', and Lohse talks of 'the theological ethics of the New Testament'.[69] Furthermore, we have seen above how Paul's understanding of what God has done in Christ dominates all of his thinking. If all of this is true, then Paul's ethical material in his letters should flow from and be a consequence of his theology, indeed of his Christology. Thus, a simple separation of his letters into theology first and ethics later does not work. Bultmann's consideration of 'the problem of ethics in Paul' demonstrated the integral connection of the imperative and indicative — that Paul's ethical instructions are to enable his readers to become in practical ways what he has said that they are theologically: 'since we live by the Spirit [indicative], let us walk by the Spirit [imperative]' (Gal. 5.25).[70] Increasingly, analyses of individual letters have sought to demonstrate the overall unity throughout their chapters and between their theology and ethics. Thus Hays and Barclay have responded to Betz' dissection of Galatians by arguing that the ethical instructions of Gal. 5–6 arise out of the themes of the earlier chapters.[71] Equally, in a South African context David Bosch has argued that the ethical instructions of Rom. 12–15, including 13.1-7 on the state, follow from the

---

66. Jack T. Sanders, *Ethics in the New Testament* (London: SCM, 1975), pp. 64-66.

67. E. P. Sanders, *Paul and Palestinian Judaism*, pp. 474-518; quotations from pp. 501, 517.

68. See R. B. Hays, 'Christology and Ethics in Galatians', pp. 271-72 and W. L. Willis, 'Pauline Ethics, 1964-1994', in Lovering and Sumney, *Theology and Ethics in Paul and His Interpreters*, pp. 313-14.

69. W. Marxsen, *New Testament Foundations for Christian Ethics* (Edinburgh: T&T Clark, 1993), p. 1; Lohse, *Theological Ethics of the NT.*

70. R. Bultmann, 'Das Problem der Ethik bei Paulus', *ZNW* 23 (1924), pp. 123-40; ET 'The Problem of Ethics in Paul', in *Understanding Paul's Ethics*, ed. Rosner, pp. 195-216; see further our discussion of the indicative and imperative below.

71. Hays, 'Christology and Ethics in Galatians'; J. Barclay, *Obeying the Truth: A Study of Paul's Ethics in Galatians* (Edinburgh: T&T Clark, 1988).

theology of the rest of the epistle, while N. T. Wright's reading of Romans inspired by the approach of Gore stresses the 'integration of Paul's ethics with his theology' and the narrative unity of the progression of the chapters as a whole.[72] Therefore Hooker is right to point out that 'the neat division into theological and ethical sections is too simple'.[73]

This understanding of the integration of theology and ethics in Paul owes much to Furnish's seminal work which maintained that the study of Pauline ethics begins with 'the theological convictions which underlie Paul's concrete exhortations and instructions'.[74] Matera agrees that 'ethics and theology are one in Paul's writings', while Schrage has pointed out the consequence of this integration that 'any presentation of the basis of Pauline ethics must perforce sketch an outline of Pauline theology'.[75] Therefore the next step is to examine whether any particular aspect of Paul's theology is central for his ethics. Achtemeier considers attempts to locate it in justification by faith and in the cross, but concludes that the 'generative center of Paul's theology' is the resurrection.[76] Hays begins his *Moral Vision of the New Testament* with a detailed chapter arguing that Paul's ethics are theologically grounded in three key images of community, cross and new creation, through which he reads not only Paul's ethics, but those of the whole New Testament.[77] However, we have already demonstrated above that Christology is at the centre of both Paul's theology and his ethics. If ethics and theology are integrated and behaviour is a consequence of a right relationship with God, then the Christological basis of this relationship will be primary in ethics. Granted the primacy of Christology, however, a brief consideration of other important aspects of Paul's theology also shows their links with ethics.

72. David Bosch, 'Paul on Human Hopes', *JTSA* 67 (1989), pp. 3-16, esp. pp. 10-11; N. T. Wright, 'Coming Home to St. Paul? Reading Romans a Hundred Years after Charles Gore', The Gore Lecture, Westminster Abbey, November 14, 2000; later published in *SJT* 55.4 (2002), pp. 392-407, quotation from p. 405.

73. M. D. Hooker, 'Interchange in Christ and Ethics', in *From Adam to Christ* (Cambridge: Cambridge University Press, 1990), pp. 56-69; quotation from p. 56.

74. Furnish, *Theology and Ethics in Paul*, p. 212.

75. Matera, *NT Ethics*, p. 122; Schrage, *The Ethics of the NT*, p. 167; see also Horrell, *Solidarity and Difference*, pp. 13-15.

76. Paul J. Achtemeier, 'The Continuing Quest for Coherence in St. Paul: An Experiment in Thought', in Lovering and Sumney, *Theology and Ethics in Paul and His Interpreters*, pp. 132-45; quotation from p. 138; Odette Mainville also concludes that the resurrection is central, 'L'éthique paulienne', *Église et Théologie* 24 (1993), pp. 391-412.

77. Hays, *Moral Vision of the NT*, pp. 16-59.

b. *Ethics and eschatology*

We noted in the previous chapter that the heart of Jesus' preaching was the kingdom of God, which was inextricably linked with eschatology. Equally for Paul, while preaching the kingdom may have become his proclamation of Christ, it is just as much connected to eschatology, which flows from his Christology. As Ridderbos has put it, 'Paul's "eschatology" is "Christ-eschatology"'.[78] This is because God has inaugurated the age to come in his saving work in Christ: 'If anyone is in Christ, there is a new creation: everything old has passed away; see, everything has become new! All this is from God, who reconciled us to himself through Christ' (2 Cor. 5.17-18). This focus on Jesus affects ethics as much as theology: as Schrage makes clear, 'Pauline eschatology, too, belongs primarily within the context of Christology, which furnishes its basis and focus'.[79] The moral life is possible only because of what God has done in Christ already; but, equally, because all is not yet complete, the moral life is even more needed as we wait for the fulfilment of the reign of God. Thus Dunn concludes, 'A Pauline ethic inevitably starts from the already and not yet and is shot through with the eschatological tension'.[80] This is why Sampley describes 'Paul's moral reasoning' as 'walking between the times'.[81]

This mixture of the already and the not yet has implications for both the present and the future. After various practical instructions answering the Corinthians' questions about marriage and sex for the present, Paul introduces the eschatological perspective that 'the appointed time (καιρός) has grown short'; therefore people should live as though they had no wives, no mourning or possessions (1 Cor. 7.29-31). Similarly, Rom. 13 begins with civic ethics, or obeying the state in the here and now (13.1-7), and goes on to other practical instructions about the law and love (13.8-10), all of which is then set in the context of the end being at hand; the 'now' is motivated by the fact that 'already (ἤδη) it is time to wake from sleep' (13.11-14). Given that the whole creation is 'groaning in labour pains' waiting for the redemption of the end time, ethics is vital during the 'sufferings of this present time' (Rom. 8.18-25). Furthermore, Paul suggests that the future dimension of reward and punishment to come at the end can help to motivate human behaviour in the present: 'For we must all appear before the judgment seat of Christ' (2 Cor. 5.10). In extreme cases, Paul recommends excommunication of a notorious offender now 'so that his spirit may be saved in the day of the Lord' (1 Cor. 5.1-5).

---

78. Ridderbos, *Paul: An Outline of His Theology,* p. 49.
79. Schrage, *The Ethics of the NT,* p. 181.
80. Dunn, *The Theology of Paul the Apostle,* p. 496.
81. Sampley, *Walking between the Times: Paul's Moral Reasoning.*

c. The response of being 'in Christ'

Jesus' preaching of God's rule being present now, yet also leading to a future climax sought a response of faith from his hearers, more than moral obedience to an ethical set of instructions. Similarly, Paul's Christology and eschatology also require a response that leads to participation in Christ: 'If anyone is in Christ, there is a new creation' (2 Cor 5.17). The concept of new life 'in Christ' is central for Paul. The first decades of the twentieth century produced a flurry of studies about this from Deissmann, Bousset and Schweitzer; however, the declining interest in mystical approaches through the middle of the century also affected such 'Christ mysticism'.[82] More recently, E. P. Sanders has redirected attention back to the importance of participation 'in Christ'.[83] Dunn helpfully provides the detailed statistics: the phrase ἐν Χριστῷ, 'in Christ', occurs eighty-three times in the Pauline corpus, of which fifty-eight come in the undisputed letters. However, in the rest of the New Testament, it only occurs in 1 Peter. Paul has forty-seven (thirty-nine undisputed) occurrences of 'in the Lord', ἐν κυρίῳ, which is also rare elsewhere. In addition, phrases like 'into Christ', 'of Christ', 'through Christ', plus the compound words expressing unity 'with Christ' and with one another, all demonstrate just how important this idea of participating in Christ is for Pauline theology.[84] Furthermore, Barcley has drawn attention to the importance of the complementary phrase 'Christ in you'.[85] Verhey argues that 'these texts are not concerned with a "mystical union" but with a moral identity'.[86] Dunn agrees that 'Paul draws immediate ethical corollaries from this being "in Christ"', while Hooker prefers to speak of the 'interchange in Christ and ethics'.[87]

Paul's fullest account of this shift of allegiance and status achieved by being in Christ comes in Rom. 5–8. After the parallel of the two ways of being in Adam or in Christ in Rom. 5, Paul goes on to argue that to be baptized into Christ is to be baptized into his death and resurrection (Rom. 6.1-5). This

82. A. Deissmann, *Die neutestamentliche Formel 'in Christo Jesu'* (Marburg: Elwert, 1892); W. Bousset, *Kyrios Christos* (1921; ET Nashville: Abingdon, 1970); A. Schweitzer, *The Mysticism of Paul the Apostle* (London: Black, 1931); for analysis see Dunn, *The Theology of Paul the Apostle*, pp. 390-96 and Brenda B. Colijn, 'Paul's Use of the "in Christ" Formula', *Ashland Theological Journal* 23 (1991), pp. 9-26.

83. E. P. Sanders, *Paul and Palestinian Judaism*, pp. 453-63.

84. Dunn, *The Theology of Paul the Apostle*, pp. 396-410.

85. W. B. Barcley, *'Christ in You': A Study in Paul's Theology and Ethics* (Lanham, MD and Oxford: University Press of America, 1999).

86. Verhey, *The Great Reversal*, p. 107.

87. Dunn, *The Theology of Paul the Apostle*, p. 411; Hooker, 'Interchange in Christ and Ethics', passim.

means that our old way of life has also died — 'our old self was crucified with him' — and so we also have new life 'with him' (6.5-10). This has immediate ethical effects, for 'How can we who have died to sin still live in it?'; therefore we must consider ourselves 'dead to sin and alive to God in Christ Jesus' (6.2, 11). On this basis, there is 'no condemnation for those who are in Christ Jesus' (8.1); therefore Paul exhorts his readers to offer the whole of their lives to God as a 'living sacrifice' (12.1). Thus we can see once again how Paul's ethical demand in Romans flows from and is bound up with his theological and Christological arguments.

Similar baptismal language, 'you were washed', also leads into ethical instructions on the grounds that we belong to Christ in 1 Cor 6.11-20. The same logic also appears in Colossians: those who have died 'with Christ' and have been 'raised with Christ' need a new way of life (Col. 2.20–3.4). In language redolent of the baptismal stripping off and being clad in new clothes, the readers are to 'put off the old nature' and 'put on' the new life in Christ, complete with very practical ethical instructions (3.5-14). As Matera says, 'This baptismal catechesis has profound ethical implications for the moral life of believers'.[88] Thus Paul does not see himself as a writer of ethical instructions any more than Jesus is primarily a moral teacher — but for both of them, responding in faith to what God is doing brings with it implications for how we live.

d. Together in the Christian community

Those who responded to Jesus' preaching found themselves in a very mixed group of others who were also following him. The same is true for Paul's converts, as being 'baptized into Christ' leads into our next Pauline theme: for such baptism breaks down all barriers between Jew and Gentile, male and female, slave and free. We are not just 'in Christ', but '*all* one in Christ', according to Gal. 3.27-28, which brings us to Paul's stress on the Christian community. Matera states that 'for Paul, one lives the moral life within the context of a nurturing community'.[89] Yet this dimension is less well covered in the secondary literature. Writing in 1994, Hays lamented that 'the standard surveys of NT ethics almost completely ignore the ecclesial context and shaping of Paul's moral vision'.[90] Hays' own *Moral Vision of the New Testament* provided some balance

---

88. Matera, *NT Ethics*, p. 212.

89. Matera, *NT Ethics*, p. 133.

90. Richard B. Hays, 'Ecclesiology and Ethics in 1 Corinthians', *Ex Auditu* 10 (Cambridge, 1994), pp. 31-43; quotation from p. 34.

with his stress on the rôle of community. More recently, Horrell has gone much further and demonstrated conclusively the importance of 'the construction of community: corporate solidarity in Christ' for Pauline ethics.[91]

Paul's setting of ethics within the community is perhaps best seen in 1 Corinthians. Here there is no suggestion of 'theological' chapters followed by later ethical instructions; instead he enters straight into the moral problems of the community with an appeal for unity, 1 Cor. 1.10-16; the theology follows, for their disunity empties the 'cross of Christ of its power' (1.17) and their 'jealousy and strife' shows that they are still 'of the flesh . . . behaving like ordinary people' (3.3). Thus the whole of chaps. 1–4 forms a major unit appealing for unity.[92] A similar contrast between immoral behaviour and life lived in the unity of the Spirit comes in Gal. 5.16–6.2.

These ethical concerns affecting the unity of the church then influence Paul's responses to the Corinthians' various questions about sexual morality, lawsuits, marriage and meat offered to idols in 1 Cor. 4–11. Here, Hays argues, 'The ethical norm is not . . . a predetermined rule. . .; rather, the right action must be *discerned* on the basis of a Christological paradigm, with a view to the need of the community and the community's identity as God's covenant people.'[93] Horrell also argues that these chapters demonstrate 'how this "other-regarding" morality has a fundamentally christological foundation'.[94] The next section, 1 Cor. 12–14, brings together morality and Christology as Paul confronts their behaviour together as 'the body of Christ' and places unity at the centre with his hymn to love in chap. 13. 'For Paul, love has its primary locus in the common life of the church.'[95] Participating 'in Christ' involves living the moral life in a community which is the 'body of Christ' with a 'variety of gifts' but all one in the Lord (1 Cor. 12.4-31). The same combination of the body of Christ and the differing gifts of individuals leading to practical instructions about unity is also found in Rom. 12.3-18 and Eph. 4.1-16.[96] Therefore, for Paul, responding to what God has done in Christ in the light of the eschaton has this

91. Horrell, *Solidarity and Difference*, chap. 4, pp. 99-132.

92. See Hays' discussion in 'Ecclesiology and Ethics', pp. 36-37 and *Moral Vision of the NT*, pp. 33-34.

93. Hays, 'Ecclesiology and Ethics', p. 38; his italics.

94. Horrell, *Solidarity and Difference*, p. 181; he develops this idea of 'other-regard' in pp. 166-245; see also Horrell's earlier work, 'Restructuring Human Relationships: Paul's Corinthian Letters and Habermas' Discourse Ethics', *ExpT* 110.10 (1999), pp. 321-25, esp. pp. 323-24 and Horrell, 'Theological Principle or Christological Praxis? Pauline Ethics in 1 Corinthians 8.1–11.1', *JSNT* 67 (1997), pp. 83-114.

95. Hays, 'Ecclesiology and Ethics', p. 40 and *Moral Vision of the NT*, p. 35.

96. See Dunn, *The Theology of Paul the Apostle*, pp. 548-64; and Ridderbos, *Paul: An Outline of His Theology*, pp. 369-76, 393-95, 446-67.

inevitably ecclesiological dimension of love in the Christian community of all who are making a similar response. In this respect, therefore, we find another important link between Paul and what we discovered about Jesus in the previous chapter, with his concern for a response to his preaching of the kingdom of God to be lived out within the community of other disciples who respond similarly.

e. Indicative and imperative

Finally, the connection between theology and ethics evident throughout these brief studies of Christology, eschatology and responding by participating in Christ in his body, the church, all come together in our last topic, in what Schrage has called 'a commonplace . . . under the catchwords "indicative" and "imperative"'.[97] Indeed, Furnish goes so far as to introduce his book by stating that 'the relation of indicative and imperative, the relation of "theological" proclamation and "moral" exhortation, is *the* crucial problem in interpreting the Pauline ethic'. Furthermore, he ends his survey of nineteenth- and twentieth-century interpretations of Paul's ethic with the conclusion that 'no interpretation of the Pauline ethic can be judged successful which does not grapple with the problem of indicative and imperative in Paul's thought'.[98]

In a nutshell, this formulation encapsulates the whole dialectic between theology and ethics in Paul, summed up in verses such as 'Since we live by the Spirit [indicative], let us walk by the Spirit [imperative]' (Gal. 5.25). If God has acted (indicative) supremely already in Christ to save us, then why does Paul need to give us moral imperatives at all? Nineteenth- and early twentieth-century scholars such as Wernle, Jacoby and Schweizer struggled to explain this apparent contradiction. However, Bultmann's article of 1924 is usually credited with making the issue central for Paul's ethics.[99] Bultmann argued that this is not a contradiction, but rather a 'paradox' or 'antinomy', in which our human indicative state of being righteous in Christ before God and the power to obey the divine imperative are both united in the gift of grace. The history of the subsequent debate — including Windisch, Bornkamm, Dodd, Goguel and Ramsey — is well documented by Furnish, Denison, Parsons and Willis.[100] For

97. Schrage, *The Ethics of the NT,* p. 167.

98. Furnish, *Theology and Ethics in Paul,* pp. 9 and 279.

99. R. Bultmann, 'Das Problem der Ethik bei Paulus'; ET 'The Problem of Ethics in Paul', in *Understanding Paul's Ethics,* ed. Rosner, pp. 195-216; see further Horrell, *Solidarity and Difference,* pp. 10-15.

100. Furnish, *Theology and Ethics in Paul,* pp. 242-79; W. D. Denison, 'Indicative and Impera-

Parsons, the imperatives are based upon the indicatives: 'Ethical behaviour, then, is a consequence, not the cause, of the newness of the believer's being'.[101] This is often summed up as 'Be what you are',[102] while others prefer the more dynamic words of Pindar's *Pythian Ode* 2.72, 'Become what you are'.[103] Whichever formulation is used, the eschatological tension of 'walking between the times' is clear as we seek to respond to the imperative and to let God work out in us, in the here and now, what we are already indicatively in Christ and will be seen to be finally at the end of all things.[104] As Paul says, 'Work out your own salvation . . . for God is at work in you' (Phil. 2.12-13; see also 1.6).

We saw above how the logic of Romans moves from being baptized into Christ's death and resurrection (6.4-7) to the instructions not to let sin reign in us (6.12-13); this too is a development from the indicative to the imperative. Parsons shows how the imperative of Rom. 12.1-2, 'present your bodies', flows from 'the mercies of God', which includes all of the earlier chapters of the letter; he also analyses Phil. 2.12-13 , Gal. 5.25 and 1 Cor. 6.12-20, to show the 'indissoluble' connection of the indicative and imperative.[105] Fowl's treatment of the Christological hymns of Phil. 2.6-11, Col. 1.15-20 and 1 Tim. 3.16b also shows how these 'foundational narratives, . . . three (indicative) stories about Christ are related to moral demands (imperative)'.[106] Equally, we demonstrated above a similar movement in Col. 2.20–3.14 from 'being' dead with Christ to 'putting on' the list of ethical imperatives.

Thus this final section has brought together all the major aspects of Paul's theology and how they are integrally connected with his ethics. Although it is true that in some letters Paul does collect his ethical material in the final chapters, nonetheless it still flows from and is a consequence of his more doctrinal teaching. His imperatives follow from his indicative statements about what God has done in Christ, whether they come later in the letter or are intimately connected throughout. Because we live in the eschatological tension 'between

---

tive: The Basic Structure of Pauline Ethics', *Calvin Theological Journal* 14 (1979), pp. 55-78; Michael Parsons, 'Being Precedes Act: Indicative and Imperative in Paul's Writing', *Evangelical Quarterly* 88.2 (1988), pp. 99-127, repr. in *Understanding Paul's Ethics*, ed. Rosner, pp. 217-47; W. L. Willis, 'Bibliography: Pauline Ethics, 1964-94', in Lovering and Sumney, *Theology and Ethics in Paul and His Interpreters*, pp. 306-19.

101. Parsons, 'Being Precedes Act', p. 229.

102. Hooker, 'Interchange in Christ and Ethics', p. 58; Kilner, 'A Pauline Approach to Ethical Decision-Making', p. 373.

103. See Dunn, *The Theology of Paul the Apostle*, p. 630; Denison, 'Indicative and Imperative', p. 72; Parsons, 'Being Precedes Act', p. 231.

104. Sampley, *Walking between the Times*; Dunn, *The Theology of Paul the Apostle*, p. 229.

105. Parsons, 'Being Precedes Act', pp. 233-47.

106. Fowl, *The Story of Christ in the Ethics of Paul*, pp. 207-8.

the times', ethics is all the more necessary as we work out the consequences of being 'in Christ' and sharing in the Christian community.

We argued in the previous chapter that, far from being a coherent set of moral instructions, Jesus' ethics were primarily concerned with a response to his preaching of the coming of the kingdom of God into our present now, undertaken within the context of a community of disciples. Paul is often contrasted with Jesus, and seen as responsible for a shift from 'the kingdom of God' to the 'King', to the person of Christ, and thus the founder of a new religious movement. In fact, this is an unfair distinction since, for Paul, the supreme act of God's sovereignty (i.e., the 'kingdom') is what he has done in Christ: this is how he has brought the whole story of Israel to a climax in Jesus of Nazareth. Therefore Paul's primary concern for an obedient response from his readers, lived out in the community of the body of Christ, may be seen as directly continuous with the preaching and ethical teaching of Jesus — and, Paul would argue, continuous with Israel's history as the people of God. In this respect, therefore, Paul is clearly a follower of Jesus rather than the founder of something new. Now we need to consider Paul's attitude to love and the law before taking up his specific ethical teaching, so that we can then return to this question of Paul's continuity with the ethics of Jesus in the final section of this chapter.

4. Paul, love and the law

a. Love as the greatest commandment

We saw in the previous chapter that the heart of Jesus' ethics was the double love command, to love God and the neighbour, given in response to a question about the greatest commandment (Mark 12.28-34 and parallels). Interestingly, Paul never quotes the double command as such, but this does not mean that love is not important for him. As Furnish points out, 'There is no Pauline letter in which the term "love" does not appear' with frequent 'exhortations to love'.[107] Collins gives the statistics: 'More than sixty per cent of the occurrences of the word "love", ἀγάπη, are to be found within the Pauline corpus', while Paul uses the verb 'to love' more frequently than the three Synoptic gospels put together and only slightly less than John.[108]

---

107. V. P. Furnish, *The Love Command in the New Testament* (Nashville: Abingdon, 1972), pp. 91-94.

108. Raymond F. Collins, *Christian Morality: Biblical Foundations* (Notre Dame, IN: University of Notre Dame Press, 1986), p. 137, taken from Collins' essay, 'Paul's First Reflections on Love',

Once again, Christology is the motivating factor as Paul describes love in the same terms he uses for Christ. Love does not seek its own (1 Cor. 13.5), even as Christ did not please himself (Rom. 15.3; Phil. 2.3-5). To 'walk', or live, 'in accord with love', κατὰ ἀγάπην (Rom. 14.15), is to live 'in accord with Christ Jesus', κατὰ Χριστὸν Ἰησοῦν (Rom. 15.5). To be 'rooted in love' is another way of being 'rooted in Christ' (compare Eph. 3.17 with Col. 2.7). Paul was supremely motivated by Christ, 'who loved me and gave himself for me' (Gal. 2.20). God's love is shown by the death of Christ 'while we were yet sinners', and 'poured into our hearts through the Holy Spirit' (Rom 5.5, 8).[109]

Thus Schrage concludes that love is 'the fundamental criterion of Pauline ethics', which 'takes precedence over all other commandments' and is 'the greatest good in the Christian life'.[110] Once again, as in our discussion of Jesus' ethic, Hays' dismissal of love seems curious. His explanation — that it does not feature significantly in Mark, Acts, Hebrews and Revelation — does not even consider Paul, while his treatment of Paul does not include love at all![111] We suggested before that this omission is caused by Hays' concern that love is 'easily debased in popular discourse . . . a cover for all manner of vapid self-indulgence'. While that may be true in the USA today, that is no reason for disregarding what Paul means by love. As Schrage says, 'Love must not be confused with a vague feeling of good will'.[112] Throughout Paul's letters, love has lots of very practical, ethical consequences. For Furnish, it is the 'eschatological-christological orientation of Paul's love ethic', which means that 'the apostle is chiefly concerned with the implications of love for life within the Christian community'.[113] In commenting upon Hays' abandonment of love, Campbell also concludes, 'In short, a participatory understanding of "love" in Paul is neither sentimental, nor culturally conditioned. It is, one suspects, powerful, difficult, and also deeply challenging.'[114]

This can be easily demonstrated in 1 Corinthians. In the first four chapters, Paul writes to 'my beloved children' to urge them to overcome their divisions in the unity of Christ, so that he might come to visit them 'in love' (1 Cor. 4.14, 21). When he then comes to the difficult ethical issue of meat which has been of-

---

pp. 137-48, an interesting analysis of Paul's first letter, 1 Thessalonians, to demonstrate how important love was for him right from the start.

109. See further Schrage, *The Ethics of the NT*, p. 211; Ridderbos, *Paul: An Outline of His Theology*, p. 293, and Furnish, *The Love Command*, p. 92.

110. Schrage, *The Ethics of the NT*, pp. 212-3; see also pp. 216-17.

111. Hays, *Moral Vision of the NT*, pp. 200-202 and 16-46.

112. Schrage, *The Ethics of the NT*, p. 211.

113. Furnish, *The Love Command*, p. 95.

114. Campbell, *The Quest for Paul's Gospel*, p. 117.

fered to idols, Paul agrees with some of the Corinthians who know that idols do not really exist; but while 'knowledge puffs up, love builds up' (1 Cor. 8.1-4). Throughout the discussion of chaps. 8–10, love for others takes precedence over the Corinthians' vaunted freedom in Christ in order to prevent behaviour which may be morally acceptable from offending others. Paul concludes, "'All things are lawful," but not all things build up. Do not seek your own advantage, but that of the other' (1 Cor. 10.23).[115] Theissen calls this attitude 'love-patriarchalism', whereby, even if social differences are still accepted, concern for the other, especially the 'weaker' or subordinate, must take priority over 'norms now superseded'.[116] In fact, Horrell goes further, arguing that Paul's stress on love challenges and even subverts the social order.[117] The next major section, chaps. 11–14, is concerned with prayer and holy communion, with spiritual gifts and worship — yet right in the middle of it all comes Paul's great hymn to love: 'the greatest of these is love' (1 Cor. 13.13). Once again, the words Paul uses to describe love are also true of the character of Christ.[118]

There is a similar stress in the final chapters of Romans. After describing God's love for us in the previous sections, Paul turns to urge his readers to 'let love be genuine' (Rom. 12.9). Such love is to extend even to enemies, picking up the teaching of Jesus (Rom. 12.17). Practical ethics about obeying the state, Rom. 13.1-7, comes in this context of 'the relationship between Christians and non-Christians on the basis of love',[119] as Paul then goes on show how love fulfils the commandments in 13.8-10. When Paul comes next to the issue of meat offered to idols in chaps. 14–15, as with the Corinthians, 'living in love' is the criterion which must take priority (14.15).[120]

Thus, we want to argue against Hays' dismissal of love; in fact, love is a central theme for both Paul's theology and his ethics, arising from his own personal experience of the love of God in Christ: 'The life I now live in the flesh I live by faith in the Son of God, who loved me and gave himself for me' (Gal. 2.20). Such love has definite ethical implications for the Christian community,

115. See Furnish, *The Love Command*, pp. 112-15; Horrell, 'Theological Principle or Christological Praxis? Pauline Ethics in 1 Corinthians 8.1–11.1', which is then reworked in Horrell, *Solidarity and Difference*, pp. 168-82; J. A. Davis, 'The Interaction between Individual Ethical Consciousness and Community Ethical Consciousness in 1 Corinthians', *Horizons in Biblical Theology* 10.2 (1988), pp. 1-18.

116. See Theissen, *The Social Setting of Pauline Christianity*, pp. 107-10 and 139-40.

117. David G. Horrell, *The Social Ethos of the Corinthian Correspondence* (Edinburgh: T&T Clark, 1996), pp. 126-98.

118. See Thiselton, 'Love, the Essential and Lasting Criterion', in his *1 Corinthians*, pp. 1026-74; and Ridderbos, *Paul: An Outline of His Theology*, pp. 295-98.

119. Schrage, *The Ethics of the NT*, p. 215.

120. Furnish, *The Love Command*, pp. 115-18.

and Paul uses it as a major criterion in handling the very practical issues facing his readers, as we shall see below shortly.

b. Love is the 'fulfilling of the law'

Given this centrality of love for Paul's ethics, we must next consider the issue of the law. Paul's relationship with the law — and with Judaism as a whole — has undergone a major revision in recent scholarship. For centuries, Protestant scholars, especially those from a German and/or Lutheran tradition, inter-preted Paul's attitude to the law as essentially negative. In many ways, this is now seen as a consequence of the debates at and since the Reformation rather than from Paul himself. The work of E. P. Sanders — especially his concept of 'covenantal nomism' and his distinction between observing the law for 'staying in' the covenant rather than 'getting in' — has been pivotal.[121] While we cannot discuss this whole debate in detail here, the relation of love and the law is very important for Pauline ethics.

Paul grapples with the law in Galatians and Romans, and, in both cases, says that love 'fulfils' the law (Gal. 5.14; Rom. 13.10). The general thrust of Galatians is against those who, under the influence of 'Judaizers', think they have to be circumcised and keep 'the works of the law' (Gal. 3.2, 10). Paul's re-sponse is that 'Christ has set us free' — so his readers should not 'submit again to a yoke of slavery. . . . If you are led by the Spirit, you are not under the law' (5.1-2, 18). It is, indeed, a generally negative picture of the law — and love is su-perior. 'For the whole law is fulfilled in a single commandment [ὁ γὰρ πᾶς νόμος ἐν ἑνὶ λόγῳ πεπλήρωται], "You shall love your neighbour as yourself"' (5.14, quoting Lev. 19.18). This statement then leads into Paul's contrast of the 'works of the flesh' and the 'fruit of the Spirit' (5.16-26). Hübner tries to avoid the negative verdict by suggesting that while 'the whole law', ὅλον τὸν νόμον, in 5.3 does refer to the Mosaic law, the different Greek of 'the whole law', ὁ πᾶς νόμος, of 5.14 means 'law as a whole' instead, and not the Torah.[122] However, as John Barclay has argued, Paul's consistent use of νόμος for the Mosaic law means that this 'ingenious' suggestion will not work.[123]

If Galatians was written in the heat of debate, Paul gives a more considered

---

121. E. P. Sanders, *Paul and Palestinian Judaism, Paul, the Law, and the Jewish People* and *Paul;* see nn. 46 and 67 above.

122. Hans Hübner, *Law in Paul's Thought: A Contribution to the Development of Pauline Theol-ogy* (Edinburgh: T&T Clark, 1984); see esp. pp. 36-42.

123. Barclay, *Obeying the Truth*, pp. 135-42 and 232-35; see also Furnish's discussion of this pas-sage in *The Love Command*, pp. 96-102.

approach in Romans in which he seems more positive about the law, asserting that it is 'holy, just and good' (Rom. 7.12). However, when we come to the ethical instructions in the later chapters, we find a similar formulation about the law and love to that in Galatians. Romans 13.8 begins with the obligation to love, 'For the one who loves another has fulfilled the law', ὁ γὰρ ἀγαπῶν τὸν ἕτερον νόμον πεπλήρωκεν. Then Paul sums up the commandments by again quoting Lev. 19.18 and concludes, 'Therefore, love is the fulfilling of the law', πλήρωμα οὖν νόμου ἡ ἀγάπη (13.9-10). This use of the abstract noun 'love' echoes his comments in 1 Cor. 13, especially vv. 4-6. Furnish draws attention to the chiastic structure of Rom. 13.10: 'Love is the first word and also the last word in the sentence — just as it is the first word and the last word Paul has to say about the meaning of the new life in Christ'.[124]

In both Gal. 5.14 and Rom. 13.10, love 'fulfils' the law — so what does 'fulfil' mean here? The situation is not helped by the fact that although the RSV translated πεπλήρωται as 'fulfilled' in Gal. 5.14, NRSV changes it to 'summed up'! This phrase is more accurately used by both RSV and NRSV for how the commandments are 'summed up', ἀνακεφαλαιοῦται, in the quotation of Lev. 19.18 in Rom. 13.9 — but it should not be used in Gal. 5.14. We noted above that often Paul says of love what he also says of Christ, and so some connect love 'fulfilling' the law with 'Christ is the end of the law', τέλος γὰρ νόμου Χριστός (Rom. 10.4). Again, translation may be a problem here, as 'end' suggests a negative finality. Thus the Lutheran bishop Anders Nygren sees it as a 'terminus': 'The day of the law is past'.[125] However, τέλος has the sense of 'end' in terms of the 'goal' or completion.[126] Robert Badenas' exhaustive treatment of Rom. 10.4 argues for a much more 'teleological' interpretation of τέλος as purpose or fulfilment.[127] Thus Michael Thompson interprets 10.4 as 'the embodiment of the righteousness promised by the law and the latter's fulfilment'.[128] Matera construes it similarly: 'Paul affirms that the law has completed its salvation-historical goal' and 'purpose' in Christ. This does not mean it is at an end, for 'those who believe in Christ do not violate it'.[129]

John Barclay notes that this mixture of 'fulfil' and 'law' is not used in the

124. Furnish, *The Love Command*, pp. 108-11.

125. Anders Nygren, *Commentary on Romans*, ET (London: SCM, 1952), p. 380.

126. Compare the similar ambiguity with the related verb in Jesus' final cry from the cross in John 19.30, τετέλεσται, it is 'finished' or 'accomplished'.

127. Robert Badenas, *Christ the End of the Law: Romans 10.4 in Pauline Perspective*, JSNTSS 10 (Sheffield: JSOT Press, 1985).

128. M. B. Thompson, *Clothed with Christ: The Example and Teaching of Jesus in Romans 12.1–15.13*, JSNTSS 59 (Sheffield: Sheffield Academic Press, 1991), p. 126.

129. Matera, *NT Ethics*, p. 201; see also pp. 169-72 on Gal. 5.

Jewish tradition, nor elsewhere even in Paul, who uses other words, such as 'keep' or 'do' for observing the law. Paul's use of 'fulfil' is deliberately ambiguous, and it does not mean that the law is 'summed up' or 'reduced' to the love command; rather, it is a way of valuing the law to 'outflank' his opponents.[130] Moule's treatment of 'fulfil' in the New Testament links this to the only other text referring to fulfilment of the law, Matt. 5.17; the word includes the sense of meeting the full requirements of God's will and the law, and fulfilling prophecy.[131] Finally, it is significant that Paul goes on from Rom. 13.8-10 to the eschatological context of vv. 11-14; as J. T. Sanders notes, 'To say that agape is the fullness of the law is to make an eschatological statement'.[132]

Thus our consideration of the way love fulfils the law takes us back to the central themes of Paul's ethics and theology. Love is not only the greatest commandment, but fulfils all the law because Christ has brought the law to its fulfilment. Therefore Christology is central to Paul's understanding of love and the law — and in an eschatological setting. For all these verses about love fulfilling the law are indicative statements; as with the rest of Paul, the demands of the law, its imperatives, can be understood only in the light of what God has done in Christ.[133]

c. 'Love and do what you like' or 'the law of the Spirit'?

Given the contingent nature of his letters to different communities, Paul's treatment of the law varies according to his readers' situation; as Sanders says, 'All of the diverse things which he said about the law were determined by circumstances'.[134] He seems to be more negative about the law in dealing with the Galatians' crisis, and more positive in his more measured handling in Romans. However, in both he sees Christ as the 'end', the goal of the law, and love as its fulfilment. This brings us, therefore, to the question of whether the law has any purpose left in ethics.

130. Barclay, *Obeying the Truth*, pp. 135-42; see also Sanders, *Paul, the Law, and the Jewish People*, p. 97.

131. C. F. D. Moule, 'Fulfilment-Words in the New Testament: Use and Abuse', *NTS* 14 (1967-68), pp. 293-320.

132. J. T. Sanders, *Ethics in the NT*, p. 52.

133. For further discussion of the relationship of these texts with Jesus and the love commandment, see E. Lohse, 'The Church in Everyday Life: Considerations of the Theological Basis of Ethics in the New Testament', ET in *Understanding Paul's Ethics*, ed. Rosner, pp. 251-65, and D. Moody Smith, 'The Love Command: John and Paul?', in Lovering and Sumney, *Theology and Ethics in Paul and His Interpreters*, pp. 207-17.

134. E. P. Sanders, *Paul*, p. 84.

While Paul is clear that the law is 'holy and just and good' (Rom. 7.12), it is through the law that sin is defined for both Jews and Gentiles, for 'all have sinned and fallen short of the glory of God' (Rom. 3.23). Since this leads to death, Paul has to face the question of why God gave the law in the first place (Gal. 3.19). Paul's answer in Gal. 3.19-29 is complex, but reveals the special relationship of Israel with God 'under the law' as a παιδαγωγός, the guardian or tutor of children in Graeco-Roman society, until the coming of Christ. This means, in Dunn's words, that 'Israel's special relation under the law was only *temporary*', one 'whose time is past'.[135]

A similar picture emerges from Paul's discussion in Rom. 5–8. Here Paul describes two ways of being: Adam is the 'one man' through whose sin and disobedience came death, where 'law came in, with the result that the trespass multiplied'; on the other hand, the 'free gift of grace' through Christ's obedience and righteous act brings 'justification and life for all' (Rom. 5.12-21). Those who are baptized into Christ are baptized into his death and raised to new life and are 'not under law but under grace' (6.1-14); since the law is not 'binding on a person' after death, 'now we are discharged from the law, dead to that which held us captive' (7.1-6). All of this puts the law in a very negative light, which is why Paul has to deny that he is saying that 'the law is sin'; instead, he stresses that the law itself is 'holy, just and good' but that sin, working through the commandment, brings death (7.7-13). As Matera sums it up, 'Sin, not the law, is the culprit'.[136]

However, there is another consequence of Paul's logic which he is also keen to avoid — that this stress on freedom from the law is a recipe for antinomian disaster, where 'anything goes'. On several occasions, Paul has to deal with questions from his hypothetical objector that we should 'continue in sin in order that grace may abound' (Rom. 6.1, 15) or use our 'freedom as an opportunity for the flesh', or, as the NRSV translates it, 'for self-indulgence' (Gal. 5.13). Augustine's dictum, *dilige, et quod vis, fac*, 'Love and do what you want',[137] has sometimes been (mis-)interpreted in this way — which, of course, leads exactly to the sort of situations which cause Hays to dismiss love as 'vapid self-indulgence'.[138]

Paul moves from his discussion of law and sin in Rom. 6–7 to his great declaration: 'There is therefore now no condemnation for those who are in Christ Jesus. For the law of the Spirit of life in Christ Jesus has set you free from the law of sin and of death' (Rom. 8.1-2). After all the negative material about sin and

---

135. Dunn, *The Theology of Paul the Apostle*, p. 143, his emphasis; see pp. 128-61 for his full discussion.

136. Matera, *NT Ethics*, p. 191.

137. Augustine, *Seventh Homily on the Letter of John*.

138. Hays, *Moral Vision of the NT*, p. 202.

death, the positive connection of the word 'law' with 'Spirit' and 'Christ' can seem surprising at first — but something similar also happens in Galatians. Paul sums up all the arguments against the law in the early chapters by stating that 'for freedom Christ has set us free'; therefore, his readers must not 'submit again to a yoke of slavery' (Gal. 5.1). But in order that freedom does not become 'an opportunity for the flesh' or 'self-indulgence', they must 'walk by the Spirit', producing 'the fruit of the Spirit' — 'love, joy, peace' etc. — and 'fulfil the law of Christ' (5.13, 16, 22-23; 6.2). It is this connection of 'love' with 'law', 'Spirit' and 'Christ' which prevents Paul's freedom from the law from becoming anti-nomian self-indulgence.

However, the meaning of the phrase 'the law of Christ', ὁ νόμος τοῦ Χριστοῦ, in Gal. 6.2 has provoked much debate. The only similar verse comes in Paul's attempt to 'become all things to all people', including becoming as though 'lawless' to those who are 'without' or 'outside the law', τοῖς ἀνόμοις ὡς ἄνομος. Here, however, Paul is quick to point out that he is not 'lawless from God', μὴ ὢν ἄνομος θεοῦ, but 'under Christ's law', ἀλλ' ἔννομος Χριστοῦ (1 Cor. 9.21-22). W. D. Davies interpreted the 'law of Christ' as a new messianic Torah, made up of the teachings of Jesus, and C. H. Dodd came to interpret ἔννομος Χριστοῦ in the same way as 'the precepts' given by Jesus.[139] We shall return to Paul's use of Jesus' teaching later, but it is unlikely that he is referring a specific collection here. Instead, Furnish sees 'the law of Christ' as the love com-mand.[140] Verhey thinks it 'certainly includes love' but takes it further as 'a prin-ciple of identity', belonging to Christ.[141] Hays similarly interprets this 'breath-taking paradox' as a 'regulative principle or structure of existence' in Christ'.[142] Heikki Räisänen also argues that the 'law of Christ' is 'not literally a law', but rather 'the way a life in Christ is to be lived'.[143] Barclay includes both aspects in his definition, 'the law as redefined and fulfilled by Christ in love'; in his de-fence against charges of lawlessness, Paul uses this term to show how the 'moral standards of the law are taken up into and fully realized in the life of the

139. W. D. Davies, *Paul and Rabbinic Judaism: Some Rabbinic Elements in Pauline Theology* (London: SPCK, 1948), pp. 142-46; see also his *Torah in the Messianic Age and/or the Age to Come* JBLMS 7 (Philadelphia: SBL, 1952), pp. 92-93; C. H. Dodd, 'ἔννομος Χριστοῦ', in *Studia Paulina in Honorem Johannis de Zwaan*, ed. J. N Sevenster and W. C. Van Unnik (Harlem: Bohn, 1953), pp. 96-110; repr. in Dodd, *More New Testament Studies* (Manchester: Manchester University Press, 1968), pp. 134-48.

140. Furnish, *Theology and Ethics in Paul*, pp. 59-65.

141. Verhey, *The Great Reversal*, pp. 112-13.

142. Hays, 'Christology and Ethics in Galatians: The Law of Christ', pp. 272-76.

143. H. Räisänen, *Paul and the Law*, WUNT 29 (Tübingen: Mohr, 1983), pp. 80-81; see also H. Räisänen, *Jesus, Paul and Torah: Collected Essays*, JSNTSS 43 (Sheffield: JSOT Press, 1992), chaps. 1-3.

Spirit'.[144] Hong also brings together love and the power of the Spirit as the way Paul tells his readers to fulfil the law.[145]

Finally, Dunn links the 'law of Christ' together with the 'law of the Spirit' and 'law of faith'. Given the negative way 'law' is viewed by most Pauline scholars, its connection with three of Paul's most positive terms is remarkable. Dunn discusses Paul's treatment of 'faith', 'the Spirit' and 'Christ' in turn and concludes that this demonstrates that Paul still saw a 'positive function' for the law 'for the first Christians'; his negative strictures are directed at the law weakened by the flesh and the power of sin and at its relation to Israel. Freed from these, the law has 'a positive role to play in the life of believer and church'; it can only be 'fulfilled out of faith' with the love command, and it is epitomised supremely in the life of Jesus himself.[146] Thus, this use of the law for moral guidance and ethical behaviour resembles both E. P. Sanders' concept of the law as a way of 'staying in' rather than 'getting in' to a covenant relationship with God, and is related to the Lutheran 'third use of the law'.

In sum, therefore, the relation of love and the law in Paul is extremely rich and takes us to the heart of his theology. As Räisänen concludes, 'The starting point of Paul's thinking about the Torah is the Christ event, not the law'[147] — or, to use Wright's phrase, in what God has done in Christ, Paul sees the 'climax of the covenant'.[148] Once again, Christology is central in that the law is fulfilled in what the love of God has done in Christ. Accordingly, such love, as exemplified in the life and teaching of Jesus, is the supreme commandment, which is to be lived out in the ethical behaviour of Christians. While they have been set free from the demands of the law, they are not lawless or immoral antinomians — for the Spirit of Christ provides both the power and the desire to live a holy life. Therefore, while Paul's understanding of the relationship of love and the law is much more fully worked out than was the case in our previous study of Jesus' attitude, once again there is continuity and agreement between them that the divine love, which is never 'vapid' or 'self-indulgent', is the key to understanding the law, a love which seeks an equally loving response from human beings, both to God and to one another.

144. Barclay, *Obeying the Truth,* pp. 126-45; quotations from pp. 134 and 141.

145. In-Gyu Hong, 'The Law and Christian Ethics in Galatians 5–6', *Neotestamentica* 26.1 (1992), pp. 113-30.

146. J. D. G. Dunn, '"The Law of Faith", "the Law of the Spirit" and "the Law of Christ"', in Lovering and Sumney, *Theology and Ethics in Paul and His Interpreters,* pp. 62-82; this material is revised and represented in Dunn's *The Theology of Paul the Apostle,* pp. 631-58.

147. Räisänen, *Paul and the Law,* p. 201.

148. N. T. Wright, *The Climax of the Covenant: Christ and the Law in Pauline Theology* (Edinburgh: T&T Clark, 1991).

5. Ethical issues in early Pauline communities

We began by arguing that Jesus' ethics are more concerned with eliciting a response to what God is doing in initiating the sovereign rule of his kingdom than in providing a list of particular moral instructions. Equally, Paul may shift the emphasis to how God has begun his sovereign rule in Christ, but he is still concerned primarily for a response of discipleship from his readers, to follow Christ within the community of the church. Nonetheless, it was noted in the previous chapter that Jesus' ethics did touch on the major human moral experiences and practical issues of money, sex, power, violence and so forth. However, his actual teaching set out a rigorous, even impractical ethic, which is difficult to follow in practice in so-called 'ordinary life'. Because of the contingent nature of Paul's letters, it is not surprising that he also has to confront many of these key human experiences. In most of these cases, Paul is traditionally seen as being rather extreme, or oppressive — often being 'against' whatever is under discussion. The 'recurring criticisms of Paul' are listed by Still: 'power-obsessed . . . prideful . . . patriarchal . . . a prude . . . perverted the teachings of Judaism and Jesus.'[149] This negative view of Paul is best demonstrated by the Peter Cook and Dudley Moore sketch on 'Religion':

> PETE: St Paul's got a bloody lot to answer for.
> DUD: He started it didn't he — all those letters he wrote.
> PETE: To the Ephiscans.
> DUD: You know, 'Dear Ephiscans, Stop enjoying yourselves, God's about the place. Signed Paul.'[150]

While this is a caricature, the impression that Paul wants people to 'stop enjoying' life and 'start flaying' themselves can often be formed by looking simply at some final instructions towards the end of his letters, or by quoting the occasional 'proof text'. Whether this is fair in the light of the wider context of Paul's writing in the light of his Christology, eschatology and emphasis on love remains to be seen.

---

149. Todd D. Still, 'Paul: An Appealing and/or Appalling Apostle?', *ExpT* 114.4 (January 2003), pp. 111-18.

150. PETE then goes off into a typical rambling description of 'a nice Ephiscan family' planning a picnic over a happy breakfast until 'a messenger bearing a letter from Paul' arrives for them, with an expanded personal message: 'Dear George and Deirdre and Family, Stop having a good time, resign yourself to not having a picnic, cover yourself with ashes and start flaying yourselves, until further notice, Signed Paul.' 'Religion', originally broadcast on *Not Only But Also*, BBC 2 (1965); script can be found in *Tragically I Was an Only Twin: The Complete Peter Cook*, ed. William Cook (London: Arrow, 2003), pp. 127-32; quotations from p. 129, punctuation etc. *sic*.

We have also argued that it is a genre mistake to read the gospels as ethical manuals; rather, the moral teaching of Jesus needs to be put in the context of the narrative of his ministry and deeds — especially his acceptance of others. Similarly, Paul's ethical comments must be put in the context of his wider theology — especially the Christological reading we have already given above. Furthermore, he is not writing in the genre of ethical treatises, but letters. The simple fact that they are correspondence means that Paul is attempting to apply his theology to the issues arising in dialogue with his early communities. Horrell has argued that such a 'discourse-ethical approach shows that Paul can be read and appropriated in other ways than as a supporter of particular ethical stances: anti-divorce, anti-gay, anti-idol-food, or whatever.'[151] Thus, before we come finally to Paul's account of the imitation of Christ, we need to consider his treatment of the main ethical issues in the light of this discourse and the application of his Christological thinking. We obviously cannot cover every subject in full detail here. Nonetheless, a careful reading suggests that Paul is trying to work out his bigger principles in practice, which means that his ethics are 'mixed' — often with at least two sides to most questions. Far from being the final moral word, often Paul's ethics are more like 'work in progress'.

a. Power and the state

A good example to demonstrate this complexity is Paul's ethical teaching on obedience and the state, where Rom. 13.1-7 immediately comes to mind: 'Let every person be subject to the governing authorities; for there is no authority except from God, and those authorities that exist have been instituted by God.' Indeed, these verses are usually quoted as encapsulating the New Testament ethic about the state. Yet this direct approach to reading them has had an enormous effect: 'These seven verses have caused more unhappiness and misery in the Christian East and West than any other seven verses in the New Testament by the licence they have given to tyrants, and the support for tyrants the Church has felt called on to offer as a result of the presence of Romans 13 in the canon.'[152] Taken on their own, these verses teach full submission by Christians to 'the powers that be' (the AV's translation), regardless of who they are, with all the concomitant problems for the German church under the Nazis, or South African Christians in the apartheid years. It is hardly surprising, therefore, that

151. Horrell, 'Restructuring Human Relationships: Paul's Corinthian Letters and Habermas' Discourse Ethics', p. 324.

152. J. C. O'Neill, *Paul's Letter to the Romans* (Harmondsworth: Penguin, 1975), p. 209.

the passage has been subjected to detailed scrutiny, as, for example, in the work of Jan Botha from Stellenbosch University.[153] Mark Reasoner's paper, 'Ancient and Modern Exegesis of Romans 13 under Unfriendly Governments', for the SBL 'Romans through History and Culture' seminar group, draws on a wide range of authors and approaches to compare the early church fathers with twentieth-century German exegesis.[154]

In South Africa, the main reaction was set in the *Kairos Document,* first issued anonymously by black theologians in September 1985 in response to the declaration of the State of Emergency by the apartheid regime on July 21, 1985. This document was critical of so-called 'State Theology', which 'assumes that in this text Paul is presenting us with the absolute and definitive Christian doctrine about the State'. However, 'in the rest of the Bible, God does not demand obedience to oppressive rulers. . . . Rom. 13:1-7 cannot contradict all of this'. In fact, Paul is talking about a state acting 'as God's servant for your good' (Rom. 13.4). 'That is the kind of State that must be obeyed.' According to the *Kairos* authors, the issue of an unjust government is not addressed in Rom. 13 but rather in Rev. 13. Therefore they were able to go on to call Christians to participate in the struggle for liberation against the apartheid regime.[155] In the next few years, this approach was used by many others, like Allan Boesak, who sought to limit the application of Rom. 13 to those governments that are beneficial.[156] Archbishop Desmond Tutu took a similar view in his famous letter to State President P. W. Botha in 1988: 'The corollary is that you must not submit yourself to a ruler who subverts your good.'[157] He has continued to maintain this exegesis, for example, in a personal recorded interview with me at the Truth and Recon-

153. Jan Botha, *Subject to Whose Authority? Multiple Readings of Romans 13* (Atlanta: Scholars Press, 1994).

154. Mark Reasoner, 'Ancient and Modern Exegesis of Romans 13 under Unfriendly Governments', in *Society of Biblical Literature 1999 Seminar Papers,* SBLSP 38 (Atlanta: Society of Biblical Literature, 1999), pp. 359-74.

155. *The Kairos Document, A Challenge to the Church: A Theological Comment on the Political Crisis in South Africa* (Johannesburg: Skotaville/Grand Rapids: Eerdmans, 2nd ed. 1986), quotations from pp. 4-5; for further discussion, see John W. de Gruchy, *The Church Struggle in South Africa: Twenty-Fifth Anniversary Edition* (Minneapolis: Fortress, 2005), pp. 196-204; also R. M. Brown (ed.), *Kairos: Three Prophetic Challenges to the Church* (Grand Rapids: Eerdmans, 1990); *KAIROS '95: At the Threshold of Jubilee: Conference Report* (Johannesburg: Institute for Contextual Theology, 1996).

156. A. A. Boesak, 'What Belongs to Caesar? Once again, Romans 13', in *A Call for an End to Unjust Rule,* ed. A. A. Boesak and C. Villa-Vicencio (Philadelphia: Westminster, 1986), pp. 138-57; first edition entitled, *When Prayer Makes News.*

157. Letter of April 8, 1988, originally published in *JTSA* 63 (June 1988), pp. 82-87; preserved in D. Tutu, *The Rainbow People of God: South Africa's Victory over Apartheid,* ed. John Allen (London: Bantam, 1995), pp. 143-52; quotation from p. 148.

ciliation Commission.[158] While Ridderbos, writing out of a Reformed tradition, is unhappy with such limiting of the text,[159] Dunn agrees that the use of Rom. 13 by a 'government . . . *not* serving God for the good of its citizens . . . as a way of maintaining their subservience would be a complete distortion and an abuse of Paul's purpose and of its continuing scriptural significance.'[160]

A different approach is taken by others such as Winsome Munro, also from South Africa, who have tried to deal with the problem by seeing the passage as an interpolation or later redaction linked to the Pastoral Epistles,[161] although this is unlikely. Significantly, a decade after the transition to democracy in South Africa, this passage was much debated in the elections in its neighbour, Zimbabwe, as the Mugabe government sought to use it for its own ends and others resisted.[162]

Many scholars also point out that Paul is repeating the common view held in society around him and drawing on all his possible sources.[163] Allegiance to the authorities is taught in the Hebrew scriptures (Ps. 72.1; Prov. 8.15-16) and later Jewish traditions (Wis. 6.3-4), as well as in Stoicism and other forms of Graeco-Roman philosophy. Winter has drawn attention to the importance of benefaction and civic honours in the society of the time in understanding this passage.[164] None of this means that Paul is just echoing contemporary *mores* without proper reflection: Botha argues that Rom. 13.1-7 can be read as 'a paradigm of order' only in isolation from its context; in fact, it is 'characteristic of a society going through a liminal experience in the second phase', moving from 'a previous social order' towards a new community.[165]

Equally, attention to the wider context of the passage within the paraenetic section of Rom. 12–15, especially 12.1–13.14, is extremely important.

158. Archbishop Desmond Tutu interview, recorded as part of the original research for this book at the Truth and Reconciliation Commission, Cape Town, March 30, 1998.

159. Ridderbos, *Paul: An Outline of His Theology*, p. 322.

160. James D. G. Dunn, *Romans 9–16*, Word Biblical Commentary 38B (Milton Keynes: Word, 1991), p. 774; his italics.

161. Winsome Munro, 'Romans 13.1-7: Apartheid's Last Biblical Refuge', *BTB* 20.4 (1990), pp. 161-68; also, idem, *Authority in Paul and Peter: The Identification of a Pastoral Stratum in the Pauline Corpus and 1 Peter*, SNTSMS 45 (Cambridge: Cambridge University Press, 1983), pp. 16-19.

162. Lovemore Togarasei, '"Let Everyone Be Subject to the Governing Authorities": The Interpretation of New Testament Political Ethics towards and after Zimbabwe's 2002 Presidential Elections', *Scriptura* 85 (2004), pp. 73-80.

163. See, for example, Dunn, *Romans 9–16*, pp. 772-73, and McDonald, *The Crucible of Christian Morality*, pp. 176-77.

164. Bruce W. Winter, *Seek the Welfare of the City: Christians as Benefactors and Citizens* (Grand Rapids: Eerdmans, 1994), pp. 26-40.

165. Botha, *Subject to Whose Authority?*, p. 225.

Thus Jonathan Draper from the University of Cape Town used such contextual exegesis to critique the appeal to Rom. 13 by the 'new constitution' brought in during the final years of the apartheid regime, while Monya Stubbs has argued for 'a three-dimensional process of empowerment' — 'subjection, reflection and resistance' — within the wider context.[166] Similarly, Karl Barth began his reading of these verses with Rom. 12.21, 'Do not be overcome by evil, but overcome evil with good.' Not only does this allow for the possibility that the state can be evil, but it also makes clear that *God*, and not the state, is the ultimate authority.[167] Barth's views on this passage were crucial for the German church in drawing up the Barmen declaration in 1934.[168] Another check on the use of Rom. 13.1-7 for tyranny is that it is surrounded by what Dunn calls the 'rubric of love';[169] it is significant that either side of this passage, Paul goes back to the same emphasis on love as we saw with Jesus: 'Let love be genuine' (12.9) and 'Owe no one anything, except to love one another. . . . love is the fulfilling of the law' (13.8-10).

Thus Rom. 13 is far from being the tyrant's charter it might seem at first sight, and Paul's view is much more complex than sometimes thought. This is even more the case when we remember that this passage comes in a letter; as Matera puts it, it is 'not necessarily the theological basis for a doctrine of church and state so much as an ad hoc response to a specific situation'.[170] McDonald suggests that this might have been the 'agitation over taxation' in the early years of Nero's reign; Paul's emphasis on paying taxes (13.6-7) is directed to Christians who may have just returned to Rome after the expulsions under Claudius and who needed to keep a low profile.[171]

Furthermore, as Wright says, 'Whereas almost all works on Paul assume that Romans 13.1-7 is his only comment on Caesar, this is far from the truth. . . .

---

166. J. A. Draper, '"Humble Submission to Almighty God" and Its Biblical Foundation: Contextual Exegesis of Romans 13.1-7', *JTSA* 63 (June 1988), pp. 30-38; Monya A. Stubbs, 'Subjection, Reflection, Resistance: A Three-Dimensional Process of Empowerment in Romans 13 and the Free-Market Economy', in *Navigating Romans through Cultures: Challenging Readings by Charting a New Course*, ed. K. K. Yeo, Romans through History and Cultures, vol. 3 (London and New York: T&T Clark International, 2004), pp. 171-97.

167. K. Barth, *The Epistle to the Romans* (Oxford: Oxford University Press, 1980), pp. 481-90.

168. See esp. Section Five: *Die erste Bekenntnissynode der Deutschen Evanglischen Kirche zu Barmen, II: Text-Dokumente-Berichte*, Arbeite zur Geschichte des Kirchenkampfes 6, ed. Gerhard Niemöller (Göttingen: Vandenhoeck & Ruprecht, 1959), pp. 200-201; see also Reasoner, 'Ancient and Modern Exegesis of Romans 13', pp. 9-12.

169. Dunn, *The Theology of Paul the Apostle*, pp. 675-76; see also Schrage, *The Ethics of the NT*, p. 236.

170. Matera, *NT Ethics*, p. 185.

171. McDonald, *The Crucible of Christian Morality*, p. 177.

The gospel of Christ upstages the gospel of Caesar'.[172] Paul is well aware that rulers and the state can be anything but 'for your good', as is evidenced in his list of beatings and mistreatments from Jews and Romans alike in 2 Cor. 11.23-25, as well as from local rulers like King Aretas (11.32-33). Elsewhere he tells the Corinthians that 'the rulers of this age . . . are doomed to perish'; they do not understand 'God's wisdom. . . ; for if they had, they would not have crucified the Lord of glory' (1 Cor. 2.6-8). Thus it is not surprising that he warns his readers against using the courts and state litigation (1 Cor. 6.1-6). Schrage sees 'a certain undeniable tension between Romans 13 and 1 Corinthians 6, which is probably a sign that Paul is somewhat tentative in addressing these questions of "political ethics".'[173] We argued in the previous section that Paul is more concerned about the relationships between his readers, which should be characterized by the love of Christ. It is that love which drives Paul's ethical comment here about avoiding litigation, in the same way that the 'rubric of love' surrounds the comment about the state in Rom. 13.1-7.

This same stress on love for another within the love of Christ is also behind Paul's argument in Phil. 2–3, which reaches its climax with the statement that 'our citizenship is in heaven' (3.20).[174] That Paul, proud of his status as a Roman citizen, could tell those living in Philippi, one of the most Romanized colonies, that his and their πολίτευμα, citizenship, belonged not to Rome but 'in heaven' is perhaps the clearest warning that a surface reading of Rom. 13.1-7 of Paul upholding the state regardless is far too simplistic. Greater attention to its literary context within the genre of a letter and its theological context within Paul's overarching theology of love and Christology is crucial to avoid its being misinterpreted as a 'tyrant's charter'; instead this will bring us again back to Paul's central Christological concern and his overarching stress upon the love of God and neighbour.

b. Women

Another area where Paul is often perceived as negative or reactionary concerns his views on women, again reflecting the views of his society. Although women

172. N. T. Wright, 'Coming Home to St. Paul? Reading Romans a Hundred Years after Charles Gore', p. 403.

173. Schrage, *The Ethics of the NT*, p. 239; see also Winter, *Seek the Welfare of the City*, pp. 105-21.

174. See Wendy Cotter, C.S.J., 'Our *Politeuma* Is in Heaven: The Meaning of Philippians 3.17-21', in *Origins and Method: Towards a New Understanding of Judaism and Christianity. Essays in Honour of John C. Hurd*, ed. Bradley H. McLean, JSNTSS 86 (Sheffield: Sheffield Academic Press, 1993), pp. 92-104.

had an honoured place in the family as homemakers, Jewish males thanked God that he had not made them women, and women were separated behind a screen in synagogues (*t. Megilla* 4:11; *b. Megilla* 23a). The Talmud says that 'every man who teaches his daughter Torah is as if he taught her promiscuity' (*m. Soṭah* 3:4; see also *y. Soṭah* 19a). Greek men similarly had three reasons to be grateful: 'that I was born a human being, and not a beast, next, a man and not a woman, thirdly, a Greek and not a barbarian' (often quoted — see Diogenes Laertius, *Lives of the Philosophers* 1.33; Plutarch, *Marius* 46.1; Lactantius, *Divine Institutes* 3.19.17). Although women in some parts of the Mediterranean did enjoy greater rights and emancipation during the Hellenistic and Roman periods, Longenecker shows that women were still excluded from education and much of life in society.[175]

George Bernard Shaw has described Paul as 'the eternal enemy of Woman'.[176] The case for Paul's misogyny rests on some negative passages which immediately spring to mind, notably 1 Cor. 11.2-16 on headship and 14.33b-36 telling women to keep silent in church.[177] As with Rom. 13, one response is to view the latter passage as a later deutero-Pauline interpolation, as is argued by scholars as notable as Schrage, Hays and Barrett.[178] Others, such as Odell-Scott,[179] interpret the passage as the view of the Corinthians being quoted by Paul (as seems to happen in 6.12 and 7.1), although this is unlikely given the typical Pauline vocabulary in these verses. Since an outright ban on women speaking in church contradicts Paul's earlier instructions (11.5), those who retain this section take it to forbid only specific situations of speaking, such as the interrogation of prophets (as in the immediately preceding verses, 14.29-33a), as is argued at length by Witherington and Thiselton.[180]

---

175. Richard N. Longenecker, *New Testament Social Ethics for Today* (Grand Rapids: Eerdmans, 1984), pp. 70-74; see also Schrage, *The Ethics of the NT*, pp. 222-23.

176. George Bernard Shaw, 'Preface on the Prospects of Christianity', from *Androcles and the Lion* (1913, 1941), extracted as 'The Monstrous Imposition upon Jesus', in *The Writings of St. Paul*, ed. Wayne A. Meeks (New York, n. p., 1972), pp. 296-302, quotation from p. 299.

177. Marlene Crüsemann, 'Irredeemably Hostile to Women: Anti-Jewish Elements in the Exegesis of the Dispute about Women's Right to Speak (1 Cor. 14.34-35)', *JSNT* 79 (2000), pp. 19-36; the whole of this issue of *JSNT* is devoted to making recent German-language feminist exegesis of Paul available in English.

178. Schrage, *The Ethics of the NT*, p. 224; Richard B. Hays, *First Corinthians*, Interpretation (Louisville: John Knox, 1997), pp. 245-49 and his *Moral Vision of the NT*, pp. 54-55; C. K. Barrett, *1 Corinthians* (London: A & C Black, 2nd edn. 1971), pp. 330-33; a full argument for this view is put forward by Horrell, *Social Ethos*, pp. 184-95.

179. D. W. Odell-Scott, 'Let the Women Speak in Church: An Egalitarian Interpretation of 1 Cor 14.33b-36', *BTB* 17 (1983), pp. 90-93.

180. B. W. Witherington, *Women in the Earliest Churches*, SNTSMS 59 (Cambridge: Cambridge University Press, 1988), pp. 90-104; Thiselton, *1 Corinthians*, pp. 1146-61.

1 Corinthians 11.2-16 has been debated at great length (Thiselton's bibliography includes some eighty publications), both for its importance about Paul's attitude to men and women and because of what Horrell terms 'its obscurity (at least to modern readers)'.[181] While, once again, some wish to excise this passage as non-Pauline, Murphy O'Connor has demonstrated its authenticity, as well as stressing that Paul is concerned with how *both* sexes, men and women, pray and conduct themselves in worship.[182] What is crucial here is that, contrary to the apparent meaning of 14.34 discussed above, women do pray and prophesy in church, as well as men (11.4-5). The problem seems to concern the way they do it, particularly with regard to their hair and head coverings — and the messages this is sending out within the Corinthians' social context. Thus the key issue here is a specific one, having to do with decorum in worship, rather than gender relationships in general. Paul uses four arguments — from the order of creation (11.7-9), 'because of the angels' (11.10), what 'nature itself' teaches (11.14-15) and the custom of the churches (11.16) — and their cogency is endlessly debated. The particular meanings of key words such as κεφαλή (head? source? preeminence? all of these and more?) are also much discussed.[183] For our purposes here, the important thing to note is that, although there is subordination in Paul's account of creation, as Horrell puts it, 'Paul's purpose seems clearly to be the establishment of "proper" distinction between men and women and not superiority or authority'.[184] Indeed, David Wenham has suggested that these 'spiritually liberated women' are acting on the consequences of Paul's general egalitarian teaching that 'we all with unveiled face' (2 Cor. 3.18) have freedom in the Spirit, and he is correcting them only by advocating 'sexual differentiation' here.[185]

Whatever one makes of these passages from Corinthians, it is clear from their epistolary genre that Paul is addressing specific situations in Corinth at the time, not seeking to give the definitive ethic about women and men. Where such a theological statement does come, however, is in the key text, Gal. 3.27-28.

181. Thiselton, *1 Corinthians*, pp. 800-848; Horrell, *Social Ethos*, p. 168; see pp. 168-95 for his full discussion.

182. J. Murphy O'Connor, 'The Non-Pauline Character of 1 Cor 11.2-16?', *JBL* 95 (1976), pp. 615-21; idem, 'Sex and Logic in 1 Cor. 11.2-16', *CBQ* 42 (1980), pp. 482-500.

183. See Thiselton's commentary ad loc. for a full and nuanced account of each.

184. Horrell, *Social Ethos*, p. 173; see also J. M. Gundry-Wolf, 'Gender and Creation in 1 Cor 11.2-16: A Study in Paul's Theological Method', in *Evangelium, Schriftauslegung, Kirche: Festschrift für Peter Stuhlmacher*, ed. J. Adna, S. J. Hafemann and O. Hofius (Göttingen: Vandenhoeck & Ruprecht, 1997), pp. 151-71.

185. David Wenham, *Paul: Follower of Jesus or Founder of Christianity?* (Grand Rapids: Eerdmans, 1995), pp. 246-50; idem, *Paul and the Historical Jesus*, Grove Biblical Series 7 (Cambridge: Grove, 1998), pp. 10-12.

This comes at the end of Paul's extensive theological argument about the relationship of the law and faith, and whether Gentiles need to be circumcised as do the Jews. It culminates with Paul's declaration that people are children of God through faith, being 'baptized into Christ'. It is this which breaks down all barriers, not just between Jew and Gentile but also slave and free, and male and female. Unlike the contingent passages in 1 Corinthians, the reference to gender is not specific to the Galatians' situation, but flows from the heart of Paul's theology. Therefore Schrage terms this 'the basic statement of Paul's position. . . . Men and women have the same value and dignity in the eyes of God; the inferior and marginal status of women is overcome "in the Lord".'[186] Longenecker also agrees that to understand the other passages about 'submission, subordination and silence of women . . . one must begin with the gospel as proclaimed by the apostles and the principles derived therefrom . . . with the confession of Galatians 3.28.'[187] Douglas Campbell notes that the use of three binary couplets is typical of Paul's thought and points out that while Paul says 'Jew nor (οὐδέ) Greek, slave nor free', the third pair reads 'there is no longer male and female', οὐκ ἔνι ἄρσεν καὶ θῆλυ. This evokes the language of the creation of human beings as 'male and female' in Gen. 1.27, which is even surpassed in the 'new creation' in Christ (see 6.14-15). He concludes: 'In Gal. 3.28a Paul baldly negates three standard bifurcations of society that include gender on the grounds of the eschatological existence of Christians in Christ — negations that he intends radically and seriously *and that his gospel is intrinsically committed to*. That is, *we now have a theological criterion from Paul's own hand of the (correct) ethical implications of his gospel* (and not merely of a putative early church confession), here specifically for questions concerning ethnicity, slavery, and/or gender.'[188]

This text is therefore a much surer insight into Paul's theological view of men and women than his contingent comment about a particular situation in Corinth. That this is his more general view is further exemplified in his relationships with women associated with his ministry, such as Euodia and Syntyche, who 'have struggled beside me in the work of the gospel' (Phil. 4.23), or by his reference to 'Chloe's people', rather than the more usual use of a man's name to denote a group or family (1 Cor. 1.11). Romans ends with Paul commending 'our sister Phoebe, deacon of the church at Cenchrea', who has been 'my helper' (προστάτις, Rom. 16.1-2), and giving his greetings to Prisc(ill)a, a 'fellow-worker (συνεργός, Rom. 16.3-5; see also 1 Cor. 16.19), Mary, 'who has worked very hard

186. Schrage, *The Ethics of the NT*, p. 223.

187. Longenecker, *New Testament Social Ethics for Today*, p. 84.

188. Campbell, 'The Witness to Paul's Gospel of Galatians 3.28', in his *The Quest for Paul's Gospel*, pp. 95-111; see pp. 97-98 on binary couplets; quotation from p. 109, his italics.

among you' (Rom. 16.6), and those 'workers in the Lord', Tryphaena and Tryphosa (Rom. 16.12). He even describes a woman as 'prominent among the apostles', assuming that 'Junia' is the correct translation in 16.7.[189] Cranfield sees this as 'highly significant evidence . . . of the falsity of the widespread and stubbornly persistent notion that Paul had a low view of women and something to which the church as a whole has not yet paid sufficient attention.'[190]

Thus, here too we must be wary of quoting simply one or two individual passages which have an apparent anti-women teaching on the surface. We must make allowances for the contingent and specific nature of such passages both within their epistolary genre and their dependency upon the particular historical situation of the original recipients. On the other hand, a closer look at how Paul works out his theology of the love of God in Christ throughout his writings and how he applies this in Gal. 3.28 to gender relationships, taken together with his actual practice in sharing ministry with women and sending them greetings, leads to a much more positive understanding of Paul's ethic concerning men and women.[191]

c. Sex and marriage

A third area where Paul is assumed to be negative is with regard to sex in general and, in some quarters at present, especially being 'anti-gay'. As Hays says, 'Paul is often castigated as a misogynistic character with pathological attitudes about sex'.[192] Dunn refers to the 'assumption that Paul's sexual ethic was basically ascetic in character' — yet Ridderbos says that Paul's pronouncements on marriage are 'positive and fundamentally anti-ascetic'.[193] So, once again, we

189. The accusative, if accented Ἰουνιᾶν, could be from the masculine name Ἰουνιᾶς, although it is not otherwise known; it is more likely Ἰουνίαν from the feminine Ἰουνία, which occurs over 250 times in ancient authors; both Dunn (*Romans 9–16*, p. 894) and C. E. B. Cranfield, *Romans IX–XVI*, ICC (Edinburgh: T&T Clark, 1979), vol. 2, p. 788, translate it in the feminine. See Richard Bauckham, *Gospel Women: Studies of the Named Women in the Gospels* (Grand Rapids: Eerdmans, 2002), pp. 165-69 for the overwhelming evidence for preferring the feminine Junia translation, and chap. 5, 'Joanna the Apostle', pp. 109-202 for his larger case that she is to be identified with the Joanna of Luke 8.3 and 24.10.

190. Cranfield, *Romans IX–XVI*, p. 789.

191. See also Willard M. Swartley, *Slavery, Sabbath, War and Women: Case Issues in Biblical Interpretation* (Scottdale: Herald, 1983), pp. 164-91; Judith M. Gundry-Volf, 'Paul on Women and Gender: A Comparison with Early Jewish Views', in *The Road from Damascus: The Impact of Paul's Conversion on His Life, Thought, and Ministry*, ed. Longenecker, pp. 184-212.

192. Hays, *Moral Vision of the NT*, p. 47.

193. Dunn, *The Theology of Paul the Apostle*, p. 693; Ridderbos, *Paul: An Outline of His Theology*, p. 308.

have a mismatch between the common view of Paul and his actual teaching, arising in part from frequent quotation from some of his particular comments directed to specific situations facing his readers.

The earliest comes in 1 Thess. 4.1-8. Here Paul stresses his concern for 'the will of God, your sanctification' (4.3), which leads to avoidance of 'immorality', πορνεία, and his commending of marriage, yet also the avoidance of passion and desire, ἐν πάθει ἐπιθυμίας (4.4-5). Dale Martin compares this with the avoidance of desire both in the Stoics and in the Aristotelian medical system. While these seek to extirpate desire through a rational self-sufficiency, Martin concludes, 'From a Christian point of view, and I think this is not just Paul's view, self-sufficiency is neither possible nor desirable' (2 Cor. 3.5-6).[194] Paul instead permits or encourages sex within marriage as a way of controlling desire or the effects of desire. The link between desire, self-indulgence and sexual immorality was commonplace in the Hebrew scriptures and Jewish moral teaching, and Paul warns against 'desire', ἐπιθυμία, regularly in his letters (e.g., Rom. 1.23-7; 6.12; 7.7-8; Gal. 5.16, 24) and tells his readers to 'flee from immorality' (πορνεία, 1 Cor. 6.18).[195]

Next, once again, we come to some specific situations in Paul's first letter to the Christians in Corinth, a city renowned for its sexual licence, arising from its temple of Aphrodite and its markets and port. Drawing upon Paul's teaching about freedom in Christ, his early Christians seem to have gone in two opposite directions, either to an ascetic avoidance of sex or to a libertine indulgence, basing both approaches upon stressing life in the Spirit and downplaying the significance of the body. First, Paul confronts the problem of one man who has taken his freedom even to the extreme of 'having relations with his father's wife', a form of πορνεία not even approved of by the pagans (5.1). Paul gives instructions for him to be disciplined by removal, so that 'his spirit may be saved in the day of the Lord' (5.2-5). It is very significant that even here, which is the only time that we have Paul calling for someone to be excluded or excommunicated, it is for the positive, pastoral purpose of eventual salvation. After going on to rule out use of the secular courts (6.1-8), Paul gives one of his lists of vices (6.9-11) and forbids sex with prostitutes (6.12-20). Against the Corinthians' slogan, 'All things are lawful for me', Paul stresses the theological importance of the body, particularly quoting the principle of one flesh (6.16, from Gen. 2.24).

This is further worked out in 1 Cor. 7, which begins with 'It is well for a

194. Dale B. Martin, 'Paul without Passion: On Paul's Rejection of Desire in Sex and Marriage', in *Constructing Early Christian Families*, ed. H. Moxnes (London: Routledge, 1997), pp. 201-15; repr. in Dale B. Martin, *Sex and the Single Savior: Gender and Sexuality in Biblical Interpretation* (Louisville: Westminster John Knox, 2006), pp. 65-76.

195. See Dunn, *The Theology of Paul the Apostle*, pp. 119-23.

man not to touch a woman.' As Hays points out, this is 'surely one of the most widely misinterpreted texts in the New Testament', for it represents not Paul's view but another of the Corinthians' slogans.[196] As in 1 Thess. 4, Paul is actually countering sexual abstinence with his instructions about the importance of sex within marriage in order to avoid πορνεία (7.2).[197] Both Hays and Schrage point out that Paul stresses the mutuality of husband and wife over against any form of sexual domination or subordination here (7.3-5).[198] Paul describes his own celibacy as a spiritual gift of grace, χάρισμα, not given to everyone (7.6-7).[199] The rest of the chapter gives further instructions for those who are unmarried and widows (7.8-9, 25-28, 36-38). Paul echoes Jesus' prohibition of divorce (7.10-11), but also gives his own views about divorce from an unbelieving partner (7.12-16) and marriage after being widowed (7.39-40).[200]

Here also, therefore, it is clear that these chapters do not contain Paul's complete theology of sex. Rather, he is answering questions contingent upon the Corinthians' situation, who were still growing in their relatively new understanding of the Christian faith. His overriding concern is for them to avoid immorality, πορνεία, particularly in the light of the eschatological dimension. Both Dunn and Schrage note how Paul stresses the shortness of the time 'in view of the impending crisis' (7.26, 29); he wants his converts not to be distracted or anxious, but to be devoted to God's work (7.17-24, 32-35).[201]

Finally, in view of some current concerns, it is notable that homosexual-

---

196. Hays, *Moral Vision of the NT*, p. 48; see Thiselton, *1 Corinthians*, pp. 498-501 for the arguments about the quotation; also, Will Deming, *Paul on Marriage and Celibacy: The Hellenistic Background of 1 Corinthians 7* (Grand Rapids: Eerdmans, 2nd edn. 2004), pp. 107-13 argues that a 'Cynic' position is being quoted by the Corinthians.

197. Collins describes the link in 'The Unity of Paul's Paraenesis in 1 Thess 4:3-8; 1 Cor 7:1-7, A Significant Parallel', in his *Christian Morality: Biblical Foundations*, pp. 211-22.

198. Hays, *Moral Vision of the NT*, pp. 49-51; Schrage, *The Ethics of the NT*, pp. 227-28.

199. See William Loader, *Sexuality and the Jesus Tradition* (Grand Rapids: Eerdmans, 2005), pp. 149-92.

200. For a full discussion of this chapter, see Deming, *Paul on Marriage and Celibacy: The Hellenistic Background of 1 Corinthians 7*, pp. 105-219; also Paul W. Gooch, 'Authority and Justification in Theological Ethics: A Study in I Corinthians 7', *Journal of Religious Ethics* 11 (1983), pp. 62-74; Judith Gundry-Volf, 'Celibacy in Corinth: Towards a Reconstruction from 1 Corinthians 7', Colloquium Biblicum Lovaniense XLIII, August 8-10, 1994, later published as 'Controlling the Bodies: A Theological Profile of the Corinthian Sexual Ascetics', in *The Corinthian Correspondence*, ed. R. Bieringer, BETL 125 (Leuven: Leuven University Press–Peeters, 1996), pp. 499-521; C. C. Caragounis, '"Fornication" and "Concession"? Interpreting 1 Cor. 7.1-7', Colloquium Biblicum Lovaniense XLIII, August 8-10, 1994, in *The Corinthian Correspondence*, ed. R. Bieringer, BETL 125 (Leuven: Leuven University Press–Peeters, 1996); Rosner, *Paul, Scripture, and Ethics: A Study of 1 Corinthians 5–7*; and the commentaries, esp. Thiselton, *1 Corinthians*, pp. 483-606.

201. Schrage, *The Ethics of the NT*, p. 229; Dunn, *The Theology of Paul the Apostle*, pp. 693-98.

ity is mentioned only here in the lists of vices, described by two terms, οὔτε μαλακοὶ οὔτε ἀρσενοκοῖται, which are difficult to translate,[202] along with another eight forms of immorality, greed, drunkenness, reviling and so forth, common to heterosexuals also, of all of whom Paul says, 'None of these will inherit the kingdom of God' (1 Cor. 6.9-11). It is also the case that ἀρσενοκοῖται recurs in the vice-list in 1 Tim. 1.10, again along with, and outnumbered by, other forms of immorality, including slave trading and lying. In Rom. 1.24-27, 'unnatural' sexual relations, τὴν παρὰ φύσιν, are another example of the problems of 'desire', ἐπιθυμία, which then leads to another list of vices, including envy, strife, insolence, boasting, and even 'being rebellious towards parents and foolish' — sins which are obviously common to all types of people, not just homosexuals. The extraordinary thing is that Paul suggests that God's decree is 'that those who practice such things deserve to die' (1.28-32).[203]

202. John Boswell, *Christianity, Social Tolerance, and Homosexuality: Gay People in Western Europe from the Beginning of the Christian Era to the Fourteenth Century* (Chicago: University of Chicago Press, 1980), provoked much debate about the meaning and translation of these terms; see, for example, among many others, David F. Wright, 'Homosexuals or Prostitutes? The Meaning of ARSENOKOITAI (1 Cor. 6:9, 1 Tim. 1:10)', *Vigiliae Christianae* 38 (1984), pp. 125-53; Richard B. Hays, 'Relations Natural and Unnatural: A Response to John Boswell's Exegesis of Romans 1', *Journal of Religious Ethics* 14.1 (1986), pp. 184-215; William L. Petersen, 'Can ARSENOKOITAI Be Translated by "Homosexuals"?', *Vigiliae Christianae* 40 (1986), pp. 187-91; L. C. Broughton, 'Biblical Texts and Homosexuality: A Response to John Boswell', *Irish Theological Quarterly* 58.2 (1992), pp. 141-53; J. B. de Young, 'The Source and Meaning of the Translation "Homosexuals" in Biblical Studies', *Evangelical Review of Theology* 19.1 (1995), pp. 54-63; Dale B. Martin, 'Arsenokoitēs and Malakos: Meanings and Consequences', in *Biblical Ethics and Homosexuality: Listening to Scripture*, ed. Robert L. Brawley (Louisville: Westminster John Knox, 1996), pp. 117-36, repr. in Martin, *Sex and the Single Savior*, pp. 37-50.

203. On Rom. 1 and homosexuality, see as examples, among many others, D. E. Malick, 'The Condemnation of Homosexuality in Romans 1:26-27', *Bibliotheca Sacra* 150 (1993), pp. 327-40; M. Davies, 'New Testament Ethics and Ours: Homosexuality and Sexuality in Romans 1:26-27', *Biblical Interpretation* 3.3 (1995), pp. 315-31; Dale B. Martin, 'Heterosexism and the Interpretation of Romans 1:18-32', *Biblical Interpretation* 3.3 (1995), pp. 332-55, repr. in Martin, *Sex and the Single Savior*, pp. 51-64; J. E. Miller, 'The Practices of Romans 1.26: Homosexual or Heterosexual?' *NovT* 37.1 (1995), pp. 1-11; M. D. Smith, 'Ancient Bisexuality and the Interpretation of Romans 1:26-27', *JAAR* 64.2 (1996), pp. 223-56; Daniel A. Helminiak, 'Ethics, Biblical and Denominational: A Response to Mark Smith', *JAAR* 65 (1997), pp. 855-59; James E. Miller, 'Pederasty and Romans 1.27: A Response to Mark Smith', *JAAR* 65 (1997), pp. 861-65; R. B. Ward, 'Why Unnatural? The Tradition behind Romans 1:26-27', *HTR* 90.3 (1997), pp. 263-84; D. L. Balch, 'Romans 1:24-27, Science and Homosexuality', *Currents in Theology and Mission* 25.6 (1998), pp. 433-40; R. H. Bell, *No One Seeks for God: An Exegetical and Theological Study of Romans 1:18–3:20* (Tübingen: Mohr-Siebeck, 1998); Douglas A. Campbell, 'Rereading Romans 1.18–3.20', chap. 11 in his *The Quest for Paul's Gospel: A Suggested Strategy*, pp. 233-61.

Given that whole books and theses have been written on this topic, let alone innumerable articles, in recent years,[204] we cannot go into such detail here, but two comments are perhaps in order. The first is that these relatively few references show that this area was not as central or dominating a concern for Paul as for some modern readers. It is puzzling why being against homosexuality, about which Jesus and the gospels have nothing to say and Paul has only these passing references alongside many other sins equally common to heterosexuals, should have become the acid test of what it means to be truly 'biblical' in a number of quarters over recent years. We noted in the previous chapter that Jesus' all-demanding ethic contains an element of hyperbole, with no one really suggesting that people should pluck out eyes or cut off their hands to enter the kingdom of God, as required in Matt. 5.29-30. Something similar seems to happen with these vice-lists since those who are 'rebellious towards parents and foolish' are not usually lined up for the death penalty in church (Rom. 1.30-32)! Like Jesus' preaching, Paul's lists of those who will not 'inherit the kingdom of God' are meant to spur us all on to respond in love and live out that response more worthily ourselves,

204. See, for example, Letha Scanzoni and Virginia Ramey Mollenkott, *Is the Homosexual My Neighbour?* (San Francisco: Harper & Row, 1978); D. J. Atkinson, *Homosexuals in the Christian Fellowship* (Grand Rapids: Eerdmans, 1979); Peter Coleman, *Christian Attitudes to Homosexuality* (London: SPCK, 1980); R. Scroggs, *The New Testament and Homosexuality: Contextual Background for Contemporary Debate* (Philadelphia: Fortress, 1983); D. F. Wright, 'Homosexuality: The Relevance of the Bible', *Evangelical Quarterly* 61.4 (1989), pp. 291-300; D. F. Greenberg, *The Construction of Homosexuality* (Chicago: University of Chicago Press, 1989); J. J. McNeill, *The Church and the Homosexual* (Boston: Beacon, 4th edn. 1993); D. A. Helminiak, *What the Bible Really Says about Homosexuality* (San Francisco: Alamo Square, 1994); J. S. Siker (ed.), *Homosexuality in the Church: Both Sides of the Debate* (Louisville: Westminster John Knox, 1994); Marion L. Soards, *Scripture and Homosexuality: Biblical Authority and the Church Today* (Louisville: Westminster John Knox, 1995); Choon-Leong Seow (ed.), *Homosexuality and Christian Community* (Louisville: Westminster John Knox, 1996); Robert L. Brawley (ed.), *Biblical Ethics and Homosexuality: Listening to Scripture* (Louisville: Westminster John Knox, 1996); Harold E. Brunson, *Homosexuality and the New Testament: What Does Christian Scripture Really Teach?* (San Francisco: International Scholars Publications, 1998); Walter Wink (ed.), *Homosexuality and the Christian Faith: Questions of Conscience for the Churches* (Minneapolis: Fortress, 1999); David L. Balch (ed.), *Homosexuality, Science, and the "Plain Sense" of Scripture* (Grand Rapids: Eerdmans, 2000); William J. Webb, *Slaves, Women & Homosexuals: Exploring the Hermeneutics of Cultural Analysis* (Downers Grove, IL: IVP, 2001); Robert A. J. Gagnon, *The Bible and Homosexual Practice: Texts and Hermeneutics* (Nashville: Abingdon, 2001); Alice Ogden Bellis and Terry L. Hufford, *Science, Scripture and Homosexuality* (Cleveland: Pilgrim, 2002); Dan O. Via and Robert A. J. Gagnon, *Homosexuality and the Bible: Two Views* (Minneapolis: Fortress, 2003); J. M. Childs, *Faithful Conversation: Christian Perspectives on Homosexuality* (Minneapolis: Fortress, 2003); Willard M. Swartley, *Homosexuality: Biblical Interpretation and Moral Discernment* (Scottdale: Herald, 2003); Douglas A. Campbell, 'A Brief Case Study in the Ethical Aspect of Paul's Gospel: The Case for Gay Ordination', chap. 6 in his *The Quest for Paul's Gospel: A Suggested Strategy* (London: T&T Clark, 2005), pp. 112-31.

rather than single out one particular group for especial condemnation. It is also notable that the Pauline epistles include many other vice-lists which do *not* refer to homosexuality; see, for example, Rom. 13.13; 1 Cor. 5.10; 2 Cor. 12.20-21; Gal. 5.19-21; Eph. 4.25-32; 5.3-5; Col. 3.5; 1 Tim. 6.4-5; 2 Tim. 3.1-9.[205]

The other point arises from our concern throughout this book with literary genre. It is significant that these three references come in the context of these lists of vices, so Thiselton provides a useful excursus on Paul's use of vice-lists and the homosexuality debate.[206] However, we want to return to the point that Paul's ethical comments are both more complex than his usual 'anti-everything', negative portrayal suggests, and that they are more like 'work in progress' than being the considered, final moral word. For such vice-lists are a common literary genre, or subgenre, in both Jewish and Graeco-Roman ethical writings, and therefore perhaps Paul's repetition of such lists derives more from his contemporary social context than from considered theological reflection upon the eschatological in-breaking of the sovereign love of God. Thus, E. P. Sanders notes that 'in Paul's discussions of sex there are two types of material in terms of form, vice lists (and related material) and substantial discussions'. The former are 'traditional Jewish homiletical material'; when Paul 'is passing on this traditional material, especially when he does so in lists, he seems inflexible and unsympathetic'. However, 'when circumstances forced him to leave his traditional lists . . . we find [the] fresh thinking' of a 'creative theologian.' The example Sanders adduces here is of the man in an incestuous relationship where 'Paul does not follow the traditional practice of roundly condemning transgressors to destruction, but proposes that the man's soul would be saved. Conceivably, had one of his parishioners engaged in homosexual activity, Paul would have re-thought that issue too. . . . This was the case with regard to topics other than sex.' According to Sanders, Paul's thinking is 'the beginnings of a code of behaviour that is founded on the Jewish principle of love of neighbour and his new principle of union with Christ'.[207] Similarly, Dunn pays tribute to Paul as 'a deeply caring pastor' drawing on his resources to deal with his readers' situation: 'Such a sensitive attempt to blend authoritative tradition, personal opinion, and pragmatic counsel which respects real-life situations, and all under the priority of faith, ought to be accorded more positive commendation.'[208]

Once again, therefore, this brief discussion has revealed a more complex and positive view of Paul's ethics of marriage and sexuality as 'work in progress' than

205. See also B. J. Oropeza, 'Situational Immorality: Paul's "Vice Lists" at Corinth', *ExpT* 110.1 (1998), pp. 9-10.

206. Thiselton, *1 Corinthians*, pp. 440-53.

207. E. P. Sanders, *Paul*, pp. 115-16.

208. Dunn, *The Theology of Paul the Apostle*, p. 698.

is sometimes popularly supposed. While Paul professes to be quite happy in his own celibate state, he seeks to help his converts bring their sex lives closer to conformity with the loving reign of God, with his primary concern to avoid immorality, πορνεία, within a much more easygoing society. His overriding concern is for the salvation of their souls, as seen in his pastoral concern even for someone in an incestuous relationship. His few references to homosexuality, which occur only in his repetition of a couple of his vice-lists, should also be read in this context, rather than singled out as a primary test for the Christian fellowship.

d. Money and property, work and slavery

Paul has remarkably little specific teaching on property and wealth[209] (unlike Jesus' ethical teaching, as we saw above); he also appears harsh on the unemployed and returns runaway slaves (2 Thess. 3.10; Phlm. 12). As Verhey puts it, 'Paul's teachings seem a good deal closer to the middle-class respectability of Stoic morality than to the tradition of Jesus.'[210] So is his teaching in this area just a reactionary regurgitation of contemporary views?

On the contrary, what Paul does say is once again driven by his eschatological Christology. This is made plain in the midst of the same chapter just studied on sex and marriage, dominated by Paul's concern for the shortness of the time. Almost as an aside, he says, '[Let] those who buy be as though they had no possessions, and those who deal with the world as though they had no dealings with it. For the present form of this world is passing away' (1 Cor. 7.29-31). As Schrage puts it, 'Eschatology does not call buying as such into question, but ownership and possession.'[211] This is then borne out in his warnings about greed or covetousness, πλεονεξία (Rom. 1.29; 1 Cor. 5.10-11; 6.10) or exploiting others (1 Thess. 4.6). Instead, Paul appeals for generosity, not least in following Christ's example of self-giving and embracing poverty: 'For you know the generous act of our Lord Jesus Christ, that though he was rich, yet for your sakes he became poor, so that by his poverty you might become rich' (2 Cor. 8.9).

Such generosity leads to sharing material possessions with the needy (Rom. 12.8, 13) and with their teachers (Gal. 6.6; Phil. 4.10-14). Sharing of this sort

209. There is even less in the secondary literature — which is remarkable when compared with how much is written about Paul's views on sexuality, as in the notes above! Most of the material written about property, poverty and wealth in the New Testament relates to Luke-Acts, as we shall see in chapter VI below. On Paul, see Justin Meggitt, *Paul, Poverty and Survival* (Edinburgh: T&T Clark, 1998).

210. Verhey, *The Great Reversal*, p. 119.

211. Schrage, *The Ethics of the NT*, p. 231.

should take place in worship and at the Lord's Supper, and not as in Corinth, where 'each of you goes ahead with your own supper, and one goes hungry and another becomes drunk,' which only shows 'contempt for the church of God and humiliate[s] those who have nothing' (1 Cor. 11.21-22). It is not coincidental that the word for the 'communion' in Christ's body and blood (1 Cor. 10.16) is Paul's favourite word for 'fellowship': κοινωνία, sharing 'in common', applies not just to fellowship with God in the Spirit (1 Cor. 1.9; 2 Cor. 13.13; Phil. 2.1) but also financially (2 Cor. 9.5-15). The most practical expression of this 'sharing' is the collection Paul organized among his congregations for those in Jerusalem, 'that there may be equality, ἰσότης' (Rom. 15.26-27; 2 Cor. 8.10-15).[212] It is quite possible that his references to practical love for fellow Christians might also refer to a community of goods so that they would need to 'be dependent on no one' (see 1 Thess. 4.9-12). The only instruction Paul accepted from the Jerusalem apostles was to 'remember the poor, which was actually what I was eager to do' (Gal. 2.10).

While Graeco-Roman society may have looked down on manual labour, the Jews derived the dignity of work from Adam's work in the garden at the creation (Gen. 2.15). Thus Paul himself worked and was proud of the fact: 'You remember our labour and toil, brothers and sisters; we worked night and day, so that we might not burden any of you while we proclaimed to you the gospel of God' (1 Thess. 2.9; see also 1 Cor. 4.12; 2 Cor. 12.14). He tells his readers to 'work with your hands' (1 Thess. 4.11) and to avoid those who 'are living in idleness, mere busybodies, not doing any work' (2 Thess. 3.6-13).[213] Such work, of course, is not to amass riches, but to enable further giving, as is developed in Eph. 4.28: 'Let them labour and work honestly with their own hands, so as to have something to share with the needy.'

Of course, within this ancient economy, it is to be expected that slaves feature regularly. Slaves were property and could be bought and sold at will by their masters. There is no doubt that their lives could be wretched, especially on the galleys, in the mines or in the chain gangs working large farms. However, household slaves could also be highly educated and earn money to buy their freedom, thereby, as Dale Martin has argued, using slavery as a way of becoming upwardly mobile socially.[214]

212. See Dunn, *The Theology of Paul the Apostle*, pp. 706-12.

213. For a discussion of Paul's work, see Margaret Davies, 'Work and Slavery in the New Testament: Impoverishments of Traditions', in *The Bible in Ethics*, ed. John W. Rogerson, Margaret Davies and M. Daniel Carroll R., JSOTSS 207 (Sheffield: Sheffield Academic Press, 1995), pp. 315-47; pp. 335-38 deal with Paul.

214. Dale B. Martin, *Slavery as Salvation: The Metaphor of Slavery in Pauline Christianity* (New Haven, CT: Yale University Press, 1990), esp. pp. 1-49; see also Longenecker, *New Testament Social Ethics for Today*, pp. 48-51 and Davies, 'Work and Slavery in the New Testament', pp. 338-40.

What is significant is that Paul does not advocate an antislavery campaign. Wayne Meeks has shown how clergy and well-trained biblical scholars in the Southern states provided 'biblical justification' for slavery in the first half of the nineteenth century. As with the Dutch Reformed Church's 'biblical justification' for apartheid, they appealed to Rom. 13.1-7 and other Pauline passages, including 1 Cor. 7.20-21 and the household codes of Col. 3.22-25, 1 Tim 6.1-6 and Titus 2.9.[215] While historical criticism can help a little here, Meeks concludes that 'it appears to provide no knock-down argument against such uses of scripture as the apologists for slavery made'.[216] Similarly, Swartley draws attention to essays and books written just before the American Civil War, stressing the biblical arguments for slavery, including various passages from Paul.[217] As Bledsoe thundered, 'The history of interpretation furnishes no examples of more willful and violent perversions of the sacred text than are to be found in the writings of the abolitionists. They seem to consider themselves above the scriptures: and when they put themselves above the law of God, it is not wonderful that they should disregard the laws of men.'[218] Particular attention was drawn to 1 Tim. 6.1-6, where Paul's instructions, 'Let all who are under the yoke of slavery regard their masters as worthy of all honour', are given additional dominical authority as 'the sound words of our Lord Jesus Christ'.

Yet we have already seen that Gal. 3.28 is the theological charter for equality not just between the sexes but also for slave and free. Furthermore, unlike the male-female pairing, the couplet on slave and free being baptized into Christ is repeated in 1 Cor. 12.13 and Col. 3.11. So Longenecker notes that it is strange that Paul 'was so relaxed and non-committal about the institution of slavery itself'

215. See esp. Iveson L. Brookes, *A Defence of the South against the Reproaches and Incroachments of the North: In Which Slavery Is Shown to Be an Institution of God Intended to Form the Basis of the Best Social State and the Only Safeguard to the Permanence of a Republican Government* (Hamburg, SC: At the Republican Office, 1850), p. 28.

216. Wayne A. Meeks, 'The "Haustafeln" and American Slavery: A Hermeneutical Challenge', in Lovering and Sumney, *Theology and Ethics in Paul and His Interpreters*, pp. 232-53; quotation from p. 245.

217. *Cotton Is King, and Pro-Slavery Arguments Comprising the Writings of Hammond, Harper, Christy, Stringfellow, Hodge, Bledsoe, and Cartwright on This Important Subject*, ed. E. N. Elliot (1860 original; repr., New York: Negro Universities Press, 1969), containing 'The Argument from the Scriptures' by Albert Taylor Bledsoe, Ll.D.; 'The Bible Argument: or, Slavery in the Light of Divine Revelation', by Thornton Stringfellow, D.D., pp. 457-521; 'The Bible Argument on Slavery', by Charles B. Hodge, D.D., pp. 841-77; similarly George D. Armstrong, D.D., *The Christian Doctrine of Slavery* (1857 original; repr., New York: Negro Universities Press, 1969) 'devotes its 148 pages almost exclusively to the exposition of pertinent New Testament texts'; see Swartley, *Slavery, Sabbath, War and Women*, pp. 31-37, 278-79.

218. Bledsoe's original is all in capital letters in his 'The Argument from the Scriptures', in *Cotton Is King*, pp. 379-80; see Swartley, *Slavery, Sabbath, War and Women*, pp. 49 and 285.

and did not use his principle 'in warfare' against it.[219] Davies is even more critical, calling the New Testament 'an impoverishment of traditions . . . which allowed gross injustice to flourish in Christian countries through the centuries.'[220] Various reasons are advanced to explain Paul's failure to call for action, usually stressing the widespread acceptance of the institution in contemporary society and the early church's lack of political muscle.[221] It is worth remembering that the muscle power of slavery in preindustrialised societies was the equivalent of our use of fossil fuels like electricity, gas and oil. Calling for it to be abolished was as difficult as contemporary attempts to save the environment!

As noted above with marriage, we need to return to Paul's central theological principles of Christology and eschatology. Paul's eschatological emphasis led him to recommend that people should 'remain in the state in which you were called', which he applies equally to both marriage and slavery (1 Cor. 7.17-24). Given that 'the appointed time has grown short' (7.29), Paul seems to expect that all institutions like marriage and slavery will soon be swept away at the coming of Christ. Nonetheless, as Horrell argues, Paul's view is 'that slavery is not a desirable institution and should be avoided if possible'.[222] Paul accepts that people who are slaves can be called by Christ, but that 'if you can gain your freedom, avail yourself of the opportunity', as the RSV translates 1 Cor. 7.21; others interpret it in accordance with Paul's basic concern to use every situation for Christ: 'Even if you can gain your freedom, make use of your present condition now more than ever' (NRSV).[223] Whichever translation is adopted, the next verse makes it clear that the primary relationship is with Christ, since 'a slave is a freed person belonging to the Lord, just as whoever was free when called is a slave of Christ' (7.22). Furthermore, Christians who were 'bought with a price' by Christ should not become 'slaves of human masters' (7.23).

Thus it is Paul's Christology which does most to undermine slavery. Dale Martin's study of the 'slave of Christ' and Paul's use of the image of the enslaved leader not only draws attention to the self-giving and humbling of Christ, but also establishes Paul's 'authority as Christ's agent and spokesperson'. It also gave hope to the 'lower-status members of the church. . . . Paul, the upwardly mobile

219. Longenecker, *New Testament Social Ethics for Today*, p. 54.

220. Davies, 'Work and Slavery in the New Testament', p. 347.

221. See, for example, Longenecker, *New Testament Social Ethics for Today*, pp. 54-58; McDonald, *The Crucible of Christian Morality*, pp. 174-75.

222. Horrell, *Social Ethos*, p. 162.

223. For full debate of this verse, see Thiselton, *1 Corinthians*, pp. 544-65, and S. Scott Bartschy, *Μᾶλλον χρῆσαι: First-Century Slavery and the Interpretation of 1 Cor. 7:21*, SBLDS 11 (Missoula: Scholars Press, 1973).

slave of Christ, was also their model, the assurance that they need not be trapped forever in the slavery of obscurity.'[224]

Finally, Paul's understanding of everyone's equal place in Christ underlies the subversive rhetoric of his letter to Philemon. On the surface level, Paul keeps the law and returns Onesimus, Philemon's runaway slave, to him (v. 12). He even offers to take responsibility for any losses or amounts owing (vv. 18-19). He goes out of his way not to command Philemon 'to do your duty', yet instead he delivers lots of rhetorical appeals to how much Philemon owes Paul (vv. 8-9, 14, 19-21). The reason for all this is that Onesimus has been converted by Paul in prison;[225] he is no longer just a slave but Paul's 'child' and 'a beloved brother' (vv. 10, 16). Paul appeals to his central ethical value of love (v. 9) that Philemon should 'welcome him as you would welcome me' (v. 17). As Schrage notes, 'The old legal relationship continues in force, but the institution does not remain unchanged. . . . we also note a love that influences the structures of property rights and society.'[226] The letter would be read out to 'the church in your house' — and doubtless both slaves and other masters listening would have been very interested in Philemon's response to Paul's emotional blackmail![227] Longenecker does not believe that Paul is asking for Onesimus to be transferred to him as his slave, or to be given emancipation, but that at least 'relations between Philemon and Onesimus be put on a basis of mutual acceptance as fellow human beings *(en sarki)* and brothers in Christ *(en kuriō)*.'[228] Similarly, Craig de Vos does not think that manumission would have made much difference, given that 'once a slave, always a slave'; in asking for this 'fundamental change in perception and relationship, Paul was actually asking for something far more radical than manumission. What he expected effectively undermined the collectivist, authoritarian and patriarchal values of Graeco-Roman society.'[229]

It can be argued that this same new relationship of slaves and masters can be seen in the household instructions in Col. 3.22–4.1. While the slaves are given fairly conventional advice about obeying and serving their masters, it is notable

224. Martin, *Slavery as Salvation,* pp. 147-49.

225. See Craig S. Wansink, *Chained in Christ: The Experience and Rhetoric of Paul's Imprisonments,* JSNTSS 130 (Sheffield: Sheffield Academic Press, 1996), esp. chap. 5 on Onesimus, pp. 175-99.

226. Schrage, *The Ethics of the NT,* p. 234; see also McDonald, *The Crucible of Christian Morality,* pp. 172-74.

227. Bieberstein also draws attention to the importance of public reading to unmask and break open the oppression in her 'Disrupting the Normal Reality of Slavery: A Feminist Reading of the Letter to Philemon', *JSNT* 79 (2000), pp. 105-16.

228. Longenecker, *New Testament Social Ethics for Today,* p. 59.

229. Craig de Vos, 'Once a Slave, Always a Slave? Slavery, Manumission and Relational Patterns in Paul's Letter to Philemon', *JSNT* 82 (2001), pp. 89-105.

that the masters are told to treat them 'justly and fairly, for you know that you also have a Master in heaven'. This concern for Christian relationships rather than changing the institution characterised most responses in the early church fathers, although there is some evidence of Christian slaves wanting the church to buy their freedom (see, e.g., Ignatius' *Letter to Polycarp* 4.3).[230]

Nonetheless, Dunn concludes, 'Above all, the repeated reference to the primary relationship to the Lord (for both slave and free) highlights a fundamental criterion of human relationships which in the longer term was bound to undermine the institution of slavery itself.'[231] Given that the 'longer term' took some eighteen hundred years before the 'institution of slavery' was abolished in countries with a Christian tradition (and still continues in many places today), Dunn's comment may seem optimistic! Nonetheless, he is surely correct to draw attention to Paul's stress on the 'primary relationship to the Lord', which once again brings us back to the basic point about Paul's contingent ethics, dependent upon the genre of the letters and the situation of his recipients and upon his main theological stress on belonging to Christ. Even here, however, careful attention to what Paul actually says and the Christological reasons motivating his moral teaching reveal evidence of his 'fresh thinking' in an increasingly radical approach to his ethics.

e. Household codes

Our last discussion on slavery began to take us into the later Pauline material particularly known as the *Haustafeln*, or household codes. The basic pattern is clear in the examples in Col. 3.18–4.1 and Eph. 5.21–6.9. In each case, a set of instructions is applied to both sides of the main constituent pairings in the household — husbands and wives, parents and children, slaves and masters.[232] Some elements also occur in 1 Tim. 2.8-15 (wives), 6.1-2 (slaves and masters), Tit. 2.1-10 (wives, younger men, slaves) and 1 Pet. 2.13–3.8 (honour the emperor and governors, slaves, wives and husbands). Horrell shows that similar codes continue into the postapostolic age and second-century writings, particularly those standing within the 'Pauline trajectory'.[233]

230. See Longenecker, *New Testament Social Ethics for Today*, pp. 60-69 for an account of the church and slavery from the New Testament to today.

231. Dunn, *The Theology of Paul the Apostle*, p. 701.

232. For discussion of these codes, see J. D. G. Dunn, 'The Household Rules in the New Testament', in *The Family in Theological Perspective*, ed. S. C. Barton (Edinburgh: T&T Clark, 1996), pp. 43-63; Matera, *NT Ethics*, pp. 223-27.

233. David G. Horrell, 'Leadership Patterns and the Development of Ideology in Early Chris-

In these lists, the keyword is 'be subject', ὑποτάσσεσθαι, applied to authority figures. Such hierarchical ethical instructions were traditional for socially inferior groups like wives, children and slaves within both Jewish and Hellenistic sources.[234] Hartman suggests that the Colossians' code is based upon the Decalogue, while Standhartinger argues the opposite, that this 'unambiguously oppressive' text comes from contemporary Hellenistic street philosophy.[235]

There are two notable points about these codes within the New Testament, which both pick up our discussion of Pauline ethics. The first is that they tend to provide a Christological basis as the reason for acting in this way, rather than just for society or on philosophical grounds. Submission is 'out of reverence for Christ' for husbands and wives, 'in the Lord' for children, 'as you obey Christ' for slaves, while masters have 'the same Master in heaven' (Eph. 5.21; 6.1, 5, 9). Similarly, everything is done 'in the Lord' in Col. 3.18, 20, 22. Secondly, the socially inferior members are now balanced with their 'other halves' — husbands, fathers, and masters. There is a mutuality and reciprocity in which both sides are to submit to or respect each other (Eph. 5.21). This is significant in that husbands are to love their wives, fathers not to provoke their children and masters to treat slaves fairly (Eph. 5.25; 6.4, 9; Col. 3.19, 21; 4.1). Hays argues that 'the conventional authority structures of the ancient household are thereby subverted even while they are left in place'.[236]

We would argue that both this Christological motivation and the subverting mutuality are typical of Paul's 'fresh thinking' in working out his ethics in practice, as was demonstrated just above with regard to slavery. Significantly, Horrell notes that 'the reciprocity evident in Colossians and Ephesians all but disappears' in the other New Testament lists and on into the later material, as the focus shifts away from the household to a more hierarchical and church-based model.[237] Elliott similarly argues that the later Pauline legacy has contributed to a reading of Paul as 'an instrument in the legitimation of oppression' of women, slaves and the poor; however, he is convinced 'that Paul himself

---
tianity', in *Social-Scientific Approaches to New Testament Interpretation*, ed. Horrell, pp. 309-37; see esp. pp. 328-30.

234. Verhey, *The Great Reversal*, p. 67; Meeks, 'The "Haustafeln" and American Slavery', pp. 242-43.

235. Lars Hartman, 'Code and Context: A Few Reflections on the Parenesis of Col. 3.6–4.1', in *Understanding Paul's Ethics*, ed. Rosner, pp. 177-91; Angela Standhartinger, 'The Origin and Intention of the Household Code in the Letter to the Colossians', *JSNT* 79 (2000), pp. 117-30.

236. Hays, *Moral Vision of the NT*, p. 64.

237. Horrell, 'Leadership Patterns and the Development of Ideology in Early Christianity', p. 330.

137

is far more an advocate of human liberation than the inherited theological tradition has led us to think.'[238]

Thus this study of Paul's treatment of various key areas of human moral experience shows that he is far from being the reactionary negative social conformist popularly imagined. Paul is not first and foremost an ethicist, nor are his letters systematic ethical treatises. Therefore, it is not enough simply to quote one or two verses taken out of their context and then applied direct to today's ethical dilemmas. Rather, they must always be read in their literary context within letters addressed to certain specific human experiences of their recipients and within Paul's wider theological concerns. Closer examination of these various topics has revealed that Paul is actually a creative and radical theologian who applies his basic theological and Christological insights to his readers' situations with care and sensitivity as he seeks to work out what a loving response to the sovereign rule of God in Christ might mean as the time grows short. This is particularly true when he has to deal with the particular or specific issues and questions facing his converts. In some areas, he can be quite liberating, while in others, especially those which were taken for granted in his society, like slavery, his careful handling sows the seeds for future transformation. Of course, it has to be recognized that not all of his disciples followed his lead, and the church still has to work out the practical implications of some of his ethical statements today.

6. The imitation of Jesus in Paul

The preliminary summaries of the above sections of this chapter so far have clustered around two basic conclusions. We have argued that there is a real continuity between Jesus' preaching for a response from disciples in community to the kingdom of God and Paul's constant appeal to his readers to respond to what God has done in Christ through their life together in the early church. Secondly, it has become increasingly apparent that the centrality of Christology for Paul's theology in general is also true for his ethics in particular. Given both of these conclusions, the apparent lack of quotations of Jesus' ethical material in Paul's letters is rather surprising — and therefore we must turn at last to the relationship of Jesus and Paul.

238. Neil Elliott, *Liberating Paul: The Justice of God and the Politics of the Apostle* (Maryknoll, NY: Orbis, 1994/Sheffield: Sheffield Academic Press, 1995), pp. 22-23.

a. Paul's knowledge of Jesus and his teaching

The debate about the relationship of Jesus and Paul was sparked off by F. C. Baur in 1831, but came to dominate much of German criticism over the next century through to Bultmann's conclusion that 'the teaching of the historical Jesus plays no role or practically none in Paul'.[239] This debate concerned not just Paul's knowledge of Jesus' life and teaching, but the extent to which Paul was a legitimate follower of Jesus, his re-interpreter — or the founder of a completely different religion.[240] Much of the argument contrasted Paul's supposed Hellenistic background with Jesus' Jewishness. W. D. Davies' *Paul and Rabbinic Judaism* reopened the issue, arguing that 'it was the words of Jesus Himself that formed Paul's primary source as ethical *didaskalos*.'[241] Dungan's study of the sayings of Jesus in Paul's churches argued that Paul did not need to quote Jesus because his readers would have recognized both his allusions and his authority in Paul's letters.[242] Academic debate was renewed through the 'Paulus und Jesus' seminar of the SNTS (1984-88), chaired by Christian Wolff and Alexander Wedderburn.[243] This has been followed by the more recent work of Witherington, Furnish and Wenham, all of whom argue for a clear continuity between Jesus and Paul.[244] Meanwhile, at a more popular level in the media, A. N. Wilson tried to resurrect the idea of Paul being the real founder of Christianity, only to be rebuffed in both print and public debate by N. T. Wright.[245]

The first problem concerns the lack of quotations of Jesus in the Pauline corpus. The clearest examples come from 1 Corinthians. In 1 Cor. 7.10-11, Paul refers to 'the Lord' for the command not to divorce or marry again, which we

239. R. Bultmann, *Theology of the New Testament* (London: SCM, 1952), vol. 1, p. 35; for a full discussion of this period, see V. P. Furnish, 'The Jesus-Paul Debate: From Baur to Bultmann', in *Paul and Jesus: Collected Essays,* ed. A. J. M. Wedderburn, JSNTSS 37 (Sheffield: Sheffield Academic Press, 1989), pp. 18-50, a revised version of Furnish's original article in *BJRL* 47 (1964-65), pp. 342-81.

240. See Bornkamm, *Paul,* pp. 228-39.

241. W. D. Davies, *Paul and Rabbinic Judaism* (London: SPCK, 2nd edn. 1962), p. 136.

242. David L. Dungan, *The Sayings of Jesus in the Churches of Paul: The Use of the Synoptic Tradition in the Regulation of Early Church Life* (Oxford: Blackwell, 1971).

243. Wedderburn's edited collection, *Paul and Jesus: Collected Essays,* includes some essays arising from the SNTS Seminar, with other papers on this topic.

244. Ben Witherington III, *Jesus, Paul and the End of the World* (Exeter: Paternoster, 1992); V. P. Furnish, *Jesus according to Paul* (Cambridge: Cambridge University Press, 1993); David Wenham, *Paul: Follower of Jesus or Founder of Christianity?* (Grand Rapids: Eerdmans, 1995); David Wenham, *Paul and Jesus: The True Story* (London: SPCK/Grand Rapids: Eerdmans, 2002).

245. A. N. Wilson, *Paul: The Mind of the Apostle* (London: Sinclair-Stevenson, 1997); N. T. Wright, *What Saint Paul Really Said: Was Paul of Tarsus the Real Founder of Christianity?* (Oxford: Lion, 1997).

can compare with Synoptic sayings such as Mark 10.2-9 and parallels.[246] Wenham argues that Paul's views on marriage, 'one flesh' and celibacy in 1 Cor. 6–7 are all derived from Jesus.[247] It is significant that Paul distinguishes his own commands from those of Jesus when giving instructions about not divorcing an unbelieving spouse and for the unmarried (7.12, 25). A couple of chapters later, Paul again refers to Jesus: 'The Lord commanded that those who proclaim the gospel should get their living by the gospel' (1 Cor. 9.14), a directive which comes in the mission instructions (see Matt. 10.10 and Luke 10.7).[248] Furthermore, in 1 Cor. 11.23-25 he quotes Jesus' sayings at the Last Supper (see Luke 22.19-20 and parallels), although this is more about liturgy than ethics.[249] Nonetheless, for a single letter, this is a significant little group of sayings.

We must also bear in mind that none of the gospels were written down when Paul wrote his letters, so Paul is referring to material in oral circulation or in collections of sayings or stories about Jesus.[250] The complexity of this can be seen in Acts 20.35, where Paul is made to quote Jesus as saying, 'It is more blessed to give than receive'. It is significant that this is the only place in Acts where a saying of Jesus is quoted. It certainly 'sounds like Jesus', as the Jesus Seminar would say (see Luke 6.38; 11.9), but it is not preserved anywhere in the gospels, although there are similar sayings in classical literature.[251] This means that we have to look not so much for quotations from Jesus as for allusions to sayings later preserved in the gospels.[252]

Most scholars agree that the ethical section of Rom. 12–15 provides the most scope for allusions, notably to material which Matthew would later locate in the Sermon on the Mount: possible echoes include Rom. 12.14, blessing persecutors (Matt 5.44); 12.17, 21, do not repay 'evil for evil', but with good (Matt 5.38-39); 13.8-10, love as fulfilling all the commandments, recalls the great commandment material (Mark 12.28-34 and parallels); 14.10 on not pass-

---

246. Dungan, *The Sayings of Jesus*, pp. 80-135; Thiselton, *1 Corinthians*, pp. 521-25, 540-43.

247. Wenham, *Paul*, pp. 240-50.

248. See David Horrell, "'The Lord commanded . . . but I have not used . . .'": Exegetical and Hermeneutical Reflections on 1 Cor 9.14-15', *NTS* 43 (1997), pp. 587-603; Horrell, *Solidarity and Difference*, pp. 214-22, which takes some of this article further; see also Dungan, *The Sayings of Jesus*, pp. 3-80; Wenham, *Paul*, pp. 190-200.

249. Wenham, *Paul*, pp. 156-59.

250. See Dunn, *The Theology of Paul the Apostle*, p. 187.

251. Horrell suggests that 'Luke has created a saying of Jesus, already known as a proverbial aphorism, in order to support Paul's stance on the question of support'; Horrell, "'The Lord commanded . . . but I have not used . . .'", p. 598.

252. For a useful table of 'explicit references and allusions', as well as 'echoes and parallels' to Jesus' teachings in Paul, see Fisk, 'Paul: Life and Letters', in *The Face of New Testament Studies*, ed. McKnight and Osborne, pp. 310-14.

ing judgement (Matt 7.1); 14.13 on a stumbling block, σκάνδαλον (Mark 9.42); and 14.14, 'nothing is unclean' (Mark 7.15). Thompson rightly begins his extremely detailed study of these chapters by defining criteria for allusions and then works his way painstakingly through each case in turn. After demonstrating which are the most likely allusions, Thompson concludes that Paul's use of the 'example of Jesus' as well as the whole Jesus event throughout his letters will be more profitable for the debate.[253] Similar conclusions are reached by Furnish: 'Paul does not understand his apostolic task to be merely handing on Jesus' teachings, or interpreting and applying them. He understands his task to be, above all, proclaiming Jesus himself'.[254] Wenham is more confident about the allusions here, but also stresses the example of Jesus.[255] In an important earlier article, Dunn argues for significant influence from the Jesus tradition on this section of Romans, but that the problems over recognizing allusions stem from 'the way in which the Jesus tradition was retained and used' as 'living tradition . . . shaping Pauline paraenesis at the level of his own thought processes'.[256]

The second issue arises from Paul's comment that even if he once knew 'Christ according to the flesh', ἐγνώκαμεν κατὰ σάρκα Χριστόν, he did so no more (2 Cor. 5.16). For much of the twentieth century, this was taken to imply that this meant that Paul may have known Jesus himself or known about Jesus in his time as a persecutor before his conversion, but now was not interested in Jesus' human life. Bultmann interprets 'Christ according to the flesh', Χριστὸς κατὰ σάρκα, as equivalent to the 'Jesus of history', something in which he thinks Paul has no interest.[257] However, more recent exegesis has argued that κατὰ σάρκα properly belongs not with Christ but with the verb, meaning a human way of knowing or seeing; thus RSV translates it, 'Even though we once regarded [or 'knew', NRSV] Christ from a human point of view, we regard him thus no longer.' Wolff's thorough analysis of the verse notes its context in Paul's quarrel with his opponents, and sees it as central to Paul's basic conviction that everything is now to be regarded from the point of view of what God's love has

---

253. Thompson, *Clothed with Christ: The Example and Teaching of Jesus in Romans 12.1–15.13*, pp. 240-41.

254. Furnish, *Jesus according to Paul*, pp. 40-65; quotation from p. 65.

255. Wenham, *Paul*, pp. 250-70.

256. J. D. G. Dunn, 'Paul's Knowledge of the Jesus Tradition', in *Christus bezeugen: Festschrift für Wolfgang Trilling zum 65 Geburtstag*, ed. Karl Kertelge, Traugott Holz and Claus-Peter Marz (Leipzig: St. Benno-Verlag, 1989), pp. 193-207; see also his *The Theology of Paul the Apostle*, pp. 189-97.

257. R. Bultmann, *The Second Letter to the Corinthians* (Minneapolis: Augsburg, 1985), pp. 155-56; see also his *Theology of the New Testament* (London: SCM, 1952), vol. 1, pp. 238-39.

done in Christ.[258] Therefore, this verse does not mean that Paul has no interest in Jesus' earthly life and ministry.[259]

Furnish's study of Paul's knowledge of Jesus and his sayings concludes that Paul stresses 'knowing Jesus' as a continuing relationship more than 'knowing certain facts about Jesus' earthly life and ministry'.[260] Meeks points out that Paul's use of the genre of letters means that we do not think of him as a story-teller; nonetheless, 'The pivotal story for Paul was simple and astounding', the account of what God had done in the life, death and resurrection of Jesus, which undergirds all of his teaching and ethics.[261] Wright also argues that the story of Jesus himself is at the centre of Paul's various interlocking stories, which enables the move from the stories of the creation and covenantal narrative from Abraham through the Jesus story to the stories of the church and the individual Christian, including Paul's own story.[262] Fowl similarly sees at the heart of the hymnic passages in Paul 'a story in which Christ is the main character', and 'Paul's aim is to present each community with a story of its founder'.[263] Wedderburn points out that Paul's 'story of Jesus . . . is clearly a narrative of events' but that it includes both a 'prehistory' of Jesus' pre-existence and what happened to him after 'this-worldly life came to an end'; he thinks that the Hellenists are the most likely source for the transmission of the story of Jesus to Paul.[264] Wenham works his way painstakingly through all the major events of Jesus' life from his birth, baptism and temptation through his ministry and miracles to his transfiguration, passion and resurrection, analysing Paul's letters for any knowledge of each in turn; while the evidence is stron-

258. Christian Wolff, 'True Apostolic Knowledge of Christ: Exegetical Reflections on 2 Corinthians 5.14ff', in Wedderburn, *Paul and Jesus*, chap. 4, pp. 81-98.

259. See further discussion in Dunn, *The Theology of Paul the Apostle*, pp. 184-85 and Wenham, *Paul*, pp. 400-402.

260. Furnish, *Jesus according to Paul*, pp. 66-92; quotation from p. 92.

261. Wayne A. Meeks, *The Origins of Christian Morality: The First Two Centuries* (New Haven, CT: Yale University Press, 1993), pp. 196-97.

262. N. T. Wright, 'A Fresh Perspective on Paul? The T. W. Manson Memorial Lecture', Westminster Abbey, October 26, 2000; Wright also uses this approach in his *Paul: Fresh Perspectives*, see esp. pp. 7-13 and 21-39. He then goes on to argue that the relationship between Jesus and Paul is not merely that of 'a second-generation rabbi determined to pass on as much as possible of what the original master had said'; it is 'much more like that between a composer and a conductor; or between a medical researcher and a doctor; or between an architect and a builder', *Paul: Fresh Perspectives*, pp. 154-61; quotation from p. 155.

263. Fowl, *The Story of Christ in the Ethics of Paul*, p. 199; see also Dunn, *The Theology of Paul the Apostle*, pp. 187-88.

264. Wedderburn, 'Paul and the Story of Jesus', in *Paul and Jesus*, chap. 8, pp. 161-89; quotations from p. 163; for transmission through the Hellenists, see his 'Paul and Jesus: Similarity and Continuity', in *Paul and Jesus*, chap. 6, pp. 117-43.

ger for the passion and resurrection than for the infancy or temptation, none-theless he concludes that 'Paul may well have been familiar with much of the gospel "story" as we know it.'[265] Such narrative approaches to Paul have become increasingly important in recent years and are much more fruitful for the ques-tion of Paul's knowledge of Jesus than previous attempts to find quotations of and references to his teaching.[266]

In other words, we are back to the vital distinction we have been making throughout this book between Jesus' words and his deeds, between his teach-ings and his activities. The old search for quotations of Jesus' teaching reflects the previous scholarly concentration upon his words as the way of understand-ing Jesus' ethic. This brief study has concluded that there are, in fact, a number of allusions to Jesus' teaching scattered throughout the epistles. However, the narrative approach to Paul arising out of the 'new' or 'fresh' perspective looks rather for Paul's assumptions about the basic story of Jesus, and therefore fits in well with our biographical reading of Jesus' deeds and activities as the proper context for his teaching. In this respect, there is a basic commitment to the story of Jesus underlying both Paul's ethical teaching and his wider theology. Given that Paul is writing letters about his communities' specific situations, rather than gospel narratives about Jesus, the absence of more references to Je-sus' life and teaching should not be surprising. Wenham points out that the purpose of the letters is 'to clarify what was unclear or disputed', not to retell the stories and teaching of Jesus, which would be well known and assumed as common knowledge.[267] Furthermore, we must not forget both the contingent nature of the letters and how dependent we are upon the accident of their sur-vival. As Wenham argues, if we did not have 1 Corinthians, it might be thought that Paul did not know about Jesus' teaching on divorce, or about the Last Sup-per or the resurrection traditions; yet because these were issues of dispute at Corinth, Paul deals with them in some detail.[268] Thus it is quite possible that Paul knew of various other Jesus traditions which do not feature in his surviv-ing letters because they were not at issue or because of the vagaries of the pres-ervation of his epistles. However, enough have survived to demonstrate that Paul is aware of both Jesus' deeds and words, and can allude or refer to the Lord's teaching in his epistles, while assuming the underlying biographical nar-rative of his activities and ministry as well as of his death and resurrection.

265. Wenham, *Paul*, pp. 338-72.

266. See Longenecker (ed.), *Narrative Dynamics in Paul*, for further discussion, and the re-sponse from Richard Hays, 'Is Paul's Gospel Narratable?' *JSNT* 27 (2004), pp. 217-39.

267. Wenham, *Paul*, pp. 402-8.

268. Wenham, *Paul and the Historical Jesus*, Grove Biblical Series 7 (Cambridge: Grove, 1998), pp. 20-22.

b. The appeal to the imitation of Christ

If Paul refers more to the story of Jesus than he alludes to his specific ethical teaching, he is even more interested in 'Jesus Christ as a paradigm for the life of the Christian believer', as Hays puts it.[269] We saw in the last chapter that the imitation of Jesus' actions and deeds, especially his open and accepting attitude to sinners and outsiders, is a crucial aspect of following him in discipleship. So too, according to Schrage, 'Paul sees a large area of overlap between the exemplary character of Jesus and of his words.'[270]

Paul stresses this theme of imitation in his earliest letters: he says of the Thessalonians that 'you became imitators of us and the Lord . . . an example to all the believers' (1 Thess. 1.6-7) and 'you became imitators of the churches of God in Christ Jesus' (1 Thess. 2.14). Between these two references to the Thessalonians' imitation, Paul describes his own example given to them in his conduct and hard work (1 Thess. 2.1-12). Such imitation is to be very practical 'you know how you ought to imitate us' — in not living off people but working, following the 'example to imitate' (τύπον μιμεῖσθαι) (2 Thess. 3.7, 9). Marxsen notes how these ideas of 'type' or 'example' (τύπος) and imitation (μιμη-) occur frequently throughout the letters and uses the words 'shape' and 'shaper' to describe how Paul is both the pattern for his converts and the one urging them to be 'shaped' in this way.[271] So Paul appeals to the Galatians also, 'I beg you, become as I am, for I also have become as you are' (Gal. 4.12). Similarly, the Corinthians are to 'learn by us to live according to scripture' so that they can be 'imitators of me' (1 Cor. 4.6, 16). After dealing with some of their queries, Paul sums up his response with, 'Be imitators of me, as I am of Christ' (1 Cor. 11.1).[272] Matera sees the 'shift to the first-person singular' in 1 Cor. 13.1-3 as indicating that the qualities of love he describes are exemplified in his own conduct — and much of 2 Corinthians is taken with Paul describing or defending his actions.[273]

269. R. B. Hays, 'Christology and Ethics in Galatians', p. 273; see also Hays, *The Faith of Jesus Christ: The Narrative Substructure of Galatians 3:1–4:11* (Grand Rapids: Eerdmans, 2nd edn. 2002), pp. 220-26 on how the Christ-story shapes Paul's ethics; Tuckett makes a similar point, 'There is a persistent theme running through Paul's letters of the importance of the person of Christ as an ethical example for the Christian to follow', Tuckett, *Christology and the New Testament*, p. 45.

270. Schrage, *The Ethics of the NT*, p. 211.

271. W. Marxsen, *New Testament Foundations for Christian Ethics*, pp. 190-200.

272. For a similar contemporary confession, see Todd Still's conclusion, 'I cannot get away from a deep-seated conviction that *imitatio Pauli* is in fact *imitatio Christi*, that is, in seeking to emulate Paul in general I am more able to follow Christ in particular, 'Paul: An Appealing and/or Appalling Apostle?', p. 118.

273. Matera, *NT Ethics*, pp. 152, 154-58; see also Hooker, 'Interchange in Christ and Ethics', pp.

Having initially studied Phil. 2.5-11 in great detail on its own, Fowl now sees that this approach to the story of Christ 'can be extended more broadly through the epistle',[274] while Matera interprets the whole letter through this theme of imitation and example.[275] Thus Paul follows his teaching about the example of Christ in 2.5-11 with an appeal to the Philippians to 'join in imitating me, and observe those who live according to the example you have in us' (Phil. 3.17). Paul begins his practical and ethical teaching in Rom. 12–15 with the instruction, 'do not be conformed to this world, but be transformed' (12.2); his various appeals to love (e.g., Rom. 12.9-21,[276] 13.8-10) show that this transformation happens as we are conformed to the example of Christ (Rom. 13.14; 15.1-7).[277] So Thompson concludes his detailed study, 'Christ is the example for the Christians in Rome to follow'. For Paul this is the conclusion of both the specific problems of the weak and the strong and 'the climax of his paraenesis in general'.[278]

Thus the imitation of Paul leads to the imitation of Christ — and eventually this means that we are also to be 'imitators of God' (Eph. 5.1). As Clarke points out, this later linking of imitation to God himself is unique within the Pauline corpus, but it is enclosed within references to the love of Christ on either side (4.32–5.2).[279] Matera notes that the notion of imitating God is 'thoroughly Jewish', being found in both the Old Testament and the gospels (Lev. 19.2; Matt. 5.48; Luke 6.36),[280] which takes us back to our conclusions at the end of the last chapter on Jesus about the reinterpretation of the Levitical Holiness Code so that we should be both perfect and merciful even as God is perfect and merciful.

But what exactly is it that we are to imitate? We saw that both the Greek idea of *mimesis* and the Jewish concept of *ma'aseh* involve imitating specific actions of the teacher. Given that Paul's epistles contain relatively little about the

---

63-65; Ernest Best, 'Paul as Model', chap. 3 in his *Paul and His Converts: The Sprunt Lectures 1985* (Edinburgh: T&T Clark, 1988), pp. 59-72.

274. Fowl, 'Christology and Ethics in Philippians 2:5-11', in *Where Christology Began: Essays on Philippians 2*, ed. R. P. Martin and B. J. Dodd (Louisville: Westminster John Knox, 1998), pp. 140-53, quotation from p. 141; for his earlier work, see his *The Story of Christ in the Ethics of Paul*, pp. 77-101.

275. Matera, *NT Ethics*, pp. 174-83.

276. See Walter T. Wilson, *Love without Pretense: Romans 12.9-21 and Hellenistic Jewish Wisdom Literature*, WUNT 2.46 (Tübingen: Mohr, 1991).

277. See A. McGrath, 'In What Way Can Jesus Be a Moral Example for Christians?' *Journal of the Evangelical Theological Society* 34 (1991), 289-98; McGrath compares this with Luther's idea of 'being conformed to Christ' and Calvin's being 'incorporated into Christ' (p. 296).

278. Thompson, *Clothed with Christ: The Example and Teaching of Jesus in Romans 12.1–15.13*, pp. 234-35.

279. Andrew D. Clarke, 'Be Imitators of Me': Paul's Model of Leadership', *Tyndale Bulletin* 49.2 (1998), pp. 329-60, esp. pp. 350-51.

280. Matera, *NT Ethics*, pp. 221-22.

life of Jesus, it is noteworthy that we still find some practical aspects being used for imitation. Thus, in Philippians, humility is taught by having the 'same mind as Christ Jesus, who humbled himself' (Phil. 2.1-13). While Käsemann rejected the use of this passage as an ethical ideal, work by Fowl, Dodd and Hooker has returned to its ethical implications.[281] What is significant is that while the hymn itself is a profound theological statement about Christ's self-emptying and exaltation, Paul is using it simply to teach that people should imitate his humility. From this text, Hays develops his stress on the focal image of the 'cross' for reading Pauline ethics — though a lot more than just Jesus' death on the cross is involved here.[282]

When we come to the pastoral problems at Corinth, again Hays notes that Paul does not appeal to the authority of the Torah or Jesus' teaching or even the Apostolic Council, but to 'follow the example of Christ'.[283] His example of self-emptying humility can be applied to several issues of practical ethics, from eating meat offered to idols to apostolic rights and the collection for the poor at Jerusalem. Through his discussion of the ethics of eating meat offered to idols (1 Cor. 8–10), Paul appeals to love and to concern for others, especially the weaker brothers and sisters, as exemplified in Christ.[284] Similarly, Paul appeals to Jesus' example, 'who, though he was rich, yet became poor for your sake', to persuade people to give generously for his collection (2 Cor. 8.9). David Horrell stresses the 'self-giving' example of Christ in both passages — and notes how this leads Paul into a discussion of his rights as an apostle, which is then backed up by an allusion to Jesus' saying that 'those who proclaim the gospel should get their living by the gospel' (1 Cor. 9.14; cp. Matt. 10.10; Luke 10.7). What is most significant is that Paul actually goes *against* Jesus' teaching in not making use of his right to be supported (9.15). Instead, he prefers to follow Jesus' example of self-giving — which leads eventually to his appeal, 'Be imitators of me, as I am of Christ', in 1 Cor 11.1. Thus, for Paul here, imitating the example of Jesus 'required the setting aside of a specific instruction, or word, of Jesus'.[285] Else-

---

281. E. Käsemann, 'Kritische Analyse von Phil. 2,5-11', *ZTK* 47 (1950), pp. 316-60; see Fowl, *The Story of Christ in the Ethics of Paul* and esp. his 'Christology and Ethics in Philippians 2:5-11', p. 140; Brian J. Dodd, 'The Story of Christ and the Imitation of Paul in Philippians 2–3', in *Where Christology Began: Essays on Philippians 2*, ed. R. P. Martin and B. J. Dodd, pp. 154-60; Hooker, 'Interchange in Christ and Ethics', pp. 62-63.

282. Hays, *Moral Vision of the NT*, pp. 27-32.

283. Hays, *Moral Vision of the NT*, p. 43.

284. See Matera, *NT Ethics*, pp. 148-51; Meeks, *The Moral World of the First Christians*, pp. 132-36; Winter, *Seek the Welfare of the City*, pp. 165-77; Dunn, *The Theology of Paul the Apostle*, pp. 701-6.

285. Horrell, '"The Lord commanded . . . but I have not used . . .", pp. 599-601; see also Horrell, *Social Ethos*, pp. 206-16, and *Solidarity and Difference*, pp. 214-22.

where, Horrell notes that 'a fundamental influence on the shape and content of Paul's ethics is not the words and teaching of Jesus but rather the self-giving of Jesus Christ, which constitutes a principal moral paradigm'; he concludes therefore, 'Paul allows the *imitatio Christi* paradigm to override all particular ethical rules and prescriptions, even when the rule is a direct command of the Lord Jesus.'[286] Dungan not only agrees about Paul's 'freedom . . . against this command of the Lord' but notes that Paul is 'nowhere . . . charged with *disobeying the command of the Lord*'.[287] Similarly, after his study of Jesus' sayings in Paul, Mike Thompson concludes that 'the example of Jesus carries more significance for the apostle than dominical logia'; 'the example of Christ does not signify for Paul any kind of mechanical reproduction of Jesus' life and words' but a 'Spirit-enabled following of Jesus' spirit and attitude'.[288] Wolff's study of Paul's acceptance of deprivation, renunciation of marriage, humble service and persecution concludes that 'his entire existence was shaped by the person and way of Jesus Christ. In all this Paul displayed himself as a true follower.'[289]

But Paul's appeals to imitate Christ go beyond simply his examples of humility and self-giving in Philippians and Corinthians to an active ethic of concern for others. In Romans, the problem once again concerns those who are 'weak' and 'strong', although this time the issue is about eating only vegetables, rather than meat offered to idols, and observing certain days (Rom. 14–15). Reasoner's detailed treatment of these chapters attempts to situate both the ascetic practices and the terms 'strong' and 'weak' within the Roman context of social relationships of *potentes* and *inferiores* as well as Jewish practices.[290] Paul's detailed handling of this problem in Rom. 14 is preceded by several instructions about love (Rom. 12.9; 13.8) and putting on Christ (13.14), and these themes recur immediately afterwards in Rom. 15. Thus, Paul instructs the Romans to 'bear with the failings of the weak' and not to please themselves 'as Christ did not please himself'. He appeals to them to welcome others 'just as Christ has welcomed you' (Rom. 15.1-7). Dunn and Thompson note the use of βαστάζειν for 'to bear' in 15.1, with its echoes of the Suffering Servant 'bearing' our infir-

286. Horrell, *Solidarity and Difference*, pp. 27 and 221.

287. Dungan, *The Sayings of Jesus*, pp. 35, 39, his italics; Horrell, *Solidarity and Difference*, pp. 218-19 suggests that 'aspects of his self-defence in 2 Cor. 10–13' might 'hint at such accusations'.

288. Thompson, *Clothed with Christ: The Example and Teaching of Jesus in Romans 12.1–15.13*, pp. 239-40.

289. Christian Wolff, 'Humility and Self-denial in Jesus' Life and Message and in the Apostolic Existence of Paul', in Wedderburn, *Paul and Jesus*, chap. 7, pp. 145-60; quotation from p. 160.

290. Mark Reasoner, *The Strong and the Weak: Romans 14.1–15.13 in Context*, SNTSMS 103 (Cambridge: Cambridge University Press, 1999); see also Dunn, *The Theology of Paul the Apostle*, pp. 680-92; Matera, *NT Ethics*, pp. 202-5.

mities and diseases (Isa. 53.4 as quoted in Matt. 8.17) as well as Jesus' own 'bearing' of his cross and his teaching that 'bearing' the cross is the mark of his disciples (John 19.17; Luke 14.27).[291] The same word occurs in Paul's appeal to 'bear one another's burdens, and so fulfil the law of Christ' (Gal. 6.2). Horrell brings these two passages together to conclude, 'Imitating this pattern of other-regarding conduct is the fundamental moral responsibility. In other words, the christological basis of Paul's moral argument here undergirds not so much an individual's stance on specific ethical matters but more *a pattern of relating, an 'other-regard', which is morally imperative*.[292] Hays, too, links Gal 6.2 with Rom. 15.1 and sees this as 'the fundamental paradigm for Christian ethics'; 'Paul understands his own life as a recapitulation of the life-pattern shown forth in Christ', which then becomes the task of all those who respond together: 'The community as a whole is given a task of burden-bearing which corresponds to and at the same time fulfils the life-pattern of Jesus Christ as portrayed in Paul's kerygmatic formulations.'[293]

This ethic and paradigm continues to be taught in the later or deutero-Pauline letters. Thus when Eph. 5.1 says that we are to be 'imitators of God', it follows from the very practical ethical teaching to 'be kind . . . forgiving one another as God in Christ has forgiven you' (Eph. 4.32–5.1). Similarly, forgiving others 'as the Lord has forgiven you' is the basis for human relationships which enables us to 'bind everything together in love' with the 'peace of Christ' in Col. 3.13-15.

Thus we may conclude that Paul's use of these images of Jesus' self-emptying or humility and the story of his incarnation and death on a cross presuppose some knowledge among his readers of the biographical narrative about Jesus beyond the bare theological fact of the Christ-event. Paul uses this knowledge to appeal to his communities to grow as disciples of Christ through imitation of his own way of following Jesus' example, more than by appeal to Jesus' sayings. To follow the example of Jesus Christ's self-giving love even to death on the cross lies at the heart of Paul's own life as well as his theology and ethics — and must be worked out in practical ways of self-denial and concern for others, especially the weaker, through the imitation of Christ. Thus, rather than referring to Jesus the great moral teacher, to his *words,* Paul seems to be asking for an imitation of Jesus' *deeds* in his accepting of others, what we have called his open pastoral practice.

291. Dunn, 'Paul's Knowledge of the Jesus Tradition', p. 199; Thompson, *Clothed with Christ: The Example and Teaching of Jesus in Romans 12.1–15.13,* pp. 208-41.

292. Horrell, *Solidarity and Difference,* p. 188, his italics; see also his earlier article, 'Solidarity and Difference: Pauline Morality in Romans 14:1–15:13', *Studies in Christian Ethics* 15.2 (2002), pp. 60-78, esp. p. 71.

293. Hays, 'Christology and Ethics in Galatians', quotations from pp. 287, 280 and 290.

c. Keeping company with 'sinners'?

Not just Paul's concern for others, but his bearing with them, especially the weaker brothers and sisters and those who cause offence or commit acts which may need to be forgiven, bring us to the crucial final element in Jesus' ethics which we noted in the previous chapter — his attitude towards so-called 'sinners' or outsiders.[294] Despite the popular negative caricature of Paul the hardliner discussed above, is it possible that in fact he also imitates Jesus' open acceptance?

Wedderburn believes that there is real 'similarity and continuity' between Jesus and Paul in this regard, with the Hellenists of Acts 6.1ff. as the means of transmission between them. He suggests that 'the example of Jesus' attitude and behaviour towards the despised outsiders of his world led them to adopt a similar welcoming attitude and behaviour towards the despised outsiders of their own, more cosmopolitan world.'[295] This led the Hellenists to being open to accepting Gentiles, with the consequent threat to the place of the temple and the law, resulting in the persecution of Stephen, Saul's involvement and his subsequent conversion (Acts 6–9). This seems to Wedderburn to be the likely 'bridge' between Jesus and Paul, both of whom 'were in their lives and ministries characterized by what might be called an openness to the outsider, and that in the name of their God'.[296] To substantiate this, Wedderburn draws on E. P. Sanders' picture of Jesus' acceptance of 'sinners', which we noted in our previous chapter, and observes that for Paul, 'Gentiles too were by definition "sinners" (Gal. 2.15)'.[297] Thus Paul's openness to Gentiles, and his acceptance of them in his mission, is in direct continuity with Jesus' attitude to 'sinners' and outsiders — even with regard to the practices of eating with such people in table fellowship. So Wedderburn concludes that 'the ministry of Jesus and the ministry of his apostle Paul were both characterized by what might appropriately be described as an *openness to the outsider*'.[298] If this is the case, then we can conclude our study of Paul's ethics as we did with Jesus', by grounding his teaching in his open pastoral practice.

But, 'some may say' — to introduce the Pauline anonymous objector! —

---

294. See Horrell, 'Ethics and Outsiders', chap. 8, in *Solidarity and Difference,* pp. 246-72 for a clear demonstration that Paul is concerned for those outside the community of faith and provides a basis for ethics in a wider society than just a sectarian ecclesial group.

295. Wedderburn, 'Paul and Jesus: Similarity and Continuity', in *Paul and Jesus*, chap. 6, pp. 117-43; quotation from p. 124.

296. Wedderburn, 'Paul and Jesus: Similarity and Continuity', pp. 130-31.

297. Wedderburn, 'Paul and Jesus: Similarity and Continuity', pp. 132-35.

298. Wedderburn, 'Paul and Jesus: Similarity and Continuity', pp. 136-43.

can we really see Paul as some kind of 'ethical liberal', happily accepting people as they are? After all, Jesus may have kept bad company while teaching good morals, but it is Paul who quotes, with approval, Menander's dictum, 'Bad company ruins good morals' (1 Cor 15.33; Menander, *Thais*, fragment 218). It is perhaps significant that this verse comes not in the middle of the debate about the Corinthians' dubious ethical practices earlier in the chapter, but in his discussion about the resurrection and may refer to complacent sceptics within the church or non-Christians from outside, according to Thiselton.[299]

Nonetheless, Paul's concern for holiness within the church leads him to require the exclusion outside the community of the 'man living with his father's wife', who is to be 'delivered to Satan' for the sake of his future salvation (1 Cor. 5.1-5). A little leaven might leaven the lump — but this is going too far, and the leaven must be cleansed out (5.6-7). This passage is much debated and contains a number of problems for the interpreter. Clearly, Paul views this form of incest as an extremely serious sin, which goes even beyond behaviour tolerated by the pagans around (5.1). E. P. Sanders suggests that the man 'is acting thus in the name of the Lord Jesus', translating the end of v. 3 and the start of v. 4 in a literal order (as NRSV also has in its alternative translation in the margin). Thus the man is simply taking Paul's logic of freedom as a new being in Christ even further, allowing him completely new relationships![300] Most other commentators take 'in the name of the Lord Jesus' with either the assembly in v. 4 or Paul's passing judgement on him in v. 3.[301] What is clear is that Paul does not tolerate this behaviour and requires the person's excommunication. Hays and Rosner believe that there is at least an implicit reference to the Torah's ban on such relationships (e.g., Lev. 18.18) and for the sanction, 'Drive out the wicked person from among you' (1 Cor. 5.13; see also Deut. 17.7 and Deut. 22.21-22, which includes the death penalty for such illicit relationships).[302] Tuckett is less convinced about the Old Testament allusions, and says that 'the primary basis for Paul's argument here is the *Christological* claim'.[303]

Harris' more sociological analysis of the passage sees this as the 'beginnings of church discipline', while Pascuzzi's extremely detailed treatment considers the historical and religious background, using rhetorical analysis to conclude that Paul includes Christological criteria for the sanction in order to preserve

299. See Thiselton, *1 Corinthians*, pp. 1253-55.
300. Sanders, *Paul*, pp. 106-7.
301. See Thiselton, *1 Corinthians*, pp. 392-94.
302. Hays, 'Ecclesiology and Ethics in 1 Corinthians', pp. 38-39; *Moral Vision of the NT*, p. 43; Rosner, *Paul, Scripture, and Ethics*, pp. 61-93.
303. Tuckett, 'Paul, Scripture and Ethics: Some Reflections', pp. 411-16; quotation from p. 415.

the unity and purity of the Christian community.[304] Both the approaches from the Old Testament background and the more sociological analyses demonstrate that Paul's concern is for the holiness and purity of his new Christian community, which must therefore exclude the incestuous man. It might be argued that this does not display an open or accepting attitude towards the 'sinner'. Yet Paul still cares for the individual, and says that the purpose of the excommunication is 'that his spirit may be saved in the day of the Lord Jesus' (5.5). He does not invoke the death penalty of Deut. 22.21-22, but has what Dunn terms 'a loving concern for the individual'.[305] Sanders even praises Paul's 'fresh thinking' in 'not roundly condemning transgressors to destruction' but trying to save him instead.[306] Thus, even in this most extreme example of exclusion, it can be argued that there is still a concern for the 'sinner'.

The following chapter contains one of Paul's frequent vice-lists of various activities (1 Cor. 6.9-10). Similar lists can be found in other letters, such as Rom. 1.29-31, or the contrast between the fruit of the Spirit and the works of the flesh in Gal. 5.19-24. Yet in all of these cases there is no call for exclusion or excommunication. Instead Paul warns his readers that those who do such things 'will not inherit the kingdom of God' (1 Cor. 6.9; Gal. 5.21), thus pleading for a change of behaviour. While the sexual immorality, πορνεία, of those joining their bodies to prostitutes is strongly criticized, again on Christological grounds, these 'sinners' are still not condemned to exclusion. Instead Paul pleads that they should 'shun' or 'flee from' πορνεία and instead glorify God in their bodies (1 Cor. 6.13-20). It is only in that one extreme case of the man 'living with his father's wife' that excommunication is called for, for the sake of saving his soul or spirit (1 Cor. 5.5).

Indeed, the very fact that Paul has to produce such lists in his letters and plead with his readers implies that the early Christian communities were much more ethically diverse. After the vice-list, Paul states 'such were some of you', but 'you were washed, you were sanctified, you were justified in the name of the Lord Jesus Christ and in the Spirit of our God' (1 Cor. 6.9-11). On the surface, the past tense here implies that all has now changed. Yet this does not mean that everyone is Corinth was now morally perfect and that all greed, drinking or reviling had gone. The rest of the correspondence suggests otherwise! We are back to the relationship between the indicative and imperative. If all those 'washed' or baptised were perfect, Paul would not need to urge his readers to

304. Gerald Harris, 'The Beginnings of Church Discipline: 1 Corinthians 5', in *Understanding Paul's Ethics*, ed. Rosner, pp. 129-51; Maria Pascuzzi, *Ethics, Ecclesiology and Church Discipline: A Rhetorical Analysis of 1 Corinthians 5*, Tesi Gregoriana Serie Teologia 32 (Rome: Editrice Pontificia Università Gregoriana, 1997).

305. Dunn, *The Theology of Paul the Apostle*, pp. 691-92.

306. Sanders, *Paul*, pp. 115-16.

live out their baptism — 'let not sin reign in your mortal bodies' (Rom. 6.12). Similarly, after contrasting 'the fruit of the Spirit' with 'the works of the flesh', Paul still has to urge people therefore to 'walk by the Spirit' and not to provoke others (Gal. 5.16, 25-26). Even Paul himself admits that he is not 'already perfect; but I press on to make it my own, because Christ Jesus has made me his own' (Phil. 3.12). Again, we note the Christological centre of Paul's ethic and his desire to bring his imitation of Christ to its perfect fulfilment.

Horrell argues that Paul's concerns for holiness and purity are part of what it means to be in Christ. Paul appeals for holiness because we are the body of Christ — and a member of that body cannot be one flesh with a prostitute (1 Cor. 6.15-16).[307] Yet that same idea of the body of Christ produces Paul's concern for unity, seen in 'look to the good of your neighbour' (1 Cor. 10.24) and a regard for others, especially the 'inferior' or less honoured among the many different members of the body of Christ in 1 Cor. 12.12-26. This means that there can be no judging of others: 'Let us therefore no longer pass judgment on one another, but resolve instead never to put a stumbling block or hindrance in the way of another' (Rom. 14.13). As Thompson concludes, 'The Christians at Rome are not to reform their standards of judgment; . . . they are to cease "judging" *altogether*.'[308] Dunn comes to a similar conclusion: 'All the while Paul sought to encourage genuine respect across the spectrum of Christian liberty.'[309]

This applies to different Christians' views on various ethical issues. As Horrell argues, in the passages about food offered to idols in 1 Cor. 8.1–11.1 and Rom. 14.1–15.13, 'here Paul more clearly develops a form of ethical relativism within which differences of conviction can remain, again in the context of a communal solidarity sustained not via ethical unanimity but through the practice of other-regarding love'.[310] Elsewhere he stresses, 'The foundation of solidarity, the basis for identity and belonging, is being "in Christ"'; in this way, 'Paul tries to create the kind of moral space within which distinctive convictions and practices can co-exist with mutual respect and love'.[311] This 'other-regard' and 'respect' do not arise out of some mutual 'let and let live' attitude, but flows from our key point about imitating Jesus: 'But the imitation in view

---

307. Horrell, *Solidarity and Difference,* pp. 140-52; Newton compares Paul's idea of purity with that of Qumran, arguing that both think that their community represents the temple: Michael Newton, *The Concept of Purity at Qumran and in the Letters of Paul,* SNTSMS 53 (Cambridge: Cambridge University Press, 1985).

308. Thompson, *Clothed with Christ: The Example and Teaching of Jesus in Romans 12.1–15.13,* p. 173; his italics.

309. Dunn, *The Theology of Paul the Apostle,* p. 712.

310. Horrell, *Solidarity and Difference,* p. 197.

311. Horrell, 'Solidarity and Difference: Pauline Morality in Romans 14.1–15.13', p. 75.

concerns an imitation of self-giving and self-lowering *for the sake of the other,* which is a practice which precisely creates the room for difference to be sustained within a context of communal solidarity'.[312] This concern for 'the other' is also central to Bonhoeffer's theology, which he derives in part from Rom. 15.7: 'When God was merciful to us, we learned to be merciful with our brethren. When we received forgiveness instead of judgment, we, too, were made ready to forgive our brethren. . . . Thus God himself taught us to meet one another as God has met us in Christ. "Wherefore receive ye one another, as Christ also has received us, to the glory of God" (Rom. 15.7).'[313] Writing just after the first democratic elections in South Africa, Smit noted that 'one of the most important challenges to South African Christians and theologians flowing from Bonhoeffer's legacy is the importance of "learning to live with the other"'.[314]

Thus the Christological centre of Paul's ethic, the tension of the indicative and imperative, and the following of Jesus' teaching combined with imitating his open acceptance of people, all come together in the fact that ethical transformation does not happen overnight. As White puts it, 'To Paul, the Christian is a saved man, and the Christian ethic is the ethic implied in the process of salvation' which takes place in people 'who steadily advance towards the goal of redemption, in Christlikeness'.[315] Paul teaches that Christ died for us 'while we were still sinners' (Rom. 5.8), and he is described as the 'foremost' of sinners (1 Tim. 1.15). This means that he, and we, need to be open and accepting of other sinners who are making their own response along the journey towards perfection in the kingdom of God. What Horrell terms Paul's 'metanorms' of 'corporate solidarity' and 'other-regard' are what hold the Christian community together, despite our differences. Some of these differences may be other ethical convictions or practices, such as which foods to eat, which are acceptable; others, which Paul thinks threaten our union with Christ, like joining the body of Christ to a prostitute, still need to be handled with the mercy which we have also received (Rom. 15.7). In this way, Paul's combination of clear and demanding ethical teaching set within the context of the diversity of the body of Christ and underscored with a self-denying concern particularly for weaker brothers and sisters is not so dissimilar after all from Jesus teaching his rigorous ethic while accepting a wide and diverse group of followers, including 'sinners'.

312. Horrell, *Solidarity and Difference,* p. 243; his italics.
313. D. Bonhoeffer, *Life Together* (London: SCM, 1954), pp. 10-13; he also returned to Rom 15.7 as the basis for living together in marriage; see *Letters and Papers from Prison* (London: SCM, 1971), p. 153.
314. Dirkie Smit, 'Dietrich Bonhoeffer and "The Other": "Accept One Another, Therefore . . ." (Rom. 15:7)', *JTSA* 93 (December 1995), pp. 3-16; quotation from p. 3.
315. R. E. O. White, *Christian Ethics,* pp. 146-48.

7. Conclusion

This study of Paul's ethics has had to be somewhat longer and more detailed than previous chapters, partly because the Pauline corpus occupies about a quarter of the New Testament, but also because there is a wide range of ethical material in Paul, dealing with many moral issues. And yet we can discern the same basic outline as was found with Jesus. It is still supremely an ethic of response, even though the preaching of the kingdom has become the event of the King, with Christology being absolutely central for both Paul's own new life and for his theology and ethics; the demand for a response to what God is doing is the same, within the eschatological tension of the now and the not yet, with the prospect of both reward and punishment; the same centrality of the love command, seen as fulfilling the law, is to be lived out within a community of other disciples in corporate solidarity as the body of Christ; the particular ethical issues handled cover the same basic topics, including obedience to the state, sex, marriage and divorce, money, property and poverty, and the various forms of human relationships. Through it all we also have the link of direct quotation and indirect allusion to Jesus' teachings which would not be written down until later, in the gospels, they were set within the context of the narrative of the story of Jesus' activities and deeds. Finally, Paul appeals to his readers to follow Christ's example of including others within an open and mixed community. In this way, far from being the founder of a new religion or ethic, Paul is applying the teaching and personal example of Christ to his readers, as the evangelists will do later in the gospels.[316]

In conclusion, Paul is often seen as uncomfortable reading for those wanting open debate in an inclusive community today. Yet we have argued that this is precisely how we should read Paul — as following the creative complementarity of Jesus' rigorous and demanding ethics together with his acceptance of sinners within his community. As the biographical genre of the gospels means that we should take Jesus' deeds and example into account as much as his words, so the epistolary genre of Paul's letters directs us to set his ethical teaching within the contingent context of his early Christian communities. As Jesus' pastoral acceptance of 'sinners' means that his extremely demanding teaching cannot be applied in an exclusive manner, so too Paul's ethical teaching must always be balanced by his appeal to the imitation of Christ — and this entails accepting others as we have been accepted.

---

316. See Matera, *NT Ethics*, 248-55 for a similar conclusion.

IV. Mark: Suffering for the Kingdom

We are setting out an account of New Testament ethics which begins with Jesus as the original event — the earliest layer in archaeological terms — and moving forwards from there. Our survey of Jesus found that he was not primarily concerned to be an ethical teacher, but rather was more like an Old Testament prophet, preaching the in-breaking of God's kingdom, or attempting to spread his rule. He sought a response from his hearers, which involved following him in community with others who made a similar response, even if they had little else in common. The love command was central to Jesus' ethic, but such ethical instructions as he gave tended to be rather rigorous and demanding. However, paradoxically, Jesus kept company with sinners, the very people who had severe ethical problems — and what seemed worse to many, he welcomed them into God's kingdom on his own authority, healed them and even saw his death as 'for' them.

Our chronological reconstruction took us next to Paul. His Christological focus stressed that God's kingdom or rule has already been inaugurated in Christ as we live 'between the times'. Like Jesus, Paul is not primarily an ethicist. First and foremost, he is a writer of letters to his readers, looking for a response within his early communities. His ethical material has the same emphasis on the love command, which he tries to apply to some key ethical and moral issues. Yet it is all couched within a similar appeal to the imitation of Christ, to live within the company of sinners.

Introduction to the four gospels

Lastly, we come to the four gospels, which we find at different depths in the last few layers, later than Paul and going forwards towards the end of the first century. Here, above all, we note the impact of the 'Jesus-event'. First, it is important to bear in mind our earlier comments about genre as a key for interpretation. In the same way that neither Jesus nor Paul is primarily an ethical teacher, so, although the gospels contain some moral teaching, they also are not ethical treatises. We have argued before, and elsewhere, that the gospels are a form of Graeco-Roman biography and therefore need to be interpreted in the light of other ancient Lives.[1] We should therefore expect their authors to include some of Jesus' ethical teaching as part of their account of his life and ministry, and also that their own views about morality might be evident in their writing as they paint their particular portrait of Jesus for their audiences. Most importantly, this is a narrative genre — and stories about people were a major method of imparting moral teaching in the ancient world.[2] Therefore we should not just try to extract any ethical material from the gospels and look at it on its own, as though they were just collections of sayings like the *Gospel of Thomas* or the assumed source, Q. Rather, we need to see how the individual evangelists develop their biographical narrative account of Jesus' life and teaching as a whole. As Hays puts it, 'The ethical significance of each Gospel must be discerned from the shape of the story as a whole'.[3]

Furthermore, it is significant that this biographical 'shape' is a Graeco-Roman genre,[4] and that the gospels are written in Greek. And yet they contain stories, anecdotes, sayings and dialogues which are very Jewish. Indeed, we can find many parallels within rabbinic literature to these gospel passages. What is striking, however, is that no one ever brought them together to compose an account of the life of a particular rabbi, such as Hillel or Shammai, despite there being ample material so to do. As Philip Alexander comments, 'There are no Rabbinic parallels to the Gospels as such. This is by far the most important single conclusion to emerge.' He concludes that this is because no rabbi held 'the central position that Jesus held in early Christianity.'[5] The point of preserving

---

1. Richard A. Burridge, *What Are the Gospels? A Comparison with Graeco-Roman Biography*, rev. and updated ed. (Grand Rapids: Eerdmans, 2004).

2. Wayne A. Meeks, *The Origins of Christian Morality: The First Two Centuries* (New Haven, CT: Yale University Press, 1993), pp. 189-92.

3. Richard B. Hays, *The Moral Vision of the New Testament* (Edinburgh: T&T Clark, 1997), p. 74.

4. See Burridge, *What Are the Gospels?* (1992), pp. 70-81 for an account of the development of ancient biography; pp. 67-77 in the second edn. (2004).

5. Philip S. Alexander, 'Rabbinic Biography and the Biography of Jesus: A Survey of the Evi-

and passing on stories and accounts of questions and answers within the rabbinic tradition is to remember what different rabbis have said about this or that point of the law. In other words, the Torah is the central focus, and the genre of the rabbinic anecdotes lends itself to legal and ethical teachings. When, however, the evangelists collect their material into the form of an account of Jesus, they are revealing that the focus on the Torah has been replaced by a focus on Jesus. Such is his impact. Thus, writing a *bios* out of a Jewish context is itself a Christological claim, for it is putting a person in the centre in a way no ordinary human being should be.[6] In writing a biographical account of Jesus, they redirect our attention to the foundation, Jesus of Nazareth and his words and deeds, his teachings and example, his beliefs and all that happened to him in his life and death and afterwards.

Then there is the question of plurality and the significance of having four gospels in the canon. The dates and settings of each gospel are simply not known. Early church traditions associate the gospels with specific authors or places, such as Papias' comments that Mark was 'Peter's interpreter' and that Matthew collected Jesus' sayings in Hebrew (Eusebius, *Historia Ecclesiastica* 3.39.15-16), or Irenaeus' association of Luke with Paul and the fourth evangelist with John as the beloved disciple, who wrote from Ephesus (*Adversus Haereses* 3.1.1). The development of the historical-critical method gave rise to all sorts of theories about the authorship and provenance of the four gospels, while redaction criticism brought back the author as theologian, which also led to hypotheses about the communities which produced these texts; more latterly, such community theories have come under serious scrutiny.[7] Perhaps all we can say is that we have these four accounts, written by different people intended for various audiences (about which we may speculate, but only from the texts themselves) but each in its own way telling the story of Jesus.[8]

What is significant is how quickly these four accounts were accepted within

---

dence', in *Synoptic Studies: The Ampleforth Conferences of 1982 and 1983*, ed. C. M. Tuckett, JSNTSS 7 (Sheffield: JSOT Press, 1984), pp. 19-50; see p. 40.

6. See further Richard A. Burridge, 'Gospel Genre, Christological Controversy and the Absence of Rabbinic Biography: Some Implications of the Biographical Hypothesis', in *Christology, Controversy and Community: New Testament Essays in Honour of David Catchpole*, ed. David G. Horrell and Christopher M. Tuckett (Leiden: Brill, 2000), pp. 137-56; also repr. in the 2nd edn. of *What Are the Gospels?* (2004), Appendix II, pp. 322-40.

7. See R. J. Bauckham (ed.), *The Gospels for All Christians: Rethinking the Gospel Audiences* (Grand Rapids: Eerdmans, 1998), esp. Richard A. Burridge, 'About People, by People, for People: Gospel Genre and Audiences', pp. 113-45.

8. For a survey of the current situation, see Richard A. Burridge, 'Who Writes, Why, and for Whom?' in *The Written Gospel*, ed. Markus Bockmuehl and Donald A. Hagner (Cambridge: Cambridge University Press, 2005), pp. 99-115.

the early church, kept together as the fourfold gospel, and yet not amalgamated into a single authoritative account (as is demonstrated by the fact that Tatian's experiment with the *Diatessaron* did not become widely accepted).[9] Their reasonable coherence within their diversity both allows the search for the historical Jesus, and yet also reveals how their redaction of Jesus' teaching and ministry applied it to their own situations. As Matera notes, 'Jesus is the focal point of these writings. To put it another way, while many speak of Markan, Matthean, Lukan, and Johannine ethics, I prefer to speak of Jesus' ethics as mediated by these writers.'[10]

Therefore, we began by outlining the basic ethical stance of the historical Jesus. There is a clear ethic common to all four gospels (though expressed in different language in John) about the coming of the kingdom as Jesus preaches for people to respond to what God is doing, with the centrality of love, teachings about life within the new community of followers, and so forth. The fact that each evangelist reinterprets this differently without losing the basic thrust suggests that the outline comes from the historical Jesus. As Harvey puts it, 'These sayings, in some form at least, go back to Jesus. They are too original, too remarkable, to have been coined by a mere follower or evangelist. The suggestion that we owe an ethic which has fascinated and challenged humanity for two thousand years to some anonymous disciple and not to Jesus at all, is surely implausible.'[11]

Having considered carefully the basic outline of the historical Jesus and how he was understood by Paul in the previous chapters, we will now consider the particular ethical concerns of each gospel in turn. In doing so, we shall follow a similar structure to that already used for both Jesus and Paul. In each case, we need to begin with Christology: given that the gospels are a form of ancient biography, we cannot just consider what ethical material each gospel may or may not include; what is crucial is how they portray Jesus and his character. It is notable that when he gets to the gospels, Hays similarly begins each chapter with a section on the evangelist's Christology,[12] and this is surely correct; however, it makes it all the more odd that he begins with Paul rather than Jesus and, even then, does not have a section on Paul's Christology. After considering each evangelist's Christology, we shall then go on to discuss the relationship of ethics

9. See Graham N. Stanton, 'The Fourfold Gospel', in idem, *Jesus and Gospel* (Cambridge: Cambridge University Press, 2004), pp. 63-91.

10. Frank J. Matera, *New Testament Ethics: The Legacies of Jesus and Paul* (Louisville: Westminster John Knox), 1996, pp. 8-9.

11. A. E. Harvey, *Strenuous Commands: The Ethic of Jesus* (London: SCM/Philadelphia: Trinity Press International, 1990), p. 27.

12. Hays, *Moral Vision of the NT,* pp. 75-80, 94-96, 114-20, 140-42.

to eschatology in each gospel. As with our treatment of Jesus and Paul, consideration of the ethical material will begin with the issue of the law and the love command and then go on to the main ethical teaching about specific human moral issues which occur. Finally, we will explore how each gospel treats our major theme of following and imitating Jesus within an inclusive community.

Introduction to Mark's gospel

We start with Mark as the first gospel to be written — or at least the earliest example to survive.[13] If Q was a written document, it seems to have been more in the genre of 'sayings' literature, a collection without a coherent narrative, while speculation about the genre of other possible sources or documents remains just hypothetical. It seems to have been Mark's contribution to bring together Jesus' sayings and stories about his life, ministry and death into a coherent biographical narrative. However, despite all Jesus' ethical teaching and material in the gospels as a whole, some scholars, like McDonald, believe that Mark 'contains relatively little moral teaching' or refer to what Houlden calls his 'paucity of ethical material'.[14] As Matera puts it, 'On first appearance, the Gospel according to Mark, the oldest of the four Gospels, is an unlikely source for moral or ethical instruction'.[15] However, we will argue, along with Verhey, that such a surface assumption about the apparent lack of ethical teaching in Mark 'needs to be challenged'.[16] Via agrees that 'its ethical import has been neglected, especially the complexity and problematics which it introduces into ethical reflection', hence his full-length study of Mark's ethics, stressing the importance of narrative.[17]

Such observations take us straight back to the issue of genre: the lack of

13. For introductions to the current start of play in studies of Mark, see Peter G. Bolt, 'Mark's Gospel', in *The Face of New Testament Studies: A Survey of Recent Research,* ed. Scot McKnight and Grant R. Osborne (Grand Rapids: Baker Academic, 2004), pp. 391-413; Carl R. Holladay, *A Critical Introduction to the New Testament: Interpreting the Message and Meaning of Jesus Christ* (Nashville: Abingdon, 2005), esp. chap. 6, 'The Gospel of Mark', pp. 104-27, or pp. 146-80 in the expanded CD version; Joel B. Green, 'The Gospel according to Mark', in *The Cambridge Companion to the Gospels,* ed. Stephen C. Barton (Cambridge: Cambridge University Press, 2006), pp. 139-57.

14. J. Ian H. McDonald, *The Crucible of Christian Morality* (London: Routledge, 1998), p. 108; J. L. Houlden, *Ethics and the New Testament* (Harmondsworth: Penguin, 1973), pp. 41-42.

15. Matera, *NT Ethics,* p. 13.

16. Allen Verhey, *The Great Reversal: Ethics and the New Testament* (Grand Rapids: Eerdmans, 1984), p. 78.

17. Dan O. Via, *The Ethics of Mark's Gospel — In the Middle of Time* (Philadelphia: Fortress, 1985), p. 3; see pp. 3-23 for an account of his methodology on the hermeneutics of narrative.

ethical material is immediately apparent if one looks for specific sayings or teachings in the manner of a document like Q, or even the way its material is preserved in the blocks of Jesus' moral teaching in Matthew, such as the Sermon on the Mount. Equally, Schrage's redaction-critical method means that having devoted so much space to a detailed study of Jesus' ethic, he is interested only in the 'ethical accents in the synoptic Gospels', looking at what makes them distinctive.[18] However, if we look at Mark's *wider* narrative, then a lot more emerges: 'Sermons and explicit moral instructions are not the only ways to communicate moral teaching. Moral and ethical traditions can also be transmitted through narrative.'[19] Furthermore, Mark's combination of Jesus' deeds and words is not just narrative but a form of ancient biography — and we have already noted how biographical stories played a crucial role in ethical development in the ancient world.[20] Here our earlier comments on the genre of the gospels have direct application to our study of Mark, as is shown by the way my previous work is used by scholars such as Bryan and Shim:[21] it is notable that Witherington begins his socio-rhetorical commentary on Mark with an introductory section on the biographical genre of Mark as the key hermeneutical tool for its interpretation, drawing upon my previous work.[22] Therefore, it is right that we begin with Mark's portrait of Jesus as a whole, and look at his wider narrative for what it reveals about his ethical perspective.

1. Mark's Christology

'It has long been recognized that Jesus' identity is a major issue in the Gospel of Mark.'[23] Tuckett recognizes that to say that 'the person of Jesus is absolutely central for Mark' is to run the risk of sounding 'bland, even trite', but argues

18. Wolfgang Schrage, *The Ethics of the New Testament* (Philadelphia: Fortress, 1988); this is also the title of his third major section, pp. 135-62.

19. Matera, *NT Ethics*, p. 13; see the same point also in Joseph Loessl, S.J., 'The Ethical Dimension of Mk. 10.17-22', *Hekima Review* (Nairobi) 6 (1991), pp. 57-82, esp. pp. 57-59, and Hays, *The Moral Vision*, pp. 73-75.

20. Wayne A. Meeks, *The Origins of Christian Morality*, pp. 189-92; compare Pieter J. J. Botha, 'Mark's Story of Jesus and the Search for Virtue', in *The Rhetorical Analysis of Scripture*, ed. S. E. Porter and T. H. Olbricht (Sheffield: Sheffield Academic Press, 1997), pp. 156-84, esp. pp. 156-64.

21. Christopher Bryan, *A Preface to Mark: Notes on the Gospel in Its Literary and Cultural Settings* (Oxford: Oxford University Press, 1993), see esp. pp. vii, 27-30; Ezra S. B. Shim, 'A Suggestion about the Genre of Text-Type of Mark', *Scriptura* 50 (1994), pp. 69-89; see esp. pp. 70-75.

22. Ben Witherington III, *The Gospel of Mark: A Socio-Rhetorical Commentary* (Grand Rapids: Eerdmans, 2001), pp. 1-9, see esp. n. 18 on p. 6.

23. Botha, 'Mark's Story of Jesus', p. 170.

nonetheless that 'the question of who Jesus is provides the central focus of Mark's narrative'.[24] Traditionally, Christological studies concentrate on the titles used to describe Jesus in the New Testament, such as 'Christ', 'Son of God', 'Lord' and so forth.[25] Norman Perrin's classic study of methodology about Mark's Christology combined consideration of such titles with an attempt to reconstruct Mark's redactional contributions.[26] Rhoads and Michie's stress on reading the narrative of Mark pioneered a literary approach to Mark's characterization of Jesus, looking at areas such as his authority, integrity and service of others even to death rather than titles, while Kingsbury similarly looked at areas such as plot and conflict.[27] As Matera summed it up, 'None of these [titles] can be understood adequately apart from Mark's narrative; for the Christology is in the story, and through the story we learn to interpret the titles.'[28] While such narrative approaches are important for any story, it is all the more so for biographical accounts like the gospels, so it is not surprising that more recent Christological debate has moved from a focus on titles to stories.[29]

The key question posed by Jesus, according to Mark, comes in the story at the centre of the gospel: 'Who do people say that I am?' (Mark 8.29). In fact, Mark told his audience the answer in his opening verse: 'The beginning of the gospel of Jesus Christ, the Son of God' (Mark 1.1). However, while the readers may know about Jesus' identity from the start, the way Mark constructs his narrative depicts a gradual unfolding of his portrait, with the characters in the story coming to understand him only slowly, if at all.[30]

24. Christopher M. Tuckett, *Christology and the New Testament: Jesus and His Earliest Followers* (Edinburgh: Edinburgh University Press/Louisville: Westminster John Knox, 2001), p. 109.

25. See, for example, Oscar Cullmann, *The Christology of the New Testament* (London: SCM, 1959); J. D. G. Dunn, *Christology in the Making* (London: SCM, 1980; 2nd edn. 1989).

26. Norman Perrin, 'The Christology of Mark: A Study in Methodology', *JR* 51 (1971), pp. 173-87; slightly rev. version repr. in *The Interpretation of Mark,* ed. William Telford (London: SPCK, 1985), pp. 95-108; 2nd edn. (Edinburgh: T&T Clark, 1995), pp. 125-40.

27. David Rhoads and Donald Michie, *Mark as Story: An Introduction to the Narrative of a Gospel* (Philadelphia: Fortress, 1982), pp. 101-16; Jack Dean Kingsbury, *The Christology of Mark's Gospel* (Philadelphia: Fortress, 1983), and idem, *Conflict in Mark: Jesus, Authorities, Disciples* (Philadelphia: Fortress, 1989).

28. Frank J. Matera, *New Testament Christology* (Louisville: Westminster John Knox, 1999), p. 26.

29. Richard A. Burridge, 'From Titles to Stories: A Narrative Approach to the Dynamic Christologies of the New Testament', in *The Person of Christ,* ed. Murray Rae and Stephen R. Holmes (London: T&T Clark, 2005), pp. 37-60; see also how Tuckett, *Christology and the New Testament,* argues for titles within a narrative approach, pp. 109-10, 116.

30. See Richard A. Burridge, *Four Gospels, One Jesus? A Symbolic Reading* (Grand Rapids: Eerdmans/London: SPCK, rev. edn. 2005), pp. 35-65 for an account of Mark's portrait of Jesus.

a. The opening movement

Analyses of the gospel abound, but many see it in a three-part structure — a bit like a symphony in three movements. The first half of the gospel is the opening movement, a fast-paced narrative with lots of scurrying violins and loud clashes on the brass, as Jesus moves around Galilee and the northern territories healing, teaching and fighting against evil at a rapid pace — there are eleven examples of 'and immediately' in Mark 1 alone! Jesus is described as a miracle worker, a healer and an exorcist. While the unclean spirits know who he is, 'Jesus of Nazareth . . . the Holy One of God', the people are simply amazed and wonder, 'What is this?' (Mark 1.23-27). Mark recounts no fewer than seventeen miracles — exorcisms (1.23-26; 5.1-20), healings (1.30-31, 40-44; 2.1-12; 3.1-5; 5.22-34, 35-43; 7.25-30, 32-37; 8.22-26) and power over nature (4.36-41; 6.35-44, 47-51; 8.1-9). Given Mark's shorter length, this is proportionally more than in any other gospel, and most occur in this first section.

Mark also characterizes Jesus as a teacher: this is a key word for Mark with the noun-verb combinations in 1.21-22 and 4.1-2, together with the stress in his summary passages (1.14; 1.39; 4.1; 6.6; 6.34). Jesus is called διδάσκαλος both by his disciples (4.38) and by those seeking his help (5.35; 9.17), while Peter (9.5; 11.21) and Judas (14.45) use the original term 'rabbi'. Yet Mark records surprisingly little actual teaching, only four parables: the sower (4.1-20), the seed growing secretly (4.26-29, unique to Mark), the mustard seed (4.30-32) and the tenants of the vineyard (12.1-12). Such direct teaching as there is comes in response to questions from the religious leaders (2.15-28; 3.23-30; and 7.1-23). This is in complete contrast to the large amounts of Jesus' teaching preserved in Matthew and Luke, mostly taken from their common source, Q.

Furthermore, this teacher is not understood by his hearers (4.9-13): his family think he is 'out of his mind' and want to take him away, while the religious leaders believe him to be possessed by Beelzebul (3.19b-35). Even his disciples seem to sink into deeper incomprehension as Jesus gets more exasperated with them (4.13, 40; 6.52; 7.18; 8.4, 17-18, 21). That the leaders of the early church should be portrayed as so stupid and slow to understand has caused no little difficulty, right from the start, the time of Matthew and Luke, both of whom 'improve' the picture of the disciples. Weeden has argued that they represent other leaders within the early church who are opponents of Mark and his group.[31] From the point of view of genre, such a theory is a wrong answer to the

---

31. Theodore J. Weeden, Sr., 'The Heresy That Necessitated Mark's Gospel', *ZNW* 59 (1968), pp. 145-58, repr. in *The Interpretation of Mark*, ed. William Telford (Edinburgh: T&T Clark, 2nd edn. 1995), pp. 89-104; idem, *Mark: Traditions in Conflict* (Philadelphia: Fortress, 1971).

wrong question being posed: their apparent stupidity is not designed to tell us anything about the disciples themselves. In a biographical narrative, everything is to be interpreted as portraying something about the main character — in this case, that Jesus is hard to understand and tough to follow, and we should not be surprised if we do not get it right immediately; after all, look at the disciples![32] In fact, throughout this first movement, questions are asked by various groups, the people, scribes and Pharisees, and the disciples alike, about who Jesus is and why he is doing what he does (1.27; 2.16, 24; 4.41; 6.2-3; 7.5)[33] — all of which go unanswered. The demons, who do know the answer, are muzzled (1.25, 34; 3.12), while those who are helped by him are bound to secrecy (1.44; 5.43; 7.36).

b. The middle section — who is this?

The answers start to emerge in the middle section, the more contemplative, slower second movement of our symphony, which is marked out at its start and finish by the healing of two different blind men (8.22–10.52). In the first story, at Bethsaida, the man does not see clearly at first and requires a second dose of treatment (8.22-26). Interestingly, both Matthew and Luke omit this story with its implication that Jesus does not get it right immediately — but for Mark, it serves as a precursor to the central scene about Jesus' identity at Caesarea Philippi (8.27-38). In response to Jesus' enquiry, 'Who do people say that I am?', Peter thinks he can see clearly — 'you are the Christ' — only to be told a few minutes later that his vision is blurred by Satan when he rebukes Jesus for predicting his own death (8.27-33). For Jesus' identity, being the Christ leads inexorably to the cross in the three passion predictions (8.31-32; 9.31-32; 10.33-34), and anyone who wants to follow him must follow a similar path of self-denial (8.34-38; 9.42-50; 10.23-31). Only after James and John have been told that their ambitions will simply lead to sharing Jesus' death, rather than earning good seats in heaven (10.35-45), do we come to the story of blind Bartimaeus, who 'immediately regained his sight and followed him on the way' (10.46-52).

Thus the quieter, reflective second movement concludes with a mixture of titles and representations of Jesus as the Christ who will go to Jerusalem, not to fight the Romans but to die, as the one whom demons recognize as the 'Son of God' but who calls himself the 'Son of Man', as the miracle worker

---

32. See further Burridge, 'About People, by People, for People', pp. 124-25; also, *What Are the Gospels?* rev. and updated edn., pp. 289-90.

33. Ben Witherington, III, *The Many Faces of the Christ: The Christologies of the New Testament and Beyond* (New York: Crossroad, 1998), p. 132.

who instructs those he helps to tell no one, and as the healer who will suffer himself. Rather than seeing these descriptions as in conflict with each other and explaining them as deriving from contrasting Markan sources in the manner of earlier form critics, a narrative approach to Mark's Christology marvels at the creative tension and complexity in his portrait as Jesus finally comes to Jerusalem.

c. Jerusalem and the final climax

The third and final section is more of a steady march as the expectant hero comes to the capital city but finds that it is not bearing fruit. The story of Jesus cursing the fig tree can sometimes be interpreted as a fit of pique on his part, damning a shrub which was not even in season. However, closer attention to Mark's narrative composition reveals yet more of his Christology: elsewhere in the gospel, Mark likes to 'sandwich' one story around another, such as Jairus' daughter around the woman with a haemorrhage (5.21-24, 35-43 around 5.25-34). In Mark 11 we have a 'double-decker' triple sandwich as the entry into Jerusalem at the start is balanced by the dispute about authority at the end, both raising the question of Jesus' identity again (11.1-11, 27-33). The fig tree's lack of fruit and its subsequent withering form the next layer in (11.12-14, 20-25), while the incident in the temple, 'the house of prayer for all nations', lies at the heart of the chapter and of Mark's Christology (11.15-19). For those still unclear, the parable of the tenants of the vineyard who are destroyed for refusing to pay their rent follows (12.1-12). Both the fig tree and the vines are symbols of Israel in the Old Testament, and Mark's narrative skill suggests that in Jesus, God has come to his people looking for fruit, to which they should respond, whether in season or not, 'to render to God the things that are God's' (12.13-17). The love of God and neighbour is the greatest commandment, 'more important than all whole burnt offerings and sacrifices' in the temple (12.28-34). Those who seek 'the best seats . . . and places of honour' receive only condemnation, while the widow who gives her all to God is commended (12.38-44).[34] No wonder that the Markan apocalypse with its prophecy of the destruction of the temple and Jerusalem itself follows: the attentive reader must 'keep awake' (13.1-37).

All the narrative threads about Jesus' identity build to a climax in the ac-

---

34. For a review of how this story has been read in various contexts, see Elizabeth Struthers Malbon, 'The Poor Widow in Mark and Her Poor Rich Readers', *CBQ* 53.4 (1991), pp. 589-604; repr. in Malbon's collection, *In the Company of Jesus: Characters in Mark's Gospel* (Louisville: Westminster John Knox, 2000), pp. 166-88; also in *A Feminist Companion to Mark*, ed. Amy-Jill Levine with Marianne Blickenstaff (Sheffield: Sheffield Academic Press, 2001), pp. 111-27.

count of his arrest, passion and death. After being the one who was rushing around in the first movement, now Jesus is passive, described as 'handed over' no fewer than ten times, from Judas to the religious leaders on to Pilate and, finally, to the soldiers (14.10, 11, 18, 21, 41, 42, 44; 15.1, 10, 15). The various titles come together in the high priest's direct question: 'Are you the Christ?' (picking up 1.1 and 8.29), 'the Son of the Blessed One?' (implying the title 'Son of God' used by the demons, and by the heavenly voice in 1.11 and 9.7 — but avoided by the priest since he is only a human being). Jesus' answer, 'I am', echoes the divine name of Exod. 3.14 but immediately returns to his self-designating 'Son of Man'. The high priest's reaction of tearing his clothes simply emphasizes how stupendous a claim has been made (14.61-63). The kingly language of the welcome from the crowd (11.10) is reinforced by Jesus' anointing, though again he turns it back to his coming death and burial (14.3-9). It rings out like a refrain through the next chapter, as Pilate asks Jesus directly if he is 'King of the Jews' and calls him that before the crowd (15.9, 12); mocked as King by soldiers and priests alike (15.16-20, 32), Jesus is executed beneath that ascription on the cross (15.26). Yet the King dies all alone, in unrelieved darkness and desolation, still misunderstood by those who hear his final cry of abandonment even by God (15.33-37). But at that very moment, when the temple veil is 'torn' in the same way as the heavens at his baptism (σχίζω, 15.38; cp. 1.10), there comes another voice which recognizes him as 'Son of God', not from heaven or a demon, but a human being, though not from his own people, the Roman centurion (15.39). It is Mark's sublime Christological achievement to bring his account of Jesus' identity to a climax at such a dark, God-forsaken place as crucifixion.[35] No wonder that Meeks concludes that what is unique here is 'this imperious and subversive assault on moral sensibilities'.[36]

Finally, Mark's conclusion is no less comfortable. The women at the cross witness Jesus' burial on the Friday evening (15.46-47) and return early on Sunday to anoint his body (16.1-8). But instead of having a nice, happy ending which ties up all the narrative threads, Mark's story simply leaves us with more questions about the empty tomb and the absent Jesus. After Jesus' earlier commands for secrecy, now a mysterious young man in white instructs the women to tell others, only for the gospel to end almost in mid-sentence with 'they said nothing to anyone, for they were afraid'! The crucial point in this most open of conclusions is the invitation to the disciples to follow the risen Jesus back to Galilee, where they

---

35. See also John Reumann's conclusion, 'The achievement of Mark was to bring together so many disparate traditions about Jesus, as teacher, wonder-worker, or apocalyptic figure, and combine them, under the overarching theme of the Cross', in his *Variety and Unity in New Testament Thought* (Oxford: Oxford University Press, 1991), p. 52.

36. Meeks, *The Origins of Christian Morality*, p. 199.

will see him (16.7) — but whether they do or not is not described as the baton, and the call to discipleship, is handed over to the reader. No wonder that later manuscripts include various longer endings in an attempt to finish the story.[37]

Such a narrative biographical account of Mark's portrait reveals a much richer Christology than any amount of dissection of mere titles. Furthermore, Mark's account of the Christ who will suffer and die for others is not just a deeply theological statement — it is packed with ethical implications. We have argued that Jesus' own preaching was more like that of an Old Testament prophet seeking a response than an ethical teacher wanting to impart moral maxims. This explains why Mark can call Jesus 'teacher' so often, yet have so little actual teaching. Instead, Mark has grasped Jesus' life and message at a very profound level with his careful construction of the Jerusalem section in particular, which is all about God in Jesus looking for a response from his people, as is made clear through the material on the fig tree, the temple, the tenants in the vineyard and so forth.

But the worrying thing for the reader is that the response being sought is one of taking up one's cross and following the same path of self-denial through darkness and desolation, even to the point of being forsaken by God. There may indeed be 'relatively little moral teaching' in Mark, but such a gospel's narrative could never be described as containing a 'paucity of ethical material'.[38] The whole of Mark's Christology is 'ethical material', uncomfortable though its ethic of suffering and self-denial may be.[39]

2. Mark's setting and eschatology

We saw at the beginning of this book that the centre of Jesus' preaching and teaching was the kingdom of God, which was inextricably connected with eschatology — that the rule of God is breaking into the here and now. Yet there is

37. For further discussion of the end of Mark's gospel, see Andrew T. Lincoln, 'The Promise and the Failure: Mark 16:7, 8', *JBL* 108 (1989), pp. 283-300, repr. in *The Interpretation of Mark*, ed. William Telford, 2nd edn. (1995), pp. 229-51; Morna D. Hooker, *The Gospel according to St Mark* (London: A & C Black, 1991), pp. 382-94; Beverly Roberts Gaventa and Patrick D. Miller (eds.), *The Ending of Mark and the Ends of God: Essays in Memory of Donald Harrisville Juel* (Louisville: Westminster John Knox, 2005); Witherington, *The Gospel of Mark*, pp. 44-49 and 411-19; Holladay, *A Critical Introduction to the New Testament*, pp. 170-73 in the expanded CD version.

38. McDonald, *Crucible of Christian Morality*, p. 108; Houlden, *Ethics and the New Testament*, pp. 41-42; see n. 14 above.

39. For more on Mark's Christology and ethics see Hays, *The Moral Vision of the NT*, pp. 75-80; Ernest Best, *Mark: The Gospel as Story* (Edinburgh: T&T Clark, 1983), pp. 79-82; Matera, *NT Christology*, pp. 5-26; Witherington, *The Many Faces of the Christ*, pp. 128-38.

also a dialectic between the now and the final end to come, as well as between the personal and the corporate, the political and the spiritual. As the earliest gospel, Mark's gospel reflects that emphasis on the kingdom, and it may be seen as an *interim eschatological ethic in suffering*.

Right at the start, after the brief announcement of 'the beginning of the gospel of Jesus Christ, the Son of God', the gospel moves straight into the preaching of John the Baptist without any infancy or childhood stories. John appears as the fulfilment of a composite quotation taken not just from Isa. 40.3 but also from Exod. 23.20 and Mal. 3.1, and then makes his own prophecy of one more powerful coming after him, which is itself fulfilled in the appearance of Jesus to be baptized (Mark 1.2-11). After his baptism and temptation, and John's arrest, Jesus himself comes 'proclaiming the good news of God, and saying, "The time is fulfilled, and the kingdom of God has come near"' (1.14-15).[40] Matera argues that 'although the phrase "kingdom of God" occurs only fourteen times in Mark's Gospel, it underlies everything that Jesus says and does'; in fact, the kingdom, or rule, of God makes up 'Mark's moral universe'.[41]

The 'nearness' of the kingdom is a constant theme for the gospel, through Jesus' teaching and preaching, but also through his mighty acts, healings and exorcisms. In this most eschatological gospel, the expectation of the imminent end is never very far away. We have already noted above Mark's narrative skill in the Jerusalem section as God in Jesus comes to the city and to the temple looking for the response of his people bearing fruit and rendering to God 'the things that are God's'; it is the commercial activity of the temple, as barren as the fig tree, and the lack of people's response which leads to Jesus' prophecy of both the destruction of Jerusalem and the final cataclysm in the so-called Markan apocalypse of chap. 13.[42]

If Mark's gospel was composed in the 60s, then this all makes good sense against the background of Nero's persecution of Christians at Rome (where Mark is traditionally associated with Peter's preaching)[43] and the Jewish revolt

40. For a stimulating account of Mark's opening section, see Morna D. Hooker, *Beginnings: Keys That Open the Gospels* (London: SCM, 1997), pp. 1-22.

41. Matera, *NT Ethics*, pp. 14-25, quotation from p. 18; see also his emphasis in Frank J. Matera, 'Ethics for the Kingdom of God: The Gospel according to Mark', *Louvain Studies* 20 (1995), pp. 187-200, an earlier draft of this material.

42. For a robust argument that this material is authentically Markan and reflects the historical Jesus, see Adela Yarbro Collins, *The Beginning of the Gospel: Probings of Mark in Context* (Minneapolis: Fortress, 1992), pp. 73-91; see also Willem S. Vorster, 'Literary Reflections on Mark 13:5-37: A Narrated Speech of Jesus', *Neotestamentica* 21 (1987), pp. 91-112, repr. in *The Interpretation of Mark*, ed. Telford, 2nd edn. 1995, pp. 269-88.

43. See, for example, Robert A. Guelich, *Mark 1–8.26*, Word Biblical Commentary 34A (Dallas:

and war in Palestine (increasingly seen by many scholars as Mark's context).[44] J. T. Sanders makes the provocative suggestion that Mark's 'imminent eschatology is so much the basis of his outlook that he cannot even pass on Jesus' command to love in its original meaning' (a claim we shall consider in the next section), and therefore Mark has little or nothing to say to us about ethics today.[45] Although not as extreme as Sanders', Kee's reconstruction for Mark's context is an apocalyptic community like other Jewish sectarian groups.[46] Schrage thinks that goes too far: traces of a delayed Parousia mean that 'the Markan community cannot be understood as an apocalyptic sect with a sectarian ethics'.[47] Despite these scholarly debates, the basic outline is clear that against such an eschatological background, it is not surprising that Mark does not contain systematic blocks of ethical teaching material in the manner of Matthew's gospel.

However, this does not mean that he has no ethical concerns; in fact, his interim eschatological ethic is more about the command to 'keep alert . . . watch . . . keep awake' (13.33-37), waiting for the Jesus who suffered and died to return to collect his people's final response.[48] In the meantime, such an ethic is a call to endure suffering for the sake of the gospel through the persecutions of Jewish and Roman authorities alike (13.9-13),[49] and, like the book of Revelation, it has meant most to those who are also suffering. Thus it should not be surprising that Blount's reading of ethics in an African American context highlights how Mark's ethic with its understanding of suffering and hope of a 'boundary-breaking transformation and liberation' appealed both to black slaves and to African American civil rights leaders of the 1960s and 1970s.[50]

Word, 1989), pp. xxix-xxxii; Best, *Mark: The Gospel as Story,* pp. 21-36, and Witherington, *The Gospel of Mark,* pp. 20-31.

44. Howard C. Kee, *Community of the New Age: Studies in Mark's Gospel* (London: SCM, 1977), see esp. pp. 100-105 and 176-77; Ched Myers, *Binding the Strong Man: A Political Reading of Mark's Story of Jesus* (Maryknoll, NY: Orbis, 1988), pp. 39-87; H. N. Roskam, *The Purpose of the Gospel of Mark in Its Historical and Social Context,* NovTSup 114 (Leiden: Brill, 2004), pp. 74-114; for further discussion, see Petr Pokorný, 'Das Markusevangelium: Literarische und theologische Einleitung mit Forschungsbericht', in *ANRW* 2.25.3, pp. 1969-2035, esp. pp. 2019-22; Hooker, *The Gospel according to St Mark,* pp. 5-8.

45. J. T. Sanders, *Ethics in the New Testament: Change and Development* (Philadelphia: Fortress, 1975), pp. 31-33.

46. See Kee, *Community of the New Age,* esp. pp. 77-105, 145-46.

47. Schrage, *The Ethics of the NT,* p. 139.

48. See Hays, *Moral Vision of the NT,* pp. 85-88; Verhey, *The Great Reversal,* pp. 75-76.

49. On the suffering of Jesus and of the disciples in Mark, see Collins, *The Beginning of the Gospel,* pp. 61-72.

50. Brian K. Blount, *Then the Whisper Put on Flesh: New Testament Ethics in an African American Context* (Nashville: Abingdon, 2001), pp. 50-63.

Thus the eschatological setting reinforces Mark's ethic of suffering and self-denial already seen in his portrait of Jesus, as the apocalyptic hope of the rule of God being at hand furnishes strength for the present.

3. The law and love

We saw that both Jesus' and Paul's attitudes to love and the law were complex. Jesus appeared to strengthen and radicalize some of the demands of the law, while not participating in the casuistic debates of his contemporaries; the love command, however, occupies a central place in his ethical teaching. Paul was engaged with debates about the law through many of his epistles and argues that love is the fulfilment of the law through what God has done in Christ.

In his massive treatment of Jesus' attitude towards the law in the gospels, Loader notes that 'Mark's Jesus is beyond being a teacher of the Law. He exercises an authority which enables him both to affirm it in parts and to supersede it.'[51] This conclusion is not unlike our observation already about the historical Jesus — but clearly Mark's account reflects his understanding and that of his audience. As Matera points out, in Mark's gospel 'the word for law *(nomos)* does not even occur' and his audience 'seems to have been composed of Gentiles who had little understanding of the Mosaic law and did not practice its many ritual prescriptions (see 7:3-4)'.[52] Verhey agrees that they had 'a significant freedom from scrupulous observance of the regulations of the Jewish authorities', which Blount sees in terms of 'boundary-breaking'.[53] Let us undertake a brief journey through the key incidents in this gospel to see how accurate these observations are.

Many of these pericopae occur in the situation of conflict. The first comes in the battle with sickness and evil, where Jesus touches the leper; normally, this would have made Jesus himself unclean until the evening — but instead, his power makes the leper clean as he heals him 'immediately'. It is also notable that he does not tell him to sacrifice first, as required by the law, and then he will be clean, but he does still tell him to go to the priest and make the offering after he has been healed (1.39-45). Loader thinks that this leaves 'the impression that Jesus upholds Torah', but Myers argues that the instruction is so that he can 'confront an ideological system'.[54]

---

51. William Loader, *Jesus' Attitude towards the Law: A Study of the Gospels* (Grand Rapids: Eerdmans, 2002), p. 123.

52. Matera, *NT Ethics*, p. 26.

53. Verhey, *The Great Reversal*, p. 79; Blount, *Then the Whisper*, pp. 50-53.

54. Loader, *Jesus' Attitude towards the Law*, p. 25; Myers, *Binding the Strong Man*, p. 153.

This is followed by a sequence of stories of conflict between Jesus and the religious authorities:[55] we begin with the healing of the paralytic where Jesus proclaims that his sins are forgiven first, thus claiming authority to act on behalf of God, which causes offence to the scribes (2.1-12). This leads into the call of a tax collector, Levi, and accusations from the scribes about Jesus eating with sinners; his reply is that he has come 'to call not the righteous but sinners' (2.13-17). A similar point is made in the debate about fasting with his claim to be 'the bridegroom' — with the dark hint that the day will come when he is 'taken away from them' (2.18-20). That something new and special is happening here is reinforced by the image of the difficulty of putting a new patch on old cloth, or new wine in old wineskins (2.21-22). The protest by the Pharisees about Jesus' disciples plucking grain on the Sabbath leads to the pronouncement, 'The sabbath was made for humankind, and not humankind for the sabbath', with its associated claim that 'the Son of Man is lord even of the sabbath' (2.23-28). The final conflict arises over the healing of the man with the withered hand on the Sabbath, which leads to the Pharisees plotting with the Herodians 'how to destroy him' (3.1-6). In this collection, Myers once again sees a challenge to the system, even 'civil disobedience', while Loader suggests that Mark sees Jesus 'as one who, in coming with eschatological authority, effectively replaces the authority of the Torah as the absolute court of appeal'.[56]

These issues then recur in the debate about keeping the traditions regarding hand-washing and the practice of Corban, setting aside resources as an offering to God, which had the advantage of making them unavailable for supporting one's parents. All of this leads to the pronouncement that it is not external things which defile, but what goes on in the heart (7.1-23). Once again, although Jesus is in conflict with the religious authorities and is accused of not keeping the traditions, Mark represents him as appealing to the real meaning of the law of Moses, to honour father and mother; in fact, these human traditions are 'making void the word of God' (7.13). So far, therefore, Jesus cannot be said to be attacking the law: the problem comes with the apparent setting aside of all purity legislation as 'he declared all foods clean' (7.19).[57] McDonald says that 'his own strength of holiness overwhelmed the impurity with which he came into contact', suggesting a link back to Jesus' cleansing of the leper rather than being contaminated by his

55. See Joanna Dewey, 'The Literary Structure of the Controversy Stories in Mark 2:1–3:6', *JBL* 92 (1973), pp. 394-401; repr. in *The Interpretation of Mark*, ed. Telford (1985), pp. 109-18; 2nd edn. (Edinburgh: T&T Clark, 1995), pp. 141-52.

56. Loader, *Jesus' Attitude towards the Law*, p. 38; Myers, *Binding the Strong Man*, p. 161.

57. For full discussion of this passage, see Roger P. Booth, *Jesus and the Laws of Purity: Tradition History and Legal History in Mark 7*, JSNTSS 13 (Sheffield: JSOT Press, 1986).

impurity.[58] Matera notes that this section comes between the two miraculous feedings, one in Jewish and one in Gentile territory (6.30-44; 8.1-10); the coming of the kingdom means that both may now share table fellowship.[59] Thus all the boundary markers which separate people — sickness, avoiding sinners, fasting, Sabbath keeping, vows, food laws — are radicalized by Jesus in Mark's presentation through an appeal to the deeper meaning of the law.

Something similar happens in the collection of material in chap. 10.[60] First the traditional Mosaic provision for divorce (with the grounds for 'something objectionable' and the certificate of divorce as in Deut. 24.1) is set aside, again by an appeal to the original word of God in 'the beginning of creation' (10.1-12). Furthermore, the rich man who wants 'to inherit eternal life' and who claims to have kept all the commandments from his youth is told to sell his possessions to gain 'treasure in heaven' and to follow Jesus (10.17-22).[61] Sandwiched between these two sections is the story about Jesus and the children, with its warning that 'whoever does not receive the kingdom of God as a little child will never enter it' (10.13-16). To reinforce this point, James and John's request for the best seats in the kingdom receives only the promise of suffering and death, turning the usual human desire for lording it over others on its head with the command to be the 'slave of all' (10.32-44). Here too, the ultimate authority for this ethic is the person of Jesus himself, who 'came not to be served but to serve, and to give his life a ransom for many' (10.45). Once again, Loader concludes that 'Jesus is pictured both as Torah faithful and as one who interprets Torah on the basis of these fundamentals', who can use even 'such principles to argue against a Torah provision'.[62]

When we come to the final section of this gospel in Jerusalem, the debates continue between Jesus and the religious leaders about his authority to interpret the law in general and specifically about paying taxes and the resurrection (11.27-33; 12.13-27). It all reaches a climax with a scribe asking Jesus the question about the greatest commandment. Given that many interpreters believed that there were some 613 commands in the law (365 negative and 248 positive), it is a fair question and one which features in rabbinic anecdotes also. We noted above in our consideration of Jesus' ethics that Furnish argues that Jesus' specific combination of Deut. 6.5 and Lev. 19.18 to produce the answer of the love of God and neighbour is not found anywhere else.[63] However, in Mark's redac-

---

58. McDonald, *Crucible of Christian Morality*, p. 111.

59. Matera, *NT Ethics*, p. 28.

60. For a full discussion of Mark 10, see Via, *The Ethics of Mark's Gospel*, pp. 67-195.

61. See further Loessl, 'The Ethical Dimension of Mk. 10.17-22'.

62. Loader, *Jesus' Attitude towards the Law*, p. 95.

63. Victor Paul Furnish, *The Love Command in the New Testament* (Nashville: Abingdon, 1972), p. 62.

tion, Furnish thinks that its application, 'this is much more important than all whole burnt offerings and sacrifice' (10.33), means that the command to love is lost in the argument about ritual worship; he argues that Mark has 'far less interest in anything like a "love ethic" than either Matthew or Luke' and that 'we must conclude that the love command and related themes play no great role in Mark's gospel'.[64] Following him, J. T. Sanders believes that Mark's account is not about love at all, 'but rather how Jesus was a better interpreter of Scripture than his contemporaries'.[65] However, not many other scholars are persuaded: Verhey says that this approach 'seems to miss the point'.[66] In fact, Mark's version of the debate about the love command forms the climax of his account of Jesus as the one who rightly interprets the law precisely because of his commitment to the love of God which seeks loving self-giving in response.

Thus Mark seems to be writing for an audience for whom the law is no longer a major issue. While Mark does not portray Jesus as abrogating the law, nonetheless he is free to interpret it radically, which results in both strengthening it and relaxing it — which is not dissimilar to our conclusions about Jesus himself. Here he goes beyond the provisions of the law for divorce to restate God's original rigorous intention of permanence, or tells the rich man to sell his possessions in addition to keeping the commandments. Yet the priority to love God and neighbour takes precedence over legal requirements, such as Corban and purity rules for food and for lepers. As Loader concludes, 'For Mark, then, Jesus is the absolute authority under God. . . . What remains is love for God, expressed in the community of faith.'[67]

4. Ethical issues in Mark

So far our treatment of Christology, eschatology and the law and love has outlined a clear interim ethic of suffering in Mark's gospel which would lead us not to expect too much specific teaching material. Nonetheless, some of the key human moral experiences we noted in our treatment of Jesus and Paul — such as sexuality and the family, money and possessions, violence and the power of the state — do appear in Mark's narrative. In each case, such issues are radicalized under the prevailing preaching of the kingdom of God, whose sovereignty grows quietly and unexpectedly from small beginnings, yet must take priority since it will end up 'the greatest of all' (Mark 4.26-32).

64. Furnish, *The Love Command*, pp. 29, 71, 74
65. J. T. Sanders, *Ethics in the NT*, p. 32.
66. Verhey, *The Great Reversal*, p. 79; see also Schrage, *The Ethics of the NT*, p. 143.
67. Loader, *Jesus' Attitude towards the Law*, pp. 134-35.

a. 'Family values'

I have already referred to Mark's penchant for 'sandwiching' one story inside another. In 3.19b-35, we have another typical triple structure: it begins with Jesus going εἰς οἶκον, which probably means more than just 'into a house'; rather, it should be translated as 'goes home', since οἱ παρ' αὐτοῦ, his family and friends, soon appear and want 'to restrain him' because they think he is 'out of his mind' (3.19-21). However, the focus then turns to opposition from the religious leaders, who believe that he is possessed by Beelzebul (3.22). For Jesus, though, the reverse is true since the central clash is between Satan and himself (3.23-27).[68] Then the narrative returns to the authorities' attack on him (3.28-30), followed by Jesus' refusal to see his mother and brothers since 'Whoever does the will of God is my brother and sister and mother' (3.31-35). This careful balancing of family — authorities — cosmic conflict — authorities — family shows how the opposition from his family and the authorities are only aspects of the central battle, that with the 'strong man', Satan. Painter holds that even the disciples are included in οἱ παρ' αὐτοῦ as another group criticized in this section.[69]

What is clear is that this story contains an explicit rejection by Jesus of his natural family, replacing it with those who are responding to the kingdom of God. This is uncomfortable reading for those who think that the Christian ethic trumpets 'family values'.[70] Even Matthew and Luke were discomforted, as they dismantle the 1-2-3-2-1 sandwich, linking the Beelzebul controversy with other material elsewhere in their narratives (Matt. 12.22-45; Luke 11.14-32) and omitting altogether the opening section about Jesus being 'out of his mind'; Matthew still places the comment about his family after the controversy, but Luke moves it earlier, well away from the conflict with evil (Matt. 12.46-50; Luke 8.19-21). But in the earliest gospel, as Schrage points out, 'Mark did not evade the breaking of family ties. In 3.31ff., he relativized the traditional understanding of the family, although it is replaced by incorporation into the new community (3.35).'[71] This is, of course, a key section for Myers: Jesus' attack is not just on 'the highest au-

---

68. See Willard M. Swartley, *Covenant of Peace: The Missing Peace in New Testament Theology and Ethics* (Grand Rapids: Eerdmans, 2006), pp. 92-100 for further discussion of Mark's depiction of 'Jesus' Kingdom Gospel as Battle against Evil'.

69. John Painter, 'When Is a House Not Home? Disciples and Family in Mark 3.13-35', *NTS* 45 (1999), pp. 498-513.

70. See further Stephen C. Barton, *Discipleship and Family Ties in Mark and Matthew*, SNTSMS 80 (Cambridge: Cambridge University Press, 1994).

71. Schrage, *The Ethics of the NT*, pp. 141-42; Painter agrees: 'Jesus clearly distances himself from his natural family . . . to make clear that his movement was not based on natural family ties', 'When Is a House Not Home?', pp. 511-12.

thorities in the land' but is a repudiation of 'kinship . . . the axis of the social world in antiquity'; instead 'the fundamental unit of "resocialization" into the kingdom will be the new family, the community of the disciples'.[72]

The same point comes later when Peter notes that following Jesus has meant forsaking everything else: again, Jesus makes explicit both the leaving of 'house or brothers or sisters or mother or father or children or fields, for my sake and for the sake of the gospel' and the promise of a hundredfold reward of a new family in the kingdom (10.28-31). Furthermore, it is worth noting that in response to the Sadducees' question about the much-married wife of seven brothers, Jesus answers that 'when they rise from the dead, they neither marry nor are given in marriage' (12.18-27) — so here, too, the eschatological perspective makes a significant difference!

Thus the in-breaking of the sovereign rule of God takes priority over all family relationships. This immediately raises the question of the implications of this for marriage and children.

b. Marriage and divorce, children

This area of 'family values' continues in Mark's largest collection of ethical material in chap. 10. Here, as Verhey notes, we have almost 'a kind of *Haustafel*' dealing with marriage and divorce, children, possessions and power: 'but it is not a code. Jesus and his words neither rely on the law nor create a new *Halakah*'.[73] Instead, Jesus refers back to God's original intention at creation and forwards to his kingdom for the basis of his comments (10.6, 14-15).[74]

The debate about marriage and divorce was as lively then as now: according to Deut. 24.1, a certificate of divorce could be issued if the husband found 'some indecency' (RSV) or 'something objectionable' (NRSV) in his wife. As indicated in the RSV's translation, the conservative school of Rabbi Shammai interpreted this as general unchastity, rather than only adultery, which demanded the death penalty anyway (Lev. 20.10). However, the NRSV's translation has a wider scope, which reflects the views of the more liberal Hillel, who said it could be 'even if she has merely ruined his dinner' or if he found someone else more attractive (*m. Giṭṭin* 9:10; see also *b. Giṭṭin* 90a-b).[75] When Jesus

72. Myers, *Binding the Strong Man*, pp. 164-68.

73. Verhey, *The Great Reversal*, p. 80.

74. See further on these sections, Via, *The Ethics of Mark's Gospel*, pp. 101-33.

75. For further discussion of the background debate, see the commentaries ad loc., for example, Craig A. Evans, *Mark 8:27–16:20*, Word Biblical Commentary 34B (Nashville: Nelson, 2001), pp. 83-84.

is asked to enter this debate, he goes beyond even Shammai, referring back to 'the beginning' with the statement about 'one flesh' (Gen. 2.24), as he then decrees, 'Therefore what God has joined together, let no one separate' (Mark 10.9). Interpreted as a 'new law' or express command of the Lord, such a total ban on divorce has been difficult for the church since the time of Matthew, who inserts a Shammai-type provision with his μὴ ἐπὶ πορνείᾳ, 'except for unchastity' (Matt. 19.9). Jesus' appeal to God's original intention in creation, McDonald suggests, means that 'the primary moral question is not "Is divorce permissible?" but rather, "To what does God call us?"'[76] What is also noticeable for Mark's particular redaction is that in his account here the kingdom presupposes an inclusive community, where women have the same rights and protection as men, so that Jesus' explanation to his disciples carefully balances both genders (10.11-12).[77] Myers notes that such equality is both 'a critique of patriarchy' and 'directly contradicted Jewish law'.[78]

Mark's narrative continues immediately with the story about Jesus rebuking the disciples for preventing children from coming to be blessed by him (10.13-16). The point of this pericope teaches another lesson about entering the kingdom — that it should be received 'as a little child' would do so (10.15). But it is also significant that the previous verse goes beyond the role of children as merely a lesson to adults: as Schrage points out, children themselves 'are members of the community'.[79]

Thus, once again it is the kingdom which takes priority. As Matera sums up this chapter, 'In the light of God's kingly rule, Jesus makes extraordinary demands upon disciples: They must not divorce their spouses; they must welcome children; . . . they must be willing to sacrifice all their possessions for the sake of the kingdom',[80] which takes us into the next area of Mark's ethical material.

c. Money and possessions

Therefore we move on in Mark's collection of ethical issues in the kingdom to the area of money and possessions.[81] In Mark's account, an individual, εἷς, comes and addresses Jesus as 'Good teacher' (10.17-22); note that at this point

---

76. McDonald, *Crucible of Christian Morality*, p. 112.

77. William Loader, *Sexuality and the Jesus Tradition* (Grand Rapids: Eerdmans, 2005), pp. 77-80, 116-17.

78. Myers, *Binding the Strong Man*, pp. 264-66.

79. Schrage, *The Ethics of the NT*, p. 141.

80. Matera, *NT Ethics*, p. 29.

81. See further Via, *The Ethics of Mark's Gospel*, pp. 134-55.

we are not even told that he is rich, nor that he is 'young' (which is found in Matt. 19.22), nor 'a ruler' (as in Luke 18.18). The address, 'teacher', takes us back to Mark's key title for Jesus — and this time we will get some teaching — but again Jesus deflects attention back to God alone as the one who is good. In reciting the commandments, Jesus quotes the second table with the prohibitions against murder, adultery, stealing and false witness, ending with the command to honour one's parents. In between, he says, μὴ ἀποστερήσῃς, 'you shall not defraud', which is omitted by Matthew and Luke. Some take this to stand for the last of the Ten Commandments, that against coveting, but Myers argues instead that it is used for 'economic exploitation', which refers to keeping back the wages of a hireling.[82]

In response to the man's zealous reply that he has kept these 'since my youth', Jesus looks at him with love, ἐμβλέψας αὐτῷ ἠγάπησεν αὐτόν, which is the only place where Mark tells us he loved someone. Therefore Jesus invites him to sell everything and become a follower. Verhey says that this additional 'commandment [10.21] may not be understood as a new regulation but as the statement of a moral posture that is freed from bondage to possessions . . . not based on law but on an heroic confidence in God'.[83] Unfortunately, the response of the man is not to love Jesus in return and follow him, but to go away grieving. We argued in the second chapter above that Jesus was more concerned for a response to his preaching than for obedience to ethical maxims. Loessl says that 'this love-relationship is not a violent force or a rigid principle. It is a gentle invitation and can be bluntly rejected'; this 'personal Christological dimension' is essential to understanding the ethics of Jesus in the gospels.[84] Only then, as the man departs, does Mark finally tell us that he had 'many possessions' (10.22).

There then follows the exchange between Jesus and his disciples about how hard it is for the rich to enter heaven with the famous saying about a camel going through the eye of a needle (10.23-31). Once again, Jesus redirects his disciples' attention back to God, for such an all-demanding ethic is impossible for human beings, but everything is possible for God (10.23-27). Not surprisingly, Peter protests about the sacrifices he and the others have made in leaving everything to follow Jesus. In reply, Jesus gives him the eschatological promise of multiple rewards of homes and families to his followers in a kingdom where 'many who are first will be last, and the last will be first' (10.28-31). Thus the

---

82. Myers, *Binding the Strong Man*, pp. 272-73; see also D. E. Nineham, *The Gospel of St. Mark* (London: Penguin, 1963), p. 274.

83. Verhey, *The Great Reversal*, p. 81.

84. Loessl, 'The Ethical Dimension of Mk. 10.17-22', pp. 76-77.

area of money and possessions is turned upside-down by the rule of God in exactly the same way as we have seen with family life, marriage and children. Everything in the sphere of 'personal ethics' is relativized by the kingdom, so now we need to move our study out into wider society.

d. Power, leadership and the state

Finally, therefore, in chap. 10, and in this section, we come to the area of power and leadership in the church and world. This is prefaced by the third passion prediction, the most explicit warning to the disciples of Jesus' coming suffering (10.32-34; see 8.31-33 and 9.30-32 for the two previous predictions). To show how little they have understood all of this, James and John come forward to request the seats of honour in heaven. When the others realize what is going on, 'they began to be angry with James and John', though one suspects that this was because they were annoyed at the attempt to outflank them, rather than any 'righteous anger' at such an un-gospel-like request! This is all part of Mark's portrayal of the disciples being slow to grasp what it means to live in the kingdom.[85] The early church's embarrassment at the behaviour of its leaders is shown by the fact that Luke leaves out this story altogether, while Matthew has their mother make the request for her boys (Matt. 20.20-23)! In any case, their reward is to be granted to share Jesus' cup and baptism, his suffering and death, for this is what leadership means in the kingdom (Mark 10.35-41). The rulers of the Gentiles might like 'to lord it over them . . . but it is not so among you'.[86] The pattern for those in the kingdom is to follow Jesus, who 'came not to be served but to serve, and to give his life a ransom for many' (10.42-45) — what Via calls 'the ethics of servanthood'.[87] Verhey describes this as an 'heroic effort in the midst of opposition to demonstrate and participate in God's reign — even politically'.[88]

What is meant by that is perhaps best seen by our final section of direct ethical teaching in Mark. After Jesus' entry into Jerusalem and all the material about the fig tree and the vineyard, representing Israel's not being ready with the appropriate response to God's arrival, comes the authorities' question about paying the census, κῆνσος, or poll-tax to Caesar (12.13-17). Once again, as

85. See on Weeden, 'The Heresy That Necessitated Mark's Gospel', and *Mark: Traditions in Conflict*, n. 31 above and sect. 5.a below for the debate about Mark's picture of the disciples.

86. See further Alberto de Mingo Kaminouchi, *'But It Is Not So Among You': Echoes of Power in Mark 10.32-45*, JSNTSS 249 (London: T&T Clark, 2003).

87. Via, *The Ethics of Mark's Gospel*, pp. 156-68.

88. Verhey, *The Great Reversal*, p. 77.

with the rich man, Jesus is flattered by being given the title 'teacher', but their question raises the key ethical issue of obedience to the state. Jesus' request for them to bring him a denarius immediately exposes their hypocrisy: as a law-obedient Jew, he did not carry on his person an imperial coin with its graven image of Tiberius and its 'blasphemous ascription of divinity to the Roman Caesar',[89] which violated the first three commandments; however, they do not seem to have any trouble producing one! Jesus' reply, 'Render to Caesar the things that are Caesar's, and to God the things that are God's', is sometimes explained as legitimating a sacred-secular divide for two parallel spheres of sovereignty by those Myers terms 'bourgois exegetes'.[90] In fact, of course, for a patriotic Jew nothing really belongs to Caesar, since everything belongs to God. So, once again, we are back to Mark's central ethical theme of the kingdom, which challenges all human areas of human life, both personal and in wider society, with the sovereign rule of God, and where 'all things are possible with God'.

We began by noting the general scholarly view of the 'paucity of ethical material' in Mark and countered this by concentrating on his portrait of Jesus throughout the gospel, noting its ethical implications. We have also seen how the breaking in of the kingdom relativizes everything and even reinterprets the law with the all-demanding love of God. However, this study of what ethical teaching Mark does contain has demonstrated that, in fact, this gospel does touch on many key ethical experiences — the family, marriage and divorce, children, money and possessions, leadership, taxes and the state — and consistently reexamines them in the light of the sovereignty of God. As Telford concludes, 'The Markan Gospel still has much to offer to contemporary ethical debate'.[91] However, rather than just extracting the different bits of ethical teaching, such as chap. 10, out of the gospel for study, as in most approaches to New Testament ethics, our method locates this material within the overall biographical narrative of Jesus' words and deeds. His ethical teaching about the way the kingdom of God impacts upon human moral experiences is only part of the overall picture of how Jesus himself lived his life in the light of God's sovereign rule, despite the cost of suffering and self-denial. Thus our reading of Mark has demonstrated that, far from having no ethics, this gospel follows the historical Jesus in making the total demand upon those who would be his disciples. Finally, therefore, we need to turn to how Mark expects us to follow and imitate his way.

89. Evans, *Mark 8:27–16:20*, p. 247; see also Hooker, The *Gospel according to St Mark*, pp. 280-81.

90. Myers, *Binding the Strong Man*, p. 312; spelling *sic*.

91. Telford, *The Theology of the Gospel of Mark*, p. 225.

5. Following and imitating Jesus, the friend of sinners

The central thesis of this book is that according to the biographical hypothesis, the genre of the gospels means taking Jesus' deeds as seriously as his words — or even more so. As has just been demonstrated, this means that we do not just look for ethical teaching and abstract it from the narrative; rather, the whole narrative itself becomes charged with ethical import. Furthermore, we have argued that the moral imitation of the subject was an important purpose of ancient biography. In the case of Jesus, we discovered that his demanding ethical teaching was delivered in the context of keeping company with outsiders and sinners, those who had ethical difficulties, yet he seems to have accepted them, ate and lived with them — which leaves us with the challenge of how imitating him requires New Testament ethics to be done within an inclusive community. Similarly with Paul, we noted his frequent appeals for the imitation of Jesus by his readers, who lived in diverse communities which actually were more inclusive than many reconstructions of Paul have previously assumed. Therefore, having looked at Mark's account of Jesus and his ethical teaching, we need to see whether he too follows a similar pattern.

a. Following in discipleship

In fact, the remarkable thing is that practically everyone agrees that the key thrust of Mark's gospel is following Jesus in an ethic of discipleship.[92] So common is this theme of discipleship that Black took it as his test-case for his analysis of how different scholars view Markan redaction.[93] As Verhey puts it, Mark 'has ordered and shaped the traditional materials to bring into prominence the call to discipleship'.[94]

92. See, for example, Ernest Best, *Following Jesus: Discipleship in the Gospel of Mark,* JSNTSS 4 (Sheffield: JSOT Press, 1981), and idem, *Disciples and Discipleship: Studies in the Gospel according to Mark* (Edinburgh: T&T Clark, 1986); Morna D. Hooker, *The Message of Mark* (London: Epworth, 1983), pp. 105-21; Larry W. Hurtado, 'Following Jesus in the Gospel of Mark — And Beyond', in *Patterns of Discipleship in the New Testament,* ed. Richard N. Longenecker (Grand Rapids: Eerdmans, 1996), pp. 9-29; Elizabeth Struthers Malbon, *In the Company of Jesus: Characters in Mark's Gospel* (Louisville: Westminster John Knox, 2000); Swartley, 'Mark: Gospel of the Way, Crucified Messiah', chap. 4 in his *Covenant of Peace,* pp. 92-120; Holladay, *A Critical Introduction to the New Testament,* pp. 119-21; Witherington, *The Gospel of Mark,* pp. 421-42; Schrage, *The Ethics of the NT,* pp. 138-43; Hays, *Moral Vision of the NT,* pp. 80-85; Rhoads and Michie, *Mark as Story,* pp. 122-29; Kee, *Community of the New Age,* pp. 87-97; Kingsbury, *Conflict in Mark: Jesus, Authorities, Disciples,* pp. 89-117.

93. C. Clifton Black, *The Disciples according to Mark: Markan Redaction in Current Debate,* JSNTSS 27 (Sheffield: Sheffield Academic Press, 1989).

94. Verhey, *The Great Reversal,* p. 75.

This call begins at the opening of the gospel with the start of Jesus' ministry: 'Jesus came to Galilee, proclaiming the good news of God, and saying, "The time is fulfilled, and the kingdom of God has come near; repent, and believe in the gospel"' (Mark 1.14-15). We have found the kingdom of God to be foundational for everything in this gospel: 'Put simply, Jesus' initial proclamation of the kingdom is the key to unlocking all that he says and does. His ministry is a constant call to repent and believe in God's good news that the kingdom of God has made its initial appearance'.[95] Thus the opening proclamation is immediately followed by the call of the first disciples (1.16-20). As Loessl puts it, 'The basis is the call to follow Jesus as a response to his love'.[96] After the collection of stories about the conflict with the religious leaders (2.1–3.11) and before the triple sandwich about Jesus' family and the Beelzebul controversy (3.19b-35), Mark places the appointment of the twelve apostles from among the wider group of disciples (3.13-19): these are the inner group who are called to follow and to share Jesus' conflict, as well as his ministry. Yet we have noted how they themselves struggle to understand what is going on. As Charry memorably puts it, it is about 'following an unfollowable God'.[97]

The real nature of discipleship is further clarified at Caesarea Philippi where Peter's confession finally gets something right in his recognition of Jesus as Messiah, only for him to be rebuked when he protests against Jesus' first prediction of his suffering and death (8.27-32). Peter and the disciples have to learn that discipleship is costly: if Jesus is going to Jerusalem to suffer and die, then anyone who wants to follow him must 'deny themselves and take up their cross and follow me' (8.34).[98] As J. T. Sanders observes, 'Left alone, this understanding possesses the possibility of providing a noble, albeit individualistic, ethics. But Mark's discipleship cannot be left with self-denial and taking up one's cross; for one must ask where Jesus is going, i.e. where one is to follow'.[99] This is clarified by the sequence of three passion predictions, becoming more detailed to make the point (8.31; 9.31; 10.32-34).[100] Hays concludes, 'The way of the cross is simply the obedience to the

95. Matera, *NT Ethics*, p. 21.

96. Loessl, 'The Ethical Dimension of Mk. 10.17-22', p. 74.

97. Ellen T. Charry, 'Following an Unfollowable God', in *The Ending of Mark and the Ends of God*, ed. Gaventa and Miller, pp. 155-63.

98. For a feminist reading of this verse which denies that it encourages any form of acceptance of victimization, see Joanna Dewey, '"Let Them Renounce Themselves and Take Up Their Cross": A Feminist Reading of Mark 8:34 in Mark's Social and Narrative World', in *A Feminist Companion to Mark*, ed. Levine, pp. 23-36.

99. J. T. Sanders, *Ethics in the NT*, p. 33.

100. Kingsbury, *Conflict in Mark: Jesus, Authorities, Disciples*, pp. 103-11.

will of God, and discipleship requires following that way regardless of cost or consequences'.[101]

Given the centrality of discipleship for Mark, it is not surprising that the failure of the disciples to understand and provide a good model of how to follow should have caused much scholarly debate. We have already noted Weeden's theory that they stand for Mark's opponents.[102] The problem is that this does not deal with the fact that there is also positive material about the disciples, which is why what Telford calls the more 'pastoral or pedagogic explanation' of Tannehill and Best is more likely[103] — namely, that Mark's purpose is to encourage his suffering readers to identify with the disciples. This is where our argument about gospel genre can make a distinct contribution, for in a biographical narrative every motif reflects on the character of the main subject, so that the disciples' failure to grasp everything immediately adds to Mark's portrayal of Jesus as hard to follow — and hence, therefore, further pastoral encouragement to struggling would-be disciples in his audience. Given the particular failure of the male disciples in this gospel, Philip Groves was inspired by his Tanzanian context to note how the women in Mark are 'models of discipleship and leadership . . . examples for all Christian disciples', citing Simon's mother-in-law, the woman with the haemorrhage, the Syrophoenician and the widow with her mite (1.31; 5.25-34; 7.25-30; 12.41-44).[104]

What is crucial is that, despite their failures and struggles, the disciples do keep following, all the way to Jerusalem. Although Peter protests about the passion prediction and James and John request the best seats in heaven with Jesus, they are still the three disciples invited to witness the transfiguration and to pray with Jesus in Gethsemane (9.2-8; 14.33). Peter may eventually be forced to deny Jesus at the fireside — but that is only because he has kept his promise and continued to follow Jesus when others fled, even into the high priest's courtyard

---

101. Hays, *Moral Vision of the NT*, pp. 84-85.

102. Weeden, 'The Heresy That Necessitated Mark's Gospel'; idem, *Mark: Traditions in Conflict*; see n. 31 above.

103. W. R. Telford, *The Theology of the Gospel of Mark* (Cambridge: Cambridge University Press, 1999), pp. 127-37, quotation from p. 131; see Robert C. Tannehill, 'The Disciples in Mark: The Function of a Narrative Role', *JR* 57 (1977), pp. 386-405, repr. in *The Interpretation of Mark*, ed. Telford (1985), pp. 134-57; 2nd edn. (Edinburgh: T&T Clark, 1995), pp. 169-95; E. R. Best, 'The Role of the Disciples in Mark', *NTS* 23 (1976-77), pp. 377-401, repr. in idem, *Disciples and Discipleship*, pp. 98-130; see also Kingsbury, *Conflict in Mark: Jesus, Authorities, Disciples*, pp. 89-117.

104. Philip Groves, 'The Least in the Community of Jesus as Examples for Leadership Today', *Anvil* 15.1 (1998), pp. 13-21, esp. pp. 17-18; Myers similarly deduces from Mark's attack on 'patriarchy and domination' that women are the 'true servant-leaders', *Binding the Strong Man*, pp. 280-81; for further discussion, see Hisako Kinukawa, 'Women Disciples of Jesus (15.40-41; 15.47; 16.1)', in *A Feminist Companion to Mark*, ed. Levine, pp. 171-90.

(14.29, 50, 54, 66-72). Thus, as Best concludes his study, 'The role of the disciples in the gospel is then to be examples to the community. Not examples by which their own worth or failure is shown, but examples through whom teaching is given to the community and the love and power of God made known'.[105]

Therefore, the general presumption in the genre of ancient biography that the narrative of the subject provides an example to follow is greatly amplified here by Mark's deliberate stress on how Jesus' preaching of the kingdom requires a total response in wholehearted discipleship. Furthermore, the disciples themselves, despite their failings, also provide a further model for Mark's audience to learn from and emulate.

b. A mixed group

So Jesus' disciples may struggle to follow, but follow they do — and what a mixed bunch they are. The list of the apostles contains names redolent of the great Jewish leaders from the period of the Maccabees, James and John and Matthew (3.13-19). Yet we also have Greek names like Andrew and Philip. Simon 'the Cananaean' does not mean he came from Canaan, but is a Greek transliteration of the Aramaic *qan'ana'*, meaning 'the Zealot' (as it is translated in Luke 6.15), a freedom fighter or terrorist depending on one's viewpoint, who must have sat uneasily alongside tax collectors like Levi son of Alphaeus (2.14). If 'Iscariot' also does not mean that Judas came from Kerioth, but rather was a *sicarius* or dagger carrier, this contributes more to the mix.[106] Add to this Jesus' habit of 'eating and drinking with tax collectors and sinners', it is not surprising that he comes in for criticism about the company he kept. Mark records his reply as, 'Those who are well have no need of a physician, but those who are sick; I have come to call not the righteous but sinners' (2.13-17).

Similarly, Kee deduces from the setting aside of ritual Jewish separateness in 7.1-30 'that this was an issue for Mark's community, but one on which a firm position had been taken: the community was open across social, economic, sexual, and ethnic barriers'.[107] We have already noted that Mark seems to presuppose equal rights and responsibilities for women among his audience and that children also have their place as members within the kingdom of God (10.11-12,

---

105. Best, 'The Role of the Disciples in Mark', in *Disciples and Discipleship*, p. 130.

106. Guelich, *Mark 1–8.26*, pp. 162-63; NRSV translates *sicarii* as 'assassins' in Acts 21.38; for a discussion of Iscariot and *sicarius*, see R. E. Brown, *The Death of the Messiah* (New York: Doubleday, 1994), pp. 1414-15; for a full account of the *sicarii*, see Crossan, *The Historical Jesus*, pp. 117-23.

107. Kee, *Community of the New Age*, p. 97.

14). Loader wants to take this further in his conclusion on Jesus and the law in Mark: 'Inclusiveness has become a hermeneutical criterion [for Mark], as it had for Paul. . . . One can even extend a Markan perspective on scripture from inclusion of Gentiles to inclusion of many others, excluded on grounds of their social status (slaves), gender, race, age, sexual orientation or disability.'[108] Another indication of Mark's inclusiveness is that the final scene is given over to the first witnesses of the resurrection, namely some women who were so frightened (doubtless about the men's reaction to their news, cp. Luke 24.11) that they did not tell anyone (Mark 16.8)! As Struthers Malbon notes, 'No one is excluded from followership; no one is protected from fallibility'.[109]

Thus Mark's narrative makes the important point that following Jesus can never be simply an individual matter. Discipleship takes place within the context of the community of all those who are also responding, though that may be a very mixed group which includes others with whom we might not normally consort. All such differences are also relativized by the sovereign call of the kingdom of God.

c. Imitating Jesus

Finally, if Mark is about 'following Jesus' and his gospel was aimed at an open and inclusive community, this leads naturally to our final issue, that of the imitation of Jesus. It is interesting that various studies of Mark's ethics also seem to come to this conclusion. For instance, McDonald says, 'Disciples of Jesus did not simply follow his teaching; rather, they "took up the cross" and followed him',[110] and Best agrees, 'This does not imply that for Mark to be a disciple simply means to imitate Christ. Jesus took up his cross, denied himself, served others; the disciple is summoned to do all these.'[111] Given that ancient biography was about deeds as much as words, and action more than teaching, this should not be surprising. Here we have a good example of how the genre of a work communicates its intention and provides a crucial clue about how to read its ethics. Even though most of these scholars are not necessarily working from

---

108. Loader, *Jesus' Attitude towards the Law*, p. 136.

109. Elizabeth Struthers Malbon, 'Fallible Followers: Women and Men in the Gospel of Mark', *Semeia* 28 (1983), pp. 29-48, repr. in Malbon's collection, *In the Company of Jesus: Characters in Mark's Gospel* (Louisville: Westminster John Knox, 2000), pp. 41-69, quotation from p. 67; see also Richard Bauckham, *Gospel Women: Studies of the Named Women in the Gospels* (Grand Rapids: Eerdmans, 2002), pp. 286-95.

110. McDonald, *Crucible of Christian Morality*, p. 108.

111. Best, *Following Jesus*, p. 248.

our biographical hypothesis, the text has communicated its intention for moral imitation to them: so Matera has a whole section entitled 'Jesus a model for moral behaviour', while Hays describes him as 'the singular pattern for faithfulness'.[112] Now that we have made the biographical genre explicit, we have a good reason for this model patterning.

Therefore, Hooker is right to sum all this up when she notes that 'commentators frequently shy away from suggestions that discipleship is seen in terms of the imitation of Christ in the New Testament, but there is no doubt that Mark sees it in these terms'.[113] Our argument from the biographical approach to the gospels and to ethics means that commentators need 'shy away' no longer! For Mark's central ethical theme, made clear in both Jesus' words and deeds, is for his audience to follow Jesus as disciples along the way of the cross, and this fits in very well with the mimetic purpose of ancient biographical narratives. The readers of this text are not called just to follow Jesus, but to imitate him in his words and deeds, life and death. This must also entail, therefore, imitating his open acceptance of others within the inclusive community of all those who are following.

6. Conclusion

We began this study by noting that some commentators think that Mark's gospel has 'relatively little moral teaching' or a 'paucity of ethical material'. However, this is the result of the basic genre mistake committed by so many who read the gospels, looking for an ethical treatise like the Sermon on the Mount or at least a collection of pithy sayings. Once we approach these texts as biographical narratives, a wealth of ethical possibilities starts to emerge. Our study of Mark's Christology and eschatology demonstrated the importance of his narrative of Jesus' own life of service and self-sacrifice in proclaiming, and eventually dying for, the sovereign rule of God; as Matera sums it up, 'The ethics of Jesus in Mark's Gospel are necessarily bound up with the story of Jesus. To know that story is to be shaped by a new ethical vision whose horizon is none other than the in-breaking kingdom of God.'[114] Furthermore, if the gospel was written in the dark days of the 60s, it is no wonder that its eschatological call to endure suffering while expecting the final cataclysm imminently has continued to speak in particular to generations of readers suffering persecution and tribulations.

112. Matera, *NT Ethics*, pp. 31-34; Hays, *Moral Vision of the NT*, p. 84.
113. Hooker, *The Message of Mark*, pp. 110-11.
114. Matera, *NT Ethics*, p. 35.

This radical vision of the kingdom also dominated Mark's account of how Jesus handles the law, both strengthening some of its demands (e.g., over divorce) or setting aside others (such as over the food purity laws); in all cases, this is the effect of Mark's placing the double love command at the centre of Jesus' teaching. Contrary to expectations, consideration of the actual ethical teaching material which Mark does contain revealed that many of our key human moral experiences — the family, marriage, divorce and children, money and possessions, power, leadership and the state — all appear, and are also treated according to the same radicalizing principles of love and the priority of the sovereign rule of God. Such demanding ethical teaching is not just given in the words of Jesus, but in his deeds, as they are portrayed in Mark's biographical account of how he himself lived. Finally, Mark's central theme of discipleship, coupled with his portrait of the disciples struggling to believe and understand, is securely located within his depiction of an open and inclusive community. Therefore, for Mark, as for Paul, following Jesus inevitably entails imitating his deeds and words, seeking to obey his ethical teachings while emulating his life of self-sacrifice in a loving acceptance of others, whoever they may be.

V. Matthew: Being Truly Righteous

Mark forms an intermediate layer in our excavation, coming between Paul's letters and the other gospels. If Mark was written in the turbulent 60s against the background of Nero's persecutions at Rome and the Jewish war, then this goes some way towards explaining his interim ethic about suffering and radical discipleship in which the kingdom takes priority over everything, including the law, in the expectation of the imminent end of all things. It is hard for us to imagine just how profound an effect the destruction of Jerusalem in AD 70 must have had upon all Jews across the ancient Mediterranean. With many of the different groups within Second Temple Judaism wiped out and the focal point of the temple (which used to unify them all) razed to the ground, the Jews who survived had to find new ways of relating to one another and to their tradition. In addition, those Jews who accepted Jesus of Nazareth as Messiah had the tension of being caught in the middle between other Jews, who did not accept him, and the growing early Christian communities, especially from the Pauline tradition, who included Gentiles. Furthermore, since the destruction of Jerusalem had not provoked the expected final apocalyptic climax of history, there was the need to reconsider how the message about Jesus' deeds and words, his proclamation of the eschatological kingdom of God, and the narrative of his life, death and resurrection could all be applied to the new postwar situation in the next decade or two.

In this way, we share the scholarly consensus that Mark was the first gospel to be written and is later followed by Matthew as his main source, together with a collection of Jesus' sayings which are referred to under the general heading of Q (for *Quelle*, or 'source' in German), although the extent to which they formed a single written document is much debated.[1] In this chapter, we turn to discover what happens when Matthew rewrites Mark for his new situation. If our argument about the genre of Mark's gospel has been more widely accepted, this is even more true for Matthew, who takes Mark's overall biographical narrative, but conforms it still more to the expectations of ancient 'lives', *bioi*, not least with the addition of his opening chapters about Jesus' ancestry and birth. Thus more recent scholarly work has increasingly accepted my arguments for the biographical genre of Matthew as a basis upon which to develop further discussion and interpretation; as Stanton concludes, 'There is little doubt that early Christian readers of the gospels did read them as biographies'.[2]

As with Mark, therefore, we shall now read Matthew's gospel as a biographical narrative of Jesus' words and deeds, his teachings, life, death and resurrection, looking at the ethical implications of this as a whole rather than merely extracting his ethical material, such as the Sermon on the Mount (which is what usually happens with studies of Matthew's ethics). In doing so, we shall follow the same basic structure as in previous chapters, beginning with Matthew's Christology and his portrait of Jesus, his setting and eschatology, before going on to look at his treatment of the law and love, followed finally by consideration of his particular ethical material; we shall then conclude by considering whether and how Matthew intends his audience to imitate Jesus, and within what sort of community of disciples.

---

1. On Matthew's sources, see, for example, W. D. Davies and Dale C. Allison, *The Gospel according to Saint Matthew*, International Critical Commentary, vol. 1 (Edinburgh: T&T Clark, 1988), pp. 97-138, and G. N. Stanton, *A Gospel for a New People: Studies in Matthew* (Edinburgh: T&T Clark, 1992), pp. 23-53; on Q, see John S. Kloppenborg, *The Formation of Q: Trajectories in Ancient Wisdom Collections* (Philadelphia: Fortress, 1987); David R. Catchpole, *The Quest for Q* (Edinburgh: T&T Clark, 1993) and James D. G. Dunn, *Jesus Remembered* (Grand Rapids: Eerdmans, 2003), pp. 147-61; we shall explore Matthew's possible setting and date shortly in sect. 2 below, pp. 199-203.

2. Graham Stanton, *The Gospels and Jesus* (Oxford: Oxford University Press, 2nd edn. 2002), p. 16-17; see also his *A Gospel for a New People*, pp. 59-71; for other examples of the use of my arguments about genre in others' interpretations of Matthew, see also David E. Garland, *Reading Matthew: A Literary and Theological Commentary on the First Gospel* (London: SPCK, 1993), pp. 5-9; Craig S. Keener, *A Commentary on the Gospel of Matthew* (Grand Rapids: Eerdmans, 1999), pp. 16-24, esp. p. 17, n. 46; Warren Carter, *Matthew: Storyteller, Interpreter, Evangelist* (Peabody, MA: Hendrickson, rev. edn. 2004), pp. 40-42, 45-46, 167-69 and 182; Dale C. Allison, Jr., 'Structure, Biographical Impulse, and the *Imitatio Christi*', in his *Studies in Matthew: Interpretation Past and Present* (Grand Rapids: Baker Academic, 2005), pp. 135-55, esp. pp. 142-47.

1. Matthew's Christology

It is not surprising that if Mark's portrait of Jesus is rather dark and riddling, Matthew has traditionally been represented by the symbol of the human face, to use the four images taken from the visions of Ezek. 1 and Rev. 4–5.[3] While he does follow Mark's basic account, his extra material tries to answer the obvious questions arising from Mark's narrative, such as where Jesus came from, what his teaching comprised and why it brought him into conflict with the religious authorities. As Gerhardsson says, 'Matthean Christology has a conspicuous ethical dimension'.[4] Thus, as with our account of Mark, rather than looking just at Christological titles, we will again trace the story of Jesus in the whole narrative, as well as Matthew's accompanying story of the developing conflict.[5] In this way, we will begin to gather some understanding of Matthew's particular approach to Jesus' ethics as portrayed in both his words and his deeds.

a. The story of Jesus

'At the center of Matthew's interest is not Jesus' message, but Jesus himself. The First Gospel is strongly Christocentric.'[6] Matthew makes this clear when he begins his story with, 'An account of the genealogy of Jesus Christ, the son of David, the son of Abraham' (Matt. 1.1). The first two Greek words, βίβλος γενέσεως, literally mean 'the book of genesis', and the intratextual referral to the opening of the Hebrew scriptures is unmistakable, especially when followed by the identification of Jesus as the son of David and the son of Abraham.[7] The actual genealogy which follows makes the same point, being structured in three groups of fourteen generations, from Abraham to David (1.2-6), David to the exile (1.6-11), and thence to Jesus himself (1.11-16), with the numerical point reiterated in his summary (1.17): given that fourteen is the sum of the numerical value of the He-

3. Richard A. Burridge, *Four Gospels, One Jesus? A Symbolic Reading* (Grand Rapids: Eerdmans/London: SPCK, rev. edn. 2005), pp. 25-33 for the four symbols and pp. 67-99 for an account of Matthew's portrait of Jesus.

4. Birger Gerhardsson, 'The Christology of Matthew', in *Who Do You Say That I Am? Essays on Christology in Honor of Jack Dean Kingsbury*, ed. David R. Bauer and Mark Allan Powell (Louisville: Westminster John Knox, 1999), pp. 14-32, quotation from p. 26.

5. See further Jack Dean Kingsbury's classic study, *Matthew as Story* (Philadelphia: Fortress, 2nd rev. edn. 1988), and his earlier book, *Matthew: Structure, Christology, Kingdom* (Philadelphia: Fortress, 1975).

6. Birger Gerhardsson, *The Ethos of the Bible* (Philadelphia: Fortress, 1981), p. 34.

7. Dale C. Allison, Jr., 'Matthew's First Two Words (Matt. 1:1)', in his *Studies in Matthew: Interpretation Past and Present*, pp. 157-62.

brew letters *d-w-d* for David, it is as though Matthew is claiming that Jesus is David three times over![8] This Hebrew Bible atmosphere continues through the birth narrative, with angels, prophecy and a miraculous birth (1.18-25), reminding us of the birth stories of Ishmael or Samson (Gen. 16; Judg. 13). Jesus shares his name with the hero Joshua, meaning 'God is salvation', and he is also Emmanuel, 'God with us' (1.21-23). The events of his birth recapitulate the story of Moses, as the baby has to be saved from an evil king's slaughtering (Exod. 1.15-20; cp. Matt. 2.16-18) and has to flee for his life to another land (Exod. 2.15-22; cp. Matt. 2.13-14), to return only after the death of the king (Exod. 2.23; cp. Matt. 2.19-20), which also involves taking wife and sons (Exod. 4.20; cp. Matt. 2.21). The narrative echoes are unmistakable.[9]

After this introduction, the main story continues to recall Moses, as Jesus goes through the river Jordan and is tested in the wilderness — but, unlike Israel, he remains faithful (3.13–4.11). Then Jesus goes 'up the mountain' to deliver his main teaching (5.1), as Moses gave the law.[10] What is more, Jesus continues to go up mountains at major points throughout this gospel: to resist temptation, 4.8; to pray, 14.23, to heal, 15.29-31 and to feed the people, 15.32-39; to be transfigured, 17.1; and finally to be worshipped and to commission his disciples, 28.16-20.[11] As Moses gave Israel the five books of the Pentateuch, so in Matthew Jesus gives his teaching in five main discourses: the Sermon on the Mount (5–7), the mission charge (10), the parables of the kingdom (13), the new community (18) and eschatological teaching (24–25); all five sermons end with the same formula, 'when Jesus had finished saying these things' (7.28; 11.1; 13.53; 19.1; 26.1). Given how little actual direct ethical teaching Mark contained, such structuring by Matthew sends a deliberate message, that Jesus is '*the* teacher of morality'.[12] Nor are the parallels just with Moses: Meeks argues that 'one of Matthew's strategies is to depict Jesus as a teacher of wisdom, a "sage" like Ben Sira or like the rabbis' own

8. See Davies and Allison, *Matthew*, vol. 1, pp. 161-90; David R. Bauer, 'The Literary and Theological Function of the Genealogy in Matthew's Gospel', in *Treasures New and Old: Recent Contributions to Matthean Studies,* ed. David R. Bauer and Mark Allan Powell (Atlanta: Scholars Press, 1996), pp. 129-59.

9. On Matthew's opening chapters, see Morna D. Hooker, *Beginnings: Keys That Open the Gospels* (London: SCM, 1997), pp. 23-42.

10. On Jesus and Moses, see Dale C. Allison, *The New Moses: A Matthean Typology* (Edinburgh: T&T Clark, 1993); Christopher M. Tuckett, *Christology and the New Testament: Jesus and His Earliest Followers* (Edinburgh: Edinburgh University Press/Louisville: Westminster John Knox, 2001), pp. 126-27.

11. Terence L. Donaldson, *Jesus on the Mountain: A Study in Matthean Theology,* JSNTSS 8 (Sheffield: JSOT Press, 1985).

12. John P. Meier, *The Vision of Matthew: Christ, Church and Morality in the First Gospel* (New York: Paulist, 1979), pp. 45-51, his italics.

prototypes'.[13] In fact, in his analysis particularly of Matt. 11.2-19, Suggs argued that Jesus does not just speak wisdom, nor speak for the figure of Wisdom herself: he is nothing less than Wisdom incarnate.[14] This has been much debated over the years,[15] and has been restated by Deutsch and Witherington.[16]

What is important is that Matthew still sets these blocks of teaching within a narrative about Jesus. In between the five discourses, we have sections about his activity, with three triplets of miracle stories in chaps. 8–9, followed by the beginnings of rejection and conflict in 11.2–12.50; more miracles and opposition come after the parables of the kingdom, but Jesus is recognized by the Syrophoenician woman and in Peter's confession and the transfiguration (14.1–17.27). After the church discourse comes the journey to Jerusalem (chaps. 19–20) and the clash with the Jewish leaders (chaps. 21–23), while the eschatological discourse is followed by the events of Jesus' arrest, passion and resurrection (26–28). For all his stress on Jesus' teaching, Matthew still does not write just a collection of moral sayings: 'Fundamental for Matthew's ethics is its foundation in the person and work of Jesus'.[17] It is therefore significant that Carter has made use of my material on the gospel genre as ancient biography to argue that for Matthew's picture of Jesus: 'The audience deduces his character from his actions, words and relationships . . . as it moves through the sequence of the story.'[18] However, before we draw together the ethical implications of this story, we have to deal with the crucial issue of the conflict between Jesus and the Jewish authorities within the narrative.

b. The story of the conflict

With all the Old Testament resonances of the opening chapters, it should be no surprise that, like a new Moses, Jesus goes up a mountain to deliver his teaching

---

13. Meeks, *The Origins of Christian Morality*, pp. 199-201; see also idem, *The Moral World of the First Christians* (Philadelphia: Westminster, 1986), pp. 138-40.

14. M. Jack Suggs, *Wisdom, Christology, and Law in Matthew's Gospel* (Cambridge, MA: Harvard University Press, 1970).

15. See Dan O. Via, Jr., 'Structure, Christology, and Ethics in Matthew', in *Orientation by Disorientation: Studies in Literary Criticism and Biblical Literary Criticism, Presented in Honor of William A. Beardslee* (Pittsburgh: Pickwick, 1980), pp. 199-215; Frances Taylor Gench, *Wisdom in the Christology of Matthew* (Lanham, MD: University Press of America, 1997).

16. Celia M. Deutsch, *Lady Wisdom, Jesus and the Sages: Metaphor and Social Context in Matthew's Gospel* (Valley Forge, PA: Trinity Press International, 1996); Witherington, *The Many Faces of the Christ*, pp. 147-50.

17. Schrage, *The Ethics of the NT*, p. 144.

18. Warren Carter, *Matthew: Storyteller, Interpreter, Evangelist* (Peabody, MA: Hendrickson, rev. edn. 2004), pp. 168-69.

about the kingdom of heaven. What is unexpected is the growing dispute which ensues between this teacher of Israel, the human face of God, and the Jewish religious authorities.[19] 'In narrating his story of Jesus, Matthew employs a plot of conflict . . . between Jesus and Israel's leadership'.[20] This unfolding narrative begins when Herod consults with 'all the chief priests and scribes of the people' to ascertain where the Christ was to be born; the ensuing warnings, dreams and massacre hint at the rejection of Jesus to come (2.3-5, 12-18). After the Sermon on the Mount and several stories of miracles and healings, the first controversy comes with the call of Matthew from his tax booth and the complaint by the Pharisees about Jesus eating with tax collectors and sinners: it is met with the warning that a repair needs new cloth, and new wine requires fresh wineskins (9.9-17). Three further healings provoke the response from the crowd, 'Never has anything like this been seen in Israel'; unfortunately, the Pharisees' response is to make their first accusation, 'By the ruler of the demons he casts out the demons' (9.33-34). This is followed by a summary of Jesus' own mission of teaching and healing and his mission charge to the disciples (9.35–10.42); significantly, only in Matthew's account are they told not to go among the Gentiles or Samaritans, but 'rather to the lost sheep of the house of Israel', even though they will be rejected and persecuted (10.5-6, 16-25).

This warning is then fulfilled in the next section of narrative, where even John the Baptist questions if he is 'the one to come' (11.2-6), 'this generation' does not want to respond (11.16-19) and its towns ignore Jesus (11.20-24). Jesus reflects on hiddenness and revelation (11.25-30) and clashes with the Pharisees over plucking grain and healing on the sabbath (12.1-14). Then Matthew uses Isaiah's Servant Song to suggest that the Teacher will bring justice and hope to the Gentiles if Israel rejects him (12.15-21; cp. Isa. 42.1-4). Further conflict ensues in the Beelzebul controversy (12.22-45) and is hinted at with Jesus' own family, although toned down from Mark's version (12.46-50; cp. Mark 3.23-30, 31-35). Thus, it is not surprising that the central discourse hides things in parables with a theme of judgement and warnings not to be hard of heart (13.13-15).

After the parables of the kingdom, further opposition from the Pharisees (15.1-20) is contrasted with the faith of the Syrophoenician woman: Matthew alone has Jesus declare that he was 'sent only to the lost sheep of the house of Israel' (15.24); the woman kneels in worship and prays to Jesus, 'Lord, help me' (15.25), and declares her faith in him, 'O Lord, Son of David' (15.22, 27). While the disciples have 'little faith', Jesus responds, 'Woman, great is your faith!', and she receives her daughter's healing (15.28). Matthew is carefully suggesting that

19. For a fuller account, see Burridge, *Four Gospels, One Jesus?*, pp. 86-93.
20. Matera, *NT Christology*, p. 27.

as Israel questions and rejects her Teacher, so the Gentiles begin to receive his benefits. Therefore Peter's confession that Jesus is 'the Christ, the Son of the living God' is met by the first use of ἐκκλησία, the church, which Jesus will build on Peter's rock (16.16-19). After the passion predictions and transfiguration, the next discourse also deals with the life of this new community, with two more occurrences of 'church' (18.1-35, see esp. vv. 15, 17). For Carter, this has to be 'a community of sustaining relationships and practices', 'a countercultural alternative' to 'the dominant society . . . of empire and synagogue'.[21]

The journey to Jerusalem (19–20) follows Mark's account fairly closely, but the ensuing clash with the Jewish leaders is sharpened (21–23). As in Mark, they ask Jesus about his authority, but Matthew answers with the parable of the two sons with its praise of tax collectors and sinners, who may not say the right things but will go into the kingdom of heaven 'ahead of you' (21.23-32). Matthew's version of the tenants in the vineyard has a unique warning in v. 43 that the kingdom will be taken away from Israel and given to Gentiles (21.33-46, see esp. vv. 41, 43). Next comes Matthew's rendering of the parable of the marriage feast (22.1-14, which is not in Mark and occurs much earlier in Luke 14.16-24); it is fuller and includes the king destroying and burning their city (22.7, which reminds us of the destruction of Jerusalem in AD 70) and the unique rejection of the person who is unprepared and not clad in the right garment (21.11-14). Thus this collection of three stories in Matthew is applicable to the controversy with the Jewish leaders as well as to the future inclusion of the Gentiles. The whole range of Jewish leaders now join the conflict (chief priests and elders, 21.23; Pharisees and Herodians, 22.15-16; Sadducees, 22.23; a lawyer, 22.35) in four controversy stories; after this, the Jewish leaders are reduced to silence, and they withdraw from questioning him (22.46). The stage is clear for Matthew's final discourse: according to this teacher of Israel, her other teachers are hypocrites, even preventing others from entering the kingdom (23).

This is strong stuff indeed and requires some explanation: how is it that this most Jewish of gospels with Jesus recapitulating Moses and David while teaching about the 'law and prophets' can end up with such a bitter denunciation of the religious authorities that some consider it 'anti-Semitic' or 'anti-Jewish'?[22] As Stanton puts it, 'Matthew's vigorous anti-Jewish polemic is

21. Warren Carter, *Matthew and the Margins: A Sociopolitical and Religious Reading* (Maryknoll, NY: Orbis, 2000), p. 361; see pp. 361-75 for his commentary on chap. 18.

22. Scot McKnight prefers to use 'anti-Semitism for irrational, personal, racial prejudice against Jews because they are Jews; anti-Judaism for the religious polemic exercised especially by early Christians who thought rejecting Jesus as Messiah was abandoning God's covenant with Israel', in his 'A Loyal Critic: Matthew's Polemic with Judaism in Theological Perspective', in *Anti-Semitism and Early Christianity: Issues of Polemic and Faith*, ed. Craig A. Evans and Donald A.

acutely embarrassing to most modern readers of this gospel'.[23] Our analysis above has revealed a careful subplot running alongside the discourses which shows Jesus beginning only with 'the lost sheep of the house of Israel' but later founding his church and turning to the Gentiles as opposition and conflict grows. The language and content of the gospel indicate that both the author and his intended audience were thoroughly Jewish, but its atmosphere suggests that a painful split has occurred — and its attitude is not designed to woo over the opponents!

Jesus was a Jew, and all his first disciples were Jews preaching the good news about Jesus among their own people. First-century Judaism was a mixed culture with different groups, such as Pharisees, Sadducees, Essenes and Zealots, existing together; the early Christians seemed like just another group within Judaism. However, the Jewish revolt of AD 66-70, culminating in the destruction of Jerusalem and the temple, brought things to a head as many of the different religious, cultural, and political groups within prewar Judaism simply disappeared or were destroyed in the war. In an attempt to provide cohesion and a renewed identity, some rabbis gathered at Yavneh/Jamnia in the mid-80s; with the focus of Jerusalem and the temple gone, they centred Jewish faith and worship around the law and the synagogue, giving rise to the rabbinic tradition which has kept Judaism alive all around the world for two millennia. In a similar way, the Jewish followers of Jesus as Messiah were developing their identity around the focus on worship of him. It used to be thought a few decades ago that the so-called *birkat ha-minim,* the 'blessing against the heretics', was included in the synagogue liturgy around this time, together with its invocation against the *notzrim.* If this meant 'Nazarenes', then from that time Jewish-Christians could no longer worship with other Jews without cursing themselves, and so this precipitated the break between 'Jews' and 'Christians'.[24] However, more recently, doubt has been cast upon the exact dating of the *birkat ha-minim* and when it included the *notzrim.* It is better to see the parting of the

---

Hagner (Minneapolis: Fortress, 1993), pp. 55-79, quotation from p. 56; similar distinctions are used in William R. Farmer (ed.), *Anti-Judaism and the Gospels* (Harrisburg, PA: Trinity Press International, 1999), see, for example, pp. 4-5 and 49; on Matthew, see its opening articles, Amy-Jill Levine, 'Anti-Judaism and the Gospel of Matthew', pp. 9-36, with Responses from Philip L. Shuler, pp. 37-46, and Warren Carter, pp. 47-62.

23. G. N. Stanton, 'The Gospel of Matthew and Judaism', chap. 6 in his *A Gospel for a New People: Studies in Matthew* (Edinburgh: T&T Clark, 1992), pp. 146-68, quotation from p. 146; see also Carter, *Matthew and the Margins,* pp. 459-61; for a Jewish reading of how Matthew feels, see Samuel Sandmel, *Anti-Semitism in the New Testament?* (Philadelphia: Fortress, 1978), pp. 49-70.

24. See, for example, W. D. Davies, *The Setting of the Sermon on the Mount* (Cambridge: Cambridge University Press, 1966), pp. 256-315.

ways between the synagogue and the church as a gradual process, taking place around the Mediterranean during the end of the first century and beginning of the second, including local disagreements at various times rather than just one sudden break across all areas.[25]

Internal rows within families are often the most bitter, and civil wars the hardest fought. Matthew's portrayal of Jesus as the Teacher of Israel reflects the bitterness and pain of this separation: it was not a polite agreement to differ, or an amicable settlement.[26] Only Matthew warns that they will be flogged in synagogues and dragged before Gentile rulers, even by their own family (10.17-25). The synagogue is now 'their synagogue' (4.23; 9.35; 10.17; 12.9; 13.54) or 'your synagogue' (23.34), opposed to 'my church' (16.18).[27] Something similar happens with the Dead Sea Scrolls, which use even harsher language about the Jewish leaders in Jerusalem — yet no one calls them 'anti-Semitic'.[28] Severe criticism is tolerated within the family alone, and, as with all families and communities, today only Jewish comedians (or rabbis!) are allowed to tell Jewish jokes, and likewise for the Irish or whoever; as Levine concedes, 'The analogy to the ethnic joke is somewhat apt'.[29] Matthew is part of an argument going on within Judaism as he seeks to explain the theological problem for

25. See further Stanton, 'Synagogue and Church', chap. 5 in his *A Gospel for a New People,* pp. 113-45, esp. pp. 118-24 and 142-45 on the *birkath ha-minim* and how this hypothesis developed and more recently has been challenged again; see also Steven T. Katz, 'Issues in the Separation of Judaism and Christianity after 70 c.e.: A Reconsideration', *JBL* 103 (1984), pp. 43-76; P. W. van der Horst, 'The *Birkat ha-minim* in Recent Research', *ExpT* 105 (1993-94), pp. 363-68; Anthony J. Saldarini, *Matthew's Christian-Jewish Community* (Chicago: University of Chicago Press, 1994), pp. 3, 18-19, 220-21; see also Craig S. Keener's detailed treatment of both the *birkat* and local disagreements in his Introduction to his *The Gospel of John: A Commentary,* 2 vols. (Peabody, MA: Hendrickson, 2003), pp. 171-214. See further our similar discussion of the setting of John's gospel in Chapter VII, sect. 3.a, pp. 313-22 below.

26. Luz also uses the image of 'family conflict' for the separation and argues that rather than a mother-daughter rivalry (with Judaism as the parent body to early Christianity), it is more like 'sibling conflict' as 'the Pharisees and the Jesus movement . . . both tried to define themselves as Israel' after the war; Ulrich Luz, 'Anti-Judaism in the Gospel of Matthew as a Historical and Theological Problem: An Outline', in his *Studies in Matthew* (Grand Rapids: Eerdmans, 2005), pp. 243-61; quotation from p. 255.

27. Carter sees 'Matthew's (largely) Jewish community committed to Jesus' as 'involved in a local fight within a synagogue over its place in a common tradition'; see 'Tension with a Synagogue', in Carter, *Matthew and the Margins,* pp. 30-36, quotation from p. 36.

28. See Stanton's comparison of Matthew with the Damascus document as representing a painful split of the Qumran community from the wider parent body of Essenes: 'Matthew's Gospel and the Damascus Document in Sociological Perspective', chap. 4 in his *A Gospel for a New People,* pp. 85-110.

29. Levine, 'Anti-Judaism and the Gospel of Matthew', p. 19, though she goes on to have some criticisms of it.

Jewish Christians of why Israel rejected her teacher, the fulfilment of her scriptures and her hopes, of why the kingdom has gone to the Gentiles, and why Jerusalem was destroyed.[30] Thus Carter concludes, 'This gospel is not anti-Jewish in the way that this term has often been understood'.[31] Similarly, McKnight ends with his 'contention that Matthew's Gospel, however harsh and unpleasant to modern sensitivities, is not anti-Semitic. It is, on the contrary, a compassionate but vigorous appeal to nonmessianic Judaism to respond to the Messiah'.[32] But when it gets read 'outside the family', as Christian scripture, it can appear 'anti-Semitic', despite all its Semitisms, and 'anti-Jewish' despite its Jewish context.

This means that in our biographical narrative reading for Matthew's ethics, we must bear all of this in mind. He is like a scribe, bringing 'out of his treasure what is new and what is old' (13.52), seeking to hold together the law and the prophets with the new wine of the kingdom of heaven. Therefore, he depicts Jesus as the one who truly fulfils the law and prophets in his life and person, so that by following his teaching and his example, Matthew's audience can live a moral life which is still different from the practice of their opponents within early rabbinic Judaism.[33]

c. The climax of both stories

Both the main plot of the story of Jesus, the true teacher of Israel, and the subplot of his conflict with the religious leaders come to their climax with the events of Holy Week — his arrest, passion and death — in which the authorities appear to have won. Matthew follows Mark's account by including nearly every verse of his passion narrative in the same order,[34] with only twenty-six

30. See further Saldarini, *Matthew's Christian-Jewish Community;* David L. Balch (ed.), *Social History of the Matthean Community: Cross-Disciplinary Approaches* (Minneapolis: Fortress, 1991); and Donald A. Hagner, 'Matthew: Christian Judaism or Jewish Christianity', in *The Face of New Testament Studies: A Survey of Recent Research,* ed. Scot McKnight and Grant R. Osborne (Grand Rapids: Baker Academic, 2004), pp. 263-82.

31. Carter, *Matthew: Storyteller, Interpreter, Evangelist,* p. 237; see further, pp. 235-40; also his response to Levine in *Anti-Judaism and the Gospels,* ed. Farmer, pp. 47-62, and that by Shuler, pp. 37-46.

32. Scot McKnight, 'A Loyal Critic: Matthew's Polemic with Judaism in Theological Perspective', p. 77.

33. See Stanton, 'Christology and the Parting of the Ways', chap. 7 in his *A Gospel for a New People,* pp. 169-91.

34. Matthew omits the details about the young man (Mark 14.51-52) and Simon of Cyrene's sons (Mark 15.21b).

verses unique to himself, but they make a huge difference (26.1-2, 25, 52-54; 27.3-10, 19, 24-25, 29, 51b-53, 62-66).[35]

It begins with a fourth prediction of Jesus' passion, unique to Matthew, to make it clear that Jesus knows exactly what is about to happen (26.1-2). At the Last Supper, only Matthew has Jesus identify Judas as the betrayer in response to Judas' address, 'Rabbi', which is never used by other disciples in Matthew (26.25). When Judas again calls him 'Rabbi' in the garden, Jesus replies with 'Friend', as though giving permission for his arrest (26.50). Only in Matthew does Jesus tell his followers to put away the sword, saying that he has the power to call up 'more than twelve legions of angels' if he wishes; it is so 'that the scriptures may be fulfilled', a common motif throughout the gospel (26.52-54).

Among the gospels, only Matthew describes Judas' death (Matt. 27.3-10; Acts 1.18-20 has a different version), having previously included the unique comment that Judas actually asked for money (Matt. 26.15). Thirty pieces of silver is the compensation value of a slave's life (Exod. 21.32) and also the redundancy payoff for the rejected shepherd-prophet in Zech. 11.12, so this Old Testament background suggests that Jesus is the servant and shepherd-prophet rejected by his people. Matthew inserts the story of Judas into Mark's flow to stress the guilt of the religious leaders as 'the sons of Israel' (27.9). Mention of the Gentile ruler, Pilate, who calls Jesus 'King of the Jews', and his wife, who has a dream, reminds us of the wise men's quest for the 'King of the Jews' and their dreams right at the start of this gospel (Matt 2.1-12). Once again, Matthew's unique additions about Pilate's hand-washing and his wife's dream that Jesus is 'righteous', δίκαιος, focus the responsibility upon the Jewish authorities; this is compounded by the reply of 'all the people', 'His blood be on us and on our children!' (27.19, 24-25). As Carter points out, this does not exonerate or absolve him of his guilt: 'Roman justice is all washed up'![36] The soldiers put the reed-staff into his hand when they mock him to enhance the irony that he really is the King of the Jews (27.29). Matthew alone records the earthquake and opening of tombs at the moment of Jesus' death, making it like a typical Old Testament theophany, so that 'the centurion and those with him' all say that Jesus is the 'Son of God', unlike Mark's quiet word from the Roman alone (27.51b-54).

Matthew deletes Mark's description of Joseph of Arimathea as 'a respected member of the Sanhedrin' (Mark 15.43), since those leaders of Israel have rejected Jesus; instead, he calls him a disciple, one of the new community of faith (27.57). The persecution of Jesus by the chief priests and Pharisees continues even after his death with the setting of the guard on the tomb, unique to Mat-

35. For a fuller account, see Burridge, *Four Gospels, One Jesus?*, pp. 93-99.
36. Carter, *Matthew and the Margins*, p. 527.

thew (27.62-66). The last chapter describes the final separation with its three-fold structure of believers (28.1-10), opponents (28.11-15) and believers (28.16-20). With yet more Old Testament phenomena at the resurrection, the women meet Jesus and worship him, while the representatives of the authorities flee and take bribes to tell lies about the disciples, and 'this story is still told among the Jews to this day' (28.15). Meanwhile, the true community of faith have gone up another mountain to worship Jesus, the Emmanuel who promises to be 'with us', 'always, to the end of the age' (28.20; cp. 1.23). Now that Israel has rejected 'God among us' in the person of Jesus, the new people of God are commanded to 'go and make disciples of all nations' (28.19).

So both stories reach their climax on this mountain: as Luz puts it, 'The Gospel of Matthew is a story that needs to be read from beginning to end. It discloses itself only when read — several times if possible — in its entirety'.[37] Matthew's portrait of Jesus is complete, as he is worshipped and revealed as the risen Son of God, who has tried to teach Israel, whose religious leaders have rejected and killed him, and who still tell lies about him. 'His Gospel is from beginning to end a Christological book'.[38] Matthew's narrative subplot about the authorities makes perfect sense in the light of our discussion above about Matthew's situation. However, not everyone reads it that carefully or in that context, with the result that it has led to all Jews being called 'Christ-killers', being blamed for Jesus' death, rather than Matthew's chief priests, scribes and leaders. Therefore, any attempt to represent Matthew's passion today can quickly lead to ethical difficulties and passionate reactions, as happened with Mel Gibson's film, *The Passion of the Christ*.[39] Any morally responsible recreation of Matthew's account today must, of course, be sensitive to how it sounds after two millennia of anti-Semitism and persecution of Jews by Christians; at the same time, it has to be faithful to the Christological account, which came out of a group of Jewish Christians being themselves persecuted in separating from the synagogue.

We concluded Mark's Christology by noting that those who look for ethical

37. Luz, *Studies in Matthew*, p. 83; his essay, 'Matthean Christology Outlined in Theses', pp. 83-96, is worth careful study.

38. Birger Gerhardsson, 'The Christology of Matthew', p. 29.

39. See Richard A. Burridge, review articles of the film in *The Times*, March 25, 2004; *The Sun*, March 24, 2004; *The Sunday Express*, March 28, 2004; *The Church of England Newspaper*, March 4, 2004; also my paper, 'Interpreting Mel Gibson's *The Passion of the Christ*', British New Testament Conference, University of Edinburgh, September 4, 2004; on the reactions, see Mark Goodacre, 'The Power of *The Passion*: Reacting and Over-reacting to Gibson's Artistic Vision', in *Jesus and Mel Gibson's* The Passion of the Christ: *The Film, the Gospels and the Claims of History*, ed. Kathleen E. Corley and Robert L. Webb (London: Continuum, 2004), pp. 28-44; on the film's portrayal of Pilate and the Jewish leaders, see the chapters by Alan F. Segal, 'The Jewish Leaders', pp. 89-102, and Helen K. Bond, 'Pilate and the Romans', pp. 103-17.

teaching in the manner of the Sermon on the Mount miss the real ethical implications of his narrative portrait of Jesus. Similarly, although this gospel does contain that Sermon, and much other ethical teaching, mere concentration on that alone will miss Matthew's principal ethic — that God has come to be 'with us' in Jesus, who is the sum of all Israel's prophets, priests and kings, and came not just to fulfil all the teachings of the law and prophets, but to build the true community of faith; religious leaders opposed him and, in association with the imperial power, were responsible for his death — but God raised him to new life to be 'with us' for ever more.[40] Religious leaders and teachers of ethics should therefore take care how they represent him!

2. Matthew's setting and eschatology

If the above reconstruction of Matthew's situation with regard to his Christology is about right, then this also helps with his possible setting and date. The most common location involves a setting in Antioch,[41] though other major centres such as Caesarea, Tyre and Sidon, or even a Galilean town like Tiberias or Sepphoris[42] have been suggested, while others prefer somewhere east of the Jordan, such as Pella, where the Jerusalem church fled in about AD 66 (Eusebius, *Historia Ecclesiastica* 3.5.3).[43] As with Mark, more recent scholarship has begun to move away from attempting to define a particular community and location to sketching out the kind of group envisaged in the text.[44] Matthew's use of the Hebrew scriptures led Stendahl and Orton to talk of a 'school',[45] while Overman and Stanton reconstruct his community as typical of the 'sectarianism' of Jewish groups towards the end of the first century.[46]

40. See Luz' stress on Immanuel Christology, *Studies in Matthew*, pp. 83-85.

41. See, for example, R. Schnackenburg, *The Gospel of Matthew* (Grand Rapids: Eerdmans, 2002), pp. 5-7; Rodney Stark, 'Antioch as the Social Setting for Matthew's Gospel', in *Social History of the Matthean Community: Cross-Disciplinary Approaches*, ed. Balch, pp. 189-210.

42. Preferred by J. A. Overman, *Matthew's Gospel and Formative Judaism* (Minneapolis: Fortress, 1990), and in his introduction to his commentary, *Church and Community in Crisis* (Valley Forge, PA: Trinity Press International, 1996), pp. 16-19.

43. A full list of suggested locations is discussed by Davies and Allison, *Matthew*, vol. 1, pp. 138-147 and in R. E. Brown, *An Introduction to the New Testament* (New York: Doubleday, 1997), pp. 208-17; see also G. N. Stanton, 'The Origin and Purpose of Matthew's Gospel', in *ANRW* 2.25.3, pp. 1889-1951, esp. pp. 1941-43.

44. See D. E. Aune (ed.), *The Gospel of Matthew in Current Study* (Grand Rapids: Eerdmans, 2001), esp. Richard S. Ascough's essay, 'Matthew and Community Formation', pp. 96-126.

45. K. Stendahl, *The School of St Matthew* (Lund: Gleerup, 2nd edn. 1967); D. E. Orton, *The Understanding Scribe* (Sheffield: Sheffield Academic Press, 1989).

46. Overman, *Matthew's Gospel and Formative Judaism: Church and Community in Crisis;*

We noted above the period of the *birkat ha-minim* insertion into the Jewish liturgy and the growing separation of church and synagogue after AD 85 as a possible background for Matthew, but this date has waxed and waned along with the popularity of that hypothesis.[47] The arguments with the synagogue predated the events around Yavneh/Jamnia, so Matthew could be prior to that, as well as later. Assuming that Mark was written first and used by Matthew as his primary source suggests that his composition is at least a decade or so later, but Hagner argues for the possibility of only a few years after Mark and still before the destruction of Jerusalem.[48] However, the majority of scholars assume a date around the 80s; since this seems the most likely hypothesis, we shall also work with it.

Given this date, then Matthew has various things to explain and deal with as he paints his portrait of Jesus. First, there are the theological questions of why the Jewish leadership rejected their Messiah and why God allowed his holy city of Jerusalem to be destroyed; we have already seen how Matthew handles that in the context of the early church's increasing self-definition of its identity over and against the synagogue. The second concerns the timing of the end: if Mark's grim eschatology reflects the dark days of the 60s with Nero's persecutions and the Jewish revolt, it is not surprising that he may have thought that the end was about to happen, hence his ethic of discipleship and suffering. However, if Matthew's gospel was written a decade or two later, the question looks different: given that the events of AD 70 did not usher in the final cataclysm, then the church might have to prepare for a longer period of existence — and therefore would require more by way of ethical teaching: 'The End is in his view sufficiently distant to enable him to envisage a continuing mission of the Church and to be concerned with its ethical and institutional problems'.[49] In his particular context, Matthew also has to deal with what is the continuing significance of the law, and how Jewish-Christians might keep it in a different way from those in the synagogue, given that 'until heaven and earth pass away, not one letter [iota], not one stroke of a letter, will pass from the law until all is accomplished' (Matt. 5.18).[50]

But 'this relaxation of eschatological urgency', to use Hays' phrase,[51] does

---

Stanton, *A Gospel for a New People,* esp. pp. 85-107; and G. N. Stanton, 'The Communities of Matthew', *Interpretation* 46 (1992), pp. 379-91.

47. See P. W. van der Horst, 'The *Birkat ha-minim* in Recent Research', and other references cited in n. 25 above.

48. Donald A. Hagner, *Matthew,* Word Biblical Commentary 33, 2 vols. (Dallas: Word, 1993 and 1995); see vol. 1, pp. lxxiii-lxxv.

49. J. L. Houlden, *Ethics and the New Testament* (Oxford: Oxford University Press, 1973), p. 52.

50. See Meier, *The Vision of Matthew,* pp. 229-34.

51. Richard B. Hays, *The Moral Vision of the New Testament: A Contemporary Introduction to*

not mean that thinking about the end is of no value. On the contrary, 'Matthew's perspective is thoroughly eschatological: in Jesus the times are fulfilled'.[52] It is precisely because we live between Jesus' human incarnation and the final judgement that Matthew contains more detailed ethics: 'The uncompromising radicalism of Christ's moral message in Matthew is a challenge to all of us to realize, in our own lives, that the word "eschatological" is more than theological jargon'.[53] There is still a real end-time expectation: thus Matthew keeps Mark 13.18, 'Pray that it may not be in winter', but his redaction replaces 'it' with ἡ φυγὴ ὑμῶν, 'your flight', and adds 'or on a Sabbath', μηδὲ σαββάτῳ (Matt. 24.20), something which would cause further problems with the synagogue.[54] The eschatological discourse of chap. 24 follows Mark's warnings: 'You also must be ready, for the Son of Man is coming at an unexpected hour' (Matt. 24.44). In fact, the eschatological discourse (chaps. 24–25), the fifth of Matthew's blocks of teaching, contains ninety-five verses, almost as many as the first discourse, the Sermon on the Mount (107 verses in chaps. 5–7), which it balances. Given the impact of the Sermon upon Matthew's ethics, eschatology deserves equal attention.

The story about faithful and wicked servants comes at the end of the apocalyptic teaching in 24.45-51, but is immediately followed in the next chapter by three parables about the end. The middle one, the parable of the Talents, has parallels in Luke's story of the Pounds (Luke 19.11-27) though with much Matthean redaction, while the other two, the Wise and Foolish Virgins[55] and the Sheep and Goats (Matt. 25.1-13, 31-46) are unique to Matthew, again demonstrating his redactional interest. The last one has been subject to enormous interpretation throughout history, as chronicled in Gray's exhaustive account.[56] Debate varies about whether 'all the nations' is universal, or just the pagans, in-

---

New Testament Ethics (San Francisco: HarperSanFrancisco/Edinburgh: T&T Clark, 1996), pp. 104-7; and J. T. Sanders, *Ethics in the New Testament* (London: SCM, 1975), pp. 40-46.

52. Allen Verhey, *The Great Reversal: Ethics and the New Testament* (Grand Rapids: Eerdmans, 1984), p. 90; for further discussion of 'the relationship of ethics to eschatology' in Matthew, see Dan O. Via, 'Narrative World and Ethical Response: The Marvelous and Righteousness in Matthew 1–2', *Semeia* 12 (1978), pp. 123-45.

53. Meier, *The Vision of Matthew*, p. 264.

54. See Stanton, "'Pray That Your Flight May Not Be in Winter or on a Sabbath': Matthew 24.20", chap. 8 in his *A Gospel for a New People*, pp. 192-206.

55. For a 'redemptive reading' of this parable, see Marie-Eloise Rosenblatt, 'Got into the Party after All: Women's Issues and the Five Foolish Virgins', *Continuum* 3 (1993), pp. 107-37; repr. in *A Feminist Companion to Matthew*, ed. Amy-Jill Levine with Marianne Blickenstaff (Sheffield: Sheffield Academic Press, 2001), pp. 171-95.

56. Sherman W. Gray, *The Least of My Brothers: Matthew 25:31-46, A History of Interpretation* (Atlanta: Scholars Press, 1989).

cluding or excluding Jews or Christians, and whether 'the least of these my brothers' also has a universal application to the sick and poor everywhere, or just to how 'the nations' have treated 'my brothers', the persecuted, poor Christians.[57] While we recognize that most scholarly opinion tends towards the more limited latter meaning as Matthew's original intention, Luz is surely right to argue from the wide appeal of the universal interpretation throughout history that it reflects the universal thrust of Jesus' teaching on love.[58] Whichever interpretation is adopted, the eschatological thrust of the parable is clear, and this expectation is what drives the ethical point.

Such motivation for ethics is central: 'In Matthew, eschatology becomes a powerful warrant for moral behaviour'.[59] Not for him, the idea that ethics are self-authenticating or good deeds should be done for their own sake. Instead, Matthew argues for ethical behaviour because of the consequences: 'For the Son of Man is to come with his angels in the glory of his Father, and then he will repay everyone for what they have done' (16.27). He constantly stresses the theme of the coming judgement (5.21-23; 7.1-2; 10.15; 11.22, 24; 12.36, 41-42; 23.33) with both the rewards (5.12, 46; 6.1-6, 16-18; 10.41-42; 25.34) and the punishments (7.23; 13.42, 50; 22.13; 24.51; 25.30, 41) in return for people's deeds. The direst warnings are about being excluded from the kingdom, 'into the outer darkness, where there will be weeping and gnashing of teeth' (8.12; 13.42, 50; 22.13; 24.51; 25.30). No wonder that Matera concludes his survey, 'The threat of judgment and the prospect of eschatological salvation in the kingdom of heaven play a major role in Jesus' teaching in Matthew'.[60]

Therefore, if we assume that Matthew writes later using Mark as his source, the apparent delay of the end has led him to formulate a more settled ethical system for his new community of faith. However, it is clear that the end is still the motivating force for this ethic in the here and now, together with a confident expectation that the final judgement will happen soon in the coming of the same Jesus who fulfilled the law and the prophets, and who will judge us for

57. See, for example, Don O. Via, 'Ethical Responsibility and Human Wholeness in Matthew 25.31-46', *HTR* 80 (1987), pp. 79-100; John R. Donahue, 'The "Parable" of the Sheep and Goats: A Challenge to Christian Ethics', *Theological Studies* 47 (1986), pp. 3-30; Stanton, 'Once More: Matthew 25.31-46', chap. 9 in his *A Gospel for a New People*, pp. 206-31; John Paul Heil, 'The Double Meaning of the Narrative of Universal Judgment in Matthew 25:31-46', *JSNT* 69 (1998), pp. 3-14.

58. Luz, 'The Final Judgment (Matthew 25.31-46): An Exercise in "History of Influence" Exegesis', in *Treasures New and Old*, ed. Bauer and Powell, pp. 271-310; see his conclusions on pp. 308-10.

59. Hays, *Moral Vision of the NT*, pp. 106-7.

60. F. J. Matera, *New Testament Ethics* (Louisville: Westminster John Knox, 1996), p. 58; see pp. 56-59 for discussion; also Houlden, *Ethics and the New Testament*, pp. 52-53; J. T. Sanders, *Ethics in the NT*, pp. 42-45; Verhey, *The Great Reversal*, pp. 90-92; Schrage, *The Ethics of the NT*, pp. 144-46.

how we have followed his teaching and example — to which topics, therefore, we must now turn.

3. The law and love

We have seen how both Jesus and Paul stress that love is the greatest commandment and that it fulfils the law, and noted the implications of this for how they handled the vexed topic of the law. For Mark, in particular, the law is radicalized by the priority of the sovereign rule of God. However, given the debate with the synagogue, especially with the religious authorities and guardians of morality, taking place in the decades after the fall of Jerusalem, it should not be surprising that Matthew's position is more complex, as he develops his ethic of a proper righteousness in the kingdom of heaven which is shown in Jesus' deeds and activities as much in his teaching and discourses.

a. The central theme: righteousness in the kingdom of heaven

Most people concentrate on the Sermon on Mount as the centre of Matthean ethics. However, our biographical approach and the above study of Matthew's Christology and eschatology have begun to suggest that to focus narrowly on the Sermon runs the risk of missing the wider point. Matthew has structured his narrative of Jesus as a new Moses around five balancing discourses, in which the Sermon on the Mount (chaps. 5–7, 107 verses), the longest with its teaching on ethics in the present, is closely matched by the eschatological discourse about the future in chaps. 24–25 (ninety-five verses). The next layer in comprises the two much shorter discourses, on the mission, and the life, of the new community (10.5-42; 18.1-35). In between, both in length (fifty-two verses) and right at the heart of the five discourses and, indeed, of the very gospel itself, comes the collection of parables of the kingdom (13.1-52). Matera points out, 'Whereas Mark has 14 references to the kingdom of God, Matthew has 50 references to the kingdom of God/heaven, 32 of which are peculiar to him'.[61] Thus we may conclude that the kingdom of heaven (which Matthew usually prefers as a respectful Semitic idiom to avoid mentioning God) is literally at the centre of his gospel and his thinking. We must bear in mind our previous discussions about the best translation, such as 'God's reign': Carter prefers to render ἡ βασιλεία τῶν οὐρανῶν as 'the empire of the heavens' or 'God's empire' to make

61. Matera, *NT Ethics*, p. 37.

the point that Jesus is talking about something which challenges all imperial systems, from Rome to today's.[62]

Right in the centre of the gospels, chap. 13 collects the parables depicting the progress of the kingdom — the Sower (vv. 1-9, 18-23), the Weeds (vv. 24-30, 36-43), the Mustard Seed (vv. 31-32), Leaven (v. 33), Hidden Treasure and the Pearl (vv. 44-46), the Net (vv. 47-50) and the Householder (vv. 51-52). They all show the slow, and often secret, growth of the kingdom from small beginnings — and that its secrets are revealed to Jesus' disciples but hidden from those who do not understand (vv. 10-17, 34-35). Even in the parables, therefore, we cannot get away from the warnings of judgement through the images of the harvest, the fire and separating good from bad. Elsewhere, the kingdom is compared to a child (18.1-4), a forgiving king (18.23-35), a king's wedding banquet (22.2-14), and the owner of a vineyard hiring labourers (20.1-16), as God's reign features at the heart of Jesus' teaching throughout this gospel.[63]

b. Righteousness and the debate with the teachers of the law

One of Matthew's key word groups is δίκαιος, 'righteous', and its cognate noun, δικαιοσύνη, 'righteousness'; the latter appears seven times in Matthew, never in Mark, once in Luke (Luke 1.75) and twice in John but in the same passage (John 16.8-10).[64] Thus at the beginning of Matthew, Joseph is introduced as 'a righteous man' (1.19), while Jesus insists on being baptized, against the Baptist's protests, 'to fulfil all righteousness' (3.15) — a phrase which becomes almost programmatic for this gospel. The extraordinary thing is that Jesus begins by saying that his followers' righteousness must 'exceed' or 'abundantly overflow', περισσεύσῃ,[65] 'more than that of the scribes and Pharisees', for them to enter the kingdom (5.20). Given that these are the experts on being righteous in keeping the law, this is a very high standard. Many scholars suggest that Matthew is concerned to steer a path between the lawkeeping of the Jewish teachers on the one hand, and certain antinomian tendencies within the Christian community, who may have been inspired by Mark's apparently freer attitude towards the law, on the other.[66]

---

62. Carter, *Matthew and the Margins*, passim, explained in n. 8, pp. 571-72.

63. See further Matera, *NT Ethics*, pp. 39-42, and his earlier article, 'The Ethics of the Kingdom in the Gospel of Matthew', *Listening* (Romeoville, IL), 24.3 (1989), pp. 241-50.

64. Robert G. Bratcher, '"Righteousness" in Matthew', *The Bible Translator* 40.2 (1989), pp. 228-35.

65. See Gerhardsson, *The Ethos of the Bible*, pp. 38-41; Willi Marxsen, *New Testament Foundations for Christian Ethics* (Minneapolis: Fortress, 1993), pp. 235-42.

66. See William Loader, *Jesus' Attitude towards the Law: A Study of the Gospels* (Grand Rapids:

Therefore Matthew makes a concerted attack throughout his gospel on externalised, hypocritical religion which does not practise what it preaches. He is careful not to criticize the law or the Pharisees' teaching of it, since, 'The scribes and the Pharisees sit on Moses' seat; therefore, do whatever they teach you and follow it; but do not do as they do, for they do not practise what they teach' (23.2-3). This is shown in his redaction of the controversy stories which we considered previously in Mark. When the Pharisees see Jesus eating with tax collectors and sinners after the call of Matthew from the tax booth, Matthew inserts into his version an appeal to Hos. 6.6, 'Go and learn what this means, "I desire mercy, not sacrifice"' (cp. Matt. 9.9-13 with Mark 2.13-17). Hays notes that 'this passage was cited by the great rabbi Yohanan ben Zakkai, the founder of the rabbinic academy at Jamnia, as a word of reassurance for Israel after the destruction of the Temple, when the prescribed sacrifices were no longer possible'.[67] Thus in Matthew, Jesus' defence is taken from the prophets, in particular a passage prominent in debate contemporary with his composition, rather than just Jesus' own word, 'I have come to call not the righteous but sinners' (Matt. 9.13).

Exactly the same strategy is used in the debate about plucking corn to eat on the Sabbath, inserting the same verse from Hosea to make Jesus 'greater than the temple' and 'guiltless' against the charge of breaking Sabbath law: 'If you had known what this means, "I desire mercy and not sacrifice," you would not have condemned the guiltless.' Furthermore, Mark's pithy saying, 'The Sabbath was made for human beings', and not vice versa, is omitted (cp. Matt. 12.1-8 with Mark 2.23-28). Mark's following story of the healing of the man's withered hand on the Sabbath is then repeated, but Jesus' question, 'Is it lawful to do good or to do harm on the Sabbath?' is answered in Matthew with an halakic argument about saving a sheep from a pit, leading to his assertion that 'it is lawful' (Matt. 12.9-14; cp. Mark 3.1-6).[68] In the divorce debate, Matthew's transposition of the sequence and his insertion, 'except for unchastity', portray Jesus as an halakic interpreter of the law, siding with the conservative Shammai; he also omits Mark's equal treatment of women (Matt. 19.1-12; cp. Mark 10.2-12). Thus Verhey concludes, 'The law holds, and Jesus is its true interpreter'.[69]

Eerdmans, 2002), pp. 137-54 for a review of scholarship on this issue; see also Verhey, *The Great Reversal*, pp. 83-85; Frank Thielman, *The Law and the New Testament: The Question of Continuity* (New York: Crossroad, 1999), pp. 47-49; Roger Mohrlang, *Matthew and Paul: A Comparison of Ethical Perspectives*, SNTSMS 48 (Cambridge: Cambridge University Press, 1984), pp. 7-23.

67. Hays, *Moral Vision of the NT*, p. 99.

68. On these passages, see further Yong-Eui Yang, *Jesus and the Sabbath in Matthew's Gospel*, JSNTSS 139 (Sheffield: Sheffield Academic Press, 1997), who argues that, for Matthew, Jesus has fulfilled the Sabbath.

69. Verhey, *The Great Reversal*, p. 85.

This plot line comes to a head in Jesus' denunciation of the scribes and Pharisees in Matt. 23. Much of this is double tradition or Q material, also occurring in Luke, but there it is spread throughout the gospel and given various narrative settings. Matthew collects it all into one of his teaching blocks, but the cumulative effect makes it very strong indeed. What is clear is that they are being attacked not for their teaching of the law, but for their failure to put it into practice (23.3), and for external show (e.g., 23.5-7, 14). Again, the issue is the interpretation of the law, being concerned for relatively minor matters such as tithing herbs and cleaning the outside of a plate, but neglecting 'weightier matters of the law: justice and mercy and faith' (23.23-26). Thus, set against Matthew's background of struggling with Pharisaic redefinition of Judaism after the loss of the temple, this approach to 'righteousness' is clear: the demands of the law are upheld, but they are interpreted by 'Matthew's image of Jesus — the teacher of the new righteousness'.[70]

c. The Sermon on the Mount — righteous living

'Classically and popularly, the Sermon on the Mount . . . has been regarded as the quintessence of the moral teaching of Jesus'.[71] While Houlden is right that this is how it has been viewed, Verhey is also correct to respond: 'The Sermon is certainly dependent on the ethic of Jesus, but it is just as certainly not to be identified with it; it is rather the quintessence of Matthew's ethic'.[72] Meeks sees it as 'an epitome of Jesus' teaching' in Matthew's account, comparable to similar statements found in biographies of other philosophers in the Graeco-Roman tradition.[73] Sublime it may be, but to treat it as 'quintessence' or 'epitome' runs the risk of abstracting this piece of teaching from its narrative context within Matthew's overall biographical portrait, and of ignoring the wider picture.[74] As Stanton puts it, 'The Sermon is the largest and most impressive of his five discourses, but it must not be separated from the rest of the gospel'.[75]

A brief survey of its content reveals how carefully Matthew has structured

---

70. Marxsen, *New Testament Foundations for Christian Ethics*, pp. 235-43.

71. Houlden, *Ethics and the New Testament*, p. 53.

72. Verhey, *The Great Reversal*, p. 85.

73. Meeks, *The Origins of Christian Morality*, p. 20; he uses the same phrase in *The Moral World*, p. 138.

74. See how the Sermon on the Mount is the basis for nearly every section of Glen H. Stassen and David P. Gushee, *Kingdom Ethics: Following Jesus in Contemporary Context* (Downers Grove, IL: IVP, 2003).

75. Stanton, 'Interpreting the Sermon on the Mount', chap. 12 in his *A Gospel for a New People*, p. 305.

this material, using patterns of threes.[76] It begins with nine Beatitudes, 'Blessed are . . .', in three groups of three (5.3-12). After describing the witness of the community of the disciples as 'salt and light' (5.13-16), we have Jesus' statement about fulfilling the law and prophets, and exceeding the righteousness of the scribes and Pharisees (5.17-20). This leads into six (two groups of three, or three pairs) so-called 'antitheses', contrasting the law, 'you have heard that it was said . . .', with Jesus' demands, 'but I say to you . . .' (5.17-47), and concluding with the call to be perfect 'as your heavenly Father is perfect' (5.48). Then the threefold practice of almsgiving, prayer (including the Lord's Prayer) and fasting is contrasted with the outward show of the Jewish leaders (6.1-18). A three-part 'sandwich' follows: trusting in riches or in God (6.19-33), judging others (7.1-6) and trusting God again (7.7-11) which leads to the Golden Rule, which is described as equivalent to the law and prophets (7.12). Finally, three warnings to put it into practice conclude: the two ways of the narrow gate and the wide road (7.13-14); the fruits of the two trees of false prophets and self-deception (7.15-23); and the two builders — the wise one on the rock, and the foolish on the sand (7.24-27). Throughout it all, Matthew stresses the same message that we have already discovered about righteousness in the kingdom of heaven which is fulfilled in Jesus' interpretation of the law, as he preaches for a response from his hearers to deny themselves in a life of discipleship. As Keck concludes, 'To sum up, Matthew does not regard Jesus' ethic (and thereby his own as well) as a new ethic at all, but as the recovery of what has been God's will all along.'[77]

The amount of detail lavished upon the Sermon on the Mount can be seen in Betz' exhaustive commentary running to 694 pages, including a comparison with Luke's Sermon on the Plain (Luke 6.20-49).[78] W. D. Davies set the tracks for much scholarly outpouring with his classic treatment of *The Setting of the Sermon on the Mount*,[79] and more recently helpfully reviewed both traditional and contemporary approaches to the Sermon.[80] The rest of the secondary literature

76. See Dale C. Allison, Jr., 'The Configuration of the Sermon on the Mount and Its Meaning', in his *Studies in Matthew: Interpretation Past and Present*, pp. 173-215, which even includes a comparison of this triadic structure with stories like 'Goldilocks and the Three Bears', pp. 199-201!

77. Leander E. Keck, 'Ethics in the Gospel according to Matthew', *Iliff Review* 41 (1984), pp. 39-56; quotation from p. 51.

78. Hans Dieter Betz, *The Sermon on the Mount*, Hermeneia (Minneapolis: Fortress, 1995); cf. the review article by B. T. Viviano, 'The Sermon on the Mount in Recent Study', *Biblica* 78.2 (1997), pp. 255-65; for other approaches, see also Davies and Allison, *Matthew*, vol. 1, pp. 429-731; Hagner, *Matthew*, vol. 1, pp. 82-194; etc.

79. W. D. Davies, *The Setting of the Sermon on the Mount* (Cambridge: Cambridge University Press, 1966).

80. W. D. Davies and Dale C. Allison, Jr., 'Reflections on the Sermon on the Mount', *SJT* 44 (1991), pp. 283-309.

is vast and too large to be treated in detail here,[81] for fear of falling into the temptation of concentrating upon it at the expense of the rest of Matthew's ethics. However, it is worth noting the debate about its ethical and political interpretation. In 1986, Sjef van Tilborg began his study by rightly observing that 'there is at the moment no dearth of studies on the Sermon on the Mount' and then set out to provide an ideological reading to balance the common individualistic approaches.[82] In particular, Matthew is often criticized for spiritualizing the Beatitudes (5.1-12), especially in comparison with Luke 6.20-26: Patte's study helpfully analyses five different ways of interpreting the Beatitudes,[83] while recently political interpretations calling for justice seem to be increasing.[84]

81. See further, for example, Matera, *NT Ethics*, pp. 42-50; Verhey, *The Great Reversal*, pp. 85-89; Eduard Lohse, *Theological Ethics of the New Testament* (Minneapolis: Fortress, 1991), pp. 61-73; Stanton, 'Interpreting the Sermon on the Mount', chap. 12, pp. 285-306 and 'The Origin and Purpose of the Sermon on the Mount', chap. 13, pp. 307-25, in his *A Gospel for a New People*; Bernard Brandon Scott and Margaret E. Dean, 'A Sound Map of the Sermon on the Mount', in *Treasures New and Old,* ed. Bauer and Powell, pp. 311-78; Christoph Burchard, 'The Theme of the Sermon on the Mount', in *Essays on the Love Commandment* by Luise Schottroff, Reginald H. Fuller, Christoph Burchard and M. Jack Suggs (Philadelphia: Fortress, 1978), pp. 57-91; Oscar Stephen Brooks, *The Sermon on the Mount: Authentic Human Values* (Lanham, MD: University Press of America, 1985); Raymond F. Collins, 'Christian Personalism and the Sermon on the Mount', in his *Christian Morality: Biblical Foundations* (Notre Dame, IN: University of Notre Dame Press, 1986), pp. 223-37; L. S. Cahill, 'The Ethical Implications of the Sermon on the Mount', *Interpretation* 41.2 (April 1987), pp. 144-56 — and the whole of that edition of *Interpretation* is devoted to the Sermon on the Mount; James G. Williams, 'Paraenesis, Excess, and Ethics: Matthew's Rhetoric in the Sermon on the Mount', *Semeia* 50 (1990), pp. 163-87; Richard J. Dillon, 'Ravens, Lilies, and the Kingdom of God (Matthew 6:25-33/Luke 12:22-31)', *CBQ* 53.4 (1991), pp. 605-27; G. Greenfield, 'The Ethics of the Sermon on the Mount', *SWJT* 35.1 (1992), pp. 13-19; H. D. Betz and William Schweiker, 'Concerning Mountains and Morals: A Conversation about the Sermon on the Mount', *Criterion* (Chicago) 36.2 (1997), pp. 12-26; Donald A. Hagner, 'Ethics and the Sermon on the Mount', *Studia Theologia* 51 (1997), pp. 44-59; H. D. Betz, 'The Portrait of Jesus in the Sermon on the Mount', *Currents in Theology and Mission* 25.3 (1998), pp. 165-75; Daniel J. Harrington, S.J., and James F. Keenan, S.J., 'The Sermon on the Mount and Virtue Ethics: How Do We Get There?', in their *Jesus and Virtue Ethics: Building Bridges between New Testament Studies and Moral Theology* (Oxford: Sheed and Ward, 2002), pp. 61-75; Charles H. Talbert, *Reading the Sermon on the Mount: Character Formation and Decision Making in Matthew 5-7* (Columbia, SC: University of South Carolina Press, 2004), see the review article of this by Leslie Houlden with a response from Talbert, *Conversations in Religion and Theology* 3.2 (2005), pp. 119-23; Francois P. Viljoen, 'Jesus' Teaching on the *Torah* in the Sermon on the Mount', *Neotestamentica* 40.1 (2006), pp. 135-55.

82. Sjef van Tilborg, *The Sermon on the Mount as an Ideological Intervention: A Reconstruction of Meaning* (Assen/Maastricht: Van Gorcum, 1986).

83. Daniel Patte, *The Challenge of Discipleship: A Critical Study of the Sermon in the Mount as Scripture* (Harrisburg, PA: Trinity Press International, 1999).

84. See, for example, Carter, *Matthew and the Margins,* pp. 128-37 on the Beatitudes, and pp. 137-95 on the rest of the Sermon; Stanley Hauerwas, 'The Sermon on the Mount, Just War and the

Rather than adding further to this outpouring of words about this section of Jesus' ethical teaching as depicted by Matthew, perhaps it would be fitting to give the last comment to Dietrich Bonhoeffer's conclusion about the Sermon on the Mount: 'The only proper response to this word which Jesus brings with him from eternity is simply to do it. Jesus has spoken: his is the word, ours the obedience'.[85]

d. Love and the righteous fulfilment of the law

We observed in the previous chapter that the very word νόμος, law, does not occur in Mark, but Matthew has it eight times (5.17, 18; 7.12; 11.13; 12.5; 22.36, 40; 23.23). Bearing in mind the above suggestion that he is trying to steer a middle path between the Scylla of post-70 Pharisaic focus on the law and the Charybdis of post-Markan antinomianism,[86] let us consider these passages to see how he navigates his way through.

Matthew begins with a statement which immediately seems to confirm a middle way between abolition and minute observance: 'Do not think that I have come to abolish the law or the prophets; I have come not to abolish but to fulfil' (Matt. 5.17). However, this is the passage (called 'an exegetical minefield' by Charles[87] and 'notoriously difficult to interpret' by Mohrlang[88]) where Jesus goes on to affirm that not even an iota 'will pass from the law until all is accomplished' and that his followers' righteousness must exceed that of the Pharisees (5.18-20). This is a clear statement against any antinomians, or even those who interpret Mark as allowing them to set aside certain aspects of the law. On the other hand, the 'exceeding' righteousness is shown by the following antitheses not to be a nit-picking or legalistic interpretation of the law; rather, his hearers are to go beyond merely avoiding murder or adultery to living a life without ha-

---

Quest for Peace', *Concilium* 195 (1988), pp. 36-43 and 'Living the Proclaimed Reign of God: A Sermon on the Sermon on the Mount', *Interpretation* 47 (1993), pp. 152-58; Michael H. Crosby, O.F.M.Cap., *House of Disciples: Church, Economics and Justice in Matthew* (Maryknoll, NY: Orbis, 1988), pp. 147-70 on the Beatitudes, and pp. 171-95 on the rest of the Sermon, and the rev. edn. of his *Spirituality of the Beatitudes: Matthew's Vision for the Church in an Unjust World* (Maryknoll, NY: Orbis, 2005).

85. Dietrich Bonhoeffer, *The Cost of Discipleship* (New York: Touchstone, 1995), p. 197; the bulk of Bonhoeffer's classic is a detailed study of the Sermon on the Mount.

86. See n. 66 above: Loader, *Jesus' Attitude towards the Law*, pp. 137-54; Thielman, *The Law and the New Testament*, pp. 47-49.

87. J. Daryl Charles, 'The Greatest or the Least in the Kingdom? The Disciple's Relationship to the Law (Matt 5:17-20)', *Trinity Journal*, n.s. 13 (1992), pp. 139-62; opening quotation, p. 139.

88. Mohrlang, *Matthew and Paul*, p. 8.

tred or lust, speaking the truth instead and loving enemies. This is what Jesus means when he says he has come to 'fulfil' the law (5.17).[89]

Towards the end of the Sermon on the Mount, we have Matthew's version of the Golden Rule, 'In everything do to others as you would have them do to you', also shared with Luke 6.31 — except that Matthew adds, 'for this is the law and the prophets' (Matt. 7.12). This is a good example of Matthew's 'both/and' middle way, demonstrating that Jesus' teaching fulfils the law. The same argument is made in his redaction of Mark's controversy passage about new wine needing new wineskins: Matthew adds the significant point, 'and so both are preserved' (Matt. 9.17; cp. Mark 2.22) — 'the law is indeed preserved, but *as interpreted by Jesus*'.[90]

Matthew's redaction of the Q-passage about the John the Baptist is also interesting. While Luke has no verb, suggesting that 'the law and the prophets [were] until John came', followed by the preaching of the gospel, Matthew inserts ἐπροφήτευσαν to make the simple statement that 'all the prophets and the law prophesied until John came', no adverse comparison (Matt. 11.13; cp. Luke 16.16). In the controversy about plucking grain on the Sabbath, Matthew omits Mark's provocative statement that the Sabbath was made for human beings and not the other way around (Mark 2.27), replacing it with an example from the law, 'Or have you not read in the law that on the sabbath the priests in the temple break the sabbath and yet are guiltless?' to make the point that 'something greater than the temple is here' (Matt. 12.5-6). Thus once again, Jesus is both the fulfilment and the interpreter of the law. This is reinforced later in his attack on the Pharisees' interpretation, that they 'tithe mint, dill, and cummin, and have neglected the weightier matters of the law: justice and mercy and faith' (23.23).

However, the concentrated denunciation of the scribes and the Pharisees in chap. 23 is preceded by Matthew's version of the Greatest Commandment (22.34-40). While the central exchange follows Mark as his source, the changes are significant: 'The way in which the Great Commandment is presented by Matthew further shows that Matthew intends to intensify the law on the basis of the command to love'.[91] In Mark it is a scribe who asks the question, and who agrees with Jesus in reply and thus is commended as being 'not far from the kingdom' (Mark 12.28-34). However, in Matthew the questioners are the Pharisees, who, when they 'heard that he had silenced the Sadducees', gathered 'to test him'. One of them, identified as 'a lawyer', specifically asks which com-

---

89. On Matt. 5.15-20, see further, Luz, 'The Fulfilment of the Law in Matthew (Matt. 5:17-20), in his *Studies in Matthew*, pp. 185-218; Thielman, *The Law and the New Testament*, pp. 49-58; Meier, *The Vision of Matthew*, pp. 222-39.

90. Donald A. Hagner, 'Balancing the Old and the New: The Law of Moses in Matthew and Paul', *Interpretation* 51.1 (1997), pp. 20-30; quotation from p. 24, his italics.

91. J. T. Sanders, *Ethics in the NT*, p. 42.

mandment 'in the law' is greatest. Jesus' reply notes that 'the greatest and first commandment' is to love God, and then adds love of neighbour, but crucially concludes, 'On these two commandments hang all the law and the prophets' (Matt. 22.40). Thus the pericope ends not with the commendation of a scribe, but with how the law and prophets depend on love.[92] In fact, as Furnish demonstrates, this stress here on love of God and neighbour dominates all of Matthew's account of Jesus throughout his gospel.[93]

Therefore, our study of the main passages about the law in this gospel has revealed this middle path between antinomianism and Pharisaic legalism: 'To Matthew's way of thinking, Jesus *neither* set aside any of the law *nor* interpreted it the way many of his contemporaries did. . . . The proper understanding of the law is attained through a "prophetic" reading of it that sees love and mercy as its real focus'.[94] Given the Jewish setting of the gospel with its echoes of Moses, it is not surprising that some scholars speak of 'Jesus' teaching as a new law'[95] or 'Jesus as a new lawgiver'.[96] However, as Mohrlang points out, Matthew never uses the word νόμος to refer to Jesus' teaching. 'The crucial point is this: Matthew presents Jesus not as a new lawgiver, but as the giver of a new interpretation of the law'.[97]

Furthermore, this interpretation is not meant to be burdensome. Jesus' invitation to those who are struggling features as 'comfortable words' in the liturgy of the Book of Common Prayer: 'Come to me, all you that are weary and are carrying heavy burdens, and I will give you rest' (Matt. 11.28). But as Stanton rightly observes, the invitation is to follow him in discipleship: 'Take my yoke upon you, and learn from me; for I am gentle and humble in heart, and you will find rest for your souls. For my yoke is easy, and my burden is light' (Matt. 11.29-30).[98] For Matthew, true righteousness is not found in lawlessness nor in keeping the law in the manner of the Pharisees with whom he was in conflict in the post–70 AD debate about the heart of Judaism. Rather, it belongs to the kingdom of heaven, proclaimed and initiated by Jesus.

92. On Matthew's account of the Love Command, see further Loader, *Jesus' Attitude towards the Law*, pp. 235-37; Gerhardsson, *The Ethos of the Bible*, pp. 45-54.

93. Victor Paul Furnish, *The Love Command in the New Testament* (Nashville: Abingdon, 1972), pp. 74-84.

94. Klyne R. Snodgrass, 'Matthew's Understanding of the Law', *Interpretation* 46.4 (1992), pp. 368-78; quotation, with his italics, from p. 369; see also his article, 'Matthew and the Law', *Treasures New and Old*, ed. Bauer and Powell, pp. 99-127.

95. See, for example, Thielman, *The Law and the New Testament*, pp. 69-71.

96. Similarly, Rudolf Schnackenburg, *The Moral Teaching of the New Testament* (New York: Herder and Herder, 1965), p. 203.

97. Mohrlang, *Matthew and Paul*, pp. 23-25; quotation from p. 24.

98. Stanton, 'Matthew 11.28-30: Comfortable Words?', chap. 16 in his *A Gospel for a New People*, pp. 364-77.

Although a surface comparison of Matthew with Paul can suggest very different approaches to the law, in fact they are not so dissimilar: 'Both Matthew and Paul manifest a deep commitment to continuity with the law, or more specifically with the righteousness articulated by the law'.[99] Matthew agrees with Paul that the law is fulfilled in Jesus, but he also portrays Jesus in his narrative account as the true interpreter of the law. His gospel begins with Jesus interpreting the law on a mountain in a way reminiscent of Moses, with the Sermon on the Mount (chaps. 5–7). But this interpretation is then carried on through the narrative of the rest of the gospel in the debates with the teachers of the law, with the parables of the kingdom in pride of place at the very centre (chap. 13). It all comes to a climax with the lawyer's question about the greatest commandment, which is rapidly followed by the severest denunciation of those who interpret the law in an unloving manner in the next chapter (chaps. 22–23). Thus, although Matthew's sublime achievement is to bring together so much of Jesus' ethical teaching in the Sermon on the Mount, he does not intend his readers to take that on its own: the rest of his narrative and the other discourses reveal that one must also imitate Jesus by fulfilling the law according to the greatest commandment — to love God and neighbour.

4. Ethical issues in Matthew

Our treatment above has already demonstrated how Matthew's view of Jesus as the true interpreter is the hermeneutical key to his ethical understanding of the law and love all the way through the gospel; this also affects his typical redaction of some key passages from Mark, such as plucking grain and healing on the Sabbath (Matt. 12.1-14; cp. Mark 2.23–3.6) and hand-washing and food (Matt. 15.1-20; cp. Mark 7.1-23). We will not repeat our study of these passages again here, therefore, but we might expect to find Matthew taking a similar approach in our other areas of human moral experience.

a. The family

In our study of Mark 3.19b-35, we noted that his 'triple sandwich' balancing Jesus' relationship to his family with the conflict with the authorities and ultimately with the cosmic battle with Satan made for uncomfortable reading for

99. Hagner, 'Balancing the Old and the New: The Law of Moses in Matthew and Paul', p. 28; for a full treatment, see Mohrlang, *Matthew and Paul,* esp. his final conclusions, pp. 126-32.

'family values'. Matthew's own discomfort is shown by the fact that he discon-nects Mark's intertwined sequence. Matthew does repeat Mark's description of 'his mother and his brothers standing outside, wanting to speak to him' and Je-sus' response that 'whoever does the will of my Father in heaven is my brother and sister and mother' (12.46-50). However, he completely omits the opening comment that they had come to restrain him because people thought he was mad (Mark 3.19b-21). Furthermore, he relates the Beelzebul controversy earlier in the same chapter simply as a debate with the Pharisees, disconnected from the family completely, thus making it simply part of the wider conflict with the religious authorities (12.22-32). He also repeats Mark's story about Jesus bless-ing the little children, 'for it is to such as these that the kingdom of heaven be-longs' (Matt. 19.13-15; cp. Mark 10.13-16). He also includes an additional use of children as an example of who is 'the greatest in the kingdom of heaven' (Matt. 18.1-5).

b. Marriage and divorce

We saw above that in Mark's version of the controversy about divorce, Jesus did not join in the debate about the interpretation of Deut. 24.1, but rather went back to God's original intention of 'one flesh' in creation. Crucially for our pur-poses, Matthew's changes reflect his interest in Jesus as the true interpreter of the law: first, Jesus is asked if divorce is lawful 'for any cause', and he replies with the appeal to 'one flesh' in Gen. 2.22-24. This then leads into a debate about Deut. 24.1, in which Jesus takes the more conservative approach of interpreters like Shammai, by providing the exception for 'unchastity', μὴ ἐπὶ πορνείᾳ; fur-thermore, everything is seen from the viewpoint of the man divorcing his wife, with no corresponding concern for the woman's position (Matt. 19.1-9, unlike Mark 10.12).[100] The same point, again with the exception for πορνεία and from the male point of view, is made in the antithesis about divorce (5.31-32).[101] However, the previous antithesis on lust and adultery (5.27-30) does broaden the issue beyond legal exceptions and is concerned for women: 'Against the ten-dency of his day to place the burden of fault on the woman, Jesus clearly places the responsibility on the man guilty of lustful desires and glances'.[102] So this

100. See William Loader, *Sexuality and the Jesus Tradition* (Grand Rapids: Eerdmans, 2005), pp. 102-7.
101. Meier, *The Vision of Matthew*, pp. 248-57 argues that Matthew's account does not make Jesus side with Shammai, but rather both passages have to do with πορνεία as 'incestuous unions'.
102. Meier, *The Vision of Matthew*, p. 246; see also Loader, *Sexuality and the Jesus Tradition*, pp. 9-20.

demonstrates that while Mark goes beyond the law in his radical intensification of 'one flesh' and equal treatment, Matthew prefers to interpret the provisions of the law — and yet can still follow Jesus' total demand for a new way of living.

c. Money and possessions

Matthew does preserve Mark's story of the man whose many possessions prevented him from becoming a disciple later in the gospel, but first we have the Sermon on the Mount. Here some of Jesus' most famous teaching about wealth uses phrases which have passed into the English language: 'treasure in heaven', 'you cannot serve God and mammon', the 'birds of the air' and the 'lilies of the field' (Matt. 6.19-34). That this is Matthew's redactional skill in collecting it all together is shown by the fact that those verses here which he shares with Luke from Q are scattered through Luke's middle section (Luke 12.33-34; 11.34-36; 16.13; 12.22-31).

The opening section on moths and treasure in heaven reflects shared material with Luke, which each evangelist has used freely (Matt. 6.19-20; cp. Luke 12.33), but both lead into exactly the same pithy statement, typical of Jesus: 'For where your treasure is, there your heart will be also' (Matt. 6.21 = Luke 12.34). Matthew's next two verses on the eye reinforce this message with the need to 'focus on God', as they lead into 'No one can serve two masters. . . . You cannot serve God and mammon' (Matt. 6.24), which Carter memorably translates as 'serve God, not materialism'.[103] The final section on not worrying, looking at the birds and the lilies of the field, which are finer than 'Solomon in all his glory', closely parallels Luke, reflecting their shared source; however, Matthew concludes by adding onto the instruction to 'seek first the kingdom of God' the final phrase with his typical concern, 'and his righteousness' (6.33).[104]

Matthew's account of the 'rich young man' mostly follows Mark, though only Matthew calls him ὁ νεανίσκος, young (Matt. 19.16-32; cp. Mark 10:17-32). To avoid any doubt that Jesus can be rightly called 'good' which may arise from Jesus' question in Mark 10.17-18, Matthew makes the young man ask, 'What good deed must I do to have eternal life?' As we would expect from our study above of Jesus as the true interpreter of the law, here Jesus tells him to 'keep the commandments'; Mark's extra phrase, 'Do not defraud', is omitted as not being properly part of the Ten Commandments; instead, Matthew inserts the com-

---

103. Carter, *Matthew and the Margins*, pp. 173-76.

104. See further Dillon, 'Ravens, Lilies, and the Kingdom of God (Matthew 6:25-33/Luke 12:22-31)', esp. pp. 614-16.

mand to 'love your neighbour as yourself' at the end. In keeping with Matthew's antagonism to Jewish leaders who do not follow Jesus, there is no mention that Jesus looks at him and loves him (Mark 10.21); instead, in an echo of the Sermon on the Mount, he challenges the young man to emulate the heavenly Father who is perfect: 'If you wish to be perfect, go, sell your possessions' (Matt. 19.21; cp. 5.48). There is also another reprise, to have 'treasure in heaven' and the challenge to 'come, follow me'.

Thus what connects both of Matthew's treatments of wealth is the call to follow; as Hagner rightly observes, 'Wealth, it happens, is only the most conspicuous example of that which can distract from true discipleship'.[105] However, it is important that such comments about the link with discipleship in these two passages do not allow us to avoid the challenge of Jesus' teaching directed at the ownership of wealth itself, a challenge which is incarnated in the intervening narrative's depiction of the Son of Man who had 'nowhere to lay his head' (8.20).

d. Violence

Matthew also contains some teaching on a key topic not mentioned in Mark with the antitheses on murder and hatred (5.21-26) and retaliation and love of enemies (5.38-48). The first, telling people to go beyond avoiding murder to not even being angry, appears only here, and reflects Matthew's concern to show Jesus' righteous interpretation of the law, with his unique stress on not offering God 'a gift at the altar' while being in dispute with a brother (cp. Matt. 5.23 with Mark 11.25).[106] As Davies and Allison put it, 'Life in strict accord with legal ordinances is not enough. God demands a radical obedience that cannot be casuistically formulated'.[107]

The two sections on the *lex talionis* and love of enemies contain material shared with Luke 6.27-36, which Matthew has separated out to form his last pair of antitheses (5.38-42, 43-48).[108] Both are introduced by the Matthean contrast

---

105. Hagner, *Matthew*, vol. 1, p. 160 on 6.19-24; see his very similar comment on 19.16-24 in *Matthew*, vol. 2, p. 562.

106. Dale C. Allison, Jr., 'Murder and Anger, Cain and Abel', in his *Studies in Matthew: Interpretation Past and Present*, pp. 65-78.

107. Davies and Allison, *Matthew*, vol. 1, p. 521.

108. See Luise Schottroff, 'Non-Violence and the Love of One's Enemies', in *Essays on the Love Commandment* by Luise Schottroff, Reginald H. Fuller, Christoph Burchard and M. Jack Suggs (Philadelphia: Fortress, 1978), pp. 9-39; William Klassen, 'The Authenticity of the Command: "Love Your Enemies"', in *Authenticating the Words of Jesus*, ed. B. Chilton and C. A. Evans (Leiden:

'you have heard that it was said . . . but I say to you' as part of his intensifying interpretation of the law. While Luke seems to envisage begging or robbery on the road, where the outer cloak, ἱμάτιον, is taken first and then the inner shirt or tunic, χιτών, is to be given up too (Luke 6:29), Matthew once again is concerned for a legal situation: here the disciple is in court being sued, κριθῆναι, for his χιτών. This is because the law did not permit taking away a man's cloak overnight, for fear he might freeze to death while sleeping (Exod. 22.26-27; Deut. 24.12-13). However, Jesus tells his hearers to hand over their ἱμάτιον also. While this has traditionally been seen as a call to being meek and submissive, interpreters like Wink and Carter see it more as 'nonviolent resistance to evil': 'By standing naked before one's creditor who has both garments in his hand, one shames and dishonors the creditor. Nakedness exposes, among other things, the greed and cruel effect of the creditor's action and the unjust system the creditor represents'.[109] Wink exclaims, 'Imagine the hilarity this saying must have evoked'.[110] Something similar happens with the blow on the cheek: while Luke suggests simply being hit in the face, Matthew's specifying 'the right cheek' (Matt. 5.39; cp. Luke 6.29) entails a more insulting back-handed blow dealt by a superior like a master to a slave or 'the religious elite with a dangerous preacher (Matt. 26.67)', as Carter likens it to Jesus' own treatment.[111] Refusing to retaliate to such legally sanctioned violence, but instead 'turning the other cheek' for yet more abuse is indeed a radical approach to the law. Strecker relates both antitheses to the Golden Rule to summarize the teaching of Jesus.[112] However, in Matthew's version, again we see his typical redactional concern as he adds, 'for this is the law and the prophets' (cp. Matt. 7.12 with Luke 6.31)

The antithesis on the love of enemies makes use of material shared with Luke (Matt. 5.43-48; cp. Luke 6.27-36), but Matthew's 'tax collectors' and 'Gentiles' (instead of Luke's simple 'sinners') again probably reflects his Jewish background. It concludes with the aphorism, 'Be perfect, therefore, as your heavenly Father is perfect' (Matt. 5.48), which sums up all of the antitheses —

Brill, 1999), pp. 385-407; John Piper, 'Love your enemies': Jesus' Love Command in the Synoptic Gospels and in the Early Christian Paraenesis. A History of the Tradition and Interpretation of Its Uses, SNTSMS 38 (Cambridge: Cambridge University Press, 1979), see esp. pp. 141-52.

109. Carter, Matthew and the Margins, p. 152.

110. Walter Wink, 'Neither Passivity nor Violence: Jesus' Third Way (Matt. 5.38-42 par.)', in The Love of Enemy and Nonretaliation in the New Testament, ed. Willard M. Swartley (Louisville: Westminster John Knox, 1992), pp. 102-25; quotation from p. 107.

111. Carter, Matthew and the Margins, pp. 151-52; see also Wink, 'Neither Passivity nor Violence', pp. 104-5.

112. Georg Strecker, 'Compliance — Love of One's Enemy — The Golden Rule', Australian Biblical Review 29 (1981), pp. 38-46.

and indeed Matthew's attitude to the law, which is 'perfected' in Jesus' totally demanding loving interpretation. To be 'perfect', τέλειος, is to be completely whole, 'holy as I the Lord your God am holy' (Lev. 19.2). This is neither antinomian nor casuistic — but fulfilling in all senses of the word. As Meier concludes, 'Jesus is the Messiah who brings consummation, not the revolutionary who brings desolation'.[113] Once again Jesus, the 'perfect' interpreter of the law, then lives out his words in his deeds at the passion, not retaliating when he is slapped in the face by his enemies and allowing them to strip him of his cloak and tunic (Matt. 26.67-68; 27.28-30).

e. The power of the state and taxes

Matthew follows Mark's pericope about paying the census tax to the emperor with only a couple of very minor changes of order (Matt. 22.15-22; cp. Mark 12.13-17). However, it is preceded several chapters earlier by the curious story of Peter being asked by tax collectors if Jesus pays the temple tax; Jesus, for his part, instructs Peter to catch a fish which has a Greek coin in its mouth sufficient to pay the tax for them both (17.24-27). Given that this pericope is unique to Matthew's gospel, there has been much speculation about why he has preserved it here.

Hagner argues that 'it is of importance to Matthew to continue to press his argument about the loyalty of the Jesus of history to fundamental Jewish realities such as the law and the temple'.[114] Van Aarde's study of the passage takes in ecology and economics as he notes Jesus' point that 'the children are free' (18.26) — but that the miraculous catch rescues Peter 'from the abuses of the temple cult' (having to pay this tax with an idolatrous Tyrian silver coin) without needing to resort to refusal like the Essenes; he concludes, 'Matthew represented Jesus as the fulfilment of the covenant . . . because he shows through his conduct and teachings that compassion is the fulfilment of the law, of the rules of the covenant'.[115] Garland explores the various possibilities, depending on the situation either in the time of the historical Jesus when the half-shekel tax went towards the daily sacrifices in the temple or after the destruction of the temple

113. Meier, *The Vision of Matthew*, p. 262, see further pp. 244-62 on the antitheses; also Willard M. Swartley, 'Matthew: Emmanuel, Power for Peacemaking', in his *Covenant of Peace: The Missing Peace in New Testament Theology and Ethics* (Grand Rapids: Eerdmans, 2006), pp. 53-91.

114. Hagner, *Matthew*, vol. 2, p. 511.

115. A. G. van Aarde, 'A Silver Coin in the Mouth of a Fish (Matthew 17:24-27) — A Miracle of Nature, Ecology, Economy and the Politics of Holiness', *Neotestamentica* 27.1 (1993), pp. 1-25; quotation from p. 21.

in AD 70 when the Romans diverted the δίδραχμα into the *fiscus Iudaicus,* which went into the temple of Jupiter on the Capitol at Rome as a sign of the Roman victory and Jewish humiliation. Whichever the background, Garland reads it for its theological 'object lesson', to demonstrate the freedom of the children of God and to avoid giving offence — which prepares the way for the discourse of chap. 18 with similar themes.[116] Carter laments that 'most readings of this enigmatic scene are apolitical and tax-free'; he also sees it as preparing for instruction for 'the marginal community' in chap. 18, and teaching that whichever empire demands tribute, in the end 'God's sovereignty will triumph'.[117] What these various readings have in common is that they all demonstrate the importance of reading Matthew, even in such apparently obscure passages, both in terms of his historical setting and in the light of his main theological concern to show how Jesus fulfils the true righteousness of God's kingdom for the new community of God's children.

Thus while Matthew's main ethical theme is the fulfilment and proper interpretation of the law in and through Jesus' life and teaching under the sovereign rule of God, it is notable that these same theological concerns also drive his individual passages on particular human moral experiences such as marriage and the family, or wealth and violence — even to the thorny question of taxes! In this way, these particular stories about Jesus' interpretations of the law fit between the large discourses of his teaching about the kingdom to provide a harmony of his words and deeds in Matthew's biographical narrative. Important though the discourses of Jesus' teaching, such as the Sermon on the Mount, are, they cannot be divorced from Matthew's bigger picture. In the light of all the above, we must now turn finally to how he expects us to imitate Jesus in the righteousness of the kingdom of heaven.

5. Imitating Jesus, the friend of sinners

We have already noted in our study of Jesus the injunction based on the traditional call to 'be holy as God is holy' (Lev. 19.2) which Matthew renders in the Sermon on the Mount as, 'Be perfect, therefore, as your heavenly Father is perfect' (Matt. 5.48). This exhorts us to emulate the perfection of God but also raises the suggestion that we are not all yet perfect. Therefore we must turn to our final area of this study, to examine as we have done with Jesus, Paul, and

116. David E. Garland, 'The Temple Tax in Matthew 17:24-25 and the Principle of Not Causing Offense', in *Treasures New and Old,* ed. Bauer and Powell, pp. 69-98.

117. Carter, *Matthew and the Margins,* pp. 356-60.

Mark, what Matthew's view is of what it means to follow and imitate Jesus, and how inclusive is the community of followers which he envisages.

a. Discipleship in Matthew

The first disciples are called by the lakeside (4.18-22, repeating Mark 1.16-20) which involves leaving everything at Jesus' command, as Peter later reminds him (19.27). Matthew's account of the stilling of the storm (8.23-27) is the classic example of Matthean redaction.[118] In Mark's account, 'they' take Jesus into the boat (Mark 4.36); in Matthew, Jesus takes the initiative to get into the boat — and 'the disciples followed him' (8.23). 'Disciples' and 'following' give the moral of the story. The disciples in Mark protest about Jesus' apparent lack of concern in the storm (Mark 4.38); in Matthew, their cry becomes a prayer: 'Lord, save us! We are perishing' (Matt. 8.25). Further, while in Mark they have 'no faith' (Mark 4.40), here Jesus calls them 'you of little faith' (8.26). This word ὀλιγόπιστοι, which does not occur in Mark, is used in Matthew when the disciples get anxious (6.30) or frightened (14.30-31), when they misunderstand him (16.8) or are unable to cast out the epileptic demon (17.20). As Luz puts it, 'Matthew has quite consistently "improved" the picture of the disciples in his elimination of the Markan motif of their failure to understand. In Matthew the disciples do understand'.[119]

Such sympathy for the disciples and their 'little faith' creates a more positive picture than in Mark. Of course, they still betray Jesus (Judas, 26.25, 47-50), deny him (Peter, 26.69-75) and forsake him (all of them, 26.31, 56) — and some still doubt even after the resurrection (28.17). However, unlike the disciples in Mark's account, they do understand Jesus' teaching (13.51; 16.12; 17.13; cp. Mark 6.52; 8.21; 9.32), and they believe and worship him (14.33). As 'disciples', they study under the 'one teacher and master' (10.24-25; 23.8-10) to become teachers themselves. Eventually they do 'as Jesus directed them' (21.6; 26.19; 28.16) as they start to become the church, the new community of God's people, built upon the rock of Peter with the keys of the kingdom of heaven (16.18-19) and the authority to bind and loose given to them all (18.18). Now that Jesus has come as the true teacher of the law, they are to teach the whole world (28.20).[120]

118. See G. Bornkamm, 'The Stilling of the Storm in Matthew', in *Tradition and Interpretation in Matthew*, ed. G. Bornkamm, G. Barth and H. J. Held (London: SCM, 1963), pp. 52-57.
119. Luz, 'The Disciples in the Gospel according to Matthew', in his *Studies in Matthew*, pp. 115-42; quotation from pp. 121-22.
120. For a full study, see Michael J. Wilkins, *The Concept of Disciple in Matthew's Gospel: As*

This at last begins to bring our themes together: Matthew's Christology is constantly concerned to depict Jesus as the truly righteous interpreter of the law in all his teaching, especially ethics, as well as in his deeds. Those whom he calls to follow him have to become 'learners', disciples, and grow in their 'little faith' and understanding, despite their difficulties, so that they too may 'learn' to teach others. Thus, Luz is clear that 'connecting being a disciple with the person of the earthly Jesus seems to be fundamental above all for the ethics of this Gospel, i.e., for the imperative'; 'in Matthew's understanding of the disciples and in his Christology we thus have an indicative and an imperative together'.[121] Discipleship in Matthew is therefore a process which begins with the call of Jesus to follow him, and is always intimately connected with learning from him as we grow towards the truly righteous perfection which reflects the character of God himself.

b. An inclusive community?

Furthermore, we have argued that Jesus does not call people to follow him individually, but within the community of other learners and followers, which can be a very mixed group of people. We have seen that in Jesus' acceptance of a wide range of backgrounds among his first disciples, in the variety of people Paul seems to envisage in the communities to which he writes and in Mark's sense of an inclusive community. Here, not only is Matthew the only gospel to use the word ἐκκλησία, church (16.18 and twice in 18.17), but the second and fourth discourses clearly envisage a community with a mission (chap. 10) and discipline (chap. 18). Some of the reconstructions of Matthew's community can seem to suggest a small, introverted group battling with the synagogue as they seek the perfect interpretation of the law[122] — which is hardly an image of an inclusive community. Against this, Donaldson is right to note that 'discipleship in Matthew's Gospel, however, is characterized not only by a relationship to Jesus and God, but also by *the disciples' relationship to other disciples* in community'.[123]

The call to 'be perfect as your heavenly Father is perfect' is the conclusion of the antitheses in general, and in particular of the one on the love of enemies,

---

Reflected in the Use of the Term μαθητής, NovTSup 59 (Leiden: Brill, 1988); also, Carter, *Matthew: Storyteller, Interpreter, Evangelist*, pp. 215-27.

121. Luz, 'The Disciples in the Gospel according to Matthew', pp. 134-36.

122. See sect. 1.b above, esp. nn. 22-33.

123. Terence L. Donaldson, 'Guiding Readers — Making Disciples', in *Patterns of Discipleship in the New Testament*, ed. Richard N. Longenecker (Grand Rapids: Eerdmans, 1996), pp. 30-49; quotation, with his italics, from p. 45.

which is certainly inclusive, based upon an open view of God's generosity: 'so that you may be children of your Father in heaven; for he makes his sun rise on the evil and on the good, and sends rain on the righteous and on the unrighteous' (5.45). This suggestion that God allows both evil and good, righteous and unrighteous to exist together is reinforced by the parable of the Wheat and Weeds. This parable and its subsequent private explanation to the disciples (Matt. 13.24-30, 36-43) is unique to Matthew's gospel and provides a good example of an inclusive community in which good and bad are allowed to live alongside each other until the judgement. Admittedly, the 'good seed' was sown by the master and the weeds by his 'enemy' — but to uproot the latter too soon might harm the former. And, of course, it is always possible that some things which look like weeds at first might turn out to be wheat after all. Nonetheless, there is a clear warning of judgement to come, when all will be harvested and the wicked weeds destroyed, so the existence of both together should not breed complacency. Some commentators want to interpret the mixed field as the life of the church — and that would certainly fit our concern for an inclusive community well. However, the explanation is quite clear: 'the field is the world' (13.38). Despite this, the background of Matthew's community still suggests that the parable can be applied to it as well as more widely. As Meier concludes, 'The field is to be interpreted universally. It refers to the world, and not simply to the church, though the situation and problems of the church are no doubt in Matthew's mind'.[124] Similarly, if 'the least of these my brothers' in the parable of the Sheep and Goats is understood in the more limited sense to represent the church, then again we note that this community includes the hungry and thirsty, the naked, sick and those in prison — as well as strangers (25.35-40).[125]

That all was not perfect in the life of the church is shown as Matthew repeats Mark's story about James and John wanting the best seats in the kingdom, with one important difference: rather than have the apostles make such a request (which might reflect badly on church leaders), according to Matthew, their mother asked for the favour! However, it still leads into Jesus' teaching that his disciples are not to go about lording it over others, but to be servants of all (Matt. 20.20-28; cp. Mark 10.35-45).

Similar themes dominate the crucial fourth discourse with all its material on the life of the church. Chapter 18 begins with the disciples asking, 'Who is the greatest in the kingdom of heaven?', to which Jesus replies with the example of a child (18.1-5). This is followed by his teaching about not causing another or oneself to stumble, and by the parable of the Lost Sheep as the example of how

---

124. Meier, *The Vision of Matthew*, p. 91.
125. See our discussion in sect. 2 above, esp. pp. 201-2, nn. 56-58.

far God is willing to go to find the lost (18.6-14). This leads neatly into the teaching about how to handle church discipline (18.15-20), all of which then comes under the rubric of unlimited forgiveness, 'seventy times seven': in response to Peter's question of how often one should forgive 'if another member of the church [as the NRSV translates ὁ ἀδελφός μου, 'my brother'] sins against me', Jesus says that we should imitate the example of God's merciful forgiveness, rather than be like the forgiven servant who refused to forgive a small debt (18.23-35). Thus the two parables of the Lost Sheep and the Unforgiving Servant suggest 'a wideness in God's mercy' which the hearers are encouraged to emulate in the life of the church. Admittedly, the material between them does allow for excommunication of the one who 'refuses to listen even to the church' (18.15-20). However, even in such a difficult situation, 'Matthew's advice here is aimed at drawing back members who are perilously close to being lost to the community';[126] one is reminded of Paul's concern to save the incestuous man's soul in 1 Cor. 5.5. The thrust of the two parables which enclose these instructions and the rest of the chapter's teaching stresses the same message as throughout the gospel, that the demands of the law are fulfilled supremely through following the example of Jesus. It is the love command which reigns supreme in the kingdom of heaven, as Carter stresses in his exposition of this chapter: 'that [God's] reign shapes practices and relationships which differ greatly from Rome's empire. Instead of the empire's arrogant privileging of the center and mistreatment of the rest, instead of its hierarchical structure whereby a few control the many, this community practices humility, includes the marginalized, and exercises care for one another. Instead of exterminating or excluding dissenters, it seeks inclusion and relationship (18:15-20), forgiveness and reconciliation (18:21-35).'[127] Therefore, reconstructions of Matthew's community as a small, embattled sectarian group of the like-minded are wide of the mark: the call to perfection is addressed to sinners who are setting out on the journey towards holiness in the mixed company of others who respond in their own way.

c. Imitating Jesus

Finally, therefore, we come to our central theme that ancient biographical narratives were written to encourage the imitation of their central subject. It is also the case that, with his Jewish background, Matthew is likely to have been aware

126. Overman, *Church and Community in Crisis*, p. 267.
127. Carter, *Matthew and the Margins*, p. 361.

of *ma'aseh* and the disciples' need to imitate their rabbi. It is thus significant that Stanton, having accepted my argument that he should take more seriously the implications of his earlier study of the genre of the gospels,[128] concludes his more recent comprehensive study of 'a gospel for a new people' thus: 'Matthew intended that his biography of Jesus, with its many strong Christological themes, would shape the convictions and lives of the recipients of his gospel.'[129] Similarly, Allison draws upon my earlier work that the 'biographical impulse' in Matthew leads to the *imitatio Christi*: 'Our evangelist, like Paul, Origen, and other early Christians, makes Jesus a model for emulation. This is why, despite the regrettable silence of many commentators, our gospel hosts a multitude of obvious connections between Jesus' words and his deeds'; it 'involves the mimetic following of Jesus, who is virtue embodied.'[130]

Of course, it was not necessarily only the central character in a biography who was a subject for *mimesis:* the other people could also give examples to follow or avoid. Therefore, the disciples, struggling with their 'little faith', yet following Jesus, provide good material for the audience to imitate. Thus Wilkins ends his exhaustive study of discipleship in Matthew with the conclusion, 'Peter and the disciples are historical examples of what Jesus, with his people, can accomplish.'[131] The disciples are a good pattern to follow, because they are fallible human beings like us, but they are to be imitated only insofar as they themselves are imitating Jesus.[132] Luz argues from his study of the second teaching block in chap. 10 that 'the disciple discourse reveals itself as a discourse on the way of life of the disciples which corresponds to that of the master'.[133] As Jesus was teaching the new righteousness in the kingdom of heaven, so he instructed his disciples to do the same. In this way, Matthew's account may be compared with Paul's exhortation, 'Be imitators of me, as I am of Christ' (1 Cor. 11.1). Thus

---

128. G. N. Stanton, *Jesus of Nazareth in New Testament Preaching*, SNTSMS 27 (Cambridge: Cambridge University Press, 1974); see my evaluation in Richard A. Burridge, *What Are the Gospels? A Comparison with Graeco-Roman Biography*, SNTSMS 70 (Cambridge: Cambridge University Press, 1992), pp. 82-84; rev. 2nd edn. (Grand Rapids: Eerdmans, 2004), pp. 78-80.

129. Stanton, *A Gospel for a New People*, p. 381; see pp. 62-64 on the biographical genre of Matthew.

130. Dale C. Allison, Jr., 'Structure, Biographical Impulse, and the *Imitatio Christi*', in his *Studies in Matthew: Interpretation Past and Present*, pp. 135-55, quotations from pp. 149 and 153; see also nn. 20, 24 and 46 for how Allison's change of view to seeing Matthew as biography is the result of my work, 'I now prefer to think that Burridge . . . is right'.

131. Wilkins, *The Concept of Disciple in Matthew's Gospel*, p. 224.

132. See Jeannine K. Brown, *The Disciples in Narrative Perspective: The Portrayal and Function of the Matthean Disciples* (Atlanta: Society of Biblical Literature, 2002), esp. 145-46.

133. Luz, 'Discipleship: A Matthean Manifesto for a Dynamic Ecclesiology', in his *Studies in Matthew*, pp. 143-64; quotation from p. 159.

it is not surprising that Matera and Gerhardsson entitle their sections on ethics in Matthew with Jesus as 'a model of righteous behaviour'.[134] Similarly, Howell's study of Matthew's 'inclusive story' notes how 'Jesus can function as a model for the disciples'; since the implied reader is included in the story, then he concludes that 'Jesus is exemplary as a model for discipleship'.[135]

Once again, I want to give the last word in this section to Bonhoeffer, who concludes his study of 'the cost of discipleship' based upon Matthew's portrait of the ethics of Jesus thus: 'The disciple looks solely at his Master. But when a man follows Jesus Christ and bears the image of the incarnate, crucified and risen Lord, when he has become the image of God, we may at last say that he has been called to be the "imitator of God." The follower of Jesus is the imitator of God.'[136]

6. Conclusion

Our study has moved from the so-called 'paucity of ethical material' in Mark to Matthew's gospel which contains what many consider to be the 'quintessence' of Jesus' moral teaching, the Sermon on the Mount. In fact, more detailed consideration has shown both those judgements to be erroneous. Our biographical reading of Mark's narrative of Jesus' deeds as well as his words revealed much more ethical material. It is true that Matthew does certainly build upon Mark's account and contains much more specific, ethical teaching. However, to concentrate on these sayings alone, and especially upon the Sermon on the Mount, is to miss the overall thrust which a biographical reading of the gospels can provide. Matthew's Christological portrait depicts Jesus as the true interpreter of righteousness under the law, steering a middle path between antinomians and legalists, as his likely audience grappled with their debate with Pharisaic-rabbinic Judaism in the developing parting of the ways between church and synagogue. As befits his probable historical setting in the decade or two after the destruction of Jerusalem, Matthew's eschatology requires more detailed ethical teaching for the present which is nonetheless still dominated by the final judgement still to come.

Rather than being singled out as the 'essence' of Jesus' ethics, the Sermon on the Mount is best interpreted as the first of Matthew's *five* discourses, bal-

134. Matera, *NT Ethics*, pp. 50-53; Gerhardsson, *The Ethos of the Bible*, pp. 54-60.
135. David B. Howell, *Matthew's Inclusive Story: A Study in the Narrative Rhetoric of the First Gospel*, JSNTSS 42 (Sheffield: Sheffield Academic Press, 1990), pp. 258-59.
136. Bonhoeffer, *The Cost of Discipleship*, p. 304.

anced by the eschatological warnings at the end of the narrative, with the parables of the Kingdom right at the heart of the gospel in the middle. True righteousness is shown in Jesus' interpretation of the law throughout the narrative of his activities, leading up to his teaching about the centrality of the double love command of God and neighbour. In this context, the major moral experiences of human life, such as marriage and the family, wealth and violence, power and the state, are also brought under this true interpretation of the law. Finally, Matthew has built upon Mark's theme of discipleship to show the followers of Jesus growing in their 'little faith' and beginning to learn how to become teachers of the new righteousness themselves. But they do so within an inclusive community, ruled by the forgiving love of God which ever seeks the lost, as supremely they seek to imitate the person of Jesus who did not just teach them the law but made them righteous through his life and ministry, death and resurrection. There is so much more to the ethics of this gospel than just the Sermon on the Mount, sublime though it may be. Matthew's particular situation and likely historical setting led him to write his biography of Jesus in this particular manner — but the remarkable thing is how, in its own way, it still reflects what our studies of Jesus, Paul and Mark have revealed.

VI. Luke-Acts: A Universal Concern

Matthew takes Mark's account, written in the difficult times of the 60s under suffering and persecution, and retells the story in such a way as to make it relevant for his readers' situation a decade or two later during the stressful period when both the synagogue and the early church were beginning to redefine themselves after the sack of Jerusalem; in response to the synagogue's concentration on the reading and interpretation of the law, Matthew shows how Jesus is the true interpreter of and himself the fulfilment of the law. The usual scholarly consensus, which we are following, is that Luke was probably writing around the same period of the 80s, and also used Mark as his main source together with another collection of teachings shared with Matthew which we know as Q (though not necessarily all written down or all one document).[1] It is significant that whereas Matthew tends to collect the Q-sayings material into his five extended teaching discourses, especially the Sermon on the Mount, Luke prefers to provide a narrative context or story which then leads up to the Q-saying or pronouncement. He also includes a substantial amount of material which is unique to himself. What is interesting is how, like Matthew, Luke retells his story of Jesus, but does so in a different way for a different audience, and yet remains true to our basic picture of combining Jesus' deeds and words so that we can imitate his open acceptance of others within an inclusive community. In fact, this is so much so that we can sum up Luke's particular redactional interest as 'a universal concern'.[2]

1. See John S. Kloppenborg, *The Formation of Q: Trajectories in Ancient Wisdom Collections* (Philadelphia: Fortress, 1987); David R. Catchpole, *The Quest for Q* (Edinburgh: T&T Clark, 1993); and James D. G. Dunn, *Jesus Remembered* (Grand Rapids: Eerdmans, 2003), pp. 147-61.
2. For recent general introductions to Luke's composition and theological concerns see Darrell L. Bock, 'Luke', in *The Face of New Testament Studies: A Survey of Recent Research*, ed. Scot

However, the most significant difference is that this is only his first volume: his second one begins, 'In the first book, Theophilus, I wrote about all that Jesus began to do and teach, until the day when he was taken up to heaven' (Acts 1.1). The use of ποιεῖν τε καὶ διδάσκειν, 'to do and teach', confirms the biographical genre of the first book, since, as we have seen, concentrating on the subject's 'deeds and words' is a central feature of ancient Lives. Furthermore, the description of the first book as ἤρξατο ὁ 'Ιησοῦς, what 'Jesus *began* to do and teach', suggests that Luke's second volume recounts what 'Jesus *goes on* to do and teach' in the continuation of the same story.[3] The problem of the genre of Luke's second book is almost as vexed as that of the gospels. The obvious generic parallel for Acts is the ancient historical monograph, a one-volume narrative work usually concentrating on one topic, place or event.[4] In my own 'first book', I raised the possibility of the two volumes being of the same or a related genre, with Luke's gospel being a biography and Acts a biographical narrative like Dicaearchus' *Life of Greece;* alternatively, Acts could be more of an historical monograph, but maintain many biographical generic features such as the focus on Peter and Paul.[5] Since then, there has been much debate, both about whether Luke and Acts have to be of the same genre to belong together, and

---

McKnight and Grant R. Osborne (Grand Rapids: Baker Academic, 2004), pp. 349-72; Carl R. Holladay, *A Critical Introduction to the New Testament: Interpreting the Message and Meaning of Jesus Christ* (Nashville: Abingdon, 2005), pp. 158-89 on Luke and pp. 225-60 on Acts, or pp. 220-68 and 317-62 in the expanded CD version; John T. Squires, 'The Gospel according to Luke', in *The Cambridge Companion to the Gospels,* ed. Stephen C. Barton (Cambridge: Cambridge University Press, 2006), pp. 158-81.

3. Cadbury's definition of Luke-Acts as 'a single continuous work' has been assumed by most scholars since his *The Making of Luke-Acts* (London: Macmillan, 1927; 2nd edn. 1958); for some recent counterarguments, see Richard Pervo, 'Must Luke and Acts Belong to the Same Genre?', in *SBL 1989 Seminar Papers* (Atlanta: Scholars Press, 1989), pp. 309-16, and M. C. Parsons and R. I. Pervo, *Rethinking the Unity of Luke and Acts* (Minneapolis: Fortress, 1993); for an assessment of this and a restatement of the consensus view for unity, see J. Verheyden, 'The Unity of Luke-Acts: What Are We Up To?' and D. Marguerat, 'Luc-Actes: Une unite à construire', both in *The Unity of Luke-Acts,* 47th Colloquium Biblicum Lovaniense, ed. J. Verheyden (Leuven: Leuven University Press, 1999), pp. 13-56 and 57-81; also more recently, C. Kavin Rowe, 'History, Hermeneutics and the Unity of Luke-Acts'; Luke Timothy Johnson, 'Literary Criticism of Luke-Acts: Is Reception-History Pertinent?'; and Markus Bockmuehl, 'Why Not Let Acts Be Acts? In Conversation with C. Kavin Rowe', all in *JSNT* 28.2 (2005), pp. 131-57, 159-62 and 163-66.

4. See, for example, Colin J. Hemer, *The Book of Acts in the Setting of Hellenistic History,* WUNT 49 (Tübingen: J. C. B. Mohr, 1989); Darryl W. Palmer, 'Acts and the Ancient Historical Monograph', in *The Book of Acts in Its Ancient Literary Setting,* ed. Bruce W. Winter and Andrew D. Clarke (Carlisle: Paternoster/Grand Rapids: Eerdmans, 1993), pp. 1-29.

5. Richard A. Burridge, *What Are the Gospels? A Comparison with Graeco-Roman Biography,* SNTSMS 70 (Cambridge: Cambridge University Press, 1992), pp. 244-46; rev. and updated edn. (Grand Rapids: Eerdmans, 2004), pp. 237-39.

about the various possible genres for Acts.[6] It is notable that more recent commentaries on Acts begin with discussions of its genre in the area of biography and historical monograph.[7] Schmidt concludes, 'It seems unlikely that attempts to settle once and for all whether Luke and/or Acts are really "history" or "biography", or something else, can be successful', although in the end he settles for 'the rather wide spectrum of "Hellenistic historiography"',[8] while Talbert continues to argue for biography.[9] Interestingly, Porter has recently brought together the 'ethics of discourse' with biography to argue that 'the ethical discourse of the ancient world, biography, may be at play, not only in the Gospels, but in the book of Acts as well'.[10]

Since monograph and biography are *genera proxima,* both being narrative genres of one person *(bios)* or one topic, but containing accounts of several people (monograph), we shall continue with our narrative account of Luke's ethics, looking mostly at his portrait of Jesus in the first volume and supplementing it with his other material from Acts. Therefore, we will follow the same approach as with Paul, Mark and Matthew, beginning with Luke's Christology

---

6. For a more detailed account of this debate, see my rev. and updated edn. of *What Are the Gospels?* (2004), pp. 275-79; see also Daniel Marguerat, *The First Christian Historian: Writing the 'Acts of the Apostles',* SNTSMS 121 (Cambridge: Cambridge University Press, 2002), esp. pp. 1-42; and Clare K. Rothschild, *Luke-Acts and the Rhetoric of History: An Investigation of Early Christian Historiography,* WUNT 2.175 (Tübingen: J. C. B. Mohr, 2004).

7. See, for example, F. Scott Spencer, *Acts* (Sheffield: Sheffield Academic Press, 1997), pp. 13-14; Joseph A. Fitzmyer, S.J., *The Acts of the Apostles: A New Translation with Introduction and Commentary,* The Anchor Bible (New York: Doubleday, 1998), pp. 47-49; Ben Witherington, III, *The Acts of the Apostles: A Socio-Rhetorical Commentary* (Grand Rapids: Eerdmans, 1998), pp. 2-39, see esp. pp. 15-21.

8. Daryl D. Schmidt, 'Rhetorical Influences and Genre: Luke's Preface and the Rhetoric of Hellenistic Historiography', in *Jesus and the Heritage of Israel: Luke's Narrative Claim upon Israel's Legacy,* ed. David P. Moessner (Harrisburg, PA: Trinity Press International, 1999), pp. 27-60; quotations from pp. 51 and 59; in the same volume, see also the articles by Richard Pervo, 'Israel's Heritage and Claims upon the Genre(s) of Luke and Acts: The Problems of a History', in *Jesus and the Heritage of Israel,* pp. 127-43; and I. Howard Marshall, '"Israel" and the Story of Salvation: One Theme in Two Parts', in *Jesus and the Heritage of Israel,* pp. 340-58, esp. p. 348 and n. 27, accepting my work on the biographical genre of Luke; more recently, Pervo has argued that the amount of direct speech in Acts is unlike historiography and more like popular narrative, Richard I. Pervo, 'Direct Speech in Acts and the Question of Genre', *JSNT* 28.3 (2006), pp. 285-307.

9. Charles H. Talbert, 'The Acts of the Apostles: Monograph or *Bios?*' in *History, Literature, and Society in the Book of Acts,* ed. Ben Witherington, III (Cambridge: Cambridge University Press, 1996), pp. 58-72; see also L. C. A. Alexander, 'Acts and Ancient Intellectual Biography', in *The Book of Acts in Its Ancient Literary Setting,* ed. Winter and Clarke, pp. 31-63.

10. Stanley E. Porter, 'The Genre of Acts and the Ethics of Discourse', in *Acts and Ethics,* ed. Thomas E. Phillips, New Testament Monographs 9 (Sheffield: Phoenix Press, 2005), pp. 1-15; quotation from p. 15.

and eschatology, and then going through the material on the law and love and other ethical issues, to see what emerges with regard to our central theme about imitating Jesus within an open community.

1. Luke's Christology

'As with all the biblical writers, Luke's ethics follows logically from his fundamental convictions about his Christ.'[11] Mark went straight into his story, but Matthew began his account with a deliberate echo of the opening book of the Torah, 'the book of the genesis of Jesus' who is also 'the Messiah' and 'son of David, son of Abraham' (Matt. 1.1), thus signalling that both his own interest and his target audience were Jewish. Luke, in contrast, begins with a typical Greek preface in a single classical Greek period, explaining his intention in writing and dedicating his work to his patron or sponsor, Theophilus (Luke 1.1-4).[12] Theophilus' name means 'Lover of God', but we know nothing about him beyond his official title, κράτιστε, 'your Excellency'; however, such dedications to a publisher or benefactor were typical in classical writings. Luke's account is a 'narrative' (διήγησις), based upon eyewitnesses 'from the beginning' (οἱ ἀπ' ἀρχῆς αὐτόπται) and 'in sequence' or 'orderly' (καθεξῆς). Thus, Luke has moved Jesus' biography to the universal stage as a Graeco-Roman 'life', and similar prefaces can be found in many other ancient biographies.[13] This immediately signals a greater universal perspective for Luke and suggests a target audience more among Gentiles. It also gives us our first clue about Luke's portrait of Jesus — that he is for all the world, and not just for audiences with a Jewish background.

Such universality is confirmed if we compare their lists of Jesus' ancestry: while Matthew begins his genealogy with Abraham and moves on to Joseph, Luke takes his genealogy (located after the baptism as Jesus begins his public ministry, Luke 3.23-38) of seventy-seven names back past Abraham and Jewish patriarchs all the way to Adam, son of God and father of the whole human race.

---

11. Robert W. Wall, 'Introduction: New Testament Ethics', *Horizons in Biblical Theology*, 5.2 (1983), pp. 49-94; quotation, p. 59.

12. For a lively account, see Morna D. Hooker, *Beginnings: Keys That Open the Gospels* (London: SCM, 1997), pp. 43-47.

13. See further Loveday C. A. Alexander, 'Luke's Preface in the Context of Greek Preface-Writing', *NovT* 28 (1986), pp. 48-74; idem, *The Preface to Luke's Gospel: Literary Convention and Social Context in Luke 1.1-4 and Acts 1.1*, SNTSMS 78 (Cambridge: Cambridge University Press, 1993) and her chapter, 'Formal Elements and Genre: Which Greco-Roman Prologues Most Closely Parallel the Lukan Prologues?', in *Jesus and the Heritage of Israel*, pp. 9-26.

As Marshall comments, 'We may be sure that the carrying back of the genealogy to Adam is meant to stress the universal significance of Jesus for the whole of the human race, and not merely for the seed of Abraham'.[14]

The preface and the genealogy also show Luke's interest in history and time, as he makes clear his place in the sequence going back to the eyewitnesses as well as Jesus' place in the history of both Israel and the world. Redactional studies on Luke ever since Conzelmann's seminal study have noted his stress on how the coming of Jesus marks out the 'centre of history' in the 'middle of time'.[15] However, Luke is also interested in geography and space:[16] at a basic level this is shown by the way he structures his gospel's main narrative in three main geographical sections (Galilee, 4.14–9.50; Jordan, 9.51–19.27; and Jerusalem, 19.28–24.53) and then radiates out from Jerusalem to the ends of the earth in Acts (1.8). However, more recent studies using the insights of social geographical theory have shown how Luke's portrait of Jesus reconfigures space as well as time.[17] Therefore, we shall follow this structure in our analysis of his Christology as we explore the universal significance of Jesus for all times and places.

a. Beginnings: infancy and childhood

To locate Jesus' birth within history, Luke goes back beyond his baptism (as in Mark), and even beyond his birth (as in Matthew), to the childless parents of his forerunner (Luke 1.5-80). Remarkably, the style changes from the quasi-classical Greek of the preface to an Old Testament atmosphere. Luke is a writer with great literary skill; changes of style happen throughout the gospel and on into Acts, where a gradual linguistic shift through the book from a Semitic style to more cosmopolitan Greek mirrors the geographical shift from Jerusalem to Rome. In the gospel's opening stories, phrases like 'the house of', 'before the face of', 'and behold', 'and it came to pass' evoke the Hebrew scriptures. Zecha-

---

14. I. Howard Marshall, *The Gospel of Luke: A Commentary on the Greek Text*, NIGTC (Grand Rapids: Eerdmans, 1978), p. 161.

15. H. Conzelmann, *Die Mitte der Zeit: Studien zur Theologie des Lukas* (Tübingen: Mohr, 1954); unfortunately, the English title does not translate the German, 'the Middle of Time', but instead is the rather tame *The Theology of St. Luke*, trans. Geoffrey Buswell (London: Faber, 1960); see also Joseph A. Fitzmyer, S.J., *The Gospel according to Luke*, Anchor Bible 28 and 28A (New York: Doubleday, 1981 and 1985), pp. 171-92.

16. On Luke and his use of geography, see further Fitzmyer, *Luke*, pp. 162-71 and Conzelmann, *The Theology of St. Luke*, pp. 18-94.

17. See Matthew Sleeman, '"Under Heaven": The Narrative-Geographical Implications of the Ascended Christ for the Believers (and Their Mission) within Acts 1:1–11:18', Ph.D. thesis, King's College London, 2006.

riah and Elizabeth are 'righteous before God' (like Noah, Gen. 6.9) and child-less (like Abraham and Sarah, Gen. 16.1; 18.11); they burst into psalms of praise (like Moses and Miriam in Exod. 15.1-21, or Hannah in 1 Sam. 2.1-10). There are angels and miraculous births, and Simeon and Anna keep the ancient faith alive in the temple (2.25-38). Throughout his narrative, Luke makes it perfectly clear: 'In Jesus Christ, God's activity in the history of Israel is manifested'.[18]

Unlike Matthew's picture of the court of King Herod, the wise men, and the powerful, Luke begins his portrait of Jesus among the pious poor and women, the meek and the lowly — Zechariah and Elizabeth, and Mary herself. While Matthew sees things through Joseph's eyes, Luke takes Mary's viewpoint, treasured in her heart (2.19, 51); the opening chapter is not about *his* genealogy but *her* family. The angel appears not in a dream to Joseph (Matt. 1.20), but visi-bly to Mary (Luke 1.26), to her kinsman (1.11) and to the shepherds (2.9). The lowly praise God in the revolutionary tones of the *Magnificat* (1.46-55) and *Benedictus* (1.68-79) for his salvation for the poor and overthrow of the power-ful. When Jesus is finally born, he is laid in a feeding trough because 'there was no place for them at the inn' (2.7). In this way, Luke sets up his basic theme that, coming out of Israel's history, Jesus is the universal bearer of burdens, con-cerned especially for women, the poor and outcasts, of all races and nations.[19] As Hurtado puts it, 'Clearly it is an important Lukan emphasis that Jesus is the Messiah of *Israel*, and precisely as such also brings *universal* redemption'.[20]

Luke alone includes a typical biographical childhood cameo which fore-shadows the adult. The twelve-year-old Jesus confounding the wise teachers in the temple is reminiscent of the early brilliance of Cicero at school (Plutarch, *Cicero* 2.2) — but it leads up to the pithy *sententia*, ἐν τοῖς τοῦ πατρός μου δεῖ εἶναί με: 'I must be about my Father's business' (2.41-52). So, despite all the Se-mitic language and Jewish atmosphere of Luke's opening sections, the universal concern of Jesus for everyone is introduced as nothing less than the mission of God: as Minear concludes, 'The first two chapters of the Gospel "set the stage" for all subsequent speeches and actions'.[21]

18. Jacob Jervell, *The Theology of the Acts of the Apostles* (Cambridge: Cambridge University Press, 1996), p. 30.

19. For a more political reading of the infancy narratives, see Richard A. Horsley, *The Libera-tion of Christmas: The Infancy Narratives in Social Context* (New York: Crossroad, 1989), and the critique by Charles H. Talbert, 'Jesus' Birth in Luke and the Nature of Religious Language', in his collection of essays, *Reading Luke-Acts in Its Mediterranean Milieu*, NovTSup 107 (Leiden: Brill, 2003), pp. 79-90, esp. pp. 89-90.

20. Larry W. Hurtado, *Lord Jesus Christ: Devotion to Jesus in Earliest Christianity* (Grand Rapids: Eerdmans, 2003), pp. 343-44; his italics.

21. Paul S. Minear, 'Luke's Use of the Birth Stories', in *Studies in Luke-Acts: Essays Presented in*

b. Ministry in the middle of space and time: Galilee and Jordan

Whereas Mark moves into a slower reflective middle section to consider Jesus' identity, and Matthew structures his gospel around the five teaching discourses, Luke prefers to handle this material in a narrative setting as he depicts Jesus going about teaching and healing, first in Galilee (4.14–9.50) and then 'he set his face to go to Jerusalem', a journey which takes most of the next ten chapters as Jesus and his disciples head down the Jordan valley (9.51–19.27). While the so-called 'Sermon on the Plain' (Luke 6.17-49) does include some of the Q-material which Matthew places in the Sermon on the Mount, Luke prefers to place many of the other sayings which appear in Matthew's Sermon into narrative contexts; similarly, instead of collecting all the negative comments about scribes and Pharisees into one vituperative chapter like Matt. 23, Luke has various stories of interactions between Jesus and the religious leaders, sometimes over a meal, which include, and usually build up to, the individual sayings.

The focus for this narrative of Jesus' ministry to all is made clear through his opening 'manifesto' delivered at the synagogue at Nazareth, which replaces Matthew and Mark's accounts of Jesus' initial preaching of the kingdom.[22] After reading from Isaiah, 'The Spirit of the Lord is upon me, because he has anointed me to bring good news to the poor. He has sent me to proclaim release to the captives and recovery of sight to the blind, to let the oppressed go free, to proclaim the year of the Lord's favour', Jesus causes consternation by his claim, 'Today this scripture has been fulfilled in your hearing' (Luke 4.14-30). Joel Green sums it up thus: 'People are not to be predetermined as insiders or outsiders by their sex, family heritage, financial position, location in the city or in rural environs, religious purity, and so on. The message of Jesus is that such status markers are no longer binding. Anyone may freely receive the grace of God. Anyone may join the community of Jesus' followers. All are welcome.'[23]

Honor of Paul Schubert, ed. Leander E. Keck and J. Louis Martyn (London: SPCK, 1968), pp. 111-30, quotation from p. 130; for a narrative reading of the opening chapters see Mark Coleridge, *The Birth of the Lukan Narrative: Narrative as Christology in Luke 1–2,* JSNTSS 88 (Sheffield: JSOT Press, 1993).

22. Similarly in Acts both Peter and Paul set out their key themes in preaching to Jews and in synagogues; see F. Neirynck, 'Luke 4,16-30 and the Unity of Luke-Acts', in *The Unity of Luke-Acts,* ed. Verheyden, pp. 357-95.

23. Joel B. Green, *The Theology of the Gospel of Luke* (Cambridge: Cambridge University Press, 1995), p. 82; for further discussion of the manifesto announcement at Nazareth, see idem, *The Theology of the Gospel of Luke,* pp. 76-84; also Christopher J. Schrek, 'The Nazareth Pericope: Luke 4:16-30 in Recent Study', in *L'Evangile de Luc — The Gospel of Luke,* rev. and enlarged edn. of *L'Evangile de Luc: Problèmes littéraires et théologiques,* ed. F. Neirynck, BETL 32 (Leuven: Leuven University Press, 1989), pp. 399-471; and David R. Catchpole, 'The Anointed One in Nazareth', in

Such a manifesto immediately directs attention to Jesus' identity: who is he to announce such things? Thus throughout the first part of Jesus' ministry, Luke shows how the questions are raised: worshippers wonder in the synagogues of Nazareth (4.22) and Capernaum (4.36); questions are asked by the scribes and Pharisees (5.21), John the Baptist (7.19), the disciples (8.25) and Herod (9.9). Jesus himself questions his disciples, and Peter confesses him as 'the Christ of God' (9.18-22): Luke does not say where this event took place, and it is earlier and briefer than Matthew (omitting Peter and the church, Matt. 16.17-19) and Mark (omitting Peter's protests and Jesus' rebuke, Mark 8.32-33). Rather than presenting a single climactic moment of revelation at Caesarea Philippi, Luke provides several suggestions for Jesus' identity.[24]

The first answer is to see Jesus as a prophet.[25] The baptism scene in Luke reminds us of a prophetic anointing; John the Baptist and Matthew's conversation about righteousness is missing, while Luke stresses the descent of the Holy Spirit and the voice addressed to Jesus, 'You are my beloved Son' (3.21-22). Equally, the prophetic atmosphere of Jesus' rejection at Nazareth is enhanced by the references to Elijah and Elisha (4.16-30). The raising of the widow's son at Nain recalls Elijah's similar miracle (Luke 7.11-17; cp. 1 Kings 17.17-24). Further, the crowd calls Jesus 'a great prophet' (7.16); however, this identification is questioned by Simon the Pharisee (7.39). Those around Herod (9.8) and the disciples both suggest that people see Jesus as a prophet (9.19).[26] Jesus compares

From *Jesus to John: Essays on Jesus and New Testament Christology in Honour of Marinus de Jonge,* ed. Martinus C. De Boer, JSNTSS 84 (Sheffield: Sheffield Academic Press, 1993), pp. 231-51.

24. Tuckett notes that Luke-Acts 'points in different directions Christologically' as Luke records various views about Jesus: C. M. Tuckett, 'The Christology of Luke-Acts', in *The Unity of Luke-Acts,* ed. Verheyden, pp. 133-64, quotation from p. 162; Lee notes three differing 'stories of Jesus' characterized from the point of view of Jesus himself, the demons and the narrator, and that 'the Lukan narrator demonstrates a way of living with these differences': David Lee, *Luke's Stories of Jesus: Theological Reading of Gospel Narrative and the Legacy of Hans Frei,* JSNTSS 185 (Sheffield: Sheffield Academic Press, 1999), quotation from p. 329.

25. On Luke's use of 'prophet' and its relation to his Christology, see further Jack Dean Kingsbury, *Conflict in Luke: Jesus, Authorities, Disciples* (Minneapolis: Fortress, 1991), pp. 48-55; David Ravens, 'Luke's View of Jesus', in his *Luke and the Restoration of Israel,* JSNTSS 119 (Sheffield: Sheffield Academic Press, 1995), pp. 110-38, esp. pp. 124-34; Ben Witherington, III, *The Many Faces of the Christ: The Christologies of the New Testament and Beyond* (New York: Crossroad, 1998), pp. 162-64; Luke Timothy Johnson, 'The Christology of Luke', in *Who Do You Say That I Am? Essays on Christology in Honor of Jack Dean Kingsbury,* ed. David R. Bauer and Mark Allan Powell (Louisville: Westminster John Knox, 1999), pp. 49-65; Christopher M. Tuckett, *Christology and the New Testament: Jesus and His Earliest Followers* (Edinburgh: Edinburgh University Press/Louisville: Westminster John Knox, 2001), pp. 138-39.

26. See E. Earle Ellis, 'Luke 9 and the Sources of Its Christology', chap. 5 in his collection of essays, *Christ and the Future in New Testament History,* NovTSup 97 (Leiden: Brill, 2000), pp. 62-69;

himself with Jonah (11.29-32) and the rejection and murder of prophets (11.47-52); he calls himself a prophet at Nazareth (4.24), and he journeys to the holy city because 'it cannot be that a prophet should perish away from Jerusalem' (13.33). Even after his death, he is called 'a prophet mighty in deed and word' by a disciple, Cleopas, on the way to Emmaus (24.19). Prophetic figures were known around the Mediterranean in both Jewish and Gentile contexts, so this description would be a good first estimate of Jesus' identity for Luke's audience — but there are hints that we need to go further.

In response to other people's ideas, Jesus uses the phrase 'Son of Man' to designate himself in front of Pharisees (5.21-24; 6.1-5), disciples (6.20-22) or crowds (7.24, 34). As in the other gospels, this teasing allusion does not reveal his identity so much as indicate his activity; he is 'the man' who suffers (7.34; 9.22, 44) and who will come in judgement to be vindicated by God (9.26; 11.30; 18.8; 21.27).[27]

Luke's own narrative voice reveals a rich Christology. First, the angel announces that there is born 'in the city of David a Saviour, who is Christ the Lord' (2.11). 'Saviour' is not used at all by Matthew and Mark, and just once, by the Samaritans, in John (John 4.42). However, in Luke, Mary first calls God 'my Saviour' (1.47), and then the same term is applied to Jesus (1.69; 2.11). Jesus often tells people that their faith has 'saved' them, once again especially the marginalized like the 'sinful woman' who anointed him (7.50), the Samaritan leper who returned with thanks (17.19) and the blind beggar (18.42); salvation comes to Zacchaeus, because 'the Son of Man came to seek and save the lost' (19.9-10). In fact, so central is this aspect for Luke's depiction of Jesus' ministry that Matera entitles his entire treatment of Luke's ethics, 'Ethics in an Age of Salvation'.[28]

Similarly, while the other gospel writers depict Jesus being addressed in the vocative as κύριε, this is simply equivalent to the deferential term 'lord', 'sir' or 'master'; they never refer to Jesus by the full title in his lifetime. Only Luke uses the definite term, ὁ κύριος, 'the Lord', for Jesus in his actual narrative: first it refers to God in narrative comments fourteen times in the first five chapters (1.6, 9, 11, 58, 66; 2.9, 22, 23a-b, 24, 26, 39; 3.4; 5.17), then a further fourteen times to refer to Jesus (7.13, 19; 10.1, 39, 41; 11.39; 12.42; 13.15; 17.5, 6; 18.6; 19.8; 22.61; 24.3).

---

originally published in *Current Issues in Biblical and Patristic Interpretation: FS M. C. Tenney,* ed. G. F. Hawthorne (Grand Rapids: Eerdmans, 1975), pp. 121-27.

27. See further Kingsbury's 'Excursus: Jesus' Use of "The Son of Man"', in his *Conflict in Luke,* pp. 73-78; Witherington, *The Many Faces of the Christ,* p. 162; Tuckett, *Christology and the New Testament,* p. 139.

28. Matera, *NT Ethics,* pp. 64-91; see also Green, *The Theology of the Gospel of Luke,* pp. 94-97; Johnson, 'The Christology of Luke', pp. 60-61.

As God is 'the Lord', so too is Jesus.[29] Given the gospels' caution about using post-Easter affirmations of faith for the human Jesus, this shift in Luke is indicative of his own view: Jesus is 'the Lord' and the Son of God, as the angel announces (1.32, 35) and the voice from heaven confirms (3.22; 9.35); demons recognize this also (4.34, 41; 8.28), and it is accepted by Jesus at his trial (22.70). Perkins takes this as her keyword, giving her chapter studying Luke's 'portrait of Jesus' as 'universal saviour' the title, 'Luke: Jesus, the Lord'.[30] Therefore, this shift of terms which were originally used for God in the Hebrew scriptures being applied now to Jesus, plus the fact that Roman emperors liked to style themselves 'Saviour' and 'Lord', means that once again Luke is using words and titles recognizable to Jews and Gentiles alike to increase their understanding of Jesus' identity as the true Lord who brings salvation to all.

The source of Jesus' power to bring universal salvation is shown by Luke to derive from his life of prayer. Time after time, Luke inserts a phrase into Mark or Q's source material to draw attention to Jesus being at prayer when things happen: at his baptism (3.21), after ministry to others (5.16), before choosing the apostles (6.12), at Peter's confession (9.18), at his transfiguration (9.29), before teaching the disciples the Lord's Prayer (11.1-3). Luke's version of the Lord's Prayer comes not in a sermon, but as a result of the disciples watching Jesus pray (11.1-4). Luke has various unique parables about prayer, such as the Friend at Midnight (11.5-8), the Persistent Widow (18.1-8) and the Pharisee and the Tax Collector in the temple (18.9-14). Luke's repeated references to prayer in Acts show how the disciples had learned the lesson (e.g., Acts 1.14, 24; 2.42; 3.1; 4.23-31; 6.4, 6; 7.59; 8.15; 9.11; 10.9, 30; 11.5; 12.5, 12; 13.3; 14.23; 16.13, 16, 25; 20.36; 21.5; 22.17; 26.29; 27.29; 28.8).

Finally, the Holy Spirit plays a crucial role in Luke's portrait of Jesus. Luke refers to the Holy Spirit eighteen times in his gospel, with a staggering fifty-seven occurrences in Acts (compared with only six references in Mark and twelve in Matthew).[31] The Holy Spirit initiates each section of Luke's gospel: at the beginning, the Holy Spirit comes upon Mary (1.34), Elizabeth (1.41), Zechariah (1.67), John (1.15, 80) and Simeon (2.25, 26, 27). At the start of the ministry, according to Luke, the Holy Spirit descends on Jesus 'in bodily form' at his baptism (3.22), and leads him both into (4.1) and out of the wilderness (4.14). We have already noted how his manifesto at Nazareth begins, 'The Spirit of the

29. See further Christopher Kavin Rowe, *Early Narrative Christology: The Lord in the Gospel of Luke*, BZNW 139 (Berlin: Walter de Gruyter, 2006).

30. Chapter 14 in Pheme Perkins, *Reading the New Testament: An Introduction* (London: Geoffrey Chapman, rev. edn. 1988), pp. 229-41.

31. See Joseph A. Fitzmyer, 'The Role of the Spirit in Luke-Acts', in *The Unity of Luke-Acts*, ed. Verheyden, pp. 165-83, esp. p. 171.

Lord is upon me' (4.18). Similarly, as Jesus sets his face to journey to Jerusalem, we have another cluster of references (10.21; 11.13; 12.10, 12). Jesus is not only supremely the man of the Spirit himself, but also the one who baptizes in the Holy Spirit (3.16). In the Q-passage about asking, seeking and knocking, Luke says that the heavenly Father will give 'the Holy Spirit to those who ask him' (11.13), as opposed to Matthew's 'good gifts' (Matt. 7.11). This promise is renewed by the risen Jesus (24.49), and fulfilled throughout the Acts of the Apostles (see Acts 2.1-4, 33 and below). So Tuckett concludes, 'Jesus is thus for Luke one who is himself anointed by the Spirit and who then dispenses the Spirit'.[32]

Therefore, Luke's middle sections on Jesus' travelling ministry give us a clear picture of Jesus' deeds and activities, interspersed with his words and teaching delivered in a narrative context. His identity as prophet and saviour, Christ and Lord is well established by both the characters and the narrator. In keeping with his universal concern, Luke depicts Jesus as having a special care throughout his ministry for the poor, women, the marginalized and the outsider: 'Universalism in Luke-Acts means a divine mercy for people of all possible sorts and conditions'.[33] We shall return to this later, but first we need to consider how Luke takes his story of Jesus forward to its climax and beyond.

c. The climax: opposition in Jerusalem

Through the middle sections of Jesus' ministry among the poor and marginalized, in Luke's account he has greater favour with the crowds, who welcome him, increase in size and rejoice at his 'wonderful' deeds (8.40; 11.29; 13.17); once he gets to Jerusalem, people are 'spellbound', hanging on his words and even getting up 'early in the morning' to listen to him (19.48; 21.38). We saw how Matthew depicts the Pharisees as Jesus' principal opponents, leading to his chapter of denunciation (23), and suggested that this approach probably reflects Matthew's own situation in debate with early rabbinic Judaism after the loss of the temple. It is instructive to compare how Luke handles the opposition to Jesus from the various religious leaders. During Jesus' ministry in Luke, the Pharisees regularly debate with Jesus about tradition and the law: they question his authority to forgive (5.21-22; 7.49), his lack of fasting (5.33-39), his activity and healing on the Sabbath (6.1-2, 6-11; 13.14; 14.1-6) and his apparent impurity (11.38), and complain about Jesus' keeping company with sinners (5.29-32; 7.39; 15.1-2).

---

32. Tuckett, *Christology and the New Testament*, p. 137; see also pp. 115-16.

33. John Reumann, *Variety and Unity in New Testament Thought* (Oxford: Oxford University Press, 1991), p. 62.

However, it is not yet confrontational: only Luke depicts Pharisees inviting Jesus to dinner for discussions as between equals. Thus, Luke's unique story of the dinner with Simon the Pharisee allows extravagant love to be shown to Jesus by the forgiven woman sinner (7.36-50). Luke uses another dinner with a Pharisee for the Q-teaching on inner and outer purity which Matthew includes in his great diatribe (cp. Luke 11.37-44 with Matt. 23.6-7, 23, 25-27). Discussion with lawyers, scribes and Pharisees (11.45, 53; 12.1) uses more of Matthew's sermon (cp. Luke 11.45–12.1 with Matt. 23.4, 29-31, 34-36, 13). Thus, instead of being in a single discourse like Matt. 23, here Jesus' criticism emerges in various conversations. Rather than plotting with the Herodians (as in Mark 3.6), some Pharisees go so far as to warn Jesus that 'Herod wants to kill you' (Luke 13.31). A further dinner debate with Pharisees about healing on the Sabbath provides the parable of the Messianic Supper and more teaching on humility and discipleship (14.1-35). A self-righteous Pharisee is contrasted with the repentant tax collector in the unique parable of 18.9-14, but, after a brief protest about the crowd's reaction to Jesus' entry into Jerusalem (19.39), the Pharisees disappear, not to be mentioned again until Acts.

Nor are the Pharisees depicted as opponents in Luke's second volume: Gamaliel, the well-known Pharisaic teacher, suggests that the early Christian movement might be 'of God' (Acts 5.34-39), and the Jerusalem community even included 'some believers who belonged to the sect of the Pharisees' (15.5). According to Luke's account, when Paul appears before the Sanhedrin, he splits them down the middle by asserting, 'I am a Pharisee, a son of Pharisees' — and, not surprisingly, the Pharisees declare there is 'nothing wrong' with him (23.6-9; see also 26.5).

Luke's picture of the Pharisees has caused no little scholarly debate. Thus Tomson analyses Luke's 'positive portrayal . . . of the Pharisees in comparison to what the other evangelists do',[34] whereas Neale speaks of Luke's 'hostility' and his treatment as 'more organized and negative than any of the other Synoptic evangelists'.[35] This is because Neale believes that Luke has made them into 'a foil against which Jesus' association with "sinners" can be cast in high relief'; it is not an historical portrait, for 'every age, every community, every individual has its own "Pharisees", its own "sinners"'.[36] Franklin thinks that Neale has

34. Peter J. Tomson, *'If this be from Heaven . . .': Jesus and the New Testament Authors in Their Relationship to Judaism* (Sheffield: Sheffield Academic Press, 2001), pp. 223-28.

35. David A. Neale, *None but the Sinners: Religious Categories in the Gospel of Luke*, JSNTSS 58 (Sheffield: Sheffield Academic Press, 1991), quotations from pp. 105-7; Brian E. Beck, *Christian Character in the Gospel of Luke* (London: Epworth, 1989), also thinks that Luke's portrayal of the Pharisees is essentially negative; see esp. pp. 127-44.

36. Neale, *None but the Sinners*, pp. 191-94.

overstated his case: Luke's portrayal of them is 'ambivalent', but they do need to take 'a radical leap forward' in following Jesus' demands in his interpretation of the law.[37] Moxnes draws particular attention to Luke's accusation that the Pharisees are 'lovers of money' who scoffed (Luke 16.14); this is confirmed by Luke's portrayal of them as rich men who invite Jesus to dinners in their houses. Once again there is a contrast, with 'the common people and the outcasts on the one side, the Pharisees on the other'.[38] Thus he concludes that 'the Pharisees in Luke's Gospel are not so much historical figures as stereotypes. His portrait of the Pharisees is designed to fit into the overall theme of his Gospel'.[39] Moxnes' view fits well into our general reading of Luke's narrative portrayal of Jesus' universal mission with especial concern for the poor and marginalized, but we can also accommodate Neale's 'foil' over against the sinners. Whichever view is adopted, Luke clearly portrays the Pharisees as in contrast with both Jesus and his disciples on the one hand, and with the poor and marginalized on the other — but despite their dinner debates with Jesus, they do not bring about his death.

According to Acts, the real opponents in the Sanhedrin are the other group, the Sadducees — and the same is true in the gospel. It is Jesus' demonstration in the temple and his 'teaching daily' there which provokes the first serious danger: 'The chief priests, the scribes, and the leaders of the people sought to destroy him' (Luke 19.45-47). Now the conflict is not with Pharisees over dinner, but with powerful leaders who control the temple and the sacrificial system, and who question him about his authority (20.1-8); only Luke says that the priests were frightened that 'all the people will stone us' (20.6). The parable of the Tenants of the Vineyard is told against them, but they can do nothing for fear of the crowd (20.9-19). As in Mark and Matthew, the question about taxes to Caesar (20.20-26) follows, but here it comes from 'chief priests, scribes, and elders' (20.1, 20) rather than Pharisees and Herodians (as in Mark 12.13 and Matt. 22.15-16). Luke continues with the Sadducees' question about the resurrection (20.27-40) and the debate about David's son (20.41-44), finishing with a brief denunciation of the scribes (20.45-47, rather than Matthew's diatribe against the Pharisees, Matt. 23). As Jesus teaches daily in the temple to those who gather early to hear him (21.37-38), the chief priests and scribes can do nothing because 'they feared the people' (22.2).

Only in Luke does Satan now intervene, inspiring Judas Iscariot to betray

37. Eric Franklin, *Luke: Interpreter of Paul, Critic of Matthew,* JSNTSS 92 (Sheffield: Sheffield Academic Press, 1994), pp. 174-97.

38. Halvor Moxnes, *The Economy of the Kingdom: Social Conflict and Economic Relations in Luke's Gospel* (Philadelphia: Fortress, 1988), pp. 17-21.

39. Moxnes, *The Economy of the Kingdom,* p. 152.

Jesus 'in the absence of the crowd' (22.3-6).[40] After his arrest, Jesus is brought to the high priest's house (22.54), from where the chief priests, elders and scribes take him to Pilate (22.66–23.2). Luke stresses Jesus' innocence at the various hearings. There are no false witnesses, nor charges of blasphemy from the high priest (22.66-71; cp. Mark 14.55-64). Jesus is declared innocent by Pilate three times (23.4, 14, 22), and in a hearing before Herod, unique to Luke (23.7-12, 15).[41] When Herod and Pilate both declare that Jesus has done 'nothing deserving death' and that they propose to release him (23.12-16), according to Luke, the chief priests and the scribes, who accused him 'vehemently' (23.10), protest so strongly that he finally delivers him 'up to their will' (23.25). Jesus' innocence is even confirmed later at the crucifixion by the penitent thief (23.40), and by the Roman centurion, who calls him δίκαιος (23.47).[42]

Here then is an important difference in Luke's narrative which has significant ethical implications: those responsible for Jesus' death are neither the Jewish authorities in general (as in Mark's situation in the 60s), nor the Pharisees (representing Matthew's debating opponents in the reconstruction of Jewish identity in the 80s), nor even the Romans themselves, with whom Luke's audience would still have to reckon.[43] Instead, it is the temple authorities, referred to by Cassidy as 'the chief-priests and their allies';[44] Jane Via objects to this phrase, preferring to stress Luke's references to the 'rulers' (23.13, 35).[45] Cassidy clarifies that the chief-priestly families were also the rulers, who controlled the selling in the temple.[46] As such, it is not surprising that they are the real opponents in Luke's account of Jesus' universal concern for the poor and marginal-

40. See Marion L. Soards, *The Passion according to Luke: The Special Material of Luke 22*, JSNTSS 14 (Sheffield: Sheffield Academic Press, 1987), for Luke's particular concerns in this chapter; on the whole narrative, see François Bovon, 'The Lukan Story of the Passion of Jesus (Luke 22-23)', in his collection of essays, *Studies in Early Christianity*, WUNT 161 (Tübingen: Mohr Siebeck, 2003), pp. 74-105.

41. See Hays, *Moral Vision of the NT*, pp. 118-20.

42. Doble argues that δίκαιος here means more than mere innocence with roots in righteous devotion to God in the Wisdom traditions: Peter Doble, *The Paradox of Salvation: Luke's Theology of the Cross*, SNTSMS 87 (Cambridge: Cambridge University Press, 1996).

43. Paul W. Walaskay, *'And so we came to Rome': The Political Perspective of St Luke*, SNTSMS 49 (Cambridge: Cambridge University Press, 1983), argues that Luke's aim is not to justify the church to the Romans, but rather to 'commend the Roman government to the Christian community', p. 48.

44. Richard J. Cassidy, *Jesus, Politics, and Society: A Study of Luke's Gospel* (Maryknoll, NY: Orbis, 1978), p. 63.

45. E. Jane Via, 'According to Luke, Who Put Jesus to Death?', in *Political Issues in Luke-Acts*, ed. Richard J. Cassidy and Philip J. Scharper (Maryknoll, NY: Orbis, 1983), pp. 122-45.

46. Richard J. Cassidy, 'Luke's Audience, the Chief Priests, and the Motive for Jesus' Death', in *Political Issues in Luke-Acts*, ed. Cassidy and Scharper, pp. 146-67.

ized. Any attempt today to imitate Jesus' identification with the lowly and outcasts must expect similar conflict with the powerful, whether religious, political or commercial.

If the opposition comes from the rich and powerful, Luke's description of the passion and crucifixion reveals again Jesus' special care for the lowly. While Matthew follows Mark's account closely, but changes it significantly with his relatively small additions confirming the responsibility of the Pharisees and religious authorities, Luke omits quite a lot of Mark, preferring instead to weave in large amounts of his own material which bring to a climax many of his narrative and ethical threads running throughout the gospel. In Luke's portrait, Jesus dies still concerned, not for himself and his abandonment (as in Mark 15.34), but for those for whom he has always cared, the lowly, poor and women. After all the women mentioned in this gospel, now women are the first to weep for Jesus on his way to be crucified; as he has been concerned for them before, so now he says, 'Daughters of Jerusalem, weep not for me, but weep for yourselves and for your children', looking ahead, beyond his own fate, to the doom of Jerusalem (23.27-31). Second, he cares for the ordinary people, the carpenters and soldiers, carrying out the orders of the powerful: 'Father, forgive them, for they know not what they do' (23.34).[47] Although missing in some ancient manuscripts, this fits Luke's picture of Jesus forgiving outcasts like the sinful woman (7.47-50); also in Acts, Luke shows his disciples following suit, as Stephen dies with a similar prayer for forgiveness (Acts 7.60). Third, only Luke tells us of forgiveness for the criminal crucified alongside him; once again, Jesus is concerned for the social outcasts (Luke 23.39-43). Finally, Jesus cries with a loud voice, not in desolate abandonment, but as the man of prayer, having prayed for others (23.34), entrusting himself to God, 'Father, into your hands I commend my spirit' (23.46).

Although the people shouted 'crucify' with the chief priests and leaders (23.13, 18), afterwards they followed Jesus to the cross, with the women lamenting (23.27); they 'stood by, watching' in silence (23.35), and went home afterwards 'beating their breasts' (23.48). Nor did the disciples forsake him, but watched with the women 'from a distance' (23.49). As the rich and powerful opponents in this gospel, the chief priests and elders plotted Jesus' death, so now it is the 'leaders' and soldiers who mock, not the people (23.35-37). The irony is in the taunt, 'He saved others; let him save himself' (23.35, 37, 39); all through the gospel, the universal Saviour (2.11, 30) has been concerned to save others, but not himself. So Luke's account of the passion may be different from Mark's and

---

47. On Luke's choice of this as the final saying of Jesus rather than Mark and Matthew's cry of abandonment, see Doble, *The Paradox of Salvation*, pp. 161-83.

Matthew's, but it skillfully brings his threads together and teaches the ethical lesson that Jesus died as he had lived, caring for others, especially the marginalized, while the powerful leaders mocked.

Mark's gospel ended with the enigma of the empty tomb and an absent Jesus, while Matthew had the supernatural happenings and the division of Israel as the Teacher commissions the new community on a mountain in Galilee. Although Luke's account of the resurrection is different again, like the other two it draws his themes together.[48] Jesus is once again walking and eating with his friends, and they stay in Jerusalem in prayer and praise in the temple. Instead of the backward journey to Galilee (cp. Mark 16.7; Matt. 28.7), impossible for the geographically minded Luke, the women at the tomb are reminded of what Jesus said 'while he was still in Galilee' (24.6); Luke names them, including Mary Magdalene and Joanna, who provided for Jesus in Galilee (24.10; see 8.1-3)[49] and with his typical understanding of women's lowly position, he points out that the men did not believe their words, 'an idle tale' (24.11)!

After the women, Luke's main resurrection story concerns two disciples, not otherwise known: with his typical interest in ordinary people, Luke recounts what happens on the Emmaus road to Cleopas and his companion (wife, perhaps, to match Luke's other male-female pairings, 24.13-35).[50] As so often in this gospel with Pharisees, disciples, and sinners alike, Jesus is invited to dinner, where 'he took the bread and blessed and broke it, and gave it to them' (24.28-30). The echo of the Last Supper is unmistakable, and they have a seven-mile dash back to Jerusalem to tell the others that Jesus can be known in the breaking of bread (24.31-35). The final section provides the climax as Jesus eats fish with his friends, shows how his suffering and resurrection fulfils 'Moses and the prophets' and commissions the disciples to be witnesses 'beginning from Jerusalem' and going 'to all nations' (24.36-48). The universal Saviour, Christ the Lord (2.11), now promises them the power of the Holy Spirit to continue his universal mission, as he ascends to heaven (24.49-52).

---

48. See Charles H. Talbert, 'The Place of the Resurrection in the Theology of Luke', in his *Reading Luke-Acts in Its Mediterranean Milieu*, pp. 121-33.

49. See Esther A. de Boer, 'The Lukan Mary Magdalene and Other Women Following Jesus', in *A Feminist Companion to Luke*, ed. Amy-Jill Levine with Marianne Blickenstaff (London: T&T Clark, Continuum, 2001), pp. 140-60; Richard Bauckham, *Gospel Women: Studies of the Named Women in the Gospels* (Grand Rapids: Eerdmans, 2002), pp. 279-83; also, Loretta Dornisch, *A Woman Reads the Gospel of Luke* (Collegeville, MN: Liturgical Press, 1996), pp. 211-28.

50. Bauckham makes her the wife of Cleopas and identifies her with 'Mary of Clopas' in John 19.25, *Gospel Women: Studies of the Named Women in the Gospels*, pp. 203-23.

d. To the ends of the earth: Christology in Acts

Luke's gospel ends, and Acts begins, with the ascension of Jesus into heaven (Luke 24.49-51; Acts 1.1-11). The fact that Jesus is 'now no longer "on earth" but "in heaven"' led Moule to speak of an 'absentee Christology' in Acts,[51] a view followed by other scholars such as Tuckett and Zwiep.[52] Franklin is more cautious: 'Jesus in Luke-Acts, though not an absent Lord, is a hidden one whose present activity and nearness have to be argued for'.[53] O'Toole goes further still: 'The risen Lord acts and is present to the whole life of his church. He leads the Christians. Their mission is Christ's mission'.[54] This is surely right: even Moule and Jervell admit that it is the 'exalted Jesus' who 'poured out the Spirit'.[55] We noted Luke's stress on the Holy Spirit in his gospel, and now Jesus' promises there (Luke 3.16; 11.13; 24.49) are fulfilled here in Acts 2.1-4, 33. Witherington describes the Spirit 'now acting on earth as Christ's agent'.[56] In fact, throughout the narrative, Luke makes clear that the Holy Spirit is the Spirit of Jesus (Acts 16.6-7) who directs and works through the apostles: as in the gospel, so again in Acts, the Holy Spirit of Jesus initiates each new advance (4.8, 30-31; 5.32; 6.3; 7.55; 8.15-20, 29, 39; 9.17; 10.19, 44-47; 11.12-16; 13.2-4; 15.8, 28; 19.2-6; 20.22-23, 28; 21.4, 11).[57]

Therefore, although the narrative of Acts is less focussed on Jesus and more on the progress of the gospel and the early Christian community, nonetheless Luke's account continues to paint the same portrait. The lack of stories about Jesus himself means that 'here Luke prefers to form his christology by the use of

51. C. F. D. Moule, 'The Christology of Acts', in *Studies in Luke-Acts,* ed. Keck and Martyn, pp. 159-85, quotations from pp. 179-80.

52. 'Luke presents Jesus as for the most part *absent* in the post-Easter period', Tuckett, *Christology and the New Testament,* p. 144; see also, 'Luke advocates an "absentee Christology", i.e. a Christology that is dominated by the (physical) absence *and present inactivity* of the exalted Lord', Arie W. Zwiep, *The Ascension of the Messiah in Lukan Christology* (Leiden: Brill, 1997), p. 182; their italics in both cases.

53. Franklin, *Luke: Interpreter of Paul, Critic of Matthew,* p. 277.

54. Robert F. O'Toole, 'Activity of the Risen Jesus in Luke-Acts', *Biblica* 62 (1981), pp. 471-98; quotation from p. 498; see also Beverly Roberts Gaventa, 'The Presence of the Absent Lord: The Characterization of Jesus in the Acts of the Apostles', SBL Annual Meeting, Atlanta, November 2003; for full discussion of the presence and absence of Jesus in Acts, see Sleeman, '"Under Heaven": The Narrative-Geographical Implications of the Ascended Christ for the Believers (and Their Mission) within Acts 1:1–11:18'.

55. The same phrase is used by Moule, 'The Christology of Acts', p. 179 and Jervell, *Theology of the Acts of the Apostles,* p. 33.

56. Witherington, *The Many Faces of the Christ,* p. 155.

57. On the activity of the Spirit in Acts, see further Jervell, *Theology of the Acts of the Apostles,* pp. 43-54 and Tuckett, 'The Christology of Luke-Acts', pp. 153-56.

titles'.[58] While the description of Jesus as 'Christ' is further developed through Acts (occurring twenty-six times), the use of the term ὁ κύριος, 'the Lord', is increasingly applied to Jesus now by the disciples and not just the narrator as in Luke's gospel; while it does refer to God the Father in the earlier chapters, as we saw with the gospel, here too it is increasingly applied to Jesus: 'Luke even within Acts seems conscious that as time went on the Lord terminology was used of Christ more and more frequently'.[59]

Furthermore, not only do the early believers serve the same Lord and Christ, but they share his same universal mission and concern for outsiders. Verhey notes how 'all the heroes give alms' (Acts 3.1-10; 10.1-4; 11.27-30; 12.25; 24.17) and share 'all things in common' to give to all 'as any had need' (2.44-45; 4.32-35).[60] As with the 'lovers of money' in the gospel, resistance once again comes from those with the 'hope of making money' (16.19; 19.23-25), while the only saying of Jesus quoted in Acts is 'remember the words of the Lord Jesus, "It is more blessed to give than to receive"' (20.35). This certainly fits Luke's portrait of Jesus — even if the saying is not actually preserved in any of the gospels![61]

Jesus has come as the Saviour for Israel (5.31; 13.23) — but not only for Israel: 'There is salvation (ἡ σωτηρία) in no one else, for there is no other name under heaven given among human beings by which we must be saved' (δεῖ σωθῆναι ἡμᾶς, 4.12). Now salvation can come to a Gentile like Cornelius, 'by which you and your entire household will be saved' (11.14). Paul and Barnabas assert, 'For so the Lord has commanded us, saying, "I have set you to be a light for the Gentiles, so that you may bring salvation to the ends of the earth,"' quoting Isaiah (Acts 13.47). In this way, Luke continues the story of Jesus' universal mission to all in his concern for the 'restoration of Israel';[62] some believe, but as others do not accept it, so through the events of Cornelius, Paul's missions and the Jerusalem Council, the universal mission comes to include Gentiles.[63] Thus

58. Jervell, *Theology of the Acts of the Apostles*, p. 26.

59. Witherington, *The Many Faces of the Christ*, p. 159; see further pp. 154-60 and Tuckett, 'The Christology of Luke-Acts', pp. 149-64.

60. Verhey, *The Great Reversal*, pp. 93-94.

61. Interestingly, *1 Clement* 2.1 says that 'giving is sweeter than receiving' for those who heed the words of Jesus, ἥδιον διδόντες ἢ λαμβάνοντες; similar sentiments can be found in classical literature, for example, Thucydides 2.97.4 and Seneca, *Epistles* 81.17. See further Witherington, *The Acts of the Apostles*, pp. 626-27 and F. F. Bruce, *The Acts of the Apostles: The Greek Text with Introduction and Commentary* (London: Tyndale, 1951), p. 383.

62. See Ravens, *Luke and the Restoration of Israel*, passim.

63. See Charles H. Talbert, 'Once Again: The Gentile Mission in Luke-Acts', in his *Reading Luke-Acts in Its Mediterranean Milieu*, pp. 161-73.

Paul's last words in Acts are: 'Let it be known to you then that this salvation of God has been sent to the Gentiles; they will listen' (28.28).[64]

We saw in Luke's gospel that the crowds (of ordinary Jewish people) were positive and the Pharisees debated with Jesus, while the real opposition came from the 'rulers', especially the powerful chief priests. The picture is similar in Acts, as crowds of ordinary Jews and synagogue members across the eastern Mediterranean become believers in Jesus as Messiah (2.41; 9.31; 12.24; 13.43; 14.1; 16.4; 17.11), including 'many of the priests' (6.7), 'believers who belonged to the sect of the Pharisees' (15.5) and 'how many thousands of believers there are among the Jews, and they are all zealous for the law' (21.20), until finally even Jews at Rome are 'convinced by what he had said' (28.24).

It is 'the priests, the captain of the temple, and the Sadducees' who arrest Peter and John and bring them before the Council, where again the stress is on the priestly rulers: 'their rulers, elders, and scribes assembled in Jerusalem, with Annas the high priest, Caiaphas, John, and Alexander, and all who were of the high-priestly family' (4.1, 5). The responsibility for the second arrest is similarly clear: 'The high priest took action; he and all who were with him (that is, the sect of the Sadducees), being filled with jealousy, arrested the apostles and put them in the public prison' (5.17), while it is King Herod who kills James and imprisons Peter (12.1-5). Out in the Diaspora, it is Jewish leaders and synagogue authorities who stir up opposition (14.2; 17.5, 13; 18.12; 19.8). They also provoke the arrest of Paul in the temple at Jerusalem (21.27), where again the chief priests, elders, Sadducees and 'leaders' take the lead against him and plot his death (23.1-15; 24.1; 25.2, 15). Thus Jervell argues that 'Israel is becoming a divided people over the issue of the Messiah',[65] but the opposition is primarily from the chief priests and rulers. Meanwhile, the Romans and local civil authorities continue to be helpful as Luke highlights the innocence of the church leaders in Acts (e.g., 3.14, 21; 5.39; 16.37-39; 18.14-15; 22.25; 23.9; 26.31). With his concern for history and geography, Luke realizes that the Roman empire and its system of justice across time and space enable the church to live and grow — and therefore his readers must understand that, although Jesus was crucified, he was no criminal, nor are his followers as they seek to continue his universal mission. Thus Acts ends with Paul at the heart of the empire in Rome as he 'welcomed all who came to him, proclaiming the kingdom of God and teaching about the Lord Jesus Christ with all boldness and without hindrance' (28.30).

---

64. See further Joel B. Green, '"Salvation to the End of the Earth" (Acts 13:47): God as the Saviour in the Acts of the Apostles', in *Witness to the Gospel: The Theology of Acts*, ed. I. Howard Marshall and David Peterson (Grand Rapids: Eerdmans, 1998), pp. 83-106.

65. Jervell, *Theology of the Acts of the Apostles*, p. 36; see further pp. 34-43.

Therefore, Luke's narrative, διήγησις, across his two books gives us a clear portrait of Jesus reconfiguring space and time in his universal mission to Jews and Gentiles alike. In particular, he highlights Jesus' especial concern for the poor and marginalized, so it is perhaps not surprising that the real opposition comes from the rich and powerful leaders in Jerusalem, who bring about his death. After his resurrection, he ascends into heaven, whence he pours out his Spirit who inspires the believers to continue the universal mission, bringing salvation to all, despite facing similar opposition from powerful rulers. As with Matthew and Mark's portraits, such a Christological narrative has clear ethical implications for our study.

2. Luke's setting and eschatology

We have noted above how Mark's imminent eschatological expectation and his consequent ethic of suffering probably reflect the circumstances of his gospel's composition in the dark days of the 60s, while Matthew's mixture of the proper interpretation of the law from a longer-term point of view with ethical warrant derived from eschatological judgement also mirrors his probable setting in debate with emerging rabbinic Judaism in the 80s. We shall come to Luke's different relationship to Judaism and the law in the next section, but Hays is right to sum up his situation and eschatology thus: 'Luke, writing in the same general time period as Matthew, confronts some of the same issues and makes some similar adaptations of the early church's apocalyptic eschatology'.[66]

Although Hemer argues for an early date of 62 for Acts, most scholars agree that a date of around the late-70s to mid-80s does seem likely for Luke-Acts, assuming his use of Mark's prior account.[67] Luke's portraits of Jesus and the early believers seem to imply a setting outside Palestine in a more Gentile environment; Antioch has been suggested, though other contenders include Achaia, Boeotia, Rome, Caesarea, the Decapolis — so it is not surprising that both Fitzmyer and Evans conclude that any suggestions are 'mere guesses'.[68] The search for the community behind Luke has followed a similar trajectory to Matthew's, though it never reached such detailed specificity: in 1979, Johnson warned of the difficulties of identifying one community, followed by Allison's

---

66. Hays, *Moral Vision of the NT,* p. 129.

67. Hemer, *The Book of Acts in the Setting of Hellenistic History,* esp. pp. 365-410; see pp. 367-70 for a list of scholars and their suggested dates from AD 57 to 135.

68. Joseph A. Fitzmyer, S.J., *Luke,* Anchor Bible 28 (New York: Doubleday, 1981), pp. 35-62, esp. p. 57; C. F. Evans, *Saint Luke* (London: SCM, 1990), pp. 1-15; see also Robert Maddox, *The Purpose of Luke-Acts* (Edinburgh: T&T Clark, 1982), pp. 6-15.

even more sceptical treatment. It is not surprising, therefore, that Moxnes preferred to talk about the 'social context' of Luke in much more general terms as 'a group of nonelite persons who are culturally and ethnically mixed'.[69] As for its purpose and occasion, Luke-Acts has been seen as part of the brief for the defending counsel at Paul's trial (hence why Acts ends before Paul's death),[70] while other suggestions include internal debate about Paul in early Christianity, external debate with the Romans about the legality and acceptability of this new religion, and many others.[71]

Central to these theories about Luke's location and date is the suggestion that one of his major purposes in writing was to deal with the delay of the Parousia, the final coming of Christ. Into Jesus' call, 'If anyone wants to come after me, let them deny themselves and take up their cross and follow me' (as recorded by Mark 8.34), Luke inserts 'take up their cross *daily*', καθ' ἡμέραν (Luke 9.23). Thus instead of Mark's invitation to imminent suffering and likely execution, taking up the cross becomes a call to persevere 'day by day'. Only Luke has Jesus tell a would-be disciple that 'no one who puts a hand to the plough and looks back is fit for the kingdom of God' (9.62). In the apocalyptic discourse, Luke replaces Mark's promise that 'the one who endures to the end will be saved' with 'by your endurance you will gain your souls' (cp. Luke 21.19 with Mark 13.13). Luke's version of the Parable of the Talents, the Pounds, is told because 'they supposed that the kingdom of God was to appear immediately' (19.11-27). Thus Hans Conzelmann proposed his highly influential concept that Luke's 'struggle is essentially an anti-apocalyptic one' which uses salvation history to explain the delay of the Parousia.[72] History is divided into three ages: the period of Israel with the law and prophets up to John the Baptist (Luke 16.16), the period of Jesus' ministry in 'die Mitte der Zeit', the centre of time, and the period of the church between the ascension and the Parousia. When the

---

69. L. T. Johnson, 'On Finding the Lukan Community: A Cautionary Essay', in *Society for Biblical Literature 1979 Seminar Papers* (Missoula, MT: Scholars, 1979), vol. 1, pp. 87-100; Dale C. Allison, 'Was There a "Lukan Community"?', *Irish Biblical Studies* 10 (1988), pp. 62-70; H. Moxnes, 'The Social Context of Luke's Community', *Interpretation* 48 (1994), pp. 379-89, quotation from p. 387; see also Barton's discussion in his essay 'Can We Identify the Gospel Audiences?', in *The Gospels for All Christians: Rethinking the Gospel Audiences*, ed. R. J. Bauckham (Grand Rapids: Eerdmans, 1998), pp. 173-94, esp. pp. 186-89.

70. A. J. Mattill, Jr., 'The Purpose of Acts: Schneckenburger Reconsidered', in *Apostolic History and the Gospel*, ed. W. Ward Gasque and R. P. Martin (Exeter: Paternoster, 1970), pp. 108-22; see also his 'The Jesus-Paul Parallels and the Purpose of Luke-Acts', *NovT* 17 (1975), pp. 15-46.

71. See further R. Maddox, *The Purpose of Luke-Acts;* W. W. Gasque, *A History of the Criticism of the Acts of the Apostles* (Tübingen: J. C. B. Mohr, 1975); Fitzmyer, *Luke*, pp. 8-11 and 57-59.

72. Conzelmann, *The Theology of St. Luke*, p. 123; the German original was entitled *Die Mitte der Zeit*, the Middle of Time.

disciples ask Jesus just before his ascension, 'Lord, is this the time when you will restore the kingdom to Israel?', he replied that it was not for disciples 'to know the times and seasons' (Acts 1.6-8); the period of 'the church in history' is therefore the period in which ethics will be necessary.[73]

In addition, it has been argued that Luke's unique parable of the Rich Man and Lazarus (Luke 16.19-31) suggests that he has moved away from a future cataclysmic judgement to a more Platonic view of the soul with immediate judgement upon death; the same point can be seen in the parable of the Rich Fool, also found solely in Luke (12.13-21). This is also implied by Jesus' promise to the penitent thief on the cross, only in Luke, that 'today you will be with me in Paradise' (23.43), and Stephen's vision of Jesus at God's right hand waiting to welcome his first martyr (Acts 7.55-56). Thus Flender argues that instead of a 'horizontal' view of waiting for the final judgement, Luke has a more 'vertical' concept: 'The transition . . . is from this world into the celestial world which exists concurrently'.[74]

While Conzelmann undoubtedly blazed the trail for Lukan redactional studies and correctly identified Luke's interest in history and time, he has been increasingly criticized for imposing his schema onto the third gospel and not doing justice to the other side of Luke's eschatology.[75] Similarly, what Mattill calls 'the Platonizing of Luke-Acts' reads those judgement texts away from 'the apocalyptic framework of intermediate and final states'.[76] Ellis' consideration of Conzelmann and Flender concludes that the 'conceptual framework of Luke's eschatology' is rather to be found 'within the context of a two-stage manifestation of the kingdom of God, present and future'.[77] His consideration of Jewish eschatological anthropology also argues against Flender's suggestion of Platonic individualism: 'For Luke, it is the person of Jesus who binds together horizontal and vertical eschatology . . . quite different from Platonic conceptions'.[78]

73. Hays, *Moral Vision of the NT*, pp. 129-35.

74. H. Flender, *St. Luke: Theologian of Redemptive History* (Philadelphia: Fortress/London: SPCK, 1967), p. 19.

75. See A. J. Mattill, Jr., *Luke and the Last Things: A Perspective for the Understanding of Lukan Thought* (Dillsboro: Western North Carolina Press, 1979); see chap. 2, 'The De-Apocalypticizing of Luke-Acts', pp. 13-24 for a discussion of Conzelmann and Luke's eschatological system.

76. Mattill, *Luke and the Last Things*, pp. 26-40; quotation from p. 40.

77. E. Earle Ellis, 'Eschatology in Luke', chap. IX in his collection of essays, *Christ and the Future in New Testament History*, pp. 105-19, quotation from p. 119; originally published in *L'Évangile de Luc: FS L. Cerfaux*, ed. F. Neirynck (Leuven: Leuven University Press, 1973), pp. 51-65.

78. E. Earle Ellis, 'Eschatology in Luke Revisited', chap. X in his collection of essays, *Christ and the Future in New Testament History*, pp. 120-28, quotation from p. 128; originally published in *L'Évangile de Luc: FS L. Cerfaux*, ed. F. Neirynck (Leuven: Leuven University Press, 2nd edn. 1989), pp. 296-303.

Thus his consideration of the three key Lukan texts (3.16-17, 9.23-36 and 23.42-43) reveals a 'juxtaposition of present and future eschatology' which has affinities with both John and Paul, because 'it is very similar to the eschatological teaching of Jesus'.[79]

This mixture of present and future can be seen throughout both the gospel and Acts. Despite the above passages suggesting delay and a longer time before the end, the expectation that it is imminent is still there, from the preaching of John the Baptist onwards (Luke 3.7-9). The cross may have to be taken up 'daily', but it is still at the coming of the Son of Man in glory that people will be ashamed or rewarded (9.23-27). There is an echo of Matthew's unique parable of the Wise and Foolish Virgins (Matt. 24.42-51) in Luke's unique, direct teaching: 'Be dressed for action and have your lamps lit; be like those who are waiting for their master to return from the wedding banquet, so that they may open the door for him as soon as he comes and knocks' (Luke 12.35-36). This call to be watchful and ready continues through the rest of that chapter (12.37-59) and other sections about the coming judgement such as Luke's unique parable of the Widow and the Unjust Judge (18.1-8) and his version of the apocalyptic discourse (21.5-36).[80] Similarly in Acts, Peter preaches to Cornelius that Jesus 'commanded us to preach to the people and to testify that he is the one ordained by God as judge of the living and the dead', while Paul tells the Athenians that God 'has fixed a day on which he will have the world judged in righteousness by a man whom he has appointed, and of this he has given assurance to all by raising him from the dead' (Acts 10.42; 17.31).[81]

Therefore for Luke, eschatology reinforces the ethical implications of his portrait of Jesus' mission to all with an especial concern for the poor. The kingdom of God has both present and future dimensions and the period of the church in history is a time to preach the universal salvation brought by Jesus to all peoples.[82] As with Matthew, the time of waiting for the Parousia, together with the imminent expectation of judgement, provide what Schrage calls 'eschatological motives for Christian conduct'.[83] In one of the stories about dinner parties found only in Luke, as people head for seats of honour, Jesus tells his host, 'When you give a banquet, invite the poor, the crippled, the lame, and the

---

79. E. Earle Ellis, 'Present and Future Eschatology in Luke', chap. XI in his collection of essays, *Christ and the Future in New Testament History*, pp. 129-46, quotation from p. 146; originally published in *NTS* 12 (1965-66), pp. 27-41.

80. For a full discussion of these passages, see Matill, *Luke and the Last Things*, pp. 55-155.

81. See Mattill, *Luke and the Last Things*, pp. 41-54.

82. See John Nolland, 'Salvation-History and Eschatology', in *Witness to the Gospel: The Theology of Acts*, ed. Marshall and Peterson, pp. 63-81.

83. Wolfgang Schrage, *The Ethics of the New Testament* (Philadelphia: Fortress, 1988), p. 155.

blind. And you will be blessed, because they cannot repay you, for you will be repaid at the resurrection of the righteous' (Lk. 14.7-14). Hays notes that this is the fulfilment of Mary's *Magnificat,* bringing down the powerful and exalting the lowly, filling the hungry and sending the rich empty away (1.52-53); such 'eschatological reversal' continues through much of Luke's special material (e.g., the endings of the parables of the Prodigal Son and the Rich Man and Lazarus, 15.11-32 and 16.19-31).[84] Any apparent delay of the Parousia in Luke is merely an opportunity for those who practise Christian ethics to continue imitating the example of Jesus in both words and deeds, preaching the kingdom of heaven with the imminent expectation of the final judgement on the one hand, while on the other releasing captives, setting the oppressed free, feeding the poor and hungry, and accepting the marginalized and outcasts.

3. The law and love

So far we have noted how each gospel's likely setting affects its attitude towards both Judaism in general and the law itself. Thus if Mark is composed during the dark days of the 60s, its imminent eschatology helps us to understand its radical approach to the law, with the love command taking priority over everything else. Matthew's probable attempt to define the identity of Jewish believers in Jesus as Messiah over against rabbinical Judaism emerging after the destruction of the temple explains his very careful depiction of Jesus as the true interpreter of the law, which depends upon the love command but does not conflict with it. We have suggested above that it is likely that Luke is writing around the same period, but out of a different context than Matthew is. His Christological portrait of Jesus therefore does not concentrate upon the law, but rather upon Jesus' universal mission to everyone, especially the marginalized. Given Luke's eschatology with a longer-term view of the community of believers, we might expect some clear treatment of the extent to which the law can guide ethical behaviour while waiting for the end. However, most commentators agree that Luke's attitude towards the law and Judaism is at best mixed, or even inconsistent: Green calls it 'one of the more pressing issues of Lukan theology, for the Gospel of Luke does not appear to speak with only one voice on this issue'.[85]

84. Hays, *Moral Vision of the NT,* pp. 132-33.
85. Green, *The Theology of the Gospel of Luke,* p. 68.

a. Luke's attitude towards Judaism

The gospel begins with an angel appearing to Zechariah in his priestly duty in the temple, and the opening chapters are full of resonances of the Hebrew scriptures and Jewish piety in Gabriel's announcement to Mary, and in the songs sung by the principal characters, the *Benedictus, Magnificat* and *Nunc Dimittis* (1.5-25, 26-38, 46-55, 67-79; 2.28-32). Both John the Baptist and Jesus are circumcised 'on the eighth day' (1.59; 2.21), and sacrifice for purification is made for Jesus 'according to the law of Moses' (2.22-24). The boy Jesus must be about his Father's business in his house, the temple (2.41-50). Jesus uses the Hebrew scriptures to defeat the tempter in the wilderness and for his inaugural sermon at Nazareth (4.1-11, 16-30). He goes around preaching in the synagogues (4.44) and tells the healed lepers to go and show themselves to the priests (17.14). Similarly, in Acts the disciples go to the temple and its porticoes for the hours of prayer and to gather and preach (Acts 3.1; 5.12, 25-26, 42). At first 'they spoke the word to no one except Jews' (11.19), while Barnabas and Paul proclaimed 'the word of God in the synagogues of the Jews' on the Sabbath, 'as was his custom' (13.4, 14-43; 14.1; 16.13; 17.1-2, 10, 17; 18.4, 19, 26; 19.8); on his return to Jerusalem, Paul went to the temple for purification and prayer (21.26; 24.18). Thus Luke sets his whole story of Jesus, his forerunner and his family, his disciples and the early believers, within the context of observant pious Jews.

On the other hand, Luke includes much of the controversy material shared with Mark and Matthew, such as the disputes about why he and his disciples were not fasting (Luke 5.33-39), plucking grain on the Sabbath (6.1-5) and healing on the Sabbath (6.6-11). Jesus is accused of using demonic power in the Beelzebul controversy, although, in Luke, it does not involve his family or the authorities (11.14-23). Despite the various discussions and dinner parties, Jesus still has harsh words to say about the Pharisees, which leads to the warning about blasphemy against the Holy Spirit (11.37–12.12; see also 16.14-15; 18.9-14). He tells parables against the chief priests and scribes (20.19) and denounces them (20.45-47). Similarly, in Acts Peter tells the Sanhedrin that 'we must obey God rather than any human authority' (5.29), while Stephen's speech is seen as an attack on the temple and Jewish traditions (7.1-53). Paul's sermon in the synagogue of Pisidian Antioch leads to his accusation that the gospel has been rejected by the Jews, and he turns to the Gentiles (13.14-52). Equally, the attack on Paul and his arrest in the temple (21.26-36) cause him to make his speech justifying going to Gentiles (22.1-21). As with Jesus in Luke, it is the Council, and especially the rulers, leaders and Sadducees, who are behind the plots against Paul and his hearings in Acts 23–25, while King Agrippa and Governor Festus say that he could have been set free (26.24-32). The two-volume work about Jesus' universal mission ends with Paul in Rome saying that the Jews are fulfilling Isaiah's prophecy of those who 'will indeed listen, but never understand' with dull hearts, ears hard of hearing and eyes shut, while 'this salvation of God has been sent to the Gentiles; they will listen' (28.24-28).[86]

How then is this mixture of 'negative and positive images'[87] to be explained? It is determinative for Conzelmann's view of history: 'The Church represents the continuity of redemptive history, and to this degree is "Israel". . . . the Church is now the people of God'.[88] Thus, for Conzelmann, the positive aspects represent the continuity with Israel's past, but the negative reflect how it is replaced by the church. Jervell prefers to talk of 'the divided people of God': Israel is split into those who reject Jesus' mission, while those Jews who accept him bring about 'the restoration of Israel and salvation for the Gentiles' as Jewish Christians form the nucleus of the church, which becomes predominately Gentile.[89] J. T. Sanders is much more negative about what he sees as Luke's 'monolithic anti-Judaism' in which 'in general, "the Jews" are roundly condemned for the crucifixion of Jesus and for similar hostile acts against the church'.[90] Tomson disagrees, arguing that Luke's 'vision of one history of salvation for Jews and non-Jews' means that 'Luke's attention for the situation of non-Jews does not entail indifference towards the Jews, let alone hostility towards them as in Matthew or John'.[91]

A wider view of Luke's purposes can help here; thus Esler looked not only at the relationship of Jews and Gentiles within Luke's community, but also at that of the rich and the poor; he concludes that Luke's aim was to provide 'an exercise in the legitimation of a sectarian movement' in which 'Christianity was the genuine fulfilment of Jewish traditions'.[92] More recent studies have questioned how much we can discern from the text about its actual sociohistorical context, but have noted that narrative and reader-response criticism can also help us understand both Luke's attitude and how his gospel has been read; thus Schmidt concludes that these texts are 'potentially anti-Jewish', even if Luke's intention was something different.[93] Perhaps the clue can be found in Luke's

---

86. See further Marguerat, 'The Enigma of the End of Acts (28.16-31)', in his *The First Christian Historian*, pp. 205-30.

87. Green, *The Theology of the Gospel of Luke*, pp. 70-72.

88. Conzelmann, *The Theology of St. Luke*, pp. 145-49, 162-67; quotations from pp. 146 and 167.

89. Jacob Jervell, *Luke and the People of God: A New Look at Luke-Acts* (Minneapolis: Augsburg, 1972), pp. 41-74; see also his *Theology of the Acts of the Apostles*, pp. 34-54.

90. J. T. Sanders, *The Jews in Luke-Acts* (London: SCM, 1987), p. 303.

91. Tomson, *'If this be from Heaven . . .'*, pp. 246-47.

92. Philip F. Esler, *Community and Gospel in Luke-Acts: The Social and Political Motivations of Lucan Theology*, SNTSMS 57 (Cambridge: Cambridge University Press, 1987), pp. 221-22.

93. Daryl D. Schmidt, 'Anti-Judaism and the Gospel of Luke', in (ed.), *Anti-Judaism and the Gospels*, ed. William R. Farmer (Harrisburg, PA: Trinity Press International, 1999), pp. 63-96, quo-

decision to write his gospel with a sequel so that Luke-Acts provides what Marguerat calls 'continuity *and* rupture'.[94] In telling how the story of Jesus emerges out of Israel's history, followed by the growth of the early church, Luke needs to have both positive and negative material about Judaism — and both must be held together. The overall theme we have identified about Luke's view of Jesus' universal mission means that his account includes both rejection, especially by the powerful leaders, and acceptance, especially by ordinary people, which leads to the formation of the new community, initially of believing Jews and then increasingly of Gentiles.[95]

b. Luke's attitude towards the law

Exactly the same happens when we turn to the law. In his monograph treatment of this topic, Wilson is clear: 'It is virtually impossible to construct a consistent pattern from this evidence, even if we agree that Luke has not attempted this himself. He presents Jesus as sometimes opposed to and sometimes in league with the law.'[96] This apparent inconsistency is best illustrated by two of the most puzzling verses from Jesus in the gospel: 'The law and the prophets were until John; since then the good news of the kingdom of God is proclaimed, and everyone tries to enter it by force. But it is easier for heaven and earth to pass away, than for one stroke of a letter in the law to be dropped' (Luke 16.16-17). The second half of v. 16 is a notorious crux: whether βιάζεται is to be translated in a negative sense (people try to force their way in, or oppose it violently)[97] or positive

---

tation from p. 96; see also the Responses from David L. Balch, pp. 97-110, and Allan J. McNichol, pp. 111-19.

94. Marguerat, *The First Christian Historian,* pp. 151-54; his italics.

95. For further discussion of combining both aspects, Jew and Gentile, positive and negative, see David L. Tiede, '"Fighting against God": Luke's Interpretation of Jewish Rejection of the Messiah Jesus', in *Anti-Semitism and Early Christianity: Issues of Polemic and Faith,* ed. Craig A. Evans and Donald A. Hagner (Minneapolis: Fortress, 1993), pp. 102-112; Franklin, *Luke: Interpreter of Paul, Critic of Matthew,* pp. 210-43; Ravens, *Luke and the Restoration of Israel,* passim; Bovon, *Studies in Early Christianity,* pp. 28-32; M. Rese, 'The Jews in Luke-Acts: Some Second Thoughts', in *The Unity of Luke-Acts,* ed. Verheyden, pp. 185-201; Michael Wolter, 'Israel's Future and the Delay of the Parousia, according to Luke'; Robert C. Tannehill, 'The Story of Israel within the Lukan Narrative'; and I. Howard Marshall, '"Israel" and the Story of Salvation: One Theme in Two Parts', all in *Jesus and the Heritage of Israel,* ed. Moessner, pp. 307-24, 325-39, 340-58.

96. S. G. Wilson, *Luke and the Law,* SNTSMS 50 (Cambridge: Cambridge University Press, 1983), p. 57.

97. As in Matthew's version, 'From the days of John the Baptist until now the kingdom of heaven has suffered violence, and men of violence take it by force' (Matt. 11.12); see Evans, *Saint*

(everyone should seize it energetically)[98] does not really affect the view of the law here, so that issue may be left to one side for our purposes.[99] The crucial thing is that v. 16 suggests that the law and prophets 'apply' or 'were in effect' (there is no verb in the Greek) only until the time of John the Baptist, since when the gospel is preached — thus implying that the law has been superseded, or is no longer valid. However, the next verse, v. 17, explicitly denies that any part of the law can 'fall', as strong a statement of its continuing validity as is possible, and apparently contradicting the previous verse.

The same mixture of positive and negative aspects can be seen throughout the gospel and Acts. Zechariah, Mary and Joseph keep 'the custom of the law' in worship, circumcision and purification (1.9, 59; 2.21, 23-24, 27, 39, 42), and Jesus similarly keeps the 'custom' of attending synagogue on the Sabbath (4.16; see also 4.31, 44; 13.10). He instructs lepers whom he has healed to show themselves to the priest and 'make an offering as Moses commanded' (5.14; 17.14). Luke does not have Matthew's contrast of the 'weightier matters of the law, justice, mercy and faith' with tithing herbs (Matt. 23.23); Jesus simply notes that the Pharisees 'ought to have done these things, without neglecting the others' (Luke 11.42). Father Abraham tells the rich man in Hades that 'Moses', that is, the law, 'and the prophets' are there to teach people how to live correctly (Luke 16.29-31). After his resurrection, Jesus explains to his disciples all that has happened as fulfilling 'the law of Moses and the prophets' (24.27, 44). Similarly in Acts, we have already noted above the 'custom' of the disciples and Paul of attending worship in the temple and the synagogues (Acts 3.1; 5.12, 25-26, 42; 13.4, 14-43; 14.1; 16.13; 17.1-2, 10, 17; 18.4, 19, 26; 19.8). The accusations that Stephen (and Jesus) are blaspheming against Moses, the law and the temple are from 'false witnesses' (6.11-14), and Paul equally denies such charges: 'Neither against the law of the Jews, nor against the temple, nor against Caesar have I offended at all' (25.8; repeated by Paul in 24.14; 28.17). Instead, Luke depicts Paul as observing the law in circumcising Timothy and keeping his vows (16.1-3; 18.18; 21.23-26).

On the other hand, while the 'rich ruler' and the 'lawyer' are both told to keep the commandments, they are also given additional instructions unique to Luke, to 'sell *everything*' and to 'do likewise', like the Good Samaritan (Luke 10.25-36; 18.18-23). Two additional disputes about healing on the Sabbath occur

---

Luke, pp. 606-8; on p. 97 Evans describes these verses as being 'to the despair of the commentator'!

98. The positive is preferred by, for example, Fitzmyer, *Luke*, pp. 1117-18 and Luke Timothy Johnson, *The Gospel of Luke*, Sacra Pagina 3 (Collegeville, MN: Liturgical Press, 1991), p. 251.

99. For further discussion, see Wilson, *Luke and the Law*, pp. 43-51; J. T. Sanders, *The Jews in Luke-Acts*, pp. 199-202; William Loader, *Jesus' Attitude towards the Law: A Study of the Gospels* (Grand Rapids: Eerdmans, 2002), pp. 337-40; Esler, *Community and Gospel in Luke-Acts*, pp. 120-21.

only in Luke, in which Jesus justifies his actions by appealing to watering or res-
cuing animals on the Sabbath (13.10-17; 14.1-6); however, as Wilson points out,
'Luke was more interested in the Christological than in the legal implications of
the Sabbath stories'.[100] At one of his dinners with a Pharisee, Jesus delivers the
pronouncement about washing the inside of a cup as well as the outside, which
also occurs in Matthew's diatribe — but characteristically for Luke's gospel, he
turns it into an instruction for almsgiving (Luke 11.39-54; cp. Matt. 23.25-26).
Luke's version of the Sermon on the Plain (6.17-49) makes use of some Q material shared with Matthew's Sermon on the Mount — but does not have anything like his antitheses in which Jesus contrasts his teaching with the law
(Matt. 5.21-43). Luke does include, however, the most challenging statement to a
would-be disciple to 'leave the dead to bury the dead' (Luke 9.60; cp. Matt.
8.22). Thus while in his gospel Luke portrays Jesus as not directly challenging
the law, there are suggestions that simply keeping it is not enough.

This is developed further in Acts. The earliest believers are shown to be
keeping the law and customs, and Stephen's speech focuses on the temple, ignoring the law. However, as the gospel spreads to Gentiles it becomes more of
an issue. Peter is depicted as having kept the purity food laws: 'I have never
eaten anything that is common or unclean' — but his vision of being instructed
to eat unclean animals leads to the pronouncement from heaven, 'What God
has cleansed, you must not call common', preparing him to preach the gospel to
Cornelius and his Gentile household (Acts 10.9-48). The lesson of this episode
is that 'God shows no partiality, but in every nation any one who fears him and
does what is right is acceptable to him' (10.34-35), and its significance is shown
by its repetition in 11.1-18 and Peter's reference to it at the Council of Jerusalem
(15.7).[101] Here Peter even describes the law and traditions as 'a yoke upon the
neck of the disciples which neither our fathers nor we have been able to bear'
(15.10). Such a negative attitude is also seen in Paul's sermon in Pisidian
Antioch, which concludes that forgiveness comes through Jesus and that 'every
one that believes is freed from everything from which you could not be freed by
the law of Moses' (13.38).

So therefore we must turn to Council of Jerusalem. The debate is more
about circumcision as a prerequisite for salvation than about keeping the law
(15.1, 5). According to Luke, it is Peter who argues from his experience with
Cornelius that no such burden or 'yoke' should be put upon them; Jews and
Gentiles alike 'shall be saved through the grace of the Lord Jesus' (15.7-11). In re-

100. Wilson, *Luke and the Law*, p. 38.
101. On the Cornelius episode, see further Wilson, *Luke and the Law*, pp. 68-73; J. T. Sanders,
The Jews in Luke-Acts, pp. 139, 255-56; Loader, *Jesus' Attitude towards the Law*, pp. 368-71.

sponse, James gives his formal 'judgement' (15.18), which leads to the letter setting out the four requirements of abstaining from 'what has been sacrificed to idols and from blood and from what is strangled and from unchastity' (15.20, 29). There has been enormous scholarly discussion of this passage, including about the textual variants and its historical plausibility in the light of the strongly worded arguments about circumcision and the law in Paul's letters — let alone what Luke's narrative actually means. Wilson's detailed treatment explores whether the debate is about table fellowship or general relations between Jewish believers and Gentiles, and whether it is primarily cultic-ritual or ethical; he argues against seeing the origins of the four demands in the requirements of Lev. 17–18 for Gentiles living among Jews, preferring to see their authority as essentially apostolic.[102] J. T. Sanders replies that the provisions do originate in Lev. 17–18, but interprets the whole Council in terms of his view about Luke's essentially negative attitude to Jews and Jewish Christians.[103] Bockmuehl has demonstrated that the four requirements are strongly reminiscent of the Noachide Commandments, drawing upon the instructions in the law for resident aliens and the children of Noah living among Jews, which were important in the Second Temple period and then crystallized in the rabbinic tradition.[104] Therefore, it does seem likely that Luke's account of the Council is actually less about observing the law and more about what Verhey calls 'a *modus vivendi* to facilitate some degree of fellowship between Jewish and Gentile Christians'.[105]

Therefore, it is perhaps not surprising that this mixed range of attitudes towards the law in Luke-Acts, like that towards Judaism itself, has produced a wide range of scholarly interpretations.[106] Conzelmann takes Luke 16.16-17 as determinative of his salvation-historical scheme, as the law and prophets are 'until John', with the early believers keeping the law and the increasingly Gentile church being in continuity with redemptive history.[107] Jervell's idea of the 'di-

102. Wilson, *Luke and the Law*, pp. 71-102.

103. J. T. Sanders, *The Jews in Luke-Acts*, pp. 114-31.

104. M. Bockmuehl, 'Public Ethics in a Pluralistic Society? Lessons from the Early Church', *Crux* 28.3 (September 1992), pp. 2-9; fuller treatment in his 'The Noachide Commandments and New Testament Ethics with Special Reference to Acts 15 and Pauline Halakhah', *Revue Biblique* 102 (1995), pp. 72-101; repr. in Bockmuehl, *Jewish Law in Gentile Churches: Halakhah and the Beginning of Christian Public Ethics* (Edinburgh: T&T Clark, 2000), pp. 145-73.

105. Verhey, *The Great Reversal*, p. 101; see also Frederick W. Danker, 'Reciprocity in the Ancient World and in Acts 15:23-29', in *Political Issues in Luke-Acts*, ed. Cassidy and Scharper, pp. 49-58.

106. For a useful discussion of the various approaches, see Loader, *Jesus' Attitude towards the Law*, pp. 273-300.

107. Conzelmann, *The Theology of St. Luke*, esp. pp. 147-48, 158-61.

vided people of God' leads him to conclude that Luke is very conservative with regard to the law, while J. T. Sanders thinks that Luke is quite the opposite and wants to 'invalidate the Jewish Christian position'.[108] Neither of these last two extreme positions takes into account all the complex and varied mixture found in Luke-Acts. Wilson makes a virtue out of a necessity with his stress on Luke's diversity, but concludes that Luke sees the law as 'the *ethos* of a particular *ethnos*'; it is all right for Jewish-Christians to be fully law-observant, but they live alongside Gentiles who have their own requirements.[109] Esler concludes that Luke's attitude to the law is more consistent and 'extremely conservative', but that his attempt to reassure the Jewish members of his community while serving the Gentiles shows how he has been 'vitally influenced by the social and ethnic, as well as the religious, pressures upon his community'.[110] Thielman is more blunt: in Luke-Acts 'both Jesus' approach to the law and the church's unity were preserved through sensible compromise'.[111]

In the end, therefore, perhaps this apparent inconsistency arises from a misreading of the genre of Luke-Acts. Marguerat concludes that 'what a survey of the Law throughout the work *ad Theophilum* makes clear is that *Luke the historian and Luke the theologian do not always say the same thing*'.[112] If the double work is read as a treatise on the Jewish law, then the varieties of emphasis and attitude are a problem. However, it is a biographical narrative, first of the life of Jesus and then of the life of the early church and its leaders. Both books begin with displays of law-observant piety, on the part of Jesus' family in the gospel and of the early believers in Jerusalem in Acts. Both books depict the main characters going to the synagogue and temple, keeping the demands of the law, and not challenging or abrogating it. But both books suggest that this is not enough in itself. If Jewish-Christians want to be zealous and still keep the law, that is an expression of their discipleship, according to Luke — but it cannot now be imposed upon Gentile believers in the expanding people of God. The requirements of the Jerusalem Council are an attempt to help Jews and Gentiles

108. Jervell, *Luke and the People of God*, pp. 133-47; idem, *Theology of the Acts of the Apostles*, pp. 54-61; J. T. Sanders, *The Jews in Luke-Acts*, pp. 115-31, quotation from p. 119.

109. Wilson, *Luke and the Law*, pp. 103-17; quotation from p. 103.

110. Esler, *Community and Gospel in Luke-Acts*, pp. 110-30; quotation from p. 130.

111. Frank Thielman, *The Law and the New Testament: The Question of Continuity* (New York: Crossroad, 1999), pp. 135-61; 'sensible compromise' appears in the title of his chapter on Luke-Acts as well as in his conclusion on p. 161; Blomberg also concludes that 'the Jerusalem Council agreed on a compromise that left Paul's law-free gospel intact: Gentile Christians should avoid unnecessarily offending Jewish brothers and sisters, and Jewish Christians were free to practice their traditional piety', Craig L. Blomberg, 'The Christian and the Law of Moses', in *Witness to the Gospel: The Theology of Acts*, ed. Marshall and Peterson, pp. 397-416.

112. Marguerat, *The First Christian Historian*, p. 63; his italics.

live together within the early community. Thus we are back to Luke's key theme of the universal mission and to his desire to hold together the two aspects which we noted above in his attitude towards Judaism. However, in the end, for Luke the law provides neither ethics nor salvation; his biographical focus shows that only Jesus can provide this — and at the heart of his life and teaching is love, to which we must now finally turn.

c. The love command

The double love command of God and neighbour is not only at the climax of Mark and Matthew's gospels as Jesus teaches in the temple prior to his arrest, but it also demonstrates their general attitude towards the law. While for Mark, obeying the radical demand of love of God and neighbour is 'much more than whole burnt offerings and sacrifices', Matthew leaves out this comment and concludes instead that 'on these two commandments depend all the law and prophets' (Mark 12.33; Matt. 22.40). Luke omits both of these concluding comments in his version of the story, which occurs much earlier in his gospel at the start of the middle travel section to set the theme for what is to come (Luke 10.25-28). First, the person who questions Jesus is neither one of the Pharisees (as in Matthew) nor a scribe (as in Mark), but simply 'a lawyer'. Nor is the question about which is the greatest or first commandment, as in the other two gospels; instead he simply asks, 'What must I do to inherit eternal life?' (10.25, the same question as asked by the rich ruler later in 18.18). It is Jesus who mentions the law by asking, 'What is written in the law? What do you read there?' In Matthew and Mark's accounts, Jesus himself brings together the two separate commandments about love in his great pronouncement, whereas here it is the *lawyer* who replies with the love of God and neighbour as a single instruction. Jesus commends his answer, and tells him, 'Do this, and you will live' (10.26-28). These changes therefore make the story more into a question about eternal life and salvation, rather than focusing on Jesus' interpretation of the law and its many commandments in the manner of a rabbinic anecdote.[113]

The pericope should end there — but as with the later story of the rich ruler, 'there is still something lacking' (18.22). Simply keeping the commandments is not enough: more is needed. So Luke has the lawyer ask a typically le-

---

113. Despite these differences, Furnish argues that this is still Luke's redaction of the same pericope as in Mark 12/Matt. 22: Victor Paul Furnish, *The Love Command in the New Testament* (Nashville: Abingdon, 1972), pp. 34-38.

gal question about the definition of 'who is my neighbour?' (10.29). Jesus' answer is to tell the parable of the Good Samaritan, which is proof that neither keeping the law nor the greatest commandment is enough: action which imitates practical love is required, 'Go and do likewise' (10.30-37). Once again, Luke's universal concerns especially for the marginalized are seen, as the priest and Levite avoid touching the man (presumably keeping the law out of fear of contracting ritual impurity for seven days from a corpse, as in Num. 5.2; 19.11-13), while the despised Samaritan is the neighbour 'who showed him mercy'. Fitzmyer comments that 'these details underlie the story's basic contrast: the pity and kindness shown by a schismatic Samaritan to an unfortunate, mistreated human victim stands out vividly against the heartless, perhaps Law-inspired insouciance of two representatives of the official cult, who otherwise would have been expected by their roles and heritage to deal with the "purification" of physically afflicted persons'.[114]

Therefore the lawyer who set out to 'test' Jesus is himself now being tested: keeping the law is about more than being able to repeat the double love command, and inheriting eternal life requires practical action. As Matera notes, 'A Gentile audience, unfamiliar with the Mosaic law, would surely have concluded that love was the essence of the law that Jesus upheld'.[115] Furthermore, the echo of Jesus' teaching on the love of enemies in the Sermon on the Plain a few chapters earlier is unmistakable (6.27-36), and drives home Luke's wider concerns.[116] Loader's analysis of Luke's attitude to the law notes here that 'making the Samaritan the hero is also loading the story with polemical intent: it effects a reversal. The lowly and marginalised are Luke's heroes. It also reflects Luke's universalism: neighbour is broader than Israelite. Luke uses the twofold commandment to sharpen a contrast between commitment to observe purity law and concern for human beings in the interpretation of Torah.'[117]

Thus this brief analysis of the Good Samaritan takes us back to the wider account of Luke's whole narrative. Furnish similarly concludes his study of the love command in Luke with the broader picture: 'In summary, Luke views Jesus' whole ministry as a mission to the world's needy, as the effective presence of the gospel of peace. The command to love is given special prominence in the Sermon on the Plain, and its practical implications for the Christian life are constantly emphasized. It means the compassionate serving of whoever stands

114. See Fitzmyer, *Luke*, pp. 883-84 and 887.
115. Matera, *NT Ethics*, p. 88.
116. See John R. Donahue, S.J., 'Who Is My Enemy? The Parable of the Good Samaritan and the Love of Enemies', in *The Love of Enemy and Nonretaliation in the New Testament*, ed. Willard M. Swartley (Louisville: Westminster John Knox, 1992), pp. 137-56.
117. Loader, *Jesus' Attitude towards the Law*, pp. 328-29.

in need, active "doing good" even to one's enemies, restraint in judging others, forgiveness, reconciliation, and sharing one's resources with all the brethren in the Christian *koinonia*.[118]

It is on this larger canvas of Luke's portrait of Jesus' life and ministry that we find his true consistency. His attitude towards both Judaism and the law can indeed appear mixed and variable, as we have noted throughout this section — but this is because he is not primarily writing a treatise about either of them. He is writing a biographical account of the life and ministry of Jesus which is thoroughly rooted in the history and traditions of Israel, but which has grown through its universal concern into a much wider community which includes the marginalized and Gentiles. This explains Luke's mix of positive and negative, as he commends all that he can about Israel's past and present, including those who try to observe the law; however, ultimately 'to inherit eternal life', one must go beyond this to a practical response to the person and teaching of Jesus, which imitates the life of love within a community which holds everyone together.

4. Ethical issues in Luke

Given how Luke's eschatology allows for a longer period of the church, J. T. Sanders says, 'It is to be expected that Luke will move in the direction of designating more adequately than Mark the marks of a Christian life this side of the Parousia — that is, of a Christian ethics which reckons with an ongoing world'. However, unfortunately, 'Luke does this only to a disappointingly slight degree'.[119] Furthermore, 'Acts adds nothing materially to the view of Christian ethics one finds in the third Gospel'.[120] In part, Sanders' view arises from a false expectation that Luke-Acts is primarily intended to provide ethical teaching for the church while waiting for the eschaton, in other words, a wrong identification of its genre. As a biographical narrative about Jesus' deeds and words, this is not its primary purpose, as we are arguing throughout this book. However, we have already noted how Matthew and Mark in fact do touch upon many of the key areas of human moral experience as part of their portrait of Jesus. Therefore, we will examine similar aspects of Luke's gospel to see if Sanders' pessimism is actually warranted.

First, however, we should note how Luke begins his account of Jesus' minis-

118. Furnish, *The Love Command*, pp. 89-90.
119. J. T. Sanders, *Ethics in the NT*, pp. 35-36.
120. J. T. Sanders, *Ethics in the NT*, p. 40.

try with his sermon in Nazareth: Luke's version is nearly three times longer than the similar story which occurs much later in Mark and Matthew's accounts (Mark 6.1-6; Matt. 13.54-58).[121] Giving an early cameo of the main themes of the hero's character is a typical biographical motif, and we saw earlier how this pericope functions as Jesus' manifesto for Luke, as he quotes Isaiah: 'The Spirit of the Lord is upon me, because he has anointed me to bring good news to the poor. He has sent me to proclaim release to the captives and recovery of sight to the blind, to let the oppressed go free, to proclaim the year of the Lord's favour' (4.18-19). The response to his statement that 'today this scripture has been ful-filled in your hearing' is initially positive as 'all spoke well of him and were amazed at the gracious words that came from his mouth' (4.21-22). But, as he warns of people's failure to appreciate a prophet from their hometown and re-fers to Elijah and Elisha's ministry to Gentiles like the widow of Sidon and Naaman the Syrian, the tone changes. Jesus' concern for the salvation of every-one provokes an angry rejection (4.23-30). Nonetheless, such care for all, espe-cially the marginalized and the outsiders, in this opening story sets the tone for Luke's treatment of specific ethical issues through the rest of his work.[122]

a. Rich and Poor

The theme for this central ethical issue is set right at the start with Mary's cele-bration about being chosen to bear Jesus, the *Magnificat*: 'He has brought down the powerful from their thrones, and lifted up the lowly; he has filled the hun-gry with good things, and sent the rich empty away' (1.52-53). Therefore, Jesus begins his ministry by preaching good news to the poor (4.18; 7.22); it is the real poor and those who are actually hungry who are blessed in Luke's Beatitudes in the Sermon on the Plain (6.20-21, unlike Matthew's 'poor in spirit' and 'those who hunger for righteousness', Matt. 5.3, 6), and the corresponding Woes to the rich are unique to Luke (6.24-26). Only in Luke does Jesus tell people not to in-vite the rich to dinner, but to welcome the 'poor, maimed and blind' (14.12-14); his version of the parable of the Messianic Banquet follows immediately in which the 'poor, maimed and blind' are to be brought in after the rich possess-ors of fields, oxen and wives have refused the invitation (14.15-24; contrast Mat-thew's inclusion of 'good and bad', Matt. 22.9-10).[123]

121. See also our earlier discussion of the Nazareth sermon in sect. 1.b above, esp. n. 23.

122. On how the Nazareth pericope relates to the rest of Luke-Acts' attitude to the poor and the rich, see Esler, *Community and Gospel in Luke-Acts*, pp. 164, 179-83 and Green, *The Theology of the Gospel of Luke* pp. 76-83.

123. On Luke's characterization of these groups as 'recipients of God's saving action', see

Luke depicts both John the Baptist and Jesus warning people about greed in comments unique to his gospel (3.11; 12.15). The man who asks about eternal life is described only by Luke as 'a ruler', and Luke inserts into Mark's account the crucial word πάντα, 'sell *all* that you have'; he goes away sad, because only Luke describes him as 'very rich' (18.18-23; cp. Mark 10.17-22; Matt. 19.16-22). Generations of preachers have sought to avoid the universal application of this principle to their congregations by pointing out that Jesus' words are specifically directed to this 'very rich' 'ruler'; however, into the Q-material about the lilies of the field, the ravens and treasure in heaven, Luke suddenly inserts the general instruction, 'sell your possessions, and give alms' (Luke 12.33; cp. Luke 12.22-34 with Matt. 6.19-21, 25-34). We noted above how Luke includes in the comment to Pharisees about cleaning the outside of the cup the slightly obscure instruction to 'give for alms those things that are within' (Luke 11.41; cp. Matt. 23.25-26). The teaching about counting the cost of discipleship, which occurs only in Luke, ends with the clear, and total, command, 'So therefore, none of you can become my disciple if you do not give up all your possessions' (Luke 14.25-33).

This is illustrated by the first disciples, Simon, James, John and Levi, who, accordingly to Luke alone, 'left *everything*' as once again he inserts his keyword, πάντα, into his Markan source material (cp. Luke 5.11, 28 with Mark 1.20; 2.14). In contrast, the very rich ruler who goes away sadly, not doing what Jesus says (Luke 18.18-23), is followed shortly by Zacchaeus, who does at least give away half of his possessions, and repays those whom he defrauded fourfold, unlike the 'one-fifth' required by the law (19.1-10).[124] Zacchaeus' positive example leads to his salvation (19.9-10),[125] unlike the judgement meted out in the parables of the Rich Fool, building his barns, and the Rich Man and Lazarus, both found only in Luke (12.13-21; 16.19-31). Luke's unique parable of the Unjust Steward also concludes with the instruction that those who have material wealth, 'unrighteous mammon', should use it eschatologically to make friends of those who can 'welcome you into the eternal homes', which may also take us back to almsgiving.[126] In this context, the Pharisees, who are characterized here as 'lovers of money', are rebuked by Jesus (16.1-9, 14-15). Thus we have here, par-

---

S. John Roth, *The Blind, the Lame, and the Poor: Character Types in Luke-Acts,* JSNTSS 144 (Sheffield: Sheffield Academic Press, 1997).

124. See Lev. 6.5 and Num. 5.6-7 for repaying the principal plus an additional fifth; however, Exod. 22.1 (21.37 in Hebrew) does require four sheep to be paid for one which has been stolen; see Fitzmyer, *Luke,* ad loc., p. 1225.

125. See Neale, 'The Story of Zacchaeus', chap. 8 in his *None but the Sinners,* pp. 179-90.

126. See Kyoung-Jin Kim, *Stewardship and Almsgiving in Luke's Theology,* JSNTSS 155 (Sheffield: Sheffield Academic Press, 1998), esp. pp. 145-67 on these parables.

ticularly in the unique sections of Luke's own source material and his redaction of others' in his gospel, a clear and consistent ethic about the 'option for the poor' with warnings for the rich and the demand for disciples to sell or give away everything in order to follow Jesus.[127]

This leads in Luke's second volume to the depiction of the early community actually putting this into practice: 'All who believed were together and had all things in common; they would sell their possessions and goods and distribute the proceeds to all, as any had need' (Acts 2.44-45; 4.32-35).[128] As in the comparison of the rich ruler with Zacchaeus in the gospel, so here Barnabas' literal obedience of selling his land to give the money to the apostles contrasts with the deceit of Ananias and Sapphira, who hold back the proceeds of their sale (4.36–5.11). Such a community is challenging for those who are affluent: it is important to note that there was no compulsion to sell and give — both the property and its proceeds continued to belong to Ananias.[129] Furthermore, Luke later depicts rich property owners joining the believers and using their homes for the church at various points in Acts (see, e.g., 12.12-18; 16.14-15; 17.12). Ananias' and Sapphira's mistake was 'to lie to the Holy Spirit' (5.4; cp. the blasphemy against the Spirit in Luke 12.10). Nonetheless, it is significant that, as Marguerat puts it, 'Luke wants to inform his readers that *the original sin in the church is a sin of money . . .* a financial crime'.[130]

The concern for the proper care of the needy, especially widows, prompted the appointment of Stephen and the other deacons (Acts 6.1-6). Those who did not sell their property, but continued to own houses, used them for gatherings of the community, such as 'the house of Mary' where they gathered to pray for Peter (12.12-18). Such hospitality would also have included the provision of food and other needs. Capper argues that while the 'community of goods' is encouraged in the early chapters of Acts, the main thrust is the replacement of the usual 'meal-fellowship' with expectation of reciprocity between social equals by

127. Esler draws attention to 'how pronounced is Luke's concern to sharpen the preference in his sources for the utterly destitute and the virtues of renouncing wealth', *Community and Gospel in Luke-Acts*, pp. 164-200, quotation from p. 168; on this topic generally, see further Cassidy, *Jesus, Politics, and Society*, esp. pp. 20-33; Beck, *Christian Character in the Gospel of Luke*, pp. 28-54; Matera, *NT Ethics*, pp. 80-86; Verhey, *The Great Reversal*, pp. 92-95; Brian K. Blount, *Then the Whisper Put on Flesh: New Testament Ethics in an African American Context* (Nashville: Abingdon, 2001), pp. 80-91.

128. On sharing possessions and the community of goods, see Luke T. Johnson, *The Literary Function of Possessions in Luke-Acts*, SBLDS 39 (Missoula, MT: Scholars Press, 1977) and *Sharing Possessions* (London: SCM, 1986).

129. See Witherington, *The Acts of the Apostles*, pp. 215-17.

130. Marguerat, *The First Christian Historian*, pp. 176 and 178, his italics; see pp. 154-78 for a full discussion of Ananias and Sapphira's 'original sin'.

'social integration' with 'very substantial support for the poor'. He concludes, 'It is inconceivable that a Christian community in which the underprivileged were regularly entertained in the houses of the rich could let them want for the essential human needs of food, clothing, and shelter through the week'.[131] The practice of almsgiving and 'good works' is mentioned with Tabitha (9.36-43) and Cornelius (10.1-4) — though the lame beggar at the Gate Beautiful received rather more than 'silver and gold' from Peter and John (3.1-11)! Meanwhile, Paul was involved in raising the collection in Antioch for famine relief in Jerusalem following the prophecy of Agabus (11.27-30; 12.25; 24.17).[132]

Thus we have throughout Luke-Acts a clear and very demanding ethic of renunciation of wealth, but it is always part of Luke's wider purpose of depicting Jesus' universal care, especially for the marginalized, running through his ministry and later through his church. As Heard concludes his study on this topic, 'The motivation behind the sharing of wealth is always love; therefore, Jesus' disciples are to be an inclusive community which always embraces the outcasts, destitute and disadvantaged. Indeed, the community of faith should exclude no one, as the parable of the banquet clearly demonstrates.'[133]

b. The marginalized: women, outsiders and non-Jews

We noted earlier how Luke begins with stories about pious women, Elizabeth, Anna and Mary. While Mary appears occasionally in the other Synoptics (Mark 3.31-35; 6.3; Matt. 1.16-20; 2.11; 13.53), Luke calls her by name thirteen times (1.27, 30, 34, 38, 39, 41, 46, 56; 2.5, 16, 19, 34; Acts 1.14) and also refers to her in 2.41-51, 8.19-21 and 11.27-28. Luke has many unique incidents involving women: the widow of Nain who lost her son (7.11-17); the sinful woman with ointment (7.36-50); the support of women disciples (8.2-3); Mary's right to sit and listen to Jesus in contrast to Martha's complaint about helping her to serve (10.38-42); a woman in the crowd calling out a blessing (11.27); the crippled woman healed on the Sabbath (13.10-17); and the 'daughters of Jerusalem' who weep for Jesus on his way to crucifixion (23.27-31). In addition, Luke includes Peter's mother-in-law (4.38-39), Jairus' daughter and the woman with the haemorrhage (8.41-56), all taken from his source in Mark (Mark 1.29-31; 5.21-43).

131. Brian Capper, 'Reciprocity and the Ethic of Acts', in *Witness to the Gospel: The Theology of Acts*, ed. Marshall and Peterson, pp. 499-518; quotation from p. 518.

132. On the almsgiving motif in Acts, see Kim, *Stewardship and Almsgiving in Luke's Theology*, pp. 218-52.

133. Warren Heard, 'Luke's Attitude toward the Rich and the Poor', *Trinity Journal*, n.s. 9 (1988), pp. 47-80; quotation from p. 74.

Women also feature regularly in Luke's teaching, often paired with a man: the woman with leaven follows the man with a mustard seed (13.18-21); a woman's lost coin pairs the man's lost sheep (15.3-10); the two women grinding, one taken at the end and one left, balance the two men in bed, one taken and one left (17.34-35). In this way, Luke's narrative portrays Jesus being inclusive in his teaching. He also seems to have a particular concern for widows: Anna, the widowed prophetess in the temple (2.37); the widow of Sidon (4.25-26); the widow of Nain (7.12); the poor widow offering her all (21.1-4, the only widow to occur in the other gospels, Mark 12.41-44). A widow provides an example of persistent prayer in Luke's unique parable (18.1-8). This special care for such vulnerable women also appears in the early community of believers (Acts 6.1; 9.39-41). Acts also shows women involved in teaching and prophecy (Priscilla, 18.26; the daughters of Philip, 21.9).

Such a clear interest on the part of Luke in women has usually been interpreted positively.[134] Arlandson's analysis of the many women in the gospel and in Acts shows how the social status of most of them rises in the kingdom of God,[135] while Quesnell argues that Luke's account assumes that women are present even at the Last Supper: 'Luke thought of the women as part of that community, sharing in all its life and actions'.[136] Therefore it is not surprising that Luke-Acts has provided plenty of scope for feminist studies.[137] More recently, a number of scholars have reacted to the interpretation of Luke as 'pro-women' because of the 'anti-Jewish' assumptions about the denigration of women in the time of Jesus in this view. Thus, Davies' provocative article describes how his attempt to argue that Luke-Acts was written by a woman actually moved him from believing that Luke-Acts 'advocated raising the social status of women' to the complete opposite![138] In response, Koperski's careful analysis of Davies and many others, both those who interpret Luke as favourable to women and those who are suspicious, has argued that the Mary and

134. See, for example, Verhey, *The Great Reversal*, pp. 95-96; also, Loretta Dornisch, *A Woman Reads the Gospel of Luke* (Collegeville, MN: Liturgical Press, 1996).

135. James Malcolm Arlandson, *Women, Class, and Society in Early Christianity: Models from Luke-Acts* (Peabody, MA: Hendrickson, 1997); see esp. pp. 120-50.

136. Quentin Quesnell, 'The Women at Luke's Supper', in *Political Issues in Luke-Acts*, ed. Cassidy and Scharper, pp. 59-79; quotation from p. 71.

137. See, for example, *A Feminist Companion to Luke*, ed. Amy-Jill Levine with Marianne Blickenstaff (Sheffield: Sheffield Academic Press, 2001), and *A Feminist Companion to the Acts of the Apostles*, ed. Amy-Jill Levine with Marianne Blickenstaff (London: T&T Clark, 2004).

138. Stevan Davies, 'Women in the Third Gospel and the New Testament Apocrypha', in *"Women like This": New Perspectives on Jewish Women in the Greco-Roman World*, ed. Amy-Jill Levine (Atlanta: Scholars Press, 1991), pp. 185-97; genre studies come into play here also, since Davies' argument includes accepting Pervo's designation of Acts as ancient romance or novel.

Martha pericope (Luke 10.38-42), together with the passage about the appointment of deacons in Acts 6.1-7, may well reflect a debate in the early church about the leadership role of women.[139] Other similarly nuanced studies of this passage have also argued that accepting Mary's right to listen at Jesus' feet need not denigrate Martha either.[140] As with Luke's attitude towards Judaism and the law, a balanced reading of his universal and inclusive concern for the dignity of women must be careful to avoid appearing to be anti-Jewish — or anti-serving at table for that matter!

The story of the sinful woman who anointed Jesus' feet while he was at dinner with Simon the Pharisee also illustrates how Luke's concern for women is part of his wider interest in sinners and outsiders (Luke 7.36-50). The connection of this pericope with the anointing of Jesus' *head* in the house of Simon the leper at Bethany (according to Mark 14.3-9/Matt. 26.6-13) or of his *feet* by Mary but also in Bethany (according to John 12.1-8) is much disputed, but the difference of context is significant for Luke. Instead of Jesus being anointed just prior to his death and arguments about the 'waste' of expensive ointment which could have been sold and given to the poor, Luke's version comes much earlier in his account of the ministry, immediately after the accusation that Jesus is 'a friend of tax collectors and sinners'; here the rejection of John the Baptist by the Pharisees is compared with the welcome given by tax collectors (7.28-35). Similarly, the anointing story contrasts the love of the sinful woman with the distaste of the Pharisee for 'what kind of woman this is',[141] rather than getting into the awkward issue of the waste of something which could have been given in alms (which would conflict with Luke's interest in almsgiving and the poor just studied above). The little parable of the Two Debtors sums up both passages: those who have been forgiven much show the greater love (7.47). Therefore, both the narrative context of Jesus as 'friend of sinners' and the parable's lesson show how Luke's concern for women is part of his wider portrayal of Jesus' ethic for the marginalized.

The connection with John the Baptist in this story also demonstrates that Luke's concern is for more than just those who are economically poor. The Bap-

---

139. Veronica Koperski, 'Luke 10.38-42 and Acts 6.1-7: Women and Discipleship in the Literary Context of Luke-Acts', in *The Unity of Luke-Acts,* ed. Verheyden, pp. 517-44; rev. and expanded version as 'Women and Discipleship in Luke 10.38-42 and Acts 6.1-7: The Literary Context of Luke-Acts', in *A Feminist Companion to Luke,* ed. Levine, pp. 161-96.

140. See, for example, Loveday C. Alexander, 'Sisters in Adversity: Retelling Martha's Story', and Warren Carter, 'Getting Martha out of the Kitchen: Luke 10.28-42 Again', both in *A Feminist Companion to Luke,* ed. Levine, pp. 197-213 and 214-31.

141. See further Neale, 'The Story of the Sinful Woman', chap. 5 in his *None but the Sinners,* pp. 135-47.

tist's earlier answers to his questioners are unique to Luke, in which he tells those who have coats or food to share with those who do not; however, he also gives instructions about fairness to tax collectors and to soldiers, neither of whom were poor (3.10-14). What connects them all is their social status. As Scheffler concludes, 'To emphasise only the economic aspect does harm to Luke's sympathy for all those who suffer and even distorts his emphasis on the poor. For the motivation behind his emphasis on the suffering of the poor is not in the first place a political or economical philosophy or ideology but a concern which he also has for rich toll-collectors or soldiers who are social outcasts'.[142] In other words, this ethic for the poor, women and outsiders is all part of Jesus' fulfilling his opening manifesto: true to his pledge in the synagogue (4.18-19), Jesus consorts with lepers (5.12-16; 7.22; 17.11-19), the crippled (5.17-26; 7.22), the blind (7.21-22; 18.35-43) and tax collectors (5.27-30; 15.1-2; 19.1-10).[143] In response to criticism about this from the Pharisees, Luke narrates three parables about the lost to justify Jesus' behaviour (15:1-32).

Such a universal concern also embraces non-Jews: we have already noted how a Samaritan acts as neighbour to the wounded man on the Jericho road, and another one, described as ὁ ἀλλογενὴς οὗτος, 'this foreigner', 'one of another kind', is the only leper to return to thank Jesus for his healing in a story unique to Luke (17.11-19). Luke alone includes Jesus' rebuke to James and John's desire to bring fire down upon a Samaritan village which would not receive Jesus (9.51-56). Donahue relates Luke's material about Samaritans in the gospel and Acts to his teaching on 'love of enemies'.[144] However, Jervell argues that Luke's interest in Samaritans is not merely part of his 'interest for the outcasts, the poor, and the down-trodden'; instead, 'from Luke's perspective, Jesus has solved the Samaritan problem; the church has brought the straying Samaritans back to Israel . . . back to be part of the restored people of God'.[145] Not surprisingly, J. T. Sanders, with his view of Luke as 'anti-Jewish', disagrees, and sees both the Samaritans and outcasts as part of the 'clearly defined periphery about Judaism through which the salvation of God passes on its way from the Jews to the Gentiles'.[146] Certainly, the centurion with the sick servant is shown on the periphery as one who 'loves

142. E. H. Scheffler, 'The Social Ethics of the Lucan Baptist (Lk. 3.10-14)', *Neotestamentica* 24.1 (1990), pp. 21-36; quotation from p. 33.
143. See Green, *The Theology of the Gospel of Luke*, pp. 76-94; also Mary Ann Beavis, '"Expecting Nothing in Return": Luke's Picture of the Marginalized', *Interpretation* 48.4 (1994), pp. 357-68.
144. John R. Donahue, S.J., 'Who Is My Enemy? The Parable of the Good Samaritan and the Love of Enemies', in *The Love of Enemy and Nonretaliation in the New Testament*, ed. Willard M. Swartley (Louisville: Westminster John Knox, 1992).
145. Jervell, *Luke and the People of God*, pp. 113-32; quotations from pp. 125 and 127.
146. J. T. Sanders, *The Jews in Luke-Acts*, pp. 132-53; quotation from p. 53.

our nation and built our synagogue for us' (7.1-10); similarly in Acts, Cornelius is a centurion who is also a God-fearer (Acts 10.1-2). However, we have already argued above against Sanders that such universalism is not necessarily anti-Jewish; this grouping of women, tax collectors and other outcasts includes both Jewish and non-Jewish examples of those who are marginalized — which is what they all have in common. Luke's version of the apocalyptic warnings does look forward to what he uniquely terms 'the times of the Gentiles', and the mission to all nations concludes the gospel (Luke 24.47), as well as framing the beginning and ending of Acts (Acts 1.8; 28.28). This sets Luke's picture of Jesus' concern for the socially downtrodden firmly within his universal ethic.

c. Family, marriage and divorce

We have already noted that Luke dismantles Mark's 'sandwich' connecting opposition to Jesus from his family with that from the authorities and the cosmic conflict (Mark 3.19b-35). Like Matthew, Luke completely omits Mark's opening verses about Jesus' family and friends thinking he is 'beside himself', and instead connects the spiritual battle section with Q-material on the Beelzebul controversy (Luke 11.14-23; cp. Matt. 12.22-30). But whereas Matthew continues with the blasphemy against the Holy Spirit and other controversies on testing and unclean spirits which eventually all lead into the saying about Jesus' mother and brothers and sisters (Matt. 12.31-50), Luke places the blasphemy against the Spirit a chapter later (Luke 12.10). Meanwhile his treatment of Mary and his brothers comes much earlier in this gospel, and omits Mark and Matthew's harsher verses about 'who are my mother and my brothers? Here are my mother and brothers' (Luke 8.19-21). Given Luke's interest in Mary, perhaps he considered Mark's construction to be too strong, but the effect is to tone down the rhetoric against the family. However, he does still have the dialogue between Jesus and Peter about those who have left 'house or wife or brothers or parents or children, for the sake of the kingdom of God' (Luke 18.28-30).

Interestingly, Luke also omits the debate about marriage and divorce (Mark 10.2-12; Matt. 19.3-12). He does preserve the single verse about adultery, though it lacks the mutuality of the man and the woman divorcing each other found in Mark: 'Anyone who divorces his wife and marries another commits adultery, and whoever marries a woman divorced from her husband commits adultery' applies simply to the man (Luke 16.18).[147] Given Luke's attitude to

147. See Wilson, *Luke and the Law*, pp. 29-31, 45-51; J. T. Sanders, *The Jews in Luke-Acts*, pp. 199-202; Schrage, *The Ethics of the NT*, pp. 95-98.

women elsewhere, this is rather curious, as is its context: the verse follows the saying about the law being 'until John', but still not passing away (Luke 16.16-17) — and all three verses come in the middle of a bigger section about money, including describing the Pharisees as 'lovers of money', in between the parables of the Unjust Steward and the Rich Man and Lazarus (16.1-31). Not wishing to follow Mark's challenge to the Mosaic law, or Matthew's concern for its proper interpretation, Luke probably preserves this Q-saying in its strongest original form and includes it here simply as part of Jesus' all-demanding ethical teaching, supremely shown by his teaching on wealth.[148]

d. Violence

We noted in the previous chapter on Matthew how his arrangement of the *lex talionis* and love of enemies forms two of his antitheses (Matt. 5.38-48). Luke has this material in one section, beginning with the love of enemies (Luke 6.27-36).[149] Unlike Matthew's legal setting of being sued in court for one's inner shirt, χιτών, Luke has the more obvious setting of someone begging or being robbed on the road, where the outer cloak, ἱμάτιον, is taken first; Jesus says that, in this case, the inner shirt or tunic, χιτών, is to be given up too. Similarly, there is no mention of Matthew's formal insult or a blow to the 'right cheek' — just offering the other cheek to anyone who hits you (Luke 6.29-30; cp. Matt. 5.39-40). The group chosen as a contrast to the behaviour of Jesus' followers is also interesting: while Matthew suggests that 'Gentiles' greet their brethren, Luke says that even 'sinners lend to sinners' and 'love those who love them' (Luke 6.32-35; cp. Matt. 5.47); Matthew's low expectations of Gentiles' behaviour would not be appreciated by Luke's wider audience! In the middle of this section, Luke includes the Golden Rule: 'Do to others as you would have them do to you' (Luke 6.31), which Matthew only has later in the Sermon on the Mount with his characteristic additional comment, 'for this is the law and the prophets' (Matt. 7.12). Given all these minor but significant differences, it is perhaps not surprising that, as we have noted several times, Luke concludes with his version of the Holiness Code as 'be merciful, just as your Father is merciful' (Luke 6.36; contrast Matthew's 'be perfect, as your heavenly Father is perfect, Matt. 5.48).[150]

148. Fitzmyer concludes his analysis in *Luke*, pp. 1119-21, with 'it is still puzzling why it has been introduced into this part of the travel narrative'; see also Evans, *Saint Luke*, pp. 609-10.

149. John Piper, 'Love your enemies': Jesus' Love Command in the Synoptic Gospels and in the Early Christian Paraenesis. A History of the Tradition and Interpretation of Its Uses, SNTSMS 38 (Cambridge: Cambridge University Press, 1979), esp. pp. 153-70.

150. See Matera, *NT Ethics*, pp. 76-77.

It is also noteworthy that Luke makes explicit Mark's description of Simon 'the Cananaean' (Mark 3.18), avoiding any confusion with 'Canaan' by translating the Aramaic *qan'ana'* as 'who was called the Zealot' (Luke 6.15). Despite all his teaching about nonviolence and love of enemies, Luke seems to depict Jesus at the Last Supper as reversing his previous instructions: 'Now, the one who has a purse must take it, and likewise a bag; and the one who has no sword must sell his cloak and buy one.' When the disciples reveal that they have 'two swords', Jesus replies, 'It is enough' (22.35-38). Walaskay comments, 'While Jesus had allowed the disciples to make their own calculations for defence, he also established a limit of active resistance'.[151] Clearly, however, two swords are not 'enough' to see off a detachment of temple police, and when they use the swords to cut off the ear of the high priest's slave, Jesus stops them, 'No more of this!' Interestingly, although all four gospels mention this incident, only Luke says that Jesus then healed the man (22.49-51); as Swartley observes, 'His healing the high priest's slave's ear demonstrates his mission and manner of ministry. Put sharply, Jesus came to heal precisely what the sword devastates'.[152] Therefore, Fitzmyer is surely right to translate Jesus' reply at the Supper, ἱκανόν ἐστιν, as an ironic dismissal, 'Enough of that!': the fact that the disciples take Jesus' comment about how bad the times ahead are as a literal instruction to go and buy swords means that 'his disillusionment is complete . . . the irony concerns not the number of the swords, but the whole mentality of the apostles. Jesus will have nothing to do with swords, even for defense'.[153] Cassidy agrees with Fitzmyer's translation and sets this incident within the whole narrative; he concludes, 'Throughout Luke's gospel, Jesus' teaching and actions relative to violence are thoroughly consistent. In particular circumstances Jesus acts and speaks aggressively, but he always does so without doing or sanctioning violence to persons, and he continually witnesses to overriding love and forgiveness.'[154] Thus, Luke's portrayal of Jesus' deeds, especially in his nonviolent and healing acceptance of his arrest and his coming passion and death, provides the narrative context within which the various teachings about peace and violence are to be understood.

---

151. Walaskay, *'And so we came to Rome'*, pp. 16-17.

152. Willard M. Swartley, *Covenant of Peace: The Missing Peace in New Testament Theology and Ethics* (Grand Rapids: Eerdmans, 2006), p. 132; see pp. 121-51 for his treatment of peace in Luke's gospel and pp. 152-76 for Acts.

153. Fitzmyer, *Luke*, pp. 1428-35.

154. Cassidy, *Jesus, Politics, and Society*, p. 47.

e. Attitude towards leadership, power and the state

O'Toole is clear that the final aspect of Luke's ethical material is also part of Luke's overall portrayal of Jesus' universal concern: 'This theme of Jesus as the savior of the disadvantaged unifies the remaining considerations of Jesus in politics and society in Luke-Acts'.[155] Thus, while James and John's own request for the best seats in heaven (Mark 10.35-45) was given by Matthew to their mother to deliver (Matt. 20.20-21), Luke omits the whole story, since it does not fit into his generally better portrait of the disciples. However, they do have a dispute about who is the greatest, which takes place at the Last Supper — of all times and places! Jesus explicitly contrasts the behaviour he expects from his followers with that of the rest of the world: 'The kings of the Gentiles lord it over them; and those in authority over them are called benefactors. But not so with you'. He then appeals to his own example, 'I am among you as one who serves' (ὡς ὁ διακονῶν, Luke 22.24-27). The same point is made in Luke's unique parable of the Pharisee and the Tax Collector at prayer, which concludes with the moral that 'all who exalt themselves will be humbled, but all who humble themselves will be exalted' (18.9-14). It is notable also in Acts that the 'deacons' who are commissioned to 'serve' at tables, διακονεῖν, to follow Jesus' example, end up both preaching the gospel and, in the case of Stephen, dying like him also (Acts 6.1–7.60).

The question to Jesus about paying tribute to Caesar comes from the Pharisees and Herodians, according to Mark and Matthew (Mark 12.13-17; Matt. 22.15-22). As we have already noted, in Luke the Pharisees do not provide the final opposition to Jesus, and here the 'they' who ask the question are the 'scribes and chief priests' of the previous verse (Luke 20.19); otherwise the story follows Mark closely, as Luke's source (20.20-26). However, as Derrett has noted, for Luke, rendering to Caesar cannot mean unquestioning obedience to civil authorities.[156]

In fact, only Luke says that 'the assembly of the elders of the people, both chief priests and scribes' accused Jesus before Pilate of such civil charges: 'We found this man perverting our nation, forbidding us to pay taxes to the emperor, and saying that he himself is the Messiah, a king' (22.66; 23.1-2, 5). However, Jesus is declared 'innocent' according to Pilate three times (23.4, 14, 22) and also by the centurion at the foot of the cross (23.47).[157] The early community in Acts were

155. Robert F. O'Toole, 'Luke's Position on Politics and Society in Luke-Acts', in *Political Issues in Luke-Acts*, ed. Cassidy and Scharper, pp. 1-17; quotation from p. 9.

156. J. Duncan M. Derrett, 'Luke's Perspective on Tribute to Caesar', in *Political Issues in Luke-Acts*, ed. Cassidy and Scharper, pp. 38-48.

157. See Daryl Schmidt, 'Luke's "Innocent" Jesus: A Scriptural Apologetic', in *Political Issues in Luke-Acts*, ed. Cassidy and Scharper, pp. 111-21.

well aware in their prayer to God, however, that it was an unholy alliance of all sides which executed Jesus: 'For in this city, in fact, both Herod and Pontius Pilate, with the Gentiles and the peoples of Israel, gathered together against your holy servant Jesus, whom you anointed' (Acts 4.27). The church leaders in Acts, especially Paul, follow a similar pattern to that of Jesus. They are accused of being against Caesar for another king (17.7), but regularly acquitted of such charges (18.12-17; 25.18; 26.31). Roman authorities view it all as internal Jewish disputes (18.15; 23.29; 24.5, 14; 25.19); the state protects Christians (18.12; 22.23-29), pays respect to Paul as a citizen (16.37; 22.25) and even apologizes to him (16.39). Like Jesus, Paul is innocent, having done nothing to deserve death (23.29; 25.25; 26.31). Despite all the trials and appearances before various authorities, Luke is keen to stress how the preaching of the gospel continues, right up to Paul's very last words, 'proclaiming the kingdom of God and teaching about the Lord Jesus Christ with all boldness and without hindrance' (Acts 28.31).

This has all provoked much debate, from the earliest scholarly work on Luke in the eighteenth and nineteenth centuries through to Conzelmann, who argued that Luke is engaged in 'political apologetic' to the Romans.[158] Against Conzelmann's approach, Cassidy's studies of both the gospel and Acts have argued that Jesus and the early believers posed a threat to the Roman authorities: 'By espousing radically new social patterns and by refusing to defer to the existing political authorities, Jesus pointed the way to a social order in which neither the Romans nor any other oppressing group would be able to hold sway'; therefore, his audience might also expect hearings and trials as they sought to 'witness before kings and governors'.[159] Meanwhile, Walaskay has argued that rather than offering an apology for the church to Romans, Luke is more interested in 'an *apologia pro imperio* which would help the Christian community live effectively with the social, political, and religious realities of the present situation until the advent of God's reign'.[160] Esler is not convinced by any of these approaches and uses his sociological analysis to show how Luke is attempting to provide 'legitimation' for the various groups, including some Jews and Romans, within his community.[161] Therefore Luke is not simply 'anti-' or 'pro-' any political system,

158. See Conzelmann, *The Theology of St. Luke,* pp. 137-44; Esler's survey in *Community and Gospel in Luke-Acts,* pp. 205-6, takes the debate back to C. A. Heumann in 1720 and K. Schrader in 1836; for a fuller discussion, see Walaskay, *'And so we came to Rome',* pp. ix, 1-14.

159. Cassidy, *Jesus, Politics, and Society,* esp. pp. 77-79, quotation from p. 70; see his Appendix 4 on Conzelmann, pp. 128-30; also, Richard J. Cassidy, *Society and Politics in the Acts of the Apostles* (Maryknoll, NY: Orbis, 1987), esp. his conclusions, pp. 158-70.

160. Walaskay, *'And so we came to Rome',* p. 67.

161. Esler, *Community and Gospel in Luke-Acts,* pp. 201-19; see also Jervell, *Theology of the Acts of the Apostles,* pp. 100-106.

Jewish or Roman. As we noted earlier about his attitude towards Judaism, in everything Luke is aiming for a more balanced and universal, inclusive approach; so Marguerat sums it up: 'Luke's theological project . . . is to integrate into the definition of Christianity, the two opposite poles, Jerusalem and Rome'.[162]

Thus we have seen that, as Pilgrim concludes, the portrait of the state in Luke and Acts is 'more complex and ambiguous', 'highly critical of those who hold political office, both Jewish and Roman'. Once again, therefore, this topic, like so many others, goes back to our key theme of Luke's portrait of Jesus' universal concern: 'Jesus envisions a new pattern of community and social relations that reverses the established order in which the rich and powerful dominate and instead welcomes the poor and marginal. . . . Rome is neither friend nor partner of the church'.[163] Surely the final word on leadership, power and the state comes from Peter when the Sanhedrin forbid him to teach and preach about Jesus: 'We must obey God rather than any human authority' (Acts 4.19; 5.29). This directs attention back to the main implication of our approach through literary genre: Luke is writing a biographical narrative about the life and ministry, death and resurrection of Jesus and what God accomplished through all of that, rather than a political tract or ethical treatise. Therefore, it is the attitude of Jesus in the gospel and the apostles in Acts which is to be emulated: their lives demonstrate that it is God who should be obeyed in all things, rather than political power, even if that means at the cost of one's own life.

In summary, we may now conclude this survey of the ethical issues which surface in Luke-Acts by agreeing that, in one sense, Sanders is right: Luke does not provide a clear ethical system to guide Christians 'this side of the Parousia'.[164] On the other hand, Sanders is wrong to be disappointed about the lack of ethics in this two-volume work. As with the complaints about the 'paucity of ethical material in Mark' and the fixation upon the Sermon on the Mount in Matthew, Sanders needs to look more widely than just for material which resembles the genre of ethical sayings or treatises. As we demonstrated in the other two Synoptic gospels, the narrative-biographical approach yields a great deal of material which has ethical implications and applications. However, at all stages, Luke's treatment of ethical issues, like his narrative, his eschatology and his attitude towards Judaism and the law, always maintains its focus upon love, developed through Luke's main biographical portrait of Jesus' universal concern for everyone, especially for the marginalized. Whether it is Jews or

162. Marguerat, *The First Christian Historian*, p. 82.

163. Walter E. Pilgrim, *Uneasy Neighbours: Church and State in the New Testament* (Minneapolis: Fortress, 1999), pp. 123-43; quotations from p. 43.

164. J. T. Sanders, *Ethics in the NT*, p. 36; see further the start of this section.

Romans, women or Samaritans, rich or poor, Luke tries to balance the positive and the negative, which entails living with a certain amount of messiness within an inclusive community while waiting for Parousia, rather than offering a simple set of ethical instructions. However, this universal concern does touch upon most of the main areas of human moral experience. Supremely, however, the centre of attention is always the person of Jesus, as depicted in his words and deeds; so we must finally turn to what it means to follow and imitate him.

5. Imitating Jesus, the friend of sinners

Finally, as with our studies of Jesus, Paul, Mark and Matthew, we must come to the questions of discipleship and imitation. In terms of the biographical genre of the gospels, this is the shift from words to deeds, from Jesus' teaching to his activity, particularly in terms of how he accepted people. However, in the case of Luke-Acts, perhaps this move is not so marked as previously, since we have already discovered at the centre of Luke's portrait of Jesus a universal mission, concerned for everyone, especially the marginalized. Furthermore, this theme of an all-embracing love has dominated how Luke has handled everything else, his eschatology, his attitude towards Judaism and the law, and his treatment of the various main areas of ethical experience. Mark's radical ethic of suffering with eschatological expectation led to his picture of discipleship as tough and difficult, but it still allowed for a mixed community seeking to imitate Jesus together. Matthew's central concern for the proper interpretation of the law was based on his depiction of a community of followers of Jesus the true interpreter, including some who were more like weeds than wheat, who had to learn to forgive one another as they sought to 'be perfect, even as your heavenly Father is perfect' (Matt 5.48). Luke's all-embracing portrait of Jesus, together with his balancing act in holding together differing approaches to our various topics, should lead even more naturally into an inclusive community — and this expectation is confirmed by his decision to write not just a biographical narrative about Jesus, but to continue it with a second volume through into the life of the early church as individually and corporately they sought to emulate Jesus' words and deeds.

a. Jesus, the 'friend of sinners'

Our consideration of Luke's Christology illustrated his central concern for the universal mission of Jesus, underscoring the truth of Matera's comment: 'One of the most distinctive aspects of the Lukan Jesus is the company he keeps'.[165] This direction was clearly signposted in his opening sermon at Nazareth with its concern for the poor, captives, blind and oppressed, as well as the subsequent mention of Gentiles (Luke 4.16-20, 26-27).[166] Our study so far has amply demonstrated how this manifesto was certainly fulfilled, so we only need to summarize it here. In Luke's gospel, Jesus spends a large amount of his time with, or concerned for, the poor (1.52-53; 6.20-21; 7.22; 12.13-21; 16.19-31; 18.22-25), the blind and the lame or crippled (5.17-26; 7.21-22; 13.10-17; 14.12-14, 15-24; 18.35-43), lepers (5.12-16; 7.22; 17.11-19), those who are possessed and oppressed by unclean spirits (4.31-37, 41; 6.18; 7.21; 8.2, 26-39; 9.37-42, 49-50) and, of course, with women (1.24-25, 26-56; 2.5-7, 36-38, 51; 7.11-17, 36-50; 4.38-39; 8.1-3, 40-56; 10.38-42; 13.10-17; 15.8-10; 18.1-8; 23.27-31). What all these groups have in common is that they were socially marginalized.

Roth argues that so far there was no problem; what he terms the 'LXX-competent audience' would expect from their reading of the scriptures the 'coming one' to associate with such obvious recipients of God's favour. The problem comes in the fact that Jesus also associates with 'sinners', and it is this for which he is criticized:[167] 'The Son of Man has come eating and drinking, and you say, "Look, a glutton and a drunkard, a friend of tax collectors and sinners!"' (7.33-34). As Neale concludes his detailed study on the subject, 'The tradition about Jesus' association with "sinners" is one of the central issues in the Gospel of Luke'.[168] The problem is that the description of Jesus as the 'friend of sinners' is so deeply embedded in the Christian tradition as a positive image that it is easy to forget that it was levelled originally as an accusation, not something which 'a great moral teacher' should be. Yet the objection is consistent, following Jesus' eating with Levi and friends, accepting the sinful woman in Simon's house, and above all receiving hospitality in the home of a renowned sinner like the tax collector Zacchaeus (5.29-32; 7.39; 19.7). It is to defend himself against such 'grumblings' that Luke depicts Jesus telling the parables of the Lost Sheep, Lost Coin, and Prodigal Son (15.1-2, 3-7, 8-10, 11-32). On the other hand, Luke also demonstrates another aspect to Jesus' inclusive attitude, as he shows him also happy to accept the hospitality of his critics among the Pharisees (7.36; 11.37; 14.1).[169] It is quite understandable that in Matthew's depiction of Jesus as

165. Matera, *NT Ethics*, p. 88.
166. See our earlier discussion of the Nazareth sermon in section 1.b above, esp. n. 23.
167. Roth, *The Blind, the Lame, and the Poor*, p. 218.
168. Neale, *None but the Sinners*, p. 191.
169. See Craig L. Blomberg, *Contagious Holiness: Jesus' Meals with Sinners* (Downers Grove, IL: InterVarsity Press, 2005), esp. chap. 5, 'Pervasive Purity', pp. 130-63, on Jesus' eating with sinners and with Pharisees in material peculiar to Luke.

the proper interpreter of the law, his version of the Q-saying on imitating God should be redacted as 'be perfect, even as your heavenly Father is perfect' (Matt. 5.48). It is even less surprising that Luke's version stresses the other dimension: 'Be merciful, just as your Father is merciful' (Luke 6.36) — for this is at the heart of his portrait of Jesus, the friend of sinners.

b. The mixed community which follows

This open attitude leads into the mixed collection of those who are shown following Jesus. 'Luke takes pains to emphasize the diversity of persons who are called to discipleship by Jesus. We meet women and men from all social categories'.[170] As Luke provides narrative settings for some of the Q-teachings which Matthew collects into his sermons and discourses, so he also explains the story behind the call of the first disciples. In Mark, Jesus simply appears without warning on the lakeside and issues his summons to Peter and Andrew, James and John, 'Follow me' (Mark 1.16-20; similarly in Matt. 4.18-22). However, in Luke, Jesus heals Peter's mother-in-law first, and then shows Peter how to find fish after an unproductive night's work (4.38-39; 5.1-11); Peter's immediate reaction is to ask Jesus to leave him alone, 'for I am a sinner' (5.8). But, as we know, Jesus is the 'friend of sinners' — and he wants this particular sinful man to lead his followers; so Peter, together with James and John, leaves *everything* (only inserted in Luke) to follow him.

Furthermore, Luke paints the disciples in a better light. While in Mark they have 'no faith' (Mark 4.40), which Matthew changes to 'you of little faith' (Matt. 8.26), in Luke they actually ask Jesus, 'Increase our faith' (Luke 17.5; cp. Matt. 17.20). We have already noted that Luke omits James and John's request for the good seats in heaven (Mark 10.35-45); he also excuses them and Peter for their panic at the transfiguration because they were 'heavy with sleep', while in Gethsemane they fall asleep 'for sorrow' (Luke 9.32; 22.45). The Twelve are called 'apostles' only once in Matthew and twice in Mark (Matt. 10.2; Mark 3.14; 6.30), but Luke uses the term for them five times in his gospel (6.13; 9.10; 17.5; 22.14; 24.10) — preparing the way for the thirty occurrences in Acts, when they have become the leaders of the early community. As Longenecker puts it, 'Luke views the disciples as modeling the essential characteristics of Christian discipleship. It is not their failures that he highlights. Rather, what he emphasizes are the new commitments, orientation, and lifestyle that they reflected in their lives by association with Jesus their Master'.[171]

170. Perkins, *Reading the New Testament*, p. 238.
171. Richard N. Longenecker, 'Taking Up the Cross Daily: Discipleship in Luke-Acts', in *Pat-*

Nor does Luke view discipleship as an exclusive club: 'To a far greater extent than either Mark or Matthew, Luke associates Jesus with diverse numbers of disciples'.[172] The twelve are sent out on mission practice as in the other gospels (9.1-6),[173] but only Luke mentions another seventy (or seventy-two in some manuscripts) being sent out in pairs (10.1-16). He even talks of 'a great crowd of his disciples' and 'the whole multitude of the disciples' (6.17; 19.37). Luke alone mentions women followers, naming Mary Magdalene, Joanna wife of Herod's steward Chuza, Susanna 'and many others' who provided financial resources for them (8.1-3).[174] Despite Martha's protests, Mary is allowed to adopt the disciple's posture, sitting at Jesus' feet, having 'chosen the better part, which will not be taken away from her' (10.38-42).

Such an inclusive approach continues into Acts, which begins with the eleven apostles 'constantly devoting themselves to prayer, together with certain women, including Mary the mother of Jesus, as well as his brothers'. However, altogether they number 'about one hundred twenty persons', which includes others 'who have accompanied us during all the time that the Lord Jesus went in and out among us', out of which Matthias is chosen by lot to be added to the 'eleven apostles' (Acts 1.13-15, 21-26). If Jesus' sermon at Nazareth acts as a manifesto for the gospel, Peter's address at Pentecost functions similarly for Acts; Jesus quotes Isaiah's concern for the poor and the marginalized, while Peter picks up Joel's inclusive attitude towards sons and daughters, young and old, male and female servants or slaves, and ends with the same universal mission: 'Then everyone who calls on the name of the Lord shall be saved' (2.16-21). As Longenecker comments on these two sermons, 'Each of these themes — the Spirit's presence, the proclamation of God's redemptive activity, and the universality of God's grace — is not only an important feature of Luke's writing, but also is presented in both his Gospel and his Acts as factors that are to characterize the self-consciousness of a follower of Jesus, and so to be accepted and worked out in Christian discipleship'.[175]

---

terns of Discipleship in the New Testament, ed. Richard N. Longenecker (Grand Rapids: Eerdmans, 1996), pp. 50-76; quotation from p. 57.

172. Kingsbury, *Conflict in Luke: Jesus, Authorities, Disciples*, p. 109; see pp. 109-39 for full discussion of 'the story of the disciples'; also, Kim, *Stewardship and Almsgiving in Luke's Theology*, pp. 89-110 on 'Luke's View of Discipleship'.

173. See Daniel J. Harrington, S.J., and James F. Keenan, S.J., 'Discipleship as Context: Who Are We?', in their *Jesus and Virtue Ethics: Building Bridges between New Testament Studies and Moral Theology* (Oxford: Sheed and Ward, 2002), pp. 49-59.

174. See Bauckham, *Gospel Women: Studies of the Named Women in the Gospels*, pp. 109-202 and pp. 203-23, for his reconstructions of 'Joanna the Apostle' and 'Mary of Clopas'.

175. Longenecker, 'Taking Up the Cross Daily: Discipleship in Luke-Acts', pp. 71-72.

Thus it is not surprising that about three thousand people were added to the early community on that day of Pentecost (2.41). The fact that 'the disciples were increasing in number' needed more than just the twelve to lead and serve the growing community, so they appointed the deacons; then 'the word of God continued to spread; the number of the disciples increased greatly in Jerusalem' (6.1-7). The use of 'disciples' twice in this passage to include everyone in the community is significant, and thereafter Luke uses both 'disciples' and ἀδελφοί, 'brothers and sisters', about thirty times each to refer to the believers.[176] He also describes them as those 'who belonged to the Way, men or women' (9.2; see also 18.25; 19.9, 23; 22.4; 24.22). Having written his 'biography' *(bios)* of Jesus' words and deeds in the gospel, in Acts Luke pens a biographical narrative of the 'life' *(bios)* of the church, including portraits of the various key individuals, especially Peter and Paul.[177] Talbert has consistently drawn attention to the 'remarkable series of correspondences between what Jesus does and says in Luke's Gospel and what the disciples do and say in the Acts'.[178]

Talbert is right to conclude, 'The disciple who is shaped by the tradition of Jesus and enabled by an ongoing experience of the Lord is no solitary individual but a participant in a community. The communal dimension of discipleship is seen both in *the way* one is called to walk and in the mission he or she is commissioned to fulfill'.[179] For Luke, it is a community which follows Jesus, and, given his universal theme, this must be a mixed and inclusive group — what Green calls 'an egalitarian community': 'it is precisely Jesus' radical openness in table fellowship in the Gospel of Luke that stands as the model and reproach to the Christian community in Acts as it struggles with crossing ethnic and religious lines at the table'.[180] Esler also picks up the theme of table

176. Note that while ἀδελφοί is the plural of the masculine ἀδελφός, it also serves as an inclusive plural of the masculine and the feminine ἀδελφή when both genders are present, so that NRSV's translation, 'brothers and sisters', is perfectly acceptable; however, the fact that NRSV also translates it by 'believers' in some places does obscure the point.

177. See further, for example, John C. Lentz, Jr., *Luke's Portrait of Paul*, SNTSMS 77 (Cambridge: Cambridge University Press, 1993), and Richard I. Pervo, *Luke's Story of Paul* (Minneapolis: Fortress, 1990).

178. Charles H. Talbert, 'Discipleship in Luke-Acts', in *Discipleship in the New Testament*, ed. Fernando F. Segovia (Philadelphia: Fortress, 1985), pp. 62-75, quotation from p. 63; see further Talbert's various writings, esp. *Literary Patterns, Theological Themes and the Genre of Luke-Acts*, SBLMS 20 (Missoula, MT: Scholars Press, 1974); *What Is a Gospel?: The Genre of the Canonical Gospels* (Philadelphia: Fortress, 1977/London: SPCK, 1978); 'Biographies of Philosophers and Rulers as Instruments of Religious Propaganda in Mediterranean Antiquity', in *ANRW* 1.16.2 (1978), pp. 1619-51.

179. Talbert, 'Discipleship in Luke-Acts', pp. 71-72; his italics.

180. Green, *The Theology of the Gospel of Luke*, p. 117.

fellowship in his sociological reconstruction of Luke's community as including law-observant Jews, God-fearing Gentiles from the proselyte fringe, outright pagans, Greeks and Romans on the 'axis of their religious affiliation prior to becoming Christians'; on the 'second axis, that of socio-economic position', Esler believes that the community included both the 'highest strata' and the 'lowest levels'.[181]

We have argued throughout this chapter that it is Luke's depiction of Jesus' universal concern to include everyone which has led to this gospel's all-embracing middle-path approach to topics such as Judaism and the law. He does this through an account of Jesus' all-demanding ethical teaching (words) within a narrative of his all-accepting attitude towards sinners (deeds). Kim notes a potential discrepancy here and seeks to solve it by introducing a distinction between 'itinerant' disciples, who were expected to renounce everything, and 'sedentary' disciples, who were not: 'What is particularly noteworthy is that, despite the strict nature of his commands to renounce *all* to follow him, Jesus does not reproach the sedentary disciples, who are shown not to have left their possessions and property, but rather appears to accept them as they are, enjoying their entertainment as they invite him and his wandering disciples to meals in their houses. This is a very significant point'.[182] Kim is absolutely right to point to this dichotomy, which lies at the heart of the argument of this book also.[183]

However, it is not obvious that Luke would recognize Kim's distinction of 'itinerant' and 'sedentary' disciples: it is reminiscent of the attempts to solve tension this through 'evangelical counsels' and 'evangelical precepts', or first-class and second-class Christians, the religious orders and ordinary believers, which we noted in our discussion of the historical Jesus' teachings earlier.[184] It is the same Luke who stresses Jesus' teaching about giving away *everything* to be his disciple (Luke 5.11, 28; 12.33; 14.33; 18.22) who depicts Jesus' actions in praising Zacchaeus, who offers to give away only *half* of his possessions (19.8). Kim is right that 'Jesus does not reproach' him, but this is not because he is in a second-class category of 'sedentary' disciples to whom the teaching does not apply. It is because, as we have consistently argued throughout this book, Jesus' ethical teaching is not a new law which he expects to be obeyed to the letter;

---

181. See Esler's concluding summary, Esler, *Community and Gospel in Luke-Acts*, pp. 220-23.

182. Kim, *Stewardship and Almsgiving in Luke's Theology*, p. 285; his italics.

183. Compare the distinction between 'wandering charismatics' and 'local sympathizers' in, for example, Martin Hengel, *The Charismatic Leader and his Followers* (Edinburgh: T&T Clark, 1968), and Gerd Theissen, *The First Followers of Jesus: A Sociological Analysis of Earliest Christianity* (London: SCM, 1977).

184. See Chapter II, sect. 2.f above, esp. pp. 58-61.

rather, it is a challenge to live in the light of the kingdom or sovereignty of God. It is the *response* to that challenge which Jesus seeks primarily, and so Zacchaeus is praised for his reaction, even if it does not fulfil the letter of Jesus' teaching.

Furthermore, the inclusion of such radical teaching within the biographical narrative of Jesus' deeds in accepting anyone who wanted to respond is at the heart of the gospel genre. Luke has understood this better than most by stressing both aspects in his gospel, the all-demanding rigorous teaching and the all-embracing inclusive acceptance. He also continues this into Acts, where those who do sell their possessions, like Barnabas, are praised, as are those who keep their houses and use them for the early community, like Mary (Acts 4.34-37; 12.12). This individual response to the gospel and acceptance of others', possibly different, responses, is what it means to follow Jesus within an inclusive community, according to Luke. The only thing which is really unacceptable is to do one thing and pretend the other, as when Ananias and Sapphira hold back their proceeds but claim to give it all, for this is to lie to Holy Spirit (Acts 5.4), which cannot be forgiven (Luke 12.10).

c. Jesus, the pattern for imitation

If Luke understands this combination of words and deeds, of Jesus' teaching and his example all within an inclusive community, better than others, he is also the evangelist who makes the role of *mimesis*, imitation, most explicit. 'Go and do likewise' may be Jesus' instruction to the lawyer to follow the example of the Good Samaritan (10.29-37), but in fact the whole of Luke-Acts is full of examples to follow or to avoid for moral conduct. This can be seen in the parables which feature only in Luke about two people, one to imitate and one not to follow, such as the Rich Man and Lazarus, the Widow and the Unjust Judge, and the Pharisee and the Tax Collector (16.19-31; 18.1-8, 9-14). Luke alone includes the explicit instruction, 'When you give a banquet, invite the poor, the crippled, the lame, and the blind', as did the man who gave a great dinner in the parable (14.13, 15-24); meanwhile, the man who wanted Jesus to arbitrate over his inheritance is told not to be like the Rich Fool, again all unique to Luke (12.13-21). The pious figures of Elizabeth and Zechariah, and the humble acceptance of Mary, 'let it be with me according to your word', provide narrative examples to imitate in the opening chapters (1–2; see 1.37), while an 'obvious paradigm of discipleship is provided by Peter'.[185]

185. Beck, *Christian Character in the Gospel of Luke*, p. 108; see further his chap. 8, 'Imitation?', pp. 105-26.

Within Acts, examples of Christian conduct abound for readers to emulate, such as Barnabas, Dorcas and Lydia (Acts 4.36-37; 9.27, 36; 16.14-15). Stephen imitates his Lord's last words and attitude in committing his spirit and praying for forgiveness for those who bring about his death, '"Lord Jesus, receive my spirit." Then he knelt down and cried out in a loud voice, "Lord, do not hold this sin against them"' (Acts 7.59-60; cp. Luke 23.33, 46). Supremely, of course, it is Luke's biographical narrative about Paul in Acts which provides another exemplar for the audience: this is made explicit in Paul's farewell to the Ephesian elders, where he brings together Jesus' words with his own deeds and life: 'In all this I have given you an example that by such work we must support the weak, remembering the words of the Lord Jesus, for he himself said, "It is more blessed to give than to receive"' (20.35). In writing his two-volume work, Luke takes his exemplary intention through to the life of the early believers; as Wall puts it, linking Acts to our previous work on Paul, 'The canonical position of Acts underscores that the true foundation of the Church is not apostolic, but Christological: to imitate the traditions and memories of the apostles is to imitate Christ (1 Cor 11:1)!'[186]

Throughout his gospel, Luke depicts Jesus as the 'friend of sinners', embracing and including all who respond to him, regardless of their social standing, ethnic or religious background, but always being especially concerned for the outcast and marginalized. This comes to its climax at the Last Supper, where Luke locates the material about how his followers are to behave. In response to their concern for who was the greatest, Jesus explicitly refers to his example, 'I am among you as one who serves' (Luke 22.27): 'as Luke in his Gospel shows, Jesus' earthly ministry has exemplified this kind of serving behaviour *par excellence*.'[187] Therefore, if Luke's particular concern has been for the marginalized, this should be at the centre of our *mimesis*: 'Christians should imitate Christ, the savior of the disadvantaged'.[188]

After all our study of Jesus' words and teaching in Luke's gospel and the book of Acts, it is to his deeds that we need to return to discover a pattern for imitation, especially concentrating on his universal concern. As Matera concludes his study of Jesus as a 'model for ethical conduct', 'in summary, Jesus' actions give those who read and hear this Gospel an important source of ethical instruction. Jesus' behaviour teaches disciples to seek God's will, to pray constantly, to listen to Moses and the prophets, to form a community that excludes

---

186. Wall, 'Introduction: New Testament Ethics', p. 70; his emphasis.

187. H. Douglas Buckwalter, 'The Divine Saviour', in *Witness to the Gospel: The Theology of Acts*, ed. Marshall and Peterson, pp. 107-23; quotation from p. 120.

188. O'Toole, 'Luke's Position on Politics and Society in Luke-Acts', p. 14.

none, and to overcome evil by doing good to one's enemies'.[189] Furthermore, Luke's organization of his gospel around the structure of the journey to Jerusalem and of Acts as the progress of the gospel out from Jerusalem to the ends of the earth, together with his description of the faith as 'the Way', reminds us that no response is perfect at the beginning; rather, to imitate Jesus is set out on a life of following him in the mixed company of others who are also trying to respond — and we have to accept and include them also. The combination of a biblical scholar and a theologian looking together at Luke's call to discipleship sums it up thus: 'The call to the moral life is a call to walk on the way of the Lord . . . the entire moral life is organized and shaped by our following of Jesus . . . that image of Jesus on the road is a dominant one in understanding the call to imitate Jesus'.[190]

6. Conclusion

Like Mark and Matthew, Luke takes the basic outline of the life and teaching of Jesus and retells it, applying it to his context. In addition, however, his decision to write a two-volume work which continues on into the life of the early Christian community has enormous implications for our study of the ethics of the New Testament. The necessity for this chapter to be rather longer than those on the other two Synoptics reflects in part that the two books of Luke and Acts are much longer, comprising together about a quarter of the total of the New Testament and about the same length as all Paul's letters. However, it is also an indication of how much ethical material there is to be found in Luke's double work.

As with the other gospels, it is Luke's Christology which is determinative, as he portrays Jesus' universal mission, going around Galilee and then along the Jordan valley to Jerusalem, being in dialogue with Jews and Gentiles, men and women, Pharisees and sinners, rich and poor alike — but always with an especial concern for the socially marginalized. The real opposition comes from the powerful leaders in Jerusalem — and the same picture of an all-embracing mission being opposed by rulers also emerges through the account of the early church in Acts. Luke's eschatological approach reckons with the delay of the Parousia as it combines present and future and seeks a way of caring for others in the light of the imminent end. True to his universal concern, Luke seeks to include both the positive and the negative in his attitude to Judaism and the law; Jesus has come out of the history and traditions of Israel, and they are still

---

189. Matera, *NT Ethics*, p. 89.
190. Daniel J. Harrington, S.J., and James F. Keenan, S.J., 'Discipleship as Context', pp. 55, 57.

to be honoured by those who wish to do so — but 'something more' is always required by the demands of love.

It is a genre mistake to look to Luke for a systematic treatment of Christian ethics while waiting for the Parousia; however, Luke's biographical narrative does contain substantial amounts of ethical material, particularly about wealth and the poor, women and the marginalized, marriage and the family, peace and violence, and how one is to relate to the state. In all cases, however, Luke's inclusive intent attempts to balance the positive and negative under the main imperative of love, especially for the marginalized. As in the other gospels, in Luke-Acts, 'Christian ethics is not presented as a checklist of commands and prohibitions. The Gospels challenge believers to adopt a way of life that emulates that of Jesus'.[191] Luke's portrait of Jesus as the 'friend of sinners' leads into his account in both the gospel and Acts of the mixed and inclusive community of those who wish to become disciples and to follow Jesus' words and deeds, teaching and example. While it may be a call to perfection eventually in the kingdom of heaven, the realities of this life must allow for a generous acceptance of others who are also engaged in following Jesus along the way, so that in all things, we might 'be merciful, just as your Father is merciful' (Luke 6.36).

191. Barbara Reid, O.P., 'The Ethics of Luke', *The Bible Today* 31.5 (1993), pp. 283-87; quotation from p. 286.

VII. John: Teaching the Truth in Love

'For God so loved the world that he gave his only Son, so that everyone who believes in him may not perish but may have eternal life' (John 3.16). This is probably the most famous verse in John's gospel, perhaps the most well-known verse in the whole Bible — but who actually says it? Jesus is talking to Nicodemus and replies to his question, 'How can these things be?' with a paragraph about his witness, likening himself to Moses and the serpent (3.9-15). Then v. 16 leads into the free-standing paragraph about light and darkness in 3.16-21: is this Jesus still speaking to Nicodemus, or over his head to the general audience, or is it a comment by the fourth evangelist? Exactly the same thing happens a little later in 3.31-36; again, is this the continuation of John the Baptist's speech, or another comment from the narrator?[1] Punctuation was inserted into the manuscripts only centuries after the originals were written, but usually it is obvious when a person starts or stops speaking — especially one whose voice and style is as instantly recognizable as Jesus in the Synoptic gospels with his pithy sayings and teasing parables. Here in the fourth gospel, however, he speaks with a different voice, one which is indistinguishable from that

---

1. For example, Westcott sees both passages as 'commentary' and 'reflections' from the evangelist, B. F. Westcott, *The Gospel according to St. John* (London: Murray, 1919), pp. 54-57, 60, while Brown argues that both are speeches from Jesus, Raymond E. Brown, S.S., *The Gospel according to John,* Anchor Bible 29 and 29A (New York: Doubleday, 1966 and 1970; 2nd edn. 1984), pp. 149, 159-60; the debate continues as Stibbe treats them as 'narrator's commentary', Mark W. G. Stibbe, *John,* Readings Series (Sheffield: JSOT Press, 1993), pp. 57-58, 61, but Keener sees them as the words of Jesus and of John the Baptist, even if they contain 'consummate Johannine Christology', Craig S. Keener, *The Gospel of John: A Commentary,* 2 vols. (Peabody, MA: Hendrickson, 2003), pp. 566-74 and 581-83.

of the narrator, and indeed in this chapter from the Baptist's as well. In fact, all the characters in this gospel, including its narrator, sound alike, in a unique style with a limited vocabulary with various keywords repeated over and over again, such as 'light', 'darkness', 'life', 'world', 'see', 'look', 'know', 'believe', 'faith', 'send', 'abide', 'hour', 'glory', 'father', 'son': John uses these words, many of them rare in the other gospels, more than the rest of the New Testament combined.[2] Someone has thought and prayed, taught and preached this material over and over again.

Two word groups in particular demonstrate this. We have noted how the kingdom of God was central to Jesus' teaching in the other gospels (occurring twenty times in Mark and around fifty in both Matthew and Luke) and how it was illuminated by his parables. However, John has the word 'kingdom' only a few times (here with Nicodemus, and later with Pilate, John 3.3, 5; 18.36), and never even mentions the word 'parable', let alone actually including any of these stories. Since so much of the ethical material in the other gospels depends upon the kingdom of God and the parables, this does not augur well for the ethics of John. On the other hand, the word for 'love' appears in the fourth gospel about fifty times, as opposed to Mark's seven mentions and fourteen each in Matthew and Luke. Similarly, the root, ἀλήθ-, for 'true' and 'truth', appears only two or three times in each Synoptic gospel, but John uses it on some forty-five occasions.[3] Yet these two word groups, 'truth' and 'love', so central to this evangelist's thought and theology, also come close to our argument about combining words and deeds, Jesus' teaching and his life; we have noted throughout how the former is often highly demanding, while the latter is all-embracing. In John's gospel in general as well as in 3.16-21 in particular, Jesus brings the 'truth' from God, even if people do not want to hear it, but he also comes as the expression of the divine love to help us 'love' one another. To borrow from one of the later Pauline letters, Eph. 4.15, in the fourth gospel Jesus comes 'teaching the truth in love'. So while the language may be very different, perhaps it might be the case that John, in his own way and style, nonetheless agrees with the same combination of words and deeds, rigorous teaching and inclusive acceptance, which we have found in Paul and the Synoptists. We shall follow this theme of truth in love through the fourth gospel as we subject it to the same analysis as in the other gospels.

Yet we must also be careful to hold our course. John's gospel has been fre-

2. See Warren Carter, 'Johnspeak', chap. 5 in his *John: Storyteller, Interpreter, Evangelist* (Peabody, MA: Hendrickson, 2006), pp. 86-106.
3. For detailed statistics and discussion, see Brown, *The Gospel according to John*, Appendix I, pp. 497-501.

quently described as 'a book in which a child can paddle and an elephant may swim deep':[4] it is a deceptively simple narrative of Jesus which is often given to new converts at evangelistic rallies, but sustains the faith of millions of ordinary Christians while keeping the theologians and mystics occupied for centuries. Using the same image of the pool for the child and the elephant, Thompson is 'tempted to add' a third phrase: 'and in which a scholar can drown'![5] This is understandable, since the huge amount of secondary scholarly literature which has been erected upon this relatively small primary base threatens to topple over and subdue everything. Nearly every possible topic with regard to this gospel has been endlessly debated, with reputable scholars on both, or all, sides. We need to be aware of the various arguments and controversies as we consider this narrative — but we must not lose sight of our main aim, to see if 'teaching the truth in love' can illuminate John's ethics for us.

We have noted the contrast of style and vocabulary between John and the other gospels, but there are many other differences. Jesus' ministry takes place over some three years (see three Passovers in John 2.13; 6.4; 12.1 and 13.1), unlike the briefer time implied elsewhere, and begins with the incident in the temple rather than ending there (John 2.13-23; cp. Mark 11.15-18). Along with the absence of the kingdom of God and parables, there are no exorcisms, no narratives of Jesus' baptism or transfiguration, no institution of the Eucharist or dereliction in Gethsemane. Instead, many of the memorable events and figures from Jesus' life appear only in John, such as the wedding at Cana (John 2.1-11), Nicodemus (3.1-15/21), the Samaritan woman (4.1-42), the man at the pool of Bethesda (5.1-16), the man born blind (9.1-41) and Lazarus (11.5-44). In addition, John also has distinctive approaches to theology, Christology, eschatology, the sacraments, the church and many other areas.[6] Some even argue, 'The gos-

---

4. See, for example, Francis J. Moloney, S.D.B., *The Gospel of John: Text and Context* (Leiden: Brill, 2005), p. 5; elsewhere I use this image as a way in to an accessible introduction to most of the key issues in the study of John's gospel: Richard A. Burridge, *John*, The People's Bible Commentary (Oxford: Bible Reading Fellowship, 1998), pp. 12-29.

5. Marianne Meye Thompson, *The God of the Gospel of John* (Grand Rapids: Eerdmans, 2001), p. ix.

6. For general surveys of John and his theology, see Robert Kysar, *The Fourth Evangelist and His Gospel: An Examination of Contemporary Scholarship* (Minneapolis: Augsburg, 1975), abbreviated and updated as 'The Fourth Gospel: A Report on Recent Research', *ANRW* 2.25.3 (1985), pp. 2389-2480; Stephen Smalley, *John: Evangelist and Interpreter* (Exeter: Paternoster, 1978); J. A. T. Robinson, *The Priority of John* (London: SCM, 1985); John Ashton (ed.), *The Interpretation of John* (London: SPCK, 1986; 2nd edn. 1997); Barnabas Lindars, *John* (Sheffield: Sheffield Academic Press, 1990); John Painter, *The Quest for the Messiah: The History, Literature and Theology of the Johannine Community* (Edinburgh: T&T Clark, 1991); John W. Pryor, *John: Evangelist of the Covenant People: The Narrative and Themes of the Fourth Gospel* (London: Darton, Longman and Todd, 1992);

pel of John seems to have come from another tradition entirely — even from another universe of thought'.[7]

Yet on the other hand, one must be careful not to overstress this from just a comparison between the fourth gospel and the other three, which makes it look very different; a wider comparison with other early Christian writings and wider ancient literature shows just how similar it is to the Synoptics. It is written in the same genre of biographical narrative, telling the same basic story about Jesus' life and ministry leading up to his death and resurrection in Jerusalem.[8] It contains some common stories even if they are narrated in a different way or context: see, for example, the feeding of the five thousand (John 6.1-15; cp. Mark 6.32-44 and pars.), the walking on water (John 6.16-21; cp. Mark 6.45-52 and pars.), the temple incident (John 2.14-22; cp. Mark 11.16-17 and pars.) and Jesus being anointed by a woman (John 12.1-8; cp. Mark 14.3-9//Matt. 26.6-13 and Luke 7.36-50). Other stories are similar to some in the Synoptics, such as the healing of an official's son at a distance (John 4.46-54; cp. Luke 7.1-10//Matt. 8.5-10), or the use of saliva to cure blindness (John 9.6-7; cp. Mark 8.22-25). There are also some sayings with shared wording, such as the abundant harvest (John 4.35; cp. Matt. 9.37-38//Luke 10.2), a prophet without honour at home

---

D. Moody Smith, *The Theology of the Gospel of John* (Cambridge: Cambridge University Press, 1995); Fernando F. Segovia (ed.), *What Is John?* vol. 1, *Readers and Readings of the Fourth Gospel* (Atlanta: Scholars Press, 1996) and vol. 2, *Literary and Social Readings of the Fourth Gospel* (Atlanta: Scholars Press, 1998); Ruth Edwards, *Discovering John* (London: SPCK, 2003); Klaus Scholtissek, 'The Johannine Gospel in Recent Research', in *The Face of New Testament Studies: A Survey of Recent Research,* ed. Scot McKnight and Grant R. Osborne (Grand Rapids: Baker Academic, 2004), pp. 444-72; Carl R. Holladay, *A Critical Introduction to the New Testament: Interpreting the Message and Meaning of Jesus Christ* (Nashville: Abingdon, 2005), pp. 190-222, or pp. 269-313 in the expanded CD version; Carter, *John: Storyteller, Interpreter, Evangelist;* Marianne Meye Thompson, 'The Gospel according to John', in *The Cambridge Companion to the Gospels,* ed. Stephen C. Barton (Cambridge: Cambridge University Press, 2006), pp. 182-200; and the introductions to the commentaries by Raymond E. Brown, *The Gospel according to John,* updated as R. E. Brown, *An Introduction to the Gospel of John,* ed. Francis J. Moloney (New York: Doubleday, 2003); Barnabas Lindars, *The Gospel of John,* New Century Bible Commentary (London: Marshall, Morgan & Scott, 1972); C. K. Barrett, *The Gospel of St. John* (London: SPCK, 1st edn. 1955, 2nd edn. 1978); Ernst Haenchen, *A Commentary on the Gospel of John,* 2 vols., Hermeneia (Philadelphia: Fortress, 1984); George R. Beasley-Murray, *John,* Word Biblical Commentary 36 (Dallas: Word, 1987); Keener, *The Gospel of John;* Andrew T. Lincoln, *The Gospel according to Saint John,* Black's New Testament Commentaries (London: Continuum/Peabody, MA: Hendrickson, 2005).

7. J. B. Gabel and C. B. Wheeler, *The Bible as Literature* (Oxford: Oxford University Press, 1986), p. 198.

8. See further Richard A. Burridge, *What Are the Gospels? A Comparison with Graeco-Roman Biography,* SNTSMS 70 (Cambridge: Cambridge University Press, 1992), pp. 220-39, rev. and updated edn. (Grand Rapids: Eerdmans, 2004), pp. 213-32, for a generic comparison of John with the Synoptics.

(John 4.44; cp. Mark 6.4 and pars.), discipleship as service (John 13.4-5; cp. Luke 22.24-27) and disciples are not greater than their masters (John 13.16; cp. Matt. 10.24//Luke 6.40). Some scholars still argue that John knew the other gospels, and thus explain his differences from them as arising from his theological concerns;[9] however, here we shall follow the larger consensus that John writes independently of the other three, but that he seems to have access to some early oral traditions which overlap with their sources.[10]

Another area in which John has been traditionally contrasted with the other gospels concerns theology and history. From earliest days, John has been viewed as the 'spiritual gospel', τὸ πνευματικὸν εὐαγγελίον, while the 'bodily facts', τὰ σωματικά, were preserved in the synoptics (originally attributed to Clement of Alexandria by Eusebius, *Historia Ecclesiastica* 6.14.7). Thus John was seen as primarily theological, and thought to be relatively late and Hellenistic, while the Synoptics were seen as earlier and more Jewish. Therefore, John was mostly ignored by the various quests for the historical Jesus. However, in recent decades this too has changed: we have seen in the last three chapters how 'theological' the other three gospels in fact are — while archaeological discoveries in Israel, plus a greater appreciation of the syncretistic world of first-century Hellenistic Judaism, have produced a greater appreciation of the historical substratum of much of John's material. Thus Smith has concluded that where John has different material from the other gospels, 'Its statements or narratives deserve serious consideration as quite possibly historically superior to the Synoptics'.[11]

9. W. G. Kümmel (*Introduction to the New Testament* [London: SCM, 1975], pp. 200-217) and Barrett (*The Gospel according to St. John*, pp. 34-45 [1st edn.] or pp. 42-54 [2nd edn.]) remain convinced that John knew at least one of the Synoptic gospels; however, more recently, see Richard Bauckham, 'John for Readers of Mark', in *The Gospels for All Christians: Rethinking the Gospel Audiences*, ed. Richard Bauckham (Grand Rapids: Eerdmans, 1998), pp. 147-72, and the reaction from Wendy Sproston North, 'John for the Readers of Mark? A Response to Richard Bauckham's Proposal', *JSNT* 25.4 (2003), pp. 449-68.

10. This consensus has developed since P. Gardner-Smith's *St. John and the Synoptic Gospels* (Cambridge: Cambridge University Press, 1938); see also P. Borgen, 'John and the Synoptics', in *Tradition and Interpretation in the New Testament*, ed. G. F. Hawthorne and O. Betz (Grand Rapids: Eerdmans, 1987), pp. 80-94; D. Moody Smith, *John among the Gospels: The Relationship in Twentieth-Century Research* (Minneapolis: Fortress, 1992; 2nd edn., 2001); A. Denaux (ed.), *John and the Synoptics*, BETL 101 (Leuven: Leuven University Press, 1992).

11. D. Moody Smith, 'Historical Issues and the Problem of John and the Synoptics', in *From Jesus to John: Essays on Jesus and New Testament Christology in Honour of Marinus de Jonge*, ed. Martinus C. De Boer, JSNTSS 84 (Sheffield: Sheffield Academic Press, 1993), pp. 252-67, quotation from p. 267; see also John A. T. Robinson, *The Priority of John*; Marianne Meye Thompson, 'The Historical Jesus and the Johannine Christ', in *Exploring the Gospel of John: In Honor of D. Moody Smith*, ed. R. Alan Culpepper and C. Clifton Black (Louisville: Westminster John Knox, 1996), pp. 21-42; Francis J. Moloney, S.D.B., 'The Fourth Gospel and the Jesus of History', *NTS* 46 (2000), pp.

Meanwhile, my own work on the biographical genre of John has also contributed to other scholars' reassessment of John's relationship to history.[12]

Finally, the approach to reading the text of the fourth gospel has also undergone substantial redirection lately. For most of the twentieth century, attention focussed on the apparent breaks and seams in the text, such as how 3.16-21 and 3.31-36 fitted in, the fact that there seem to be two endings to the account of Jesus' ministry (10.40-42 or 12.44-50), why the instruction, 'Rise, let us be on our way', in 14.31 is not carried out until 18.1, and the two conclusions to the gospel (20.30-31 and 21.24-25), suggesting that the last chapter is a later addition or appendix. Various theories were put forward to explain all these difficulties involving possible multiple sources behind the gospel, and likely displacement and rearrangement of the text, of which Rudolf Bultmann's is perhaps the most famous.[13] Other solutions suggested that the text had gone through various versions, especially as it was edited to fit the needs of a developing 'Johannine community' in the process of a painful separation from the synagogue, often attempting also to fit the three Johannine epistles into the presumed scenario.[14] Such community theories were popular through the 1960s to the 1980s, but then waned so that by start of this century Kysar could speak of the 'rise and decline' of this hypothesis as an object lesson in scholarly fashions and trends.[15]

42-58, repr. in his collection, *The Gospel of John: Text and Context* (Leiden: Brill, 2005), pp. 45-65; Craig L. Blomberg, *The Historical Reliability of John's Gospel: Issues and Commentary* (Downers Grove, IL: InterVarsity Press, 2001); J. Louis Martyn, *History and Theology in the Fourth Gospel* (Louisville: Westminster John Knox, 1st edn. 1968; 3rd edn. 2003); Paul N. Anderson, *The Fourth Gospel and the Quest for Jesus: Modern Foundations Reconsidered* (London: T&T Clark, 2006). The topic has also been debated in recent years through the 'John, Jesus and History Consultation' section at the annual meetings of the SBL.

12. See Keener, 'Genre and Historical Considerations', in his *The Gospel of John*, pp. 1-52, or Lincoln, *The Gospel according to Saint John*, pp. 14-17, both of which draw upon my previous work on gospel genre.

13. Rudolf Bultmann, *The Gospel of John: A Commentary*, trans. G. R. Beasley-Murray, R. W. N. Hoare and J. K. Riches (Oxford: Blackwell, 1971; German original, 1941).

14. Martyn, *History and Theology in the Fourth Gospel*; see how Brown refines his version over the years: R. E. Brown, *The Gospel according to John* (New York: Doubleday, 1966), pp. xxiv-xl; R. E. Brown, *The Community of the Beloved Disciple* (New York: Paulist, 1979); R. E. Brown, *An Introduction to the New Testament* (New York: Doubleday, 1997), pp. 368-78; R. E. Brown, *An Introduction to the Gospel of John* (New York: Doubleday, 2003), pp. 58-86 and 189-219; on any possible 'Johannine Community', see our discussion in sects. 2 and 3.a below, pp. 307-22.

15. R. Kysar, 'Expulsion from the Synagogue: The Tale of a Theory', Johannine Literature Section, Session S25-62, SBL, Toronto, Monday, 25th November 25, 2002, later published as chap. 15 in Robert Kysar, *Voyages with John: Charting the Fourth Gospel* (Waco, TX: Baylor University Press, 2005), pp. 237-45; fascinating responses were given by J. Louis Martyn and D. Moody Smith; see also R. Kysar, 'The Whence and Whither of the Johannine Community', in *Life in Abundance:*

Thus, Edwards concludes, 'Attempts to use social-scientific analysis to delineate the character of his "community" have proved unsuccessful'.[16] Instead, attention has shifted from ingenious attempts to reconstruct the prehistory of the text towards reading its final form, increasingly through literary, rhetorical, feminist, narrative, reader-response, postmodern and even deconstructionist approaches.[17] While we cannot possibly delve into all of these in this study, we will also tend to concentrate our study upon the final form of the gospel's text as we have it. Because of the theological and linguistic resonances between the fourth gospel and the three Johannine letters, we shall also make occasional reference to them.[18]

Given this brief survey of some of the main issues in Johannine studies, particularly in relation to the other gospels, it is perhaps not surprising that some scholars think that a search for John's ethics is difficult or impossible. Thus Meeks states, 'It offers no explicit moral instruction', and Blount's opening words are even more direct: 'John does not do ethics. Or so it seems.'[19]

Studies of John's Gospel in Tribute to Raymond E. Brown, ed. John R. Donahue (Collegeville, MN: Liturgical Press, 2005), pp. 65-81.

16. Edwards, *Discovering John,* p. 49.

17. The shift from Bultmann's History of Religions approach in 1923 to such contemporary approaches is well documented in the collection *The Interpretation of John,* ed. John Ashton (Edinburgh: T&T Clark, 2nd edn. 1997); see also R. Alan Culpepper, *Anatomy of the Fourth Gospel: A Study in Literary Design* (Philadelphia: Fortress, 1983); Jeffrey Lloyd Staley, *The Print's First Kiss: A Rhetorical Investigation of the Implied Reader in the Fourth Gospel,* SBLDS 82 (Atlanta: Scholars Press, 1988); *The Fourth Gospel from a Literary Perspective,* ed. R. Alan Culpepper and Fernando F. Segovia, *Semeia* 53 (Atlanta: Scholars Press, 1991); Margaret Davies, *Rhetoric and Reference in the Fourth Gospel,* JSNTSS 69 (Sheffield, JSOT Press, 1992); Mark W. G. Stibbe, *John as Storyteller: Narrative Criticism and the Fourth Gospel,* SNTSMS 73 (Cambridge: Cambridge University Press, 1992); Mark W. G. Stibbe, (ed.), *The Gospel of John as Literature: An Anthology of Twentieth-Century Perspectives* (Leiden: Brill, 1993); Derek Tovey, *Narrative Art and Act in the Fourth Gospel,* JSNTSS 151 (Sheffield: Sheffield Academic Press, 1997); Segovia, *What Is John?* vol. 2, *Literary and Social Readings of the Fourth Gospel* (Atlanta: Scholars Press, 1998); Colleen M. Conway, *Men and Women in the Fourth Gospel: Gender and Johannine Characterization,* SBLDS 167 (Atlanta: SBL, 1999); Francis J. Moloney, S.D.B., 'Where Does One Look? Reflections of Some Recent Johannine Scholarship', *Salesianum* 62 (2000), pp. 223-51, repr. in his collection, *The Gospel of John: Text and Context,* pp. 137-66; Patrick Chatelion Counet, *John, A Postmodern Gospel: An Introduction to Deconstructive Exegesis Applied to the Fourth Gospel* (Leiden: Brill, 2000); James L. Resseguie, *The Strange Gospel: Narrative Design and Point of View in John* (Leiden: Brill, 2001).

18. On the relationship of the Johannine epistles and the gospel, see Holladay, *A Critical Introduction to the New Testament,* pp. 753-55 in the expanded CD version; Raymond E. Brown, S.S., *The Epistles of John,* Anchor Bible 30 (New York: Doubleday, 1982); Keener, *The Gospel of John,* pp. 122-26.

19. Wayne A. Meeks, 'The Ethics of the Fourth Evangelist', in *Exploring the Gospel of John,* ed. Culpepper and Black (Louisville: Westminister John Knox, 1996), pp. 317-26, quotation from p. 318;

Schrage asks himself 'whether a chapter on the Johannine writings even belongs in a book on the ethics of the New Testament', while Matera starts his study thus: 'For anyone interested in the study of New Testament ethics, the Gospel according to John is a major challenge. . . . In a word, there appears to be remarkably little ethical content in the Gospel according to John, and its most explicit ethical teaching raises a host of questions.'[20] However, here we will concentrate on our generic reading of the fourth gospel in its final form as a biographical narrative about the person, life and teaching of Jesus and see what we can learn about its ethics from this point of view. What is interesting is how John, despite all his differences and particular concerns, nonetheless takes the same basic story of Jesus' deeds and words and retells it for his purposes and his audience. We will use the same analysis as before of Christology, eschatology and setting, law and love, ethical issues and the imitation of Jesus' inclusive acceptance of others, to see what are the ethical implications of John's portrait of the divine love bringing us ultimate truth.

1. John's Christology

Most studies of the fourth gospel begin by asserting the centrality of Christology for John — what Kysar terms 'the heartbeat of the theology of the Fourth Gospel'.[21] For all John's high theology, his gospel remains a biographical narra-

Brian K. Blount, *Then the Whisper Put on Flesh: New Testament Ethics in an African American Context* (Nashville: Abingdon, 2001), p. 93.

20. Schrage, *The Ethics of the NT*, p. 297; Matera, *NT Ethics*, p. 92.

21. Kysar, 'The Fourth Gospel: A Report on Recent Research', *ANRW* 2.25.3, p. 2443; for fuller discussion of John's Christology, see further Jacob Jervell, *Jesus in the Gospel of John* (Minneapolis: Augsburg, 1984); Robert Kysar, *John's Story of Jesus* (Philadelphia: Fortress, 1984); William Loader, *The Christology of the Fourth Gospel: Structure and Issues*, BETL 23 (Frankfurt: Peter Lang, 2nd rev. edn., 1992); Maarten J. J. Menken, 'The Christology of the Fourth Gospel: A Survey of Recent Research', in *From Jesus to John: Essays on Jesus and New Testament Christology*, ed. M. C. De Boer (Sheffield: Sheffield Academic, 1993), pp. 292-320; D. Moody Smith, *The Theology of the Gospel of John* (Cambridge: Cambridge University Press, 1995), pp. 80-135; Paul N. Anderson, *The Christology of the Fourth Gospel: Its Unity and Disunity in the Light of John 6*, WUNT 2.78 (Tübingen: Mohr Siebeck, 1996); Ben Witherington, III, *The Many Faces of the Christ: The Christologies of the New Testament and Beyond* (New York: Crossroad, 1998), pp. 169-84; R. Alan Culpepper, 'The Christology of the Johannine Writings', in *Who Do You Say That I Am? Essays on Christology in Honor of Jack Dean Kingsbury*, ed. David R. Bauer and Mark Allan Powell (Louisville: Westminster John Knox, 1999), pp. 66-87; Christopher M. Tuckett, *Christology and the New Testament: Jesus and His Earliest Followers* (Edinburgh: Edinburgh University Press/Louisville: Westminster John Knox, 2001), pp. 151-71; Larry W. Hurtado, *Lord Jesus Christ: Devotion to Jesus in Earliest Christianity* (Grand Rapids: Eerdmans, 2003), pp. 349-426.

tive in which Jesus is almost always centre stage, being the subject of most of the narrative and delivering most of the discourse; on the rare occasions when he is absent, the characters present are found discussing who he is and what to do about him (1.19-28; 3.25-26; 7.45-52; 9.13-33; 10.19-21; 11.45-53, 55-57; 12.9-11; 20.24-25). Drawing upon my earlier work, Culpepper has shown how 'the conclusion that John is biography has fueled several significant analyses of its plot'.[22] Therefore it is no surprise that this concentration upon Jesus also dominates its ethics: as Matera puts it, 'In a word, the Gospel of John exemplifies a christological implosion so that ethics becomes Christology'.[23] Even Schrage, who normally prefers to begin his approach to the 'ethical accent' via anthropology, is forced to admit, 'Since christology is the dominant theme and clear focus of John, the ethics of the Johannine writings is exclusively christological in a way not encountered elsewhere'.[24] Therefore, as in the other gospels, we begin with the depiction of the subject, as John's biographical narrative portrays Jesus as the divine love entering into our world to bring the truth.

a. The Prologue (John 1.1-18)

Many biographies begin with the person's origins, who they are and where they have come from. Mark starts his story with Jesus' public debut as he comes from Nazareth to be baptized (Mark 1.9). Matthew takes the story back to Jesus' birth in Bethlehem (Matt. 1.18–2.12), whereas Luke begins even before that with the annunciation of Jesus' birth and that of his forerunner, John the Baptist (Luke 1.5-80). However, it is John who takes the high-flying, all-seeing perspective: Jesus comes not from Bethlehem or Nazareth but from above, before all space and time, from being with God and being himself God (John 1.1-4). The opening words, 'in the beginning', recall the first words of the Hebrew scriptures, the book of Genesis, picking up the Jewish background, while the dualistic world-view of the realm 'above' and the world 'below', contrasting the spiritual with the physical, light with darkness, was common in the Hellenistic-Roman world of the eastern Mediterranean among Jews as well as Gentiles. The words 'light' and 'life' are keywords, occurring as often in John's gospel as in the

22. R. Alan Culpepper, 'The Plot of John's Story of Jesus', in *Gospel Interpretation: Narrative-Critical and Social-Scientific Approaches*, ed. Jack Dean Kingsbury (Harrisburg, PA: Trinity Press International, 1997), pp. 188-99; quotation from p. 192.

23. Matera, *NT Ethics*, p. 93.

24. Schrage, *The Ethics of the NT*, p. 298; see also how both Hays and Blount use Christology as their way into John's ethics: Hays, *Moral Vision of the NT*, pp. 140-42 and Blount, *Then the Whisper Put on Flesh*, pp. 93-108.

other three put together — and the Prologue tells us that they are to be found in Jesus (1.4).

Except that, unusually for an ancient biography, he is not named at this point: instead John simply calls him the 'Word', λόγος, which resonates in both Jewish and Greek cultures. The Word of the Lord was something living and active in the Old Testament (Isa. 55.11) from the creation when God had only to speak for things to come into existence ('And God said, "Let there be . . .", Gen. 1.3, 6, 9, 11, 14, 20, 24, 26) through to the prophetic refrain, 'the Word of the Lord came to me'. In Greek philosophy, the *logos* was the logical rationality behind the cosmos; alongside this masculine principle, the Hebrews placed the feminine figure of Lady Sophia, the Wisdom of God, present with God at the creation (Prov. 8.22-31; see also the intertestamental Wisdom literature, such as Wisdom 7.22–10.21).[25] John brings all these images together in his Prologue as he fills out his portrait of this divine person: as Evans concludes, 'Unlike Moses, Jesus is the *shaliach par excellence,* in whom God's Word, Torah, Wisdom and Glory have taken up residence and are revealed'.[26]

However, the amazing thing is that this is the Prologue to a biography of a human being. The divine *logos,* in whom is light and life (1.4), was coming into the world (1.9) to become incarnate: 'The Word became flesh and lived among us' (1.14). It is a daring claim to make, especially within monotheistic Judaism. The word for 'lived among us', ἐσκήνωσεν, alludes to God dwelling in the tent, σκήνη, in the wilderness (Exod. 25.8-9), and the prophets longed for God to encamp in Zion again (Joel 3.17; Zech. 2.10). Furthermore, in the intertestamental Wisdom of Ben Sirach, the Creator tells Lady Wisdom to place her tent in Jacob (Ecclesiasticus 24.8-10). No wonder that John says, 'we have seen his glory, the glory as of the Father's only Son, full of grace and truth' (1.14b). 'Grace and truth' reflect the Hebrew *chesed* and *'emet,* God's continuing gracious love and faithfulness seen throughout Israel's history (e.g., Exod. 34.6). However, this is

25. On the Jewish roots of wisdom in the Prologue, see Rudolf Bultmann, 'The History of Religions Background of the Prologue in the Gospel of John', in *The Interpretation of John,* ed. Ashton, pp. 27-46 (German original in *ΕΥΧΑΡΙΣΤΗΡΙΟΝ: Studien zur Religion und Literatur des Alten und Neuen Testaments, Festschrift für H. Gunkel,* ed. Hans Schmidt [Göttingen: Vandenhoeck und Ruprecht, 1923], vol. 2, pp. 3-26); Brown, *The Gospel according to John,* Appendix II, 'The "Word"', pp. 519-24; John Ashton, *Studying John: Approaches to the Fourth Gospel* (Oxford: Oxford University Press, 1994), pp. 5-35; Sharon H. Ringe, *Wisdom's Friends: Community and Christology in the Fourth Gospel* (Louisville: Westminster John Knox, 1999), pp. 29-45.

26. Craig A. Evans, *Word and Glory: On the Exegetical and Theological Background of John's Prologue,* JSNTSS 89 (Sheffield: Sheffield Academic Press, 1993), p. 145 — *shaliach* is the Hebrew verbal noun for 'the one who is sent' as someone's representative or agent; on John's use of this background in his prologue, see further Ringe, *Wisdom's Friends,* pp. 46-63 and Witherington, *The Many Faces of the Christ,* pp. 86-89, 169-73.

contrasted with the law 'given through Moses'; 'grace and truth came through Jesus Christ' (1.17). Here at last, in contrast to Moses, we get the first mention of Jesus' actual name — and it is to inform us that 'grace and truth' come through him. This takes us straight into our key theme, that Jesus comes as the divine love to bring truth; the choice of grace, χάρις, rather than 'love' probably reflects this Jewish background of *chesed* and *'emet*. Although χάρις is used four times in these verses (1.14-17), it does not appear again in the gospel, where John prefers to use one of his favourite words, ἀγάπη, and its cognate verb. 'No one has ever seen God', but as the divine love bringing truth, Jesus now reveals him as 'God the only Son' (1.18).

Grace, χάρις, gives way to 'love' in the remaining narrative of the gospel, as the 'Word' similarly is not mentioned again, being replaced by the person of Jesus; but the themes of this Prologue echo through the rest of John's account.[27] Furthermore, the Prologue also warns us of the plot of the story to come. Jesus comes as the divine love to bring truth to 'his own', his own world and his own people, but neither recognized him or accepted him. Those who received and believed him became the 'children of God' (1.10-13). Thus, despite the divine heights and the cosmic scale of this gospel, the essential storyline is the same as in the others: it is the mission of Jesus, how he was rejected by the Jewish leaders and accepted by the disciples. For John, this is all part of the cosmic conflict of light against darkness. Darkness, however, can neither understand it nor overcome it (κατέλαβεν, 1.5) as the divine love comes to bring us the truth.[28]

b. Jesus' ministry — the Book of Signs (John 1.19–12.50)

The overall structure of the fourth gospel is essentially in two parts, Jesus' ministry and his passion. The first half, often called 'the Book of Signs', is shaped around Jesus' miracles or 'signs', σημεῖα, as they are called here (e.g., 2.11; 4.54); it begins with the witness of John the Baptist (1.19-34) and concludes by referring to the Baptist and to Jesus' signs in a summary statement (10.40-42). The

27. See Elizabeth Harris, *Prologue and Gospel: The Theology of the Fourth Evangelist*, JSNTSS 107 (Sheffield: Sheffield Academic Press, 1994); Edwards, *Discovering John*, pp. 84-97.

28. On the Prologue, see further: Paul Lamarche, 'The Prologue of John', *Recherches de Science Religieuse* 52 (1964), pp. 497-537, trans. and repr. in *The Interpretation of John*, ed Ashton, pp. 47-65; Werner H. Kelber, 'The Birth of a Beginning: John 1.1-18', *Semeia* 52 (1990), pp. 120-44, repr. in *The Gospel of John as Literature*, ed. Stibbe, pp. 209-30; Lindars, *John*, pp. 73-78; Painter, *The Quest for the Messiah*, pp. 107-28; Davies, *Rhetoric and Reference in the Fourth Gospel*, pp. 126-29; Morna D. Hooker, *Beginnings: Keys That Open the Gospels* (London: SCM, 1997), pp. 64-83; Keener, *The Gospel of John*, pp. 333-63.

second part, the passion story, is 'the Book of Glory', running from the Last Supper (13.1) to a final conclusion (20.30-31). Although the Book of Signs seems to conclude at 10.42, another sign follows, the raising of Lazarus (11), with another summary (12.44-50), which suggests that chaps. 11 and 12 form an 'interlude' between the two halves, or possibly were inserted in a later edition.[29]

Mark has little actual teaching, but depicts Jesus' activity through his miracles; Matthew sandwiches the action in between his five extended sermons, while Luke provides narrative settings for his sayings. John, however, skilfully interweaves word and deeds throughout the first half of his gospel as the miracles lead into lengthy discourses. The 'signs' are not performed to show Jesus' compassion, nor is there any attempt to keep them secret:[30] the first sign, the turning of water into wine at Cana, 'revealed his glory, and his disciples believed in him' (2.11); the second sign brought not just the official and his son (who was healed) to faith, but the 'whole household' (4.53). The healing of the man at the pool of Bethesda on a Sabbath (5.1-9) leads into the eschatological debate about Jesus' work on his Father's behalf (5.19-47). The multiplication of loaves and fishes to feed five thousand (6.1-12) is the perfect foil to produce the discourse on 'the bread of life' (6.25-58). On the other hand, the discourse on 'the light of the world' (8.12-58) comes first and then leads into the sign of the healing of the man born blind (9.1-12), which in turn is followed by further debate about faith and true seeing (9.13-41). Finally, the raising of Lazarus (11.1-44) demonstrates the truth of Jesus' claim to be 'the resurrection and the life' (11.25). Culpepper stresses the link of words and deeds in John's portrait: 'These sayings function as aphoristic summaries of the narrative pictures John paints of Jesus'.[31] In terms of the theme we are pursuing through the gospel, the signs demonstrate Jesus' identity as 'divine love', but they also provide opportunities for him to teach 'the truth' from above in the discourses. The Book of Signs concludes that John the Baptist did 'no sign', but now many believe in Jesus (10.41-42). The purpose of the 'signs' is again made explicit in the final comment that the author has selected these examples from the 'many other signs' which Jesus did so that the reader might 'come to believe that Jesus is the Christ, the Son of God' (20.30-31).[32]

29. See Brown, *The Gospel according to John,* pp. 413-15.

30. Brown, *The Gospel according to John,* Appendix III, 'Signs and Works', pp. 525-32.

31. Culpepper, 'The Christology of the Johannine Writings', p. 85; see also Smith, *The Theology of the Gospel of John,* pp. 106-15.

32. Robert T. Fortna argued strongly for a 'Gospel of Signs' as one of John's sources in his *The Gospel of Signs: A Reconstruction of the Narrative Source Underlying the Fourth Gospel,* SNTSMS 11 (Cambridge: Cambridge University Press, 1970) and *The Fourth Gospel and Its Predecessor: From Narrative Source to Present Gospel* (Edinburgh: T&T Clark, 1989); however, the way in which the

Furthermore, while Jesus is often called teacher or rabbi (1.38, 49; 13.13), the truth which he has come to teach is not about the kingdom of God, but himself as representing the King, God himself,[33] as his representative or agent.[34] John uses all his literary skill with different levels, misunderstandings and symbols to bring this out. Thus, feeding the multitude moves beyond the surface level of bread through manna and Moses down to the identity of Jesus: 'We have come to believe and know that you are the Holy One of God' (6.1-69). In typically Johannine style, the healing of the blind man progresses from the level of physical sight down to a deeper spiritual blindness or insight of faith, depending on the characters' differing assessments of Jesus. The Pharisees are quite sure that Jesus is 'a sinner . . . not from God' (9.16, 24) and, ironically, this makes them blind (9.39-41). In contrast, the blind man not only receives his physical sight (9.7), but confesses his ignorance about Jesus (9.12, 25), asks for further insight and so comes to faith (9.36-38). Jesus raises Lazarus so that God his Father, and himself as Son of God, might be glorified (11.4). John's typical use of symbolism and misunderstanding, confusing sleep and death (11.11-13), is seen when Martha misunderstands Jesus' assurance that her brother will live as referring to 'the last day' (11.24). First, she comes to believe that Jesus is 'the Christ, the Son of God' (11.27), and then Jesus asks God to answer his prayer and raise Lazarus so that the crowd might believe (11.42), which they do when Lazarus emerges from the tomb (11.45).[35]

This typical biographical combination of signs and discourses, deeds and words, also provides *indirect* characterization of Jesus, filling out what it means for him to be the divine love which teaches the truth. John builds on this symbolism with the seven *direct* 'I am' statements: 'I am . . . the bread of life' (6.35, 41, 51), 'the light of the world' (8.12; 9.5), 'the door of the sheepfold' (10.7, 9), 'the good shepherd' (10.11, 14), 'the resurrection and the life' (11.25), 'the way, the truth and the life' (14.6) and 'the true vine' (15.1, 5). These 'I am' sayings all have

signs are so closely woven into the narrative with the discourses makes this seem unlikely to more recent scholarship; see, for example, Ashton, *Studying John*, pp. 90-113.

33. 'The reinterpretation of Jesus' kingship is given in terms of divine Sonship, understood in a typically Johannine way. Jesus is prophet and king because he is the Son sent by the Father, and only as Son of the Father.' Marinus de Jonge, 'Jesus as Prophet and King in the Fourth Gospel', *Ephemerides Theologicae Lovanienses* 49 (1973), pp. 161-77, repr. in his collection of essays, *Jesus: Stranger from Heaven and Son of God; Jesus Christ and the Christians in Johannine Perspective* (Missoula, MT: Scholars Press, 1977), pp. 49-76, quotation from p. 69.

34. See Peder Borgen, 'God's Agent in the Fourth Gospel', in *Religions in Antiquity*, ed. J. Neusner (1968), pp. 137-48; repr. in *The Interpretation of John*, ed. Ashton, pp. 83-95.

35. For an exploration of the background and composition of John. 11, see Wendy Sproston North, *The Lazarus Story within the Johannine Tradition*, JSNTSS 212 (Sheffield: Sheffield Academic Press, 2001).

a rich Jewish background. Bread and light are images of the Law and Wisdom (Ecclus. 15.3; Ps. 119.105); the vine is a symbol of Israel itself (Isa. 5.1-10; Jer. 2.21; Hos. 10.1), while sheep and shepherds describe the people and their leaders (Ps. 100.3; Ezek. 34). By applying such redolent images to Jesus, John suggests that he is the culmination of Israel's faith and history. Used on its own without a predicate, 'I am' recalls God's own revelation of his name to Moses (Exod. 3.14), used regularly by Isaiah (43.10, 13, 25); so, when Jesus says, 'before Abraham was, I am', it is not surprising that they pick up missiles to stone him for blasphemy (8.24, 28, 58-59). Ball concludes his detailed treatment of this phrase by linking it back to the start of the gospel: 'The suggestion that the "I am" sayings imply an ontological identification of Jesus with God in the Fourth Gospel calls to mind the words of the prologue'.[36]

John's Christology is advanced further through titles. As Edwards puts it, 'John's faith-confessions themselves serve as "narrative theology", reinforcing and developing the message of the "signs"'.[37] Initial speculation as to whether John the Baptist is 'the Christ' is neatly redirected to Jesus (from 1.20 to 1.41, and again in 3.28-30). The Samaritans discover that Jesus is the Christ (4.25-26, 29, 42), followed by further Jewish speculation (7.26-27, 31, 41-42; 10.24). This is dangerous, for anyone who confesses Jesus as Messiah will be 'put out of the synagogue' (9.22; 12.42), but Martha is not afraid to state her belief that Jesus is 'the Christ, the Son of God' (11.27). In fact, John's purpose in writing is so that the reader might come to share this faith that 'Jesus is the Christ, the Son of God', for such belief brings life (20.30-31; 17.3). While Jesus is described as the Son of God, or the Son, eight times in Mark, ten times in Luke and fifteen times in Matthew, John uses this term twenty-five times; meanwhile God is referred to as 'Father' about a hundred times. Jesus is not only called the Son by the narrator (1.14, 18; 3.16-18, 35-36; 20.30-31), but he also uses it happily for himself, in debate and in the discourses (5.19-26; 6.40; 8.36; 10.36; 11.4; 14.13; 17.1). The Jewish leaders complain to Pilate that 'he ought to die because he claimed to be the Son of God' (19.7). Furthermore, John uses the title 'lord' for Jesus more often than even 'son'; sometimes it means simply the honorific 'sir', but often, in both narrative and dialogue, it implies that Jesus shares God's divine lordship — even to being worshipped (6.23; 9.38; 11.2, 27; 13.13-14; 20.18, 28). Pryor concludes, 'John has given them a sure proof that he whom they confess as Lord is

36. David Mark Ball, 'I Am' in John's Gospel: Literary Function, Background and Theological Implications, JSNTSS 124 (Sheffield: Sheffield Academic Press, 1996), p. 279; see also Brown, The Gospel according to John, Appendix IV, 'Ego Eimi — "I Am"', pp. 533-38; J.-A. Bühner, 'The Exegesis of the Johannine "I-Am" Sayings', in The Interpretation of John, ed. Ashton, pp. 207-18, and Harris, Prologue and Gospel, pp. 130-54.

37. Edwards, Discovering John, p. 73.

truly the Christ, the Son of God, and through faith in him eternal life is se-cured'.[38] No wonder, therefore, that John portrays Jesus even going so far as to state, 'I and the Father are one' (10.30).[39]

On the broader scale of the whole story, John's picture may begin with the high perspective of the Prologue, but throughout the narrative proper Jesus never loses this divine knowledge: he is aware of his own preexistence with God (6.38, 62; 17.5); he knows who sent him into the world and why he was sent (6.39), when his hour has not yet come (2.4) and when it does arrive (12.23; 13.1; 17.1), what he will do when human resources run out (6.6), where he has come from and where he is going (7.33; 8.14, 21; 13.3), how he will get there (12.32-33), and the eventual destiny of all his people to be with him in his Father's glory which he had at the beginning (17.5, 24; 20.17).

Finally, many of the signs also lead to the division and opposition pres-aged in the Prologue (1.10-13). The healing of the man at the pool leads first to debate about the Sabbath, but then quickly into opposition about Jesus' iden-tity (5.18). After the miraculous feeding, some found the 'bread of life' dis-course too indigestible: 'Because of this many of his disciples turned back and no longer went about with him' (6.66). Jesus' claim to be 'the 'light of the world' provokes a sharp dispute about who are the true descendants of Abra-ham, with both Jesus and 'the Jews' demonizing each other (8.44, 52); its asso-ciated sign, healing the blind man, leads again to bitter opposition and threats of being 'put out of the synagogue' (9.22, 34, 40). Finally, the raising of Lazarus ends with John's typical irony, as the Jewish leaders plot to kill the one who gives life (11.46-53, 57). We shall return to John's portrait of 'the Jews' and their leaders in another section; from the point of view of his Christology, the teaching of the truth by the divine love produces both faith and antagonism, disciples and opponents.

38. Pryor, *John: Evangelist of the Covenant People*, p. 142; see pp. 117-42 on Jesus as the Messiah and pp. 143-56 on 'lord'.

39. On the various titles and descriptions of Jesus in the fourth gospel, see further Marinus de Jonge, 'Jewish Expectations about the "Messiah" according to the Fourth Gospel', *NTS* 19 (1972-73), pp. 246-70, repr. in his collection, *Jesus: Stranger from Heaven and Son of God*, pp. 77-116; Smalley, *John: Evangelist and Interpreter*, pp. 210-19; John Ashton, *Understanding the Fourth Gospel* (Oxford: Oxford University Press, 1991), pp. 238-336; Davies, *Rhetoric and Reference in the Fourth Gospel*, pp. 129-39; Harris, *Prologue and Gospel*, pp. 155-72; Smith, *The Theology of the Gospel of John*, pp. 85-101 and 124-33; Culpepper, 'The Christology of the Johannine Writings', pp. 72-85; Tuckett, *Christology and the New Testament*, pp. 156-68; Hurtado, *Lord Jesus Christ*, pp. 358-89; Edwards, *Discovering John*, pp. 61-73.

c. Jesus' Passion — the Book of Glory (John 13.1–19.42)

Through the Book of Signs, reactions to Jesus are polarized between those who come to believe and follow him, and those who oppose him and his teaching. After the raising of Lazarus, Jesus is anointed by Mary and then enters Jerusalem to the crowd's delight and the Pharisees' disgust (12.1-19). It is when some Greeks want to see Jesus that he realizes that his 'hour' has come 'to be glorified' (12.20-23). 'Glory' has been one of John's themes from seeing the glory of the incarnation in the Prologue and which has been revealed through the 'signs' (1.14; 2.11). However, now we learn that the way to be glorified is through death, like a grain of wheat falling into the earth, and to be 'lifted up from the earth' means upon a cross, not a throne (12.24, 28-33). It is part of John's theological genius that the one who has 'the glory as of a father's only son' should not just come from glory and return to glory, but that his path to exaltation and glorification should be through a painful and humiliating death which further demonstrates the truth of the divine love among us.[40] The interlude concludes with a warning about light and darkness, with 'many, even of the authorities', believing in him, while others did not, having their eyes blinded and hearts hardened (12.34-50).

The pace changes dramatically as John slows narrative time right down for the Book of Glory: after the several years of the Book of Signs, now seven chapters describe just the twenty-four hours of Jesus' farewell, arrest, trial and passion. First, for the next five chapters (13–17), Jesus' 'focus of attention is exclusively directed to the disciples':[41] his divine love is shown by the way he cares for his disciples and tries to reassure them and forewarn them about what is going to happen, while he continues to teach the sublime truth through what he says in the farewell discourses over the Last Supper. The institution of the Eucharist is omitted; instead Jesus washes his disciples' feet in a final action to explain his deeper meaning, to prepare them not just for his betrayal, death and departure but also for the whole history of the church. He keeps telling them things *now* for their *future* guidance (13.19; 14.29; 15.11; 16.1, 4, 33).

Chapter 13 provides the context for the content of the farewell discourses (14–17): having come to 'his own' and been rejected (1.11-12), Jesus shows his divine love for 'his own' ultimately, 'to the end' (13.1). The footwashing is a symbol of Jesus' ministry (13.8-10), but also an example of loving service for his disciples to

40. On John's use of glory and exaltation language, see Loader, *The Christology of the Fourth Gospel*, pp. 107-21; Smalley, *John: Evangelist and Interpreter*, pp. 220-23; Smith, *The Theology of the Gospel of John*, pp. 115-20.

41. Pryor, *John: Evangelist of the Covenant People*, p. 55; see pp. 54-72 for a full discussion of the farewell discourses.

follow (13.14-17), which is not understood 'now . . . , but later' (13.7).[42] They do not understand his warning of betrayal (13.22), nor going away (13.33); first Peter (13.36), then Thomas (14.5), Philip (14.8), and the other Judas (14.22) ask where he is going and what he means. Jesus' promise that they will see him again brings yet more confusion (16.17-19). When finally they claim to understand, Jesus warns them that they are about to be scattered, in a last attempt to give them peace and courage (16.29-33) before turning to pray for them and the church (17).

The content of the farewell discourse is an extended meditation on the unity and divine love between Jesus and his Father in the Spirit, as it applies to his disciples, but it also highlights our other theme of truth.[43] As noted previously, there have been various attempts to reconstruct the prehistory of earlier versions of these chapters,[44] but here we are dealing with the final form of the text. As Segovia puts it, 'The present text of the farewell speech undoubtedly did represent to someone, somewhere, at some time, not only a unified and coherent literary whole but also a proper and meaningful form of communication with an audience — an artistic and strategic whole'; therefore we prefer his 'properly integrative approach'.[45]

Like all farewells, there is a last wish, that after Jesus' demonstration of footwashing, they should 'love one another, as I have loved you' (13.34-35; 15.12-17). Jesus and his Father dwell in each other through love (14.10-11, 20; 16.28), and through the Spirit they will dwell in love in the believer who abides in them (14.15-17, 23, 26; 15.1-11). Although Jesus is going to leave his beloved disciples, he tells them 'the truth' that it is to their advantage so that the Father can give them ἄλλος παράκλητος, 'another Paraclete' (14.16). 'Paraclete' is someone 'called alongside' to help as an advocate, counsellor or comforter, and it is used to describe Jesus in 1 John 2.1. In addition to these traditional translations, Tricia Gates Brown argues for 'mediator' or 'broker', providing access for Graeco-Roman clients to a powerful patron.[46] Also, ἄλλος is 'another of the

42. See further John Christopher Thomas, *Footwashing in John 13 and the Johannine Community*, JSNTSS 61 (Sheffield: Sheffield Academic Press, 1991) and our discussion of this passage in sect. 5.c below, pp. 343-45.

43. George L. Parsenios compares the discourse to other contemporary ancient literature, especially drama and the symposium, in his *Departure and Consolation: The Johannine Farewell Discourses in Light of Greco-Roman Literature*, NovTSup 117 (Leiden: Brill, 2005).

44. See, for example, Brown, *The Gospel according to John*, pp. 581-604; Painter, *The Quest for the Messiah*, pp. 349-69; Pryor, *John: Evangelist of the Covenant People*, pp. 102-6.

45. Fernando F. Segovia, *The Farewell of the Word: The Johannine Call to Abide* (Minneapolis: Fortress, 1991), quotations from pp. 48-49; see the whole book passim for a full discussion of the farewell discourse.

46. Tricia Gates Brown, *Spirit in the Writings of John: Johannine Pneumatology in Social-scientific Perspective* (London: T&T Clark, 2003), pp. 170-234.

same type', so the Spirit, 'the one whom John calls "another Paraclete" is another Jesus' to the disciples.[47] In the same way that Jesus has been divine love living among them, the Spirit will continue in that love. Furthermore, to pick up our other theme of truth, Jesus describes himself as 'the way, the truth and the life' and the 'true vine' (14.6; 15.1), and prays to his Father as 'the only true God' (17.3). Equally, the Spirit is the 'Spirit of truth' who will guide them 'into all the truth' (14.26; 15.26; 16.7-15). Therefore, the Holy Spirit will function as divine love bringing truth in exactly the same way as Jesus; to make the point even clearer, John depicts the resurrected Jesus appearing to his frightened disciples in the upper room to enable them to 'receive the Holy Spirit' (20.19-23). '*The Paraclete makes it possible for Jesus to continue to function as broker to God for the disciples.* Because of the Paraclete, Jesus can continue to be a paraclete himself, the ultimate broker between God and his clients.'[48]

Although he warns of troubles and sufferings ahead (14.1, 27, 30; 15.18-25; 16.1-4, 20-22, 32), Jesus encourages the disciples with his peace and the promise of future security (14.1-3, 18, 27; 15.18; 16.20-24, 33). Finally, he returns to the themes of glory, truth and love with an extended threefold prayer: for 'the only true God' to be glorified in himself (17.1-5); for the disciples, in whom he has been glorified, to be protected and 'sanctified in the truth' (17.6-19); and for all those who will believe in the future 'through their word' to come at the end to share the glory which he had at the beginning with the Father within the divine love (17.20-26).[49]

At the passion, Mark's Jesus becomes increasingly passive, which is explained by Matthew as fulfilment of scripture, and by Luke as divine necessity. However, John's Jesus is active throughout his trial and passion. The nearest we get to the agony in Gethsemane is in his soul being 'troubled' (12.27). Jesus is in control, and he chooses to lay down his life of his own volition (10.18). Knowing what is going to happen (13.1-3), he explains it all to his disciples in the Farewell Discourses of chaps. 14–17. He carries his own cross 'by himself' with no mention of Simon of Cyrene (19.17), and his suffering is not stressed; instead, he continues to direct affairs from the cross (19.26-30). Smalley notes that 'much

---

47. R. E. Brown, *The Gospel according to John*, Appendix V, 'The Paraclete', pp. 1135-44; quotation from p. 1141.

48. Tricia Gates Brown, *Spirit in the Writings of John*, p. 262, her italics; on the Spirit and Paraclete, see further Jervell, *Jesus in the Gospel of John*, pp. 69-76; Smalley, *John: Evangelist and Interpreter*, pp. 228-33; Davies, *Rhetoric and Reference in the Fourth Gospel*, pp. 139-53; Smith, *The Theology of the Gospel of John*, pp. 139-44; and Hurtado, *Lord Jesus Christ*, pp. 396-402.

49. For a fresh approach to this chapter, see Fernando F. Segovia, 'Inclusion and Exclusion in John 17: An Intercultural Reading', in *What Is John?* vol. 2, *Literary and Social Readings of the Fourth Gospel*, ed. Segovia, pp. 183-210.

more than the synoptic writers, John *has* a theology of the cross . . . he views the cross christologically'.[50] As the divine love bringing truth, Jesus remains in control even at his death.

Jesus waits for Judas and the soldiers in an unnamed garden, which is not a place of agonized prayer. Here too, Jesus is in charge, knows everything and takes the initiative with his question, 'Whom are you seeking?' (18.4). When they reply, 'Jesus of Nazareth', he answers, 'I am' (18.5), the phrase of divine revelation, linked to all the other 'I am's in this gospel. Therefore it is no surprise that the soldiers, instead of seizing him, fall to the ground in awe (18.6). Harris notes, 'Traditionally the arrest is the "handing over" of Jesus into the power and authority of his enemies, so that he ceases to be a free agent and becomes the subject of the actions of others. Here, however, these others prove to be powerless, and Jesus, who is in complete control, has to do their work for them and bring about his own arrest'.[51] So now Jesus takes charge and encourages them to arrest him and let the disciples go (18.7-9).

After the hearing before the high priest and Jewish leaders, Jesus appears before Pilate, who tries to save him several times, but his opponents are insistent on his death (18.31, 38b; 19.4, 6, 12, 15). Jesus may have come as divine love to bring the truth, but Pilate cannot recognize it: 'What is truth?' (18.38). Lincoln draws upon my work on the biographical genre of the gospel to argue here for 'the truth of the narrative of the trial of truth'; to confuse this with 'the modern era's standards of historical accuracy' is to commit a genre mistake.[52] They discuss true kingship (18.33-39; 19.3, 15) as Jesus informs Pilate that real power comes 'from above' (18.36; 19.11). The irony is that Jesus, mocked with a crown of thorns and a purple robe (19.2), really is 'King of the Jews', as Pilate's superscription for the cross declares in all languages (19.19-22). As he prophesied, the divine love is now 'lifted up' for all to see (3.14; 12.32).

Even on the cross, he remains in charge, arranging for the beloved disciple to care for his mother (19.26-27). He says, 'I am thirsty', simply in order to fulfil scripture (19.28; see Ps. 69.21). Similarly, the piercing of his side instead of his bones being broken fulfils the law about the paschal lamb and other prophecy (19.36-37; see Exod. 12.46; Num. 9.12; Zech. 12.10). At Jesus' death, the beloved disciple witnesses blood and water flowing from the spear wound, and as with his master, 'His testimony is true, and . . . he tells the truth' (19.34-35). The final

50. Smalley, *John: Evangelist and Interpreter*, pp. 223-34; his italics.

51. Harris, *Prologue and Gospel*, p. 182.

52. Andrew T. Lincoln, *Truth on Trial: The Lawsuit Motif in the Fourth Gospel* (Peabody, MA: Hendrickson, 2000), pp. 370-78; Lincoln also supervised Stibbe's Ph.D. in which he undertakes genre criticism of John 18–19, arguing for a 'narrative-historical approach'; see Stibbe, *John as Storyteller*, esp. pp. 121-47 and 168-99.

irony is that, although Jesus' last cry, τετέλεσται, might suggest that all is 'finished' at the surface level, the truth is that now the divine love has 'accomplished' all he came to do (19.30). As Smith puts it, 'John makes the astonishing claim that Jesus' death reveals the glory of God — the revelatory manifestation of God — and that this glory has existed from the foundation of the world (17:5, 24)'.[53]

d. The Resurrection and Epilogue (John 20.1–21.25)

John's resurrection stories have neither Mark's enigma nor Matthew's supernaturalism; Jesus is as much in control as he has always been. He appears when *he* wishes, to Mary in the garden (20.14), to the disciples in the locked upper room (20.19), to Thomas in his doubts (20.26) and to the disciples back in their old way of life, fishing (21.4). He knows what kind of death Peter will die (20.18-19), and what will happen to his Beloved Disciple (20.22-23). This control, knowledge and direction of events is not new, not a product of the resurrection; it has been the character of John's Jesus from the very start, 'in the beginning' in the Prologue. Furthermore, it is a consequence of Jesus' coming as divine love. As throughout his ministry in the Book of Signs, so now in risen glory, Jesus brings his love to those in need: as Mary weeps, he whispers her name and brings comfort (20.11-17); to the disciples locked into fear and locked in by fear, he comes with peace and joy (20.19-21); for Thomas trapped in doubt, he offers his hands and side in tangible proof (20.24-29). Supremely, in a narrative echo of the opening stories, now he comes to Peter painfully mindful of his triple denial, bringing threefold restitution as the divine love makes him face, and admit, the truth (21.1-17).

The divine love also brings the same challenge. To Mary, who can barely see through her tears and supposes that the mysterious figure is the gardener, Jesus repeats his first words in this gospel, 'Whom are you seeking?' (20.15; cp. 1.38). Also, in another balancing echo from the first chapter to the last, the call is the same, 'Follow me' (1.43; 21.19, 22). Throughout the gospel, Jesus calls God 'the one who sent me'; now he commissions them, 'As the Father has sent me, so I send you' (20.21). Unlike Mark's silent, frightened women, Mary obediently goes to announce the resurrection to the disciples immediately, 'I have seen the Lord' (20.17-18).[54] When they 'see' the Lord in the locked room, the

53. Smith, *The Theology of the Gospel of John*, p. 122.
54. See Richard Bauckham, *Gospel Women: Studies of the Named Women in the Gospels* (Grand Rapids: Eerdmans, 2002), pp. 283-86.

disciples rejoice (20.20). Thomas refuses to believe unless he 'sees' the wounds; after he finally sees and believes, Jesus blesses 'those who have not seen and yet have come to believe' (20.24-29). This takes us into the purpose of the gospel, which is written so that 'you may come to believe that Jesus is the Christ' (20.30-31). Similarly, in the Epilogue, the disciples do not recognize the stranger on the shore; only when they see the miraculous catch of fish in their net does the deeper realization come, 'It is the Lord!' (21.7). In each case, seeing leads to a recognition of the truth of Jesus' identity as Lord, with Thomas making the fullest confession, 'My Lord and my God!' (20.28). Bultmann argues that 'if Jesus' death on the cross is already his exaltation and glorification, *his resurrection* cannot be an event of special significance. No resurrection is needed to destroy the triumph which death might be supposed to have gained in the crucifixion.'[55] While this may be true theologically, John's biographical narrative does require something more; as Smith says, 'None of it would count as revelation and deliverance apart from Jesus' resurrection from the dead. The resurrection allows Jesus' ministry and message to be seen for what they were, and are. Jesus' resurrection means for John, as for other early Christians and the New Testament writers generally, that God authenticates Jesus as his Son.'[56] It is the resurrection which demonstrates that Jesus came to bring the divine love into the world and which confirms the truth of all his words and deeds.

e. Is it too divine to be true?

We cannot conclude this brief study of John's Christology as the divine love coming to bring the truth among us without noting Käsemann's assessment arising from his study of the theme of 'glory', especially in John 17. He argues that it leads to a portrait of Jesus which is 'naively Docetic', that John is so determined to present Jesus as the divine love among us that he is no longer really human: 'Those features of his lowliness rather represent the absolute minimum of the costume designed for the one who dwelt for a little while among men'.[57] Elsewhere, Käsemann describes John's portrait of Jesus memorably as, 'God striding across the earth'.[58] Brilliant though Käsemann's study is, most scholarly

55. Rudolf Bultmann, *Theology of the New Testament* (London: SCM, 1955), vol. 2, p. 56.

56. Smith, *The Theology of the Gospel of John*, p. 123; Loader agrees, 'It is resurrection that makes the story of revelation possible', *The Christology of the Fourth Gospel*, p. 124

57. Ernst Käsemann, *The Testament of Jesus: A Study of the Gospel of John in the Light of Chapter 17* (London: SCM, 1966), p. 10.

58. Ernst Käsemann, 'The Structure and Purpose of the Prologue to John's Gospel', in his *New

responses consider that it only tells half the story: 'His presentation, strikingly uncompromising as it is, is too one-sided to give an accurate account of the Gospel's peculiar dialectic'.[59] Thus Thompson sets out to examine how the fourth evangelist treats Jesus' humanity in his earthly origin, the incarnation, his signs and his death.[60] In a similar way to Käsemann, Casey argues that 'this Gospel's presentation of Jesus is seriously false'.[61] Given all that we have said about John's concern for truth, this too is a serious charge. Lincoln's answer is to go back to the gospel's biographical genre and to argue that Casey has confused truth and falsehood with 'the modern era's standards of historical accuracy'.[62] John's portrait of Jesus is certainly more divine than the Synoptics' accounts, but this does not necessarily mean that it is not true, either theologically or historically, provided that the latter is properly understood as the ancients understood ἱστορία, enquiry, within both history and biography. As both Robinson and Ellis argue separately, the fourth gospel makes 'explicit' what is 'implicit' in the other three.[63]

Therefore, let us return to our main theme of John's Christology, that Jesus is divine love bringing us truth. The fourth gospel is a biographical narrative of Jesus' life and teaching, his words and deeds. Thompson is right to point to the divine source of both: 'The actions attributed to God in the Gospel are made known to the reader by the words of Jesus and are embodied in the deeds of Jesus'.[64] As the divine *Logos,* Jesus comes to show us God's love by his very incarnation among us, which is 'full of grace and truth' (1.14, 17). Throughout his ministry, he showed God's love through his 'signs' and taught his truth in the dialogues and discourses. At the Last Supper, he loved 'his own' even 'to the end' (13.1), while lovingly explaining the truth in the farewell discourses. Finally, he demonstrated God's love by his death on the cross (3.16), which love cannot be defeated by death as the truth of all that he said and did was vindicated in his

---

Testament Questions of Today, trans. W. J. Montague (Philadelphia: Fortress/London: SCM, 1969), pp. 138-67, esp. pp. 159, 161.

59. Günther Bornkamm, 'Towards the Interpretation of John's Gospel: A Discussion of *The Testament of Jesus* by Ernst Käsemann', *EvT* 28 (1968), pp. 8-25; trans. and repr. in *The Interpretation of John,* ed. Ashton, pp. 97-119, quotation from p. 114.

60. M. M. Thompson, *The Humanity of Jesus in the Fourth Gospel* (Philadelphia: Fortress, 1988).

61. Maurice Casey, *Is John's Gospel True?* (London: Routledge, 1996), p. 62.

62. Lincoln, *Truth on Trial,* pp. 376-77.

63. John A. T. Robinson, *The Priority of John,* pp. 343-97; E. Earle Ellis, 'Background and Christology of John's Gospel: Selected Motifs', chap. 6 in his collection of essays, *Christ and the Future in New Testament History,* NovTSup 97 (Leiden: Brill, 2000), pp. 70-88, esp. his conclusion on p. 88; originally published in *SWJT* 31.1 (1988), pp. 24-31.

64. Thompson, *The God of the Gospel of John,* p. 237.

resurrection. Therefore, while John may not have all the parables and teachings of the kingdom as in the Synoptics, this does not mean that his biographical account 'offers no moral instruction', to use Meeks' words. The whole portrait of the divine love bringing us truth is full of ethical implications if we want to know that truth and live in that love. As we shall explore at the end of this chapter, John's ethical challenge is for us to imitate Jesus' self-sacrificial example of the divine love.

2. John's eschatology and setting

In the previous chapters on the other gospels, we noted how Jesus' preaching about the kingdom of God was linked to both ethics and eschatology. However, the phrase 'the kingdom of God' occurs in this gospel only as Jesus warns Nicodemus that only those 'born from above . . . born of water and Spirit' can 'see' or 'enter' the kingdom (John 3.3, 5). In conversation with Pilate, Jesus admits, 'My kingdom is not from [or 'of'] this world' (18.36). However, Nathanael and the crowds recognize Jesus as 'King of Israel' (1.49; 6.15; 12.13-15), and this lies behind both Pilate's questions and Jesus' eventual crucifixion as 'the King of the Jews' (18.33, 36-37, 39; 19.3, 12, 14, 15, 19-21). This gospel's shift from Jesus' preaching of the coming of the kingdom to a focus on him now as King has often been seen as evidence of a later date for John and for his replacement of a future eschatological consummation with a relationship with Jesus in the here and now. Certainly, John's frequent use of language about time, 'now' and 'already', reinforces this, with his twenty-eight uses of νῦν (compared to Matthew's four, Mark's two and Luke's twelve), twelve of ἄρτι (with seven in Matthew and none in Mark and Luke), and sixteen for ἤδη (about twice as frequent as the seven each in Matthew and Mark, and nine in Luke). This interest is compounded by his particular use of 'hour' and 'day'.[65]

Even early church tradition sees the fourth gospel as the last to be written. Irenaeus claims to have received from Polycarp the tradition that 'John, disciple of the Lord, who leaned on his breast' published it in Ephesus (*Adversus Haereses* 3.1.1), while we have already noted Clement of Alexandria's famous comment that John wrote his 'spiritual gospel', τὸ πνευματικὸν εὐαγγελίον, last of all, recognizing that the 'bodily facts', τὰ σωματικά, were in the other gospels (Eusebius, *Historia Ecclesiastica* 6.14.7). While critical scholars in the twentieth century mostly did not accept the apostolic authorship, the absence of the kingdom of God and the concentration on the present led many of them to agree

---

65. See further Brown, *The Gospel according to John*, Appendix I, pp. 517-18.

that the fourth gospel was written later, possibly even into the second century, coming under Hellenistic philosophical and religious influence and being even proto-Gnostic or naively Docetic.

Thus Rudolf Bultmann used eschatology as a key to his reconstruction of the composition of John with some older apocalyptic eschatology typical of Jesus there in the earliest stages of Johannine material; however, the fourth evangelist demythologizes all of this, writing the gospel with his stress that all the benefits of Christ in the eschatological kingdom are realized here and now in experiencing Christ as king. Finally, the later 'ecclesiastical redactor' reinstates future ideas in his editing of the gospel to make it more acceptable to the church.[66] Meanwhile, Bultmann's pupil, Ernst Käsemann, a generation later picks up the idea that the original future eschatology faded in the light of the delay of the Parousia, so the fourth evangelist stresses Jesus' preexistence more than his final judgement, as 'protology, a doctrine of first things, was placed beside the eschatology'.[67] Thus John 5.19-24 makes it abundantly clear that judgement is realized in the present: 'he who hears my word and believes him who sent me has eternal life; he does not come into judgment, but has passed from death to life'. Similarly, the summary passage of 3.16-21 stresses that 'those who do not believe are condemned already', as salvation is in the present here and now (see also 3.36).[68] Therefore, Jesus can say in his high-priestly prayer at the end of the farewell discourses, 'This is eternal life, that they may know you, the only true God, and Jesus Christ whom you have sent' (John 17.3).

Clearly, if we were to accept such a realized eschatology according to Bultmann and Käsemann, this would have radical ethical implications. If the decision about salvation and judgement is fully realized in the present, and the final judgement, eternal life and death have already taken effect, then there is less need for detailed ethical instructions, moral teachings or anything like the Sermon on the Mount in the fourth gospel. People are already saved or condemned and need no ethical guidance beyond the command to love the others who are similarly saved within the small circle of the beloved disciple and his followers.

Such a shift to a realized eschatology also played its part in the various attempts to describe the development of the so-called 'Johannine Community'. Such approaches suggested that the gospel can be read on two levels at the same time, namely the original story of Jesus and his ministry overlaid with

66. See Bultmann, *The Gospel of John: A Commentary* and *Theology of the New Testament*, vol. 2.

67. Käsemann, *The Testament of Jesus*, p. 21.

68. See Käsemann, *The Testament of Jesus*, p. 14.

the story of the development of the community which produced the gospel. Both J. L. Martyn and R. E. Brown reconstruct the various stages by which the Johannine Community came into being and developed, from the early Jewish disciples, through the addition of others such as Samaritans, to a crisis around their expulsion from the synagogue in the mid-80s (as seen in the material about being put 'out of the synagogue', ἀποσυνάγωγος, in John 9.22; 12.42; 16.22); this was followed by periods of subsequent debate both with those who remained within Judaism and with heterodox believers who split away from the community, especially over the reality of the incarnation, which led in turn to the production of the Johannine epistles.[69] Brown first works out the sequence of his reconstruction in the introduction to his Anchor Bible commentary in 1966, which is then refined in his *Community of the Beloved Disciple* (1979); this is further revised in his *Introduction to the New Testament* in 1997 and finally in what would have been the *Introduction* to his revised Anchor Bible commentary, which was edited and published after his sudden death in August 1998.[70] Brown agrees with Bultmann and Käsemann that John does include the best example of realized eschatology in the New Testament, but he prefers to talk of it as a 'vertical' versus 'horizontal' dimension rather than merely present versus future. He believes that Jesus himself combined these two dimensions and both temporal aspects in his teaching, and therefore argues against Bultmann's view that the main 'future' passages are late insertions to appear more orthodox; in Brown's understanding, they could just as easily be early.[71] In his revised *Introduction*, he thinks it is 'too simple' to assign present and future sayings to pre- and postresurrection stages and talks instead of a 'blending of horizons'.[72]

We noted in the introduction to this chapter that there has been some hesitation over the questions of authorship, editions and audience in more recent scholarship: thus Beasley-Murray talks of 'more caution' and that such issues are 'less capable of precise determination than is frequently represented'.[73] This

69. Martyn, *History and Theology in the Fourth Gospel*; R. E. Brown, *The Gospel according to John*; Brown, *The Community of the Beloved Disciple*; another good example of such sociological analysis of John's community is Wayne Meeks' important article, 'The Man from Heaven in Johannine Sectarianism', *JBL* 91.1 (1972), pp. 44-72, and repr. in *The Interpretation of John*, ed. J. Ashton, pp. 141-73; see also, for further discussion, Barton's treatment, 'Can We Identify the Gospel Audiences?', in *The Gospels for All Christians*, pp. 189-93.

70. Brown, *An Introduction to the New Testament*, pp. 368-78; Brown, *An Introduction to the Gospel of John*, ed. F. J. Moloney, pp. 58-86 and 189-219.

71. Brown, *The Gospel according to John*, vol. 2, pp. cxv-cxxi.

72. Brown, *An Introduction to the Gospel of John*, pp. 234-48, esp. pp. 247-48.

73. Beasley-Murray, *John*, pp. lxvi-lxxxi, quotation from p. lxxviii; see also Ben Witherington, III, *John's Wisdom* (Cambridge: Lutterworth, 1995), pp. 11-35 with its more tentative conclusions.

change was perhaps best demonstrated in the Johannine Literature session at SBL in 2002 at Toronto, where Robert Kysar's paper, 'Expulsion from the Synagogue: A Tale of a Theory', outlined the 'rise and decline' of Johannine community theory,[74] looking at how an initial hypothesis came to be accepted by the scholarly consensus for a couple of decades before the more recent questioning. This paper received positive responses from, among others, D. Moody Smith and J. L. Martyn, despite their own involvement in producing the initial theory. This is a salutary reminder that 'scholarly consensus' and 'working hypotheses' about these texts need constantly to be reevaluated.[75]

This applies as much to Johannine eschatology as to the possible setting, within a community or not, of the gospel. In the intervening decades between Brown's original commentary in the mid 1960s and his revisions of the *Introduction* at his death in 1998, scholars from various backgrounds reconsidered Johannine eschatology and came to similar conclusions. Thus in 1975, de Jonge pointed to the more future eschatology of the First Epistle of John (seen as later than the gospel) and argues against Bultmann for a similarly future strand in the gospel, which provides motivation for 'ethics in the interim'.[76] Similar conclusions about the combination of present and future elements in Johannine eschatology, with reservations about Bultmann's approach, were reached by Smalley in 1978, Robinson in 1985 and Davies in 1992.[77] Like Brown, they all point to an inevitable future dimension there in Johannine eschatology, which cannot simply be excised or attributed to later redaction.

Brown notes that some of the future tenses refer to things still in the future for the disciples from the narrative's point of view, such as the forward references to baptism and the Eucharist, if one accepts his sacramental interpretation of 3.5 and 6.54.[78] Equally, the verses about the coming of the Spirit in 6.63, 7.38-39, 16.7 and 19.30 look forward to the so-called 'Johannine Pentecost' in 20.22. However, the various references to the 'last day', especially in the Bread of Life discourse where it acts like a refrain (6.39, 40, 44, 54), must refer to a future

74. R. Kysar, 'Expulsion from the Synagogue: A Tale of a Theory', Johannine Literature section, Session S25-62, SBL, Toronto, Monday, November 25, 2002, later published as chap. 15 in Kysar, *Voyages with John: Charting the Fourth Gospel*, pp. 237-45.

75. For a similarly radical, positive reevaluation of the claim that the fourth gospel is written by the Beloved Disciple as eyewitness testimony, see Richard Bauckham, *Jesus and the Eyewitnesses: The Gospels as Eyewitness Testimony* (Grand Rapids: Eerdmans, 2006), pp. 358-411.

76. Marinus de Jonge, 'Eschatology and Ethics in the Fourth Gospel', Dutch original 1975, trans. in his collection, *Jesus: Stranger from Heaven and Son of God*, pp. 169-91.

77. Smalley, *John: Evangelist and Interpreter*, pp. 235-41; Robinson, *The Priority of John*, pp. 339-42; Davies, *Rhetoric and Reference in the Fourth Gospel*, pp. 158-61.

78. Brown, *The Gospel according to John*, vol. 1, p. cxviii.

consummation still to come. Martha also accepts 'the resurrection on the last day' outside her brother's tomb in 11.24; while Lazarus is then raised from the dead, it is clear that this is a resuscitation rather than the final resurrection — otherwise the chief priests could not plot to kill him again in 12.10! Presumably, Lazarus still has to face the final judgement 'on the last day' as prophesied by Jesus in 12.48. It is Jesus' high-priestly prayer that 'those also, whom you have given me, may be with me where I am, to see my glory, which you have given me because you loved me before the foundation of the world' (17.24) which links protology with eschatology, so that future generations who are yet to believe may come on that last day to see his preexistent glory.

Probably the best place to see this combination of present and future is to return to the discourse after the healing of the paralytic. As Bultmann notes, in 5.19-24 Jesus argues that through his present activity as Son, not just the sick are raised, but judgement is given to him by the Father for both death and life as people are 'astonished'. However, exactly the same themes then occur in the next paragraph, which repeats it all in the future: 'the hour is coming when all who are in their graves will hear his voice and will come out' to judgement, again given by the Father to the Son, to grant life or death, about which we should not be 'astonished' (5.25-29). Of course, Bultmann argues that this section is an interpolation from the later ecclesiastical redactor, but Brown and the others prefer to see it as much earlier, reflecting an authentic combination of present and future, both in the fourth evangelist and in Jesus himself. The linking verse brings the two aspects together in a combination of present and future: 'Very truly, I tell you, the hour is coming, and is now here' (5.25).

If we apply this eschatological combination of 'now and not yet', of present and future, to our overall Johannine theme of the divine truth bringing us God's love, we can see how this provides a richer dimension to our exploration of the ethics of the fourth gospel. It opens up the possibility of present living in the divine love, with all its benefits being realized in the here and now. However, because even this evangelist depicts the importance of waiting for the consummation of this love at the 'last day', there is also a need for the divine truth to guide us in the here and now, which truth Jesus has not just brought and taught us, but which he has incarnated among us. In this way, John's eschatology has ethical relevance in his profound combination of truth and love, seeking to 'keep my commandments' (14.15, 21; 15.10) while loving one another as he loved us (13.34-35; 15.12), as we wait for the final consummation together: 'I am giving you these commands so that you may love one another' (15.17). But these observations take us beyond eschatology and into John's understanding of the law and the ethics of love.

3. Judaism, the law and love

John is one of the most Jewish of the canonical gospels. The writer is obviously steeped in the Hebrew scriptures and Jewish beliefs. Many of the stories are set against the background of the great Jewish festivals, as the ministry of Jesus in the first half, the Book of Signs, takes place on significant occasions:[79] it begins with Jesus clearing out the temple at Passover (2.13-25), while the healing of the paralytic happens on the Sabbath (5.9-10), leading to debate and discourse (5.15-47). The feeding of the five thousand is at the time of the next Passover (6.4), and its subsequent debate is full of allusions to the Exodus (6.25-59). Chapters 7 and 8 are set during Tabernacles (7.2, 14), which included ceremonies of both water and light; when Jesus appears in the temple during the festival, he claims to be both 'living water' (7.37-39) and 'the light of the world' (8.12-59), which leads in turn to the healing of the man born blind (9.1-41). Chapter 10 on sheep and the Good Shepherd reflects its setting at the Feast of Dedication, or Hanukkah (10.22), commemorating the rededication of the temple by the Maccabean leaders in 164 BC. Finally, the Last Supper with its farewell discourses and Jesus' arrest and death occurs once again at Passover (13–20; see especially 13.1 and 18.28).

As this brief analysis shows, many of the events take place in and around the temple in Jerusalem; as Jesus says to the high priest at his trial, 'I have always taught in synagogues and in the temple, where all the Jews come together' (18.20). The debates between Jesus and his opponents are conducted according to Jewish customs about witnesses and evidence (see 5.30-47), and great heroes like Moses and Abraham are brought into the arguments. The themes of the law, the prophets and the scriptures run constantly just below the surface, and particular quotations and prophecies are used through the passion (see, e.g., 12.15; 19.24, 28, 36).

Nonetheless, Bultmann and many others in the first half of the twentieth century thought that the fourth gospel was very Hellenistic and reflected a world of later thought and ideas as the church moved out into the eastern Mediterranean. However, the publication of the Dead Sea Scrolls and more recent study of groups like the Essenes and the Qumran community and of the development of the rabbinic traditions have all shown many links with the ideas and beliefs described in this gospel.[80] Lieu sums up the current scholarly view thus: 'While not

79. See G. A. Yee, *Jewish Feasts and the Gospel of John* (Wilmington, DE: Michael Glazier, 1989); Stephen Motyer, 'The Fourth Gospel and the Salvation of Israel: An Appeal for a New Start', in *Anti-Judaism and the Fourth Gospel: Papers of the Leuven Colloquium, 2000*, ed. R. Bieringer, D. Pollefyt and F. Vandecasteele-Vanneuville (Assen: Royal Van Gorcum, 2001) pp. 92-110, esp. pp. 97-103.

80. See C. K. Barrett, *Das Johannesevangelium und das Judentum* (Stuttgart: Kohlhammer,

denying the validity of appealing to "parallels" within Graeco-Roman thought, John's conceptual framework, his "culture", is unreservedly "Jewish".[81]

Given all of this Jewish background, framework and atmosphere, we might reasonably expect a very positive attitude towards Judaism and the law — yet in fact this area poses one of the greatest ethical challenges relating to the fourth gospel, provoking enormous scholarly debate. The twenty-five collected papers of the Leuven Colloquium in 2000 on *Anti-Judaism and the Fourth Gospel* run to some 550 published pages, while their 'Select Bibliography' contains around 400 items![82] As with the other gospels, there is the usual debate about whether this is best described as 'anti-Semitism', 'anti-Jewishness' or 'anti-Judaism'.[83] Furthermore, there is the question of whether the author himself can be 'anti-Jewish' at the same time as being so Jewish, or whether 'the text itself can generate anti-Jewish prejudice, even if this prejudice was not present in the mind of the author';[84] in addition, there is the entire *Wirkungsgeschichte*, the history of the influence of this text, down to and including the use of it made by the Nazis, and how we might interpret it today. Since this enormous debate affects Johannine scholarship in general, it is not surprising that it is also one of the most difficult areas to handle in any treatment of John's ethics.[85]

a. Attitude towards "the Jews"

Apart from a few Samaritans (4.7, 39), some Greeks (12.20) and Romans like Pilate (18.28), everyone in this gospel is Jewish — Jesus, the disciples, the crowds,

---

1970), ET as *The Gospel of John and Judaism* (London: SPCK, 1975); Barrett, 'John and Judaism', in *Anti-Judaism and the Fourth Gospel,* ed. Bieringer, Pollefyt and Vandecasteele-Vanneuville, pp. 401-17; J. H. Charlesworth (ed.), *John and Qumran* (London: Geoffrey Chapman, 1972); Brown, *The Gospel according to John*, pp. lii-lxii; Brown, *An Introduction to the Gospel of John,* pp. 115-50.

81. Judith M. Lieu, 'Anti-Judaism in the Fourth Gospel: Explanation and Hermeneutics', in *Anti-Judaism and the Fourth Gospel,* ed. Bieringer, Pollefyt and Vandecasteele-Vanneuville, pp. 126-43, quotation from p. 127.

82. *Anti-Judaism and the Fourth Gospel: Papers of the Leuven Colloquium, 2000,* ed. R. Bieringer, D. Pollefyt and F. Vandecasteele-Vanneuville; 'Select Bibliography', pp. 549-70.

83. See Lieu, 'Anti-Judaism in the Fourth Gospel', pp. 128-31; J. D. G. Dunn 'The Question of Anti-Semitism in the New Testament Writings of the Period', in *Jews and Christians: The Parting of the Ways AD 70 to 135,* ed. J. D. G. Dunn, WUNT 66 (Tübingen: Mohr Siebeck, 1992), pp. 177-211.

84. See the editors' introduction to *Anti-Judaism and the Fourth Gospel,* ed. Bieringer, Pollefyt and Vandecasteele-Vanneuville, pp. 5-17 on the levels of author, text and interpreter; quotation from p. 8.

85. See the treatment given it by Verhey, *Great Reversal,* pp. 142-3; Hays, *Moral Vision of the NT,* pp. 146-47; Blount, *Then the Whisper Put on Flesh,* pp. 112-17; significantly Schrage and Matera mostly avoid it with only a brief mention in *The Ethics of the NT,* pp. 317-18 and *NT Ethics,* p. 103.

the leaders, the priests. Jesus is explicitly addressed as 'you, a Jew' by the Samaritan woman (4.9). In their ensuing dialogue, Jesus tells her that 'salvation is from the Jews' (4.22), a crucial comment which is often overlooked in discussions of John's anti-Jewishness, or excised as an 'editorial gloss' in Bultmann's terms.[86] Van Belle notes that such approaches already assume John's anti-Jewishness, and argues instead that 'this positive statement' is 'originally Johannine'.[87] While this term "the Jews" comes only five or six times in each of the Synoptic gospels, John uses it some seventy times. Some of these, like 4.22 just discussed, can be seen as 'positive', especially those which refer to believing Jews: in 8.30-31, Jesus addresses 'the Jews who had believed in him'. Similarly, a number 'of the Jews' had been present to console Mary and Martha and witnessed the raising of Lazarus (11.19, 31, 36), which led to 'many of the Jews' believing in Jesus (11.45); later, the chief priests are worried that 'many of the Jews were going away and believing in Jesus' because of Lazarus (12.11); Other usages are more 'neutral' descriptions, where 'of the Jews' is another way of saying 'Jewish', as in festivals 'of the Jews' (2.13; 5.1; 6.4; 7.2; 11.55; 19.42) or their purification and burial customs (2.6; 19.40), or in the phrase 'King of the Jews' (18.33, 39; 19.3, 19-21).

However, the majority of the uses of this phrase are hostile, denoting people who become more and more opposed to Jesus: 'the Jews' send people to question John the Baptist and Jesus (1.19; 2.20) at the start, and they also interrogate those healed by Jesus (5.10-18; 9.18-34). The conflict grows through various debates with Jesus (6.42-52; 7.11-24; 8.22-29, 57), leading to acrimonious accusations that Jesus is a Samaritan and demon-possessed, while he says, 'You are of your father, the devil' (8.44-48, 52).[88] 'The Jews' seek to kill him (5.18; 7.1), stone him (10.31; 11.8), plot against him and Lazarus (11.47-53; 12.10-11), send officers to arrest him (18.12), interrogate him (18.19-23), hand him over to Pilate (18.28-31) and demand his death (18.38–19.15).[89]

There have been various attempts to solve the problem of these hostile ref-

86. Bultmann, *The Gospel of John*, pp. 189-90, see also his n. 6 there defending his claim.

87. Gilbert Van Belle, '"Salvation is from the Jews" : The Parenthesis in John 4:22b', in *Anti-Judaism and the Fourth Gospel*, ed. Bieringer, Pollefyt and Vandecasteele-Vanneuville, pp. 370-400, quotation from p. 400.

88. See Urban C. von Wahlde, '"You Are of Your Father the Devil" in Its Context: Stereotyped Apocalyptic Polemic in John 8:38-47', in *Anti-Judaism and the Fourth Gospel*, ed. Bieringer, Pollefyt and Vandecasteele-Vanneuville, pp. 418-44.

89. For differing analyses of which verses might be seen as positive, neutral and hostile, see Edwards, *Discovering John*, pp. 112-16, and Francis J. Moloney, S.D.B., '"The Jews" in the Fourth Gospel: Another Perspective', *Pacifica* 15 (2002), pp. 16-36, repr. in his collection, *The Gospel of John: Text and Context*, pp. 20-44, esp. pp. 36-42; Moloney regards the references to feasts 'of the Jews', for example, 'as a negative statement, as Jesus perfects those limited celebrations'.

erences. The Leuven Colloquium's *Anti-Judaism and the Fourth Gospel* devoted a section of no fewer than six papers of 127 pages to the two little words 'the Jews'![90] Lowe's initially appealing suggestion was to translate οἱ ᾽Ιουδαῖοι by its literal meaning of 'the Judaeans', as John refers also to Jesus going εἰς τὴν ᾽Ιουδαίαν γῆν, 'into the Judaean land' (3.22; see also 4.3, 47, 54).[91] However, by no means all the uses of the term can be applied to such a geographically restricted area as Judaea; for instance, the crowd of 'the Jews' in 6.41 and 53 are in Galilee. Therefore this solution does not seem to work.

Another approach uses the fact that it was Jewish authorities or leaders who first sent enquiries of John the Baptist and Jesus, and that once again it is the religious leadership who have him arrested and brought before Pilate. Therefore, other scholars, such as von Wahlde, have preferred to translate the term as 'Jewish leaders' or even 'Judaean leaders',[92] which makes better sense of the blind man's parents (presumably Jewish people themselves) being frightened of 'the Jews' in 9.22. As Charlesworth puts it, 'It is imperative to translate ᾽Ιουδαῖοι, wherever possible, as 'some Judean leaders' and not the equivalent of "Jews"'.[93] While this reflects the opposition of the authorities in the gospel and appears to get us off the anti-Jewish hook, it too has not found universal acceptance, not least because once again there are other uses of the term in the gospel where the authorities are not particularly in view, such as the general terms 'festival of the Jews' or 'King of the Jews', or the ordinary crowds in 6.41, 52, or those who accompanied Martha and Mary in 11.19, 33.[94] As Brown concludes, 'To translate some instances of *Ioudaioi* as "the Jewish authorities" and other instances as "Jewish people" or "the Jewish crowd" is unwarranted to clarify texts

90. See the editors' introduction 'Who Are "the Jews" in John?' pp. 17-23; plus the papers by Johannes Beutler, 'The Identity of "the Jews" for the Readers of John', pp. 229-38; Henk Jan de Jonge, 'The "Jews" in the Gospel of John', pp. 239-59; M. C. de Boer, 'The Depiction of "the Jews" in John's Gospel: Matters of Behavior and Identity', pp. 260-80; Raymond F. Collins, 'Speaking of the Jews: "Jews" in the Discourse Material of the Fourth Gospel', pp. 281-300; Peter J. Tomson, '"Jews" in the Gospel of John as Compared with the Palestinian Talmud, the Synoptics and Some New Testament Apocrypha', pp. 301-40; Adele Reinhartz, '"Jews" and Jews in the Fourth Gospel', pp. 341-56; all in *Anti-Judaism and the Fourth Gospel*, ed. Bieringer, Pollefyt and Vandecasteele-Vanneuville.

91. See M. Lowe, 'Who were the *Ioudaioi*?', *NovT* 18 (1976), pp. 101-30; Von Wahlde, '"You Are of Your Father the Devil" in Its Context: Stereotyped Apocalyptic Polemic in John 8:38-47', in *Anti-Judaism and the Fourth Gospel*, ed. Bieringer, Pollefyt and Vandecasteele-Vanneuville, pp. 443-44.

92. U. C. von Wahlde, 'The Johannine "Jews": A Critical Survey', *NTS* 28 (1982), pp. 33-60.

93. James H. Charlesworth, 'The Gospel of John: Exclusivism Caused by a Social Setting Different from That of Jesus (John 11:54 and 14:6)', in *Anti-Judaism and the Fourth Gospel*, ed. Bieringer, Pollefyt and Vandecasteele-Vanneuville, pp. 478-513; see esp. pp. 482-92, quotation from p. 490.

94. See Casey's rejection of such attempts by Lowe and von Wahlde to limit the term in his *Is John's Gospel True?*, pp. 116-23.

that John has left vague and cloaks the fact that by calling them both "the Jews", John deliberately joins them together in their hostility to Jesus'.[95]

What is clear is that neither of these simple solutions really works, yet both are on to something with the attempt to restrict the meaning either geographically or to the authorities. After all, John's phrase οἱ Ἰουδαῖοι cannot just mean all Jews everywhere, at all times, then and now, given the fact that Jesus, the disciples and other positive characters are Jews, and the general Jewishness of the gospel. Therefore, it is clear that John is using the phrase 'the Jews' in some form to denote the main opposition to Jesus.[96]

Most proposed solutions utilise the concept of internal debate within first-century Judaism, which was very factional, especially prior to the destruction of Jerusalem and the temple by the Romans in AD 70. Dunn points out that it is anachronistic to think of the later surviving rabbinic tradition (as in the Mishnah, Talmuds, etc.) as being 'normative Judaism' for the first century. Such concepts were swept away by the discovery of the Dead Sea Scrolls and the realization that the whole period of Second Temple Judaism was much more diverse, with so many groups and approaches that is it better to talk of 'Judaisms' in the plural. Furthermore, the polemic employed by different sects against each other and especially opposing the religious-political leadership in Jerusalem was extremely bitter: 'The character of denunciation and quality of vituperation are remarkably consistent across the range of literature'.[97] This is the context for John's use of language and rhetoric which should be seen as *intra*-Jewish debate going on within the wider Jewish family,[98] as we suggested in our discussion of Matthew's use of language about the Pharisees in Chapter V above.

Furthermore, this is not just internal argument within a family which agrees to stay together, despite their propensity to abuse each other. Although it may have begun like that, most reconstructions of the historical setting of the fourth gospel are set against the background of the 'parting of the ways' between what later became normative rabbinic Judaism and the early Christian church, as most of the other factions disappeared in the Jewish revolts of AD 66-70 and 132-35. Therefore, as with Matthew's gospel, what may have begun as

95. Brown, *An Introduction to the Gospel of John*, pp. 157-72; quotation from pp. 165-66.

96. See also John Ashton's discussion of the term 'The Jews in John', in his *Studying John*, pp. 36-70; also Ashton, *Understanding the Fourth Gospel*, pp. 131-37.

97. J. D. G. Dunn, *Jesus Remembered* (Grand Rapids: Eerdmans, 2003), pp. 255-325, quotation from pp. 283-84.

98. See J. D. G. Dunn, 'The Embarrassment of History: Reflections of the Problem of 'Anti-Judaism' in the Fourth Gospel', in *Anti-Judaism and the Fourth Gospel*, ed. Bieringer, Pollefyt and Vandecasteele-Vanneuville, pp. 47-67, esp. pp. 59-60; Lieu discusses the same issue in her 'Anti-Judaism in the Fourth Gospel', pp. 131-33.

intra-familial ends up being read very differently from an *external* perspective after the separation.

We have already noted the importance of the emergence in the 1960s and 70s of a two-level approach to the gospel in which the story of Jesus is overlaid with the developing history of the Johannine community. In the major reconstructions of scholars like Martyn, Brown, Ashton and Lindars, the growing conflict with 'the Jews' in the gospel is crucial.[99] Thus the early stages of the community are traced from the first disciples coming to Jesus from John the Baptist (1.35-51), through conversations with Jewish enquirers at Jerusalem such as Nicodemus, following the temple incident (chaps. 2–3), to a Samaritan mission (symbolized by the woman at the well, 4.1-27, and her testimony 4.28-30, 39-42). This then leads to the arguments with 'the Jews' of chaps. 5–10, which reach a climax with the threat of being put 'out of the synagogue', ἀποσυνάγωγος (9.22; 12.42; 16.2). While people could be punished by being barred from the synagogue for a week, or a month, or occasionally even totally excommunicated in the Old Testament (see Ezra 10.8), this does not seem to have happened to Jesus and his disciples, who, according to the other gospels and Acts, went to synagogue regularly as good Jews. Of course, there was opposition and conflict (cp. Luke 6.22 for talk of exclusion), but this technical term, ἀποσυνάγωγος, seems to belong to a later period, usually identified, as we discussed with regard to Matthew above, as the 80s and 90s, with the Council of Yavneh and the *birkat ha-minim,* 'the blessing against the heretics' and the *notzrim.* If *notzrim* meant 'Nazarenes', then this illuminates the difficulty for Johannine Christians to attend synagogue and pray against themselves, and hence the split developed rapidly after this, simultaneously explaining both John's essential Jewishness and his 'anti-Jewish' rhetoric.

There was widespread general acceptance of a reconstruction along these lines through most of scholarship during the 1980s and 1990s. In particular, such reconstructions were used to explain John's use of the term 'the Jews' and to deal with his supposed 'anti-Jewishness'.[100] Thus in 1993, Kysar outlined the various versions of the attempted reconstruction and concluded, 'An increasingly clear picture emerges from all these studies grounded in the hypothesis that the Gospel was written in response to the exclusion of the Johannine

99. Martyn, *History and Theology in the Fourth Gospel;* Brown, *The Gospel according to John,* pp. xxiv-xl; Brown, *The Community of the Beloved Disciple;* Brown, *An Introduction to the New Testament,* pp. 368-78; Brown, *An Introduction to the Gospel of John,* pp. 58-86 and 189-219; Ashton, *Understanding the Fourth Gospel,* pp. 124-204; Lindars, *John,* pp. 45-66.

100. See, for instance, Pryor's 'Epilogue — An Anti-Semitic Gospel?', in his *John: Evangelist of the Covenant People,* pp. 181-84; also Smith, *The Theology of the Gospel of John,* pp. 48-56 for the setting of the gospel and pp. 169-73 about the charge of anti-Semitism.

church from the synagogue and the subsequent dialogue between these two religious parties. . . . But most important for our purposes is how this hypothesis for the historical origin of the Gospel informs the anti-Jewish tone of the text.'[101] Similarly, Rensberger rehearsed the material about 'the Jews' and the historical reconstruction to argue that 'the Gospel of John is not anti-Jewish in the sense of intending hostility toward Jewish people in general' because 'it is still fundamentally the language of a Jewish sect employed against other Jews in positions of authority'. However, because of the subsequent anti-Semitic use of John, he suggested that 'rendering Ἰουδαῖοι by "Jewish authorities" or the like may be the best of a bad set of choices in translating John', and his approach was welcomed by his respondents Goodwin and Lea.[102]

More recent scholarship has questioned the detailed reconstructions of the development of the Johannine community, and Kysar himself has now reminded us that it is still only an hypothesis.[103] Even Brown simplified his account of five stages down to only three in his final version for his revised *Introduction*.[104] He also included a new updated section on the use of 'the Jews' in the fourth gospel, in which he analyses the various solutions as discussed above and comes to the conclusion that the gospel contains apologetic against 'Jewish crypto-Christians' who did not confess their faith in Jesus publicly.[105] We noted with regard to Matthew that there has been some reassessment of the *birkat ha-minim*, and this has been applied to John as well, suggesting that perhaps too much emphasis has been placed upon it.[106] However, while there is more doubt about whether there was a universal expulsion from the synagogue arising from such an agreed blessing, the concept of a split has been retained in most approaches, even if on a more local scale: as Moloney concludes, 'One cannot explain the Johannine story without accepting that it was written against a background (however recent or remote) of a painful breakdown between two groups in the larger Jewish community'.[107] Adele Reinhartz's Jewish reading of John has

101. Robert Kysar, 'Anti-Semitism and the Gospel of John', in *Anti-Semitism and Early Christianity: Issues of Polemic and Faith*, ed. Craig A. Evans and Donald A. Hagner (Minneapolis: Fortress, 1993), pp. 113-27, quotation from pp. 120-21.

102. David Rensberger, 'Anti-Judaism and the Gospel of John', in *Anti-Judaism and the Gospels*, ed. William R. Farmer (Harrisburg, PA: Trinity Press International, 1999), pp. 120-57, with Responses by Mark Goodwin, pp. 158-71, and Thomas D. Lea, pp. 172-75.

103. Kysar, 'Expulsion from the Synagogue: The Tale of a Theory'; see nn. 15 and 74 above.

104. Brown, *An Introduction to the Gospel of John*, pp. 58-86; see esp. p. 64.

105. Brown, *An Introduction to the Gospel of John*, pp. 157-75.

106. See, for example, P. W. van der Horst, 'The *Birkat ha-minim* in Recent Research', *ExpT* 105 (1993-94), pp. 363-68; see also Keener's detailed treatment on both the *birkat* and local disagreements in the Introduction to his *The Gospel of John*, pp. 171-214.

107. Moloney, '"The Jews" in the Fourth Gospel', p. 41; see also Peter J. Tomson, 'If this be from

also reexamined the Martyn-Brown reconstruction based on the *birkat ha-minim* and its difficulties; she is cautious about such two-level approaches, but argues that the exclusion passages 'may provide an etiology in the time of Jesus for the estranged relations between the Johannine and Jewish communities at the end of the first century CE'.[108] These issues of 'the Jews', the expulsions, the *birkat ha-minim* and the Martyn-Brown two-level hypothesis have all been subject to two major recent treatments from Scandinavia: Fuglseth accepts the difficulties over the *birkat ha-minim* and the details of some reconstructions; but he challenges the 'sectarian' interpretation, preferring a 'cultic' description which still preserves the essential element of John's community being in 'serious conflict' with its Jewish 'parent body'.[109] Hakola thinks that there are many more 'fallacies in the scholarly consensus' and is much less confident about how much John is reacting to external pressure from Jewish sources; nonetheless, the clear ambivalence about Judaism is there, and he prefers to explain it as evolving a new 'identity', working out both continuity and discontinuity with their Jewish past in the light of the dominance of Johannine Christology.[110]

It is highly significant that this survey of interpretations of John's attitude towards Judaism and 'the Jews' has brought us back to Christology, for it is here that our stress on the centrality of the person of Jesus and the importance of genre and biography as the key to the interpretation of the gospels makes its contribution. Interestingly, in his paper at the Leuven Colloquium appealing for 'a new start in our approach to the "anti-Judaism" of the Fourth Gospel', Motyer argued for a shift from such author/community-centred historical reconstructions to more reader/receiver-centred concerns. In putting forward this case, he drew upon both my work on the gospels as biography and upon the articles by Bauckham, Alexander, Barton and myself in *The Gospels for All Christians*.[111] He then returns to where we started in this section, with John's

---

Heaven . . .': Jesus and the New Testament Authors in Their Relationship to Judaism (Sheffield: Sheffield Academic Press, 2001), pp. 290-332.

108. Adele Reinhartz, *Befriending the Beloved Disciple: A Jewish Reading of the Gospel of John* (New York: Continuum, 2001), p. 51; see also her essay, '"Jews" and Jews in the Fourth Gospel', in *Anti-Judaism and the Fourth Gospel*, ed. Bieringer, Pollefyt and Vandecasteele-Vanneuville, pp. 341-56.

109. Kåre Sigvald Fuglseth, *Johannine Sectarianism in Perspective: A Sociological, Historical, and Comparative Analysis of Temple and Social Relationships in the Gospel of John, Philo, and Qumran*, NovTSup 119 (Leiden: Brill, 2005); quotations from pp. 373-74.

110. Raimo Hakola, *Identity Matters: John, the Jews and Jewishness*, NovTSup 118 (Leiden: Brill, 2005).

111. Motyer, 'The Fourth Gospel and the Salvation of Israel: An Appeal for a New Start', in *Anti-Judaism and the Fourth Gospel*, ed. R. Bieringer, D. Pollefyt and F. Vandecasteele-Vanneuville, pp. 92-110, esp. pp. 93-95 and nn. 9 and 11.

interest in the temple and Jewish festivals to show how this reinforces 'the message of the gospel's Christology', 'namely that Jesus Christ constitutes the theological essence of the Temple as the locus of the presence of God in Israel, and the focus of the means of atonement'.[112] He next analyses John's use of 'the Jews' and argues that the negative and hostile instances are to be read along with the more positive portraits of Jesus as Jewish and the others of 'the Jews' who believe in him in the gospel. John's appeal is for a new start, and Motyer hopes for a similar new approach to Jewish-Christian dialogue arising out of a shared experience of Jewish, Christian and Arab suffering.[113] Not everyone is likely to share Motyer's conclusion that John is still appealing to Jews, but his general thrust on the central Christological message of this gospel is greatly to be welcomed, along with his stress on a reading strategy.

If we relate this to our Christological reading of the fourth gospel through the theme of the divine love coming to dwell among us and teach us God's truth, this might help explain both the essential Jewishness of this gospel and its 'anti-Jewish' elements. Right from the prologue, John portrays Jesus as the one who 'came to what was his own' (εἰς τὰ ἴδια, neuter plural) but 'his own [people]' (οἱ ἴδιοι, masculine plural) 'did not receive him'; however, immediately John notes that there were those 'who received him, who believed in his name', to whom 'he gave power to become children of God' (John 1.11-12). These people would have been Jews, but Jews who follow him and accept him, and become his disciples; they are then also called 'his own', τοὺς ἰδίους, at the Last Supper (13.1). In between John shows how Jesus goes to the temple with great 'zeal', yet prophesies that his own death and resurrection will fulfil it (2.13-21), and how the temple is the setting for much of the gospel. In a similar fashion, Jesus fulfils all the various feasts, healing on the Sabbath (5.1-18), giving his own body and blood as the true bread from heaven at Passover (6.1-14, 25-58), offering 'the living water' and 'the light of the world' at Tabernacles (7.37-39; 8.12-59),[114] and being the Good Shepherd to care for God's people like the Maccabean leaders at the Dedication, in contrast to the current leadership's attempt to exclude people like the blind man (9.34-41; 10.1-23).[115]

112. Motyer, 'The Fourth Gospel and the Salvation of Israel: An Appeal for a New Start', pp. 97-103, quotations from pp. 100 and 103.

113. See Motyer, 'The Fourth Gospel and the Salvation of Israel: An Appeal for a New Start', pp. 103-8 on 'the Jews', and pp. 109-10 on the implications for dialogue today.

114. For a full treatment, see Francis J. Moloney, S.D.B., 'Narrative and Discourse at the Feast of Tabernacles: John 7:1–8:59', in *Word, Theology and Community in John*, ed. J. Painter, R. A. Culpepper and F. F. Segovia (St. Louis: Chalice, 2002), pp. 155-72, repr. in his collection, *The Gospel of John: Text and Context*, pp. 193-213.

115. For further discussion of John 10 and the shepherds of Israel, see *The Shepherd Discourse*

In each case, the debates lead into what is the real offence, namely the person of Jesus and his claims to have come from God and to fulfil all Israel's hopes, in other words, John's central Christology (1.14-18; 2.19-21; 5.17-18, 43-47; 6.14, 40-45; 7.15-27, 35-39; 8.13-17, 54-59; 9.28-41; 10.19-25, 31-39). It is as these claims become more explicit that there arises 'a division in the crowd because of him' (7.43), with some Jews believing in Jesus (8.30-31, 11.45) and others wanting to arrest, kill or stone him (5.18; 7.1, 43; 10.31; 11.45-53). Out of this basic division within the text itself comes the hostility, which may well be further fuelled by the author's own later experience of persecution and suffering within his community or group, according to the various historical reconstructions surveyed above — but it remains at heart Christologically driven. As the Leuven editors conclude, 'It seems undeniable that the conflict has its roots in the core of John's message, in his christology'.[116]

Of course, it is a short step from saying that Jesus 'fulfils' all the Jewish traditions, festivals, themes and customs to the idea that we have here a wholesale 'replacement' of Judaism, and the accusation of being supersessionist.[117] The Leuven Colloquium was divided, with those contributors who argued that John was anti-Jewish also considering it to be supersessionist, while those who did not accept entirely the charge of being anti-Jewish rejected supersessionism as well.[118] However, here too, Christology is central. Even Adele Reinhartz's argument, for example, that the gospel does contain anti-Jewish elements concludes, 'This is not to say that the principal goal of the gospel is to promote anti-Judaism. Rather, the gospel's anti-Judaism is a by-product of the evangelist's strong convictions regarding the identity and salvific role of Jesus on the one hand, and his tendency to view not only attributes and actions but also communities in a polarized way'.[119]

Therefore we are back to our basic argument about genre. If one reads the fourth gospel as a tract about Jewish-Christian relations (as some Nazis wanted to do), it is hard not to see it as principally anti-Jewish — and therefore not a document which could be usefully employed in Christian ethics. However, in

---

of John 10 and Its Context, ed. Johannes Beutler, S.J., and Robert T. Fortna, SNTSMS 67 (Cambridge: Cambridge University Press, 1991).

116. The editors' introduction to *Anti-Judaism and the Fourth Gospel,* ed. R. Bieringer, D. Pollefyt and F. Vandecasteele-Vanneuville, p. 30.

117. See Edwards, '"Replacement Theology" and Jewish Monotheism', in her *Discovering John,* pp. 122-35.

118. See the editors' introduction to *Anti-Judaism and the Fourth Gospel,* ed. R. Bieringer, D. Pollefyt and F. Vandecasteele-Vanneuville, pp. 30-33.

119. Reinhartz, '"Jews" and Jews in the Fourth Gospel', in *Anti-Judaism and the Fourth Gospel,* ed. Bieringer, Pollefyt and Vandecasteele-Vanneuville, p. 354.

fact, it must be read as a biography about the love of God breaking into our world in the person of Jesus the Jew who was accepted by some Jews and rejected by others, a biography which was written by and for others who had also shared that experience of rejection. Therefore most scholars are surely correct to conclude that we cannot exonerate either the author or the text of its anti-Jewish elements, which arise out of its central story of Jesus — but this does not mean that the author, editors and the text itself can be held responsible for all the later use to which it has been put. In interpreting John in general, and especially in applying this gospel to Christian ethics, we must be very aware of this dimension and allow for it — but that is no reason for giving up on, or ignoring, this gospel. Furthermore, its basic message about the coming of divine life itself demands this. As the Leuven editors themselves conclude, 'Even if we cannot help but admit that the entire gospel is affected by an anti-Jewish attitude, the text projects an alternative world of all-inclusive love and life which transcends its anti-Judaism. It is the world of the text, and not the world of the author that is a witness to divine revelation.'[120] Therefore, we now need to move away at long last from John's attitude to 'the Jews' to what he says about the law and love.

b. Attitude towards the law

Even a cursory reading of the fourth gospel reveals that it differs from the other three in many ways, one of which is the absence of the controversy stories between Jesus and Jewish religious leaders about the interpretation of the law with regard to specific issues, such as marriage, food and so forth. The Synoptics share similar stories in common with the rabbinic traditions about other teachers of the time — but they are absent from John. On the other hand, John refers to Moses more often than does any other gospel, and arguments about the law continue through the narrative, so it is obviously important to him, if in a different way. As with his attitude towards the Jews, there is, not surprisingly, an ambivalence here, with John being very concerned about the law and its observance at one level even though at another it also is finally eclipsed by his Christology, since the law serves to testify to the person of Jesus. This was demonstrated comprehensively in Pancaro's massive treatment, over 550 pages.[121] However, Kotila's account is more linked into the attempted reconstructions of

120. The editors' introduction to *Anti-Judaism and the Fourth Gospel*, ed. R. Bieringer, D. Pollefyt and F. Vandecasteele-Vanneuville, p. 44.

121. Severino Pancaro, *The Law in the Fourth Gospel: The Torah and the Gospel, Moses and Jesus, Judaism and Christianity according to John*, NovTSup 42 (Leiden: Brill, 1975).

the Johannine community, analysing how the law was seen at the different stages of its development.[122] Given all that has been said above about such developmental theories, we shall concentrate here on the actual texts about the law in the final form of the gospel.

The first and crucial point to emerge is that John views the law as valid and God-given. This emerges right at the start with the Prologue, which informs us that 'the law was given through Moses' (1.17). The use of the divine passive here makes its ultimate origin clear: as Keener notes, 'Most Jewish sources concur that the law was given through Moses — that God was the author and Moses the mediator'.[123] Jesus himself picks this up with his question to the Jews at Tabernacles, 'Did not Moses give you the law?' (7.19). The Pharisees claim to be 'disciples of Moses' who know 'that God has spoken to Moses' in their dispute with the blind man (9.28-29). Given this divine origin for the law mediated through Moses, it is not surprising that much of the argument between Jesus and 'the Jews' refers to the law. The healing of the paralysed man at the pool leads to arguments about carrying a mat and healing on the Sabbath, where Jesus has to defend his actions (5.10-12, 16-18). He does so later by again appealing to the Mosaic origin of the law and arguing from the permission to circumcise on the Sabbath to healing a whole body (7.21-24). In response, Jesus even accuses his opponents of lawbreaking themselves (7.19, 22-23).[124] Thus Lincoln sees the lawsuit motif as running throughout as 'the narrative of the Fourth Gospel portrays both Jesus and his opponents against the background of legal patterns found in the Jewish scriptures'.[125]

When the scribes and the Pharisees want to test Jesus, they bring him a woman taken 'in the very act of committing adultery' (so where has the man gone?), citing that 'in the law Moses commanded us to stone such women. Now what do you say?' (8.5). While he escapes that particular trap, the Pharisees' concern for the law is also seen in their contempt for the ordinary crowd 'which does not know the law — they are accursed' (7.49). Therefore, Nicodemus appeals to the law for Jesus to receive a hearing before being condemned; however, he receives the reply to 'search and you will see that no prophet is to arise from Galilee', where it is assumed that the law is what is to be searched, and its silence about a prophet from Galilee is sufficient (7.50-52).

---

122. M. Kotila, *Umstrittene Zeuge: Studien zur Stellung des Gesetzes in der johanneischen Theologiegeschichte*, Annales Academiae Scientiarum Fennicae Diss. 48 (Helsinki: Suomalainen Tiedeakatemia, 1988).

123. Keener, *The Gospel of John*, vol. 1, p. 422.

124. See Hakola, 'Jesus, the Sabbath and Circumcision', in his *Identity Matters: John, the Jews and Jewishness*, pp. 113-45.

125. Lincoln, *Truth on Trial*, passim; quotation from p. 37.

Jesus also appeals to the law in its provision for 'the testimony of two witnesses' (8.17) and in the debate about his claim to be the Son of God (10.34-36). What is significant is that in both cases he refers them to 'your law', and this distancing is also repeated in the farewell discourses when he talks to his disciples about 'their' law (15.25). The various references to people wanting to stone Jesus (8.59; 10.31-33) imply that they see him as a lawbreaker, but it is not until the appearance before Pilate that we get the full allegation: 'We have a law, and according to that law he ought to die because he has claimed to be the Son of God' (19.7). Lincoln notes that this refers to Lev. 24.16 and says, 'This statement of "the Jews" encapsulates the main issue in the continuing conflict and trial between the synagogue, with its Torah, and Johannine Christians, with their Christology'.[126]

If both sides of the conflict accept the divine origin and validity of the law, their disagreement takes us to the second main feature of John's approach to the law, namely that it points to Jesus. In the opening chapter, Philip tells Nathanael, 'We have found him about whom Moses in the law and also the prophets wrote, Jesus son of Joseph from Nazareth'. Nathanael is as sceptical as the Pharisees later about the possibility of 'anything good' coming out of Nazareth in Galilee, but is more easily convinced (1.45-51). Jesus himself appeals to Moses and the scriptures, who 'testify on my behalf' (5.39-47). This explicit appeal to the witness of the law to Jesus provides a clue to understanding the Jewish atmosphere of John's narrative, centred around the feasts, and the various implicit allusions to Jewish hopes and traditions. As Loader notes, 'This makes sense of the fourth gospel's complex use of typological symbolism and explains why it is so extensive within the gospel'.[127] This implicit witness to Jesus then becomes more explicit in the use of fulfilment formulae through the passion narrative, such as 'this was to fulfil the word spoken by the prophet' (12.38) or 'it was to fulfil the word that is written in their law' (15.25; see also 13.18; 17.12; 19.24, 36).[128]

Thirdly, the crucial dimension to John's understanding of the law is not only that it is of divine origin and witnesses to Jesus, but that he is superior and replaces it as he fulfils it. This dichotomy is clear from the Prologue: 'The law indeed was given through Moses; grace and truth came through Jesus Christ' (1.17).[129] Nicodemus may be 'a teacher of Israel', but he needs something more than his scriptural learning — to be born again (3.1-10). In the end, the scrip-

---

126. Lincoln, *Truth on Trial*, p. 131.

127. William Loader, *Jesus' Attitude towards the Law: A Study of the Gospels* (Grand Rapids: Eerdmans, 2002), p. 484.

128. See further Hakola, 'Jesus, the Jews and Moses', in his *Identity Matters: John, the Jews and Jewishness*, pp. 146-76.

129. On this crucial verse, see Pancaro, *The Law in the Fourth Gospel*, pp. 534-46.

tures may be appealed to for their witness, but it is to Jesus as the Son that all judgement has been and will be given by his Father (5.19-47). The law may have a divine origin and been mediated through Moses, but 'no one has even seen God'. It is Jesus as 'the only Son, in the bosom of the Father, who has made him known' (1.18). As Loader notes, 'The passage seems also to suggest strongly that the Law no longer has relevance; it has been replaced, since what Moses originally sought has now been made possible'.[130] Edwards makes the same point from χάριν ἀντὶ χάριτος, 'grace upon grace' (1.16): 'John acknowledges Torah as God's gracious gift; but he sees the revelation provided by Jesus as even greater'.[131]

Thus we discover that we are back to the centrality of John's Christological interpretation as the key here as everywhere else: 'John's Christology is, therefore, the ultimate basis for understanding the way John has Jesus approach the Law'.[132] This Christology is not of Jesus as the correct interpreter of the law as in Matthew, but as 'the fulfillment of and replacement for the Mosaic law'.[133] As with 'the Jews', John's ambivalent attitude means that he can be simultaneously very Jewish in his acceptance of the law and its validity, which is never actually challenged in the fourth gospel, and yet end up by no longer needing it in the light of the fuller revelation of the divine love in the person of Jesus. If this is so, then what he has to teach and command about God's love will be superior and take priority over everything else, even the law.

c. A new commandment

We saw how the double commandment to love God and neighbour was at the heart of Jesus' teaching in the Synoptic gospels. John's stress on love is also well known, as is seen in the tradition, quoted by Jerome, that the apostle John in his old age had nothing to say to his followers except, 'My little children, love one another' (Jerome, *Commentary on Galatians* 6.10). Thus Gerhardsson comments that 'John is in complete agreement with the synoptics in making the love *(agape)* commandment the central one, linking in the process love for God with love for one's fellow human beings'.[134] While this may be explicitly true of

---

130. Loader, *Jesus' Attitude towards the Law*, p. 450.

131. Edwards, *Discovering John*, p. 124; see also her article, '*Charin anti Charitos*: Grace and the Law in the Johannine Prologue', *JSNT* 32 (1988), pp. 3-15.

132. Loader, *Jesus' Attitude towards the Law*, p. 487; see his conclusions, pp. 483-91.

133. Frank Thielman, *The Law and the New Testament: The Question of Continuity* (New York: Crossroad, 1999), p. 103.

134. Birger Gerhardsson, *The Ethos of the Bible* (Philadelphia: Fortress, 1981), p. 104.

the Johannine epistles (e.g., 1 John 4.20-21) and feels implicitly central to the gospel's theology, it is an interesting fact that the fourth gospel nowhere talks of our love for God,[135] despite the emphasis on the divine love in Jesus. There is a lot about God's love for the world (e.g., John 3.16; 16.27), Jesus' love for people (11.5, 36; 13.1, 23; 19.26; 20.2) and the love of the Father and the Son for each other (3.35; 5.20; 10.17; 14.31; 15.9; 17.23-26). But Jesus' love command in the fourth gospel is horizontal, 'I give you a new commandment, that you love one another', with no equivalent vertical dimension towards God (13.34-35). This 'new commandment' is given to his disciples at the Last Supper, after washing their feet, unlike the story in the other gospels of Jesus being asked in public debate about the greatest commandment. 'Nothing in the context suggests that Jesus is setting it in relation to the commands of Torah, not even to its commands to love'.[136] There is no scribe, no mention of Matthew's 'the law and prophets' and no Good Samaritan as in Luke (Matt. 22.39; Luke 10.29-37). J. T. Sanders even goes so far as to conclude provocatively: 'Johannine Christianity is interested only in whether he believes. "Are you saved, brother?" the Johannine Christian asks the man bleeding to death on the side of the road. "Are you concerned about your soul?" "Do you believe that Jesus is the one who came down from God?" "If you believe, you will have eternal life," promises the Johannine Christian, while the dying man's blood stains the ground.'[137]

However, Matera responds that 'a comparison between the Johannine and Synoptic teaching on love is like comparing apples and oranges; they have several features in common, but they are different kinds of fruit. To appreciate Jesus' "new commandment" one must examine it within the context of the Johannine Gospel rather than compare it with the teaching of the Synoptic Gospels.'[138] This means that we need to explore what exactly is 'new' about this commandment to 'love one another'. Interestingly, John does not use this adjective, καινός, 'new', elsewhere in the gospel, except of the garden tomb which was 'new' or 'unused' in 19.42. But the command to love is hardly 'new' or 'unused'; after all, this is at the heart of the Jewish law: 'You shall love your neighbour as yourself' (Lev. 19.18).[139] Even the writer of 1 John is forced to explain

135. See Victor Paul Furnish, *The Love Command in the New Testament* (Nashville: Abingdon, 1972), pp. 133-34; also, Werner H. Kelber, 'Metaphysics and Marginality in John', in *What Is John?* vol. 1, ed. Segovia, pp. 129-54, especially p. 152.

136. Loader, *Jesus' Attitude towards the Law*, p. 478.

137. J. T. Sanders, *Ethics in the NT*, p. 100.

138. Matera, *NT Ethics*, pp. 105-6.

139. See the surprise expressed about the 'new' commandment by various exegetes, for example, Schrage, *The Ethics of the NT*, pp. 314-16; Furnish, *The Love Command in the New Testament*, pp. 138-39; Gerhardsson, *The Ethos of the Bible*, pp. 100-101; David Rensberger, 'Love for One An-

this: 'Beloved, I am writing you no new commandment, but an old commandment that you have had from the beginning; the old commandment is the word that you have heard. Yet I am writing you a new commandment that is true in him and in you, because the darkness is passing away and the true light is already shining' (1 John 2.7-8). It is interesting that his explanation of the 'newness' is because of the eschatological context of darkness and light, and many scholars agree with him.

On the other hand, John's own reasoning is made explicit in the second part of the verse: 'I give you a new commandment, that you love one another. Just as I have loved you, you also should love one another' (John 13.34). The love we are to have one for another is based on the prior love of Jesus himself, as 1 John also notes later: 'We love because he first loved us' (1 John 4.19). Jesus' love for his disciples was shown in the footwashing which preceded it as 'an example, that you also should do as I have done to you' (John 13.1-15). Furthermore, when the love command is repeated later in the discourse, it looks forward to the crucifixion to follow: 'This is my commandment, that you love one another as I have loved you. No one has greater love than this, to lay down one's life for one's friends' (15.12-13). Thus the love command in the fourth gospel is not based upon fulfilling the law and the prophets, or on altruism as with a good Samaritan, but upon the prior love of Jesus, demonstrated either side of the command by his servant-like washing of the disciples' feet and his self-sacrificial love even to death on the cross.[140]

This takes us back to the principal argument of this book. The full picture of what love means in the fourth gospel can be found only in its portrait of Jesus. As Collins concludes, 'It is, in fact, the Christological reference which constitutes the essential novelty of the Johannine new commandment'.[141] What is 'new' in John is that Jesus provides a new motive and power for the love command. We do not love others simply to fulfil an ethical demand or to keep the Sermon on the Mount, but as a consequence of what Jesus has done, 'as I have loved you'. Thus Hartin concludes his study of these verses, 'The ethical life of

---

other and Love for Enemies in the Gospel of John', in *The Love of Enemy and Nonretaliation in the New Testament*, ed. Willard M. Swartley (Louisville: Westminster John Knox, 1992), pp. 297-313, esp. p. 304; Raymond F. Collins, '"A New Commandment I Give to You, That You Love One Another . . ." (Jn 13:34)', repr. in his collection, *Christian Morality: Biblical Foundations* (Notre Dame, IN: University of Notre Dame Press, 1986), pp. 101-36, esp. 102-3.

140. See Johannes Nissen, 'Community and Ethics in the Gospel of John', in *New Readings in John: Literary and Theological Perspectives*, ed. J. Nissen and S. Pedersen (Sheffield: Sheffield Academic Press, 1999), pp. 194-212, esp. pp. 201-3; Blount, *Then the Whisper Put on Flesh*, pp. 101-4; Hays, *Moral Vision of the NT*, pp. 144-46.

141. Collins, 'A New Commandment I Give to You', p. 116.

the Christian always remains a response to what Jesus has done on their be-half'.[142] This is precisely what we argued about the teaching of the historical Jesus, that rather than giving ethical instructions to be followed, he sought a response to how God was bringing in his reign through his deeds and words. Paul appealed to his readers similarly, and while the other gospels may preserve more of Jesus' ethical teaching than John, the fourth gospel coheres with them in looking for this response of faith in action. Empowered by Jesus' example and his prior love, such extreme love is the mark of the Christian life: 'By this everyone will know that you are my disciples, if you have love for one another' (13.35). In the centuries of poverty, oppression and persecution which followed, this was the characteristic which the world could not ignore: 'See how these Christians love one another', says Tertullian (*Apology* 39.7). Over succeeding centuries, this has remained the acid test, whether it is said admiringly about Christian caring in practice, or sarcastically in frustration at the church's internal wranglings. If the historical reconstructions of the development of the Johannine community have any truth behind them, then John's theology was forged in such conflict — but he was still able to rise above it with this call to imitate Jesus' example of love.

However, there remains the issue of just how widely this command to love is to be applied. While the Synoptic gospels pick up Leviticus' command to 'love your neighbour', the command here is to 'love one another' (13.34-35; 15.12, 17).[143] Does this restrict Jesus' universalising of love down to only loving brothers and sisters in Christ? Käsemann's famous depiction of the Johannine community as 'a conventicle with gnosticizing tendencies' means that he sees this command as 'an unmistakable restriction' of the divine love: 'The love of God cannot be connected with the love of the world . . . it is only the believers, the elect, his own, who are in fact saved'.[144] Others who agree that John has narrowed the scope of the love command simply to other members of the community include such luminaries as Montefiore, J. T. Sanders, Schrage, Rensberger and Meeks.[145] Certainly, John contains nothing like the Q-passage on loving

---

142. Patrick J. Hartin, 'Remain in Me (John 15:5): The Foundation of the Ethical and Its Consequence in the Farewell Discourses', *Neotestamentica* 25.2 (1991), pp. 341-56; quotation from p. 355.

143. See Schrage, *The Ethics of the NT,* pp. 73-79 for further discussion of the debate about how universally the term 'neighbour' was used in Jesus' time.

144. Käsemann, *The Testament of Jesus,* pp. 56-73; quotations from pp. 73, 59 and 62.

145. Hugh Montefiore, 'Thou Shalt Love the Neighbour as Thyself', *NovT* 5 (1962), pp. 157-70; J. T. Sanders, *Ethics in the NT,* pp. 91-100; Schrage, *The Ethics of the NT,* pp. 316-18; David Rensberger, *Overcoming the World: Politics and Community in the Gospel of John* (London: SPCK, 1989), pp. 124-30; Rensberger, 'Love for One Another and Love for Enemies in the Gospel of John', pp. 304-9; Wayne Meeks, 'The Ethics of the Fourth Evangelist', in *Exploring the Gospel of John: In*

one's enemies (Matt. 5.43-44; Luke 6.32-36), which may have something to do with the persecution and suffering being endured by his community according to most of the reconstructions.

On the other hand, it is notable that John does not give any licence to the natural reaction to hate one's enemies, in the vituperative manner of the Qumran material (see, e.g., *Hymns*, XIV; *Manual of Discipline*, IX, 15-22).[146] Nor is everyone convinced that John has restricted the scope of the love command. Thus while Furnish agrees with Käsemann that 'love in John is no mere emotion or ethical feeling', he goes on to argue that 'if we are correct in concluding that the Fourth Evangelist regards God's love and the Son's mission of love to be extended to all who will receive it (him), then we must also acknowledge that the commandment to "love one another" need not be regarded in itself as *excluding* love for "neighbours" and "enemies". In fact it is hard to fit such terms into the framework of this writer's theology'.[147] He then analyses the first epistle to demonstrate that 'the more accurate conclusion is that, for this writer, the term "brother" can be used as a synonym for "neighbour" and that in I John there is indeed some specific acknowledgment of one's responsibility to love all men'.[148] Robinson makes a similar direct response to Montefiore, also arguing that 'brother' can include 'neighbour', and that John wants us to love others 'whether he be Christian or not. The one love is not a perversion or narrowing down of the other'.[149] Rensberger accepts that the material about Samaritans in John 4 suggests that Johannine love could embrace former enemies.[150] Perhaps the last word should go to one of Hays' typically laconic turns of phrase: 'John's emphasis on intracommunal love is sometimes construed as a license for sentimental complacency in the church.' However, Hays responds that this 'underestimates the seriousness of John's call to costly service within the community. We should also note that John unmistakably understands the death of Jesus as being for the sake of the whole world (1:29; 3:16)'.[151]

Honor of D. Moody Smith, ed. R. A. Culpepper and C. C. Black (Louisville: Westminster John Knox, 1996), pp. 317-26.

146. See Verhey, *Great Reversal,* p. 144; Collins, 'A New Commandment I Give to You', pp. 122-23; also F. C. Fensham, 'Love in the Writings of Qumran and John', *Neotestamentica* 6 (1972), pp. 67-77, esp. pp. 69, 75.

147. Furnish, *The Love Command in the New Testament,* pp. 143-48, quotations from pp. 145 and 148, his italics.

148. Furnish, *The Love Command in the New Testament,* pp. 148-58, quotation from p. 154.

149. Robinson, *The Priority of John,* pp. 329-39; quotation from p. 337.

150. Rensberger, 'Love for One Another and Love for Enemies in the Gospel of John', pp. 308-9; see also Nissen, 'Community and Ethics in the Gospel of John', pp. 211-12.

151. Hays, *Moral Vision of the NT,* p. 145.

We shall return to look at the wider picture of John's understanding of the 'world' in the next section. Here it remains only to note that once again 'the quest for John's ethic proves to be a quest for his Christology'.[152] The love command in the fourth gospel is 'new' because it is based not on Torah, or other ethical systems, but on a practical response to the loving example of Jesus himself, who washed his disciples' feet and laid down his life for them. This is why it is a mistake to look for detailed ethical instructions in this gospel: 'The Johannine ethic of love is strictly oriented to its christology'.[153] Its biographical account of Jesus tells the story of how the love of God entered our world in the person of Jesus, who showed his Father's love in the most practical ways. From this demonstration, only one simple command is necessary — to love others as he loved us. Such divine love fulfils and perhaps even replaces Jewish customs, festivals and the law, and ultimately overcomes any hostility on the part of both the author and his opponents as it needs to be shared among the believing community as well as with the wider world.

4. Ethical issues in John

We began this chapter by noting that many scholars bemoan the absence of general ethical material in John: as Meeks laments, 'It offers no explicit moral instruction'.[154] However, our biographical approach to John has provided a rich narrative of the divine love entering our world in the self-sacrificial example of Jesus which has many ethical implications about how best to follow his example, which we shall explore in the next section; unfortunately, this narrative also gives rise to the major moral dilemma arising from his attitude towards Judaism and the Jews. However, when we come to consider specific moral issues, as we did with the other gospels, we find that they are nearly all completely missing. It is true that, in the farewell discourses, Jesus does stress that his followers should 'keep my commands' (14.15, 21; 15.10, 14, 17). However, it is never specified what those commands might be, apart from the 'new commandment' to love another (13.34; 15.12). If we look for such ethical commands, or even discussion or debate about the various key areas, which we studied in the other gospels, of family, marriage and children, war and violence, wealth and poverty,

152. Willi Marxsen, *New Testament Foundations for Christian Ethics* (Minneapolis: Fortress, 1993), p. 290.
153. Eduard Lohse, *Theological Ethics of the New Testament* (Minneapolis: Fortress, 1991), p. 170; see, similarly, Furnish's conclusion, *The Love Command in the New Testament*, pp. 157-58.
154. Meeks, 'The Ethics of the Fourth Evangelist', p. 318; see our discussion above, pp. 291-92 and nn. 18-20.

power, leadership and the state, we find practically none of them here in the fourth gospel.

There is nothing about the **family**, nor any teaching on **divorce**, while **marriage** is mentioned only as the backdrop to Jesus' first miracle at 'a wedding in Cana of Galilee' to which Jesus, his mother and his disciples were invited (2.1-11). After the Synoptics' material about **children**, the only use of the word here refers to the 'children of God' (1.12; 8.39-41; 11.52; 12.36) and Jesus' way of addressing his disciples (13.33; 21.5); real children are absent. Given the other gospels' teachings about **wealth and poverty**, it is a surprise that the words 'rich', 'wealth' or 'wealthy' never appear, and the only times money is mentioned are when Jesus overturns the moneylenders' tables in the temple (2.14-15) and the anointing of Jesus by Mary. Judas complains that the 'costly perfume' should have been sold 'and the money given to the poor' (12.1-8); the only other reference to 'the poor' is when Judas leaves the Last Supper, actually to betray Jesus, although some think that he is going to give alms to the poor (13.29). Neither reference is much help in financial ethics!

With regard to **violence**, Jesus does make 'a whip of cords' to drive the money changers out of the temple (2.15). However, when Peter draws a sword to cut off the high priest's servant's ear in the garden, Jesus rebukes him and heals the man (18.10-11). His own example throughout the passion is of passive non-resistance, as he explains to Pilate that his kingdom is not one for which his followers should fight (18.36). At the Last Supper, instead of teaching about **leadership** and **humility**, Jesus washes his disciples' feet as an example, which we shall discuss in the next section. The only times that **power** and the **state** occur come in Jesus' discussions with Pilate, when he explains that his kingdom is not 'of' or 'from' this world (18.36);[155] however, he does point out to Pilate that earthly power such as he wields is only permitted 'from above', ἄνωθεν; Pilate might think this refers to the emperor, but Jesus probably means 'by God' (19.10-11; cp. ἄνωθεν in 3.3, 7). All the other connected issues, like taxes, often mentioned in the other gospels, do not appear at all.

Some scholars have argued that Jesus' words to Pilate and this gospel's generally negative attitude to the 'world' explain this lack of wider ethical concerns. This is especially so for Käsemann and others who believe that John has restricted or narrowed down the divine love just to the community as a result of persecution, as just discussed above. For Lindars, 'The Johannine church is a

155. Nissen notes that 'Jesus' kingship will inevitably come into conflict with the kingships of this world, but precisely because it is 'not of this world' the conflict is not carried out on the world's terms. Jesus' followers do not fight, and his enthronement is on the cross. John 18.36 means that the values of the kingdom are different from, and opposed to, the values of this world.' Nissen, 'Community and Ethics in the Gospel of John', p. 208.

beleaguered sect, alienated from the local society, intensely loyal internally, but hostile to those outside'.[156] This criticism, that John views the world with sectarian hostility, is so common that it bears some further examination as the other major ethical issue in his gospel, in addition to his attitude towards 'the Jews', already discussed.

In fact, the fourth evangelist is much more subtle than this 'anti-world' criticism often allows: he refers to 'the world' on nearly eighty occasions, about four times as often as all the references in the three Synoptic gospels put together. Matera notes that '"the world" has many shades of meaning in John's Gospel, and while there are times when one or the other predominates, these meanings often overlap'.[157] Closer analysis demonstrates that these references can be grouped into three categories of roughly the same size, neutral, positive and negative. Sometimes the words ὁ κόσμος, 'the world', are simply neutral, meaning 'the earth', as in 'coming into the world' (1.9; 16.21), 'before the world existed' (17.5, 24) or 'the world could not contain all the books' (21.25). It can also refer to 'everyone', as does the French tout le monde, when the Pharisees complain that 'the world has gone after him' (12.19). These 'neutral' references are spread throughout the whole gospel, from the Prologue to the Epilogue (1.9, 10; 7.4; 8.26; 9.32; 11.9; 12.25; 14.22, 31; 17.6, 13, 21, 23; 18.20; 21.25).

However, beyond this neutral use, John views the world as essentially positive, the good creation of the loving God which he sent his Son to save, not to condemn it or judge it (3.16-17, 19; 10.36; 12.47). Jesus is introduced by the Baptist as the 'Lamb of God who takes away the sin of the world' (1.29), and the Samaritans recognize him as 'the Saviour of the world' (4.42). Jesus 'gives life to the world' as the 'bread of God' and 'light of the world' (6.33, 51; 8.12; 9.5; 12.46). Jesus has come into the world as a prophet and Messiah, according to the crowd and Martha (6.14; 11.27), and he tells Pilate that he came 'into the world to testify to the truth' (18.37). Jesus is very conscious of his divine mission to the world, referring to God as 'the one who sent me', ὁ πέμψας με, over thirty times (e.g., 4.34; 5.23-24; 6.38-40; 8.16-18; 9.4; 11.42; 12.44-45; 13.20; 17.21-25). Finally, Jesus prays for his disciples as he passes his divine mission to the world on to them: 'As you have sent me into the world, so I have sent them into the world' (17.18; see also 20.21). It is notable, and appropriate, that the majority of these 'positive' references come in the first section of the gospel about Jesus' ministry.

On the other hand, the first half of the gospel contains very few of the 'negative' references which contrast 'the world' with Jesus or his followers: there are

156. Lindars, John, pp. 58-59; see also Rensberger's assessment, 'a sectarian group with introversionist tendencies', Overcoming the World, p. 138.
157. Matera, NT Ethics, p. 95.

three contrasting references in the debates of 7.7, 8.23 and 9.39. However, it is when the time comes for 'the judgement of this world' and for Jesus to 'depart' from it (12.31; 13.1) that these negatives really start to appear, mostly in the farewell discourses.[158] The world cannot receive the Spirit (14.17) or see Jesus (14.19); it is dominated by 'the ruler of this world' and hates Jesus and his followers (14.30; 15.18-19; 16.20, 33; 17.14-15) because they do not 'belong to the world' (15.19; 16.28; 17.11, 16). However, the world and its ruler will be judged by the Spirit (16.8-11) because they do not know the Father (17.25); things are so bad that Jesus does not even pray 'on behalf of the world' (17.9). It is perhaps not unconnected that Käsemann's book is subtitled 'A Study of the Gospel of John in the Light of Chapter 17',[159] and this leads him to such a negative assessment both of the world and of John's sectarianism. Furthermore, even some of those who do consider John to be sectarian still think he has something to offer to Christian ethics with political consequences. Despite his opening lament about the absence of 'moral instruction', Meeks concludes that John's 'voice is sharply sectarian, and culturally and politically subversive' but that 'ironically, in a time when Christianity has been domesticated into a polite hobby or a cheering section for vested social interests, the sectarian stance may be just what "the world" needs as well. . . . Only a candid and contextually sensitive confrontation between the Fourth Gospel's subversive challenge to "this world" and the more accommodating, conversionist, or transformative modes of engagement with the world, represented elsewhere in the canon, can enable the Bible to guide and usefully to complicate — and not merely to decorate — Christian ethical discourse.'[160]

Therefore we have these three attitudes to the world in the fourth gospel. It begins as either merely a neutral location, or positively as the object of God's love and the mission upon which he sends Jesus. It is only as the conflict grows, and when the world rejects Jesus, that the term becomes negative and stands for the source of opposition, especially later in the farewell discourses. This is foreshadowed as the Prologue actually uses all three senses programmatically in one verse: 'He was in the world [neutral, for Jesus' presence on the earth], and the world came into being through him [positive assessment of the creation]; yet the world did not know him [negative refusal to recognize Jesus]' (1.10).

158. See Segovia, *The Farewell of the Word*, esp. his section 'The World Will Hate You! John 15:18—16.4a', pp. 169-212.

159. Käsemann, *The Testament of Jesus: A Study of the Gospel of John in the Light of Chapter 17*; the German original is similar, *Jesu letzter Wille nach Johannes 17* — one wonders how it might have been different had he chosen a different chapter!

160. Meeks, 'The Ethics of the Fourth Evangelist', pp. 324-25; see similarly, Rensberger's conclusions at the end of *Overcoming the World*, pp. 144-52.

Nonetheless, while such opposition may lead 'the world' to hate the new community which has been formed by the divine love, there is nothing in John to suggest that Christians should reciprocate the antagonism (in the way which was true, say, of the sectarianism of the Qumran community in their attitude in the Dead Sea Scrolls). The command to 'love one another' may have its immediate location in the internal relationships within the community — but that love is also the only answer to the world's negativity and hatred. It is significant that, writing from his African-American experience of oppression as his interpretative 'lens', Blount observes, 'Perhaps John already understood that the "love for one another" that enabled his believing community to sustain itself and simultaneously resist the hostile world around it would also, by energizing an alternative reality and a competing force for change, transform that world.'[161]

This brief survey of specific ethical issues in John may appear to confirm the prejudices of those who think that he has little or no moral instruction. In fact, this takes us back to our main argument about recognizing the genre of the gospels as not being ethical treatises; rather, we should look for the ethical implications of their biographical narratives. The previous section on the law and the love command concluded that John's Christology brings with it an ethic of the divine love, to love others as Jesus loved us. This section has demonstrated John's wider concern for the world as the object of the mission of God's love. Rather than providing specific ethical teachings, a Johannine approach to ethics has to apply this understanding of the divine love to any individual moral issues, guided by the example of Jesus, to which we finally turn.

5. Imitating Jesus, the friend of sinners

Given the many differences between the fourth gospel and the other three, together with the general impression of John writing for an introverted sectarian community in the midst of bitter wrangling against 'the Jews' with no specific ethical instruction other than for an internal love for other members of his group, one might not expect too much as we turn to our final area about imitating Jesus' openness within an inclusive community! However, we have argued throughout this chapter that this general impression is somewhat of a caricature, and closer analysis has demonstrated that the fourth gospel is much more complex, and infinitely richer, than this stereotype might indicate. The overriding theme has been the love of God, coming to dwell among human be-

161. Blount, *Then the Whisper Put on Flesh*, p. 108.

ings in the person of Jesus of Nazareth and to teach his divine truth. The incarnation inaugurates the eschatological age and makes eternal life present in the here and now, but there is still a period of time to await the final 'last day'. During that time, the community was defining itself over against its fellow Jews, both in the local area and against the religious authorities. Out of this conflict come harsh words about 'the Jews' and 'the world' alike, yet we have discovered that John can also be very positive about both of them as the objects of God's love as Jesus is sent to save *all* the world. This love is the fulfilment of all the Jewish practices and hopes, festivals and the law, and it is the dominating theme of John's ethics as much as his wider theology. In the light of this more careful picture, perhaps we will find an example of inclusivity to follow here also.

a. Jesus, the friend of sinners

We have already noted that the flow of narrative in the fourth gospel, mixing miraculous 'signs' with extended discourses and debate, is very different from the Synoptics' sequence of stories and pericopae containing Jesus' teaching. The suggestion that Jesus is the 'friend of sinners' in the Synoptics arises out of such anecdotes, and is missing therefore in the fourth gospel. Instead, Jesus is accused of many things here, such as having a demon, being a Samaritan, committing blasphemy and making himself 'equal with God' (e.g., 5.18; 7.20; 8.48-53; 10.20-21, 30-36). However, 'the Jews' do tell the healed blind man that 'we know that this man is a sinner', even if they do not like his reply (9.24-34)! The fourth gospel is not so much about 'eating and drinking with sinners', but it is a narrative which is immensely personal and full of well-known and beloved characters: Nathanael (1.45-51); Nicodemus (3.1-10); the Samaritan woman (4.7-26); the paralysed man at the pool (5.2-14); the woman caught in adultery (8.3-11); the blind man (9.1-38); Martha, Mary and Lazarus (11.1-44); and Peter (13.6-10; 21.15-22). In each case, Jesus accepts the individual where they are and lovingly enters into their story, in an attempt to evoke a response of faith from them. As John says at the outset, Jesus 'knew all people and needed no one to testify about anyone; for he himself knew what was in everyone' (2.24-25).

He does not seem to care about social barriers, treating in the same way both a fellow ordinary Galilean who had a prejudice about Nazareth like Nathanael, and also a Pharisee and Jewish leader who came secretly with a theological issue like Nicodemus, gently teasing them with further questions to elicit their interest and response (1.45-51; 3.1-10). He also accepts the plea from 'a royal official', τις βασιλικός. This phrase probably means an administrative official of Herod Antipas, although he could also be an Herodian soldier (compare the Roman centurion of the similar story in Matt. 8.5-13 and Luke 7.1-10);[162] whichever he was, this was unlikely to have endeared him to the local people — but Jesus still heals his son in Capernaum (4.46-54).

It is at Jacob's well in the Samaritan city of Sychar that Jesus really shows his disdain for the divisions of gender, race, belief and moral reputation as he asks the Samaritan woman for a drink. Her reaction shows how unusual this request from a 'Jewish man', Ἰουδαῖος ὤν, is to 'a woman of Samaria' (4.8). Not only is she the wrong gender and race, but her beliefs about where God can be found are as unorthodox as her marital arrangements (4.16-20). It is therefore not at all surprising that, when his disciples return, they are similarly 'astonished' (4.27). However, Jesus' attitude is quite different, again gently teasing her over the double meaning of ὕδωρ ζῶν, seeming to offer 'running water' as opposed to the well's standing (if not stagnant) contents, but really encouraging her towards the 'water of life',[163] enquiring of her husband and answering her attempts at theological deflection until she comes to a confession of faith in him as Messiah (4.29). Such is his approach that many have seen echoes here of the famous betrothal scenes at wells in the Old Testament (Gen. 24; 29.1-12; Exod. 2.16-21).[164] Others draw attention to the woman's 'apostleship' in going to tell others and bringing about the conversion of the Samaritans (John 4.28-30, 39-42), as explained by Jesus' words about sowing and reaping to the disciples (4.35-38).[165] Rensberger sees here 'indications of concern for outsiders penetrating the barriers of Johannine sectarianism' to include 'former Samaritan enemies'.[166] It is significant that Spina's study of 'the faith of the outsider',

162. See Keener, *The Gospel of John*, vol. 1, pp. 630-33; Brown, *The Gospel according to John*, vol. 1, pp. 190-93.

163. For a typically fascinating exposition, see Stephen D. Moore, 'Are There Impurities in the Living Water That the Johannine Jesus Dispenses? Deconstruction, Feminism, and the Samaritan Woman', *Biblical Interpretation* 1 (1993), pp. 207-27; repr. in *The Interpretation of John*, ed. Ashton, pp. 279-99.

164. See, for example, Lyle Eslinger, 'The Wooing of the Woman at the Well: Jesus, the Reader and Reader-Response Criticism', *Journal of Literature and Theology* 1.2 (1987), pp. 167-83; repr. in *The Gospel of John as Literature*, ed. Stibbe, pp. 165-82; also Luise Schottroff, 'The Samaritan Woman and the Notion of Sexuality in the Fourth Gospel', in *What Is John?* vol. 2, ed. Segovia, pp. 157-81.

165. See, for example, Sandra M. Schneiders, 'Women in the Fourth Gospel and the Role of Women in the Contemporary Church', *BTB* 12.2 (1982), pp. 35-45; repr. in *The Gospel of John as Literature*, ed. Stibbe, pp. 123-43, esp. pp. 132-34; see also Sandra M. Schneiders, 'A Case Study: A Feminist Interpretation of John 4:1-42', in *The Revelatory Text: Interpreting the New Testament as Sacred Scripture* (San Francisco: HarperSanFrancisco, 1991), pp. 180-99, repr. in *The Interpretation of John*, ed. Ashton, pp. 235-59.

166. Rensberger, 'Love for One Another and Love for Enemies in the Gospel of John', pp. 308-9.

which concentrates mostly on stories from the Hebrew scriptures, takes this passage for his only chapter on the New Testament and concludes: 'Typically, insiders do the planting, hoping to transform outsiders into insiders. But that process has been reversed in this instance. A Samaritan woman takes on the role of one of Jesus' best Jewish disciples and performs not only admirably, but spectacularly. She is the crown jewel outsider of John's Gospel.'[167]

There is no similar apostolic result in the story of the woman taken in adultery (8.1-11), which is not found in the earliest manuscripts.[168] However, it is a well-loved part of the tradition, and it shows Jesus' attitude to be the same: once again, he is unconcerned for his own reputation, or how this might appear to others, and treats her with the usual gentle questioning to elicit her response, which in turn causes him to say, 'Neither do I condemn you. Go your way, and from now on do not sin again' (8.11).[169] Other significant women treated respectfully in the fourth gospel include his mother Mary (2.1-12; 19.25-27), Martha and Mary in Bethany (11.1-44), Mary at Jesus' anointing (12.1-8) and Mary Magdalene at the cross and the empty tomb (19.25-27; 20.1-2, 11-18). Again we see the same attitude from Jesus, a loving acceptance (11.23, 33; 12.3, 7; 19.26-27; 20.16), gently teasing questioning which seeks a response (2.4; 11.25, 34; 20.15) and similar results in Martha's confession of faith and Mary Magdalene's role as the first apostle of the resurrection (11.27; 20.18), not to mention male complaints like Judas' (12.5). Altogether, John's gospel gives us 'a picture of a first century community in which original and loving women played a variety of unconventional roles which the Fourth Evangelist presents as approved by Jesus and the community despite the grumblings of some men'.[170]

Important though these insights are for the role of women both in the early Christian communities and the church today, our primary interest at this

167. Frank Anthony Spina, *The Faith of the Outsider: Exclusion and Inclusion in the Biblical Story* (Grand Rapids: Eerdmans, 2005), pp. 137-59; quotation from p. 159.

168. For further discussion, see the commentaries, for example, Lincoln, *The Gospel according to Saint John*, who deals with it in an Appendix, pp. 524-36; both Brown, *The Gospel according to John*, pp. 332-38, and Keener, *The Gospel of John*, vol. 1, pp. 735-38, consider it inauthentic, but still include it within their main commentary.

169. For an interesting collection of essays on this, see Larry J. Kreitzer and Deborah W. Rooke (eds.), *Ciphers in the Sand: Interpretations of the Woman Taken in Adultery* (John 7.53–8.11) (Sheffield: Sheffield Academic Press, 2000).

170. Schneiders, 'Women in the Fourth Gospel and the Role of Women in the Contemporary Church', p. 142; for further discussion of the role of women in the fourth gospel, see Edwards, *Discovering John*, pp. 106-12; Martin Scott, *Sophia and the Johannine Jesus*, JSNTSS 71 (Sheffield: Sheffield Academic Press, 1992), esp. pp. 174-252; Robert Gordon Maccini, *Her Testimony Is True: Women as Witnesses according to John*, JSNTSS 125 (Sheffield: Sheffield Academic Press, 1996); Conway, *Men and Women in the Fourth Gospel*.

point is in John's depiction of the character of Jesus in his treatment of women. But it is the same for men — or at least for marginalized and excluded ones. After the encounters with Nicodemus and the Samaritan woman, Jesus goes to the pool by the Sheep Gate in Jerusalem where there was a paralyzed man who had been ill for thirty-eight years (5.1-5). Jesus' knowledge is demonstrated, as John tells us that he 'knew that he had been there a long time' (5.6). Culpepper notes that unlike the two previous signs where the suppliant made the request (2.3; 4.47), here 'Jesus initiates the exchange with the question, "Do you want to be healed?"' To us this may seem like a daft question — but it fits in with his gently teasing questioning to elicit a response which we noticed with the women. As Culpepper concludes, 'From what Jesus says and does we gain a distinct impression of his sovereign manner and his concern for the physical and spiritual needs of the man at the pool'.[171] This care for the individual takes priority over the fact that it was a Sabbath (5.9-10), and when this causes difficulties for the healed man carrying his mat, once again it is Jesus who takes the initiative in going to find him in the temple (5.14).

The same pattern emerges with the blind man, coming after the woman taken in adultery, and Jesus' claim to be 'the light of the world' during Tabernacles (8.1-11, 12).[172] The themes of light and blindness echo through the chapter as the blind man sees for the first time and the Pharisees refuse to accept it, journeying into their own blindness at the end (9.1-41).[173] For our purposes here, once again we note how Jesus takes the initiative, refusing to be distracted by the disciples' theological discussion of sin and healing the man instead to demonstrate that 'as long as I am in the world, I am the light of the world' (9.5). The way the man then witnesses for Jesus to the Pharisees 'parallels the Samaritan woman . . . in terms of his emerging faith, he functions as the woman's male counterpoint in the narrative'.[174] From the point of view of the character of Jesus, John notes that 'Jesus heard that they had driven him out, and when he found him' he continues his gentle questioning to elicit the final response of faith, 'Lord, I believe' (9.35-38).

After this consistent depiction of Jesus undertaking his mission to bring

171. R. Alan Culpepper, 'John 5.1-18: A Sample of Narrative Critical Commentary', in *The Gospel of John as Literature*, ed. Stibbe, pp. 193-207, quotations from p. 203.

172. For another comparison of these two stories, see Jeffrey L. Staley, 'Stumbling for the Dark, Reaching for the Light: Reading Character in John 5 and 9', in *The Fourth Gospel from a Literary Perspective*, ed. Culpepper and Segovia, *Semeia* 53, pp. 55-80.

173. See James L. Resseguie, 'John 9: A Literary-Critical Analysis', in *Literary Interpretations of Biblical Narratives*, ed. K. Gros Louis, vol. 2 (Nashville: Abingdon, 1982), repr. in *The Gospel of John as Literature*, ed. Stibbe, pp. 115-22; also Rensberger, *Overcoming the World*, pp. 41-49.

174. Conway, *Men and Women in the Fourth Gospel*, p. 135.

the divine love to individual men and women, especially going to find those who are marginalized, John's biographical narrative brings this to a climax with the debate about leadership in chap. 10, which is set during the festival of Dedication, commemorating the Maccabean leaders from the mid–second century BC (10.22).[175] Jesus' claim is to be the Good Shepherd, who knows his own sheep and cares for them, even to the point of laying down his life (10.3-4, 11-15). This is exactly what he has shown in his knowledge and treatment of the various marginalized characters in the first half of the gospel. Such caring leadership is then contrasted with others who are 'thieves and robbers' and the 'hired hand' who 'does not care for the sheep' (10.1, 8, 10, 12-13); it is hard not to see John contrasting Jesus' care for individuals with the Jewish leaders who oppose him and 'cast out' those whom he helps.

Thus although John's narrative is very different from the Synoptics' pericopae about Jesus as 'friend of sinners', in fact his biographical portrait of Jesus, and especially the way he seeks out and helps those in need on the margins, is very consonant with it, as the incarnate divine love reaches out to everyone.

b. Discipleship in a mixed community?

The popular image of the Johannine community as a small, narrow sect is hardly a good model for our inclusive community, but once again it may be that there is more to it on further investigation. John uses the term 'disciple' nearly eighty times, more often than any other gospel, but, like Luke, he has a broader interest: 'the twelve' occur on only two occasions (6.67-71; 20.24), and 'apostle' never appears. The first people to 'follow' (a keyword for John's understanding of discipleship) Jesus are disciples of John the Baptist, one of whom, Andrew, also brings his brother, Simon Peter; similarly, after Jesus calls Philip, Philip brings Nathanael (1.35-51). As just noted above, throughout John's account of Jesus' ministry thereafter we have a sequence of individuals who make their varying responses of faith in Jesus, and presumably therefore count as 'disciples'. In the middle of the first half of the gospel we are told that 'a large crowd kept following him' and are then fed (6.1-14). However, Jesus' teaching about being the bread of life provokes a major crisis of decision: 'Because of this many of his disciples turned back and no longer went about with

175. See *The Shepherd Discourse of John 10 and Its Context,* eds. Beutler and Fortna; and Robert Kysar, 'Johannine Metaphor — Meaning and Function: A Literary Case Study of John 10:1-18', in *The Fourth Gospel from a Literary Perspective,* ed. Culpepper and Segovia, *Semeia* 53, pp. 81-111.

him'. In the only time when the 'twelve' are mentioned during Jesus' ministry, it is Peter who speaks for them in declaring his faith in Jesus as 'the Holy One of God' (6.66-71). Despite this mention of the faithful following of the twelve, the disciples play little role during the rest of his ministry until the last supper, where Jesus washes their feet and gives them his farewell discourses (13–17). After his resurrection, Jesus again takes the initiative to comfort Mary (20.11-18), to give them all his peace when they are frightened of 'the Jews' (20.19-23), to rekindle faith in Thomas (20.24-29) and to restore Peter after his denial (21.15-19).[176]

It is significant that Jesus' last words to Peter are the same as in his opening call, 'Follow me' (21.19, 22; cp. 1.43). If Peter acts as the group's spokesman in 6.68-69 and is restored to leadership at the end, there is also the shadowy figure of the disciple 'whom Jesus loved' who appears reclining next to Jesus' bosom at the Last Supper (13.23-26), gets Peter into the high priest's house (18.15-17), is the only disciple at the crucifixion and the one to whom Jesus commits his own mother (19.25-27, 35), and is the first to reach the empty tomb and believe (20.2-8); Jesus even tells Peter at the end that this disciple's fate is none of his business (21.20-23). Furthermore, he is the eyewitness of the crucifixion and the author or authority behind the gospel (21.24-25). Traditionally, this disciple has been identified with John, son of Zebedee, never named here but only referred to in 21.2. Much has been made in Johannine scholarship of a possible rivalry between Peter and the Beloved Disciple, even standing for competition between the 'Johannine community' and 'apostolic Christians': after all, Peter has to ask him to ask Jesus who is the betrayer (13.23-26), and is only admitted to the high priest's courtyard at his instigation (18.16). He is present at the crucifixion when Peter is absent after his denial (18.15-18, 25-27), outruns Peter to reach the tomb and is the first to believe (20.4, 8).[177] On the other hand, both are shown together as significant disciples among the group of Jesus' followers. Edwards is typically forthright in dismissing some supposed reconstructions: 'The idea of

176. For further discussion of discipleship in John, see Edwards, *Discovering John*, pp. 98-112; Fernando F. Segovia, '"Peace I Leave with You; My Peace I Give to You": Discipleship in the Fourth Gospel', in *Discipleship in the New Testament*, ed. Fernando F. Segovia (Philadelphia: Fortress, 1985), pp. 76-102; Melvyn R. Hillmer, 'They Believed in Him: Discipleship in the Johannine Tradition', in *Patterns of Discipleship in the New Testament*, ed. Richard N. Longenecker (Grand Rapids: Eerdmans, 1996), pp. 77-97.

177. See, for example, Bultmann, *The Gospel of John: A Commentary*, pp. 484-85, 685; Brown, *The Community of the Beloved Disciple*, pp. 82-85; Conway, *Men and Women in the Fourth Gospel*, pp. 163-99; G. F. Snyder, 'John 13:16 and the Anti-Petrinism of the Johannine Tradition', *Biblical Research* 16 (1971), pp. 5-15; T. V. Smith, *Petrine Controversies in Early Christianity*, WUNT 15 (Tübingen: Mohr Siebeck, 1985).

the Johannine 'community' at loggerheads with other Christians is a scholarly construct arising from a surfeit of sociological speculation'![178]

In fact, not only does the group of disciples contain Peter and the Beloved Disciple, but the others who follow or respond in faith make interesting bedfellows if we follow the sequence from a Pharisee like Nicodemus to the Samaritan woman, from the woman in taken in adultery and the blind man who stands up for Jesus against the Jewish authorities to a good Jewish family like Mary, Martha and Lazarus. Such a broad social mixture, together with the absence of any obvious concern for hierarchy, has led Rensberger to note how 'the community thus appears as an egalitarian brotherhood, without distinctions of rank or dignity'. Rather than 'brotherhood', John's positive treatment of women means that Nissen prefers to talk of 'an egalitarian fellowship', Hays of 'the egalitarian character of the Johannine community' and Anderson of 'the egalitarian presentation of women in John'.[179] Ringe's treatment of the 'social composition' of the community adds to the mix of ethnicity and gender the important dimension of economic status and the marginalized.[180] Thus Blount sees in John's gospel hope 'for the African American community and all oppressed communities like it that true change begins with faith'.[181] If the discourse about the Good Shepherd is taken as programmatic for John's understanding of Jesus' concern for his flock, it is significant that he also says: 'I have other sheep that do not belong to this fold. I must bring them also, and they will listen to my voice. So there will be one flock, one shepherd' (10.16). After the inclusion of Samaritans, women, the paralyzed and blind, the outcast and the marginalized, it all comes to a head when some Greeks approach Philip and Andrew (note their Greek names) to ask, 'Sir, we wish to see Jesus' (12.20-22). What is interesting is that Jesus sees this as somehow the culmination, the trigger which means that 'the hour has come for the Son of Man to be glorified'; it takes us straight to his death which will 'bear much fruit' (12.23-26). Despite the popular caricature of the introverted Johannine sect, in fact this gospel depicts a multi-ethnic, socially variegated and all-inclusive community as both the object and achievement of Jesus in his mission to bring the divine love into the world.[182]

178. Edwards, *Discovering John*, p. 102.

179. Rensberger, *Overcoming the World*, p. 148; Nissen, 'Community and Ethics in the Gospel of John', p. 210; Hays, *Moral Vision of the NT*, p. 155; Anderson, *The Fourth Gospel and the Quest for Jesus*, p. 166.

180. Ringe, *Wisdom's Friends*, pp. 14-18.

181. Blount, *Then the Whisper Put on Flesh*, p. 118; see also Rensberger, 'The Gospel of John and Liberation', in *Overcoming the World*, chap. 6, pp. 107-34.

182. For another treatment of this area, see Fernando F. Segovia, 'Inclusion and Exclusion in John 17: An Intercultural Reading', in *What Is John?* vol. 2, ed. Segovia, pp. 183-209.

Thus we have an apparent contradiction between the fourth gospel's exclusive sectarianism and hostility to outsiders like 'the Jews' on the one hand, and his depiction of the mixed community which is brought into being in response to God's love in Jesus on the other. For Kysar, this poses the obvious question as it 'focuses on the exclusive versus inclusive tension of the Gospel's narrative. In a remarkable way, this Gospel often sounds so very exclusive and sectarian (e.g., love only *one* another). But it also witnesses to a radical inclusion of at least some of the socially marginalized (for instance, the Gospel's attention to women and Samaritans). But in this ironic contradiction the Fourth Gospel may provide sanction and empowerment for *either* the church's inclusive stance *or* exclusive posture toward others. Which will it be?'[183] Similarly, Lieu concludes her study of anti-Judaism with the challenge: 'How can the convictions of Christology, of the reality of good and evil, of divine sovereignty and guidance, be affirmed in a way which respects the 'otherness' of others; how can the Church maintain its true identity when it has access to power as well as when it is oppressed?'[184]

The answer to this, like everything else in this gospel, must lie in Lieu's opening phrase, 'the convictions of Christology', which takes us back to our own insistence on John's biographical portrait of Jesus as the divine love which brings truth. The previous section noted the tension between the negative attitude to 'the world', when it opposes the one whom God has sent, and the positive fact that it is still 'the world' which God loves and sends his Son and his church to save. The 'radically inclusive' and socially mixed community which the divine love brings into being can only fall into 'exclusive sectarianism' when it forgets the divine love which is its life, as depicted in John's narrative. Carter concludes his study, 'I would add that this gospel, even at times despite itself, provides the central criterion by which we might do this discernment. Consistent with its central theological and Christological affirmations, what manifests God's life-giving, loving, and liberating purposes should guide our thinking

183. Robert Kysar, 'Coming Hermeneutical Earthquake in Johannine Interpretation', in *What Is John?* vol. 1, ed. Segovia, pp. 185-89, quotation from p. 188, his italics; similarly, writing on the tendency to 'label "other" groups instruments of evil', as in the stigmatization of "the Jews" in John's gospel and the opponents in the epistles, Kysar says, 'The most serious issue facing the church and our culture is how we perceive and relate to those "others" who are in one way or another different from us — i.e. what we take to be the majority', Kysar, 'The "Others" in Johannine Literature', chap. 14 in Kysar, *Voyages with John: Charting the Fourth Gospel*, pp. 227-35, quotations from pp. 233-35; see, similarly, R. Alan Culpepper, 'Inclusivism and Exclusivism in the Fourth Gospel', in the collection to honour Robert Kysar edited by John Painter, R. Alan Culpepper, and Fernando F. Segovia, *Word, Theology, and Community in John*, pp. 85-108.

184. Lieu, 'Anti-Judaism in the Fourth Gospel', in *Anti-Judaism and the Fourth Gospel*, ed. Bieringer, Pollefyt and Vandecasteele-Vanneuville, p. 143.

and shape our practices. This gospel offers, then, both an affirmation of the distinctive identity of the Christian community and an active embracing of the world so as to manifest God's love and life'.[185] It is not enough for the mixed community simply to 'love one another' within the divine love: our central argument about the biographical narrative requires us to respond to the example of Jesus by imitating his love for the community and for the world. Finally, therefore, we must turn to this *mimesis*.

c. Jesus as an example for imitation

John is the only gospel to use the actual word 'example', ὑπόδειγμα, which occurs in the famous story about Jesus washing his disciples' feet: 'So if I, your Lord and Teacher, have washed your feet, you also ought to wash one another's feet. For I have set you an example, that you also should do as I have done to you' (13.14-15). The context for this action and the saying come at the start of the chapter with Jesus' knowledge of his impending death and his love for his disciples: 'Now before the festival of the Passover, Jesus knew that his hour had come to depart from this world and go to the Father. Having loved his own who were in the world, he loved them to the end' (13.1). It is interesting to note how this verse picks up so many of the themes we have noticed throughout this study, including a festival of 'the Jews', namely Passover, John's interest in time and 'the hour', his attitude towards 'the world', his use of 'his own' — and most importantly, the stress on Jesus as the bringer of divine love, who loves even to the ultimate sacrifice. As the supreme demonstration of his love, he then takes a towel and basin and washes his disciples' feet in the manner of a servant.[186]

For our purposes here, what is crucial is the interpretation Jesus gives to his action afterwards as 'an example', ὑπόδειγμα, for his followers to emulate in their behaviour. Like most interpreters, Léon-Dufour connects it to the 'new commandment' to 'love one another as I have loved you' which follows shortly (13.34; 15.12); he also draws attention to the root meaning of the word from (ὑπο)δείκνυμι, to show, reveal or explain, so that this is a 'showing' of Jesus' love, and he then suggests that 'we might paraphrase Jesus' words this way: "By

185. Carter, *John: Storyteller, Interpreter, Evangelist*, p. 222.
186. See John Christopher Thomas, *Footwashing in John 13 and the Johannine Community*, JSNTSS 61 (Sheffield: Sheffield Academic Press, 1991) for a thorough treatment of the footwashing, its antecedents in the Jewish and Graeco-Roman environment, an historical reconstruction and its implications for the church and the sacraments of baptism and the Eucharist; interestingly, however, it appears not to contain any discussion of the ethical implications for the imitation of Jesus!

acting in this way, I enable you to act the same".[187] This fits in with our suggestion about the new commandment, that what was 'new' was how Jesus provides both a 'motive and power' for ethical action. While this may be the only time John mentions 'example' explicitly, it gives a clue to the interpretation of his biographical portrait of Jesus throughout the gospel. Thus Schrage notes that 'other soteriological and christological passages in John also introduce a call to *mimesis* (see, e.g., 12:25-26 following 12:24)'.[188] This is true not only of the gospel, but also into the letters (e.g., 1 John 2.6; 3.3, 7, 16). As Collins concludes, 'Thus it would seem not only legitimate but exegetically imperative to speak of an ethics of imitation with respect to the Johannine formulation of the love commandment. The ethics of imitation is not foreign to Johannine thought.'[189]

Nor is the example to be imitated merely the physical act of washing people's feet. Culpepper's analysis shows how ὑπόδειγμα is used particularly in the Septuagint as an 'example of how to die a good death' (2 Macc. 6.28; see also 2 Macc. 6.31 and 4 Macc. 17.22-23) or of Enoch as 'an example of repentance to all generations' (Sir. 44.16): 'The occurrence of the term in these significant passages shows that one of the established contexts in which it was used was in accounts of exemplary deaths which served as models for others to follow.'[190] This passage about the footwashing and Jesus' instruction to his disciples to 'do as I have done to you' leads naturally into the 'new commandment' to 'love one another, just as I have loved you' (13.34-35). Peter shows how he has understood this, and the hints about death, by offering to lay down his life for his master, even if Jesus' response is to warn him of his coming denial (13.36-38). In this respect, the example seen in John's biographical portrait of the love of God becoming incarnate in Jesus even to the point of the ultimate sacrifice reminds us of Paul; he also used a biographical narrative about Jesus' incarnation for the purpose of ethical imitation: 'Have the same mind which is yours in Christ Jesus, who, though he was in the form of God, . . . humbled himself and became obedient to the point of death — even death on a cross' (Phil. 2.1-8).

The explication of the example as self-sacrificial reappears in the second version of the love command, which again gives the definition of such love as 'to lay down one's life for one's friends' (John 15.12-13). Jesus goes on to define 'friends' as 'you are my friends if you do what I command you' (15.14-15). This

187. Xavier Léon-Dufour, *To Act according to the Gospel* (Peabody, MA: Hendrickson, 2005), p. 127.

188. Schrage, *The Ethics of the NT*, p. 307.

189. Collins, 'A New Commandment I Give to You', p. 118.

190. R. Alan Culpepper, 'The Johannine *Hypodeigma*: A Reading of John 13', in *The Fourth Gospel from a Literary Perspective*, ed. Culpepper and Segovia, *Semeia* 53, pp. 133-52; quotations from pp. 142-43.

takes us back to our previous discussion about John's attitude to the law and 'keeping my commands' when we noted above that such commands were never defined. Now we can see that we do not need a definition, or any specific ethical commandments, since they are now explicated by his example of footwashing and self-sacrificial love. According to Hartin, this 'becomes the paradigm for the way in which believers of all ages are called to keep Jesus' command and remain in his love'. Furthermore, Hartin stresses how 'the ethical model which the farewell discourses emphasise is one of relationship-response'. This fits well into our basic argument that both the historical Jesus and the rest of the New Testament are more about seeking a response of faith than in giving moral instructions. John's portrait of how Jesus handled the various individuals, especially the vulnerable, which we studied above, provides the surrounding biographical narrative to demonstrate this 'example'. Thus Hartin concludes, 'The ethical dimension is at the very heart of the narrative. . . . The ethical life of the Christian always remains a response to what Jesus has done on their behalf. . . . In this way they imitate the self-sacrificing love of Jesus and it is this self-sacrifice which gives content to the love that is required.'[191]

Therefore this mimetic purpose is at the heart of John's biographical account of Jesus as the one who brings God's love into the world as he teaches the divine truth and ultimately lives out that love in the ultimate sacrifice. Even if the Synoptics' phrase 'friend of sinners' is absent, John's careful portrait of how Jesus treats individuals and encourages them to respond in faith coheres with it. Furthermore, the community of the disciples is made of a disparate group who respond and follow. Some historical and sociological reconstructions of John's community may appear sectarian and exclusive, but following Jesus' example in the footwashing and obeying his 'new commandment' mean that the community who 'love one another' must always be inclusive and open to the rest of the world. For John, Jesus is the revealer who not only teaches us the truth of God, but also shows us what the divine love is like, so that we can imitate him and so participate in the divine life.

6. Conclusion

At first sight, John appears very different from the Synoptic gospels with the absence of the kingdom of God and Jesus' parables and exorcisms, and no great blocks of ethical teaching in the manner of the Sermon on the Mount. Instead,

191. Hartin, 'Remain in Me (John 15:5). The Foundation of the Ethical and Its Consequence in the Farewell Discourses', pp. 354-55.

this is all replaced by John's high Christology and a realized eschatology, which seems to result in an introverted exclusive sectarian group which is opposed both to Judaism and the world, and which has no ethical instruction beyond a narrow love for other members of the community. Therefore it is little wonder that many people seem to think that John has no moral teachings and little relevance for Christian ethics today.

However, studying John at a little more depth has shown quite the opposite to be the case. Yes, the fourth gospel is very different, and yet at the same time we have discovered just another reinterpretation of our basic thesis. Like the other gospels, John is a biographical narrative, where Christology is absolutely central. In the fourth gospel, Jesus is depicted as the love of God, coming to dwell among human beings to bring them his divine truth. He teaches the crowds and seeks out individuals, especially among the marginalized who respond to him in faith. Unfortunately, this mission also provokes hostile reactions which lead to his death on the cross. Most historical reconstructions of the circumstances of the gospel's production and first circulation consider that this was also true for the evangelist's community, who suffered persecution, particularly as they were undergoing the painful separation from the synagogue after the Jewish war and the destruction of Jerusalem. Such circumstances help to explain both the gospel's stress on realized eschatology and its attitude towards Judaism and the world. Nonetheless, this can be overemphasized, as the gospel still has both a future dimension and a positive attitude towards all people and the world as the object of God's saving love in Jesus. Although the gospel is highly Jewish in its background, such is the impact of the new life brought by Jesus that it fulfils and replaces all the former ways, painful though that might be for some. Everything is now subordinated under the 'new commandment' to love one another as he has loved us, which is why the gospel does not need specific ethical instruction. Finally, John's careful portrait of how Jesus treated individuals and the mixed, inclusive nature of his community form the perfect backdrop for his ultimately mimetic purpose in writing this biographical narrative that we should follow Jesus' example of self-sacrificial love within a mixed inclusive community of others who are also responding to his call and reaching out to his world.

In this respect, John is very much in line not only with the other three gospels, but also with the rest of the New Testament, in Luke's portrait of Paul's example in Acts 20.35, Paul's own appeals to 'be imitators of me, as I am of Christ' (1 Cor. 11.1) and Peter's concern both for the example of Jesus' own suffering and for the example of church leaders (1 Pet. 2.21; 5.1-4). An inclusive approach to New Testament ethics through the imitation of Jesus embraces all the canonical witnesses that we might know the divine truth and love and share it with the whole of creation.

VIII. Apartheid: An Ethical and Generic Challenge to Reading the New Testament

Throughout this book, we have been arguing for the importance of genre in the interpretation of texts in general, and especially for the books of the New Testament. None of them are written in the genre of ethical treatises, and it has been suggested that the common practice of quoting just the ethical teachings or Jesus' and Paul's sayings about moral issues without regard to their context within the gospels and letters is a genre mistake. Instead, we have privileged a biographical reading on the grounds that this is the genre of the four gospels, which have pride of place at the start of the New Testament canon, even if they were written towards the end of its period. Also, it is this biographical genre which gives us access to the person of the historical Jesus through the evangelists' making use of the Graeco-Roman interest in preserving a narrative account of a person's words and deeds, their teachings and their activities. A similar concern for a teacher's pronouncements and his behaviour can be found in the rabbinic material, especially with their interest in *ma'aseh*, or precedent. Since the whole of the New Testament, as well as the history of Christianity itself, flows from the 'Jesus-event', his life and ministry, death and resurrection, this is where any investigation has to be begin, by reporting on the earliest archaeological layer. By undertaking such an ancient biographical reconstruction of Jesus' words and deeds, we discovered that his rigorous and demanding teaching was actually set within a narrative of his open acceptance of those who responded to his preaching of the sovereign rule of God and, as a consequence, joined the inclusive community of those who were also seeking to follow and imitate his example as his disciples.

Our later analysis of the four canonical gospels has demonstrated how each evangelist retells that story to fit their particular redactional interests and to

347

form their portrait of Jesus. Therefore, *Christology* is crucial to their interpretation, arising directly from the biographical genre of the gospels. However, it is significant that this same combination of deeds and words, teaching and open acceptance within an inclusive community, was found to be common to all four accounts. The aim of *mimesis,* to imitate the central character in his deeds and words, was a common purpose in classical biography; for the gospels, this becomes the call to discipleship, keeping Jesus' teachings and following his example within the new, mixed community of all who respond. Paul comes between Jesus and the gospels, both in historical sequence and in the course of our study, but we have argued that he does not interrupt it. While his letters may be written in a different epistolary genre, they also presume the basic biographical narrative of the whole Jesus-event, what God has accomplished through his life, death and resurrection. Here too, therefore, Christology is central for interpreting Paul's teaching in his letters. Furthermore, Paul himself models the same combination of deeds and words, giving his readers demanding teaching, while appealing to them to follow his example of imitating Jesus by accepting each other within his early communities.

We noted in the opening survey in the first chapter that it was surprisingly rare for writers on New Testament ethics to include Jesus. J. T. Sanders, Schrage and Verhey are the three main exceptions, all of whom begin with Jesus; they are also the only scholars who then go on to consider all the books of the New Testament, including the other letters and Revelation.[1] The other major exponents, such as Hays, Matera, Houlden, Marxsen, Gerhardsson and Blount, not only exclude Jesus, but they also concentrate upon the gospels and Paul.[2] We have agreed fervently with the former about the importance of starting with Jesus, but we shall not follow their example into the rest of the canon. Like the gospels and Paul, these books are also not written in ethical genres: in addition to the various letters, Hebrews is more like a theological treatise or sermon,

1. J. T. Sanders, *Ethics in the New Testament* (London: SCM, 1975; 2nd edn. 1986); W. Schrage, *The Ethics of the New Testament* (German edn. Göttingen: Vandenhoeck & Ruprecht, 1982; trans. David E. Green, Philadelphia: Fortress, 1988); Allen Verhey, *The Great Reversal: Ethics and the New Testament* (Grand Rapids: Eerdmans, 1984).

2. Richard B. Hays, *The Moral Vision of the New Testament: A Contemporary Introduction to New Testament Ethics* (San Francisco: HarperSanFrancisco/Edinburgh: T&T Clark, 1996); F. J. Matera, *New Testament Ethics* (Louisville: Westminster John Knox, 1996); J. L. Houlden, *Ethics and the New Testament* (Oxford: Oxford University Press, 1973, and frequent reprints, e.g., Edinburgh: T&T Clark, 1992); W. Marxsen, *New Testament Foundations for Christian Ethics,* trans. O. C. Dean, Jr. (Minneapolis: Fortress/Edinburgh: T&T Clark, 1993); B. Gerhardsson, *The Ethos of the Bible,* trans. S. Westerholm (Philadelphia: Fortress, 1981/London: DLT, 1982); Brian K. Blount, *Then the Whisper Put on Flesh: New Testament Ethics in an African American Context* (Nashville: Abingdon, 2001); Houlden does include James, while Revelation features in Hays and Blount.

while Revelation is an example of apocalyptic writing. Therefore, it is more difficult to find biographical narrative therein.

Of course, they are not without some ethical material: thus Schrage notes, 'No other New Testament document is as dominated by ethical questions as the Epistle of James'[3] — but Jesus is mentioned only twice (Jas. 1.1; 2.1). The *haustafel* tradition recurs in 1 Peter with instructions about the emperor, governors, slaves, wives and husbands (1 Pet. 2.13–3.7), while the risen Christ's letters to the seven churches of Asia Minor include various comments about morality (Rev. 2-3). With the exception of James, they contain a range of Christologies, from 'the apostle and high priest of our confession' and 'pioneer and perfecter of our faith' (Heb. 3.1 and 12.2) to the suffering Jesus, the victim who shed his blood for us (Heb. 9.11-14; 1 Pet. 2.21-25; Rev. 5.6, 7.14; 19.13). The other epistles are too small to enable us to build up as clear a picture of their assumed underlying narrative as is possible with Paul. Nonetheless, there is still the same call for the imitation of Jesus: Hebrews appeals to its readers to 'consider Jesus', to respond and follow his example (12.2-3; see also 3.7-14), as well becoming 'imitators of those who through faith and patience inherit the promises' (6.12; 13.7). In the manner of *ma'aseh*, 1 Peter points to the 'example' of Christ who suffered for us, and draws upon the Holiness Code for imitation, 'be holy for I am holy' (1 Pet. 2.21-25; 1.15-16). Revelation comforts and strengthens those who are being persecuted with the vision of the martyrs who have followed Jesus' example of self-sacrifice as 'they have washed their robes and made them white in the blood of the Lamb' (Rev. 7.9-17). Thus, while we cannot apply our method to these books in its entirety, we can still demonstrate the same concentration upon the person of Jesus, a similar concern for his deeds and words, and also the appeal to emulate his example as part of Christian discipleship, all of which will lead to the later tradition of the *imitatio Christi*.

This book has provided a different and distinctive approach to New Testament ethics. Rather than merely abstracting verses of ethical teaching from the wider context, which particularly misses the surrounding narrative component, our approach requires the text to be read holistically within an equally open and inclusive community of disciples who are prepared both to grapple with Jesus' teaching and to follow his example in accepting others. This takes us straight into hermeneutics, the science of interpreting texts, named after Hermes, the messenger of the gods who interpreted between the divine and the human realms. Such a task raises many issues of interpretation, cultures, approaches and methodologies, involving the use of texts and contexts, issues and principles, themes and worldviews, as people seek to claim to be 'biblical' or

---

3. Schrage, *Ethics of the NT*, p. 281.

'scriptural'. This claim is central to many major ethical debates today, not least those about the ordination and consecration of women to the offices of church leadership, and about human sexuality which are going on in governing bodies of the Anglican church such as the General Synod of the Church of England, the General Convention of the Episcopal Church of the USA, or the Lambeth Conference of Anglican Bishops.

However, it is not confined either to these topics nor to the Anglican church: any church or group of Christians who claim to follow Jesus and to be faithful to the Bible have to face this hermeneutical challenge in dealing with any ethical or moral issue. To illustrate this point, we will examine the use of the Bible under apartheid in South Africa as a 'test-case' or 'thought-laboratory' for ethical hermeneutics. There are three main reasons for adopting this as a case study.

The first is that interpreting the Bible really mattered in this context. About the only thing that both or all sides agreed upon was the importance of the Bible, even if they could not agree on what they thought it was saying! South Africa had developed as a deeply Christian country, with about three quarters of the population involved in some form of church. The dominant tradition, among the Afrikaners at least, was Reformed, most obviously in the Dutch Reformed Church (DRC or NGK in Afrikaans), but also including many other reformed groups. Therefore the Bible was at its heart, along with the centrality of debate about the law in Lutheran tradition. It was important that apartheid had a 'biblical' basis, as is seen in the official DRC Report.[4] The Nationalist Government saw themselves as Christians, called and chosen by God, and a bastion against atheistic communism. However, Willem Vorster argued that often the pro-apartheid thinking demonstrated in publications like the newspaper *Beeld* claimed to be 'biblical' or 'scriptural' 'without argumentation or substance'; this was treating the Bible as a 'coat-hanger' onto which any view was hung — but the Bible is 'just not that kind of book'. The use of terms like 'biblical' is often just a useful way of raising the noise level and claiming authority for one's own point of view.[5] On the other hand, the principal voices of opposition came from the churches, notably Desmond Tutu, Archbishop of Cape Town 1986-96,

---

4. *Human Relations and the South African Scene in the Light of Scripture,* Dutch Reformed Church, Cape Town–Pretoria, 1976. Afrikaans report entitled *Ras, Volk en Nasie en Volkerever-houdinge in die lig van die Skrif,* approved and accepted by the General Synod of the Dutch Reformed Church in October 1974.

5. Willem S. Vorster, 'The Use of Scripture and the NG Kerk: A Shift of Paradigm or of Values?', in *New Faces of Africa: Essays in Honour of Ben (Barend Jacobus) Marais,* ed. J. W. Hofmeyr and W. S. Vorster (Pretoria: UNISA, 1984), pp. 204-19, quotations from pp. 210-12; see also the discussion by D. J. Smit, 'The Ethics of Interpretation — and South Africa', *Scriptura* 33 (1990) 29-43.

but also through many exponents of liberation theology, such as Allan Boesak. In addition, the worldwide condemnation of apartheid was fuelled by the churches and Christians, including the controversial Programme to Combat Racism of the World Council of Churches. All of these also used the Bible to critique apartheid and justify the struggle for liberation. It remains to be seen in this chapter whether their arguments were any more 'biblical' than the government's.

Secondly, the personal and political implications of how one read the Bible were exceptional: it was quite literally a matter of life-and-death, or, in the views of those who gave their lives for the struggle, even more important than that! Beyond the level of individual lives and destinies, the struggle for and against apartheid affected an entire country, and the fate of its many and varied peoples and communities. Internationally, it had an enormous effect upon the rest of Africa, especially neighbouring countries, as well upon international relations and trade, involving multinational companies and the various UN agencies and NGOs. It is hard to think of any other example where the consequences of interpreting the scriptures were more momentous for all concerned personally and for the wider world.

Thirdly, it is a recent contemporary illustration still in living memory, but which is no longer as contentious as it used to be. It was not long ago that it was all over our TV screens, and the research for this book was begun in the mid-1990s in the early years of the new democracy. Those who taught the Bible on both sides of the argument are still alive and active, and I was privileged to meet and interview many of them. However, the extraordinary thing is that everyone, with the exception of a few white supremacists, now accepts that apartheid, and its biblical justification, was wrong. In that respect it is rather like slavery, which all consider now to be wrong and unbiblical; however, the issue was resolved so long ago that no one today really understands how for centuries it was supported by Christian leaders, teachers and biblical experts, who argued against the liberationists' use of the Bible. Yet Meeks and Swartley have demonstrated how the leading interpreters of the Bible in both universities and churches alike were united in providing 'biblical' support for the 'scriptural' doctrine of slavery.[6] In this respect, it is very reminiscent of the situation under apartheid; as Swartley concludes, 'Appeal to the Bible does not in itself guarantee correctness of position. . . . Both sides in the slavery debate used the Bible to

---

6. Wayne A. Meeks, 'The "Haustafeln" and American Slavery: A Hermeneutical Challenge', in E. H. Lovering and J. L. Sumney, *Theology and Ethics in Paul and His Interpreters: Essays in Honor of Victor Paul Furnish* (Abingdon: Nashville, 1996), pp. 232-53; Willard M. Swartley, *Slavery, Sabbath, War and Women: Case Issues in Biblical Interpretation* (Scottdale: Herald, 1983), pp. 31-64.

support their positions.'⁷ Unfortunately, Simon Schama's fascinating account of the history and politics of slavery does not deal with either the biblical justification for slave owning, nor the role scripture played among the abolitionists.⁸ On the other hand, today we have issues like the role of women and homosexuality in the churches, which are extremely contentious: usually, both sides are arguing that they are 'biblical' and that their opponents are merely 'conservatives' or 'liberals', so there is no meeting of minds to debate it, much less agreement. Sadly, suggestions about bringing the different groups together to work out what the scriptures really teach tend to fall on deaf ears!

Given these reasons for using South Africa and the transition from apartheid as our example, we now need finally to turn from our study of the New Testament writings themselves to how we might apply them to today in the light of our study driven by genre and our two main conclusions about imitating Jesus within an open and inclusive community. The bulk of this chapter will examine in turn the different ways in which the Bible was used by all sides under apartheid in South Africa before finally considering the implications of imitating Jesus within an 'open and inclusive community' for those who interpret the scriptures. However, before we can start on the test-case itself and go to the South African example, we need to consider the various scholarly proposals for how we can bridge the gap between the New Testament and today.

1. Using the New Testament today

a. Traditional and authorial controls

Suggestions about the interpretation of scripture go back to the early church with Origen's four levels — the literal, allegorical, moral, and anagogical or mystical — which were also used by John Cassian (360-430). This was later developed in the mediaeval period and can be summed up in Nicholas of Lyra's rhyme:

littera gesta docet
quid credas allegoria
moralis quid agas
quo tendas anagogia.

7. Swartley, *Slavery, Sabbath, War and Women*, pp. 58-59.
8. Simon Schama, *Rough Crossings: Britain, The Slaves and The American Revolution* (London: BBC Worldwide, 2005).

('The literal teaches what was done, the allegorical what you should believe, the moral what you should do, and the anagogical where you are headed'.)[9]

The Reformers were unhappy with anything other than the literal meaning of scripture, and therefore rejected the other levels. So began the development which would lead into the historico-critical method — to find out what the text actually meant in its historical context, drawing on the author's intention if possible. This produced the great stress on *exegesis* — literally, a 'leading out' what is actually there in the text. As Spohn puts it, 'The conversation should begin with the best results of historical method in presenting the original meaning of the text. The meaning of a specific scriptural passage *then* has a controlling influence on its meaning *now*'.[10] This approach treats the text like a 'window' through which we look to see that which lies 'beyond' or 'behind' the text, and it privileges the author and his intention as the proper hermeneutical key to what makes a valid reading.[11] However, this method is now being challenged. Fowl and Jones liken the traditional process to a 'relay race', with people passing on the baton from 'then' to 'now'. However, is it all only in one direction, from then to now? It is more likely to be a dialectic process — developing meaning as we move backwards and forwards between the text and today, in reading and rereading in the light of our experiences.[12]

Furthermore, we have become aware of how difficult it is to ascertain the original meaning. Can we recover the author's intention at all? Many doubt that we can really get back behind the text, to look through the 'window' onto that which lies beyond, such as the author, or the historical Jesus or early church situation. Instead, perhaps the reality is that all we can know is ourselves and the text. Therefore what we think we see *behind* the text through the 'window' is actually just the reflection of our concerns *in front of* the text, like a 'mirror'. This produces *eisegesis*, not exegesis — leading our concerns *into* the text, which is why we find them there. In today's postmodern world, we are all too aware that there is no neutral Archimedian external point from which we read: we all have our presuppositions and ideologies and theological assumptions. Hence, the hermeneutical circle can become a vicious circle, as we read our own prior con-

---

9. See further Stephen Fowl (ed.), *The Theological Interpretation of Scripture: Classic and Contemporary Readings* (Oxford: Blackwell, 1997), chaps. 1–2, esp. p. 29.

10. William C. Spohn, *What Are They Saying about Scripture and Ethics?* (New York: Paulist, 1995, rev. edn.), p. 6, his italics.

11. E. D. Hirsch, Jr., *Validity in Interpretation* (New Haven, CT: Yale University Press, 1967) and *The Aims of Interpretation* (Chicago: University of Chicago Press, 1976).

12. S. E. Fowl and L. G. Jones, *Reading in Communion: Scripture and Ethics in Christian Life* (London: SPCK, 1991), pp. 57-58.

cerns, beliefs and ideas into and then out of text; however, this reading back now enables us to claim that these views are 'scriptural', 'biblical' and so on.[13] Accusations that others were doing precisely this were made by all sides during the apartheid debate, while claiming that they were the ones who were truly 'biblical'. Thus, at the very least we have to begin with self-critical awareness of our starting point, our concerns and presuppositions, and be very careful about claiming to find those reflected in the text as the author's — or even, God's — intentions.

b. From author to reader to audience

Recognizing this, some scholars reject using authorial intention as determinative for meaning and concentrate on ourselves in front of the text. Thus Roland Barthes wrote that 'the birth of the reader must be at the cost of the death of the author'.[14] From this has developed a whole range of 'reader-response criticism' where the reader is determinative of the meaning of a text.[15] There is great debate about the 'ideal' reader who can interpret the text perfectly, the 'real' or actual reader, and the 'implied' reader, a mediating concept of a reader with a certain amount of competence able to recognize the clues to the reading encoded in the text. Thus, the reader may be seen as completely 'in' the text, put there by the author, or 'over' the text and able to impose any reading he or she wishes upon it; a middle position envisages a dialogue between text and reader. Such approaches draw heavily on the work of Wolfgang Iser and Stanley Fish.[16] In response, Kevin Vanhoozer has attempted both to 'resurrect' the author and 'reform' the reader.[17] Once again, this raises questions about what may be considered a 'valid' reading: are all meanings discovered by a reader equally acceptable — and if so, how can one talk of any-

13. See Spohn, *What Are They Saying about Scripture and Ethics?*, pp. 8-9.

14. Roland Barthes, 'La Mort de l'auteur', *Manteia* 5 (1968), ET 'The Death of the Author', in *Image, Music, Text,* trans. Stephen Heath (London: Fontana, 1977), pp. 142-48; quotation from the final words.

15. See *Reader-Response Approaches to Biblical and Secular Texts,* ed. R. Detweiler, *Semeia* 31 (Decatur: Scholars Press/SBL, 1985); Stephen D. Moore, *Literary Criticism and the Gospels: The Theoretical Challenge* (New Haven, CT: Yale University Press, 1989).

16. See Wolfgang Iser, *The Implied Reader: Patterns of Communication in Prose Fiction from Bunyan to Beckett* (Baltimore: Johns Hopkins University Press, 1974); Iser, *The Art of Reading* (Baltimore: John Hopkins University Press, 1978); Stanley Fish, *Is There a Text in This Class? The Authority of Interpretive Communities* (Cambridge, MA: Harvard University Press, 1980).

17. Kevin J. Vanhoozer, *Is There a Meaning in This Text? The Bible, The Reader and the Morality of Literary Knowledge* (Grand Rapids: Zondervan, 1998).

thing being 'biblical' at all? This takes us back to Vorster's criticism of pro-apartheid readings as 'coat-hangers'. One is sometimes reminded of Humpty-Dumpty: "'When I use a word,'" Humpty Dumpty said in a rather scornful tone, "it means just what I choose it to mean — neither more nor less'", and also of Alice's response, "'The question is,'" said Alice, "whether you *can* make words mean so many different things.'"[18]

To guard against such individual interpretations arising from a particular reader's whim, others locate the validity of an interpretation within a particular audience, community or culture. When African biblical scholars were invited to contribute to the first meeting of the SNTS in Africa, they stressed such community readings of the Bible for interpretation. Thus Teresa Okure argued for 'exegetical hermeneutics' rather than for 'hermeneutical exegesis', placing 'the exegesis at the service of the hermeneutics, the application of text to life' to 'marry the best fruits of the historical-critical method with the more liberational and reader response approaches'.[19] Justin Ukpong has developed 'inculturation hermeneutics', which 'does not consider that the meaning of a text is that intended by the author. Rather, it sees meaning as produced in a process whereby the reader *with* his/her community interacts with the text'; the emphasis is not on a personal whim since 'readers are not seen as isolated individuals, but as communities, or as individuals reading *with* communities'.[20] Such methods are an appealing contrast to traditional historical-critical readings, but they are still open to the 'coat-hanger' criticism. After all, the pro-apartheid reading of the New Testament was not an isolated individual reading, but produced within a particular community and validated by that community, namely the Dutch Reformed Church. We will therefore have to return to consider community readings of scripture in more detail in sect. 6 below.

18. Lewis Carroll, *Through the Looking-Glass* (Penguin: Harmondsworth, 1994), p. 87.

19. Teresa Okure, SHCJ, "'I will open my mouth in parables" (Matt. 13.35): A Case for a Gospel-Based Biblical Hermeneutics', *NTS* 46 (2000), pp. 445-63, paper originally given at the SNTS meeting in Pretoria, 4/8/99; see our further discussion, pp. 402-3 below, nn. 172-74.

20. Justin S. Ukpong, 'Reading with the Community: The Workers in the Vineyard Parable (Matt. 20.1-16)', paper given at the SNTS Post Conference, Hammanskraal, 9/8/99, later published in a revised form as 'Bible Reading with a Community of Ordinary Readers', in *Interpreting the New Testament in Africa*, ed. Mary Getui, Tinyiko Maluleke and Justin Ukpong (Nairobi: Acton, 2001), pp. 188-212, see esp. pp. 188-89; see also Justin S. Ukpong, 'Rereading the Bible with African Eyes: Inculturation and Hermeneutics', *JTSA* 91 (June 1995), pp. 3-14.

c. Bringing the two horizons together

Thus we have a gulf between the New Testament and our world today. Looking for the author's intention locates validity of interpretation back behind the text on one side, while stressing the reader or interpreting community keeps us in front of it on this side. To bridge a gap, a suspension bridge needs cables sunk deep into bedrock at both ends. The same is true for hermeneutics: we need to be deeply rooted in both the world of the text and in our own world to bring the two of them together. Some people are engaged in historical analysis at one end, digging up all the foundations, but they may never come back across with any results to use or apply in the modern world. On the other hand, others are deeply committed to contemporary issues and ethical problems, which are then found 'reflected' in the text without recourse to historical reconstruction. Moxnes comments that it is 'more difficult to relate to the New Testament in ethical issues; its statements can not be directly applied to our situation. . . . Instead of a traditional method of "application", it may be more appropriate to speak of "dialogue" with the New Testament as a "significant other".'[21]

Various suggestions have been made about how to bridge this gap. Thus Curran and McCormick propose a fourfold task: to determine the original meaning; to ascertain the meaning in our contemporary world; to relate it to the different levels or approaches in moral theology concerning the use of scripture; and consider how it relates to other sources of ethical or moral knowledge, especially tradition, reason and experience.[22] Nicholas Lash argues for a dialectical process back and forth across the bridge, rather than the model of 'passing on the relay race baton': 'We do not *first* understand the past and *then* proceed to understand the present. The relationship between these two dimensions of our quest for meaning and truth is dialectical: they mutually inform, enable, correct and enlighten each other'.[23]

Thiselton has done us all a great service with his *The Two Horizons*, following Gadamer on the distinct horizons of the text and the horizon of the reader.[24]

---

21. Halvor Moxnes, 'New Testament Ethics — Universal or Particular? Reflections on the Use of Social Anthropology in New Testament Studies', *Studia Theologia* 47 (1993), pp. 153-68; quotation from pp. 163-64.

22. C. E. Curran and R. A. McCormick (eds.), *Readings in Moral Theology No. 4* (New York: Paulist, 1984), pp. vif.

23. N. Lash, 'Interpretation and Imagination', in *Incarnation and Myth: The Debate Continued*, ed. M. D. Goulder (London: SCM, 1979), p. 25.

24. Anthony C. Thiselton, *The Two Horizons: New Testament Hermeneutics and Philosophical Description with Special Reference to Heidegger, Bultmann, Gadamer and Wittgenstein* (Exeter: Paternoster, 1980); see p. 16.

The fusion of the horizons, a real encounter of reader and text, can only take place if the reader recognizes the separate horizons of both the text and his own situation. Premature assimilation, where the reader assimilates the text into his own prior horizons without recognizing its distinctiveness, will leave him trapped in his own perspectives, but under the illusion of having been addressed by the text. No one who takes the Bible at all seriously would want to domesticate it in this way. However, this is precisely Vorster's criticism of the apartheid use of the Bible already described above. To counter this, Thiselton proposes ten models for using the Bible in pastoral theology at the end of his *New Horizons in Hermeneutics,* including narrative, symbols, reader-response, speech-act and socio-critical theory. He argues that we cannot impose any one model onto the Bible and thus concludes with a study of the cross and resurrection to deal with hermeneutical pluralism. An 'anything goes' relativism is not inevitable. The cross and resurrection of Jesus Christ stand as a critique of all of our readings and traditions, and offer us 'the universal horizon of eschatological promise', which transforms believing readers.[25]

Ogletree similarly makes use of Gadamer in his attempt to produce a fusion of the two horizons in three stages. First we have to understand the dominant 'preunderstandings' of ethics or 'the conceptualisations of the moral life in Western thought', which he believes to be three: deontological (universal moral rules, Kant, etc.), consequentialist (utilitarian) and perfectionist (Aristotle and the virtues). Second, we need to subject these preunderstandings to 'the pivotal themes of biblical faith', and only then can we finally move to a 'fusion of the horizons'.[26] However, it can be argued that Ogletree decides his three 'preunderstandings' of ethics first, and then he imposes them onto the biblical text and reads the text in the light of them, 'ordered with reference to these preunderstandings'. This certainly helps them to fuse together!

Finally, Hays draws these sorts of approaches together in proposing a four-fold method of bridging the gap between the New Testament and today:

- *the descriptive task:* this provides a full exegesis of all the relevant texts in the New Testament to explicate them without any premature harmonization.
- *the synthetic task:* this entails bringing all of these texts together; it needs to be comprehensive across the whole canon, and not selective and it will

25. Anthony C. Thiselton, *New Horizons in Hermeneutics* (San Francisco: HarperCollins, 1992), chaps. XV and XVI, esp. pp. 611-19.

26. Thomas W. Ogletree, *The Use of the Bible in Christian Ethics* (Philadelphia: Fortress, 1983), pp. 3-5, 15-18)

need to grapple with the tensions between different texts. Hays uses three focal images to assist this synthesis — community, cross, and new creation.

- *the hermeneutic task:* this is where the gap is crossed, bringing what we have discovered from the first two stages across to our world today; it will involve looking carefully at the different types of texts, with their different modes of appeal, plus how they are used along with other authorities such as tradition, reason and experience.
- *the pragmatic task;* this is when all the above can finally be applied to specific ethical issues today.[27]

Hays' fourfold method is probably the best current account of the method used by many people, although it is not without critics.[28] Therefore, it merits further discussion. Hays' first stage is the descriptive task, but we have already questioned whether he is sufficiently comprehensive in his description of the ethical material in the New Testament in the first part of the book, given his omission of Jesus himself. Equally, in his 'descriptive' sections in the final part of his book where he describes the New Testament's witness on pragmatic issues like divorce, homosexuality, violence, and so forth, he seems ambivalent about the role of historical criticism in exegesis. Thus he begins his descriptive section on 'anti-Judaism' with historical background (pp. 409-11), yet tends to eschew such historical reconstruction elsewhere, stressing the canonical setting instead.[29]

Secondly, Hays' method of taking such contemporary ethical issues to be addressed by the New Testament witnesses can be problematic: Martin questions whether it is really the text which speaks, or Hays' interpretation of the text.[30] Our discussion of exegesis above suggested that it is much more of a dialectical process between text and interpreter. Furthermore, Hays' separate treatment of divorce (which he accepts despite the New Testament's witness against it) and homosexuality (which he rejects despite showing how little New Testament material there is on it) opens his method to charges of inconsistency. If we look instead at the whole area of human sexuality in the New Testament before coming to our modern questions on homosexuality or divorce, we may have a more consistent ethic. This would also allow for further application to other contemporary issues such as polygamy, singleness, and so forth. Similarly, Hays

---

27. Hays, *Moral Vision of the NT,* pp. 3-7.

28. For reviews and discussions, see n. 55 on p. 15 above.

29. See Hays, *Moral Vision of the NT,* pp. 409-11; this criticism is also noted by Watson's review in *Studies in Christian Ethics* 10.2 (1997), pp. 94-99, esp. pp. 96 and 98.

30. See the review by Dale Martin in *JBL* 117 (1998), pp. 358-60, and also Dale B. Martin, *Sex and the Single Savior: Gender and Sexuality in Biblical Interpretation* (Louisville: Westminster John Knox, 2006), pp. 29-31.

recognizes that the five topics chosen do not reflect the main ethical concerns of the New Testament;[31] they arise from his own North American context, with his opening stories in each chapter all rooted in the USA. It is significant that, despite the huge importance of financial issues in the New Testament, Hays has very little on money, poverty and debt beyond a brief consideration of sharing possessions within the church in his concluding chapter.[32]

Furthermore, our discussions of Jesus, Paul and the gospels have all raised questions about Hays' too easy dismissal of 'love' as a key element for New Testament ethics. In the face of plurality and variety within the canon, Hays uses the 'focal images' of community, cross and new creation to pull things together for his second stage of synthesis. In doing so, he is in danger of imposing prior principles upon the text. It is a common criticism from scholars like Hauerwas that such 'mediating principles' stop us from actually hearing the text itself; we shall return to this issue of the use of principles in sect. 3 below. If we must have a 'focal image', perhaps Christology would be better because it arises directly out of the biographical genre of the gospels and fits into the central concerns of all the New Testament writers. The gospels' picture of Jesus as the one who brings the love of God among us saves 'love' from lapsing into Hays' objection that it is 'vapid', and instead incarnates it in a human life.

An alternative response to plurality and variety could use an image from mathematics and the sciences. Faced with a set of various data or results, we can plot them all on a graph as a 'scattergram' and then seek the 'best line fit' which includes as many of the results as possible. In other words, rather than imposing a hypothetical image upon the various data, or reading them in the light of a prior theory, it is better to look for the 'underlying trend', or the 'emerging trajectory', as the 'best line' which connects the greatest majority of the evidence. Then one needs to explain or comment on any results which appear to be particularly far from the line. This suggests that it might be better to look at what the New Testament says about key human moral experiences (rather than specific modern 'problems'). Having gathered together all the relevant material, in all its variety and contradiction, we should not look at it through a predetermined focal image or lens, but look instead for any emerging consensus, or best line fit which connects the majority of the texts — and then give some attention to those verses or passages which seem to deviate from the trajectory.

These various suggestions all recognize the reality of the gulf between the world of the New Testament and our world and the importance of understanding both sides of the gap properly and in their own right. Therefore, we must be

---

31. Hays, *Moral Vision of the NT,* pp. 313-14.
32. Hays, *Moral Vision of the NT,* pp. 464-68.

prepared for some hard work in any attempt to work out what is a truly 'biblical' perspective on something, and build into the process proper dialectic provision which will enable our conclusions to be checked and rechecked. We also have to recognize the variety within the various texts themselves and that different texts in the New Testament may function in different ways, which takes us back to our preoccupation with genre. Therefore it is time to turn to this in more detail to consider the various modes and methods for considering the use of the New Testament in ethics today.

d. Genre and types of ethical material

We have argued throughout this book that genre is the key to the understanding of texts, providing a kind of agreement, often unspoken or even unconscious, between author and audience, to guide their proper interpretation.[33] This is most obviously true for the genre of works taken as a whole — but it is also possible to analyze the genre of smaller sections of text, particularly here with regard to ethics. Many scholars have noted that there are various different genres, types, modes, or methods of ethical material in the New Testament, and they have proposed different lists of them. In recent times, they all seem to go back to Gustafson's 1970 seminal article which distinguished between the use of the 'variety of materials in Scripture' in four main ways, thus:

- *revealed morality:* scripture as moral law to be obeyed — or disobeyed;
- *moral ideals:* which we strive to attain or of which we fall short;
- *analogy:* looking at actions judged right or wrong 'in similar circumstances in the scriptures' as a guide for our behaviour;
- *'a witness to a variety of moral values, moral norms and principles through many different kinds of biblical literature'.*[34]

This last is not a recognition of a particular genre of material, nor a general approach to all the material through an overriding genre, but rather treats scrip-

---

33. See Richard A. Burridge, *What Are the Gospels? A Comparison with Graeco-Roman Biography*, SNTSMS 70 (Cambridge: Cambridge University Press, 1992), esp. pp. 26-54 on genre theory; rev. 2nd edn. (Grand Rapids: Eerdmans, 2004), pp. 25-52.

34. James M. Gustafson, 'The Place of Scripture in Christian Ethics: A Methodological Study', *Interpretation* 24 (1970), 430-55, see esp. pp. 439-44; interestingly, when Gustafson returned to this topic himself in 1997, he decided on a 'reversal of the direction' by beginning with the types of questions which ethics asks and considering how the Bible can be used to answer them, James M. Gustafson, 'The Use of Scripture in Christian Ethics', *Studia Theologia* 51 (1997), pp. 15-29.

ture as a loose collection of moral witnesses to be used alongside other ethical resources such as 'other principles and experiences'; as such it is rather vague.

John Goldingay drew on these distinctions of material to interpret the Old Testament in different ways as *explicit commands, examples* of behaviour, values and principles, an *overall view of reality,* or a *shaping of character.*[35] Thereafter, he returned to this use of genre with four 'models' to approach scripture itself as *witnessing tradition, authoritative canon, inspired word* and *experienced revelation.* These four models reflect the different major genres within the scriptures of narrative, law/torah, prophecy and responses to God in poetry, epistle and apocalyptic, although he does not simply confine the use of each model to its own specific genre.[36] He followed this by arguing that scripture as a whole can also be interpreted as witnessing tradition, authoritative canon, inspired word and experienced revelation.[37] Such an approach to the genres in and of scripture fits in with our concern for the interpretation of the gospels in terms of their genre as ancient biographies with the person of Jesus as the hermeneutical key to their reading, which we have now applied across the New Testament.

W. C. Spohn similarly uses five different ways of reading scripture from the point of view of genre to structure his book: *the command of God,* where the divine call is prescriptive; *a moral reminder* to make us aware of what God created us to be as human beings; *a call to liberation,* to act in commitment for the oppressed; *a call to discipleship,* stressing the character of the moral agent through narrative theology and transforming our 'moral psychology' to a Christian way of acting in community; and *a basis for responding in love,* using the narrative of scripture, especially about Jesus Christ as a normative guide or paradigm for Christian experience and moral practice. In each case, he uses this generic approach as a way of analyzing and critiquing how different theologians and moral philosophical traditions have handled the scriptures.[38]

Richard Longenecker also has a fourfold scheme involving *prescriptive laws,* commandments and ordinances; *universal principles* beneath the laws, applied to changing situations; *scripture as an encounter through the Spirit* to guide a person's ethical direction for the particular moment; and *tactical suggestions* for individual's response in this situation, a 'contextual' or situational ethic. He then analyses these four models on the basis of seven further 'biblical perspectives' in a brave attempt to try to bring them all together into 'prescrip-

---

35. John Goldingay, *Approaches to Old Testament Interpretation* (Leicester: IVP, 1981), chap. 2.

36. John Goldingay, *Models for Scripture* (Grand Rapids: Eerdmans/Exeter: Paternoster, 1994).

37. John Goldingay, *Models for Interpretation of Scripture* (Grand Rapids: Eerdmans/Exeter: Paternoster, 1995).

38. Spohn, *What Are They Saying about Scripture and Ethics?*

tive principles . . . applied to specific situations by the direction and enablement of the Holy Spirit', but which succeeds rather in blurring the different modes.[39]

It is significant that this approach of distinguishing the different types of ethical material in the New Testament also came into South African New Testament scholarship through Jan Botha, who developed them into a similar fourfold model: *a prescriptive approach,* finding propositions, precepts and laws in scripture; looking for *principles or ideals,* which is more of a liberal Protestant approach; *'revealed reality' rather than 'revealed morality',* which he related to Barth's method; and *relationality and responsibility,* which is closer to Niebuhr and Gustafson. The problem which Botha then identified, perhaps drawing on his experience in South Africa, is that 'the results of historical-critical scholarship have shown that what might have been a valid norm in the context of the biblical world does not necessarily mean that it has equal reference and validity today'.[40]

Finally, Hays adapts Gustafson's four types slightly to use in his third stage, that of the hermeneutical task:

- *rules:* 'direct commandments or prohibitions of specific behaviors'.
- *principles:* 'general frameworks of moral consideration'.
- *paradigms:* 'stories or summary accounts of . . . exemplary conduct or negative paradigms'.
- *a symbolic world:* 'through which we interpret reality'.[41]

Furthermore, Hays insists that 'New Testament texts must be granted authority (or not) in the mode in which they speak'. Therefore uncongenial rules must not be avoided by finding a different underlying principle, nor individual examples turned into general rules.[42]

These are all rather similar, with some scholars explicitly acknowledging Gustafson's influence.[43] What is interesting is the way they reinterpret and reapply them to the various forms of literature found in the New Testament. The

39. R. N. Longenecker, *New Testament Social Ethics for Today* (Grand Rapids: Eerdmans, 1984); see his opening chapter, pp. 1-15, quotation from p. 15.

40. Jan Botha, 'The Bible and Ethics', in *Doing Ethics in Context: South African Perspectives,* ed. C. Villa-Vicencio and J. de Gruchy (Cape Town: David Philip/Maryknoll, NY: Orbis, 1994), pp. 36-45; see pp. 40-41.

41. Hays, *Moral Vision of the NT,* p. 209.

42. Hays, *Moral Vision of the NT,* p. 294.

43. Other new versions have continued to appear; see, for example, Charles H. Cosgrove, *Appealing to Scripture in Moral Debate: Five Hermeneutical Rules* (Grand Rapids: Eerdmans, 2002), which develops the five rules of purpose, analogy, countercultural witness, nonscientific scope and moral-theological adjudication.

first three — rules, principles and examples — are common to many of them; Gustafson's rather vaguer fourth grouping is helpfully refined by Goldingay and Hays into an overall biblical worldview. Therefore, we will now try to use this as an amalgamated list to guide our case-study of South Africa:

- Obeying rules and prescriptive commands
- Looking for principles and universal values
- Following examples and paradigms
- Embracing an overall symbolic worldview.

In each mode we will include how they relate to Ogletree's 'preunderstandings of moral philosophy', such as deontological, consequentialist and character and virtue ethics approaches. In particular, our genre-based analysis will consider what sort of texts each approach best suits and how they handle the different genres of ethical material. Then we shall discuss the kinds of problems or difficulties encountered with each type, before going on to examine how the New Testament was used in South Africa in each instance as an example or test-case. Finally, all four of these modes and methods will need to be brought together under the overall umbrella of way of reading together in an open and inclusive community, in order to imitate the example of Jesus as we have seen it develop throughout this book.

2. Obeying rules and prescriptive commands

a. Ethical approach

This approach treats the New Testament as a kind of moral handbook and looks for specific material in prescriptive form or the genre of commands. It is often introduced with the idea of 'for best results, follow the maker's instructions'. Such a rule-based reading of the Bible fits into a deontological approach to ethics, to do with moral duty in terms of Ogletree's analysis. This can be linked back to the moral philosophy of Kant, with his great stress on duty. In New Testament ethics, this attitude has been seen in the approaches of Bonhoeffer and Barth:[44] 'The concept of the command of God includes the concepts: the command of God the Creator, the command of God the Recon-

---

44. Dietrich Bonhoeffer, *Ethics*, ed. Eberhard Bethge (New York: Macmillan, 1955); idem, *The Cost of Discipleship* (New York: Macmillan, 1963); see Spohn's discussion of both Bonhoeffer and Barth, *What Are They Saying about Scripture and Ethics?*, pp. 21-37.

ciler and the command of God the Redeemer'.[45] Here, God is seen as the divine commander: our task is to obey his instructions — or if we disobey, at least, that too is clear. The morality of an action is thus determined by God's commands which it is right to obey and wrong to ignore or flout.

b. Genre and texts

Such an approach works best with material from the Torah and halakhah, law and commandment. These do at least have the genre of direct command. In New Testament terms, such material will be found in the direct instructions, such as Sermon on the Mount, or Pauline injunctions. However, the problem is that these texts then get taken out of their general setting and in particular their generic context. As we saw in the chapter on Matthew, treating the Sermon on the Mount as *the* ultimate section of ethical material not only privileges it above the rest of the gospel, but also misses out on the role this particular discourse plays within the biographical narrative of the gospel. To treat the gospels as though they are a kind of 'new law', or sets of ethical commands, is to make a serious genre mistake. Furthermore, while they do contain some direct moral commands, the interpretation and application of them must always be within the overall biographical genre. Similarly with Paul, we noted that the tendency to treat the 'ethical' material in the chapters at the end of certain epistles separately from his earlier 'theological' chapters led equally to its abstraction on the one hand, and missed its intrinsic connection to the rest of his theology, especially his Christology, on the other.

c. Problems

In taking such a prescriptive approach, we immediately hit the problem of contingency. The ethical material in the Bible is dependent upon the interests, issues and concerns of the time; for example, the Old Testament includes instructions about grazing and water rights, boundary stones, crop rotation and many other issues of concern to a pastoral or an agrarian society. However, the same is also true of the New Testament: the gospels include things like being compelled to carry a Roman legionary's pack one or two miles (Matt. 5.41), while the epistles

---

45. Karl Barth, *Church Dogmatics*, II/2 (Edinburgh: T&T Clark, 1957), p. 549; see Hays' discussion, 'Karl Barth: Obedience to the Command of God', in Hays, *Moral Vision of the NT*, pp. 225-39 and p. 293.

have lots about eating meat offered to idols (Acts 15.20; 1 Cor. 8; 10.18-33; Rev. 2.14, 20) — neither of which is the most pressing concern for Western Christians today. On the other hand, this is matched by an absence of our concerns, such as nuclear war, abortion, embryo research and euthanasia. This reinforces our basic point about the genre of the scriptures: the New Testament is not a general answer book, with all the answers to our ethical dilemmas. However, many of the key issues of human moral experience do appear, such as issues of violence, the state, obedience, power, war and peace; human sexuality, marriage, divorce, relationships; money, wealth and poverty, debt; life and death and the value and meaning of life. We will therefore need to be cautious about applying biblical commands about these areas directly to our contemporary moral debates.

In addition, we have to face the issue of the variety of commands, and any (apparent?) contradictions between them. The sheer breadth of the different cultures and settings in time and space across a millennium provides plenty of scope for variation and contradiction. Before we can use the biblical material, we have to deal with differences between the New Testament and Old Testament over, for example, violence (holy wars versus 'turn the other cheek'), or whether all the laws are now binding on Christians, including things like ceremonial or purity law or circumcision. Similarly, polygamy is accepted in the patriarchal narratives, yet Jesus refers to Gen. 2 on 'one flesh' as God's original intention (Mark 10.6). Even within the New Testament itself, the much smaller time span still is sufficient for variation and contradiction between different books, such as the debate about faith and works in Rom. 4 and Jas. 2. There are even contradictions within one letter, for example, the place of women who are to wear something on their heads to speak in church (1 Cor. 11.5), yet apparently not allowed to speak in church at all (14.34)!

Finally there is the question of which laws are still to be obeyed, and which are no longer relevant. This process is already going on in the New Testament over Old Testament laws such as circumcision, food laws, Sabbaths and festivals; if these are no longer valid in the new situation following the life, death and resurrection of Jesus of Nazareth, how do we decide between such superseded commands and moral instructions which have continuing force for today?

d. South Africa

The use of the Bible to defend apartheid is a good example of the problem of the selectivity of texts, especially those of rules, norms or commands.[46] Back

46. For an account of the history of the rise of apartheid and the churches' involvement in it,

in 1947, Prof. E. P. Groenewald of Pretoria University, writing on 'apartheid and guardianship in the light of Holy Scripture', was clear that apartheid was the will of God as taught in the Bible.[47] This was later set out clearly in the official report of the Dutch Reformed Church. At its heart is God's command in Gen. 1.28 to 'be fruitful and multiply', which, the report argued, included the diversity of peoples, as confirmed in Deut. 32.8-9 and Acts 17.26-27 with 'the boundaries of their territories'.[48] Similarly, Old Testament commands forbidding the marriage of Israelites with other peoples were then used to prohibit mixed marriages in South Africa under article 16 of the Immorality Act.[49] The combination of these instructions and other passages came together over many years to form what Loubser calls 'the Apartheid Bible': 'the totality of biblical texts and presuppositions by means of which people inside and outside the official churches legitimised the policy of apartheid or are still continuing to do so'.[50]

A relatively early attempt to handle racism from a black South African perspective had little to say about scripture, except for a paragraph on 'eccentric biblical exegesis'. Here Mbali criticized the Dutch Reformed Church as 'a Bible-based Reformed Church' whose 'church leaders on the right find enough Bible texts to justify any aspect of apartheid under criticism', such as the command in Gen. 1.28 being used 'as a basis for the argument that ethnic diversity is in origin in accordance with the will of God for this dispensation'.[51]

---

see John W. de Gruchy, *The Church Struggle in South Africa: Twenty-Fifth Anniversary Edition* (Minneapolis: Fortress, 2005), chap. 1, 'Historical Origins', pp. 1-50 and chap. 2, 'Apartheid and the Churches', pp. 51-100; see also Chris Loff, 'The History of a Heresy', chap. 2 in *Apartheid Is a Heresy*, ed. J. de Gruchy and C. Villa-Vicencio (Cape Town: David Philip/Guildford: Lutterworth, 1983), pp. 10-23.

47. E. P. Groenewald, 'Apartheid en voogdyskap in die lig van die Heilige Skrif', in *Regverdige rasse-apartheid*, ed. G. Cronjé (Stellenbosch, 1947), p. 65; see Willem Vorster, 'The Bible and Apartheid 1', chap. 8 in *Apartheid Is a Heresy*, ed. Gruchy and Villa-Vicencio, pp. 94-111, esp. pp. 96-97 and 110. It should be noted that Groenewald stressed the spiritual unity of all in Christ, and that his theological argument for the separate development of peoples did not necessarily justify the later racist oppression. It is also significant that those who later argued against this biblical justification included some of his successors at Pretoria, such as Prof. Andre du Toit. I have been privileged to lecture on this material in the Theology Faculty in Pretoria under the glare of photographs of both Groenewald and du Toit!

48. *Human Relations and the South African Scene in the Light of Scripture;* see pp. 14-15 on Gen. 1.28.

49. *Human Relations and the South African Scene in the Light of Scripture*, pp. 93-99.

50. J. A. Loubser, *The Apartheid Bible: A Critical Review of Racial Theology in South Africa* (Cape Town: Maskew, Miller, Longman, 1987), pp. ix-x.

51. Zolile Mbali, *The Churches and Racism: A Black South African Perspective* (London: SCM, 1987), p. 191.

A more detailed critique came from Willem Vorster, Professor of New Testament at the University of South Africa, Pretoria, in which he argued that in the Report, 'the Bible simply becomes an 'oracle book' of proof texts' or 'a book of norms'; 'the Bible has the function of a book of rules and regulations, norms and principles by which church and society are organized in a plural society where the rulers have opted for "separate development".'[52] Bax's contribution to *Apartheid Is a Heresy* analysed the same texts as in the DRC's Report to demonstrate the opposite conclusions in his discussion of the 'Bible and apartheid'.[53] He also criticized the Report for its misuse of the genre of ethical material as it 'seeks to turn a statement about God's providence into a commandment for men, which as we have seen is such a fundamentally wrong way of thinking'.[54] However, Vorster later went on to argue that, in fact, 'both apartheid and anti-apartheid theologians in the NGK undoubtedly operate with exactly the same view of Scripture. The main difference is the (political) grid though which the Bible is read. . . . In essence there is no difference in the use and appeal to the Bible between apartheid and anti-apartheid theologians.'[55] Similarly, Combrink surveyed the very different uses of passages from Matthew's gospel in the South African context, both to justify and to critique separate development of peoples and churches.[56]

A decade later, a major research project at Stellenbosch on the influence of different contexts of social transformation on biblical interpretation produced a number of articles reviewing how the scriptures were interpreted in the Report. Jonker concluded, 'It is clear from the report of the Dutch Reformed Church *Ras, Volk en Nasie* that Biblical interpretation was done according to the mode of legitimization. The present order of political apartheid was accepted uncritically, and Biblical interpretation served the purpose of reinforcing and strengthening this order. The report consciously or unconsciously

---

52. Originally published in *Ekumene onder die Suiderkruis*, ed. A. C. Viljoen (Pretoria: UNISA, 1979), later rewritten as Willem Vorster, 'The Bible and Apartheid 1', chap. 8 in *Apartheid Is a Heresy*, pp. 94-111, quotations from pp. 96, 101 and 106.

53. Douglas Bax, 'The Bible and Apartheid 2', chap. 9 in *Apartheid Is a Heresy*, pp. 112-43.

54. Douglas Bax, 'The Bible and Apartheid 2', p. 133.

55. Willem S. Vorster, 'The Use of Scripture and the NG Kerk: A Shift of Paradigm or of Values?', pp. 210 and 212; see also the discussion by D. J. Smit, 'The Ethics of Interpretation — and South Africa', *Scriptura* 33 (1990), pp. 29-43.

56. H. J. Bernard Combrink, 'The Use of Matthew in the South African Context during the Last Few Decades', *Neotestamentica* 28.2 (1994), pp. 339-58; see also his other articles, Bernard Combrink and Bethel Müller, 'The Gospel of Matthew in an African Context', *Scriptura* 39 (1991), pp. 43-51; Bernard Combrink, 'Rhetoric and Reference in the Gospel of Matthew', *Scriptura* 40 (1992), pp. 1-17; idem, 'Translating or Transforming — Receiving Matthew in Africa' and 'The Reception of Matthew in Africa', *Scriptura* 58 (1996.3), pp. 273-84 and 285-303.

wanted to provide Biblical "proofs" or "arguments" that could legitimize this policy, as well as the practical implementation of it in society.'[57]

Therefore the experience of approaching the Bible for the genre of rules or commands which can be directly applied to today seems fraught with difficulties. What happened in South Africa stands as a warning about the temptation to choose or interpret such prescriptions according to the reader's own prejudices or presuppositions, with both sides using similar passages and commands to justify their own previously held positions. It may even call this entire approach to the Bible of 'looking for rules for today' into question. Therefore, next we must examine whether moving from such prescriptive approaches to those of principles will be any better.

3. Looking for principles and universal values

a. Ethical approach

This second approach may draw on texts which enunciate principles, but it also recognizes the difficulty over specific commands by stepping back from the direct rules to look for the principles and universal values lying behind the commands. First, therefore, one needs to find out what the principles might be, perhaps selecting from several possible options. We might include the 'call to love', which is the crucial principle for Reinhold Niebuhr,[58] and which led to Situation Ethics. A common alternative is 'liberation', which came out of Latin America, particularly through the work of Gutiérrez,[59] but now is used as the

---

57. Louis Jonker, 'The Biblical Legitimization of Ethnic Diversity in Apartheid Theology', *Scriptura* 77 (2001), pp. 165-83, quotation from p. 181; see also Alec Basson, 'Israel en die Nasies: 'N Kritiese Nadenke oor die Dokument *Ras, Volk en Nasie*', *Scriptura* 77 (2001), pp. 185-92, and similar articles in that volume of *Scriptura*. Jonker is renowned as the Afrikaner theologian who made the first apology for apartheid in response to a plea from Archbishop Tutu at the conference of South African church leaders in Rustenburg in November 1990, which was subsequently endorsed by the main DRC the next day, much to the anger of then State President P. W. Botha; see John Allen, *Rabble-Rouser for Peace: The Authorised Biography of Desmond Tutu* (London: Rider, 2006), pp. 342-43.

58. See, for example, Reinhold Niebuhr, *An Interpretation of Christian Ethics* (New York: Seabury, 1979; original edn., 1935); see Hays' discussion of Niebuhr's eschewing of rules and preference for principles, *Moral Vision of the NT*, pp. 215-25 and p. 293, and also Spohn, *What Are They Saying about Scripture and Ethics?*, pp. 104-6.

59. See, for example, Gustavo Gutiérrez, *A Theology of Liberation: History, Politics and Salvation* (London: SCM, 1974) and his *We Drink from Our Own Wells: The Spiritual Journey of a People* (London: SCM, 1984).

approach to scripture by a variety of liberation theologies, including race (black theology), gender (feminist), or sexual orientation (gay liberation).[60] In South Africa, the work of Itumeleng Mosala has particularly stressed the principle of liberation,[61] but it has also widely influenced the development of black theology there. As opposed to the deontological approach of rules and duties, this approach through biblical principles will tend to be more consequentialist from an ethical perspective, to see how the possible consequences of any action will fulfil or frustrate the universal principle: actions are not necessarily intrinsically right or wrong, but their morality is determined by which action leads to the most 'love' or 'liberation'.

b. Genre and texts

This approach works best with texts of revelation, epistles and sermons where theology is being expounded in more general terms, which can then be applied to our situation. Hays argues against turning commands into principles in order to avoid the direct sense of the command; principles can only be used with principle-texts. 'Legalists and antinomians are equally guilty of hermeneutical gerrymandering to annex New Testament texts to foreign modes of ethical discourse. Christian preachers, at least since the time of Clement of Alexandria, have preached hundreds of thousands of disastrous sermons that say, in effect, "Now the text *says* x, but of course it couldn't really mean that, so we must see the underlying principle to which it points, which is y."'[62] This raises the immediate question of how one derives the principle. Our approach through genre might help here, if the principle can be shown to be central to the genre of the biblical text; thus the call to the imitation of Jesus is a principle which is embedded in the biographical genre of the gospels. However, other principles may be forced upon the genre from outside sources.

c. Problems

Immediately, questions arise about which principles or themes should be adopted, and how we derive them from the text. It would be important to

60. See Spohn, *What Are They Saying about Scripture and Ethics?*, pp. 56-76.
61. Itumeleng J. Mosala, *Biblical Hermeneutics and Black Theology in South Africa* (Grand Rapids: Eerdmans 1989); for some analysis and full bibliography, see Gerald West, 'The Work of Itumeleng Mosala', *Bulletin for Contextual Theology in Southern Africa and Asia* 1 (1995), pp. 1-6.
62. Hays, *Moral Vision of the NT*, p. 294.

demonstrate that the theme is really there all the way through the text and that it can be read out from the text in order to claim that it is a 'biblical' principle. There is always the danger of imposing an external principle from outside the Bible onto the text and reading it in that light, but claiming to be 'biblical'. As we have just seen above, Hays suggests that this approach can sometimes be a way of getting around the plain meaning of a text which we do not like. However, one can be equally subjective in the choice of principle, to get around the implications of a principle which we do not like. For instance, Hays argues that 'love and liberation are not sufficient' for the key principles with which to interpret the Bible. While he argues that this is because they are not found sufficiently frequently across all the New Testament writers, it is also clear that he is dissatisfied with love as a key biblical principle: 'Love covers a multitude of sins in more ways than one. The term has become debased in popular discourse; it has lost its power of discrimination, having become a cover for all manner of vapid self-indulgence'.[63] Instead, he prefers to speak of 'focal images' and uses the three images of community, cross and new creation.[64] It is true that these 'focal images' are not exactly the same as principles; however, Hays' use of them to help the variety of contrasting commands, stories and examples come into focus does function in a similar way to principles. The immediate question arises of where he derives these images from. It is significant that Hays begins his study with a concentration on Paul first and then moves to the gospels, but not the historical Jesus. It can be argued that Hays' three images are more Pauline and do actually work well for that material. However, do these images apply equally well across the whole of the New Testament to satisfy his first criterion of 'a textual basis in all of the canonical witnesses' any more than 'love'? Greater use of 'love and liberation' would have brought Hays to different conclusions than he finds via the community, cross, and new creation.[65] Thus how one chooses the original principle(s) or 'focal image', and where they are derived from, is vital.

d. South Africa

The importance of biblical 'principles' for the Dutch Reformed Church is stressed by John de Gruchy: 'The position of the NGK in all its major pro-

---

63. Hays, *Moral Vision of the NT*, pp. 200-204, quotation from p. 203.
64. Hays, *Moral Vision of the NT*, pp. 193-200.
65. See further our discussion of Hays, pp. 357-59 and 362 above, nn. 27-32 and 41-42.

nouncements invariably begins with a statement of principle, and it is made clear that principles must arise from Scripture. In true Reformed Church style, the Word of God is the norm by which we test our opinions and our actions. That the Bible "contains guiding principles for all spheres of life" is a constant refrain in the documents.'[66] The key question therefore becomes how one decides which are the important biblical principles, and the source from which they are derived.

Differing exegeses of the same creation stories could lead to the contrasting 'principles' of either 'separate development' (God made us all different) or 'unity' (God made us one in our diversity). This was particularly important because of the DRC's use of Gen. 1.28 in its report.[67] Bax argues that this 'is not an ethical command, however, not a commandment'; even at the level of principle, the apartheid attempt to argue that 'the differentiation of mankind' was 'not theologically a much less fundamental characteristic of mankind than the unity and homogeneity described and emphasized in Gen. 1–10' required special reading back into the creation account.[68] Something similar happens with the story of the Tower of Babel, Gen. 11.1-9, which the DRC Report interpreted to require the principle of different language groups and different cultures in separate development.[69] Again, Bax argues that 'the Report's exegesis is a misinterpretation that depends on incorrect assumptions'; instead, he ends up with the principle of 'the *unity* of the *volke*, but a unity based on the grace of God'.[70] By now, it should not be surprising that the same thing happens with the story of Pentecost, Acts 2.6-11. The pro-apartheid reading produced the principle of everyone hearing 'God's great deeds in our own language' — and thus justified separate racial church services, according to language groups. On the other hand, Bax criticises the DRC Report's handling of the Pentecost story for this exegesis; instead, he produced the opposite principle of 'breaking down the barriers that separate humanity'.[71] Thus the same method of looking for a principle applied to the same text produced two contrasting principles. No wonder

---

66. John W. de Gruchy, *The Church Struggle in South Africa: Twenty-Fifth Anniversary Edition* (Minneapolis: Fortress, 2005), p. 69; see also, for example, the report of the DRC Conference of Church Leaders, 'Christian Principles in a Multi-Racial South Africa', Pretoria, November 1953.

67. *Human Relations and the South African Scene in the Light of Scripture*, pp. 14-15.

68. Douglas Bax, 'The Bible and Apartheid 2', chap. 9 in *Apartheid Is a Heresy*, pp. 116-17.

69. *Human Relations and the South African Scene in the Light of Scripture*, pp. 15-19.

70. Douglas Bax, 'The Bible and Apartheid 2', chap. 9 in *Apartheid Is a Heresy*, pp. 117-24, quotations from pp. 120 and 124; for an exegetical sermon on Babel which turns the DRC reading around, see G. D. Cloete and D. J. Smit, '"Its Name Was Called Babel . . .": Gen. 11:9 and Acts 2:8, 11-12', *JTSA* 86 (March 1994), pp. 81-87.

71. Bax, 'The Bible and Apartheid 2', pp. 128-30.

Smit criticises Vorster's idea of interpretation just being 'in-line' with scripture or its principles as too vague.[72]

Therefore, given this difficulty of extracting a principle from within the text itself, the alternative is to bring a principle from elsewhere as a means to interpret the text. Thus, Jan Botha acknowledges that he now takes 'human rights' as his 'starting point outside the New Testament' and then uses it to critique and reject 'those Biblical stories and cultural values which function as a stumbling block in the way of this vision' while retelling 'those stories that are suitable'.[73] Similarly, Mosala is clear that the Bible is an ideological text and that those involved with black theology who oppose apartheid are still enslaved to Western biblical hermeneutics; therefore he seeks 'to develop a distinctive biblical hermeneutics of liberation for black theology'.[74] Thus the 'liberation' reading is first imposed onto the texts from outside, rather than being read from within them. Allan Boesak is equally interesting, coming as he does out of the Reformed, biblical tradition but being one of the key leaders of the 'struggle'. While his various collections of his sermons and speeches are steeped in biblical material,[75] it is significant that his original thesis for his Doctor of Divinity from the Theological Academy of the John Calvin Foundation, Kampen, Holland, was in Liberation Theology; although it begins with a discussion of Yahweh as Liberator in Exodus and Jesus' manifesto in Luke 4.18-21, the bulk of the book is actually a study of black power and black theology, which concludes with a peroration on 'love, liberation and justice'.[76] His commitment to the principle of liberation is also seen in the subtitle and opening essay of *Black and Reformed*.[77] Therefore, it seems that, like Mosala, he brings his principle of liberation from his studies of black theology and reads the scriptures in that light.[78]

---

72. D. J. Smit, 'The Ethics of Interpretation', pp. 36-37.

73. Jan Botha, 'The Bible in South African Public Discourse — with Special Reference to the Right to Protest', *Scriptura* 58 (1996), p. 329.

74. Mosala, *Biblical Hermeneutics and Black Theology in South Africa*, p. 3.

75. See, for example, Allan Boesak, *Walking on Thorns: The Call to Christian Obedience* (Grand Rapids: Eerdmans, 1984); idem, *If This Is Treason, I Am Guilty* (Grand Rapids: Eerdmans, 1987).

76. Allan Boesak, *Farewell to Innocence: A Socio-ethical Study of Black Theology and Black Power* (Johannesburg: Raven, 1977), pp. 20-26, 115-19.

77. Allan Boesak, 'The Courage to Be Black: Black Theology and the Struggle for Liberation', in his *Black and Reformed: Apartheid, Liberation and the Calvinist Tradition* (Braamfontein: Skotaville, 1984), pp. 1-21; see also *A Call for an End to Unjust Rule*, ed. Allan Boesak and Charles Villa-Vicencio (Philadelphia: Westminster, 1986).

78. Although note that Mosala criticizes Boesak for still appealing to the same ideology of biblical hermeneutics as the oppressors; see Mosala, *Biblical Hermeneutics and Black Theology in South Africa*, pp. 26-37.

Archbishop Emeritus Desmond Tutu, however, is a more complex case. His commitment to the principle of 'justice' as he constantly stresses God's love for everyone regardless of their race, colour or the 'shape of their nose' (his frequent example, provoking laughter at his own expense, often while defusing tense situations)[79] is well known. Here, too, we might ask whether it was originally derived from his reading of the Bible or whether it arose from a theology of liberation, or from his spirituality and personal experiences, and he read the Bible subsequently in that light. His commitment to the 'struggle' and 'liberation' is seen early on in a letter to the Dean of King's College London, asking to stay on to be allowed to take a Master's degree: 'I would, I think, want to have a shot at it. In a sense it is part of the struggle for our liberation. Please, I hope it does not sound big-headed or, worse, downright silly. But if I go back home as highly qualified as you can make me, the more ridiculous our Government's policy will appear to be to earnest and intelligent people.'[80]

Boulay writes of 'his growing involvement with black theology', 'which is liberation theology in South Africa' and which 'reached South Africa around 1970', while he was teaching in Roma in Lesotho: 'Tutu espoused the cause of black theology instantly and enthusiastically. Though his opposition to apartheid stems from a simple awareness of the dignity of man, he could not but be attracted by the opportunity of giving his instincts theological backing. . . . Black theology has little difficulty in arguing that the God of the Bible is on the side of the oppressed.'[81] What is interesting about Boulay's analysis is that she sees Tutu's views stemming from 'a simple awareness of the dignity of man', after which he espoused black or liberation theology, which in turn looks to the Bible for support. Certainly a concern for the dignity of all human beings is at the heart of Tutu's message, often seen as derived from the African idea of *ubuntu* in Nguni (or *botho* in Sotho languages), as explained by the Archbishop in the Johannesburg *Star* as early as 1981.[82]

On the other hand, Tutu himself stresses that his belief about the unique status of every human being as a beloved child of God is essentially grounded

79. For the one occasion where Tutu used this example seriously, in Rwanda, where Hutus and Tutsis have different-shaped noses, see John Allen, *Rabble-Rouser for Peace: The Authorised Biography of Desmond Tutu* (London: Rider, 2006), pp. 380-81.

80. D. M. Tutu to the Dean of King's College London, October 27, 1964, KCL Archives; also quoted in Shirley du Boulay, *Tutu: The Voice of the Voiceless* (London: Hodder and Stoughton, 1988), p. 62.

81. Boulay, *Tutu: The Voice of the Voiceless*, pp. 84-85.

82. *Star*, August 12 1981; SACC Archives AC6235.7, quoted in Allen, *Rabble-Rouser for Peace*, pp. 346-47; for full analysis, see Michael Battle, *Reconciliation: The Ubuntu Theology of Desmond Tutu* (Cleveland: Pilgrim, 1997).

in the Bible. The heart of his defence before the Eloff Commission in September 1982 is full of biblical quotations. Thus Tutu begins his defence, 'I want to show that the SACC and its member churches have their agenda and their programmes in this matter determined by what the scriptures have revealed as the will of God, the God and Father of our Lord Jesus Christ'.[83] He then begins with the creation narrative in Genesis, continues through the Tower of Babel, on to Paul's understanding of reconciliation in 2 Cor. 5.18-21, breaking down the dividing wall in Eph. 2.11-22, leading to unity and the end of divisions in 1 Cor. 12.12-13 and Gal. 3.26-28, and Jesus' universal concern for unity in John 12.32; 17.11, 20-23; the need for practical action is thus required by 1 John 3.15-18; 4.19-21 and Jas. 1.27; 2.14-17, which is why the SACC is persecuted as prophesied in John 15.18-21 and Matt. 10.17-22.[84] Equally, his eight-page rejoinder to P. W. Botha in March 1988 is packed with similar scriptural references.[85] His contribution to *Apartheid Is a Heresy* was also predominantly a Bible study, arguing that 'apartheid contradicts the testimony of the Bible categorically'.[86] Thus Timothy Stanton says of Tutu's speeches and writings: 'Those were the days of Liberation Theology, Black Theology, African Theology, Contextual Theology, but it's not from the exponents of these that the Archbishop quotes. The only book that the Archbishop quotes from extensively is the Bible. So we thank God for the Bible and for God's revelation of Himself that it contains.'[87]

Pieterse and colleagues have undertaken a qualitative analysis of various speeches by Tutu, counting his use of biblical quotations, theological themes and various phrases, like 'God is on the side of the oppressed'. In the introduction, they state several times that Tutu is 'the foremost representative of South African liberation theology'.[88] The tables of the results of their analysis certainly show

---

83. Archbishop Desmond Tutu, *The Rainbow People of God: South Africa's Victory over Apartheid,* ed. John Allen (London: Bantam, 1995), p. 59.

84. See Tutu, *The Rainbow People of God,* pp. 53-78 for the full text of his Eloff submission, and Allen, *Rabble-Rouser for Peace,* pp. 197-98 for discussion of it; Archbishop Tutu himself reiterated these biblical passages in a private interview I recorded with him as part of the original research for this book at the offices of the Truth and Reconciliation Commission, March 30, 1998.

85. See Tutu, *The Rainbow People of God,* pp. 141-52 for the full text, and Allen, *Rabble-Rouser for Peace,* p. 292 for comment.

86. Desmond Tutu, 'Christianity and Apartheid', chap. 4 in *Apartheid Is a Heresy,* ed. de Gruchy and Villa-Vicencio, pp. 39-47.

87. Fr. Timothy Stanton, C.R., sermon at the Thanksgiving Service twenty-five years after Desmond Tutu's consecration as a Bishop, St. Mary's Cathedral, Johannesburg, July 2001, extracted in *Tutu As I Know Him,* ed. Lavinia Browne (Roggebaai: Umuzi, 2006), pp. 155-58, quotation from p. 156.

88. Hendrik J. C. Pieterse (ed.), *Desmond Tutu's Message: A Qualitative Analysis* (Leiden: Brill, 2001), pp. 12 and 34-36.

that he refers to both themes of liberation theology and what they term 'general theology', Christian values, biblical quotations and themes.[89] However, elsewhere they demonstrate several significant differences between liberation theology's use of civil disobedience and demands such as unbanning groups, release of prisoners, repatriation of exiles and dismantling of apartheid as preconditions on the one hand, and Tutu's unconditional message and more peaceful approach towards civil unrest on the other.[90] They conclude that 'Desmond Tutu is therefore a very sensitive and profound contextual theologian who could read the Bible in his context in such a way that he could fulfil his prophetic ministry without shrinking from this immense task. . . . Desmond Tutu is a committed pastor, church leader and theologian with a remarkably clear understanding of the essence of the gospel of Jesus Christ in the unique South African situation', without mentioning liberation theology at all![91] Indeed, their analysis of the variation of his speeches over time reveals how from his earliest days through to the early 1980s and again in the 1990s he 'put more emphasis on theological themes', while 'political themes' were stronger in the mid-1980s.[92]

Despite the claims, or accusations (as they were under apartheid!) of Tutu being simply a liberationist, this closer analysis suggests that his use of liberation theology becomes congruent with Tutu's reading of the Bible in the most difficult days of his ministry as Archbishop of Cape Town towards the end of apartheid. However, this essential commitment to a biblical principle of the love of God for everyone, regardless of status, is there in his beliefs and message from the start, going right back to his earliest influence, the monks of the Community of the Resurrection.[93] This is demonstrated in the famous story of the young Tutu being amazed to see a CR father, Trevor Huddleston, in his own words, 'doffing his hat to my mother', giving him that 'sense of the worth of a person'.[94]

---

89. See Pieterse (ed.), *Desmond Tutu's Message: A Qualitative Analysis*, Appendix 2 with five tables of results, and Appendix 3's list of keywords, pp. 136-49.

90. Pieterse (ed.), *Desmond Tutu's Message: A Qualitative Analysis*, pp. 42-43.

91. Pieterse (ed.), *Desmond Tutu's Message: A Qualitative Analysis*, p. 55.

92. Pieterse (ed.), *Desmond Tutu's Message: A Qualitative Analysis*, p. 55 and Table 2, p. 138.

93. 'The speeches and sermons of Archbishop Desmond Mpilo Tutu reveal a life spent in continuing reflection on the Bible. The Bible informs his world view and often shapes his vocabulary. But this reflection on the Bible is determined by his conviction that liberation is its central theme, its hermeneutical key. It was a conviction he and other key South African leaders, lay as well as clerical, learnt from the Community of the Resurrection at St Peter's Rosettenville and developed further.' Jonathan Draper, 'Archbishop Tutu and the Bible', in *Archbishop Tutu: Prophetic Witness in South Africa*, ed. Leonard Hulley, Louise Kretzschmar and Luke Lungile Pato (Cape Town: Human and Rousseau, 1996), pp. 222-29, quotation from p. 222.

94. I was privileged to record Archbishop Tutu's own description of this in a private interview at his Soweto home on July 12, 2001; these quotations are taken from that interview. He went on to

This understanding is then further reinforced by the spiritual discipline of the CR with frequent prayer and Bible reading several times a day in which Tutu received his formation and which still determines his daily routine now.

Therefore this analysis of looking for ethical principles in the biblical texts has taken us a little further on from the prescriptive mode. As with rules, so too looking for principles can be open to abuse, as the contrast of the pro-apartheid readings of the creation, Babel and Pentecost with Bax's anti-apartheid riposte shows. Moving from specific texts and stories to wider biblical principles such as love or liberation can seem a like a promising strategy, although they are subject to Hays' critique; however, it is not clear that his 'focal images' are any more biblical in their totality or avoid the charge of becoming a 'mediating principle' themselves. The South Africa experience shows that a reader's 'location' or prior commitments can significantly affect which principles they choose, or 'find' in the Bible. Therefore, a more honest approach may be simply to impose one's principles onto the text from outside, as Botha's use of human rights does, and, it can be argued, so do certain liberation theologians. However, the example of Desmond Tutu does suggest that being immersed in the totality of scripture over many years can lead to truly biblical principles driving someone's ethical position.

4. Following examples and paradigms

a. Ethical approach

Given the difficulties we have noted with interpreting commands and prescriptive material, as well as discerning the correct principles, it is not surprising that others look to the scriptures to provide narratives which can provide examples for us today. Spohn argues that such an approach among Catholics draws on a natural law view of how God created human beings as moral creatures; scriptural stories thus serve as 'moral reminders' by giving us examples of how others behaved in similar circumstances.[95] As we read in the Bible how God approves or disapproves of people's conduct, so we are reminded how to live as moral beings ourselves. In terms of moral philosophy, this approach links with

observe drily, 'I wasn't aware that it was something that was going to make such an indelible impression on me'; see also Allen, *Rabble-Rouser for Peace*, pp. 25-26, quoting Tutu's interview with Trevor McDonald, "Paths of Inspiration," BBC Radio 2, 1996. Allen discusses the confusion over the dates of Huddleston's ministry and Tutu's presumed young age; however, it is a typical gesture from Huddleston, who also bought Hugh Masekela his first trumpet!

95. Spohn, *What Are They Saying about Scripture and Ethics?*, pp. 38-45.

perfectionist theories or virtue-based approaches, which from Aristotle onwards have seen the moral life as being more about developing a moral character which does the right thing than about blind obedience to commands. 'Character ethics' has become increasingly significant in recent years, not least as a
forum where biblical scholars, theologians and ethicists can interact, as is demonstrated by the meetings of the 'Character Ethics and Biblical Interpretation'
group within the Society of Biblical Literature over the last decade.[96] The role
of biblical narrative and story in forming ethical character has also been important for other ethicists and theologians who do not necessarily follow a natural
law approach, like Hauerwas and Yoder.[97] It is certainly true that teaching morals by way of narrative examples was very common in the ancient world; as we
have noted several times in this book, it was one of the major aims of biographical writings in particular. In using this method today, as Hays puts it, 'we will
have to formulate imaginative *analogies* between the stories told in the texts and
the story lived out by our community in a very different historical setting.'[98]

b. Genre and texts

This approach obviously works best with narrative, story-based texts, so in the
New Testament all the gospel stories and parables are well used here, in the
same way that Old Testament narratives, especially from the Pentateuch, play
their part. As we have traced the basic story of Jesus of Nazareth in the gospels,
we have seen how each evangelist is able to retell the narrative in a particular
way to emphasize his own understanding of Jesus; thus we get Matthew's account of the interpreter of the law alongside Luke's narrative of the friend of
the outcasts. There is clearly going to be less narrative material in the letters of
Paul, although we have argued that Paul does have a basic narrative of the life,
death and resurrection of Jesus underlying all his theology and writing. At first
sight, therefore, looking for examples in the biblical story might seem potentially very productive for using the Bible in ethics today.

---

96. Some of the key papers have been published in *Character and Scripture: Moral Formation,
Community, and Biblical Interpretation* (Grand Rapids: Eerdmans, 2002), ed. William P. Brown; see
esp. the chapter by L. Gregory Jones, 'Formed and Transformed by Scripture: Character, Community, and Authority in Biblical Interpretation', in *Character and Scripture*, pp. 18-33; an early version
of our Chapter III on Paul was given to this group as part of its work at the SBL Annual Meeting in
Nashville, November 20, 2000.

97. See Hays' discussion of their approaches in *Moral Vision of the NT*, pp. 239-66 and 293;
also Spohn, *What Are They Saying about Scripture and Ethics?*, pp. 77-93.

98. Hays, *Moral Vision of the NT*, p. 298.

c. Problems

Here the first and obvious problem is that of the cultural relativism gap. Quarrying the Bible for examples for us to follow today is a typical refuge of many a preacher, or of radio 'thought for the day' presenters, who describe some obscure story in the Bible and then say, 'and I thought I am just like that — and so are you! We should be like so-and-so and do such a thing'. But can people today really be like anybody in such a different time, culture, philosophical and religious world, and so forth?

Nineham argued that everything is culturally bound; one cannot talk of what an ancient text 'means' today. 'People of different periods and cultures differ very widely; in some cases so widely that accounts of the nature and relations of God, men and the world put forward in one culture may be unacceptable, as they stand, in a different culture, even though they may have expressed profound truth in their time and expressed it in a form entirely appropriate to the original situation'.[99] The text is culturally bound in its day; we are culturally bound in our day — and a great gulf lies between the two. We simply cannot bridge the gap. We might, by careful historical study, get over to the other side and see what it looks like in its own context — that is, to talk of what the text meant *then* — but we cannot bring it back to our side and talk of what it means *now*. There is no unique revelation of God in only one culture. The Bible is more like a river, containing the 'water of life' but which has flowed a long way from its clear source and picked up things along the way which make it undrinkable for us.[100]

Cultural relativism has been further developed in work by Gadamer and MacIntyre, but Nineham's extreme view is a good example of the problem. In its hard form it is totally destructive of any attempt to use the Bible in ethics — or for that matter, any other reason; this would allow no communication across the ages or the around the world. Either we read a text in its own terms, which we cannot understand in our culture, or we read it in our terms, but we do not know if this has anything to do with what it meant originally. We may just as well be back to mediaeval flights of fancy.

However, it may be argued that cultural relativism is itself culturally relative, produced by the liberal culture of the 1960s and bound by it; therefore it can have no objective claim to apply to us in the third millennium, to anywhere and any time else. If Nineham really believed it, he would not have bothered to write and publish his book at all, as no one else in any other place or time

99. D. Nineham, *The Use and Abuse of the Bible: A Study of the Bible in an Age of Rapid Cultural Change* (London: Macmillan, 1976), p. 1.

100. Nineham, *The Use and Abuse of the Bible*, p. 232.

would be able to understand it! In fact, the very fact of writing his book is an attempt to communicate across cultures, which indicates that he believed it is at least possible. Secondly, we have suggested above that there are common human experiences which are basic to all cultures, such as food, love, sex, fear, violence, power, wealth or poverty, sickness and death, God and so forth. Indeed, we have noted material about such topics in each of our studies of Jesus, Paul and the gospels. Ethical questions gather around such experiences, and people in all cultures tell stories about them in a desire to communicate to others. Therefore, we can at least try to understand each others' stories, but Nineham warns us that this is hard work and fraught with difficulties.

Eschatology in the New Testament is a good example. J. T. Sanders argues that New Testament ethics are so bound up in eschatology that we cannot 'use' it or apply it today. The eschatological framework of Jesus and Paul and the evangelists may differ from each other, but that is nothing compared with the difference today: 'The ethical positions of the New Testament are the children of their own times and places, alien and foreign to this day and age'; thus we are 'relieved of the need or temptation to begin with Jesus . . . or the New Testament'.[101] However, we would argue that this is rather an overstatement. It may indeed be true that we have to struggle to understand first-century eschatology to read these texts. However, it can also be argued that those raised in the shadow of the bomb or the total ecological disaster of pollution or global warming may not be totally unexperienced in issues of eschatology! Similarly, the way the book of Revelation seems to come 'alive' to those suffering persecution or oppression in cultures different from first-century Asia Minor again hints at this link through common human experiences.

Therefore any attempt to use biblical texts for examples or paradigms will need to begin with good exegesis, to find out what the text really says, taking into account its own historical background; equally, the reader needs to be aware of their own background to try to make allowances for both sets of 'filters'. Even if this is then achieved, the issue becomes one of validity in the application of the stories for today: who decides who represents whom in the story? These issues can be exemplified in the use of example and story in South Africa.

d. South Africa

The paradigmatic claim to be emulating the example of a central biblical narrative lay at the heart of both the justification for apartheid and the Afrikaner

---

101. J. T. Sanders, *Ethics in the NT*, p. 130.

mind-set.[102] The early European settlers saw themselves as similar to the ancient Israelites, making an exodus from oppression and being guided on the journey by God, eventually following their example of entering into the promised land. This analogy might seem rather far-fetched from the point of view of an academic's armchair — but there can be no doubt how beautiful and fertile the valleys of Stellenbosch and Franschoek must have appeared to weary travellers after months at sea in a small boat! For the French Huguenot settlers in particular, the experience of escaping persecution in Europe through such an arduous journey to find 'a land flowing with milk and honey' must have reminded them of the exodus. However, this led them to view the local peoples like the natives of Canaan as 'hewers of wood and drawers of water', and to begin to interpret the material in Joshua and Judges as applying to their relations with the Bantu; from these biblical narratives, they derived the prohibition against mixed marriages, and justified the oppression and slavery of the native peoples.[103]

When the British authorities in the Cape began to work towards the abolition of slavery in the early nineteenth century, the Boers saw this as yet more oppression of their way of life, and so they made the Great Trek up into the interior, again emulating the Israelites' journey through the wilderness. Eventually, this reached its climax in the battle of December 16, 1838, when 500 Afrikaners defeated 20,000 Zulus at Blood River. The Voortrekker Monument, which still dominates the Pretoria skyline, celebrates this apparently miraculous victory; their deliverance became forever linked with the idea of the 'Covenant', which was ceremonially enacted every year on December 16, between God and the Afrikaners,[104] modelled on that of the ancient Israelites.[105]

The paradox is, of course, that this exodus narrative from slavery and oppression to freedom in the promised land is exactly the same story which un-

102. See Michael Prior, *The Bible and Colonialism: A Moral Critique* (Sheffield: Sheffield Academic Press, 1997), chap. 3, 'Colonialism and South Africa', pp. 71-105.

103. See, for example, de Gruchy, *The Church Struggle in South Africa*, pp. 171-74, and Battle, *Reconciliation: The Ubuntu Theology of Desmond Tutu*, pp. 31-32.

104. See Mbali, *The Churches and Racism*, pp. 191-93; on a research visit to the University of Pretoria, I was moved by the way Prof. Jan van der Watt of its Theology Faculty was able to tell me the story of Blood River twice, once from the Afrikaner perspective, and again from the Zulus'.

105. The South African comedian/-enne, Evita Bezuidenhout, played by Pieter-Dirk Uys, can now joke that 'the Afrikaners are the Chosen People of the Southern Hemisphere, just as the Jews are of the North' (as s/he did at the special seventy-fifth birthday concert for Archbishop Desmond Tutu in Cape Town Cathedral on September 29, 2006) — but it is funny only because it was so strongly believed. It is arguable that the same paradigm of escaping persecution into a promised land, with the corollary of destruction of the native peoples, equally drove the colonial expansion across North America, and continues to fuel the self-understanding particularly of elements of the Republican Right in the USA today.

derlies and motivates most liberation theology,[106] and its expression in South African black theology. The difference merely serves to emphasize the central difficulty in applying biblical stories to today. In the first version, the Afrikaners are the victims of oppression (in Europe, or by the British in the Cape) being set free by God; in the second, they are the oppressors of others, the native peoples in South Africa. Writing as a member of the 'colonial remnant' a decade after the fall of apartheid and the transition to the new democracy, Snyman also links the hermeneutics of the Afrikaans-speaking churches with that of Liberation Theology: 'For the one, God is a God of deliverance. For the other, he is a conquering god. Same texts, two views, two experiences.'[107]

On the other hand, those seeking a biblical exemplary basis against apartheid were also able to find suitable narratives to use as paradigms. We noted above how Jan Botha wants to use the Bible as 'a powerful means of promoting a culture of human rights and democracy in South Africa'. Therefore he cites the story of the triumphal entry into Jerusalem to argue for the 'right for peaceful protest', against the shootings at Bisho on September 6, 1992, which left thirty dead and 200 wounded.[108] This massacre came after a number of others where government involvement in 'black on black' violence was suspected, including that at Boipatong; Archbishop Tutu had tried unsuccessfully to avert the march on Bisho, but these tragic events did at least subsequently provoke renewed multiparty negotiations.[109] Writing during the same period of extreme violence in the townships, Patrick Hartin argued similarly that to 'get from there to here', from the New Testament to today's ethical issues, the use of analogy is very important. He also finished with a study of passages about violence in search of an example to follow: 'Faced with our own problems stemming from violence in our society, the Scriptures do not give us direct answers. What they have given us is an analogy that the way in which Jesus responded to the violence within his society was to place his trust in God. He turned away from violence to meet it with other means.'[110]

106. It is, of course, not surprising that Palestinian liberation theologians have difficulty with the exodus model, since the Israelite occupation of Canaan was used to justify early Zionist settlement and still drives the continuing Israeli occupation of Palestinian territories; see Michael Prior, *The Bible and Colonialism: A Moral Critique* (Sheffield: Sheffield Academic Press, 1997), chap. 4, 'Colonialism and Palestine', pp. 106-74; it is notable that Palestinians are tending to look more towards the model of the exile.

107. Gerrie Snyman, 'Social Identity and South African Biblical Hermeneutics: A Struggle against Prejudice?' *JTSA* 121 (March 2005), pp. 34-55; quotation from p. 39.

108. Jan Botha, 'The Bible in South African Public Discourse — with Special Reference to the Right to Protest', *Scriptura* 58 (1996), pp. 329-43; quotation from p. 330.

109. Allen, *Rabble-Rouser for Peace*, pp. 330-32.

110. P. J. Hartin, 'Ethics and the New Testament: How Do We Get from There to Here?' in *The*

Thus we have seen that, as with prescriptive material and biblical princi-ples, so too the use of scriptural narratives to provide examples for today was common on both sides of the apartheid debate. While the method of applying such stories to current issues to guide ethical behaviour can be very attractive, it runs the risk of being extremely subjective, especially in its comparison of bibli-cal heroes with people now alive. The apartheid example stands as a warning to those who wish to use biblical narratives as a guide for ethical behaviour today, that it has been used in the past to justify actions which we now find ethically repugnant. Therefore, if none of three generic modes of commands, principles nor examples can provide a secure way into using biblical material in an ethical issue like apartheid, let us turn to the fourth, more comprehensive way of using the whole Bible to see if that is any more successful.

5. Embracing an overall symbolic worldview

a. Ethical approach

Drawing upon his looser fourth category of ethical material in the Bible, Gustafson concludes that 'scripture *alone* is never the final court of appeal for Christian ethics. Its understanding of God and his purposes, of man's condi-tion and needs, of precepts, events, human relationships, however, do provide the basic *orientation* toward particular judgements.'[111] This leads to the devel-opment of a 'biblical theology'. The introduction to Karl Barth's *Church Dog-matics*, II/2, sect. 36, is entitled 'Ethics as a Task of the Doctrine of God'.[112] Such a Barthian approach therefore argues that dogmatics is equivalent to ethics and ethics to dogmatics.[113] Here we take the whole biblical story of creation-fall-redemption-eschatology and use that as the overall guide, as proposed by ethicists like Oliver O'Donovan and Michael Banner. So O'Donovan argues, 'We will read the Bible seriously only when we use it to guide our thought to-wards a comprehensive moral viewpoint, and not merely to articulate discon-nected moral claims. We must look within it not only for moral bricks, but for

Relevance of Theology for the 1990's, ed. J. Mouton and B. C. Lategan (Pretoria: Human Sciences Re-search Council, 1994), pp. 511-25; quotation from p. 523.

111. Gustafson, 'The Place of Scripture', p. 455; his italics.

112. Karl Barth, *Church Dogmatics*, II/2 (Edinburgh: T&T Clark, 1957), p. 510.

113. See Michael Banner, 'Turning the World Upside Down — and Some Other tasks for Dog-matic Christian Ethics', The F. D. Maurice Professor of Moral and Social Theology Inaugural Lec-ture, King's College London, October 16, 1996; subsequently published in M. Banner, *Christian Ethics and Contemporary Moral Problems* (Cambridge: Cambridge University Press, 1999), pp. 1-46.

the indications of the order in which the bricks belong together'. Thus he takes 'the resurrection of Jesus Christ from the dead' as the key to his 'moral order'.[114] Similarly, O'Donovan's next book, *The Desire of the Nations,* was an attempt to provide an overarching political theology from a reading of the Bible.[115]

b. Genre and texts

This holistic approach works with the entire canon of scripture, read as a whole and interpreted theologically. It builds upon the canonical criticism pioneered by Brevard Childs and developed by Francis Watson, arguing for a theological reading of the Bible.[116] However, from the point of view of genre, it can only do this by overriding the genre of the individual books. The prescriptive approach down at the level of specific commands of the Sermon on the Mount interprets them as law or norms and misses the biographical genre of the rest of the gospel of Matthew operating above the level of individual verses. However, this canonical approach goes further up beyond the gospel to the ultimate level of the entire Bible and views it as a single book with an overarching metanarrative.

c. Problems

It is true that from both a literary and ecclesiastical view, the Bible is often interpreted as a single book, with all the individual books bound together in one set of covers: witness the common comment, 'The Bible *says*', in the singular. However, this obscures the fact that τὰ βιβλία is actually plural in the Greek, and it is questionable whether the genre of the individual books can be ignored in this way. The New Testament alone contains twenty-seven different books, written by a number of different authors over a period of time (at least fifty years?) in a number of different genres: four gospels, stories of Jesus in ancient biographical genre with his words and deeds; the book of Acts as a biographical-historical monograph; a whole set of letters, some addressed to specific congregations about specific issues, others more general with a wider

114. O. O'Donovan, *Resurrection and Moral Order* (Leicester, UK: IVP, 1986), pp. 200, 13.
115. O. O'Donovan, *The Desire of the Nations* (Cambridge: Cambridge: University Press, 1995); this was then followed by his Bampton Lectures, *The Ways of Judgment* (Grand Rapids: Eerdmans 2005).
116. Francis Watson, *Text, Church and World* (Edinburgh: T&T Clark, 1994); idem, *Text and Truth: Redefining Biblical Theology* (Edinburgh: T&T Clark, 1997).

audience in mind; and the book of Revelation in an apocalyptic genre. Different audiences are presumed, from the original hearers of Jesus in Galilee, through groups of Jews in the Diaspora, to the communities in great cities of Roman empire. They are written by many different authors, many of whom we do not know, and Paul's letters witness to divisions and arguments within the early church. The books are written in different literary styles: compare the different styles of the Synoptics with John, or even of the Synoptics themselves, or of James with Paul, or of Revelation with everybody else! Whatever were the authors' intentions, they were writing for different people and reasons, and almost certainly they never expected that these writings would all be in one book. Perhaps plural phrases like 'the New Testament writings' or 'the scriptures' should always be used to remind us of this plurality.

Therefore, this overall worldview approach is a long way from the actual text of the Bible and is in danger of imposing a doctrinal or theological framework onto the text. As with other theme-based approaches, the question has to be asked whether the framework is really found in the text; alternatively, the text could be just a convenient peg from which to hang the argument, which is actually driven by dogmatics and systematic theology. Thus, while O'Donovan's stress on 'resurrection' is central to the Pauline epistles, is it really the key to understanding all the rest of the New Testament — let alone the Old Testament? Similarly, Christopher Rowland criticizes *The Desire of the Nations* because of its 'need to move beyond the particular genres and stories to a theological "meta-narrative".'[117] Once again, the dangers and benefits of this approach can be illustrated from the South African experience.

d. South Africa

Such a general theological approach could bring with it the temptation to spiritualize things; it helps to 'keep theology out of politics' by stressing the overall theology of creation-fall-redemption nexus, which can then be applied to the life of an individual believer rather than to tricky socio-political issues. During the apartheid years this was a useful strategy to keep out of trouble with the authorities. Reacting against such approaches, Patrick Hartin set out to undo the tragedy of 'the use that was made of Bible to justify the political ideology of apartheid'. He uses Curran's five themes of 'creation-sin-incarnation-

---

117. C. Rowland, 'Response to *The Desire of the Nations*', *Studies in Christian Ethics* 11.2 (1998), p. 78; the entire volume is given over to Responses and Discussion of O'Donovan's book, with a reply from the author himself.

redemption-resurrection' to provide an 'underlying Christian vision' against which any interpretation of the scriptures can be tested. 'Whatever is faithful to that vision is a valid interpretation; whatever runs counter to that vision is a distortion and is to be rejected.'[118] However, it is not immediately clear that this fivefold theological vision necessarily provides the values of 'equality, freedom and justice' which he wants. Hartin argues that 'the virtue of equality emanates from the vision of creation'[119] — and yet, as we have already seen, the story of creation could suggest that God has created variety, and then we are back to separate development! Against this, Hartin uses his fivefold vision and his values of equality, freedom and justice to hold fast to his 'basic Christian vision'. However, his approach is open to the charge of having imported these values from outside the text, as we saw above with the principle of liberation in Botha and Mosala.

Smit's discussion in 1990 of Vorster's analysis of the similar approach by pro- and anti-apartheid scholars noted that biblical specialists tended to concentrate on rhetoric and the 'literary-aesthetic paradigm' to avoid socio-political issues. As a result, 'few black, and feminist, theologians in South Africa have so far completed doctoral degrees in New Testament, compared to ethics, systematic theology, historical studies and practical theology. . . . During this time, it is remarkable to see that almost no biblical scholar wrote anything on the New Testament and ethics'.[120] To borrow Villa-Vicencio's phrase, they were 'trapped in apartheid'.[121]

However, that was all about to change. Writing at the same time as Hartin, Jan Botha analysed the developments in South African New Testament scholarship over the period of transition and showed how biblical specialists began to grapple with the relationship of the New Testament to wider theology and ethics.[122] In 1990 a conference organized by UNISA and Stellenbosch deliberately sought to bring together the debates about biblical studies and methodology with issues about theology and society to debate 'the relevance of theology for the 1990s'.[123] Meanwhile, the annual Congress of the Biblical Studies Society of

118. P. J. Hartin, 'Towards a Christian Vision as the Basis for Ethical Decisions', *Scriptura* 42 (1992) pp. 65-73, esp. p. 66.

119. Hartin, 'Towards a Christian Vision as the Basis for Ethical Decisions', p. 71.

120. D. J. Smit, 'The Ethics of Interpretation', pp. 38 and 42.

121. Charles Villa-Vicencio, *Trapped in Apartheid: A Socio-Theological History of the English-Speaking Churches* (Cape Town: David Philip/Maryknoll, NY: Orbis, 1988).

122. Jan Botha, 'Aspects of the Rhetoric of South African New Testament Scholarship anno 1992', *Scriptura* 46 (1993), pp. 80-99; Botha took this forward himself with his article, 'The Ethics of New Testament Interpretation', *Neotestamentica* 26.1 (1992), pp. 169-94.

123. Subsequently published as J. Mouton and B. C. Lategan (eds.), *The Relevance of Theology for the 1990's* (Pretoria: Human Sciences Research Council, 1994).

Southern Africa in May 1990 considered 'the actuality of the Bible in a new South Africa'.[124] Similarly, the Hermeneutics Group of the New Testament Society of South Africa was beginning to shift its focus away from just methodology.[125] While many of the papers at the 1994 Pretoria Conference on 'Rhetoric, Scripture and Theology' were still about the rhetoric *in* the New Testament, others, like Craffert and Smit, wanted to talk about the rhetoric *of* the New Testament.[126] This all received a further stimulus with the changes over the period of transition to majority rule. Now that Biblical Studies no longer had a privileged place as a compulsory subject in the school curriculum, New Testament scholars had to find ways of making their study 'relevant' or applicable to today, partly to justify their positions and to stop departments or posts being closed, but mainly to contribute to the wider debate about the new South Africa.[127]

Inevitably this has brought New Testament scholarship into conversation with wider theology and especially Christian ethics. Thus Gerald West's contribution to *Doing Theology in Context* noted 'repeated attempts to construct a

---

124. The papers were subsequently published in *Scriptura* 37 (1991), ed. P. J. Hartin; see esp. D. J. Smit's article, 'The Bible and Ethos in a New South Africa', pp. 51-67.

125. See D. J. Smit, 'A Story of Contextual Hermeneutics and the Integrity of New Testament Interpretation in South Africa', *Neotestamentica* 28.2 (1994), pp. 265-89.

126. *Rhetoric, Scripture and Theology: Essays from the 1994 Pretoria Conference,* ed. Stanley E. Porter and Thomas H. Olbricht, JSNTSS 131 (Sheffield: Sheffield Academic Press, 1996); see esp. Pieter F. Craffert, 'Reading and Divine Sanction: The Ethics of Interpreting the New Testament in the New South Africa', pp. 54-71, and D. J. Smit, 'Theology as Rhetoric? Or: Guess Who's Coming to Dinner', pp. 393-422.

127. See the frequent articles in *Scriptura* and elsewhere during the 1990s, especially the consultation papers published in *The Integrity of Theological Education,* ed. B. C. Lategan, *Scriptura,* Special Issue S11 (1993); also those from the Congress of the South African Biblical Studies Society in May 1993, published in *Scriptura* 49 (May 1994); Izak J. J. Spangenberg, 'Paradigm Changes in the Bible Sciences and the Teaching of Biblical Studies in the New South Africa', *Scriptura* 52 (1995), pp. 1-10; McGlory T. Speckman, 'Beyond the Debate: An Agenda for Biblical Studies in the New South Africa', *Religion and Theology* 3.2 (1996), pp. 135-51; Jeremy Punt, 'Biblical Studies in South Africa? The Case for Moral Values' and 'Biblical Studies in South Africa? The Case for Hermeneutics', *Scriptura* 60 (1997), pp. 1-14 and 15-30; Cornelia Roux, 'Biblical Values and Multi-Religious Education in the Primary School: Problems and Proposals', *Scriptura* 60 (1997), pp. 63-69; J. N. Vorster, 'The Study of Religion as the "Multi-Versity": Probing Problems and Possibilities', *Neotestamentica* 32.1 (1998), pp. 203-40; Jeremy Punt, 'New Testament Interpretation, Interpretive Interests, and Ideology: Methodological Deficits amidst South African Methodolomania?' *Scriptura* 65 (1998), pp. 123-52; J. N. J. (Klippies) Kritzinger and Louise Kretzschmar, 'Transforming the Undergraduate Teaching of Theology at the University of South Africa', *Religion and Theology* 6.2 (1999), pp. 240-57; J. Eugene Botha, 'The (Ir)Relevancy of the Academic Study of the Bible', *Scriptura* 73 (2000), pp. 121-40; for a further perspective after a decade of democracy, see Piet Naudé, 'Is There a Future for Scholarship? Reformed Theological Scholarship in a Transforming Higher Education Environment', *JTSA* 119 (July 2004), pp. 32-45.

biblical theology', but argued, 'This task has proved to be so problematic that it has been abandoned by most biblical scholars and theologians', because of the difficulty of locating 'the centre or trajectory of the Bible'. Instead, therefore, he explored 'the relationship between the Bible and theology' drawing upon his work with the 'ordinary reader', which we shall consider in the next section.[128] Meanwhile, its companion volume, *Doing Ethics in Context,* included the article already noted from Jan Botha on the Bible and Ethics, which distinguished Gustafson's four approaches (prescriptive commands, principles, revealed reality and relationality) similar to those we are using here.[129] Smit repeated his point that for previous decades, 'There has been almost no meaningful dialogue in South Africa between biblical scholars and ethicists on the legitimate and responsible use of the Bible in Christian ethics' — but went on to analyse three recent doctoral theses which attempted to bridge this gap.[130]

As the dialogue intensified during the transition to democracy, Richardson looked to a wider African context, while Hartin related it to the pluralistic society of the new South Africa.[131] However, within a couple of years, an entire issue of *Scriptura* could be devoted to 'Christian Ethics in South Africa', including discussion about the use of the Bible.[132] This was edited by Etienne de Villiers, an ethicist from Pretoria, who also drew on Gustafson's distinguishing of the different approaches to demonstrate the narrow scope of ethical issues discussed in the apartheid years and the new challenges of the process of transformation.[133] Thereafter biblical scholars and ethicists continued to work together on a variety of topics.[134]

128. Gerald West, 'The Bible and Theology', in *Doing Theology in Context: South African Perspectives,* Theology and Praxis, ed. John de Gruchy and C. Villa-Vicencio (Cape Town: David Philip/Maryknoll, NY: Orbis, 1994), vol. 1, pp. 15-25, quotations from p. 15.

129. Jan Botha, 'The Bible and Ethics', in *Doing Ethics in Context: South African Perspectives,* Theology and Praxis, ed. C. Villa-Vicencio and J. de Gruchy (Cape Town: David Philip/Maryknoll, NY: Orbis, 1994), vol. 2, pp. 36-45; see esp. pp. 40-41.

130. Dirk J. Smit, 'Saints, Disciples, Friends? Recent South African Perspectives on Christian Ethics and the New Testament', *Neotestamentica* 30.1 (1996), pp. 169-85, quotation from p. 175.

131. Neville Richardson, 'Can Christian Ethics Find Its Way, and Itself, in Africa?' *JTSA* 95 (July 1996), pp. 37-54; Patrick J. Hartin, 'Christian Ethics in a Pluralistic Society: Towards a Theology of Compromise', *Religion and Theology* 4.1 (1997), pp. 21-34.

132. See *Christian Ethics in South Africa (1),* ed. Etienne de Villiers, *Scriptura* 62.3 (1997), esp. Elna Mouton, 'The (Trans)formative Potential of the Bible as Resource for Christian Ethos and Ethics', *Scriptura* 62.3 (1997), pp. 245-57; the rest of the volume included articles on virtue ethics, belief and action, Christianity and democracy, sexuality, patriarchy, community and being in business.

133. D. E. de Villiers, 'Challenges to Christian Ethics in the Present South African Society', *Scriptura* 69 (1999), pp. 75-91.

134. See, for example, the collaboration of a philosopher and a biblical scholar in Deane-Peter

Therefore, it can be seen that attempts earlier in this period in South Africa to develop an entire 'biblical theology' or to use the whole system of doctrine for biblical ethics ran into the same problems with this approach as elsewhere. However, it is clear that the transformation from the end of apartheid into the new democracy did begin to allow a fruitful interchange to grow up around the wider use of the Bible in ethics. This was coupled with a realization that the approach to the Bible under apartheid had relied too much upon ethical material interpreted in the form of norms, principles and examples. Our analysis above has shown how all four of these approaches to using the Bible, based on the various genres of different ethical material, were used in South Africa on both sides of the debate. It is interesting that Loubser's own assessment ten years after he wrote *The Apartheid Bible* also utilized these distinctions of proofs, norms and principles, as well as its overall message: 'I am still convinced that not only the scriptural proofs for apartheid were finally discarded, but also that the neo-Calvinist hermeneutic that determined the deployment of the so-called apartheid texts was also abandoned. Diversity was no longer to be regarded as "a Scriptural principle." Incidental facts were no longer confused with "norms," neither was diversity confused with segregation. The remnants of the old thinking that remained in the document *Church and Society* were disempowered by a new emphasis on justice and the unity of the church, as well as the willingness to evaluate the apartheid system in the light of this. . . . The mere admission that the Bible does not lend itself to be a blueprint for any political agenda, may seem vague and commonplace to outsiders, but within the ranks of the Church it represented a seismic shift in theological thinking.'[135]

6. Reading together in an inclusive community

The use of the Bible in South Africa, both to support apartheid and to critique it in the struggle for liberation, has thus provided a salutary 'test-case' or 'thought-laboratory' in which to examine the common fourfold distinction of ethical material, stemming from Gustafson onwards, according to its genre as rules, principles, examples and symbolic worldview. What is significant is that all four genres or approaches were used by both sides, often using the same method applied to the same passage(s), to argue that their case was 'biblical'

Baker and Jonathan More, 'Taking the Quandary out of Christian Ethics', *JTSA* 115 (March 2003), pp. 5-17.

135. Bobby Loubser, 'The Apartheid Bible Revisited', *Bulletin for Contextual Theology in Southern Africa and Asia* 3.1 (February 1996), pp. 8-10.

against the other position; this suggests that merely identifying these generic approaches will not guarantee proper biblical interpretation or protect the interpreters from readings which may appear subsequently as abusive or morally repugnant.

Therefore, if simply reading the New Testament's ethical material according to its genre will not secure a good or reliable result, something else is needed as a further safeguard. Hays is surely right to argue both that each genre (or 'mode', as he prefers to call them) must be interpreted in its own terms, as command, principle, or whatever, and also that we must use all four genres or modes, not merely one or two (although Hays does suggest that narrative has hermeneutical primacy).[136] The combination of all four approaches certainly does allow for an element of accountability, where 'the results obtained from one mode can help check the others'. Our examination of the 'overall symbolic worldview' approach just completed shows how eventually it began to call into question some of the support for apartheid which had come more from rules, principles and examples, but really this was too little, too late. Therefore the use of all four genres or modal approaches in South Africa under apartheid suggests that merely combining them all together will not necessarily prevent abuses either.

Our own genre-based approach to reading the New Testament has produced several key results which have recurred at the end of each of our studies of Jesus, Paul and the gospels: given that the various books are not written in the genre of ethical writings, it is a genre mistake to approach them as an ethical handbook, looking for rules, principles or examples which can be extracted from the surrounding overall narrative. This narrative is explicitly biographical in the four gospels, while there is an implicit narrative of the significance of Jesus' life, death and resurrection underlying all of Paul's writings. It begins with Jesus' preaching of the sovereign rule of God, which is then seen as fulfilled by Paul and the evangelists in their proclamation of what God has done in Jesus. In all cases, what is being sought is a response from the hearer or reader, rather than mere obedience to moral instructions. This response is formed around following and imitating the example of Jesus himself, according to the mimetic purpose of ancient biography and the Jewish custom of *ma'aseh*. Crucially, one cannot respond alone; rather, it is to be lived out within an open and inclusive community of others who are also seeking to follow and imitate him. Now therefore we must bring this approach to bear upon our South Africa test-case to see how these twin aspects of imitating Jesus and the context of an inclusive community might be applied to the way in which scripture was read under apartheid.

136. Hays, *Moral Vision of the NT,* pp. 293-95.

First, if the imitation of Jesus is the hermeneutical and ethical key, it could serve as a critical test against which each use of the four different genres of ethical material should be measured. We have seen that while Jesus' ethical teaching could be extremely demanding and rigorous, it was given within the context of his action in maintaining an open and inclusive community. No matter how correct some of the pro-apartheid readings of biblical norms, principles and examples might have seemed to the biblical scholars and church leaders who produced them, the fact that they resulted in a violent society in which the majority of people were excluded and oppressed, suffering violence and even death, should have been a clear indicator that something was wrong with this biblical interpretation. This therefore takes us into our second criterion regarding the community who produce the reading to see what the South African example might have to teach us here also. It is important to stress at this point that this is not simply a 'fifth mode' as an alternative to the four genre approaches of rules, principles, examples and worldview derived from scholars like Gustafson and Hays. It is rather the *overall context* within which the other four are all employed, the umbrella which needs to protect the community from abusive or morally repugnant readings.

a. Ethical approach

Our ethical approach starts as the New Testament does, with Jesus, rather than as Hays does, with Paul, and takes the biographical genre of the narrative seriously. Therefore, it is clear that the task of interpretation is not just about extracting individual passages of ethical teaching; rather, it involves the whole story of the New Testament and our own story, as we seek to imitate Jesus within an inclusive community. It is not unreasonable at this point to ask whether this theme is also vulnerable to the same critique as mentioned above in sect. 3.c, pages 369-70 about the problems with principles and Hays' 'focal images': from where is our 'key' of the imitation of Jesus derived, and is it truly biblical across the canon of the New Testament?

In response, we must return to our starting point, the biographical genre of the gospels. Following the genre of classical biography, we noted the importance of both words and deeds, ethical teaching and personal example, in accounts of ancient philosophers, leaders and statesmen — all with the express aim of *mimesis,* imitation. Therefore the ethical approach which we are advocating is embedded within the actual genre of the texts themselves and derived from there, not imposed from outside the text. Furthermore, this mimetic aim is made explicit in the rest of the New Testament through the frequent instructions in Paul and the other epistles to 'be imitators of me, as I am of Christ' (cf. 1 Cor. 11.1; Eph. 5.1; Phil. 3.17; 1 Thess. 1.6; Heb. 6.12; 12.1-3; 13.7; 1 Pet. 1.15-16; 2.21-25; 1 John 2.6; 3.3, 7; 3 John 1.11).

In our outline of the ethic of Jesus, Paul and the gospels, we saw that the New Testament demands a response in, to, and through the person of Jesus of Nazareth. The New Testament is not an ethical manual, nor is it just about providing moral instructions; instead, it challenges the reader with its central Christological claim and the consequent call to follow Jesus in discipleship. In this way, the text affects the audience in putting its stress on the moral agency of the reader. Through the cycle of reading and responding, rereading and re-responding, growth takes place which begins to 'form' Christian identity and moral character, as is stressed by the work of Hauerwas.[137] We are not to be 'conformed to this world', but 'transformed by the renewal of your mind' (Rom. 12.2), so that we are 'conformed to the image of his Son' (Rom. 8.29; see also 1 Cor. 15.49; 2 Cor. 3.18). As Rowan Williams has put it, 'The Christian life is . . . the repetition or recapitulation of the act and the narrative of God, primarily but not exclusively in the incarnate Christ'.[138] This requires the active role of the Holy Spirit, guiding the reading, challenging it, and directing the interpretative community, as portrayed in the Johannine Paraclete in the farewell discourses. The indwelling of the Holy Spirit produces the fruit of 'conformity to Christ' in the narrative of our lives, rather than just obeying certain texts of ethical teaching. This is another reason for insisting on an inclusive community, for no one becomes perfect overnight. It takes time to develop moral character and to grow in virtues, so we must not expect everyone to agree immediately. Responding to Jesus and following his example within the inclusive community entails our own growing in Christian character along the way. As Hauerwas says, 'The Christian claim that life is a pilgrimage is a way of indicating the necessary and never-ending growth of the self in learning to live into the story of Christ'.[139] However, if our own 'self' has to grow, this requires a recognition

---

137. On character ethics, see Stanley Hauerwas, *Character and the Christian Life* (Notre Dame, IN: University of Notre Dame Press, 1975; 3rd repr., 1994); idem, *A Community of Character: Towards a Constructive Christian Social Ethic* (Notre Dame, IN: University of Notre Dame Press, 1981); cp. Hays' discussion, 'Stanley Hauerwas: Character Shaped by Tradition', in *Moral Vision of the NT,* pp. 253-66; see also N. Richardson, 'Ethics of Character and Community', in *Doing Ethics in Context: South African Perspectives,* ed. C. Villa-Vicencio and J. de Gruchy (Cape Town: David Philip/Maryknoll, NY: Orbis, 1994), pp. 89-101.

138. Rowan D. Williams, 'Interiority and Epiphany: A Reading in New Testament Ethics', *Modern Theology* 13.1 (January 1997), pp. 29-51; quotation from p. 41.

139. Stanley Hauerwas, *The Peaceable Kingdom: A Primer in Christian Ethics* (Notre Dame, IN: University of Notre Dame Press, 1983), p. 95.

that others will also have their areas for growth — but that does not make them any less part of the community.

Therefore, there is an inevitable corporate dimension which arises from following Jesus alongside others who have also responded by joining the community of disciples. The corporate nature of the New Testament means that any reading of the text takes place in communities. The primary method of publication in the ancient world was through reading a text out loud to a group, after dinner perhaps, or gathered together for this particular purpose.[140] The reading of gospels or epistles within the context of early Christian corporate worship would have been very similar. Discussion about the text, its meaning and its relevance would then occur naturally among members of the group. Any attempt to do New Testament ethics must take into account the centrality of community. Therefore, ecclesiology is important as the church becomes the community of interpretation. This picks up Hauerwas' other great theme of community ethics.[141]

However, it is vital that such a communitarian or ecclesiological approach allows for the example of Jesus' openness as 'friend of sinners', since we are all growing in response to his love and grace and forgiveness. We have argued consistently that Jesus' strict and rigorous ethical teaching must be held in tension with his open acceptance of sinners without expecting any preconditions or prior changes. Thus his rigorous teaching about money, violence, sex, power, and so forth, all appears in the narrative context of his associating with tax gatherers and Zealots, prostitutes and Pharisees, healing Samaritans and Romans and dying in the place of a murderer. The rest of the New Testament not only appeals regularly to the example of Jesus, but instructs us to 'accept others as Christ has accepted you' and 'forgive one another as God in Christ has forgiven you . . . to live in love as Christ loved us' (Rom. 15.1-7; Eph. 4.32–5.2; Col. 3.13-15; 1 John 3.11-24). Others may make a similar response and thus join us on the journey; they also are to be accepted as they are, even though they may change later as their response to Jesus develops and their moral character is formed.

140. See Loveday Alexander, 'Ancient Book Production and the Circulation of the Gospels', in *The Gospels for All Christians: Rethinking the Gospel Audiences,* ed. R. J. Bauckham (Grand Rapids: Eerdmans/Edinburgh: T&T Clark, 1998), pp. 71-111; see esp. pp. 86-87 and 93-94.

141. For summaries and discussion of Hauerwas' approach, see J. S. Siker, 'Stanley Hauerwas: The Community Story of Israel and Jesus', in his *Scripture and Ethics: Twentieth Century Portraits* (Oxford: Oxford University Press, 1997), pp. 97-125; S. Wells, *Transforming Fate into Destiny: The Theological Ethics of Stanley Hauerwas* (Carlisle: Paternoster, 1998); David G. Horrell, *Solidarity and Difference: A Contemporary Reading of Paul's Ethics* (London: T&T Clark, 2005), see especially his section, 'Stanley Hauerwas' Ecclesial Ethics', and his 'reactions' thereto, pp. 63-82.

Fowl and Jones argue that it is important to listen to the 'voice of the outsiders' to prevent the danger of the church becoming a closed community.[142] While they are absolutely correct in making this point, this is an unhelpful term since it already alienates other people, placing them 'outside' the community. Equally, while 'sinners' has many possibilities from the description of Jesus as 'friend of sinners', it too will not work here unless it is recognized that we are all sinners, accepted as we are. Another possibility might be to pick up Hauerwas' use of 'strangers', but again that still speaks the language of 'them and us' — with 'them' as the 'strange' ones.[143] As we shall see shortly, Gerald West, from Pietermaritzburg, involves 'ordinary readers' alongside professional scholars, and this may be a more helpful term, particularly in the light of West's stress on the poor and marginalized. It has the added advantage of bringing 'ordinary' people in from the margins to the centre, while making scholars the more unusual, 'extraordinary' readers!

Whichever term is used, we will be able to read and begin to apply the ethical teaching of Jesus only in a community which also practises his open acceptance. Despite Hays' openness and understanding, his sections on 'living the text' in his 'pragmatic' fourth stage describe how the Christian community should live out the New Testament ethic of nonviolence, or being against homosexuality or abortion, in a rather sectarian manner, with a great stress on being 'counter-cultural' communities.[144] Again, this may reflect Hays' own ecclesiological background and upbringing, or his training and starting point as a Pauline scholar. However, our reading of Paul earlier in this book also pointed out that the early Pauline communities were more open and inclusive than is sometime imagined. It is clear that in the contemporary situation, there is a need for Christian communities, based around reading and interpreting the Biblical stories, to be a primary locus of resistance to the current 'globalization' of the world. Thus Katongole called for the church to act as 'a community of resistance and hope within the playful nihilism of a post-modern culture', centred on the biblical story.[145] However, such counter-cultural reading communi-

---

142. S. E. Fowl and L. G. Jones, *Reading in Communion: Scripture and Ethics in Christian Life* (London: SPCK, 1991), pp. 110-34.

143. See, for example, Stanley Hauerwas and William H. Willimon, *Preaching to Strangers: Evangelism in Today's World* (Louisville: Westminster John Knox, 1992).

144. Hays, *Moral Vision of the NT,* pp. 343-44, 374-76, 400-403, 438-41, 457-60.

145. Emmanuel M. Katongole, 'African Hermeneutics and Theology in the Twenty First Century: On Surviving Postmodernism', paper given at the SNTS Post Conference, Hammanskraal, University of Pretoria, 8/8/99, pp. 25-29; later published in *Interpreting the New Testament in Africa,* ed. Mary Getui, Tinyiko Maluleke and Justin Ukpong (Nairobi: Acton, 2001), pp. 253-73, see esp. 269.

ties must never become fellowships of the like-minded. Our approach to New Testament ethics requires the interpretative community always to be open and diverse, inclusive of those who might disagree with us, but who are still making their response of discipleship as we follow Christ together.

b. Genre and texts

This open and inclusive approach will work best with narratives and other genres, which can be interpreted prophetically. It sees them not just as tales giving moral instructions or examples, but as becoming our story also, as we enter into them and they into the shared life of the reading community. We have just noted that texts were primarily received orally and aurally by being read aloud in communal gatherings in the ancient world. This context may have assisted them in recognizing the correct genre of the text being read, and in the case of the New Testament encouraged them in responding together in faith. Therefore, an interpretative community reading according to the genre of the text today may also be enabled to recover clues about the original intention and meaning as they seek to respond in faith and follow the path of discipleship together.

c. Problems

One problem with such 'community-based' readings of the text is that history is full of examples where biblical interpretations with apparently proper exegesis and validation by the reading community were later seen to be erroneous or even oppressive. The obvious examples include the use of the Conquest of Canaan narratives by the Conquistadores in Latin America,[146] or the biblical justification for slavery in the eighteenth century,[147] or for Nazi anti-Semitism in the mid-twentieth century. According to most reader-response theory or community- or inculturation-type hermeneutics, it is hard to see how such readings, validated by

146. See Michael Prior, *The Bible and Colonialism: A Moral Critique* (Sheffield: Sheffield Academic Press, 1997), chap. 2, 'Colonialism and Latin America', pp. 48-70; also chap. 3, 'Colonialism and South Africa', pp. 71-105, and chap. 4, 'Colonialism and Palestine', pp. 106-74; John Riches, 'Reading the Bible Contextually: Some Consideration of the Canonical Context from a Post-Colonial Perspective', paper given at the SNTS Conference, University of Pretoria, 6/8/99.

147. See Wayne Meeks, 'The "Haustafeln" and American Slavery: A Hermeneutical Challenge', in Lovering and Sumney, *Theology and Ethics in Paul and His Interpreters*, pp. 232-53; Swartley, *Slavery, Sabbath, War and Women*, pp. 31-64; see earlier comments at nn. 6-7 above.

the interpreting community, could be considered 'invalid' or plain 'wrong', yet many would still want to argue that they are. There is a tension in Hauerwas' ecclesial ethics between locating the community of interpretation in the church and its tradition, which has the right to interpret the text, and yet his wanting to be able to criticize that community for its unchristian interpretations, such as not being pacifist. Thus Hays argues that 'the logic of Hauerwas' hermeneutical position should require him to become a Roman Catholic', but Hauerwas cannot accept its 'positions on major ethical issues'; he concludes that 'thus, in the end, Hauerwas' hermeneutical position comes unraveled'.[148]

Perhaps only a combination of traditional historical-critical studies with such open and inclusive community- or culture-based readings can avoid such oppressive conclusions. We have suggested that it is better to start with common human moral experiences, such as poverty, sexuality, violence and so forth, rather than particular modern ethical problems. The first stage is to collect all the New Testament material on the chosen topic, to describe it through careful exegesis and, secondly, to see if there is some consensus, or 'best line fit', running through it all, preferably without the potential distortion of any prior principles or 'focal images'. The third step involves Hays' hermeneutical task of analysing how the different texts function according to their genre or mode, as rule, principle, example or worldview. Only then can we turn to the difficult task of applying this to our ethical dilemmas today — and this is where the context of a community-based reading is vital. Our study of Jesus, Paul and the gospels has concluded that the New Testament must be read within an open and inclusive community. Without such openness, we run the risk of becoming an exclusive community reading in a closed circle, and just finding our ideas and prejudices reflected back from the text. In practical terms, a group discussing the New Testament's material on wealth and poverty should include bank managers of financial investors alongside campaigners for relief of world debt and poverty, while a debate on war and violence would require both pacifists and serving military officers. It is particularly important that those who will be affected, or even oppressed, by possible readings should be able to make their voices heard, so that women must be involved in discussions about gender, homosexuals about sexuality, and ethnic minorities about race. As Tomson observes, 'Reading the Bible in an exclusive manner within a closed community is not a Christian patent, but is based on the general human tendency of self-protection'.[149] Only a diverse inclusive group may help to pro-

148. Hays, *Moral Vision of the NT,* p. 265; see also Horrell's discussion of Hauerwas' position in *Solidarity and Difference*, pp. 73-77.

149. See Peter J. Tomson's section, 'Reading in an Open Community', in his *'If this be from*

tect against such self-serving community readings, such as the colonialist or Nazi interpretations.

Such an approach will not give easy or straight answers. There is bound to be an element of provisionality as the response grows and develops. There may also be disagreement within the community between those who hold different views. The attempt to move from the New Testament accounts of human experiences to our ethical dilemmas today means that we are some way back from a simple surface application of the biblical text. Thus any demands for prescriptive rules and clear principles may have to be set aside. The text might be subordinated to the development of the character of individual members or the community as a whole. The contribution of the biblical exegete is not to provide the 'correct answers' of the 'biblical teaching', but to offer the Christian community some expertise and methods to enable them to grapple with the text themselves, while at the same time listening to their 'ordinary readings'.

This reading of the biblical material will need to be set alongside other sources of moral guidance such as reason, tradition and experience, as well as all our modern resources from the human sciences, medicine, psychology and the like. The view which emerges needs to be challenged by and in prayer, or by listening to the experience of others, particularly those outside our situation who can help to prevent it from becoming *eisegesis* and merely reflecting our own desires. The provisionality of decisions and the tendency to 'fudge' will frustrate those who want 'clear moral guidance'. The toleration of a variety of views, or the acceptance of 'sinners', will not be easy for those who want 'everyone to sing from the same hymn sheet'. We have argued throughout this book for Jesus' teaching his rigorous and demanding ethic within the context of an open and inclusive community. However, admitting so-called 'outsiders' or those with different views as full participants might mean that the rigorous ethic will get watered down. Furthermore, there is the problem of continuing to include persistent 'sinners' within the church; for instance, can an unreformed (or unreformable?) paedophile be fully included? It is significant that the only time Paul called for someone to be excluded from the church was regarding the man living in an incestuous relationship. The reason for his horrified reaction seems to be that this immorality was 'of a kind that is not found even among pagans'. However, as we saw in our discussion of this in Chapter III above, even then Paul's concern was primarily pastoral, to save the man's spirit (1 Cor. 5.1-5).

Heaven . . .': Jesus and the New Testament Authors in Their Relationship to Judaism (Sheffield: Sheffield Academic Press, 2001), pp. 415-22 for a discussion of how both Jews and Christians engaged in open and closed readings of scripture with and without each other, both in the early church and today; quotation from p. 419.

d. South Africa

The Dutch Reformed Church thought it was doing its interpretation of the scriptures in a Spirit-guided, prayerful community, supported by excellent university faculties of theology with biblical scholars very experienced in the area of hermeneutics. Despite all of this, the attempt to justify apartheid as being 'biblical' is now seen as incorrect, even within the DRC itself. This therefore raises the question of how they got it so wrong — and this also acts as a challenge to other communities who believe that their particular views or doctrines are 'biblical'. The Truth and Reconciliation Commission's process of enabling victims and oppressors alike to tell their stories was crucial for South Africa to move forward after apartheid.[150] Less well known are their hearings from the Faith Communities held in East London, November 17-19, 1997, as detailed in a report by the Research Institute on Christianity in South Africa (RICSA).[151]

I have undertaken an analysis of the transcripts of these hearings to examine where witnesses referred to their use of the Bible. The representatives of the Church of England in South Africa, an evangelical offshoot from the main Anglican Church of the Province of Southern Africa, were among the first to make their submission, and are particularly interesting. Bishop Frank Retief described CESA as 'a denomination that was very small but committed to the Bible as the word of God'. He admitted that 'when the government made legislation that accorded with our moral or biblical understanding, we supported them. However, on the great issue of justice for all, we were often insensitive. We had not made the connection between gospel and society.' CESA's attempt 'to be a-political . . . failed to adequately understand the suffering of our many black members who were victims of apartheid. Our failure to be involved in the political struggles of our land was a major error in both understanding and judgement, and this mistake has caused us a great deal of embarrassment, heartache and pain. . . . We do not apologise for our stand on the central message of the Bible. However, we do want to express our apology, our sorrow and regret at the things we left undone.' He refers to the use of the Bible by both sides: 'We were a witness to how the Bible and its message can be misused to

---

150. The final report can be found at http://www.info.gov.za/otherdocs/2003/trc; see also *To Remember and to Heal: Theological and Psychological Reflections on Truth and Reconciliation*, eds. H. Russel Botman and Robin M. Petersen (Cape Town: Human & Rousseau, 1996).

151. *Facing the Truth: South African Faith Communities and the Truth & Reconciliation Commission*, ed. James Cochrane, John de Gruchy and Stephen Martin (Cape Town: David Philip, 1998), which contains details of the written submissions, oral testimony and witnesses, as well as a number of reflective essays; see also Denise M. Ackermann, 'Faith Communities Face the Truth', *JTSA* 103 (March 1999), pp. 88-93.

support an evil ideology. National government used the Bible to support its policies, to give the impression that they were a Christian government. But then so did some liberation theologians who finally supported violence as a means of continuing the struggle.' However, he remained committed to being biblical: 'Where we have been negligent, careless and insensitive to biblical injunctions and mandates as we have been, may the Lord graciously forgive us. . . . The fact that the Bible was used in the past to condone injustice does not mean its true message may be ignored today. . . . It is our belief that this day and hour calls for men and women of conviction and integrity to apply the message of the Bible more accurately and faithfully to our emerging society.' This point was reinforced by his colleague, Bishop Martin Morrison, who commented that 'although we are firmly committed to the Bible as the word of God as our source of truth for all of life, there have been times, certainly in our past and I'm sure even in our present, when we don't read it properly or obey it as we ought.'[152]

What is significant here is the frank admission that misreading of the Bible in the past had caused suffering, linked with a commitment to apply it 'more accurately and faithfully' today, without necessarily explaining how the mistakes of the past can be avoided in future use of the Bible. The Evangelical Alliance of South Africa were equally keen to stress that 'the primary value and distinguishing mark of the Evangelical community is the place given to the authority and inspiration of scripture. A high view of scripture is believed to provide a perspective which safeguards the church from worldly thinking and keeps it faithful to its mission'. Regarding the struggle against apartheid, Dr. Derek Morphew noted that 'there were individuals and congregations who courageously exemplified a truly biblical witness. However, in general, our testimony is one of failure to be faithful to the word of God we so highly value. . . . The future calls us to discover a practice of missions and evangelism where biblical discipleship takes on new meaning. It will need to include biblical teaching on social ethics, human rights, the empowering of disadvantaged communities and nation building'.[153] Here, therefore, to be 'truly biblical' is linked with the human rights principles of the new South African society. Pastor Ray McCauley of the International Fellowship of Christian Churches made a similar point: 'The Bible may have been abused in the past to bolster a man-made ideology, but let's get back to what God intended for his people, and that is peace, joy and the Spirit of Christ'.[154] Despite his admission of 'past transgressions', Pastor

152. Extracts taken from the RICSA transcripts, pp. 83-93; I am grateful to Stephen Martin, Research Coordinator of RICSA, for making these available to me. See also the RICSA website at the University of Cape Town, http://web.uct.ac.za/depts/ricsa/commiss/trc/
153. RICSA transcripts, pp. 212-15.
154. RICSA transcripts, p. 221.

Izak Burger of the Apostolic Faith Mission was even more confident: 'We proclaim fearlessly that what we are doing today, we believe, is in line with the word of God and have no doubt that the future will prove us correct.'[155]

Comments about the supposed scriptural basis for apartheid and biblical hopes for the future also featured in comments from Douglas Bax of the Presbyterian Church of Southern Africa, Archbishop Tutu himself in the chair, Dr. Z. E. Mokgoebo of the Belydende Kring, a group working for the unification of the racially divided Reformed churches, Peter Hollness from the Baptist Union of Southern Africa, and James Buys and Marcus Maphoto from the Uniting Reformed Church.[156] Furthermore, Imam Gassan Solomon, representing the Muslim Judicial Council, drew attention to 'the relevant scriptural support from the holy Koran' for the struggle against apartheid.[157]

Perhaps most important were the representatives from the Dutch Reformed Church. Dominee Freek Swanepoel was clear in his admission: 'I wish to testify to the struggle that the DRC had to wage within itself in order to reject apartheid and to do away with apartheid in its decisions. In 1982 the Synod rejected apartheid as sin, rejected racism as sin. The Dutch Reformed Church stands by its admission in 1986 that the church had erred seriously with the Biblical foundation of the forced segregation of people. . . . We have indeed taught our people wrongly with regard to apartheid as a Biblical instruction.' Nico Smith agreed that 'we admit and confess that we too were blinded by an ideology which presented itself as justifiable from the Bible'. Interestingly, Ponti Venter noted that no DRC 'theologian [was] called to book for voting for this policy or providing biblical support for this doctrine'.[158]

Therefore these submissions and oral testimonies from the faith communities to the TRC included numerous references to the use of the Bible during the apartheid years, with several moving apologies for the consequences of this for those who suffered under the system. Nonetheless, many speakers remained confident in their biblical calling and mission, now that they had learned to read the Bible aright. However, the basis of this renewed confidence was never fully explained, nor was there any detailed suggestion about how the mistakes of the past came to be made in the first place, or how they could be avoided in the new application of scripture in the future.

---

155. RICSA transcripts, p. 236.

156. RICSA transcripts, pp. 113, 130, 188, 228, 242-46.

157. RICSA transcripts, p. 197.

158. RICSA transcripts, pp. 246-65; further review of the role of the Dutch Reformed Church during the end of apartheid can be found in the special volume *The Dutch Reformed Church (DRC) and Transition in SA*, ed. Wolfram Weisse, *Scriptura* 76 (2001), pp. 1-151, and during the period around the TRC in the companion volume, *Scriptura* 83 (2003), pp. 189-347.

In personal conversations, South African scholars, especially some from a Afrikaner/DRC background whose frankness is impressive, have explained to me that the biblical and theological justification for apartheid happened because the church leaders and authorities did not listen to the voices of 'outsiders' in the rest of the world and stifled the protests of people 'inside' the church. It is significant that the RICSA report lists 'active suppression of dissidents within their ranks' as one of the 'acts of commission and legitimisation' committed by faith communities under apartheid.[159]

At the end of his account of *The Apartheid Bible* in 1986, Loubser stressed how important it was that 'the Bible must be read correctly': in order for this to happen, the first requirement is 'self-criticism'. 'One of the outstanding features of any ideological interpretation of the Bible is the complete lack of any self-criticism . . . by making others aware of one's uncritical presuppositions, people with different theologies (as the "people's theology", "church theology" and liberation theology) can creatively interact with one another.'[160] The importance of this can be gauged by the fact that his plea for self-criticism and listening to others' views was resisted even in 1986: as he put it in his reflections ten years later, 'When the book finally appeared, it met with mixed reaction. While the regular Afrikaans press ignored it completely, right wing reviews labelled it as one more liberal assault on Afrikaner values.' What surprised him more was the 'unusual indignant reaction from the left' accusing him of 'trying to whitewash the DRC, while actually re-enforcing a conservative, middle of the road, *status quo* theology.'[161] Thus both sides of the debate were not willing to listen to the other, or anything other than their own view.

Fowl and Jones also use apartheid as an example of how things can go wrong: 'When distortions of character enter and deeply permeate the life of any Christian community, that community loses its ability to read Scripture in ways that would challenge and correct its character. Scripture simply becomes a mirror reflecting a community's self-deceptions back to itself disguised as the word of God. This is what happened to the DRC. It lost the ability to read Scripture over against itself; it lost the ability to hear the critical, prophetic voice of Scripture.' Likening the situation to the people of Judah in the time of Jeremiah, they conclude, 'Christians need to cultivate active dialogues with outsiders so as to avoid the interpretive self-deception into which the people of Judah and the DRC fell.'[162]

159. 'Faith Communities and Apartheid: The RICSA Report', in *Facing the Truth: South African Faith Communities and the Truth & Reconciliation Commission*, ed. James Cochrane, John de Gruchy and Stephen Martin, pp. 15-80; see pp. 36-37 for this section.

160. Loubser, *The Apartheid Bible*, p. 163.

161. Loubser, 'The Apartheid Bible Revisited', p. 8.

162. Fowl and Jones, *Reading in Communion*, pp. 96-104; quotations from pp. 99 and 104.

Shortly after the first democratic elections in South Africa, the Seventh International Bonhoeffer Congress took place in Cape Town. Smit noted that it is 'obvious that one of the most important challenges to South African Christians and theologians flowing from Bonhoeffer's legacy is the importance of "learning to live with the other". Today, this challenge is perhaps more urgent than ever before.' He concluded, 'One important characteristic of the kind of Christians, the kind of human beings, the kind of South Africans, and the kind of moral communities that we need in South Africa in order for the church *to be* the church, with truthfulness and integrity, is the ability . . . to live together. . . . We shall have to become people who can learn to live with strangers, who are willing to accept others, who are able to understand people who speak different languages (real, natural languages, like Afrikaans or Zulu, but also ideological languages, like socialist, capitalist, or nationalist, or liberal) and to cooperate, to live and to work with them'.[163]

There were two main developments in South African New Testament scholarship during the decade of transition from apartheid to democracy which reflect this need for an open and inclusive reading community. First, various New Testament scholars began to develop new community-based approaches, looking at issues like context, readers and socio-political questions, in order to avoid repeating the old mistakes. Combrink and Lategan were involved in setting up the Centre for Contextual Hermeneutics at Stellenbosch,[164] which organized its first Consultation on Contextual Hermeneutics in April 1991,[165] with several others over following years.[166] These provoked various debates about differing forms of contextual theologies.[167] Thus, Smit's study of 'contextual hermeneutics' speaks of the development of 'interpretative communities' seeking to understand the New Testament in dialogue with one another.[168]

Such approaches received additional support from developments in biblical scholarship elsewhere in Africa with its concern for inculturation. Justin

163. Dirkie Smit, 'Dietrich Bonhoeffer and "The Other": "Accept One Another, Therefore . . ." (Rom. 15:7)', *JTSA* 93 (December 1995), pp. 3-16; opening and closing quotations from pp. 3 and 15.

164. Bernard Lategan, 'Introducing a Research Project on Contextual Hermeneutics', *Scriptura* 33 (1990), pp. 1-5.

165. Papers published as *Issues in Contextual Hermeneutics*, ed. Johann Kinghorn, *Scriptura* Special Issue S9 (1991); see also D. J. Smit, 'The Ethics of Interpretation', p. 41.

166. The papers from the second and third consultations are published as *The Integrity of Theological Education*, ed. B. C. Lategan, *Scriptura*, Special Issue S11 (1993).

167. See the account in Pieter G. R. de Villiers, 'The Bible and the Struggle (for Power)', *Scriptura* 45 (1993), pp. 1-28; also F. A. Swanepoel, 'Popularising Contextual Theology', *Scriptura* 45 (1993), pp. 67-78.

168. D. J. Smit, 'A Story of Contextual Hermeneutics and the Integrity of New Testament Interpretation in South Africa', *Neotestamentica* 28.2 (1994), 265-89.

Ukpong, from Nigeria, has particularly developed an 'inculturation hermeneutic' in which the socio-cultural setting of the interpreter and their community plays a crucial role in reading: 'inculturation hermeneutic is participatory. It demands the involvements of the interpreter and his/her world in the world of the text.' African cultures with their unitive view of reality and 'the interconnectedness between God, humanity and the cosmos' together with their sense of community have much to offer this process.[169] Gerald West's analysis of the state of play in the mid-1990s concluded that it was not so much 'on the eve of an African biblical studies' as 'well into its dawn'.[170] This was given a further boost by the visit of SNTS to hold its annual conference for the first time in Africa (indeed anywhere in the southern hemisphere) in Pretoria in 1999, to which they brought biblical scholars from across Africa to join in a post-conference on African hermeneutics and theology.[171] This demonstrated the importance of contextual and incultural approaches within African biblical studies; thus Eric Anum highlighted the 'collaborative/dialogical reading process' as the way forward for readings in Africa in the new millennium,[172] while Tinyiko Maluleke overcame his 'initial hesitance' in stressing the importance of 'reading-with' theologies.[173] As the new South Africa began to look to the rest of the continent, this became an increasingly fruitful relationship.[174] Further-

169. Justin S. Ukpong, 'Rereading the Bible with African Eyes: Inculturation and Hermeneutics', *JTSA* 19 (June 1995), pp. 3-14; quotations from pp. 6, 9.

170. Gerald O. West, 'On the Eve of an African Biblical Studies: Trajectories and Trends', *JTSA* 99 (November 1997), pp. 99-115.

171. See Bernard C. Lategan, 'The *Studiorum Novi Testamenti Societas* Comes to Africa', *Scriptura* 67 (1998), pp. 419-27.

172. Eric Anum, 'Suggestions for Effective Scholarly Readings of the Bible in a Post-2000 Africa', paper given at the SNTS Post Conference, Hammanskraal, University of Pretoria, 9/8/99, pp. 5-11; later published in a revised form as 'Effective Scholarly Readings of the Bible in Africa', in *Interpreting the New Testament in Africa*, ed. Mary Getui, Tinyiko Maluleke and Justin Ukpong (Nairobi: Acton, 2001), pp. 104-22, see esp. pp. 107-17.

173. Tinyiko S. Maluleke, 'African Theologies/Christianities and the Bible — Some Hermeneutical Issues at Stake', paper given at the SNTS Post Conference, Hammanskraal, University of Pretoria, 8/8/99, p. 6; later published in a revised form as 'The Bible and African Theologies', in *Interpreting the New Testament in Africa*, ed. Mary Getui, Tinyiko Maluleke and Justin Ukpong (Nairobi: Acton, 2001), pp. 165-76.

174. See, for example, Jeremy Punt, 'Reading the Bible in Africa: Accounting for Some Trends, Part I', *Scriptura* 68 (1999), pp. 1-11; Jeremy Punt, 'Reading the Bible in Africa: Accounting for Some Trends, Part II', *Scriptura* 71 (1999), pp. 313-29. For an account of the historical background and developments up to 2000, see Justin S. Ukpong, 'Developments in Biblical Interpretation in Africa: Historical and Hermeneutical Directions', *JTSA* 108 (November 2000), pp. 3-18; the rest of that volume contains various articles demonstrating the relationship. For a fuller collection, see Gerald O. West and Musa W. Dube (eds.), *The Bible in Africa: Transactions, Trajectories, and Trends* (Leiden: Brill, 2000).

more, Ukpong sees this mixture of a contextual approach in an inculturated setting as providing both 'challenges and possibilities' which can draw upon the African experience in a postcolonial world to provide a way of 'reading with ethical accountability'.[175] This is all a long way from the closed reading of the apartheid texts which refused to hear the dissenting voices.

West himself has played a crucial role in this African renaissance in general, but has also contributed the second major factor in the new South African hermeneutics. As the first factor, the stress on context, began to get under way, West argued that 'something is missing in contextual biblical hermeneutics in South Africa. The voice(s) of the "people" or what I have called "the ordinary reader" is missing.'[176] In his larger treatment of the 'biblical hermeneutics of liberation', West argued that under apartheid the academy either used the Bible to justify apartheid, or took refuge in interpretive studies which produced nothing of relevance for South Africa's political situation; meanwhile the so-called 'ordinary reader' experienced the scriptures as an instrument of both liberation and oppression. In his contextual reading, therefore, West set out to pioneer new modes of reading the Bible in his local context.[177] He then put this into practice with his *Institute for the Study of the Bible* at the University of Natal in Pietermaritzburg to undertake contextual theology in partnership between 'ordinary' and 'trained' readers: 'The primary aim of the ISB is to establish an interface between biblical studies and ordinary readers of the Bible in the church and community that will facilitate social transformation'.[178] This experience enabled him to develop a methodology for studying the Bible which gave 'shape to the discourse of the dominated'.[179] He was concerned for the way in which such stories were being told in the TRC and the genre of their narra-

175. Justin S. Ukpong, 'New Testament Hermeneutics in Africa: Challenges and Possibilities', *Neotestamentica* 35 (2001), pp. 147-67; as an example of how this has developed further, see also Jeremy Punt, 'Current Debates in Biblical Hermeneutics in South Africa and the Postcolonial Matrix', *Religion and Theology* 11.2 (2004), pp. 139-60.

176. Gerald West, 'The Relationship between Different Modes of Reading (the Bible) and the Ordinary Reader', in *Issues in Contextual Hermeneutics*, ed. Johann Kinghorn, *Scriptura* Special Issue S9 (1991), pp. 87-110, opening quotation from p. 87.

177. Gerald O. West, *Biblical Hermeneutics of Liberation; Modes of Reading the Bible in the South African Context* (Maryknoll, NY: Orbis, 2nd rev. edn. 1995; original edn., Petermaritzburg: Cluster, 1991).

178. Gerald West, 'Some Parameters of the Hermeneutic Debate in the South African Context', *JTSA* 80 (September 1992), pp. 3-13; quotation from p. 10.

179. Gerald West, 'Reading the Bible Differently: Giving Shape to the Discourse of the Dominated', in *'Reading with . . .': An Explanation of the Interface between Critical and Ordinary Readings of the Bible*, ed. Gerald West and Musa W. Dube, *Semeia* 73 (1996), pp. 21-41; the rest of the volume looks at 'Reading with . . .' South African readers, women, inculturation readers and ordinary readers.

tive within the legal context,[180] so he continued to work for dialogue with the poor.[181] The work of the ISB has expanded and been renamed the Ujamaa Centre for Biblical and Theological Community Development and Research.[182] This method of contextual Bible study is now being widely used to handle the many, different concerns of 'ordinary readers', such as violence against women.[183] West has also begun to use this method with 'ordinary readers' to address the issues of social exclusion and stigma arising from HIV/Aids.[184] While West's method is now known worldwide, it is a mark of the concern for 'ethically sound interpretations of the Bible' and 'responsible ways of using the Bible' in the new South Africa in reaction to the apartheid use of the scriptures that it has been criticized and analysed in its turn, with Craffert attempting to redress the balance back towards the original historical and cultural contexts, and Akper wanting to ensure that the 'ordinary readers' are really reading for themselves.[185]

Therefore the development of contextual hermeneutics in general, and West's use of it for partnership with 'ordinary readers' may both be seen as reactions to the 'closed-shop', exclusive reading of the Bible which gave rise to the justification for apartheid. They are also good examples of reading communities imitating the example of Jesus in seeking to put forward ethical readings within an inclusive community. The revised situation in the new South Africa calls for biblical scholars to be involved in reconstructing society and public policy.[186]

180. Gerald West, 'Don't Stand on My Story: The Truth and Reconciliation Commission, Intellectuals, Genre and Identity', *JTSA* 98 (1997), pp. 3-12.

181. Gerald West, 'The Bible and the Poor: A New Way of Doing Theology', in *The Cambridge Companion to Liberation Theology*, ed. Christopher Rowland (Cambridge: Cambridge University Press, 1999), pp. 129-52; Gerald O. West, *The Academy of the Poor: Towards a Dialogical Reading of the Bible* (Sheffield: Sheffield Academic Press, 1999).

182. Gerald West, *Doing Contextual Bible Study: A Resource Manual* (Pietermaritzburg: Ujamaa Centre, 2005).

183. See Gerald O. West, 'The Historicity of Myth and the Myth of Historicity: Locating the Ordinary African "Reader" of the Bible in the Debate', *Neotestamentica* 38.1 (2004), pp. 127-44; idem, 'Articulating, Owning and Mainstreaming Local Theologies: The Contribution of Contextual Bible Study', *JTSA* 122 (2005), pp. 23-35.

184. Gerald O. West, 'Reading the Bible in the Light of HIV/Aids in South Africa', *The Ecumenical Review* 55.4 (2003), pp. 335-44; Gerald West and Bongi Zengele, 'The Medicine of God's Word: What People Living with HIV and AIDS Want (and Get) from the Bible', *JTSA* 125 (July 2006), pp. 51-63.

185. Pieter F. Craffert, 'From Apartheid Readings to Ordinary Readings of the Bible', *Scriptura* 64 (1998), pp. 65-79; Godwin I. Akper, 'The Role of the 'Ordinary Reader' in Gerald O. West's Hermeneutics', *Scriptura* 88 (2005), pp. 1-13.

186. See, for example, James R. Cochrane, 'Theological Reflection on Public Policy: The Church and the Reconstruction of South African Society', *JTSA* 97 (March 1997), pp. 1-15.

Paradoxically, the very success of contextual theology as originally linked into the liberation struggle has meant that 'it sowed the seeds of its own demise' and decline with 'the successes of the new regime'. However, Balcomb's analysis of contextual theology ten years into democracy, delivered at the Theological Society of South Africa's Conference in 2004, argued that its need 'is as urgent now as it has always been' if a withdrawal 'from prophetic engagement with the government and from society' is to be avoided.[187] Interestingly, Richardson's otherwise exciting look into the future of South African theology at the same conference does not seem to mention any issues about reading or interpreting the Bible![188] Meanwhile, a symposium to mark Archbishop Tutu's seventy-fifth birthday and the tenth anniversary of the TRC reunited various members of the Commission to assess how much the promises made at the TRC, particularly concerning the role of the churches in promoting healing and reconciliation, had been fulfilled — and called for holding the faith communities to account to encourage them to play their part in the new society.[189]

Therefore, this final stage in the use of South Africa as our 'test-case' has re-affirmed the importance of reading the New Testament within an inclusive community. It was precisely the lack of this openness which contributed significantly to the Dutch Reformed Church developing the scriptural justification of apartheid in the first place, and the excluding of dissident voices enabled the political and religious authorities to continue to claim that separate development was a 'biblical' teaching. While some church leaders were willing to confess this misreading of the Bible at the faith communities hearings of the TRC, they seem equally confident that they can now read it properly and continue to claim the authority of scripture for their current concerns. Over the decade or so of the transition to majority rule and democracy, the development of contextual hermeneutics within New Testament scholarship and the involvement of as wide a group of people as possible, including especially the 'ordinary reader', the poor and marginalized might well have helped that confidence not to be misplaced and to avoid false claims to being 'biblical' in the future.

187. Anthony Balcomb, 'Negotiating the Crisis of Success: Contextual Theology Ten Years into Democracy', *Scriptura* 89 (2005), pp. 482-94; quotations from pp. 486 and 494.

188. Neville Richardson, 'The Future of South African Theology: Scanning the Road Ahead', *Scriptura* 89 (2005), pp. 550-62.

189. 'The Role of the Faith Communities in Promoting Healing and Reconciliation in the RSA', a symposium jointly sponsored by the SACC, UNISA and the University of Pretoria, held at UNISA on October 6, 2006.

Conclusion

We began this book by noting that debates about the best way to read the Bible and how to apply its teaching to moral issues and ethical debate have raged throughout the history of the Christian church, plaguing its internal relationships between different Christians and its external attitude to the world. A good recent example is the doctrine of 'separate development', or apartheid, which dominated South Africa for most of the twentieth century, causing untold misery and loss of life especially to the black majority in that beautiful land, not to mention conflicts and wars across southern Africa as a whole, as well as enormous international debates and controversy affecting everything from economics to sport. Yet the extraordinary thing is that apartheid was a 'biblical' doctrine, justified 'in the light of Scripture' within a predominantly Christian country and supported by excellent university faculties of theology and biblical studies. Add to this example, the use of the Bible to support colonial conquest, to justify slavery and to oppress women, ethnic minorities, untouchables and outcasts of all sorts, and it all seems a very sorry history indeed. No wonder that Trible talks of 'texts of terror', while Carroll described it as a 'wolf in the sheepfold'. It all seems to lead to only one conclusion: 'If the Bible is really so much a problem for Christianity, and specifically for theology, would it not be better for theology to abandon the book altogether?'[190]

Not surprisingly, there has been a strong temptation to do this in the new democratic South Africa, which has removed much of the Christian basis of society and replaced it with a constitution based on human rights and a supreme constitutional court which can hold the government to account. We saw above that the renowned South African biblical scholar Jan Botha, who wrote his doctorate on the use of Rom. 13.1-7 to promote obedience to the state, acknowledged after liberation that he now takes 'human rights' as his 'starting point outside the New Testament'. This is the ultimate authority which he uses to critique and reject 'those Biblical stories and cultural values which function as a stumbling block in the way of this vision' while re-telling only 'those stories that are suitable'.[191] What is really surprising, however, is that millions of South Africans remain deeply committed to reading the Bible, while the churches are flourishing in all the ethnic and cultural communities of that land.

The situation in the rest of the world is equally complex. While the spectres

190. Robert P. Carroll, *Wolf in the Sheepfold: The Bible as a Problem for Christianity* (London: SPCK, 1991), quotation from p. 144; Phyllis Trible, *Texts of Terror: Literary Feminist Readings of Biblical Narratives* (London: SCM, 1992).

191. Jan Botha, 'The Bible in South African Public Discourse — with Special Reference to the Right to Protest', *Scriptura* 58 (1996), p. 329.

of mass starvation, international conflicts, HIV/AIDS and global warming stalk us like four modern horsemen of the Apocalypse, many Christian churches around the world are overwhelmed by internal wranglings about women in leadership and homosexuality. What it means to be 'biblical' lies at the heart of these debates, with each side claiming to be right and dismissing their opponents as bigoted conservatives or godless liberals. Here too, therefore, the temptation is to give up on the Bible, and just go for a human rights or liberationist agenda.

Yet the expectations of the secularist thesis have been dumbfounded: far from fading away, religion is a more potent force in the world at the start of the twenty-first century than ever could have been imagined fifty years ago. The two largest and strongest groups in world are Christians (dominated by evangelicals and Roman Catholics) and Muslims — both of which are known collectively as 'the people of the book'. Meanwhile, the third group which also makes up 'the people of book', the Jews, may not be particularly numerous — but their commitment to their scriptures and belief that God gave them this particular land lies at the heart of the most intractable problems of the world. The Berlin Wall and the iron curtain between East and West may have come down, but another form of apartheid grows ever stronger in the Middle East as the wall of separation goes up in the occupied Palestinian territories.

Thus we cannot ignore the Bible, or tame the wolf, or revisit the canon to remove the 'texts of terror' as some suggest among the so-called 'liberal mainline denominations' — even if we wanted to. Nor am I prepared to do so. Speaking personally, this book is the word of life, which changed everything around for me when I was an undergraduate and which has directed my personal life, ministry and academic career ever since.

So I want to grapple with it, read it and try ever to get a better understanding of it, so that I can make sense of it and, yes, apply it to my life and the life of the world in these complex and perplexing times. I am simply not prepared to let the fundamentalist lobby, or even the so-called conservatives, have the monopoly on what it means to be 'biblical' any more than I am willing to allow so-called 'liberals' to dismiss it.

While this book has not been yet another tome about 'women bishops' or 'the gay issue', it cannot be denied that such topics have been 'the elephant in the room' lurking behind so much of our discussion. By looking at the example of apartheid, we have been able to consider a test-case or thought-experiment to try to understand how biblical Christians came up with that doctrine of separate development which we all find so abhorrent now.

However, we could not have undertaken the analysis of the Bible under apartheid without the extensive study which preceded it. Our method has been driven throughout by literary genre, arising from my previous studies on the genre of the gospels. Their form of biographical narrative means that we have to start with Jesus, who is universally regarded as one of the great moral teachers of humankind. Yet he was not an ethicist, nor are the gospels collections of moral instructions. They are literary and theological portraits which combine his deeds and words according to the conventions of ancient biography to provide an example for others to imitate. Admittedly, they do contain some of his ethical teaching, but it is so strict and rigorous that most people find it impossible to keep in any practical way. Furthermore, it was actually only part of his overall preaching of the kingdom of God, the sovereign rule of divine love to which he wanted people to respond in whatever way they could. Paradoxically, this meant that Jesus continued giving his all-demanding ethical teaching within the context of an open and inclusive community comprised of those who responded and wanted to follow him. Clearly, such a state of affairs would not be allowed to continue for long, and the guardians of morality soon had him executed.

Further study revealed that the same was true of Paul and the gospel writers. While Paul is often portrayed as a negative moralist, perverting the simple faith of Jesus, our analysis demonstrated that he was in fact a faithful follower of the risen Christ. At the heart of his theology was the conviction that God's rule was being achieved in the whole event of Jesus' life, death and resurrection through which the end of the ages was inaugurated and love became the fulfilling of the law. While his letters also do contain varying amounts of ethical instruction, it all flows from his Christology and is set within the context of his loving concern for his converts within their mixed and inclusive early Christian communities to imitate his example, as he imitated Jesus.

In a similar way, each of the four evangelists takes the deeds and words of Jesus, his teaching and his story and retells it all for his own audience. Thus Mark portrays the self-denying ethic of Jesus who was misunderstood and who died for us in terrible darkness, while Matthew recasts this story within the wider history of Israel, depicting Jesus as the true interpreter of the law who brought and taught the real righteousness. Luke broadened it still further with his account of Jesus' universal concern and especial care for the outcast and marginalized, which he continued through into the narrative of the early church. Finally, John, who is often castigated for narrow sectarianism, was found to be the one who paints his picture of the divine love entering our world to bring us the truth on a cosmic scale. All four evangelists share a mimetic purpose that their audience should follow Jesus within an open community of all those who become disciples.

Building upon these two key results — the imitation of Jesus and an open, inclusive community of followers — this last chapter began by considering the various key issues in interpreting the Bible about how we can interpret it today, 'getting from there to here'. This led to another study of genre, analysing the four types of ethical material — rules, principles, paradigms and an overall worldview. Detailed attention to South Africa under apartheid and the transition to democracy revealed that the Bible was used by all sides in all four aspects. Finally, this last section applied our key idea of imitating Jesus in an inclusive community to South Africa — and discovered that this was the one thing which the pro-apartheid theology did NOT do. No imitation of Jesus could justify such violence and oppression, while had they listened to the 'voices of protest' and opened up the interpretative community to include those who were suffering under it, they could never have arrived at such a doctrine as separate development. Fortunately, in the new South Africa much more open and inclusive contextual readings are taking place which involve 'ordinary readers'; this provides hope for the future of reading the Bible in that extraordinary land — and for the rest of the world.[192]

If the history of biblical interpretation includes the dark days of oppressive readings and of exploitation of others, perhaps we can learn from the struggles of South Africa for our own debates in the future about what it means to be 'biblical'. Whenever we are presented with a choice between being biblical and being inclusive, it is a false dichotomy — for to be truly biblical is to be inclusive in any community which wants to follow and imitate Jesus.

192. It is significant that the Archbishop of Canterbury has invited Prof. Gerald West from the University of Kwa-Zulu Natal to lead the Bible studies at the worldwide conference of Anglican bishops at Lambeth in 2008.

Bibliography

Abbott, Walter M., S.J. (ed.). *The Documents of Vatican II.* London: Geoffrey Chapman, 1966.

Achtemeier, Paul J. 'The Continuing Quest for Coherence in St. Paul: An Experiment in Thought'. In *Theology and Ethics in Paul and His Interpreters: Essays in Honor of Victor Paul Furnish,* edited by E. H. Lovering, Jr. and J. L. Sumney. Nashville: Abingdon, 1996, pp. 132-45.

Ackermann, Denise M. 'Faith Communities Face the Truth', *JTSA* 103 (March 1999), pp. 88-93.

Akper, Godwin I. 'The Role of the "Ordinary Reader" in Gerald O. West's Hermeneutics', *Scriptura* 88 (2005), pp. 1-13.

Alexander, Loveday C. A. 'Luke's Preface in the Context of Greek Preface-Writing', *NovT* 28 (1986), pp. 48-74.

————. *The Preface to Luke's Gospel: Literary Convention and Social Context in Luke 1.1-4 and Acts 1.1.* SNTSMS 78. Cambridge: Cambridge University Press, 1993.

————. 'Acts and Ancient Intellectual Biography'. In *The Book of Acts in Its Ancient Literary Setting,* edited by Bruce W. Winter and Andrew D. Clarke. Carlisle: Paternoster/ Grand Rapids: Eerdmans, 1993, pp. 31-63.

————. 'Formal Elements and Genre: Which Greco-Roman Prologues Most Closely Parallel the Lukan Prologues?' In *Jesus and the Heritage of Israel: Luke's Narrative Claim upon Israel's Legacy,* edited by David P. Moessner. Harrisburg, PA: Trinity Press International, 1999, pp. 9-26.

————. 'Sisters in Adversity: Retelling Martha's Story'. In *A Feminist Companion to Luke,* edited by Amy-Jill Levine and Marianne Blickenstaff. Sheffield: Sheffield Academic Press, 2001, pp. 197-213.

Alexander, Philip S. 'Rabbinic Biography and the Biography of Jesus: A Survey of the Evidence'. In *Synoptic Studies: The Ampleforth Conferences of 1982 and 1983,* edited by C. M. Tuckett. JSNTSS 7. Sheffield: JSOT Press, 1984, pp. 19-50.

————. 'Jesus and the Golden Rule'. In *Hillel and Jesus: Comparative Studies of Two Major*

Religious Leaders, edited by J. H. Charlesworth and L. L. Johns. Minneapolis: Fortress, 1997, pp. 363-88; also reprinted in James D. G. Dunn and Scot McKnight (eds). *The Historical Jesus in Recent Research*. Sources for Biblical and Theological Study. Winona Lake, IN: Eisenbrauns, 2005, pp. 489-508.

Allen, John (ed.). *The Rainbow People of God: South Africa's Victory over Apartheid*. London: Bantam, 1995.

Allison, Dale C., Jr. 'Was There a "Lukan Community"?', *Irish Biblical Studies* 10 (1988), pp. 62-70.

————. *The New Moses: A Matthean Typology*. Edinburgh: T&T Clark, 1993.

————. *Studies in Matthew: Interpretation Past and Present*. Grand Rapids: Baker Academic, 2005.

Allsopp, Michael E. 'The Role of Sacred Scripture in Richard A. McCormick's Ethics', *Chicago Studies* 35.2 (1996), pp. 185-96.

Anderson, Paul N. *The Christology of the Fourth Gospel: Its Unity and Disunity in the Light of John 6*. WUNT 2.78. Tübingen: Mohr Siebeck, 1996.

————. *The Fourth Gospel and the Quest for Jesus: Modern Foundations Reconsidered*. LNTS 321. London: T&T Clark, 2006.

Anderson Scott, C. A. *New Testament Ethics: An Introduction*. Cambridge: Cambridge University Press, 1930.

Anon. *The Kairos Document, A Challenge to the Church: A Theological Comment on the Political Crisis in South Africa*. Second edn. Johannesburg: Skotaville/Grand Rapids: Eerdmans, 1986.

Anum, Eric. 'Suggestions for Effective Scholarly Readings of the Bible in a Post-2000 Africa'. SNTS Post Conference. Hammanskraal: University of Pretoria, August 9, 1999. Later published in a revised form as 'Effective Scholarly Readings of the Bible in Africa'. In *Interpreting the New Testament in Africa*, edited by Mary Getui, Tinyiko Maluleke and Justin Ukpong. Nairobi: Acton, 2001, pp. 104-22.

Arlandson, James Malcolm. *Women, Class, and Society in Early Christianity: Models from Luke-Acts*. Peabody, MA: Hendrickson, 1997.

Arnal, William E., and Michel Desjardins (eds.). *Whose Historical Jesus?* Studies in Christianity and Judaism 7. Waterloo, ON: Wilfrid Laurier University Press, 1997.

Ascough, Richard S. 'Matthew and Community Formation'. In *The Gospel of Matthew in Current Study*, edited by D. E. Aune. Grand Rapids: Eerdmans, 2001, pp. 96-126.

Ashton, John. *Understanding the Fourth Gospel*. Oxford: Oxford University Press, 1991.

————. *Studying John: Approaches to the Fourth Gospel*. Oxford: Oxford University Press, 1994.

———— (ed.). *The Interpretation of John*. London: SPCK, 1986. Second edn. Edinburgh: T&T Clark, 1997.

————. *The Religion of Paul the Apostle*. New Haven, CT: Yale University Press, 2000.

Atkinson, D. J. *Homosexuals in the Christian Fellowship*. Grand Rapids: Eerdmans, 1979.

Aune, D. E. (ed.). *The Gospel of Matthew in Current Study*. Grand Rapids: Eerdmans, 2001.

Badenas, Robert. *Christ the End of the Law: Romans 10.4 in Pauline Perspective*. JSNTSS 10. Sheffield: JSOT Press, 1985.

Baker, Deane-Peter, and Jonathan More. 'Taking the Quandary out of Christian Ethics', *JTSA* 115 (March 2003), pp. 5-17.

Balch, David L. 'Household Codes'. In *Greco-Roman Literature and the New Testament: Selected Forms and Genres,* edited by D. E. Aune. SBLSBS 21. Atlanta: Scholars Press, 1988, pp. 25-50.

——— (ed.). *Social History of the Matthean Community: Cross-Disciplinary Approaches.* Minneapolis: Fortress, 1991.

———. 'Romans 1:24-27, Science and Homosexuality', *Currents in Theology and Mission* 25.6 (1998), pp. 433-40.

———. 'Response to Daryl D. Schmidt'. In *Anti-Judaism and the Gospels,* edited by William R. Farmer. Harrisburg, PA: Trinity Press International, 1999, pp. 97-110.

——— (ed.). *Homosexuality, Science and the "Plain Sense" of Scripture.* Grand Rapids: Eerdmans, 2000.

Balcomb, Anthony. 'Negotiating the Crisis of Success: Contextual Theology Ten Years into Democracy', *Scriptura* 89 (2005), pp. 482-94.

Ball, David Mark. *'I Am' in John's Gospel: Literary Function, Background and Theological Implications.* JSNTSS 124. Sheffield: Sheffield Academic Press, 1996.

Banks, Robert. *Jesus and the Law in the Synoptic Tradition.* SNTSMS 28. Cambridge: Cambridge University Press, 1975.

Banner, Michael. *Christian Ethics and Contemporary Moral Problems.* Cambridge: Cambridge University Press, 1999.

Barclay, J. *Obeying the Truth: A Study of Paul's Ethics in Galatians.* Edinburgh: T&T Clark, 1988.

Barcley, W. B. *'Christ in You': A Study in Paul's Theology and Ethics.* Lanham, MD and Oxford: University Press of America, 1999.

Barnett, Paul W. *Jesus and the Logic of History.* Grand Rapids: Eerdmans, 1997.

Barrett, C. K. *A Commentary on the First Epistle to the Corinthians.* Second edn. London: A & C Black, 1971.

———. *A Commentary on the Second Epistle to the Corinthians.* London: A & C Black, 1973.

———. *Das Johannesevangelium und das Judentum.* Stuttgart: Kohlhammer, 1970. ET *The Gospel of John and Judaism.* London: SPCK, 1975.

———. *The Gospel according to St John: An Introduction with Commentary and Notes on the Greek Text.* First edn. 1995, Second edn. 1978. London: SPCK.

———. 'John and Judaism'. In *Anti-Judaism and the Fourth Gospel: Papers of the Leuven Colloquium, 2000,* edited by R. Bieringer, D. Pollefyt and F. Vandecasteele-Vanneuville. Assen: Royal Van Gorcum, 2001, pp. 401-17.

Barth, Karl. *Church Dogmatics.* Edinburgh: T&T Clark, 1957.

———. *The Epistle to the Romans.* Oxford: Oxford University Press, 1980.

Barthes, Roland. 'La Mort de l'auteur', *Manteia* 5 (1968). ET 'The Death of the Author'. In *Image, Music, Text,* edited by Stephen Heath. London: Fontana, 1977, pp. 142-48.

Barton, Stephen C. *Discipleship and Family Ties in Mark and Matthew.* SNTSMS 80. Cambridge: Cambridge University Press, 1994.

———. 'Can We Identify the Gospel Audiences?' In *The Gospels for All Christians: Rethinking the Gospel Audiences,* edited by Richard J. Bauckham. Grand Rapids: Eerdmans, 1998, pp. 173-94.

————— (ed.). *The Cambridge Companion to the Gospels*. Cambridge: Cambridge University Press, 2006.

Bartschy, S. Scott. Μᾶλλον χρῆσαι: *First-Century Slavery and the Interpretation of 1 Cor. 7:21*. SBLDS 11. Missoula: Scholars Press, 1973.

Basson, Alec. 'Israel en die Nasies: 'N Kritiese Nadenke oor die Dokument *Ras, Volk en Nasie*', *Scriptura* 77 (2001), pp. 185-92.

Battle, Michael. *Reconciliation: The Ubuntu Theology of Desmond Tutu*. Cleveland: Pilgrim, 1997.

Bauckham, Richard J. (ed.). *The Gospels for All Christians: Rethinking the Gospel Audiences*. Grand Rapids: Eerdmans/Edinburgh: T&T Clark, 1998.

—————. *Gospel Women: Studies of the Named Women in the Gospels*. Grand Rapids: Eerdmans, 2002.

—————. *Jesus and the Eyewitnesses: The Gospels as Eyewitness Testimony*. Grand Rapids: Eerdmans, 2006.

Bauer, David R., and Mark Allan Powell (eds.). *Treasures New and Old: Recent Contributions to Matthean Studies*. Atlanta: Scholars Press, 1996.

Bax, Douglas. 'The Bible and Apartheid 2'. Chapter 9 in *Apartheid Is a Heresy*, edited by J. de Gruchy and C. Villa-Vicencio. Cape Town: David Philip/Guildford: Lutterworth, 1983, pp. 112-43.

Beasley-Murray, George R. *Jesus and the Kingdom of God*. Grand Rapids: Eerdmans, 1986.

—————. *John*. Word Biblical Commentary 36. Dallas: Word, 1987.

Beavis, Mary Ann. '"Expecting Nothing in Return": Luke's Picture of the Marginalized', *Interpretation* 48.4 (1994), pp. 357-68.

Beck, Brian E. *Christian Character in the Gospel of Luke*. London: Epworth, 1989.

Becker, Jürgen. *Paul: Apostle to the Gentiles*. Louisville: Westminster John Knox, 1993.

Beker, J. Christiaan. *Paul the Apostle: The Triumph of God in Life and Thought*. Edinburgh: T&T Clark, 1980.

Bell, R. H. *No One Seeks for God: An Exegetical and Theological Study of Romans 1:18–3:20*. Tübingen: Mohr Siebeck, 1998.

Bellis, Alice Ogden, and Terry L. Hufford. *Science, Scripture and Homosexuality*. Cleveland: Pilgrim, 2002.

Best, Ernest R. *The First and Second Epistles to the Thessalonians*. London: A & C Black, 1972.

—————. 'The Role of the Disciples in Mark', *NTS* 23 (1976-77), pp. 377-401.

—————. *Following Jesus: Discipleship in the Gospel of Mark*. JSNTSS 4. Sheffield: JSOT Press, 1981.

—————. *Mark: The Gospel as Story*. Edinburgh: T&T Clark, 1983.

—————. *Disciples and Discipleship: Studies in the Gospel according to Mark*. Edinburgh: T&T Clark, 1986.

—————. *Paul and His Converts: The Sprunt Lectures 1985*. Edinburgh: T&T Clark, 1988.

Betz, Hans Dieter. *Galatians*. Hermeneia. Philadelphia: Fortress, 1979.

—————. *The Sermon on the Mount: A Commentary on the Sermon on the Mount, including the Sermon on the Plain (Matthew 5:3–7:27 and Luke 6:20-49)*. Hermeneia. Minneapolis: Fortress, 1995.

————, and William Schweiker, 'Concerning Mountains and Morals: A Conversation about the Sermon on the Mount', *Criterion* 36.2 (Chicago, 1997), pp. 12-26.

————. 'The Portrait of Jesus in the Sermon on the Mount', *Currents in Theology and Mission* 25.3 (1998), pp. 165-75.

Beutler, Johannes, S.J., and Robert T. Fortna (eds). *The Shepherd Discourse of John and Its Context.* SNTSMS 67. Cambridge: Cambridge University Press, 1991.

Beutler, Johannes, S.J. 'The Identity of "The Jews" for the Readers of John'. In *Anti-Judaism and the Fourth Gospel: Papers of the Leuven Colloquium, 2000*, edited by R. Bieringer, D. Pollefyt and F. Vandecasteele-Vanneuville. Assen: Royal Van Gorcum, 2001, pp. 229-38.

Bieberstein, Sabine. 'Disrupting the Normal Reality of Slavery: A Feminist Reading of the Letter to Philemon', *JSNT* 79 (2000), pp. 105-16.

Bieringer, R., D. Pollefyt and F. Vandecasteele-Vanneuville (eds.). *Anti-Judaism and the Fourth Gospel: Papers of the Leuven Colloquium, 2000.* Assen: Royal Van Gorcum, 2001.

Birch, Bruce C., and Larry L. Rasmussen. *Bible and Ethics in the Christian Life.* Revised and expanded edn. Minneapolis: Augsburg, 1989.

Black, C. Clifton. *The Disciples according to Mark: Markan Redaction in Current Debate.* JSNTSS 27. Sheffield: Sheffield Academic Press, 1989.

Blank, Josef. 'Unity and Plurality in New Testament Ethics'. In *Christian Ethics: Uniformity, Universality, Pluralism,* edited by J. Pohier and R. Mieth. *Concilium* 150. New York: Seabury, 1981, pp. 65-71.

Blomberg, Craig L. 'The Christian and the Law of Moses'. In *Witness to the Gospel: The Theology of Acts,* edited by I. Howard Marshall and David Peterson. Grand Rapids: Eerdmans, 1998, pp. 397-416.

————. *The Historical Reliability of John's Gospel: Issues and Commentary.* Downers Grove, IL: InterVarsity Press, 2001.

————. *Contagious Holiness: Jesus' Meals with Sinners.* Downers Grove, IL: InterVarsity Press, 2005.

Blount, Brian K. *Then the Whisper Put on Flesh: New Testament Ethics in an African American Context.* Nashville: Abingdon, 2001.

Bockmuehl, Markus. 'Public Ethics in a Pluralistic Society? Lessons from the Early Church', *Crux* 28.3 (September 1992), pp. 2-9.

————. *This Jesus: Martyr, Lord, Messiah.* Edinburgh: T&T Clark, 1994.

————. 'The Noachide Commandments and New Testament Ethics with Special Reference to Acts 15 and Pauline Halakhah', *Revue Biblique* 102 (1995), pp. 72-101.

————. *The Epistle to the Philippians.* Fourth edn. London: A & C Black, 1997.

————. *Jewish Law in Gentile Churches: Halakhah and the Beginning of Christian Public Ethics.* Edinburgh: T&T Clark, 2000.

————. 'Why Not Let Acts Be Acts? In Conversation with C. Kavin Rowe'. *JSNT* 28.2 (2005), pp. 163-66.

Boesak, Allan. *Farewell to Innocence: A Socio-ethical Study of Black Theology and Black Power.* Johannesburg: Raven, 1977.

————. *Black and Reformed: Apartheid, Liberation and the Calvinist Tradition.* Braamfontein: Skotaville, 1984.

————. *Walking on Thorns: The Call to Christian Obedience.* Grand Rapids: Eerdmans, 1984.

————. 'What Belongs to Caesar? Once Again, Romans 13'. In *A Call for an End to Unjust Rule,* edited by Allan Boesak and Charles Villa-Vicencio. Philadelphia: Westminster, 1986, pp. 138-56. First edition entitled *When Prayer Makes News.*

————. *If This Is Treason, I Am Guilty.* Grand Rapids: Eerdmans, 1987.

Bolt, Peter G. 'Do You Not Care That We Are perishing?' Ph.D. King's College London, 1997.

————. '". . . With a View to the Forgiveness of Sins": Jesus and Forgiveness in Mark's Gospel', *The Reformed Theological Review* 57.2 (Victoria, Australia, 1998), pp. 53-69.

————. *Jesus' Defeat of Death: Persuading Mark's Early Readers.* SNTSMS 125. Cambridge: Cambridge University Press, 2004.

Bonhoeffer, Dietrich. *Life Together.* London: SCM, 1954.

————. *Ethics.* Edited by Eberhard Bethge. New York: Macmillan, 1955.

————. *Letters and Papers from Prison.* Edited by Eberhard Bethge. London: SCM, 1971.

————. *The Cost of Discipleship.* New York: Macmillan, 1963/Touchstone, 1995.

Booth, Roger P. *Jesus and the Laws of Purity: Tradition History and Legal History in Mark 7.* JSNTSS 13. Sheffield: JSOT Press, 1986.

Borg, Marcus J. *Conflict, Holiness and Politics in the Teachings of Jesus.* Studies in the Bible and Early Christianity, vol. 5. New York: Edwin Mellen, 1984.

————. *Jesus, A New Vision: Spirit, Culture, and the Life of Discipleship.* San Francisco: Harper, 1987.

————, and N. T. Wright, *The Meaning of Jesus: Two Visions.* San Francisco: HarperSanFrancisco, 1999.

Borgen, Peter. 'John and the Synoptics'. In *Tradition and Interpretation in the New Testament,* edited by G. F. Hawthorne and O. Betz. Grand Rapids: Eerdmans, 1987, pp. 80-94.

————. 'God's Agent in the Fourth Gospel'. In *Religions in Antiquity,* edited by J. Neusner. Leiden: Brill, 1968, pp. 137-48. Reprinted in *The Interpretation of John,* edited by John Ashton. Edinburgh: T&T Clark, second edn. 1997, pp. 83-95.

Borgman, Paul. *The Way according to Luke: Hearing the Whole Story of Luke-Acts.* Grand Rapids: Eerdmans, 2006.

Bornkamm, Günther. 'Endwartung und Kirche im Matthäus-evangelium'. In *The Background of the New Testament and Its Eschatology: Studies in Honour of C. H. Dodd,* edited by W. D. Davies and D. Daube. Cambridge: Cambridge University Press, 1956. ET 'End Expectation and Church in Matthew'. In *Tradition and Interpretation in Matthew,* edited by G. Bornkamm, G. Barth and H. J. Held. London: SCM, 1963, pp. 15-51.

————. 'The Stilling of the Storm in Matthew'. In *Tradition and Interpretation in Matthew,* edited by G. Bornkamm, G. Barth and H. J. Held. London: SCM, 1963, pp. 52-57.

————. 'Towards the Interpretation of John's Gospel: A Discussion of *The Testament of Jesus* by Ernst Käsemann', *EvT* 28 (1968), pp. 8-25. Translated and reprinted in *The Interpretation of John,* edited by John Ashton. Edinburgh: T&T Clark, second edn. 1997, pp. 97-119.

————. *Paul.* London: Hodder and Stoughton, 1971.

Bosch, David. 'Paul on Human Hopes', *JTSA* 67 (1989), pp. 3-16.

Boswell, John. *Christianity, Social Tolerance, and Homosexuality: Gay People in Western Europe from the Beginning of the Christian Era to the Fourteenth Century*. Chicago: University of Chicago Press, 1980.

Botha, Jan. 'Aspects of the Rhetoric of South African New Testament Scholarship anno 1992', *Scriptura* 46 (1993), pp. 80-99.

———. 'The Ethics of New Testament Interpretation', *Neotestamentica* 26.1 (1992), pp. 169-94.

———. *Subject to Whose Authority? Multiple Readings of Romans 13*. Atlanta: Scholars Press, 1994.

———. 'The Bible and Ethics'. In *Doing Ethics in Context: South African Perspectives*, edited by C. Villa-Vicencio and J. de Gruchy. Cape Town: David Philip/Maryknoll, NY: Orbis, 1994, pp. 36-45.

———. 'The Bible in South African Public Discourse — with Special Reference to the Right to Protest', *Scriptura* 58 (1996), pp. 329-43.

Botha, J. Eugene. 'The (Ir)Relevancy of the Academic Study of the Bible', *Scriptura* 73 (2000), pp. 121-40.

Botha, Pieter J. J. 'Mark's Story of Jesus and the Search for Virtue'. In *The Rhetorical Analysis of Scripture*, edited by S. E. Porter and T. H. Olbricht. Sheffield: Sheffield Academic Press, 1997, pp. 156-84.

Botman, H. Russel, and Robin M. Petersen (eds.). *To Remember and to Heal: Theological and Psychological Reflections on Truth and Reconciliation*. Cape Town: Human & Rousseau, 1996.

Bousset, W. *Kyrios Christos*. ET Nashville: Abingdon, 1970.

Bovon, François. *Studies in Early Christianity*. WUNT 161. Tübingen: J. C. B. Mohr Siebeck, 2003.

Boyarin, Daniel. *A Radical Jew: Paul and the Politics of Identity*. Berkeley: University of California Press, 1994.

Bratcher, Robert G. '"Righteousness" in Matthew', *The Bible Translator* 40.2 (1989), pp. 228-35.

Brawley, Robert L. (ed.). *Biblical Ethics and Homosexuality: Listening to Scripture*. Louisville: Westminster John Knox, 1996.

Bretzke, James T., S.J. 'Scripture: The "Soul" of Moral Theology? — The Second Stage', *Irish Theological Quarterly* 60.4 (1994), pp. 259-71.

Brookes, Iveson L. *A Defence of the South against the Reproaches and Incroachments of the North: In Which Slavery Is Shown to Be an Institution of God Intended to Form the Basis of the Best Social State and the Only Safeguard to the Permanence of a Republican Government*. Hamburg, SC: At the Republican Office, 1850.

Brooks, Oscar Stephen. *The Sermon on the Mount: Authentic Human Values*. Lanham, MD: University Press of America, 1985.

Broughton, L. C. 'Biblical Texts and Homosexuality: A Response to John Boswell', *Irish Theological Quarterly* 58.2 (1992), pp. 141-53.

Brown, Jeannine K. *The Disciples in Narrative Perspective: The Portrayal and Function of the Matthean Disciples*. Atlanta: Society of Biblical Literature, 2002.

Brown, R. M. (ed.). *Kairos: Three Prophetic Challenges to the Church*. Grand Rapids: Eerdmans, 1990.

Brown, Raymond E., S.S. *The Gospel according to John*. Anchor Bible 29 and 29A. New York: Doubleday, 1966 and 1970; second edn., 1984.

———. *The Community of the Beloved Disciple*. New York: Paulist, 1979.

———. *The Epistles of John*. Anchor Bible 30. New York: Doubleday, 1982.

———. *The Death of the Messiah*. New York: Doubleday, 1994.

———. *An Introduction to the New Testament*. New York: Doubleday, 1997.

———. *An Introduction to the Gospel of John*, edited, updated, introduced and concluded by Francis J. Moloney, S.D.B. New York: Doubleday, 2003.

Brown, Tricia Gates. *Spirit in the Writings of John: Johannine Pneumatology in Social Scientific Perspective*. London: T&T Clark, 2003.

Brown, William P. (ed.). *Character and Scripture: Moral Formation, Community, and Biblical Interpretation*. Grand Rapids: Eerdmans, 2002.

Bruce, F. F. *The Acts of the Apostles: The Greek Text with Introduction and Commentary*. London: Tyndale, 1951.

———. *Paul: Apostle of the Free Spirit*. Exeter: Paternoster, 1977.

———. *1 and 2 Thessalonians*. Word Biblical Commentary 45. Waco, TX: Word, 1982.

———. *The Epistle to the Galatians: A Commentary on the Greek Text*. NIGTC. Exeter: Paternoster, 1982.

Brunson, Harold E. *Homosexuality and the New Testament: What Does Christian Scripture Really Teach?* San Francisco: International Scholars Publications, 1998.

Bryan, Christopher. *A Preface to Mark: Notes on the Gospel in Its Literary and Cultural Settings*. Oxford: Oxford University Press, 1993.

Buckwalter, H. Douglas. 'The Divine Saviour'. In *Witness to the Gospel: The Theology of Acts*, edited by I. Howard Marshall and David Peterson. Grand Rapids: Eerdmans, 1998, pp. 107-23.

Bühner, J. A. 'The Exegesis of the Johannine "I-Am" Sayings'. In *The Interpretation of John*, edited by John Ashton. Edinburgh: T&T Clark, second edn. 1997, pp. 207-18.

Bultmann, Rudolf. 'The History of Religions Background of the Prologue in the Gospel of John'. In *The Interpretation of John*, edited by John Ashton. Edinburgh: T&T Clark, second edn. 1997, pp. 27-46. German original in *EYXAPIΣTHPION: Studien zur Religion und Literatur des Alten und Neuen Testaments, Festschrift für H. Gunkel*, edited by Hans Schmidt. Göttingen: Vandenhoeck und Ruprecht, 1923, vol. 2, pp. 3-26.

———. 'Das Problem der Ethik bei Paulus'. *ZNW* 23 (1924), pp. 123-40. ET 'The Problem of Ethics in Paul'. In *Understanding Paul's Ethics*, edited by B. S. Rosner. Grand Rapids: Eerdmans, 1995, pp. 195-216.

———. *The Gospel of John: A Commentary*. Translated by G. R. Beasley-Murray, R. W. N. Hoare and J. K. Riches. Oxford: Blackwell, 1971; German original 1941.

———. *Theology of the New Testament*. London: SCM, 1955, 2 vols.

———. *Jesus and the Word*. London: Collins, 1958.

———. *The Second Letter to the Corinthians*. Minneapolis: Augsburg, 1985.

Burridge, Richard A. *What Are the Gospels? A Comparison with Graeco-Roman Biography*. SNTSMS 70. Cambridge: Cambridge University Press, 1992.

———. *John*. The People's Bible Commentary. Oxford: Bible Reading Fellowship, 1998.

———. 'Gospel Genre, Christological Controversy and the Absence of Rabbinic Biography: Some Implications of the Biographical Hypothesis'. In *Christology, Controversy and Community: New Testament Essays in Honour of David Catchpole,* edited by David G. Horrell and Christopher M. Tuckett. Leiden: Brill, 2000, pp. 137-56; reprinted in the second edition of Richard A. Burridge, *What Are the Gospels?* (2004), Appendix II, pp. 322-40.

—————. *What are the Gospels? A Comparison with Graeco-Roman Biography.* Revised and updated second edn. Grand Rapids: Eerdmans, 2004.

—————. 'Interpreting Mel Gibson's *The Passion of the Christ*'. British New Testament Conference. Edinburgh: University of Edinburgh Press, September 4, 2004.

—————. *Four Gospels, One Jesus? A Symbolic Reading.* London: SPCK/Grand Rapids: Eerdmans, 1994. Revised and updated second edn. 2005.

—————. 'From Title to Stories: A Narrative Approach to the Dynamic Christologies of the New Testament'. In *The Person of Christ,* edited by Murray Rae and Stephen R. Holmes. London: T&T Clark, 2005, pp. 37-60.

—————. 'Who Writes, Why, and for Whom?' In *The Written Gospel,* edited by Markus Bockmuehl and Donald A. Hagner. Cambridge: Cambridge University Press, 2005, pp. 99-115.

—————. 'Praying at 125mph'. In *Tutu As I Know Him: On a Personal Note,* edited by Lavinia Crawford-Browne. Roggebaai: Umuzi, Random House, 2006, pp. 89-93.

—————. 'Imitating Mark's Jesus: Imagination, Scripture, and Inclusion in Biblical Ethics Today'. *Sewanee Theological Review* 50:1 (Christmas 2006), pp. 11-31.

Burrows, Millar. 'Old Testament Ethics and the Ethics of Jesus'. In *Essays in Old Testament Ethics: In Memory of J. Phillip Hyatt,* edited by J. L. Crenshaw and J. T. Willis. New York: Ktav, 1974, pp. 227-43.

Cadbury, Henry J. *The Making of Luke-Acts.* London: Macmillan, 1927; second edn. 1958.

—————. *The Peril of Modernizing Jesus.* London: SPCK, 1937.

Cahill, L. S. 'The Ethical Implications of the Sermon on the Mount', *Interpretation* 41.2 (April 1987), pp. 144-56.

Campbell, Douglas A. *The Quest for Paul's Gospel: A Suggested Strategy.* London: T&T Clark, 2005

Capper, Brian. 'Reciprocity and the Ethic of Acts'. In *Witness to the Gospel: The Theology of Acts,* edited by I. Howard Marshall and David Peterson. Grand Rapids: Eerdmans, 1998, pp. 499-518.

Caragounis, C. C., '"Fornication" and "Concession"? Interpreting 1 Cor. 7.1-7', Colloquium Biblicum Lovaniense XLIII, August 8-10, 1994. In *The Corinthian Correspondence.* Ed. R. Bieringer. BETL 125. Leuven: Leuven University Press–Peeters, 1996.

Carapiet, M. 'Jesus and Christian Ethics Today', *Jeevadhara* 23 (Kottayam, Kerala, India, 1993), pp. 437-55.

Carleton Paget, James. 'Quests for the Historical Jesus'. In *The Cambridge Companion to Jesus,* edited by Markus Bockmuehl. Cambridge: Cambridge University Press, 2001, pp. 138-55.

Carroll, Lewis. *Through the Looking-Glass.* Penguin: Harmondsworth, 1994.

Carroll, Robert P. *Wolf in the Sheepfold: The Bible as a Problem for Christianity.* London: SPCK, 1991.

Carter, C. W., and R. D. Thompson. *The Biblical Ethic of Love.* American University Studies Series 7: Theology and Religion 79. New York: P. Lang, 1990.

Carter, Warren. 'Response to Amy-Jill Levine'. In *Anti-Judaism and the Gospels,* edited by William R. Farmer. Harrisburg, PA: Trinity International Press, 1999, pp. 47-62.

———. *Matthew and the Margins: A Sociopolitical and Religious Reading.* Maryknoll, NY: Orbis, 2000.

———. 'Getting Martha out of the Kitchen: Luke 10.28-42 Again'. In *A Feminist Companion to Luke,* edited by Amy-Jill Levine and Marianne Blickenstaff. Sheffield: Sheffield Academic Press, 2001, pp. 214-31.

———. *Matthew: Storyteller, Interpreter, Evangelist.* Revised edn. Peabody, MA: Hendrickson, 2004.

———. *John: Storyteller, Interpreter, Evangelist.* Peabody, MA: Hendrickson, 2006.

Casey, Maurice. *Is John's Gospel True?* London: Routledge, 1996.

Cassidy, Richard J. *Jesus, Politics, and Society: A Study of Luke's Gospel.* Maryknoll, NY: Orbis, 1978.

———, and Philip J. Scharper (eds.). *Political Issues in Luke-Acts.* Maryknoll, NY: Orbis, 1983.

———. *Society and Politics in the Acts of the Apostles.* Maryknoll, NY: Orbis, 1987.

Catchpole, David R. 'The Anointed One in Nazareth'. In *From Jesus to John: Essays on Jesus and New Testament Christology in Honour of Marinus de Jonge,* edited by Martinus C. De Boer. JSNTSS 84. Sheffield: Sheffield Academic Press, 1993, pp. 231-51.

———. *The Quest for Q.* Edinburgh: T&T Clark, 1993.

Charles, J. Daryl. 'The Greatest or the Least in the Kingdom?: The Disciple's Relationship to the Law (Matt 5:17-20)', *Trinity Journal* n.s.13 (1992), pp. 139-62.

Charlesworth, James H. (ed.). *John and Qumran.* London: Geoffrey Chapman, 1972.

———. 'The Gospel of John: Exclusivism Caused by a Social Setting Different from That of Jesus (John 11:54 and 14:6)'. In *Anti-Judaism and the Fourth Gospel: Papers of the Leuven Colloquium, 2000,* edited by R. Bieringer, D. Pollefyt and F. Vandecasteele-Vanneuville. Assen: Royal Van Gorcum, 2001, pp. 478-513.

Chester, S. J. *Conversion at Corinth.* London: T&T Clark, 2003.

Childs, J. M. *Faithful Conversation: Christian Perspectives on Homosexuality.* Minneapolis: Fortress, 2003.

Chilton, B. D. 'Regnum Dei Deus Est', *SJT* 31 (1978), pp. 261-70.

———. *God in Strength: Jesus' Announcement of the Kingdom.* Sheffield: JSOT Press, 1987.

———, and J. I. H. McDonald. *Jesus and the Ethics of the Kingdom.* London: SPCK, 1987.

———. *Pure Kingdom: Jesus' Vision of God.* Grand Rapids: Eerdmans, 1996.

Clarke, Andrew D. 'Be Imitators of Me': Paul's Model of Leadership', *Tyndale Bulletin* 49.2 (1998), pp. 329-60.

Cloete, G. D., and D. J. Smit. '"Its Name Was Called Babel . . .": Gen. 11:9 and Acts 2:8, 11-12', *JTSA* 86 (March 1994), pp. 81-87.

Cochrane, James R. 'Theological Reflection on Public Policy: The Church and the Reconstruction of South African Society', *JTSA* 97 (March 1997), pp. 1-15.

———, John W. de Gruchy and Stephen W. Martin (eds.). *Facing the Truth: South African Faith Communities and the Truth & Reconciliation Commission.* Cape Town: David Philip, 1998.

Coleridge, Mark. *The Birth of the Lukan Narrative: Narrative as Christology in Luke 1–2.* JSNTSS 88. Sheffield: JSOT Press, 1993.

Colijn, Brenda B. 'Paul's Use of the "in Christ" Formula', *Ashland Theological Journal* 23 (1991), pp. 9-26.

Coleman, Peter. *Christian Attitudes to Homosexuality.* London: SPCK, 1980.

Collins, Adela Yarbro. *The Beginning of the Gospel: Probings of Mark in Context.* Minneapolis: Fortress, 1992.

Collins, Raymond F. *Christian Morality: Biblical Foundations.* Notre Dame, IN: University of Notre Dame, 1986.

―――. 'Speaking of the Jews: "Jews" in the Discourse Material of the Fourth Gospel'. In *Anti-Judaism and the Fourth Gospel: Papers of the Leuven Colloquium, 2000,* edited by R. Bieringer, D. Pollefyt and F. Vandecasteele-Vanneuville. Assen: Royal Van Gorcum, 2001, pp. 281-300.

Combrink, Bernard, and Bethel Müller. 'The Gospel of Matthew in an African Context', *Scriptura* 39 (1991), pp. 43-51.

Combrink, H. J. Bernard. 'Rhetoric and Reference in the Gospel of Matthew', *Scriptura* 40 (1992), pp. 1-17.

―――. 'The Use of Matthew in the South African Context during the Last Few Decades', *Neotestamentica* 28.2 (1994), pp. 339-58.

―――. 'Translating or Transforming — Receiving Matthew in Africa', *Scriptura* 58.3 (1996), pp. 273-84.

―――. 'The Reception of Matthew in Africa', *Scriptura* 58.3 (1996), pp. 285-303.

Conway, Colleen M. *Men and Women in the Fourth Gospel: Gender and Johannine Characterization.* SBLDS 167. Atlanta: SBL, 1999.

Conzelmann, H. *Die Mitte der Zeit: Studien zur Theologie des Lukas* (Tübingen: Mohr, 1954). ET *The Theology of St. Luke,* translated by Geoffrey Buswell. London: Faber, 1960.

Cook, William (ed.). *Tragically I Was an Only Twin: The Complete Peter Cook.* London: Arrow, 2003.

Corley, Kathleen E., and Robert L. Webb (eds.). *Jesus and Mel Gibson's* The Passion of the Christ: *The Film, the Gospels and the Claims of History.* London: Continuum, 2004.

Cosgrove, Charles H. *Appealing to Scripture in Moral Debate: Five Hermeneutical Rules.* Grand Rapids: Eerdmans, 2002.

Cotter, Wendy, C.S.J. 'Our *Politeuma* Is in Heaven: The Meaning of Philippians 3.17-21'. In *Origins and Method: Towards a New Understanding of Judaism and Christianity. Essays in Honour of John C. Hurd,* edited by Bradley H. McLean. JSNTSS 86. Sheffield: Sheffield Academic Press, 1993, pp. 92-104.

Counet, Patrick Chatelion. *John, A Postmodern Gospel: An Introduction to Deconstructive Exegesis Applied to the Fourth Gospel.* Leiden: Brill, 2000.

Countryman, L. William. *Dirt, Greed and Sex: Sexual Ethics in the New Testament and Their Implications for Today.* Minneapolis: Fortress, 1988/London: SCM, 1989. Second rev. edn. Minneapolis: Fortress, 2007.

Craffert, Pieter F. 'From Apartheid Readings to Ordinary Readings of the Bible', *Scriptura* 64 (1998), pp. 65-79.

Cranfield, C. E. B. *The Epistle to the Romans,* ICC, 2 vols. Edinburgh: T&T Clark, 1975, 1979.

Crawford-Browne, Lavinia (ed.). *Tutu As I Know Him: On a Personal Note.* Roggebaai: Umuzi, Random House, 2006.

Crosby, Michael H., O.F.M.Cap. *House of Disciples: Church, Economics and Justice in Matthew.* Maryknoll, NY: Orbis, 1988.

———. *Spirituality of the Beatitudes: Matthew's Vision for the Church in an Unjust* World. Revised edn. Maryknoll, NY: Orbis, 2005.

Crossan, J. D. *Jesus Parallels: A Workbook for the Jesus Tradition.* Second Edn. Philadelphia: Fortress, 1991.

———. *The Historical Jesus: The Life of a Mediterranean Jewish Peasant.* San Francisco: HarperCollins/Edinburgh: T&T Clark, 1991.

———. *Jesus: A Revolutionary Biography.* San Francisco: HarperSan Francisco, 1994.

———, and Jonathan L. Reed. *In Search of Paul: How Jesus' Apostle Opposed Rome's Empire with God's Kingdom.* New York: Harper Collins/London: SPCK, 2005.

Crüsemann, Marlene. 'Irredeemably Hostile to Women: Anti-Jewish Elements in the Exegesis of the Dispute about Women's Right to Speak (1 Cor. 14.34-35)', *JSNT* 79 (2000), pp. 19-36.

Cullmann, Oscar. *The Christology of the New Testament.* London: SCM, 1959.

Culpepper, R. Alan. *Anatomy of the Fourth Gospel: A Study in Literary Design.* Philadelphia: Fortress, 1983.

———. 'The Johannine *Hypodeigma:* A Reading of John 13'. In *The Fourth Gospel from a Literary Perspective,* edited by R. Alan Culpepper and Fernando F. Segovia. *Semeia* 53. Atlanta: Scholars, 1991, pp. 133-52.

———, and Fernando F. Segovia (eds.). *The Fourth Gospel from a Literary Perspective. Semeia* 53. Atlanta: Scholars, 1991.

———. 'John 5.1-18: A Sample of Narrative Critical Commentary'. In *The Gospel of John as Literature: An Anthology of Twentieth Century Perspectives,* edited by Mark W. G. Stibbe. Leiden: Brill, 1993, pp. 193-207.

———, and C. C. Black. *Exploring the Gospel of John: In Honor of D. Moody Smith.* Louisville: Westminster John Knox, 1996.

———. 'The Plot of John's Story of Jesus'. In *Gospel Interpretation: Narrative-Critical & Social-Scientific Approaches,* edited by Jack Dean Kingsbury. Harrisburg, PA: Trinity Press International, 1997, pp. 188-99.

———. 'The Christology of the Johannine Writings'. In *Who Do You Say That I Am? Essays on Christology in Honor of Jack Dean Kingsbury,* edited by David R. Bauer and Mark Allan Powell. Louisville: Westminster John Knox, 1999, pp. 66-87.

———. 'Inclusivism and Exclusivism in the Fourth Gospel'. In *Word, Theology, and Community in John,* edited by John Painter, R. Alan Culpepper, and Fernando F. Segovia. St Louis: Chalice, 2002, pp. 85-108.

Curran, Charles E., and Richard A. McCormick, S.J. (eds.). *Readings in Moral Theology No. 4: The Use of Scripture in Moral Theology.* New York: Paulist, 1984.

Daly, Robert J., S.J. (ed.) *Christian Biblical Ethics. From Biblical Revelation to Contemporary Christian Praxis: Method and Content.* New York: Paulist, 1984.

Danker, Frederick W. 'Reciprocity in the Ancient World and in Acts 15:23-29'. In *Political Issues in Luke-Acts,* edited by Richard J. Cassidy and Philip J. Scharper. Maryknoll, NY: Orbis, 1983, pp. 49-58.

Davies, Margaret. *Rhetoric and Reference in the Fourth Gospel.* JSNTSS 69. Sheffield: JSOT Press, 1992.

———. 'Work and Slavery in the New Testament: Impoverishments of Traditions'. In *The Bible in Ethics,* edited by John W. Rogerson, Margaret Davies and M. Daniel Carroll R. JSOTSS 207. Sheffield: Sheffield Academic Press, 1995, pp. 315-47.

———. 'New Testament Ethics and Ours: Homosexuality and Sexuality in Romans 1:26-27'. *Biblical Interpretation* 3.3 (1995), pp. 315-31.

Davies, Stevan. 'Women in the Third Gospel and the New Testament Apocrypha'. In *"Women Like This": New Perspectives on Jewish Women in the Greco-Roman World,* edited by Amy-Jill Levine. Atlanta: Scholars Press, 1991, pp. 185-97.

Davies, W. D. *Paul and Rabbinic Judaism: Some Rabbinic Elements in Pauline Theology.* London: SPCK, 1948; 3rd edn. 1970.

———. *Torah in the Messianic Age and/or The Age to Come.* JBLMS 7. Philadelphia: SBL, 1952.

———. *The Setting of the Sermon on the Mount.* Cambridge: Cambridge University Press, 1966.

———, and Dale C. Allison, *A Critical and Exegetical Commentary on the Gospel according to Saint Matthew.* ICC, 3 vols. Edinburgh: T&T Clark, 1988, 1990, 1997.

———, and Dale C. Allison, Jr., 'Reflections on the Sermon on the Mount', *SJT* 44 (1991), pp. 283-309.

Davis, J. A. 'The Interaction between Individual Ethical Consciousness and Community Ethical Consciousness in 1 Corinthians', *Horizons in Biblical Theology* 10.2 (1988), pp. 1-18.

de Boer, Esther A. 'The Lukan Mary Magdalene and Other Women Following Jesus'. In *A Feminist Companion to Luke,* edited by Amy-Jill Levine with Marianne Blickenstaff. Sheffield: Sheffield Academic Press, 2001, pp. 140-60.

De Boer, Martinus C. (ed.). *From Jesus to John: Essays on Jesus and New Testament Christology in Honour of Marinus de Jonge.* JSNTSS 84. Sheffield: Sheffield Academic Press, 1993.

De Boer, M. C. 'The Depiction of "the Jews" in John's Gospel: Matters of Behavior and Identity'. In *Anti-Judaism and the Fourth Gospel: Papers of the Leuven Colloquium, 2000,* edited by R. Bieringer, D. Pollefyt and F. Vandecasteele-Vanneuville. Assen: Royal Van Gorcum, 2001, pp. 260-80.

de Gruchy, John, and C. Villa-Vicencio (eds.). *Apartheid Is a Heresy.* Cape Town: David Philip/Guildford: Lutterworth, 1983.

———, and ——— (eds.). *Doing Theology in Context: South African Perspectives.* Theology and Praxis, vol. 1. Cape Town: David Philip/Maryknoll, NY: Orbis, 1994.

———. *The Church Struggle in South Africa: Twenty-Fifth Anniversary Edition.* Minneapolis: Fortress, 2005.

de Jonge, Henk Jan. 'The "Jews" in the Gospel of John'. In *Anti-Judaism and the Fourth Gospel: Papers of the Leuven Colloquium, 2000,* edited by R. Bieringer, D. Pollefyt and F. Vandecasteele-Vanneuville. Assen: Royal Van Gorcum, 2001, pp. 239-59.

de Jonge, Marinus. 'Jewish Expectations about the "Messiah" according to the Fourth Gospel', *NTS* 19 (1972-73), pp. 246-70.

———. 'Jesus as Prophet and King in the Fourth Gospel', *Ephemerides Theologicae Lovanienses* 49 (1973), pp. 161-77.

————. *Jesus: Stranger from Heaven and Son of God: Jesus Christ and the Christians in Johannine Perspective*. Missoula, MT: Scholars Press, 1977.

de Mingo Kaminouchi, Alberto. *'But It Is Not So among You': Echoes of Power in Mark 10:32-45*. JSNTSS 249. London: T&T Clark, 2003.

de Villiers, Etienne (ed.). "Christian Ethics in South Africa (1)," *Scriptura* 62.3 (1997).

de Villiers, Pieter G. R. 'The Bible and the Struggle (for Power)', *Scriptura* 45 (1993), pp. 1-28.

de Vos, Craig. 'Once a Slave, Always a Slave? Slavery, Manumission and Relational Patterns in Paul's Letter to Philemon', *JSNT* 82 (2001), pp. 89-105.

de Young, J. B. 'The Source and Meaning of the Translation "Homosexuals" in Biblical Studies', *Evangelical Review of Theology* 19.1 (1995), pp. 54-63.

Deissmann, A. *Die neutestamentliche Formel 'in Christo Jesu'*. Marburg: Elwert, 1892.

Denaux, A. (ed.). *John and the Synoptics*. BETL 101. Leuven: Leuven University Press, 1992.

Deming, Will. *Paul on Marriage and Celibacy: The Hellenistic Background of 1 Corinthians 7*. Second edn. Grand Rapids: Eerdmans, 2004.

Denison, W. D. 'Indicative and Imperative: The Basic Structure of Pauline Ethics', *Calvin Theological Journal* 14 (1979), pp. 55-78.

Derrett, J. Duncan M. 'Luke's Perspective on Tribute to Caesar'. In *Political Issues in Luke-Acts*, edited by Richard J. Cassidy and Philip J. Scharper. Maryknoll, NY: Orbis, 1983, pp. 38-48.

Deutsch, Celia M. *Lady Wisdom, Jesus and the Sages: Metaphor and Social Context in Matthew's Gospel*. Valley Forge, PA: Trinity Press International, 1996.

Dewey, Joanna. 'The Literary Structure of the Controversy Stories in Mark 2:1–3:6', *JBL* 92 (1973), pp. 394-401. Reprinted in *The Interpretation of Mark*, edited by William Telford. London: SPCK, 1985, pp. 109-118; 2nd edn., Edinburgh: T&T Clark, 1995, pp. 141-52.

————. '"Let Them Renounce Themselves and Take Up Their Cross": A Feminist Reading of Mark 8:34 in Mark's Social and Narrative World'. In *A Feminist Companion to Mark*, edited by Amy-Jill Levine with Marianne Blickenstaff. Sheffield: Sheffield Academic Press, 2001, pp. 23-36.

Dibelius, M. *A Fresh Approach to the New Testament and Early Christian Literature*. London: Ivor Nicholson and Watson, 1936.

Dibelius, Martin, and Hans Conzelmann. *The Pastoral Epistles*. Hermeneia. Philadelphia: Fortress, 1972.

Dillmann, Rainer. 'Aufbruch zu einer neuen Sittlichkeit: Biblisch-narrative Begründung ethischen Handelns', *Theologie und Glaube* 82.1 (Paderborn, 1992), pp. 34-45.

Dillon, Richard J. 'Ravens, Lilies, and the Kingdom of God (Matthew 6:25-33/Luke 12:22-31)', *CBQ* 53.4 (1991), pp. 605-27.

Doble, Peter. *The Paradox of Salvation: Luke's Theology of the Cross*. SNTSMS 87. Cambridge: Cambridge University Press, 1996.

Dodd, Brian J. 'The Story of Christ and the Initiation of Paul in Philippians 2–3'. In *Where Christology Began: Essays on Philippians 2*, edited by R. P. Martin and B. J. Dodd. Louisville: Westminster John Knox, 1998, pp. 154-60.

Dodd, C. H. *Gospel and Law*. Bampton Lectures in America 3. New York: Columbia University Press, 1951.

————. Ἔννομος Χριστοῦ'. In *Studia Paulina in Honorem Johannis de Zwaan,* edited by J. N. Sevenster and W. C. Van Unnik. Harlem: Bohn, 1953, pp. 96-110. Reprinted in C. H. Dodd. *More New Testament Studies.* Manchester: Manchester University Press, 1968, pp. 134-48.

Donahue, John R., S.J. 'The "Parable" of the Sheep and Goats: A Challenge to Christian Ethics', *Theological Studies* 47 (1986), pp. 3-30.

————. 'Who Is My Enemy? The Parable of the Good Samaritan and the Love of Enemies'. In *The Love of Enemy and Nonretaliation in the New Testament,* edited by Willard M. Swartley. Louisville: Westminster John Knox, 1992.

Donaldson, Terence L. *Jesus on the Mountain: A Study in Matthean Theology.* JSNTSS 8. Sheffield: JSOT Press, 1985.

————. 'Guiding Readers — Making Disciples'. In *Patterns of Discipleship in the New Testament,* edited by Richard N. Longenecker. Grand Rapids: Eerdmans, 1996, pp. 30-49.

————. *Paul and the Gentiles: Remapping the Apostle's Convictional World.* Minneapolis: Fortress, 1997.

Dornisch, Loretta. *A Woman Reads the Gospel of Luke.* Collegeville, MN: Liturgical Press, 1996.

Downing, F. Gerald. 'Cynics and Christians', *NTS* 30 (1984), pp. 584-93.

————. 'Ears to Hear', in *Alternative Approaches to New Testament Study,* edited by A. E. Harvey. London: SPCK, 1985, pp. 97-121.

————. 'The Social Contexts of Jesus the Teacher: Construction or Reconstruction', *NTS* 33 (1987), pp. 439-51.

————. *Christ and the Cynics: Jesus and Other Radical Preachers in First-Century Tradition.* JSOT Manuals 4. Sheffield: Sheffield Academic Press, 1988.

Draper, J. A. '"Humble Submission to Almighty God" and Its Biblical Foundation: Contextual Exegesis of Romans 13.1-7', *JTSA* 63 (June 1988), pp. 30-38.

Du Boulay, Shirley. *Tutu: The Voice of the Voiceless.* London: Hodder and Stoughton, 1988.

Dungan, David L. *The Sayings of Jesus in the Churches of Paul: The Use of the Synoptic Tradition in the Regulation of Early Church Life.* Oxford: Blackwell, 1971.

Dunn, James D. G. *Christology in the Making.* London: SCM, 1980, second edn. 1989.

————. *The Evidence for Jesus.* London: SCM, 1985.

————. 'Paul's Knowledge of the Jesus Tradition'. In *Christus bezeugen: Festschrift für Wolfgang Trilling zum 65 Geburtstag,* edited by Karl Kertelge, Traugott Holtz and Claus-Peter Marz. Leipzig: St. Benno-Verlag, 1989, pp. 193-207.

————. *Romans.* Word Biblical Commentary 38 and 38A. Milton Keynes: Word, 1991.

————. 'The Question of Anti-Semitism in the New Testament Writings of the Period'. In J. D. G. Dunn (ed.). *Jews and Christians: The Parting of the Ways AD 70 to 135.* WUNT 66. Tübingen: Mohr Siebeck, 1992, pp. 177-211.

————. *Jesus' Call to Discipleship.* Cambridge: Cambridge University Press, 1992.

————. '"The Law of Faith", "the Law of the Spirit" and "the Law of Christ"'. In *Theology and Ethics in Paul and His Interpreters: Essays in Honor of Victor Paul Furnish,* edited by E. H. Lovering, Jr. and J. L. Sumney. Nashville: Abingdon, 1996, pp. 62-82.

————. 'The Household Rules in the New Testament'. In *The Family in Theological Perspective,* edited by S. C. Barton. Edinburgh: T&T Clark, 1996, pp. 43-63.

————. *The Theology of Paul the Apostle.* Grand Rapids: Eerdmans, 1998.

————. 'The Embarrassment of History: Reflections of the Problem of 'Anti-Judaism' in the Fourth Gospel'. In *Anti-Judaism and the Fourth Gospel: Papers of the Leuven Colloquium, 2000,* edited by R. Bieringer, D. Pollefyt and F. Vandecasteele-Vanneuville. Assen: Royal Van Gorcum, 2001, pp. 47-67.

————. *Jesus Remembered.* Grand Rapids: Eerdmans, 2003.

————. *A New Perspective on Jesus: What the Quest for the Historical Jesus Missed.* Grand Rapids: Baker/London: SPCK, 2005.

————, and Scot McKnight, eds. *The Historical Jesus in Recent Research.* Sources for Biblical and Theological Study. Winona Lake, IN: Eisenbrauns, 2005.

Dutch Reformed Church. *Human Relations and the South African Scene in the Light of Scripture.* Cape Town–Pretoria: Dutch Reformed Church, 1976.

Edwards, Ruth. '*Charin anti Charitos:* Grace and the Law in the Johannine Prologue'. *JSNT* 32 (1988), pp. 3-15.

————. *Discovering John.* London: SPCK, 2003.

Elliott, Neil. *Liberating Paul: The Justice of God and the Politics of the Apostle.* Maryknoll, NY: Orbis, 1994/Sheffield: Sheffield Academic Press, 1995.

Ellis, E. Earle. 'Background and Christology of John's Gospel: Selected Motifs', *SWJT* 31.1 (1988), pp. 24-31.

————. *Christ and the Future in New Testament History.* NovTSup 97. Leiden: Brill, 2000.

Ellis, Simon. 'All You Need Is Love', *New Directions* 2.28. London: Forward in Faith, 1998.

Engberg-Pedersen, Troels (ed.). *Paul beyond the Judaism/Hellenism Divide.* Louisville: Westminster John Knox, 2001.

Epstein, I. (trans. and ed.), *The Babylonian Talmud.* London: Soncino, 1958.

Esler, Philip F. *Community and Gospel in Luke-Acts: The Social and Political Motivations of Lucan Theology.* SNTSMS 57. Cambridge: Cambridge University Press, 1987.

Eslinger, Lyle. 'The Wooing of the Woman at the Well: Jesus, the Reader and Reader-Response Criticism', *Journal of Literature and Theology* 1.2 (1987), pp. 167-83. Reprinted in *The Gospel of John as Literature: An Anthology of Twentieth-Century Perspectives,* edited by Mark W. G. Stibbe. Leiden: Brill, 1993, pp. 165-82.

Evans, C. F. *Saint Luke.* London: SCM, 1990.

Evans, Craig A. *Word and Glory: On the Exegetical and Theological Background of John's Prologue.* JSNTSS 89. Sheffield: Sheffield Academic Press, 1993.

————, and Donald A. Hagner. *Anti-Semitism and Early Christianity: Issues of Polemic and Faith.* Minneapolis: Fortress, 1993.

————. *Mark 8:27–16:20.* Word Biblical Commentary 34B. Nashville: Nelson, 2001.

Fensham, F. C. 'Love in the Writings of Qumran and John', *Neotestamentica* 6 (1972), pp. 67-77.

Fish, Stanley. *Is There a Text in This Class? The Authority of Interpretive Communities.* Cambridge, MA: Harvard University Press, 1980.

Fisk, Bruce N. 'Paul: Life and Letters'. In *The Face of New Testament Studies: A Survey of Recent Research,* edited by Scot McKnight and Grant R. Osborne. Grand Rapids: Baker Academic, 2004, pp. 283-325.

Fitzmyer, Joseph A., S.J. *The Gospel According to Luke.* Anchor Bible 28 and 28A. New York: Doubleday, 1981 and 1985.

————. *The Acts of the Apostles: A New Translation with Introduction and Commentary.* Anchor Bible 31. New York: Doubleday, 1998.

————. *Romans: A New Translation with Introduction and Commentary.* Anchor Bible 33. New York: Doubleday 1993.

————. 'The Role of the Spirit in Luke-Acts'. In *The Unity of Luke-Acts, 47th Colloquium Biblicum Lovaniense,* edited by J. Verheyden. Leuven: Leuven University Press, 1999, pp. 165-83.

Flender, H. *St. Luke: Theologian of Redemptive History.* Philadelphia: Fortress/London: SPCK, 1967.

Fortna, Robert T. *The Gospel of Signs: A Reconstruction of the Narrative Source Underlying the Fourth Gospel.* SNTSMS 11. Cambridge: Cambridge University Press, 1970.

————. *The Fourth Gospel and Its Predecessor: From Narrative Source to Present Gospel.* Edinburgh: T&T Clark, 1989.

Forward, Martin. *Jesus: A Short Biography.* Oxford: Oneworld, 1998.

Fowl, Stephen E. *The Story of Christ in the Ethics of Paul.* JSNTSS 36. Sheffield: Academic Press, 1990.

————, and L. G. Jones. *Reading in Communion: Scripture and Ethics in Christian Life.* London: SPCK, 1991.

———— (ed.). *The Theological Interpretation of Scripture: Classic and Contemporary Readings.* Oxford: Blackwell, 1997.

————. 'Christology and Ethics in Philippians 2:5-11'. In *Where Christology Began: Essays on Philippians 2,* edited by R. P. Martin and B. J. Dodd. Louisville: Westminster John Knox, 1998, pp. 140-53.

Franklin, Eric. *Luke: Interpreter of Paul, Critic of Matthew.* JSNTSS 92. Sheffield: Sheffield Academic Press, 1994.

Freyne, Sean. *Jesus, A Jewish Galilean: A New Reading of the Jesus-Story.* London: T&T Clark, 2004.

Fuglseth, Kåre Sigvald. *Johannine Sectarianism in Perspective: A Sociological, Historical, and Comparative Analysis of Temple and Social Relationships in the Gospel of John, Philo and Qumran.* NovTSup 119. Leiden: Brill, 2005.

Fuller, Reginald H. 'The Double Commandment of Love: A Test Case for the Criteria of Authenticity'. In *Essays on the Love Commandment* by Luise Schottroff, Reginald H. Fuller, Christoph Burchard and M. Jack Suggs. Translated by Reginald H. and Ilse Fuller. Philadelphia: Fortress, 1978, pp. 41-56.

Funk, R. W., R. W. Hoover and the Jesus Seminar. *The Five Gospels: The Search for the Authentic Words of Jesus.* New York: Macmillan, 1993.

Funk, Robert W. *Honest to Jesus: Jesus for a New Millennium.* San Francisco: HarperSanFrancisco, 1996.

Furnish, V. P. 'The Jesus-Paul Debate: From Baur to Bultmann', *BJRL* 47 (1964-65), pp. 342-81.

————. *Theology and Ethics in Paul.* Nashville: Abingdon, 1968.

————. *The Love Command in the New Testament.* Nashville: Abingdon, 1972.

————. *Jesus according to Paul.* Cambridge: Cambridge University Press, 1993.

Gabel, J. B., and C. B. Wheeler. *The Bible as Literature.* Oxford: Oxford University Press, 1986.

Gagnon, Robert A. J. *The Bible and Homosexual Practice: Texts and Hermeneutics.* Nashville: Abingdon, 2001.

Gardner-Smith, P. *St. John and the Synoptic Gospels.* Cambridge: Cambridge University Press, 1938.

Garland, David E. *Reading Matthew: A Literary and Theological Commentary on the First Gospel.* London: SPCK, 1993.

———. 'The Temple Tax in Matthew 17:24-25 and the Principle of Not Causing Offense'. In *Treasures New and Old: Recent Contributions to Matthean Studies,* edited by David R. Bauer and Mark Allan Powell. Atlanta: Scholars Press, 1996, pp. 69-98.

Garrison, Roman. *The Graeco-Roman Context of Early Christian Literature.* JSNTSS 137, Sheffield: Sheffield Academic Press, 1997.

Gasque, W. W. *A History of the Criticism of the Acts of the Apostles.* Tübingen: J. C. B. Mohr, 1975.

Gaventa, Beverly Roberts. 'The Presence of the Absent Lord: The Characterization of Jesus in the Acts of the Apostles', S22-59, SBL Annual Meeting, Atlanta, November 22, 2003.

———, and Patrick D. Miller (eds.). *The Ending of Mark and the Ends of God: Essays in Memory of Donald Harrisville Juel.* Louisville: Westminster John Knox, 2005.

Gench, Frances Taylor. *Wisdom in the Christology of Matthew.* Lanham, MD: University Press of America, 1997.

Gerhardsson, B. *The Ethos of the Bible.* Translated by S. Westerholm. Minneapolis: Fortress, 1981/London: DLT, 1982.

———. 'The Christology of Matthew'. In *Who Do You Say That I Am? Essays on Christology in Honor of Jack Dean Kingsbury,* edited by David R. Bauer and Mark Allan Powell. Louisville: Westminster John Knox, 1999, pp. 14-32.

Getui, Mary, Tinyiko Maluleke and Justin Ukpong (eds.). *Interpreting the New Testament in Africa.* Nairobi: Acton, 2001.

Goldingay, John. *Approaches to Old Testament Interpretation.* Leicester: IVP, 1981.

———. *Models for Scripture.* Grand Rapids: Eerdmans/Exeter: Paternoster, 1994.

———. *Models for Interpretation of Scripture.* Grand Rapids: Eerdmans/Exeter: Paternoster, 1995.

Goldsmith, Dale. *New Testament Ethics: An Introduction.* Elgin, IL: Brethren Press, 1988.

Gooch, Paul W. 'Authority and Justification in Theological Ethics: A Study in 1 Corinthians 7', *Journal of Religious Ethics* 11 (1983), pp. 62-74.

Goodacre, Mark. 'The Power of *The Passion:* Reacting and Over-reacting to Gibson's Artistic Vision'. In *Jesus and Mel Gibson's* The Passion of the Christ: *The Film, the Gospels and the Claims of History,* edited by Kathleen E. Corley and Robert L. Webb. London: Continuum, 2004, pp. 28-44.

Gorman, Michael J. *Apostle of the Crucified Lord: A Theological Introduction to Paul and His Letters.* Grand Rapids: Eerdmans, 2004.

Gray, Sherman W. *The Least of My Brothers: Matthew 25:31-46, A History of Interpretation.* SBLDS 114 Atlanta: Scholars Press, 1989.

Green, Joel B. *The Theology of the Gospel of Luke.* Cambridge: Cambridge University Press, 1995.

———. '"Salvation to the End of the Earth" (Acts 13:47): God as the Saviour in the Acts of the Apostles'. In *Witness to the Gospel: The Theology of Acts,* edited by I. Howard Marshall and David Peterson. Grand Rapids: Eerdmans, 1998, pp. 83-106.

―――. 'The Gospel according to Mark'. In *The Cambridge Companion to the Gospels,* edited by Stephen C. Barton. Cambridge: Cambridge University Press, 2006, pp. 139-57.

Greenberg, D. F. *The Construction of Homosexuality.* Chicago: University of Chicago Press, 1989.

Greenfield, G. 'The Ethics of the Sermon on the Mount', *SWJT* 35.1 (1992), pp. 13-19.

Groves, Philip. 'The Least in the Community of Jesus as Examples for Leadership Today', *Anvil* 15.1 (1998), pp. 13-21.

Guelich, Robert A. *Mark 1–8.26.* Word Biblical Commentary 34A. Dallas: Word, 1989.

Guillemette N., S.J. 'The Sermon on the Mount: Feasible Ethics?', *Landas* 9 (1995), pp. 209-36.

Gundry-Volf, Judith M. 'Celibacy in Corinth: Towards a Reconstruction from 1 Corinthians 7'. Colloquium Biblicum Lovaniense XLIII, August 8-10, 1994. Later published as 'Controlling the Bodies: A Theological Profile of the Corinthian Sexual Ascetics'. In *The Corinthian Correspondence.* Ed. R. Bieringer. BETL 125. Leuven: Leuven University Press–Peeters, 1996, pp. 499-521.

―――. 'Gender and Creation in 1 Cor 11.2-16: A Study in Paul's Theological Method'. In *Evangelium, Schriftauslegung, Kirche: Festschrift für Peter Stuhlmacher,* edited by J. Adna, S. J. Hafemann and O. Hofius. Göttingen: Vandenhoeck & Ruprecht, 1997, pp. 151-71.

―――. 'Paul on Women and Gender: A Comparison with Early Jewish Views'. In *The Road from Damascus: The Impact of Paul's Conversion on His Life, Thought, and Ministry,* edited by Richard N. Longenecker. Grand Rapids: Eerdmans, 1997, pp. 184-212.

―――. 'Putting the *Moral Vision of the New Testament* into Focus: A Review', *Bulletin for Biblical Research* 9 (1999), pp. 277-87.

Guroian, Vigen. 'Bible and Ethics: An Ecclesial and Liturgical Interpretation', *Journal of Religious Ethics* 18.1 (Atlanta: 1990), pp. 129-57.

Gustafson, James M. 'The Place of Scripture in Christian Ethics: A Methodological Study', *Interpretation* 24 (1970), pp. 430-55.

―――. 'The Use of Scripture in Christian Ethics', *Studia Theologia* 51 (1997), pp. 15-29.

Gutiérrez, Gustavo. *A Theology of Liberation: History, Politics and Salvation.* London: SCM, 1974.

―――. *We Drink from Our Own Wells: The Spiritual Journey of a People.* London: SCM, 1984.

Haenchen, Ernst. *The Acts of the Apostles: A Commentary.* Philadelphia: Westminster, 1971.

―――. *A Commentary on the Gospel of John.* Translated by Robert W. Funk. Edited by Robert W. Funk with Ulrich Busse. Hermeneia, 2 vols. Philadelphia: Fortress, 1984.

Hagner, Donald A. *Matthew.* Word Biblical Commentary 33, 2 vols. Dallas: Word, 1993, 1995.

―――. 'Balancing the Old and the New: The Law of Moses in Matthew and Paul', *Interpretation* 51.1 (1997), pp. 20-30.

―――. 'Ethics and the Sermon on the Mount', *Studia Theologia* 51 (1997), pp. 44-59.

―――. 'Matthew: Christian Judaism or Jewish Christianity'. In *The Face of New Testament*

Studies: A Survey of Recent Research, edited by Scot McKnight and Grant R. Osborne. Grand Rapids: Baker Academic, 2004, pp. 263-82.

Hakola, Raimo. *Identity Matters: John, the Jews and Jewishness.* NovTSup 118. Leiden: Brill, 2005.

Harrington, Daniel J., S.J., and James F. Keenan, S.J. *Jesus and Virtue Ethics: Building Bridges between New Testament Studies and Moral Theology.* Oxford: Sheed and Ward, 2002.

Harris, Elizabeth. *Prologue and Gospel: The Theology of the Fourth Evangelist.* JSNTSS 107. Sheffield: Sheffield Academic Press, 1994.

Harris, Gerald. 'The Beginnings of Church Discipline: 1 Corinthians 5'. In *Understanding Paul's Ethics,* edited by B. S. Rosner. Grand Rapids: Eerdmans, 1995, pp. 129-51.

Hartin, Patrick. 'New Testament Ethics: Some Trends in More Recent Research', *JTSA* 59 (1987), pp. 35-41.

———. 'Remain in Me (John 15:5). The Foundation of the Ethical and Its Consequence in the Farewell Discourses', *Neotestamentica* 25.2 (1991), pp. 341-56.

———. 'Towards a Christian Vision as the Basis for Ethical Decisions', *Scriptura* 42 (1992), pp. 65-73.

———. 'Ethics and the New Testament: How Do We Get from There to Here?' In *The Relevance of Theology for the 1990's,* edited by J. Mouton and B. C. Lategan. Pretoria: Human Sciences Research Council Pretoria, 1994, pp. 511-525.

———. 'Christian Ethics in a Pluralistic Society: Towards a Theology of Compromise', *Religion and Theology* 4.1 (1997), pp. 21-34.

Hartman, Lars. 'Code and Context: A Few Reflections on the Parenesis of Col. 3.6–4.1'. In *Understanding Paul's Ethics,* edited by B. S. Rosner. Grand Rapids: Eerdmans, 1995, pp. 177-91.

Harvey, A. E. *Jesus and the Constraints of History.* London: Duckworth, 1982.

———. *Strenuous Commands: The Ethic of Jesus.* London: SCM/Philadelphia: Trinity Press International, 1990.

———. 'Genesis versus Deuteronomy? Jesus on Marriage and Divorce'. In *The Gospels and the Scriptures of Israel,* edited by Craig A. Evans and W. Richard Stegner. JSNTSS 104. Sheffield: Sheffield Academic Press, 1994, pp. 55-65.

Hauerwas, Stanley. *Character and the Christian Life.* Notre Dame, IN: University of Notre Dame Press, 1975; 3rd repr. 1994.

———. *A Community of Character: Towards a Constructive Christian Social Ethic.* Notre Dame, IN: University of Notre Dame Press, 1981.

———. *The Peaceable Kingdom: A Primer in Christian Ethics.* Notre Dame, IN: University of Notre Dame Press, 1983/London: SCM, 1984.

———. 'The Sermon on the Mount, Just War and the Quest for Peace', *Concilium* 195 (1988), pp. 36-43.

———, and William H. Willimon. *Preaching to Strangers: Evangelism in Today's World.* Louisville: Westminster John Knox, 1992.

———. 'Living the Proclaimed Reign of God: A Sermon on the Sermon on the Mount', *Interpretation* 47 (1993), pp. 152-58.

Hawthorne, Gerald F. *Philippians.* Word Biblical Commentary 43, revised by Ralph P. Martin. Nashville: Nelson, 2004.

429

Hays, Richard B. 'Recent Books on New Testament Ethics', *Quarterly Review* 6.4 (1986), pp. 13-30.

———, 'Relations Natural and Unnatural: A Response to John Boswell's Exegesis of Romans 1'. *Journal of Religious Ethics* 14.1 (1986), pp. 184-215.

———. 'Christology and Ethics in Galatians: The Law of Christ', *CBQ* 49 (1987), pp. 268-90.

———. *Echoes of Scripture in the Letters of Paul*. New Haven, CT: Yale University Press, 1989.

———. 'Ecclesiology and Ethics in 1 Corinthians', *Ex Auditu* 10 (Cambridge, 1994), pp. 31-43.

———. *The Moral Vision of the New Testament: A Contemporary Introduction to New Testament Ethics*. San Francisco: HarperSanFrancisco/Edinburgh: T&T Clark, 1996.

———. Review of *Paul, Scripture, and Ethics*, by B. S. Rosner, in *Westminster Theological Journal* 58 (1996), pp. 313-16.

———. 'The Role of Scripture in Paul's Ethics'. In *Theology and Ethics in Paul and His Interpreters: Essays in Honor of Victor Paul Furnish*, edited by E. H. Lovering, Jr. and J. L. Sumney. Nashville: Abingdon, 1996, pp. 30-47.

———. *First Corinthians*. Interpretation. Louisville: John Knox, 1997.

———. *The Faith of Jesus Christ: The Narrative Substructure of Galatians 3:1–4:11*. Chico: Scholars Press, 1983; 2nd edn., Grand Rapids: Eerdmans, 2002.

———. 'Is Paul's Gospel Narratable?' *JSNT* 27 (2004), pp. 217-39.

Heard, Warren. 'Luke's Attitude toward the Rich and the Poor', *Trinity Journal* n.s. 9 (1988), pp. 47-80.

Heil, John Paul. 'The Double Meaning of the Narrative of Universal Judgment in Matthew 25:31-46', *JSNT* 69 (1998), pp. 3-14.

Helminiak, Daniel A. *What the Bible Really Says about Homosexuality*. San Francisco: Alamo Square, 1994.

———. 'Ethics, Biblical and Denominational: A Response to Mark Smith', *JAAR* 65 (1997), pp. 855-59.

Hemer, Colin J. *The Book of Acts in the Setting of Hellenistic History*. WUNT 49. Tübingen: J. C. B. Mohr, 1989.

Hengel, Martin. *The Charismatic Leader and His Followers*. Edinburgh: T&T Clark, 1981.

———. *The Pre-Christian Paul*. London: SCM, 1991.

———, and Anna Maria Schwemer. *Paul between Damascus and Antioch: The Unknown Years*. London: SCM, 1997.

Hiers, Richard H. *Jesus and Ethics: Four Interpretations*. Philadelphia: Westminster, 1968.

Hillmer, Melvyn R. 'They Believed in Him: Discipleship in the Johannine Tradition'. In *Patterns of Discipleship in the New Testament*, edited by Richard N. Longenecker. Grand Rapids: Eerdmans, 1996, pp. 77-97.

Holladay, Carl R. *A Critical Introduction to the New Testament: Interpreting the Message and Meaning of Jesus Christ*. Nashville: Abingdon, 2005.

Holtz, T. 'Zur Frage der inhaltlichen Weisungen bei Paulus', *Theologische Literaturzeitung* 106 (1981), pp. 385-400. ET 'The Question of the Content of Paul's Instructions'. In *Understanding Paul's Ethics*, edited by B. S. Rosner. Grand Rapids: Eerdmans, 1995, pp. 51-71.

Hong, In-Gyu. 'The Law and Christian Ethics in Galatians 5–6', *Neotestamentica* 26.1 (1992), pp. 113-30.

Hooker, Morna D. *The Message of Mark*. London: Epworth, 1983.

———. *From Adam to Christ*. Cambridge: Cambridge University Press, 1990.

———. The *Gospel according to St Mark*. London: A & C Black, 1991.

———. *Beginnings: Keys That Open the Gospels*. London: SCM, 1997.

———. *Endings: Invitations to Discipleship*. London: SCM/Peabody, MA: Hendrickson, 2003.

Horn, F. W. 'Ethik des Neuen Testaments 1982-1992', *Theologische Rundschau* 60 (Tübingen, 1995), pp. 32-86.

Horrell, David G. *The Social Ethos of the Corinthian Correspondence*. Edinburgh: T&T Clark, 1996.

———. 'Theological Principle or Christological Praxis? Pauline Ethics in 1 Corinthians 8.1–11.1', *JSNT* 67 (1997), pp. 83-114.

———. '"The Lord commanded . . . but I have not used . . .": Exegetical and Hermeneutical Reflections on 1 Cor 9.14-15', *NTS* 43 (1997), pp. 587-603.

——— (ed.). *Social-Scientific Approaches to New Testament Interpretation*. Edinburgh: T&T Clark, 1999.

———. 'Restructuring Human Relationships: Paul's Corinthian Letters and Habermas' Discourse Ethics', *ExpT* 110.10 (1999), pp. 321-25.

———. 'Boundy Memorial Lectures'. University of Exeter, May 2000.

———. 'Solidarity and Difference: Pauline Morality in Romans 14.1–15.13', *Studies in Christian Ethics* 15.2 (2002), pp. 60-78.

———. *Solidarity and Difference: A Contemporary Reading of Paul's Ethics*. London: T&T Clark, 2005.

———. *An Introduction to the Study of Paul*. London: T&T Clark, 2000; 2nd edn. 2006.

Horsley, Richard A. *Jesus and the Spiral of Violence: Popular Jewish Resistance in Roman Palestine*. San Francisco: Harper, 1987.

———. *The Liberation of Christmas: The Infancy Narratives in Social Context*. New York: Crossroad, 1989.

Houlden, J. L. 'Paul, Ethical Teaching of'. In *A New Dictionary of Christian Ethics,* edited by J. Macquarrie and J. Childress. London: SCM, 1967, second edn. 1986, p. 457.

———. *Ethics and the New Testament*. Oxford: Oxford University Press, 1973. Penguin, 1973. Reprinted Edinburgh: T&T Clark, 1992.

———. 'Review article of Charles H. Talbert, *Reading the Sermon on the Mount: Character Formation and Decision Making in Matthew 5–7*', *Conversations in Religion and Theology* 3.2 (2005), pp. 119-12.

Howell, David B. *Matthew's Inclusive Story: A Study in the Narrative Rhetoric of the First Gospel*. JSNTSS 42. Sheffield: Sheffield Academic Press, 1990.

Hübner, Hans. *Law in Paul's Thought: A Contribution to the Development of Pauline Theology*. Edinburgh: T&T Clark, 1984.

Hulley, Leonard, Louise Kretzschmar and Luke Lungile Pato (eds.). *Archbishop Tutu: Prophetic Witness in South Africa*. Cape Town: Human and Rousseau, 1996.

Hurtado, Larry W. 'Convert, Apostate, or Apostle to the Nations: The "Conversion" of Paul in Recent Scholarship', *Studies in Religion/Sciences Religieuses* 22 (1993), pp. 273-84.

————. 'Following Jesus in the Gospel of Mark — and Beyond'. In *Patterns of Discipleship in the New Testament,* edited by Richard N. Longenecker. Grand Rapids: Eerdmans, 1996, pp. 9-29.

————. *Lord Jesus Christ: Devotion to Jesus in Earliest Christianity.* Grand Rapids: Eerdmans, 2003.

Iser, Wolfgang. *The Implied Reader: Patterns of Communication in Prose Fiction from Bunyan to Beckett.* Baltimore: John Hopkins University Press, 1974.

————. *The Art of Reading.* Baltimore: John Hopkins University Press, 1978.

Jeremias, J. *The Eucharistic Words of Jesus.* London: SCM, 1966.

————. *New Testament Theology 1: The Proclamation of Jesus.* New York: Scribner's/London: SCM, 1971.

Jervell, Jacob. *Luke and the People of God: A New Look at Luke-Acts.* Minneapolis: Augsburg, 1972.

————. *Jesus in the Gospel of John.* Minneapolis: Augsburg, 1984.

————. *The Theology of the Acts of the Apostles.* Cambridge: Cambridge University Press, 1996.

Johnson, Luke T. *The Literary Function of Possessions in Luke-Acts.* SBLDS 39. Missoula, MT: Scholars Press, 1977.

————. 'On Finding the Lukan Community: A Cautionary Essay'. In *Society for Biblical Literature 1979 Seminar Papers.* Missoula, MT: Scholars Press, 1979, vol. 1, pp. 87-100.

————. *Sharing Possessions.* London: SCM, 1986.

————. *The Gospel of Luke.* Sacra Pagina 3. Collegeville, MN: Liturgical Press, 1991.

————. 'Why Scripture Isn't Enough', *Commonweal* 124.11 (1997), pp. 23-25.

————. 'The Christology of Luke'. In *Who Do You Say That I Am? Essays on Christology in Honor of Jack Dean Kingsbury,* edited by David R. Bauer and Mark Allan Powell. Louisville: Westminster John Knox, 1999, pp. 49-65.

————. 'Literary Criticism of Luke-Acts: Is Reception-History Pertinent?' *JSNT* 28.2 (2005), pp. 159-62.

Jones, D. C. *Biblical Christian Ethics.* Grand Rapids: Baker, 1994.

Jones, L. Gregory. *Embodying Forgiveness: A Theological Analysis.* Grand Rapids: Eerdmans, 1995.

Jonker, Louis. 'The Biblical Legitimization of Ethnic Diversity in Apartheid Theology', *Scriptura* 77 (2001), pp. 165-83.

Kähler, M. *The So-Called Historical Jesus and the Historic, Biblical Christ.* ET Philadelphia: Fortress, 1964. German original, 1892.

Käsemann, Ernst. 'Kritische Analyse von Phil. 2,5-11', *ZTK* 47 (1950), pp. 316-60.

————. *The Testament of Jesus: A Study of the Gospel of John in the Light of Chapter 17.* London: SCM, 1966.

————. *New Testament Questions of Today.* Translated by W. J. Montague. Philadelphia: Fortress/London: SCM, 1969.

Katongole, Emmanuel M. 'African Hermeneutics and Theology in the Twenty-First Century: On Surviving Postmodernism'. SNTS Post Conference. Hammanskraal: University of Pretoria, August 9, 1999. Later published in a revised form. In *Interpreting the New Testament in Africa,* edited by Mary Getui, Tinyiko Maluleke and Justin Ukpong. Nairobi: Acton, 2001, pp. 253-73.

Katz, Steven T. 'Issues in the Separation of Judaism and Christianity after 70 c.e.: A Reconsideration'. *JBL* 103 (1984), pp. 43-76.

Keck, Leander E., and J. Louis Martyn (eds.). *Studies in Luke-Acts: Essays Presented in Honor of Paul Schubert.* London: SPCK, 1968.

———. 'Ethics in the Gospel according to Matthew', *Iliff Review* 41 (1984), pp. 39-56.

———. 'Rethinking "New Testament Ethics"', *JBL* 115.1 (1996), pp. 3-16.

Kee, Howard C. *Community of the New Age: Studies in Mark's Gospel.* London: SCM, 1977.

Keener, Craig S. *A Commentary on the Gospel of Matthew.* Grand Rapids: Eerdmans, 1999.

———. *The Gospel of John: A Commentary.* 2 vols. Peabody, MA: Hendrickson, 2003.

Kelber, Werner H. 'The Birth of a Beginning: John 1.1-18', *Semeia* 52 (1990), pp. 120-44.

———. 'Metaphysics and Marginality in John'. In *What Is John?* vol. 1, *Readers and Readings of the Fourth Gospel,* edited by Fernando F. Segovia. Atlanta: Scholars Press, 1996, pp. 129-54.

Kilner, John F. 'A Pauline Approach to Ethical Decision-Making', *Interpretation* 43 (1989), pp. 366-79.

Kim, Kyoung-Jin. *Stewardship and Almsgiving in Luke's Theology.* JSNTSS 155. Sheffield: Sheffield Academic Press, 1998.

Kinghorn, Johann (ed.). *Issues in Contextual Hermeneutics. Scriptura,* Special Issue S9 (1991).

Kingsbury, Jack Dean. *Matthew: Structure, Christology, Kingdom.* Philadelphia: Fortress, 1975.

———. *The Christology of Mark's Gospel.* Philadelphia: Fortress, 1983.

———. *Matthew as Story.* Second revised edn. Philadelphia: Fortress, 1988.

———. *Conflict in Mark: Jesus, Authorities, Disciples.* Philadelphia: Fortress, 1989.

———. *Conflict in Luke: Jesus, Authorities, Disciples.* Minneapolis: Fortress, 1991.

Kinukawa, Hisako. 'Women Disciples of Jesus (15.40-41; 15.47; 16.1)'. In *A Feminist Companion to Mark,* edited by Amy-Jill Levine with Marianne Blickenstaff. Sheffield: Sheffield Academic Press, 2001, pp. 171-90.

Klassen, William. 'The Authenticity of the Command: "Love Your Enemies"'. In *Authenticating the Words of Jesus,* edited by B. Chilton and C. A. Evans. Leiden: Brill, 1999, pp. 385-407.

Kloppenborg, John S. *The Formation of Q: Trajectories in Ancient Wisdom Collections.* Philadelphia: Fortress, 1987.

Knight, George W., III. *The Pastoral Epistles: A Commentary on the Greek Text* NIGTC. Grand Rapids: Eerdmans, 1992.

Koperski, Veronica. 'Luke 10.38-42 and Acts 6.1-7: Women and Discipleship in the Literary Context of Luke-Acts'. In *The Unity of Luke-Acts, 47th Colloquium Biblicum Lovaniense,* edited by J. Verheyden. Leuven: Leuven University Press, 1999, pp. 517-44. Revised and expanded version, 'Women and Discipleship in Luke 10.38-42 and Acts 6.1-7: The Literary Context of Luke-Acts'. In *A Feminist Companion to Luke,* edited by Amy-Jill Levine with Marianne Blickenstaff. Sheffield: Sheffield Academic Press, 2001, pp. 161-96.

Kotila, M. *Umstrittene Zeuge: Studien zur Stellung des Gesetzes in der johanneischen Theologiegeschichte.* Annales Academiae Scientiarum Fennicae Diss. 48. Helsinki: Suomalainen Tiedeakatemia, 1988.

433

Kreitzer, Larry J., and Deborah W. Rooke (eds.). *Ciphers in the Sand: Interpretations of the Woman Taken in Adultery (John 7.53–8.11)*. Sheffield: Sheffield Academic Press, 2000.

Kümmel, W. G. *Introduction to the New Testament*. London: SCM, 1975.

Kvalbein, Hans. 'The Kingdom of God in the Ethics of Jesus', *Studia Theologia* 51 (1997), pp. 60-84.

Kysar, Robert. *The Fourth Evangelist and His Gospel: An Examination of Contemporary Scholarship*. Minneapolis: Augsburg, 1975.

――――. *John's Story of Jesus*. Philadelphia: Fortress, 1984.

――――. 'The Fourth Gospel: A Report on Recent Research', *ANRW* 2.25.3. Berlin: Walter de Gruyter, 1985, pp. 2389-2480.

――――. 'Johannine Metaphor — Meaning and Function: A Literary Case Study of John 10:1-18'. In *The Fourth Gospel from a Literary Perspective*, edited by R. Alan Culpepper and Fernando F. Segovia. *Semeia* 53. Atlanta: Scholars Press, 1991, pp. 81-111.

――――. 'Anti-Semitism and the Gospel of John'. In *Anti-Semitism and Early Christianity: Issues of Polemic and Faith*, edited by Craig A. Evans and Donald A. Hagner. Minneapolis: Fortress, 1993, pp. 113-27.

――――. 'Coming Hermeneutical Earthquake in Johannine Interpretation'. In *What Is John?* vol. 1, *Readers and Readings of the Fourth Gospel*, edited by Fernando F. Segovia. Atlanta: Scholars Press, 1996, pp. 185-89.

――――. 'The Expulsion from the Synagogue: The Tale of a Theory', *Johannine Literature Section*, Session S25-62, SBL Conference, Toronto, Monday, November 25, 2002. Later published as 'The Expulsion from the Synagogue: The Tale of a Theory'. In Robert Kysar. *Voyages with John: Charting the Fourth Gospel*, Waco, TX: Baylor University Press, 2005, chap. 15, pp. 227-35.

――――. 'The Whence and Whither of the Johannine Community'. In *Life in Abundance: Studies of John's Gospel in Tribute to Raymond E. Brown*, edited by Paul N. Anderson. Collegeville, MN: Liturgical Press, 2005, pp. 65-81.

――――. *Voyages with John: Charting the Fourth Gospel*. Waco, TX: Baylor University Press, 2005.

Lapide, Pinchas, and Peter Stuhlmacher. *Paul: Rabbi and Apostle*. Minneapolis: Augsburg, 1984.

Lamarche, Paul. 'The Prologue of John', *Recherches de Science Religieuse* 52 (1964), pp. 497-537. Translated and reprinted in *The Interpretation of John*, edited by John Ashton. Edinburgh: T&T Clark, second edn. 1997, pp. 47-65.

Lash, N. 'Interpretation and Imagination'. In *Incarnation and Myth: The Debate Continued*, edited by M. D. Goulder. London: SCM, 1979, p. 25.

Lategan, Bernard C. 'Introducing a Research Project on Contextual Hermeneutics', *Scriptura* 33 (1990), pp. 1-5.

――――ed.). *The Integrity of Theological Education*. *Scriptura*, Special Issue S11 (1993).

――――. 'The *Studiorum Novi Testamenti Societas* Comes to Africa', *Scriptura* 67 (1998), pp. 419-27.

Lee, David. *Luke's Stories of Jesus: Theological Reading of Gospel Narrative and the Legacy of Hans Frei*. JSNTSS 185. Sheffield: Sheffield Academic Press, 1999.

Léon-Dufour, Xavier. *To Act according to the Gospel*. Peabody, MA: Hendrickson, 2005.

Lentz, John C., Jr. *Luke's Portrait of Paul.* SNTSMS 77. Cambridge: Cambridge University Press, 1993.

Levine, Amy-Jill. 'Anti-Judaism and the Gospel of Matthew'. In *Anti-Judaism and the Gospels,* edited by William R. Farmer. Harrisburg, PA: Trinity Press International, 1999, pp. 9-36.

————, and Marianne Blickenstaff (eds.). *A Feminist Companion to Matthew.* Sheffield: Sheffield Academic Press, 2001.

———— and ———— (eds.). *A Feminist Companion to Luke.* Sheffield: Sheffield Academic Press, 2001.

———— and ———— (eds.). *A Feminist Companion to Mark.* Sheffield: Sheffield Academic Press, 2001.

———— and ———— (eds.). *A Feminist Companion to the Acts of the Apostles.* London: T&T Clark, 2004.

Lieu, Judith M. 'Anti-Judaism in the Fourth Gospel: Explanation and Hermeneutics'. In *Anti-Judaism and the Fourth Gospel: Papers of the Leuven Colloquium, 2000,* edited by R. Bieringer, D. Pollefyt and F. Vandecasteele-Vanneuville. Assen: Royal Van Gorcum, 2001, pp. 126-43.

Lincoln, Andrew T. *Truth on Trial: The Lawsuit Motif in the Fourth Gospel.* Peabody, MA: Hendrickson, 2000.

————. *The Gospel according to Saint John.* Black's New Testament Commentaries. London: Continuum/Peabody, MA: Hendrickson, 2005.

Lindars, Barnabas. *The Gospel of John.* New Century Bible Commentary. London: Marshall, Morgan & Scott, 1972.

———— *John.* Sheffield: Sheffield Academic Press, 1990.

Loader, William. *The Christology of the Fourth Gospel: Structure and Issues.* BETL 23. Second revised edn. Frankfurt: Peter Lang, 1992.

————. *Jesus' Attitude towards the Law: A Study of the Gospels.* Grand Rapids: Eerdmans, 2002.

————. *Sexuality and the Jesus Tradition.* Grand Rapids: Eerdmans, 2005.

Loessl, Joseph S.J., 'The Ethical Dimension of Mk. 10.17-22', *Hekima Review* (Nairobi) 6 (1991), pp. 57-82.

Lohse, Eduard. *Colossians and Philemon,* Hermeneia. Philadelphia: Fortress, 1971.

————. *Theological Ethics of the New Testament.* Translated by M. Eugene Boring. Minneapolis: Fortress, 1991.

————. 'The Church in Everyday Life: Considerations of the Theological Basis of Ethics in the New Testament'. ET in *Understanding Paul's Ethics,* edited by Brian S. Rosner. Grand Rapids: Eerdmans, 1995, pp. 251-65.

Longenecker, Bruce W. (ed.). *Narrative Dynamics in Paul: A Critical Assessment.* Louisville: Westminster John Knox, 2002.

Longenecker, Richard N. *New Testament Social Ethics for Today.* Grand Rapids: Eerdmans, 1984.

———— (ed.). *Patterns of Discipleship in the New Testament.* Grand Rapids: Eerdmans, 1996.

———— (ed.). *The Road from Damascus: The Impact of Paul's Conversion on His Life, Thought, and Ministry.* Grand Rapids: Eerdmans, 1997.

———— (ed.). *Contours of Christology in the New Testament*. Grand Rapids: Eerdmans, 2005.

Loubser, Bobby. 'The Apartheid Bible Revisited', *Bulletin for Contextual Theology in Southern Africa and Asia* 3.1 (February 1996), pp. 8-10.

Loubser, J. A. *The Apartheid Bible: A Critical Review of Racial Theology in South Africa*. Cape Town: Maskew, Miller, Longman, 1987.

Louw, J. D., and E. A. Nida (eds.), *Greek-English Lexicon of the New Testament Based on Semantic Domains*, vol. 1. New York: United Bible Societies, 1988.

Lovering, E. H., Jr. and J. L. Sumney. *Theology and Ethics in Paul and His Interpreters: Essays in Honor of Victor Paul Furnish*. Nashville: Abingdon, 1996.

Lowe, M. 'Who Were the *Ioudaioi?*', *NovT* 18 (1976), pp. 101-30.

Lüdemann, Gerd. *Paul, Apostle to the Gentiles: Studies in Chronology*. London: SCM, 1984.

Luz, Ulrich. 'The Final Judgment (Matthew 25.31-46): An Exercise in "History of Influence" Exegesis'. In *Treasures New and Old: Recent Contributions to Matthean Studies*, edited by David R. Bauer and Mark Allan Powell. Atlanta: Scholars Press, 1996, pp. 271-310.

————. *Studies in Matthew*. Grand Rapids: Eerdmans, 2005.

Maccini, Robert Gordon. *Her Testimony Is True: Women as Witnesses according to John*. JSNTSS 125. Sheffield: Sheffield Academic Press, 1996.

Mack, Burton L. *A Myth of Innocence: Mark and Christian Origins*. Philadelphia: Fortress, 1988.

————. *The Lost Gospel: The Book of Q and Christian Origins*. San Francisco: HarperCollins, 1993.

————. 'Q and a Cynic-Like Jesus'. In *Whose Historical Jesus?*, edited by William E. Arnal and Michel Desjardins. Studies in Christianity and Judaism 7. Waterloo, ON: Wilfrid Laurier University Press, 1997, pp. 25-36.

Maddox, Robert. *The Purpose of Luke-Acts*. Edinburgh: T&T Clark, 1982.

Mainville, Odette. 'L'éthique paulienne', *Église et Théologie* 24 (1993), pp. 391-412.

Malick, D. E. 'The Condemnation of Homosexuality in Romans 1:26-27', *Bibliotheca Sacra* 150 (1993), pp. 327-40.

Maluleke, T. S. 'African Theologies/Christianities and the Bible — Some Hermeneutical Issues at Stake'. SNTS Post Conference. Hammanskraal: University of Pretoria, August 9, 1999. Later published in a revised form as 'The Bible and African Theologies'. In *Interpreting the New Testament in Africa*, edited by Mary Getui, Tinyiko Maluleke and Justin Ukpong. Nairobi: Acton, 2001, pp. 165-76.

Marguerat, Daniel. 'Luc-Actes: Une unite à construire'. In *The Unity of Luke-Acts, 47th Colloquium Biblicum Lovaniense*, edited by J. Verheyden. Leuven: Leuven University Press, 1999, pp. 57-81.

————. *The First Christian Historian: Writing the 'Acts of the Apostles'*. SNTSMS 121. Cambridge: Cambridge University Press, 2002.

Marshall, I. Howard. 'Using the Bible in Ethics'. In *Essays in Evangelical Social Ethics*, edited by David F. Wright. Exeter: Paternoster, 1978, pp. 39-55.

————. *The Gospel of Luke: A Commentary on the Greek Text*. NIGTC. Grand Rapids: Eerdmans, 1978.

————. 'The Use of the New Testament in Christian Ethics', *ExpT* 105 (1993/94), pp. 131-36.

————, and David Peterson (eds.). *Witness to the Gospel: The Theology of Acts.* Grand Rapids: Eerdmans, 1998.

————. '"Israel" and the Story of Salvation: One Theme in Two Parts'. In *Jesus and the Heritage of Israel: Luke's Narrative Claim upon Israel's Legacy,* edited by David P. Moessner. Harrisburg, PA: Trinity Press International, 1999, pp. 340-58.

Martin, Dale B. *Slavery as Salvation: The Metaphor of Slavery in Pauline Christianity.* New Haven: Yale University Press, 1990.

————. 'Heterosexism and the Interpretation of Romans 1:18-32', *Biblical Interpretation* 3.3 (1995), pp. 332-55. Reprinted in Dale B. Martin. *Sex and the Single Savior: Gender and Sexuality in Biblical Interpretation.* Louisville: Westminster John Knox, 2006, pp. 51-64.

————. '*Arsenokoitēs* and *Malakos:* Meanings and Consequences'. In *Biblical Ethics and Homosexuality: Listening to Scripture,* edited by Robert L. Brawley. Louisville: Westminster John Knox, 1996, pp. 117-36. Reprinted in Dale B. Martin. *Sex and the Single Savior: Gender and Sexuality in Biblical Interpretation.* Louisville: Westminster John Knox, 2006, pp. 37-50.

————. 'Paul without Passion: On Paul's Rejection of Desire in Sex and Marriage'. In *Constructing Early Christian Families,* edited by H. Moxnes. London: Routledge, 1997, pp. 201-15.

————. Review of R. B. Hays, *The Moral Vision of the New Testament,* in *JBL* 117 (1998), pp. 358-60.

————. *Sex and the Single Savior: Gender and Sexuality in Biblical Interpretation.* Louisville: Westminster John Knox, 2006.

Martyn, J. Louis. *History and Theology in the Fourth Gospel.* Louisville: Westminster John Knox, 1968, first edn.; third edn. 2003.

Marxsen, Willi. *New Testament Foundations for Christian Ethics.* Translated by O. C. Dean, Jr. Minneapolis: Fortress/Edinburgh: T&T Clark, 1993.

Matera, Frank J. 'The Ethics of the Kingdom in the Gospel of Matthew', *Listening* 24.3 (Romeoville, IL, 1989), pp. 241-50.

————. 'Ethics for the Kingdom of God: The Gospel according to Mark', *Louvain Studies* 20 (1995), pp. 187-200.

————. *New Testament Ethics: The Legacies of Jesus and Paul.* Louisville: Westminster John Knox, 1996.

————. *New Testament Christology.* Louisville: Westminster John Knox, 1999.

Mattill, A. J., Jr. 'The Purpose of Acts: Schneckenburger Reconsidered'. In *Apostolic History and the Gospel,* edited by W. Ward Gasque and R. P. Martin. Exeter: Paternoster, 1970, pp. 108-22.

————. 'The Jesus-Paul Parallels and the Purpose of Luke-Acts', *NovT* 17 (1975), pp. 15-46.

————. *Luke and the Last Things: A Perspective for the Understanding of Lukan Thought.* Dillsboro: Western North Carolina Press, 1979.

McDonald, J. Ian H. *Biblical Interpretation and Christian Ethics.* Cambridge: Cambridge University Press, 1993.

————. 'The Crucible of Pauline Ethics', *Studies in World Christianity* 3.1 (1997), pp. 1-21.

————. *The Crucible of Christian Morality.* London: Routledge, 1998.

McGaughy, Lane C. 'Words before Deeds: Why Start with the Sayings?' *Forum* n.s. 1.2 (Fall 1998), pp. 387-99.

McGrath, A. 'In What Way Can Jesus Be a Moral Example for Christians?', *Journal of the Evangelical Theological Society* 34 (1991), pp. 289-98.

McKnight, Scot. 'A Loyal Critic: Matthew's Polemic with Judaism in Theological Perspective'. In *Anti-Semitism and Early Christianity: Issues of Polemic and Faith*, edited by Craig A. Evans and Donald A. Hagner. Minneapolis: Fortress, 1993, pp. 55-79.

————, and Grant R. Osborne (eds.). *The Face of New Testament Studies: A Survey of Recent Research*. Grand Rapids: Baker Academic, 2004.

McNeill, J. J. *The Church and the Homosexual*. Fourth edn., Boston: Beacon, 1993.

McNichol, Allan J. 'Response to Daryl D. Schmidt'. In *Anti-Judaism and the Gospels*, edited by William R. Farmer. Harrisburg, PA: Trinity Press International, 1999, pp. 111-19.

Macquarrie, J., and J. Childress. *A New Dictionary of Christian Ethics*. London: SCM, 1967, second edn. 1986.

Mbali, Zolile. *The Churches and Racism: A Black South African Perspective*. London: SCM, 1987.

Mealand, David L. *Poverty and Expectation in the Gospels*. London: SPCK, 1980.

Meeks, Wayne A. 'The Man from Heaven in Johannine Sectarianism', *JBL* 91.1 (1972), pp. 44-72. Reprinted in *The Interpretation of John*, edited by J. Ashton. London: SPCK, 1986, pp. 141-73.

———— (ed.). *The Writings of St. Paul*. New York: Norton, 1972.

————. *The First Urban Christians: The Social World of the Apostle Paul*. New Haven, CT: Yale University Press, 1983.

————. 'Understanding Early Christian Ethics', *JBL* 105.1 (1986), pp. 3-11.

————. *The Moral World of the First Christians*. Philadelphia: Westminster, 1986/London: SPCK 1987.

————. *The Origins of Christian Morality: The First Two Centuries*. New Haven, CT: Yale University Press, 1993.

————. 'The "Haustafeln" and American Slavery: A Hermeneutical Challenge'. In *Theology and Ethics in Paul and His Interpreters: Essays in Honor of Victor Paul Furnish*, edited by E. H. Lovering, Jr. and J. L. Sumney. Nashville: Abingdon, 1996, pp. 232-53.

————. 'The Ethics of the Fourth Evangelist'. In *Exploring the Gospel of John: In Honor of D. Moody Smith*, edited by R. A. Culpepper and C. C. Black. Louisville: Westminster John Knox, 1996, pp. 317-26.

Meier, John P. *The Vision of Matthew: Christ, Church and Morality in the First Gospel*. New York: Paulist, 1979.

————. *A Marginal Jew: Rethinking the Historical Jesus*: vol. 1, *The Roots of the Problem and the Person*. New York: Doubleday, 1991.

————. *A Marginal Jew: Rethinking the Historical Jesus*: vol. 2, *Mentor, Message and Miracles*. New York: Doubleday, 1994.

————. *A Marginal Jew: Rethinking the Historical Jesus*: vol. 3, *Companions and Competitors*. New York: Doubleday, 2001.

Menken, Maarten J. J. 'The Christology of the Fourth Gospel: A Survey of Recent Research'. In *From Jesus to John: Essays on Jesus and New Testament Christology in Hon-*

our of Marinus de Jonge, edited by Martinus C. De Boer. JSNTSS 84. Sheffield: Sheffield Academic Press, 1993, pp. 292-320.

Merklein, H. *Die Gottesherrschaft als Handlungsprinzip: Untersuchung zur Ethik Jesu*. Würzburg: Echter, 1981.

———— (ed.). *Neues Testament und Ethik*. Freiburg: Herder, 1989.

Miller, James E. 'The Practices of Romans 1.26: Homosexual or Heterosexual?' *NovT* 37.1 (1995), pp. 1-11.

————. 'Pederasty and Romans 1.27: A Response to Mark Smith', *JAAR* 65 (1997), pp. 861-65.

Minear, Paul S. *Commands of Christ*. Edinburgh: Saint Andrew Press, 1972.

————. 'Luke's Use of the Birth Stories'. In *Studies in Luke-Acts: Essays Presented in Honor of Paul Schubert*, edited by Leander E. Keck and J. Louis Martyn. London: SPCK, 1968, pp. 111-30.

Mohrlang, R. *Matthew and Paul: A Comparison of Ethical Perspectives*. SNTSMS 48. Cambridge: Cambridge University Press, 1984.

Moloney, Francis J., S.D.B. 'The Fourth Gospel and the Jesus of History', *NTS* 46 (2000), pp. 42-58.

————. 'Where Does One Look? Reflections of Some Recent Johannine Scholarship', *Salesianum* 62 (2000), pp. 223-51.

————. '"The Jews" in the Fourth Gospel: Another Perspective', *Pacifica* 15 (2002), pp. 16-36. Reprinted in *The Gospel of John: Text and Context*, by Francis J. Moloney. Leiden: Brill, 2005, pp. 20-44.

————. 'Narrative and Discourse at the Feast of Tabernacles: John 7:1–8:59'. In *Word, Theology and Community in John*, edited by J. Painter, R. A. Culpepper and F. F. Segovia. St Louis: Chalice, 2002, pp. 155-72. Reprinted in *The Gospel of John: Text and Context*, by Francis J. Moloney. Leiden: Brill, 2005, pp. 193-213.

————. *The Gospel of John: Text and Context*. Leiden: Brill, 2005.

Moltmann, J. *Theology of Hope*. London: SCM, 1967.

————. *God in Creation: An Ecological Doctrine of Creation*. London: SCM, 1985.

Montefiore, H. 'Thou Shalt Love the Neighbour as Thyself', *NovT* 5 (1962), pp. 157-70.

Moore, Stephen D. *Literary Criticism and the Gospels: The Theoretical Challenge*. New Haven, CT: Yale University Press, 1989.

————. 'Are There Impurities in the Living Water that the Johannine Jesus Dispenses? Deconstruction, Feminism, and the Samaritan Woman', *Biblical Interpretation* 1 (1993), pp. 207-27. Reprinted in *The Interpretation of John*, edited by J. Ashton. Second edn. Edinburgh: T&T Clark, 1997.

Mosala, I. T. *Biblical Hermeneutics and Black Theology in South Africa*. Grand Rapids: Eerdmans, 1989.

Mott, Stephen C. *Biblical Ethics and Social Change*. Oxford: Oxford University Press, 1982.

Motyer, Stephen. 'The Fourth Gospel and the Salvation of Israel: An Appeal for a New Start'. In *Anti-Judaism and the Fourth Gospel: Papers of the Leuven Colloquium, 2000*, edited by R. Bieringer, D. Pollefyt and F. Vandecasteele-Vanneuville. Assen: Royal Van Gorcum, 2001, pp. 92-110.

Moule, C. F. D. 'Fulfilment-Words in the New Testament: Use and Abuse', *NTS* 14 (1967-68), pp. 293-320.

————. 'The Christology of Acts'. In *Studies in Luke-Acts: Essays Presented in Honor of Paul Schubert,* edited by Leander E. Keck and J. Louis Martyn. London: SPCK, 1968, pp. 159-85.

Mouton, Elna 'The (Trans)formative Potential of the Bible as Resource for Christian Ethos and Ethics', *Scriptura* 62.3 (1997), pp. 245-57.

Moxnes, Halvor. *The Economy of the Kingdom: Social Conflict and Economic Relations in Luke's Gospel.* Philadelphia: Fortress, 1988.

————. 'Eskatologisk eksistens: Nytestamentlige bidrag til etikken', *Norsk Teologisk Tidsskrift* 92 (Oslo, 1991), pp. 1-13.

————. 'New Testament Ethics — Universal or Particular?', *Studia Theologia* 47 (1993), pp. 153-68.

————. 'The Social Context of Luke's Community', *Interpretation* 48 (1994), pp. 379-89.

Munro, Winsome. *Authority in Paul and Peter: The Identification of a Pastoral Stratum in the Pauline Corpus and 1 Peter.* SNTSMS 45. Cambridge: Cambridge University Press, 1983.

————. 'Romans 13.1-7: Apartheid's Last Biblical Refuge', *BTB* 20.4 (1990), pp. 161-68.

Murphy-O'Connor, Jerome. 'The Non-Pauline Character of 1 Cor. 11.2-16?', *JBL* 95 (1976), pp. 615-21.

————. 'Sex and Logic in 1 Cor. 11.2-16', *CBQ* 42 (1980), pp. 482-500.

————. *Paul: A Critical Life.* Oxford: Clarendon, 1996.

————. *Paul: His Story.* Oxford: Oxford University Press, 2004.

Myers, Ched, *Binding the Strong Man: A Political Reading of Mark's Story of Jesus.* Maryknoll, NY: Orbis, 1988.

Naudé, Piet. 'Is There a Future for Scholarship? Reformed Theological Scholarship in a Transforming Higher Education Environment', *JTSA* 119 (July 2004), pp. 32-45.

Neale, David A. *None but the Sinners: Religious Categories in the Gospel of Luke.* JSNTSS 58. Sheffield: Sheffield Academic Press, 1991.

Neirynck, F. 'Luke 4,16-30 and the Unity of Luke-Acts'. In *The Unity of Luke-Acts, 47th Colloquium Biblicum Lovaniense,* edited by J. Verheyden. Leuven: Leuven University Press, 1999, pp. 357-95.

Newton, Michael. *The Concept of Purity at Qumran and in the Letters of Paul.* SNTSMS 53. Cambridge: Cambridge University Press, 1985.

Niemöller, Gerhard (ed.). *Die erste Bekenntnissynode der Deutschen Evangelischen Kirche zu Barmen: 2, Text–Dokumente–Berichte, Arbeite zur Geschichte des Kirchenkampfes 6.* Göttingen: Vandenhoeck & Ruprecht, 1959.

Nineham, D. E. *The Gospel of St. Mark.* London: Penguin, 1963.

————. *The Use and Abuse of the Bible: A Study of the Bible in an Age of Rapid Cultural Change.* London: Macmillan, 1976.

Nissen, Johannes. 'Community and Ethics in the Gospel of John'. In *New Readings in John: Literary and Theological Perspectives,* edited by J. Nissen and S. Pedersen. Sheffield: Sheffield Academic Press, 1999, pp. 194-212.

Nolland, John. 'Salvation-History and Eschatology'. In *Witness to the Gospel: The Theology of Acts,* edited by I. Howard Marshall and David Peterson. Grand Rapids: Eerdmans, 1998, pp. 63-81.

Nygren, Anders. *Commentary on Romans.* Translated by Carl C. Rasmussen. London: SCM, 1952.

O'Brien, Peter T. *Commentary on Philippians.* NIGTC. Grand Rapids: Eerdmans, 1991.

O'Donovan, Oliver M. T. 'The Possibility of a Biblical Ethic', *Theological Students Fellowship Bulletin* 67 (1973), pp. 15-23.

―――. 'Towards an Interpretation of Biblical Ethics: The Tyndale Biblical Theology Lecture 1975', *Tyndale Bulletin* 27 (1976), pp. 54-78.

―――. *Resurrection and Moral Order: An Outline for Evangelical Ethics.* Leicester: IVP, 1986.

―――. *The Desire of the Nations.* Cambridge: Cambridge University Press, 1995.

―――. *Ways of Judgment: The Bampton Lectures, 2003.* Grand Rapids: Eerdmans, 2005.

O'Malley, W. J., S.J. 'The Moral Practice of Jesus', *America* 170.14 (April 23, 1994), pp. 8-11.

O'Neill, J. C. *Paul's Letter to the Romans.* Harmondsworth: Penguin, 1975.

O'Toole, Robert F. 'Activity of the Risen Jesus in Luke-Acts', *Biblica* 62 (1981), pp. 471-98.

―――. 'Luke's Position on Politics and Society in Luke-Acts'. In *Political Issues in Luke-Acts,* edited by Richard J. Cassidy and Philip J. Scharper. Maryknoll, NY: Orbis, 1983, pp. 1-17.

Odell-Scott, D. W. 'Let the Women Speak in Church: An Egalitarian Interpretation of 1 Cor 14.33b-36', *BTB* 17 (1983), pp. 90-93.

Ogletree, Thomas W. *The Use of the Bible in Christian Ethics.* Philadelphia: Fortress, 1983.

Okure, Teresa. '"I will open my mouth in parables" (Matt. 13.35): A Case for a Gospel-Based Biblical Hermeneutics'. SNTS Conference: University of Pretoria, August 4, 1999. Revised published version in *NTS* 46 (2000), pp. 445-63.

Oropeza, B. J. 'Situational Immorality: Paul's "Vice Lists" at Corinth', *ExpT* 110.1 (1998), pp. 9-10.

Orton, D. E. *The Understanding Scribe.* Sheffield: Sheffield Academic Press, 1989.

Overman, J. A. *Matthew's Gospel and Formative Judaism.* Minneapolis: Fortress, 1990.

―――. *Church and Community in Crisis.* Valley Forge, PA: Trinity Press International, 1996.

Painter, John. *The Quest for the Messiah: The History, Literature and Theology of the Johannine Community.* Edinburgh: T&T Clark, 1991.

―――. 'When Is a House Not Home? Disciples and Family in Mark 3.13-35', *NTS* 45 (1999), pp. 498-513.

Palmer, Darryl W. 'Acts and the Ancient Historical Monograph'. In *The Book of Acts in Its Ancient Literary Setting,* edited by Bruce W. Winter and Andrew D. Clarke. Carlisle: Paternoster/Grand Rapids: Eerdmans, 1993, pp. 1-29.

Pancaro, Severino. *The Law in the Fourth Gospel: The Torah and the Gospel, Moses and Jesus, Judaism and Christianity according to John.* NovTSup 42. Leiden: Brill, 1975.

Parsenios, George L. *Departure and Consolation: The Johannine Farewell Discourses in Light of Greco-Roman Literature.* NovTSup 117. Leiden: Brill, 2005.

Parsons, Michael. 'Being Precedes Act: Indicative and Imperative in Paul's Writing', *Evangelical Quarterly* 88.2 (1988), pp. 99-127. Reprinted in *Understanding Paul's Ethics,* edited by B. S. Rosner. Grand Rapids: Eerdmans, 1995, pp. 217-47.

Parsons, M. C., and R. I. Pervo. *Rethinking the Unity of Luke and Acts.* Minneapolis: Fortress, 1993.

Pascuzzi, Maria. *Ethics, Ecclesiology and Church Discipline: A Rhetorical Analysis of 1 Corinthians 5.* Tesi Gregoriana Serie Teologia 32. Rome: Editrice Pontificia Università Gregoriana, 1997.

Patte, Daniel. *The Challenge of Discipleship: A Critical Study of the Sermon on the Mount as Scripture.* Harrisburg, PA: Trinity Press International, 1999.

Perkins, Pheme. 'New Testament Ethics: Questions and Contexts', *Religious Studies Review* 10.4 (1984), pp. 321-27.

———. *Reading the New Testament: An Introduction.* London: Geoffrey Chapman, revised edn. 1988.

———. 'Jesus and Ethics', *Theology Today* 52.1 (1995), pp. 49-65.

Perrin, Norman. *The Kingdom of God in the Teaching of Jesus.* London: SCM, 1963.

———. *Rediscovering the Teaching of Jesus.* London: SCM, 1967.

———. 'The Christology of Mark: A Study in Methodology', *JR* 51 (1971), pp. 173-87. Slightly revised version reprinted in *The Interpretation of Mark,* edited by William Telford. London: SPCK, 1985, pp. 95-108; 2nd edn., Edinburgh: T&T Clark, 1995), pp. 125-40.

Pervo, Richard I. 'Must Luke and Acts Belong to the Same Genre?'. In *SBL 1989 Seminar Papers.* Atlanta: Scholars, 1989, pp. 309-16.

———. *Luke's Story of Paul.* Minneapolis: Fortress, 1990.

———. 'Israel's Heritage and Claims upon the Genre(s) of Luke and Acts: The Problems of a History'. In *Jesus and the Heritage of Israel: Luke's Narrative Claim upon Israel's Legacy,* edited by David P. Moessner. Harrisburg, PA: Trinity Press International, 1999, pp. 127-43.

———. 'Direct Speech in Acts and the Question of Genre', *JSNT* 28.3 (2006), pp. 285-307.

Petersen, William L. 'Can ARSENOKOITAI Be Translated by "Homosexuals"?' *Vigiliae Christianae* 40 (1986), pp. 187-91.

Phillips, Thomas E. (ed.). *Acts and Ethics.* New Testament Monographs 9. Sheffield: Phoenix, 2005.

Pieterse, Hendrik J. C. (ed.). *Desmond Tutu's Message: A Qualitative Analysis.* Leiden: Brill, 2001.

Pilgrim, Walter E. *Uneasy Neighbours: Church and State in the New Testament.* Minneapolis: Fortress, 1999.

Piper, John. *'Love your enemies': Jesus' Love Command in the Synoptic Gospels and in the Early Christian Paraenesis. A History of the Tradition and Interpretation of Its Uses.* SNTSMS 38. Cambridge: Cambridge University Press, 1979.

Platten, Stephen. 'The Biblical Critic and Moral Theologian', *King's Theological Review* 12.1 (1989), pp. 11-17.

Pokorný, Petr. 'Das Markusevangelium: Literarische und theologische Einleitung mit Forschungsbericht', *ANRW* 2.25.3. Berlin: Walter de Gruyter, 1985, pp. 1969-2035.

Porter, Stanley E., and Thomas H. Olbricht (eds.). *Rhetoric, Scripture and Theology: Essays from the 1994 Pretoria Conference,* JSNTSS 131. Sheffield: Sheffield Academic Press, 1996.

Porter, Stanley E. (ed.). *The Pauline Canon, Pauline Studies,* Vol. 1. Leiden: Brill, 2004.

———. 'The Genre of Acts and the Ethics of Discourse'. In *Acts and Ethics,* edited by Thomas E. Phillips. New Testament Monographs 9. Sheffield: Phoenix, 2005, pp. 1-15.

Powell, Mark Allan, and David R. Bauer (eds.). *Who Do You Say That I Am? Essays on Christology in Honor of Jack Dean Kingsbury.* Louisville: Westminster John Knox, 1999.

Prior, Michael. *The Bible and Colonialism: A Moral Critique.* Sheffield: Sheffield Academic Press, 1997.

Pryor, John W. *John: Evangelist of the Covenant People: The Narrative and Themes of the Fourth Gospel.* London: Darton, Longman and Todd, 1992.

Punt, Jeremy. 'Biblical Studies in South Africa? The Case for Moral Values', *Scriptura* 60 (1997), pp. 1-14.

———. 'Biblical Studies in South Africa? The Case for Hermeneutics', *Scriptura* 60 (1997), pp. 15-30.

———. 'New Testament Interpretation, Interpretive Interests, and Ideology: Methodological Deficits amidst South African Methodolomania?' *Scriptura* 65 (1998), pp. 123-52.

———. 'Reading the Bible in Africa: Accounting for Some Trends, Part I', *Scriptura* 68 (1999), pp. 1-11.

———. 'Reading the Bible in Africa: Accounting for Some Trends, Part II', *Scriptura* 71 (1999), pp. 313-29.

———. 'Current Debates in Biblical Hermeneutics in South Africa and the Postcolonial Matrix', *Religion and Theology* 11.2 (2004), pp. 139-60.

Quesnell, Quentin. 'The Women at Luke's Supper'. In *Political Issues in Luke-Acts,* edited by Richard J. Cassidy and Philip J. Scharper. Maryknoll, NY: Orbis, 1983, pp. 59-79.

Räisänen, H. *Paul and the Law.* WUNT 29. Tübingen: Mohr, 1983.

———. *Jesus, Paul and Torah: Collected Essays.* JSNTSS 43. Sheffield: JSOT Press, 1992.

Rauschenbusch, W. 'The Kingdom of God'. In *The Social Gospel in America 1870-1920: Gladden, Ely, Rauschenbusch,* edited by Robert T. Handy. Oxford: Oxford University Press, 1966, pp. 264-67.

Ravens, David. *Luke and the Restoration of Israel.* JSNTSS 119. Sheffield: Sheffield Academic Press, 1995.

Reasoner, Mark. *The Strong and the Weak: Romans 14.1–15.13 in Context.* SNTSMS 103. Cambridge: Cambridge University Press, 1999.

———. 'Ancient and Modern Exegesis of Romans 13 under Unfriendly Governments', AAR/SBL Annual Meeting. Boston, November 21 1999. In *Society of Biblical Literature 1999 Seminar Papers.* SBLSP 38. Atlanta: Society of Biblical Literature, 1999, pp. 359-74.

Reid, Barbara, O.P. 'The Ethics of Luke', *The Bible Today* 31.5 (1993), pp. 283-87.

Reinhartz, Adele. '"Jews" and Jews in the Fourth Gospel'. In *Anti-Judaism and the Fourth Gospel: Papers of the Leuven Colloquium, 2000,* edited by R. Bieringer, D. Pollefyt and F. Vandecasteele-Vanneuville. Assen: Royal Van Gorcum, 2001, pp. 341-56.

———. *Befriending the Beloved Disciple: A Jewish Reading of the Gospel of John.* New York: Continuum, 2001.

Rensberger, David. *Overcoming the World: Politics and Community in the Gospel of John.* Philadelphia: Westminster, 1988/London: SPCK, 1989.

——— 'Love for One Another and Love for Enemies in the Gospel of John'. In *The Love of Enemy and Nonretaliation in the New Testament,* edited by Willard M. Swartley. Louisville: Westminster John Knox, 1992, pp. 297-313.

————. 'Anti-Judaism and the Gospel of John'. In *Anti-Judaism and the Gospels,* edited by William R. Farmer. Harrisburg, PA: Trinity Press International, 1999, pp. 120-57.

Rese, M. 'The Jews in Luke-Acts: Some Second Thoughts'. In *The Unity of Luke-Acts, 47th Colloquium Biblicum Lovaniense,* edited by J. Verheyden. Leuven: Leuven University Press, 1999, pp. 185-201.

Resseguie, James L. 'John 9: A Literary-Critical Analysis'. In *Literary Interpretations of Biblical Narratives,* vol. 2, edited by K. Gros Louis. Nashville: Abingdon, 1982. Reprinted in *The Gospel of John as Literature: An Anthology of Twentieth Century Perspectives,* edited by Mark W. G. Stibbe. Leiden: Brill, 1993, pp. 115-22.

————. *The Strange Gospel: Narrative Design and Point of View in John.* Leiden: Brill, 2001.

Reumann, John. *Variety and Unity in New Testament Thought.* Oxford: Oxford University Press, 1991.

Rhoads, David, and Donald Michie, *Mark as Story: An Introduction to the Narrative of a Gospel.* Philadelphia: Fortress, 1982.

Richards, E. Randolph. *Paul and First-Century Letter Writing: Secretaries, Composition and Collection.* Downers Grove, IL: IVP, 2004.

Richardson, Neville. 'Ethics of Character and Community'. In *Doing Ethics in Context: South African Perspectives,* edited by C. Villa-Vicencio and J. de Gruchy. Cape Town: David Philip/Maryknoll, NY: Orbis, 1994, pp. 89-101.

————. 'Can Christian Ethics Find Its Way, and Itself, in Africa?' *JTSA* 95 (July 1996), pp. 37-54.

————. 'The Future of South African Theology: Scanning the Road Ahead', *Scriptura* 89 (2005), pp. 550-62.

Riches, John K. *Jesus and the Transformation of Judaism.* London: DLT, 1980.

————. 'The Social World of Jesus', *Interpretation* 50.4 (1996), pp. 383-93.

————. 'Reading the Bible Contextually: Some Considerations of the Canonical Context from a Post-Colonial Perspective'. SNTS Conference. University of Pretoria, August 6 1999.

Ridderbos, Herman. *Paul: An Outline of His Theology.* London: SPCK, 1977.

Riesner, Rainer. *Paul's Early Period: Chronology, Mission Strategy, Theology.* Grand Rapids: Eerdmans, 1998.

Riley, Gregory J. *One Jesus, Many Christs: How Jesus Inspired Not One True Christianity, but Many.* San Francisco: HarperSanFrancisco, 1997.

————. 'Words and Deeds: Jesus as Teacher and Jesus as Pattern of Life'. *HTR* 90.4 (1997), pp. 427-36.

Ringe, Sharon H. *Wisdom's Friends: Community and Christology in the Fourth Gospel.* Louisville: Westminster John Knox, 1999.

Ritschl, A. *Three Essays.* Translated by Philip Hefner. Philadelphia: Fortress, 1972.

Robinson, J. A. T. *The Priority of John.* London: SCM, 1985.

Robinson, J. M. *A New Quest of the Historical Jesus.* Studies in Biblical Theology 25. London: SCM, 1959.

Rosenblatt, Marie-Eloise. 'Got into the Party after All: Women's Issues and the Five Foolish Virgins', *Continuum* 3 (1993), pp. 107-37.

Roskam, H. N. *The Purpose of the Gospel of Mark in Its Historical and Social Context.* NovTSup 114. Leiden: Brill, 2004.

Rosner, Brian S. *Paul, Scripture, and Ethics: A Study of 1 Corinthians 5–7.* Leiden: Brill, 1994.

———. (ed.). *Understanding Paul's Ethics: Twentieth-Century Approaches.* Grand Rapids: Eerdmans, 1995.

Roth, S. John. *The Blind, the Lame, and the Poor: Character Types in Luke-Acts.* JSNTSS 144. Sheffield: Sheffield Academic Press, 1997.

Rothschild, Clare K. *Luke-Acts and the Rhetoric of History: An Investigation of Early Christian Historiography.* WUNT 2.175. Tübingen: J. C. B. Mohr, 2004.

Roux, Cornelia. 'Biblical Values and Multi-Religious Education in the Primary School: Problems and Proposals', *Scriptura* 60 (1997), pp. 63-69.

Rowe, Christopher Kavin. 'History, Hermeneutics and the Unity of Luke-Acts'. *JSNT* 28.2 (2005), pp. 131-57.

———. *Early Narrative Christology: The Lord in the Gospel of Luke.* BZNW 139. Berlin: Walter de Gruyter, 2006.

Rowland, Christopher. 'Response to *The Desire of the Nations*', *Studies in Christian Ethics* 11.2 (1998), pp. 77-85.

——— (ed.). *The Cambridge Companion to Liberation Theology.* Cambridge: Cambridge University Press, 1999.

——— and Christopher Tuckett (eds.). *The Nature of New Testament Theology: Essays in Honour of Robert Morgan.* Oxford: Blackwell, 2006.

Saldarini, Anthony J. *Matthew's Christian-Jewish Community.* Chicago: University of Chicago Press, 1994.

Sampley, J. P. *Walking between the Times: Paul's Moral Reasoning.* Minneapolis: Fortress, 1991.

Sanders, E. P. *Paul and Palestinian Judaism.* London: SCM, 1977.

———. *Paul, the Law, and the Jewish People.* Philadelphia: Fortress, 1983.

———. *Jesus and Judaism.* London: SCM, 1985.

———. *Paul.* Oxford: Oxford University Press, 1991.

———. *The Historical Figure of Jesus.* London: Penguin, 1993.

Sanders, Jack T. *Ethics in the New Testament: Change and Development.* Philadelphia: Fortress/London: SCM Press, 1975; second edn. 1986.

———. *The Jews in Luke-Acts.* London: SCM, 1987.

Sandmel, Samuel. *Anti-Semitism in the New Testament?* Philadelphia: Fortress, 1978.

Scanzoni, Letha, and Virginia Ramey Mollenkott. *Is the Homosexual My Neighbour?* San Francisco: Harper & Row, 1978.

Schama, Simon. *Rough Crossings: Britain, the Slaves and the American Revolution.* London: BBC Worldwide, 2005.

Scheffler, E. H. 'The Social Ethics of the Lucan Baptist (Lk. 3.10-14)', *Neotestamentica* 24.1 (1990), pp. 21-36.

Schmidt, Daryl D. 'Luke's "Innocent" Jesus: A Scriptural Apologetic'. In *Political Issues in Luke-Acts,* edited by Richard J. Cassidy and Philip J. Scharper. Maryknoll, NY: Orbis, 1983, pp. 111-21.

———. 'Anti-Judaism and the Gospel of Luke'. In *Anti-Judaism and the Gospels,* edited by William R. Farmer. Harrisburg, PA: Trinity Press International, 1999, pp. 63-96.

———. 'Rhetorical Influences and Genre: Luke's Preface and the Rhetoric of Hellenistic Historiography'. In *Jesus and the Heritage of Israel: Luke's Narrative Claim upon Israel's*

Legacy, edited by David P. Moessner. Harrisburg, PA: Trinity Press International, 1999, pp. 27-60.

Schnackenburg, R. *The Moral Teaching of the New Testament.* Translated by J. Holland-Smith and W. J. O'Hara from the German second edn. of 1962. New York: Herder and Herder, 1965.

——. *The Gospel of Matthew.* Grand Rapids: Eerdmans, 2002.

Schneiders, Sandra M. 'Women in the Fourth Gospel and the Role of Women in the Contemporary Church', *BTB* 12.2 (1982), pp. 35-45. Reprinted in *The Gospel of John as Literature: An Anthology of Twentieth Century Perspectives,* edited by Mark W. G. Stibbe. Leiden: Brill, 1993, pp. 123-43.

——. 'A Case Study: A Feminist Interpretation of John 4:1-42'. In *The Revelatory Text: Interpreting the New Testament as Sacred Scripturem,* by Sandra M. Schneiders. San Francisco: HarperSanFrancisco, 1991, pp. 180-99. Reprinted in *The Interpretation of John,* edited by J. Ashton. Second edn. Edinburgh: T&T Clark, 1997, pp. 235-59.

Schnelle, Udo. *Apostle Paul: His Life and Theology.* Grand Rapids: Baker Academic, 2005.

Schöni, M. 'What More Are You Doing than Others? The Radical Ethics of Jesus', *Near East School of Theology Theological Review* 16.2 (1995), pp. 75-97.

Schottroff, Luise. 'Non-Violence and the Love of One's Enemies'. In *Essays on the Love Commandment* by Luise Schottroff, Reginald H. Fuller, Christoph Burchard and M. Jack Suggs. Translated by Reginald H. and Ilse Fuller. Philadelphia: Fortress, 1978, pp. 9-39.

——. 'The Samaritan Woman and the Notion of Sexuality in the Fourth Gospel' in Segovia (ed.), *What Is John?* vol. 2, *Literary and Social Readings of the Fourth Gospel,* edited by Fernando F. Segovia. Atlanta: Scholars Press, 1998, pp. 157-81.

Schrage, Wolfgang. *The Ethics of the New Testament.* Translated by David E. Green from the German edn. of 1982. Philadelphia: Fortress, 1988.

Schrek, Christopher J. 'The Nazareth Pericope: Luke 4:16-30 in Recent Study'. In *L'Evangile de Luc — The Gospel of Luke,* revised and enlarged edn. of *L'Evangile de Luc: Problèmes littéraires et théologiques,* edited by F. Neirynck. BETL 32. Leuven: Leuven University Press, 1989, pp. 399-471.

Schulz, S. *Neutestamentliche Ethik.* Zurich: TVZ, 1987.

Schweitzer, Albert. *Geschichte der Leben–Jesu–Forschung.* Tübingen: Mohr, 1906. ET *The Quest of the Historical Jesus.* London: A & C Black, 1954.

——. *The Mystery of the Kingdom of God: The Secret of Jesus' Messiahship and Passion.* Translated with an Introduction by Walter Lowrie, D.D. London: A & C Black, 1914. Reprinted New York: Macmillan, 2004.

——. *The Mysticism of Paul the Apostle.* Translated by W. Montgomery. London: Black, 1931.

Scott, Bernard Brandon, and Margaret E. Dean. 'A Sound Map of the Sermon on the Mount'. In *Treasures New and Old: Recent Contributions to Matthean Studies,* edited by David R. Bauer and Mark Allan Powell. Atlanta: Scholars Press, 1996, pp. 311-78.

Scott, Martin. *Sophia and the Johannine Jesus.* JSNTSS 71. Sheffield: Sheffield Academic Press, 1992.

Scroggs, R. *The New Testament and Homosexuality: Contextual Background for Contemporary Debate.* Philadelphia: Fortress, 1983.

Segal, Alan F. *Paul the Convert: The Apostolate and Apostasy of Saul the Pharisee.* New Haven, CT: Yale University Press, 1990.

Segalla, G. *Introduzione all' etica del Nuovo Testamento.* Biblioteca Biblica 2. Brescia: Queriniana, 1989.

Segovia, Fernando F. "'Peace I Leave with You; My Peace I Give to You': Discipleship in the Fourth Gospel'. In *Discipleship in the New Testament,* edited by Fernando F. Segovia. Philadelphia: Fortress, 1985, pp. 76-102.

————— (ed.). *Discipleship in the New Testament.* Philadelphia: Fortress, 1985.

—————. *The Farewell of the Word: The Johannine Call to Abide.* Minneapolis: Fortress, 1991.

—————. (ed.). *What Is John?* vol. 1, *Readers and Readings of the Fourth Gospel.* Atlanta: Scholars Press, 1996.

————— (ed.). *What Is John?* vol. 2, *Literary and Social Readings of the Fourth Gospel.* Atlanta: Scholars Press, 1998.

Seow, Choon-Leong (ed.), *Homosexuality and Christian Community.* Louisville: Westminster John Knox, 1996.

Shim, Ezra S. B. 'A Suggestion about the Genre of Text-Type of Mark'. *Scriptura* 50 (1994), pp. 69-89.

Shriver, Donald W., Jr. *An Ethics for Enemies: Forgiveness in Politics.* Oxford: Oxford University Press, 1995.

Shuler, Philip L. 'Response to Amy-Jill Levine'. In *Anti-Judaism and the Gospels,* edited by William R. Farmer. Harrisburg, PA: Trinity Press International, 1999, pp. 36-47.

Siker, J. S. (ed.). *Homosexuality in the Church: Both Sides of the Debate.* Louisville: Westminster John Knox, 1994.

—————. *Scripture and Ethics: Twentieth-Century Portraits.* Oxford: Oxford University Press, 1997.

Sleeman, Matthew. "'Under Heaven": The Narrative-Geographical Implications of the Ascended Christ for the Believers (and Their Mission) within Acts 1:1–11:18', Ph.D. thesis, King's College London, 2006.

Smalley, Stephen. *John: Evangelist and Interpreter.* Exeter: Paternoster, 1978.

Smit, Dirk. J. 'The Ethics of Interpretation — and South Africa', *Scriptura* 33 (1990), pp. 29-43.

—————. 'The Bible and Ethos in a New South Africa', *Scriptura* 37 (1991), pp. 51-67.

—————. 'A Story of Contextual Hermeneutics and the Integrity of New Testament Interpretation in South Africa', *Neotestamentica* 28.2 (1994), pp. 265-89.

—————. 'Dietrich Bonhoeffer and "The Other": "Accept One Another, Therefore . . ." (Rom. 15:7)', *JTSA* 93 (December 1995), pp. 3-16.

—————. 'Saints, Disciples, Friends? Recent South African Perspectives on Christian Ethics and the New Testament', *Neotestamentica* 30.1 (1996), pp. 169-85.

Smith, D. Moody. 'Historical Issues and the Problem of John and the Synoptics'. In *From Jesus to John: Essays on Jesus and New Testament Christology in Honour of Marinus de Jonge,* edited by Martinus C. De Boer. JSNTSS 84. Sheffield: Sheffield Academic Press, 1993, pp. 252-67.

—————. *The Theology of the Gospel of John.* Cambridge: Cambridge University Press, 1995.

—————. 'The Love Command: John and Paul?' In *Theology and Ethics in Paul and His In-*

terpreters: Essays in Honor of Victor Paul Furnish, edited by E. H. Lovering, Jr. and J. L. Sumney. Nashville: Abingdon, 1996, pp. 207-17.

———. *John among the Gospels: The Relationship in Twentieth-Century Research.* Minneapolis: Fortress, 1992, second edn. 2001.

Smith, M. D. 'Ancient Bisexuality and the Interpretation of Romans 1:26-27', *JAAR* 64.2 (1996), pp. 223-56.

Smith, T. V. *Petrine Controversies in Early Christianity.* WUNT 15. Tübingen: Mohr Siebeck, 1985.

Snodgrass, Klyne R. 'Matthew's Understanding of the Law', *Interpretation* 46.4 (1992), pp. 368-78.

———. 'Matthew and the Law'. In *Treasures New and Old: Recent Contributions to Matthean Studies,* edited by David R. Bauer and Mark Allan Powell. Atlanta: Scholars Press, 1996, pp. 99-127.

Snyder, G. F. 'John 13:16 and the Anti-Petrinism of the Johannine Tradition', *Biblical Research* 16 (1971), pp. 5-15.

Snyman, Gerrie. 'Social Identity and South African Biblical Hermeneutics: A Struggle against Prejudice?' *JTSA* 121 (March 2005), pp. 34-55.

Soards, Marion L. *The Passion according to Luke: The Special Material of Luke 22.* JSNTSS 14. Sheffield: Sheffield Academic Press, 1987.

———. *Scripture and Homosexuality: Biblical Authority and the Church Today.* Louisville: Westminster John Knox, 1995.

Spangenberg, Izak J. J. 'Paradigm Changes in the Bible Sciences and the Teaching of Biblical Studies in the New South Africa', *Scriptura* 52 (1995), pp. 1-10.

Speckman, McGlory T. 'Beyond the Debate: An Agenda for Biblical Studies in the New South Africa', *Religion and Theology* 3.2 (1996), pp. 135-51.

Spencer, F. Scott. *Acts.* Sheffield: Sheffield Academic Press, 1997.

———. *What Did Jesus Do? Gospel Profiles of Jesus' Personal Conduct.* Harrisburg, PA: Trinity Press International, 2003.

Spina, Frank Anthony. *The Faith of the Outsider: Exclusion and Inclusion in the Biblical Story.* Grand Rapids: Eerdmans, 2005.

Spohn, William C. *What Are They Saying about Scripture and Ethics?* New York: Paulist, 1984, second revised edn. 1995.

———. 'Jesus and Christian Ethics', *Theological Studies,* 56 (1995), pp. 92-107.

———. *Go and Do Likewise: Jesus and Ethics.* New York: Continuum, 1999.

Sproston North, Wendy E. *The Lazarus Story within the Johannine Tradition.* JSNTSS 212. Sheffield: Sheffield Academic Press, 2001.

———. 'John for the Readers of Mark? A Response to Richard Bauckham's Proposal', *JSNT* 25.4 (2003), pp. 449-68.

Staley, Jeffrey Lloyd. *The Print's First Kiss: A Rhetorical Investigation of the Implied Reader in the Fourth Gospel.* SBLDS 82. Atlanta: Scholars Press, 1988.

———. 'Stumbling for the Dark, Reaching for the Light: Reading Character in John 5 and 9'. In *The Fourth Gospel from a Literary Perspective,* edited by R. Alan Culpepper and Fernando F. Segovia. *Semeia* 53. Atlanta: Scholars Press, 1991, pp. 55-80.

Standhartinger, Angela. 'The Origin and Intention of the Household Code in the Letter to the Colossians', *JSNT* 79 (2000), pp. 117-30.

Stanton, Graham N. 'The Origin and Purpose of Matthew's Gospel', *ANRW* 2.25.3. Berlin: Walter de Gruyter, 1985, pp. 1889-1951.

―――. *A Gospel for a New People: Studies in Matthew.* Edinburgh: T&T Clark, 1992.

―――. 'The Communities of Matthew', *Interpretation* 46 (1992), pp. 379-91.

―――. *The Gospels and Jesus.* Second edn. Oxford: Oxford University Press, 2002.

―――. *Jesus and Gospel.* Cambridge: Cambridge University Press, 2004.

Stark, Rodney. 'Antioch as the Social Setting for Matthew's Gospel'. In *Social History of the Matthean Community: Cross-Disciplinary Approaches,* edited by David L. Balch. Minneapolis: Fortress, 1991, pp. 189-210.

Stassen, Glen H., and David P. Gushee. *Kingdom Ethics: Following Jesus in Contemporary Context.* Downers Grove, IL: IVP, 2003.

Stendahl, Krister. *The School of St Matthew.* Second edn. Lund: Gleerup, 1967.

―――. *Paul among Jews and Gentiles.* London: SCM, 1977.

Stibbe, Mark W. G. *John as Storyteller: Narrative Criticism and the Fourth Gospel.* SNTSMS 73. Cambridge: Cambridge University Press, 1992.

―――. *John.* Readings Series. Sheffield: Sheffield: JSOT Press, 1993.

――― (ed.). *The Gospel of John as Literature: An Anthology of Twentieth-Century Perspectives.* Leiden: Brill, 1993.

Still, Todd D. 'Paul: An Appealing and/or Appalling Apostle?', *ExpT* 114.4 (January 2003), pp. 111-18.

Strecker, Georg. 'The Importance of New Testament Ethics Today', *JTSA* 25 (1978), pp. 31-40.

―――. 'Compliance — Love of One's Enemy — The Golden Rule', *Australian Biblical Review* 29 (1981), pp. 38-46.

Struthers Malbon, Elizabeth. 'The Poor Widow in Mark and Her Poor Rich Readers', *CBQ* 53.4 (1991), pp. 589-604.

―――. *In the Company of Jesus: Characters in Mark's Gospel.* Louisville: Westminster John Knox, 2000.

Stubbs, Monya A. 'Subjection, Reflection, Resistance: A Three-Dimensional Process of Empowerment in Romans 13 and the Free-Market Economy'. In *Navigating Romans through Cultures: Challenging Readings by Charting a New Course,* edited by K. K. Yeo. Vol. 3 in Romans through History and Cultures. London and New York: T&T Clark International, 2004, pp. 171-97.

Stuhlmacher, Peter. 'Jesus' Readiness to Suffer and His Understanding of His Death'. In *The Historical Jesus in Recent Research,* edited by James D. G. Dunn and Scot McKnight. Sources for Biblical and Theological Study. Winona Lake, IN: Eisenbrauns, 2005, pp. 392-412.

Suggs, M. Jack. *Wisdom, Christology, and Law in Matthew's Gospel.* Cambridge, MA: Harvard University Press, 1970.

Swanepoel, F. A. 'Popularising Contextual Theology', *Scriptura* 45 (1993), pp. 67-78.

Swartley, Willard M. *Slavery, Sabbath, War and Women: Case Issues in Biblical Interpretation.* Scottdale: Herald, 1983.

――― (ed.). *The Love of Enemy and Nonretaliation in the New Testament.* Louisville: Westminster John Knox, 1992.

————. *Homosexuality: Biblical Interpretation and Moral Discernment.* Scottdale: Herald, 2003.

————. *Covenant of Peace: The Missing Peace in New Testament Theology and Ethics.* Grand Rapids: Eerdmans, 2006.

Talbert, Charles H. *Literary Patterns, Theological Themes and the Genre of Luke-Acts.* SBLMS 20. Missoula, MT: Scholars Press, 1974.

————. *What Is a Gospel? The Genre of the Canonical Gospels.* Philadelphia: Fortress, 1977/ London: SPCK, 1978.

————. 'Biographies of Philosophers and Rulers as Instruments of Religious Propaganda in Mediterranean Antiquity', *ANRW* 1.16.2 (Berlin: Walter de Gruyter, 1978), pp. 1619-51.

————. 'Discipleship in Luke-Acts'. In *Discipleship in the New Testament,* edited by Fernando F. Segovia. Philadelphia: Fortress, 1985, pp. 62-75.

————. 'The Acts of the Apostles: Monograph or Bios?' In *History, Literature, and Society in the Book of Acts,* edited by Ben Witherington, III. Cambridge: Cambridge University Press, 1996, pp. 58-72.

————. 'Reading Luke-Acts in Its Mediterranean Milieu', NovTSup 107. Leiden: Brill, 2003.

————. *Reading the Sermon on the Mount: Character Formation and Decision Making in Matthew 5–7.* Columbia: University of South Carolina Press, 2004/Grand Rapids: Baker Academic, 2006.

Tannehill, Robert C. 'The Disciples in Mark: The Function of a Narrative Role', *JR* 57 (1977), pp. 386-405; reprinted in *The Interpretation of Mark,* edited by W. Telford. London: SPCK, 1985, pp. 134-57. Second edn. Edinburgh: T&T Clark, 1995, pp. 169-95.

————. 'The Story of Israel within the Lukan Narrative'. In *Jesus and the Heritage of Israel: Luke's Narrative Claim upon Israel's Legacy,* edited by David P. Moessner. Harrisburg, PA: Trinity Press International, 1999, pp. 325-39.

Telford, William. *The Interpretation of Mark.* London: SPCK, 1985; second edn., Edinburgh: T&T Clark, 1995.

————. *The Theology of the Gospel of Mark.* Cambridge: Cambridge University Press, 1999.

Thielman, Frank. *The Law and the New Testament: The Question of Continuity.* New York: Crossroad, 1999.

Theissen, Gerd. *The First Followers of Jesus: A Sociological Analysis of Earliest Christianity.* London: SCM, 1977.

————. *The Social Setting of Pauline Christianity.* Edinburgh: T&T Clark, 1982.

————. *The Shadow of the Galilean: The Quest of the Historical Jesus in Narrative Form.* London: SCM, 1987.

————. *Social Reality and the Early Christians: Theology, Ethics and the World of the New Testament.* Translated by M. Kohl. Minneapolis: Fortress/Edinburgh: T&T Clark, 1993.

————, and Annette Merz. *The Historical Jesus: A Comprehensive Guide.* Translated by John Bowden. London: SCM, 1998.

Thiselton, Anthony C. *The Two Horizons: New Testament Hermeneutics and Philosophical Description with Special Reference to Heidegger, Bultmann, Gadamer and Wittgenstein.* Exeter: Paternoster, 1980.

———. *New Horizons in Hermeneutics.* San Francisco: HarperCollins, 1992.

———. *1 Corinthians.* NIGTC. Grand Rapids: Eerdmans, 2000.

Thomas, John Christopher. *Footwashing in John 13 and the Johannine Community.* JSNTSS 61. Sheffield: Sheffield Academic Press, 1991.

Thompson, James W. 'The Ethics of Jesus and the Early Church'. In *Christian Social Ethics,* edited by Perry C. Cotham. Grand Rapids: Baker, 1979, pp. 45-59.

Thompson, M. B. *Clothed with Christ: The Example and Teaching of Jesus in Romans 12.1– 15.13.* JSNTSS 59. Sheffield: Sheffield Academic Press, 1991.

Thompson, Marianne Meye. *The Humanity of Jesus in the Fourth Gospel.* Philadelphia: Fortress, 1988.

———. 'The Historical Jesus and the Johannine Christ'. In *Exploring the Gospel of John: In Honor of D. Moody Smith,* edited by R. Alan Culpepper and C. Clifton Black. Louisville: Westminster John Knox, 1996, pp. 21-42.

———. *The God of the Gospel of John.* Grand Rapids: Eerdmans, 2001.

Tiede, David L. '"Fighting against God": Luke's Interpretation of Jewish Rejection of the Messiah Jesus'. In *Anti-Semitism and Early Christianity: Issues of Polemic and Faith,* edited by Craig A. Evans and Donald A. Hagner. Minneapolis: Fortress, 1993, pp. 102-12.

Togarasei, Lovemore. 'Let Everyone Be Subject to the Governing Authorities': The Interpretation of New Testament Political Ethics towards and after Zimbabwe's 2002 Presidential Elections', *Scriptura* 85 (2004), pp. 73-80.

Tomson, Peter J. *'If this be from Heaven . . .': Jesus and the New Testament Authors in Their Relationship to Judaism.* Sheffield: Sheffield Academic Press, 2001.

———. '"Jews" in the Gospel of John as Compared with the Palestinian Talmud, the Synoptics and Some New Testament Apocrypha'. In *Anti-Judaism and the Fourth Gospel: Papers of the Leuven Colloquium, 2000,* edited by R. Bieringer, D. Pollefyt and F. Vandecasteele-Vanneuville. Assen: Royal Van Gorcum, 2001, pp. 301-40.

Tovey, Derek. *Narrative Art and Act in the Fourth Gospel.* JSN SS 151. Sheffield: Sheffield Academic Press, 1997.

Trible, Phyllis. *Texts of Terror: Literary Feminist Readings of Biblical Narratives.* London: SCM, 1992.

Tuckett, Christopher M. 'The Christology of Luke-Acts'. In *The Unity of Luke-Acts, 47th Colloquium Biblicum Lovaniense,* edited by J. Verheyden. Leuven: Leuven University Press, 1999, pp. 133-64.

———. 'Paul, Scripture and Ethics: Some Reflections', *NTS* (2000), pp. 403-24.

———. *Christology and the New Testament: Jesus and His Earliest Followers.* Edinburgh: Edinburgh University Press/Louisville: Westminster John Knox, 2001.

———. 'Sources and Methods'. In *The Cambridge Companion to Jesus,* edited by Markus Bockmuehl. Cambridge: Cambridge University Press, 2001, pp. 121-37.

———. 'Does the "Historical Jesus" Belong within a "New Testament Theology"?' In *The Nature of New Testament Theology: Essays in Honour of Robert Morgan,* edited by Christopher Rowland and Christopher Tuckett. Oxford: Blackwell, 2006, pp. 231-47.

Tutu, Archbishop Desmond. *The Rainbow People of God: South Africa's Victory over Apartheid.* Edited by John Allen. London: Bantam, 1995.

Ukpong, Justin S. 'Rereading the Bible with African Eyes: Inculturation and Hermeneutics', *JTSA* 91 (June 1995), pp. 3-14.

———. 'Reading with the Community: The Workers in the Vineyard Parable (Matt. 20.1-16)'. SNTS Post Conference. Hammanskraal: University of Pretoria, August 9, 1999. Later published in a revised form as 'Bible Reading with a Community of Ordinary Readers'. In *Interpreting the New Testament in Africa*, edited by Mary Getui, Tinyiko Maluleke and Justin Ukpong. Nairobi: Acton, 2001, pp. 188-212.

———. 'Developments in Biblical Interpretation in Africa: Historical and Hermeneutical Directions', *JTSA* 108 (November 2000), pp. 3-18.

———. 'New Testament Hermeneutics in Africa: Challenges and Possibilities', *Neotestamentica* 35 (2001), pp. 147-67.

van Aarde, A. G. 'A Silver Coin in the Mouth of a Fish (Matthew 17:24-27) — A Miracle of Nature, Ecology, Economy and the Politics of Holiness', *Neotestamentica* 27.1 (1993), pp. 1-25.

Van Belle, Gilbert. '"Salvation is from the Jews": The Parenthesis in John 4:22b'. In *Anti-Judaism and the Fourth Gospel: Papers of the Leuven Colloquium, 2000*, edited by R. Bieringer, D. Pollefyt and F. Vandecasteele-Vanneuville. Assen: Royal Van Gorcum, 2001, pp. 370-400.

van der Horst, Pieter W. 'The *Birkat ha-minim* in Recent Research', *ExpT* 105 (1993-94), pp. 363-68.

van Tilborg, Sjef. *The Sermon on the Mount as an Ideological Intervention: A Reconstruction of Meaning*. Assen/Maastricht: Van Gorcum, 1986.

Vanhoozer, Kevin J. *Is There a Meaning in This Text? The Bible, the Reader and the Morality of Literary Knowledge*. Grand Rapids: Zondervan, 1998.

Verdes, L. A. 'Las Eticas Bíblicas del Nuevo Testamento', *Estudios Bíblicos* 48.1 (Madrid, 1990), pp. 113-36.

Verhey, Allen. *The Great Reversal: Ethics and the New Testament*. Grand Rapids: Eerdmans, 1984.

———. *Remembering Jesus: Christian Community, Scripture, and the Moral Life*. Grand Rapids: Eerdmans, 2002.

———. *Reading the Bible in the Strange World of Medicine*. Grand Rapids: Eerdmans, 2003.

Verheyden, J. (ed.). *The Unity of Luke-Acts, 47th Colloquium Biblicum Lovaniense*. Leuven: Leuven University Press, 1999.

Vermes, G. *Jesus the Jew*. London: Collins, 1973.

Via, Dan O., Jr. 'Narrative World and Ethical Response: The Marvelous and Righteousness in Matthew 1-2', *Semeia* 12 (1978), pp. 123-45.

———. 'Structure, Christology, and Ethics in Matthew'. In *Orientation by Disorientation: Studies in Literary Criticism and Biblical Literary Criticism, Presented in Honor of William A. Beardslee*. Pittsurgh: Pickwick, 1980, pp. 199-215.

———. *The Ethics of Mark's Gospel — In the Middle of Time*. Philadelphia: Fortress, 1985.

———. 'Ethical Responsibility and Human Wholeness in Matthew 25.31-46', *HTR* 80 (1987), pp. 79-100.

———. and Robert A. J. Gagnon. *Homosexuality and the Bible: Two Views*. Minneapolis: Fortress, 2003.

Via, E. Jane. 'According to Luke, Who Put Jesus to Death?' In *Political Issues in Luke-Acts*, edited by Richard J. Cassidy and Philip J. Scharper. Maryknoll, NY: Orbis, 1983, pp. 122-45.

Viljoen, Francois P. 'Jesus' Teaching on the *Torah* in the Sermon on the Mount', *Neotestamentica* 40.1 (2006), pp. 135-55.

Villa-Vicencio, Charles. *Trapped in Apartheid: A Socio-Theological History of the English-Speaking Churches.* Cape Town: David Philip/Maryknoll, NY: Orbis, 1988.

————, and J. de Gruchy (eds.). *Doing Ethics in Context: South African Perspectives.* Theology and Praxis, vol. 2. Cape Town: David Philip/Maryknoll, NY: Orbis, 1994

Viviano, B. T. 'The Sermon on the Mount in Recent Study', *Biblica* 78.2 (1997), pp. 255-65.

von Harnack, Adolf. 'Das Alte Testament in den paulinischen Briefen und in den paulinischen Gemeinden', *Sitzungsberichte der Preussischen Akademie der Wissenschaften* (Berlin, 1928), pp. 124-41. ET 'The Old Testament in the Pauline Letters and in the Pauline Churches'. In *Understanding Paul's Ethics*, edited by B. S. Rosner. Grand Rapids: Eerdmans, 1995, pp. 27-49.

von Wahlde, Urban C. 'The Johannine "Jews": A Critical Survey', *NTS* 28 (1982), pp. 33-60.

————. '"You Are of Your Father the Devil" in Its Context: Stereotyped Apocalyptic Polemic in John 8:38-47'. In *Anti-Judaism and the Fourth Gospel: Papers of the Leuven Colloquium, 2000*, edited by R. Bieringer, D. Pollefyt and F. Vandecasteele-Vanneuville. Assen: Royal Van Gorcum, 2001, pp. 418-44.

Vorster, J. N. 'The Study of Religion as the "Multi-Versity": Probing Problems and Possibilities', *Neotestamentica* 32.1 (1998), pp. 203-40.

Vorster, Willem S. 'The Bible and Apartheid 1'. Chap. 8 in *Apartheid Is a Heresy*, edited by J. de Gruchy and C. Villa-Vicencio. Cape Town: David Philip/Guildford: Lutterworth, 1983, pp. 94-111.

————. 'The Use of Scripture and the NG Kerk: A Shift of Paradigm or of Values?' In *New Faces of Africa: Essays in Honour of Ben (Barend Jacobus) Marais*, edited by J. W. Hofmeyr and W. S. Vorster. Pretoria: UNISA, 1984, pp. 204-19.

————. 'Literary Reflections on Mark 13:5-37: A Narrated Speech of Jesus', *Neotestamentica* 21 (1987), pp. 91-112. Reprinted in *The Interpretation of Mark*, edited by W. Telford. Edinburgh: T&T Clark, 2nd edn. 1995, pp. 269-88.

Ward, R. B. 'Why Unnatural? The Tradition behind Romans 1:26-27', *HTR* 90.3 (1997), pp. 263-84.

Walaskay, Paul W. *'And so we came to Rome': The Political Perspective of St. Luke.* SNTSMS 49. Cambridge: Cambridge University Press, 1983.

Wall, Robert W. 'Introduction: New Testament Ethics', *Horizons in Biblical Theology* 5.2 (1983), pp. 49-94.

Walton, Steve. *Leadership and Lifestyle: The Portrait of Paul in the Miletus Speech and 1 Thessalonians.* SNTSMS 108. Cambridge: Cambridge University Press, 2000.

Wansink, Craig S. *Chained in Christ: The Experience and Rhetoric of Paul's Imprisonments.* JSNTSS 130. Sheffield: Sheffield Academic Press, 1996.

Watson, Francis. *Paul, Judaism and the Gentiles: A Sociological Approach.* SNTSMS 56. Cambridge: Cambridge University Press, 1986.

————. *Text, Church and World.* Edinburgh: T&T Clark, 1994.

————. *Text and Truth: Redefining Biblical Theology.* Edinburgh: T&T Clark, 1997.

————. 'The Triune Divine Identity: Reflections on Pauline God Language, in Disagreement with J. D. G. Dunn', *JSNT* 80 (2000), pp. 99-124.

Webb, William J. *Slaves, Women and Homosexuals: Exploring the Hermeneutics of Cultural Analysis*. Downers Grove, IL: IVP, 2001.

Wedderburn, A. J. M. (ed.). *Paul and Jesus: Collected Essays*. JSNTSS 37. Sheffield: Sheffield Academic Press, 1989.

Weeden, Theodore J., Sr. 'The Heresy That Necessitated Mark's Gospel', *ZNW* 59 (1968), pp. 145-58.

————. *Mark: Traditions in Conflict*. Philadelphia: Fortress, 1971.

Weiss, J. *Die Predigt Jesu vom Reiche Gottes*. Göttingen: Vandenhoeck & Ruprecht, 1892. ET *Jesus' Proclamation of the Kingdom of God*. London: SCM, 1971.

Weisse, Wolfram (ed.). *The Dutch Reformed Church (DRC) and Transition in SA*, edited by Weisse, *Scriptura* 76 (2001), pp. 1-151, and *Scriptura* 83 (2003), pp. 189-347.

Wells, S. *Transforming Fate into Destiny: The Theological Ethics of Stanley Hauerwas*. Carlisle: Paternoster, 1998.

Wenham, David. *Paul: Follower of Jesus or Founder of Christianity?* Grand Rapids: Eerdmans, 1995.

————. *Paul and the Historical Jesus*. Grove Biblical Series 7. Cambridge: Grove, 1998.

————. *Paul and Jesus: The True Story*. London: SPCK/Grand Rapids: Eerdmans, 2002.

West, Gerald O. 'The Relationship between Different Modes of Reading (the Bible) and the Ordinary Reader'. In *Issues in Contextual Hermeneutics*, edited by Johann Kinghorn, *Scriptura*, Special Issue S9 (1991), pp. 87-110.

————. 'Some Parameters of the Hermeneutic Debate in the South African Context', *JTSA* 80 (September 1992), pp. 3-13.

————. 'The Bible and Theology'. In *Doing Theology in Context: South African Perspectives*, edited by John de Gruchy and C. Villa-Vicencio. Theology and Praxis, vol. 2. Cape Town: David Philip/Maryknoll, NY: Orbis, 1994, pp. 15-25.

————. *Biblical Hermeneutics of Liberation: Modes of Reading the Bible in the South African Context*. Maryknoll, NY: Orbis, second revised edn. 1995 (original edn., Pietermaritzburg: Cluster, 1991).

————. and Musa W. Dube (eds.). *'Reading with . . .'*, *Semeia* 73 (1996).

————. 'Don't Stand on My Story: The Truth and Reconciliation Commission, Intellectuals, Genre and Identity', *JTSA* 98 (1997), pp. 3-12.

————. *The Academy of the Poor: Towards a Dialogical Reading of the Bible*. Sheffield: Sheffield Academic Press, 1999.

————, and Musa W. Dube (eds.). *The Bible in Africa: Transactions, Trajectories and Trends*. Leiden: Brill, 2000.

————. 'Reading the Bible in the Light of HIV/Aids in South Africa', *The Ecumenical Review* 55.4 (2003), pp. 335-44.

————. 'The Historicity of Myth and the Myth of Historicity: Locating the Ordinary African "Reader" of the Bible in the Debate', *Neotestamentica* 38.1 (2004), pp. 127-44.

————. *Doing Contextual Bible Study: A Resource Manual*. Pietermaritzburg: Ujamaa Centre, 2005.

————. 'Articulating, Owning and Mainstreaming Local Theologies: The Contribution of Contextual Bible Study', *JTSA* 122 (2005), pp. 23-35.

————, and Bongi Zengele. 'The Medicine of God's Word: What People Living with HIV and AIDS Want (and Get) from the Bible', *JTSA* 125 (July 2006), pp. 51-63.

Westcott, B. F. *The Gospel according to St. John*. London: Murray, 1919.

White, R. E. O. *Biblical Ethics*. Exeter: Paternoster, 1979.

————. *The Insights of History*. Exeter: Paternoster, 1981.

————. *Christian Ethics*. Leominster: Gracewing/Macon, GA: Mercer University Press, 1994.

Wiebe, B. 'Messianic Ethics: Response to the Kingdom of God', *Interpretation* 45.1 (1991), pp. 29-42.

Wilkins, Michael J. *The Concept of Disciple in Matthew's Gospel: As Reflected in the Use of the Term μαθητής*. NovTSup 59. Leiden: Brill, 1988.

Willis, W. L. 'Pauline Ethics, 1964-1994'. In *Theology and Ethics in Paul and His Interpreters: Essays in Honor of Victor Paul Furnish*, edited by E. H. Lovering, Jr. and J. L. Sumney. Nashville: Abingdon, 1996, pp. 313-14.

Williams, James G. 'Paraenesis, Excess, and Ethics: Matthew's Rhetoric in the Sermon on the Mount', *Semeia* 50 (1990), pp. 163-87.

Williams, Rowan D. 'Interiority and Epiphany: A Reading in New Testament Ethics', *Modern Theology* 13.1 (January 1997), pp. 29-51.

Wilson, A. N. *Paul: The Mind of the Apostle*. London: Sinclair-Stevenson, 1997.

Wilson, S. G. *Luke and the Law*. SNTSMS 50. Cambridge: Cambridge University Press, 1983.

Wilson, Walter T. *Love without Pretense: Romans 12.9-21 and Hellenistic Jewish Wisdom Literature*. WUNT 2.46. Tübingen: Mohr, 1991.

Windisch, Hans. *The Meaning of the Sermon on the Mount*. Philadelphia: Westminster Press, 1951.

Wink, Walter. 'Neither Passivity nor Violence: Jesus' Third Way (Matt. 5.38-42 par.)'. In *The Love of Enemy and Nonretaliation in the New Testament*, edited by Willard M. Swartley. Louisville: Westminster John Knox, 1992, pp. 102-25.

———— (ed.). *Homosexuality and the Christian Faith: Questions of Conscience for the Churches*. Minneapolis: Fortress, 1999.

Winter, Bruce W. *Seek the Welfare of the City: Christians as Benefactors and Citizens*. Grand Rapids: Eerdmans, 1994.

Witherington, Ben, III. *Women in the Earliest Churches*. SNTSMS 59. Cambridge: Cambridge University Press, 1988.

————. *Jesus, Paul and the End of the World*. Exeter: Paternoster, 1992.

————. *Paul's Narrative Thought World: The Tapestry of Tragedy and Triumph*. Louisville: Westminster John Knox, 1994.

————. *John's Wisdom*. Cambridge: Lutterworth, 1995.

————. *The Acts of the Apostles: A Socio-Rhetorical Commentary*. Grand Rapids: Eerdmans, 1998.

————. *The Paul Quest: The Renewed Search for the Jew of Tarsus*. Downers Grove, IL: IVP, 1998.

————. *The Many Faces of the Christ: The Christologies of the New Testament and Beyond*. New York: Crossroad, 1998.

————. *The Gospel of Mark: A Socio-Rhetorical Commentary.* Grand Rapids: Eerdmans, 2001.

Wolff, Christian. 'Humility and Self-denial in Jesus' Life and Message and in the Apostolic Existence of Paul'. In *Paul and Jesus: Collected Essays,* edited by A. J. M. Wedderburn. JSNTSS 37. Sheffield: Sheffield Academic Press, 1989, pp. 145-60.

————. 'True Apostolic Knowledge of Christ: Exegetical Reflections on 2 Corinthians 5.14ff'. In *Paul and Jesus: Collected Essays,* edited by A. J. M. Wedderburn. JSNTSS 37. Sheffield: Sheffield Academic Press, 1989, pp. 81-98.

Wolter, Michael. '"Reich Gottes" bei Lukas', *NTS* 41.4 (1995), pp. 541-63.

————. 'Israel's Future and the Delay of the Parousia, according to Luke'. In *Jesus and the Heritage of Israel: Luke's Narrative Claim upon Israel's Legacy,* edited by David P. Moessner. Harrisburg, PA: Trinity Press International, 1999, pp. 307-24.

Wright, Chris. 'Biblical Ethics: A Survey of the Last Decade', *Themelios* 18 (1993), pp. 15-19.

Wright, David F. 'Homosexuals or Prostitutes? The Meaning of ARSENOKOITAI (1 Cor. 6:9, 1 Tim. 1:10)', *Vigiliae Christianae* 38 (1984), pp. 125-53.

————. 'Homosexuality: The Relevance of the Bible', *Evangelical Quarterly* 61.4 (1989), pp. 291-300.

Wright, N. T. *The Climax of the Covenant: Christ and the Law in Pauline Theology.* Edinburgh: T&T Clark, 1991.

————. *Christian Origins and the Question of God:* vol. 1, *The New Testament and the People of God.* London: SPCK, 1992.

————. *Christian Origins and the Question of God:* vol. 2, *Jesus and the Victory of God.* London: SPCK, 1996.

————. *The Original Jesus: The Life and Vision of a Revolutionary.* Oxford: Lion/Grand Rapids: Eerdmans, 1996.

————. *What Saint Paul Really Said: Was Paul of Tarsus the Real Founder of Christianity?* Oxford: Lion, 1997.

————. 'A Fresh Perspective on Paul?', *The T. W. Manson Memorial Lecture.* Westminster Abbey, October 26, 2000.

————. 'Coming Home to St. Paul? Reading Romans a Hundred Years after Charles Gore'. *The Gore Lecture* (Westminster Abbey, November 14, 2000). *SJT* 55.4 (2002), pp. 392-407.

————. *Christian Origins and the Question of God:* vol. 3, *The Resurrection of the Son of God.* London: SPCK, 2003.

————. *Paul: Fresh Perspectives.* London: SPCK, 2005.

Yang, Yong-Eui. *Jesus and the Sabbath in Matthew's Gospel.* JSNTSS 139. Sheffield: Sheffield Academic Press, 1997.

Yee, G. A. *Jewish Feasts and the Gospel of John.* Wilmington, DE: Michael Glazier, 1989.

Zwiep, Arie W. *The Ascension of the Messiah in Lukan Christology.* Leiden: Brill, 1997.

Index of Subjects

References in **boldface** denote substantial discussion of these topics.

Index of Modern Authors

References in **boldface** denote substantial discussion of these authors.

Index of Biblical References and Ancient Sources

References in **boldface** denote substantial discussion of these texts.

471